P9-EMK-085

Fodor's

TURKEY

7th Edition

Fodor's Travel Publications   New York, Toronto, London, Sydney, Auckland
www.fodors.com

Be a Fodor's Correspondent

Share your trip with Fodor's

Our latest guidebook to Turkey—now in full color—owes its success to travelers like you. Throughout, you'll find photographs submitted by members of Fodors.com to our "Show Us Your...Turkey" photo contest. Facing this page is a photograph of a fishmonger near the Sea of Marmara, taken by pvd, a Fodor's member since 2004, as she waited to catch a car ferry. On page 1 you'll find our grand prize–winning photograph, taken by DoreenD as she floated over the rock formations of Cappadocia in a hot-air balloon at sunrise. We've also included "Word of Mouth" quotes from travelers who shared their experiences with others on our forums.

We are especially proud of this color edition. No other guide to Turkey is as up to date or has as much practical planning information, along with hundreds of color photographs and illustrated maps. If you're inspired and can plan a better trip because of this guide, we've done our job.

We invite you to join the travel conversation: Your opinion matters to us and to your fellow travelers. Come to Fodors.com to plan your trip, share an experience, ask a question, submit a photograph, post a review, or write a trip report. Tell our editors about your trip. They want to know what went well and how we can make this guide even better. Share your opinions at our feedback center at fodors.com/feedback, or email us at editors@fodors.com with the subject line "Turkey Editor." You might find your comments published in a future Fodor's guide. We look forward to hearing from you.

Iyi yolculuklar! (Happy Traveling!)

Tim Jarrell, Publisher

FODOR'S TURKEY

Editor: Caroline Trefler

Contributors: Stephen Brewer, Richard Carriero, Evin Doğu, Robert Fisher, Joel Hanson, Vanessa Larson, Catherine Marshall, Scott Newman, Yigal Schleifer

Production Editor: Astrid deRidder

Maps & Illustrations: Mark Stroud and Henry Colomb, Moon Street Cartography; David Lindroth Inc., *cartographers*; Bob Blake, Rebecca Baer, *map editors*; William Wu, *information graphics*

Design: Fabrizio La Rocca, *creative director*; Guido Caroti, Siobhan O'Hare, *art directors*; Tina Malaney, Chie Ushio, Ann McBride, Jessica Walsh, *designers*; Melanie Marin, *senior picture editor*

Cover Photo: Zubin Shroff/The Image Bank/Getty Images

Production Manager: Angela L. McLean

COPYRIGHT

Copyright © 2009 by Fodor's Travel, a division of Random House, Inc.

Fodor's is a registered trademark of Random House, Inc.

All rights reserved. Published in the United States by Fodor's Travel, a division of Random House, Inc., and simultaneously in Canada by Random House of Canada, Limited, Toronto. Distributed by Random House, Inc., New York.

No maps, illustrations, or other portions of this book may be reproduced in any form without written permission from the publisher.

7th Edition

ISBN 978–1–4000–0815–5

ISSN 0071–6618

SPECIAL SALES

This book is available at special discounts for bulk purchases for sales promotions or premiums. Special editions, including personalized covers, excerpts of existing books, and corporate imprints, can be created in large quantities for special needs. For more information, write to Special Markets/Premium Sales, 1745 Broadway, MD 6-2, New York, New York 10019, or e-mail specialmarkets@randomhouse.com.

AN IMPORTANT TIP & AN INVITATION

Although all prices, opening times, and other details in this book are based on information supplied to us at press time, changes occur all the time in the travel world, and Fodor's cannot accept responsibility for facts that become outdated or for inadvertent errors or omissions. So **always confirm information when it matters,** especially if you're making a detour to visit a specific place. Your experiences—positive and negative— matter to us. If we have missed or misstated something, **please write to us.** We follow up on all suggestions. Contact the Turkey editor at editors@fodors.com or c/o Fodor's at 1745 Broadway, New York, NY 10019.

PRINTED IN SINGAPORE

10 9 8 7 6 5 4 3 2 1

CONTENTS

MAPS

ABOUT THIS BOOK

OUR RATINGS

Sometimes you find terrific travel experiences and sometimes they just find you. But usually the burden is on you to select the right combination of experiences. That's where our ratings come in.

As travelers we've all discovered a place so wonderful that its worthiness is obvious. And sometimes that place is so unique that superlatives don't do it justice: you just have to be there to know. These sights, properties, and experiences get our highest rating, **Fodor's Choice**, indicated by orange stars throughout this book.

Black stars highlight sights and properties we deem **Highly Recommended**, places that our writers, editors, and readers praise again and again for consistency and excellence.

By default, there's another category: any place we include in this book is by definition worth your time, unless we say otherwise. And we will.

Disagree with any of our choices? Care to nominate a place or suggest that we rate one more highly? Visit our feedback center at www. fodors.com/feedback.

BUDGET WELL

Hotel and restaurant price categories from ¢ to $$$$ are defined in the opening pages of each chapter. For attractions, we always give standard adult admission fees; reductions are usually available for children, students, and senior citizens. Want to pay with plastic? **AE, D, DC, MC, V** following restaurant and hotel listings indicate whether American Express, Discover, Diners Club, MasterCard, and Visa are accepted.

RESTAURANTS

Unless we state otherwise, restaurants are open for lunch and dinner daily. We mention dress only when there's a specific requirement and reservations only when they're essential or not accepted—it's always best to book ahead.

HOTELS

Hotels have private bath, phone, TV, and air-conditioning and operate on the European Plan (aka EP, meaning without meals), unless we specify that they use the Continental Plan (CP, with a Continental breakfast), Breakfast Plan (BP, with a full breakfast), or Modified American Plan (MAP, with breakfast and dinner) or are all-inclusive (AI, including all meals and most activities). We

always list facilities but not whether you'll be charged an extra fee to use them, so when pricing accommodations, find out what's included.

Many Listings
★	Fodor's Choice
★	Highly recommended
⊠	Physical address
✛	Directions
⌂	Mailing address
☎	Telephone
🖷	Fax
⊕	On the Web
✍	E-mail
✍	Admission fee
☉	Open/closed times
Ⓜ	Metro stations
▭	Credit cards

Hotels & Restaurants
🏨	Hotel
🛏	Number of rooms
⌂	Facilities
⑪	Meal plans
✕	Restaurant
⌂	Reservations
⤳	Smoking
🕮	BYOB
✕🏨	Hotel with restaurant that warrants a visit

Outdoors
🏌	Golf
⛺	Camping

Other
⌂	Family-friendly
⇨	See also
⊠	Branch address
☞	Take note

Experience
Turkey

1

WHAT'S WHERE

The following numbers refer to chapters.

2 Istanbul. Straddling Europe and Asia, Istanbul is the undisputed cultural, economic, and historical capital of Turkey. There are enough monuments and attractions, as well as enticing restaurants, shops, and museums to keep you busy for days.

3 The Sea of Marmara and the North Aegean. The battlefields of Gallipoli are one of the main reasons travelers visit this part of Turkey, but the area is also a destination for beach lovers and those looking for pleasant places to hike. The archaeological site of ancient Troy is here, too.

4 The Central and Southern Aegean Coast. The heart of what was once known by the ancient Greeks as Asia Minor, this area has been drawing visitors since the time of, well, Homer. The heavyweight attraction these days is the Roman city of Ephesus but there are also many beach destinations, ranging from glitzy to relaxed.

5 The Turquoise Riviera. The beaches along Turkey's southern shores—dubbed the Turquoise Riviera— are some of the best in the country, and the ruins here are spectacular. With unspoiled seaside villages and charming hotels and *pansiyons*, this is very close to paradise. Steer clear of the megaresorts though, which have started to invade, particularly around Antalya.

| Location markers on map: |
| BLACK SEA |
| GEORGIA |
| ARMENIA |
| IRAN |
| IRAQ |
| SYRIA |

Inebolu · Sinop · Gerze · Kastamonu · Bafra · Samsun · Terme · Unye · Ordu · Gorele · Trabzon · Rize · Batumi · Tbilisi

Iskilip · Merzifon · Amasya · Niksar · Giresun · Cankiri · Turhal · Zile · Susehri · Kirikkale · Kars · Yerevan

Kaman · Sivas · Erzincan · Erzurum · Karakose · Igdir · Divrigi · Dogubeyazit

Kayseri · Elazig · Van

Goreme · Urgup · Uchisar · Afsin · Kahramanmaras · Diyarbakir · Sivarek · Şanlıurfa

Eregli · Tarsus · Adana · Osmaniye · Mersin · Iskenderun · Dortyol · Antakya (Antioch) · Samandagi · Mosul

Route numbers: 765, 100, 785, 200, 260, 300, 750, 805, 010, 100, 200, 300, 010, 950, 957, 100, 957, 965, 975, 950

6 Cappadocia, Ankara and the Turkish Heartland. In magical Cappadocia, wind and rain have shaped soft volcanic rock into a fairy-tale landscape, where conical outcroppings were centuries ago turned into churches and homes. Southwest of Cappadocia is Konya, home to a museum and tomb dedicated to the 13th-century founder of the whirling dervishes. Ankara, Turkey's capital, is also here, though it ranks fairly low on most visitors' itineraries.

7 The Far East and Black Sea Coast. It may not have the resorts, boutique hotels, and upscale restaurants of western Turkey, but there are impressive sites—both natural and manmade—to be found, including picturesque mountain villages; historic monasteries; the ancient city of Ani and towering Mt. Ararat; and fascinating Nemrut Dağı. In all these places, you're certain to get a taste of a different and rewarding Turkey.

TURKEY TODAY

Politics

In July 2007, Turks, in overwhelming numbers, reelected the Justice and Development Party (AKP). This led to Abdullah Gul's ascension as president, where he joined fellow-conservative Prime Minister Recep Tayyip Erdogan to govern the country. In Istanbul, die-hard secularists have been alarmed by AKP's increasing power and continue to assert that the party seeks to erode the secular legacy of Mustafa Kemal Atatürk. Some even contend that the AKP seeks to impose Sharia law (strict Islamic day-to-day religious law) on the country, though party leadership vehemently denies such aims. Secularists point to laws limiting the sale of alcohol, tobacco, pornography, and pork as well as a 2007 law to lift the constitutional ban on headscarves at universities.

Turkey's biggest foreign policy goal continues to be accession to the European Union. Most member states are in favor of Turkey joining, though there are some strong opponents, and accession talks have made only halting progress as Turkey faces criticism on several issues. Continued Turkish occupation of Northern Cyprus (which only Turkey recognizes as a sovereign nation) is one stumbling block, another is the Turkish government's refusal to label the death of several hundred thousand Armenian citizens during World War I as genocide. Domestically, critics cite Turkey's headscarf ban and criminal laws that punish anyone found guilt of insulting "Turkishness" as undemocratic as further obstructions.

The Economy

The AKP's greatest bargaining chip in recent elections was the upsurge of the Turkish economy since the aftermath of the 1999 earthquake. The country enjoys a diverse economy: self-sufficient agricultural production, a massive textile industry, and a growing electronics sector. Turkish annual GDP growth this decade, at 7.4% per year, is among the fastest in the world. The rest of the world has taken a greater interest in Turkey in the past 10 years, as evidenced by the consistent 10% growth rate of the tourist industry. International faith in the economy has driven considerable foreign investment, which has strengthened the Turkish Lira. Inflation, which for 30 years led to the counting of the Lira in millions, has dropped to single digit levels and allowed the government to lop six zeroes from the old Lira in 2005. Turkey's greatest economic liability is a sizable trade deficit, driven largely by the country's need to import foreign oil. Until the 2008 credit crunch, however, foreign investment more than compensated for these deficits.

Religion

In Istanbul they sell a T-shirt with the name of the city spelled using a crescent, a cross, and a Star of David. Turks pride themselves on their secularism and tolerance of other religions, a legacy of the Ottoman Empire, which governed people of all faiths. While Turkey is a secular republic, however, its population is overwhelming (99%) comprised of Muslims; the remaining 1% are Christians (Greek Orthodox and Armenian Apostolic) and Jews. One reason for the relative harmony between people of different faiths may be the relaxed approach that many Turks take toward religion. In addition to having a secular government, many Turks drink alcohol and smoke cigarettes, and on any given day in Istanbul you are as liable to find as many scantily clad fashionistas walking down the street as women wearing headscarves.

The Arts

Turkey has made many recent contributions to the art world—no surprise from a country that boasts such stunning antiquity—and Istanbul has been chosen as the 2010 European Capital of Culture. The country's most well-known creative mind may be novelist Orhan Pamuk, who garnered the country's first Nobel Prize in 2006 for his dreamy yet historic novels, but the Istanbul Film Festival is currently in its 26th year: held every April, the festival awards prizes for both Turkish and International films. Additionally, Turkey's status as a large textile exporter has helped ensure the nation a place in fashion design, and Istanbul's Nişantaşı district is literally a maze of small boutiques selling imported and Turkish clothing. In the visual arts, Turkey is most famous for its ceramics and porcelain, especially handmade Kütahya and İznik tiles.

Sports

Turkey is a die-hard soccer nation (they call it football), and heated rivalries run strong. Turkey's clubs boast lots of homegrown talent along with some players imported from Europe and South America. The Turkish national football team has enjoyed sporadic success in international play. In this decade, the team reached the semifinals in the 2002 World Cup and 2008 European Cup. Other popular sports in Turkey are basketball (the NBA has a growing fan base in Turkey) and Turkish Grease Wrestling. Edirne is famous for its annual Kırkpinar oil wrestling festival.

Media

Turkish media seems always to be on people's lips, mainly because of Article 301 and the Turkish government's penchant for closing down outlets that offend its conservative moral code. Article 301 forbids anyone from insulting "Turkishness," under pain of criminal prosecution. Most cases are dropped but many notable Turks, including Orhan Pamuk, have been prosecuted. Another issue was the 2007 shutdown of the popular video site YouTube after the government discovered videos insulting Atatürk. Despite these controversies, freedom of speech is mostly unlimited in Turkey and writers and journalists can criticize the government and people as long as they don't cross the line to insult.

Smoking

In an effort to curb rampant tobacco addiction, the Turkish government introduced a ban on smoking in enclosed public places, which took effect in May of 2008. Some bars and clubs simply ignore the ban, but the Turkish Health Ministry estimates that Turks are smoking 500 million fewer cigarettes per month.

And Looking Forward . . .

2009 marks the return of the Rock N' Coke music festival after a hiatus in 2008. This is Turkey's largest music festival attracts big names in local and international music; the 2007 festival drew Franz Ferdinand and Smashing Pumpkins. 2010 will also be a proud year for Turkey, since Istanbul has been chosen as the European Capital of Culture for the year. The Turkish government sees this as an opportunity to showcase Istanbul's wealth of art, culture, and history to the rest of the world.

TURKEY PLANNER

When to Go

Most tourists visit Turkey between April and the end of October. July and August are the busiest and hottest months. April through June and September to October offer more temperate weather, and crowds are smaller.

Istanbul tends to be hot in summer, cold and rainy in winter. The Mediterranean (Turquoise) and Aegean coasts have mild winters and hot summers; you can swim along either coast from late April into October. The Black Sea coast is mild and damp, with a rainfall of 90 inches per year. Central and eastern Anatolia can be extremely cold in winter, with roads and mountain passes closed by snow; summers bring hot, dry weather, but cool evenings.

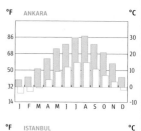

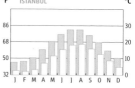

Getting Around

In Turkey you can travel by plane, car, bus, or train. With the advent of several new domestic airline companies in recent years, competition has increased and the cost of domestic flights has come down, so if your aim is to see several different areas of the country in a short time, you may want to fly between destinations.

Turkey has an extensive bus network, with buses serving all the major cities and even the smallest towns. Buses are generally safe, reliable, and surprisingly comfortable, making them an excellent way to travel around the country.

Renting a car allows you greater flexibility than traveling by bus, and the chance to see to places that are more off the beaten path, as well a glimpse of small-town Turkish life. Although major roads are generally in good condition, minor roads can be rough and badly paved, and it's wise to avoid driving at night. If you don't want a stick shift, reserve well in advance and specify automatic transmission.

Although cheaper than buses, trains tend to be far slower and do not serve many areas of the country. A high-speed rail line between Istanbul and Ankara is set to open in 2009 or 2010, but for other routes it's not usually worth taking the train.

For more detailed information, see the Travel Smart chapter and the specific regional chapters.

What to Pack

For women, it's advisable to bring a scarf or shawl that will cover the hair (and shoulders, if you are wearing a sleeveless shirt) so as to dress appropriately when entering mosques. If you're planning to visit Cappadocia, a flashlight can be extremely useful for exploring cave churches and underground cities. If you're going anywhere with beaches or archaeological ruins, it's wise to have sunscreen, as the Turkish sun can be intense. An umbrella is a good idea if you're visiting Istanbul during the rainy winter months.

Hotels in Turkey

Turkey has a variety of different types of accommodation, from simple inns to boutique hotels and luxury international chains. *Pansiyons,* found especially throughout the coastal areas and in small towns, tend to be small, family-run, and offer inexpensive but clean lodgings, usually with a typical Turkish breakfast included. The designation of "special-class hotels" includes restored Ottoman mansions and villas, cave hotels in Cappadocia, and other establishments with unique historic, cultural, and/or architectural character.

Hotels in Turkey are officially classified as HL (Luxury) and H1 to H5 (first- to fifth-class). These designations can be misleading though, as they're based on quantity of facilities rather than the quality of the service and decor, and a lack of restaurant or lounge automatically relegates the establishment to the bottom of the ratings. In reality, a lower-grade hotel may actually be far more charming and comfortable than one with a higher rating.

Restaurants in Turkey

Turkey has restaurants to suit your every mood and budget.

Bufe. These are great for cheap and simple *döners*—meat grilled on a vertical spit—or *tost,* a panini-like grilled cheese sandwich.

Lokanta. This name is given to a range of traditional restaurants that serve homey dishes like soups, stews, and casseroles. Most *lokantalar* offer a variety of fresh food that's displayed in long steam tables. Point to what looks good and a waiter will bring it to your table.

Meyhane. Tavern-like *meyhanes* are the place to go for meze, to drink raki, and perhaps sing the night away with your fellow diners. Meyhanes usually also serve fish.

Balıkci. Balık means "fish" in Turkish, and seafood restaurants tend to be more sedate than *meyhanes.* Though they serve many of the same mezes as *meyhanes,* these restaurants will have a larger selection of fish and more creative ways to cook them.

Kebabci. Kebab restaurants usually stick to the basics: skewered meat (usually a selection of lamb, beef, and chicken) served sizzling off the grill, and a few side dishes.

Muhallebi/Pastane. Indulging your sweet tooth isn't a problem in Turkey. *Muhallebis* specialize in milk-based desserts like *sutlac,* a rich rice pudding. *Pastanes* have European-style cakes and cookies.

Mosque Etiquette

The Turks are quite lenient about tourists visiting mosques and most are open to the public during the day, but there are some rules of etiquette:

It's best not to enter a mosque during the five daily prayer sessions, or at midday on Fridays, when attendances are higher—it's sort of the equivalent of Sunday morning for Christians or Saturday morning for Jews.

Immodest clothing is not allowed but an attendant by the door will lend you a robe if he feels you aren't dressed appropriately. For women, bare arms and legs aren't acceptable, and men should also avoid wearing shorts. Women should cover their heads before entering a mosque, though this is sometimes overlooked.

Shoes must be removed before entering a mosque; there's usually an attendant who watches over them. If you're uncomfortable leaving your shoes, put them in your backpack or handbag.

It's considered offensive for a non-Muslim to sit down in a mosque (though you may see tourists who do, despite signs requesting them not to).

Don't take photographs inside the mosque, particularly of people praying.

A small donation is usually requested for the upkeep of the mosque. The equivalent of approximately $3 is appropriate.

TURKEY
TOP ATTRACTIONS

Edirne

(A) Edirne is home to the undisputed masterpiece of Ottoman architecture, the Selimiye Mosque, built by the architect Sinan in 1574. A former Ottoman capital, the Sultans gave Edirne a rich collection of architecture, which can be enjoyed in the relaxed atmosphere of this leafy provincial center. Edirne is also home to Turkey's annual Grease Wrestling tournament.

Aya Sofya

(B) Aya Sofya was, for nearly a thousand years, the greatest church in Christendom. Built by the emperor Justinian in the 6th century, it's one the few buildings of this age, size, and grandeur to survive today. Its giant dome shelters numerous historic artworks, from Byzantine mosaics to Islamic calligraphy.

Yerebatan Sarnıcı

(C) Dark basements with serious damp problems aren't normally tourist attractions, unless they happen to be evocative Byzantine cisterns, held up by ancient columns that are reflected in water teaming with fish. Built 1,500 years ago to preserve the city's water supply through siege and drought, it's a peaceful, surreal escape from the heat of an Istanbul summer.

The Blue Mosque

(D) Elegant, cascading curves and a central location make the Blue Mosque (aka Sultan Ahmet Camii), the most famous mosque in Istanbul. Inside is a spectacular coating of blue İznik tiles, which give it its nickname.

Ephesus

(E) Ephesus was the metropolis of Asia and archaeologists have revealed a treasure trove of ancient streets once walked by Alexander the Great and St. Paul. There are houses, theaters, temples, toilets, even a brothel, and the columned facade of the Library of Celsus.

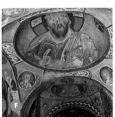

Topkapı Sarayı

Topkapı Palace was the home of the Ottoman Sultans and the heart of the empire. Its grassy courtyards once buzzed with the comings and goings of soldiers, ambassadors, eunuchs, and Pashas, while in the private chambers of the Harem, dripping with lovely blue tiles, the Sultan's women schemed to bring a son to the throne. Former storerooms overflow with gold thrones, gigantic diamonds, and the holiest relics of Islam.

Göreme Open-air Museum

(F) The unique lunar landscape of Cappadocia is honeycombed with Byzantine churches cut from the rock in the Middle Ages, many decorated with beautiful frescoes. The most famous and easily accessible place to visit is the collection of churches and dwellings known as the Göreme Open-air Museum.

Pamukkale

(G) Stunning white travertine pools of water cascade down a hillside in the hinterland of the Aegean coast: this unique rock formation was created over eons by mineral-rich water and has attracted tourists for millenia.

Mt. Nemrut

(H) Atop a lonely mountain overlooking the Euphrates, this ancient shrine to the megalomania of one man is an extraordinary archaeological site. The oversize heads of King Antiochos and his fellow gods litter the ground beside a great burial mound.

Olympos

These jungle-entangled ruins in a valley by one of the Mediterranean's most beautiful beaches are overlooked by the natural eternal flame of the Chimaera. Few places combine Turkey's many attractions as does Olympos.

TOP TURKEY EXPERIENCES

Take a Boat up the Bosphorus

A boat ride along the Bosphorus is one of the most enjoyable ways to see the sprawling, magnificent city of Istanbul. From the ferry's vantage point, you'll see landmarks like the Dolmabahçe and Çırağan Palaces; Ortaköy Mosque, perched right on the water's edge; and exquisite waterfront mansions, called *yalıs*, that were summer homes for the Ottoman elite. You'll also pass under the waterway's two suspension bridges, which connect Asia and Europe. While onboard, sip a glass of Turkish tea and listen to the calls of the seagulls as you contemplate this beautiful meeting of two continents.

Scrub Down in a Turkish Bath

Before the era of indoor plumbing, going to a hamam, or public bath, was a central element of Turkish life. Today many beautiful centuries-old hamams are still in use, by both locals and tourists. Most have separate facilities for men and women. In the hamam's steam room, you can relax on the heated marble platform in the center and rinse yourself at one of the marble washbasins. If you choose, you'll also be lathered, scrubbed, and massaged by a hamam attendant, whose goal seems to be to remove every last dry skin cell from the surface of your body. You'll emerge ultra-clean, refreshed, and having taken part in an age-old Turkish tradition.

Stay in a Cave Hotel

Where but in Cappadocia can you sleep like the Flintstones while having all of your creature comforts? While few of Cappadocia's inhabitants still live in traditional homes carved out of the soft tufa stone, in recent years the area's hoteliers have been converting more and more of these "cave" dwellings into hotels, which range from basic inns for backpackers to upscale lodgings with plush furnishings, modern lighting, and fully equipped bathrooms, some even with Jacuzzis. Surrounded by Cappadocia's magical landscape, tucked cozily into your cave room at night, you'll feel almost like you're on another planet.

Watch the Dervishes Whirl

Turkey is famous for its "whirling dervishes," a sect of Sufi mystics, the Mevlevi, who believe that ritual spinning in circles will bring them to union with God. This trance-like whirling is just one element of the *sema*, a highly symbolic religious ceremony that also includes music and Koranic recitation. Despite the fact that these dervish ceremonies have become increasingly tourist-oriented in recent years, attending a *sema* is still a powerful and mesmerizing experience. Seeing the dervishes whirl is one of the main draws of the festival commemorating Rumi in Konya each December; there are also regular dervish performances in Istanbul and elsewhere in Turkey.

Take a Blue Cruise

One of the most popular and relaxing ways to experience Turkey's Aegean and Mediterranean coasts is to take a Blue Cruise aboard a *gulet,* or wooden fishing vessel. Usually lasting several days (or longer), these cruises take passengers along the rugged coastline, with stops to visit ruins or villages. Away from the beach crowds, you'll enjoy the simple pleasures of swimming in remote coves, eating fresh caught fish, and sleeping on your boat in a wooded inlet.

Quench Your Thirst Like the Locals

A trip to Turkey isn't complete without sampling certain quintessentially Turkish beverages. You can barely go anywhere without being offered a glass of çay, or

tea: the lubricant for every social and business encounter, it's consumed in Turkey at one of the world's highest rates per capita. The famous Turkish coffee, a thick brew made with extremely finely ground coffee beans, is in fact drunk far less often: primarily just on special occasions and as a digestive after meals. For something cold, try the ubiquitous ayran, a frothy, salted, yogurt drink that's a refreshing accompaniment to a spicy meal of kebabs. Another unique beverage is sahlep, a sweet, milk-based hot drink served during the winter months. And don't forget to taste the anise-flavored national liquor rakı.

See Cappadocia from Above

Taking a trip in a hot-air balloon is a thrilling way to see the amazing scenery of Cappadocia; for many people this is the highlight of their trip to the area. As your balloon follows the natural contours of the terrain, you'll look down into scenic valleys and sail right past "fairy chimneys" and unusual rock formations that seem almost close enough to touch. Flights leave at dawn, when the air is calmest and safest for flying, and end with a champagne toast.

Wander Among Ruins

With so many civilizations having occupied the land that is now Turkey, it's no surprise that the country is sprinkled with ancient ruins. The remains of Roman and Greek cities, with their impressive theaters, temples, stadiums, and colonnaded streets compete with even older sites dating back to the Hittites. From beachside Patara and Olympos, to Termessos high up in the mountains, to the inland Aphrodisias, each spot is uniquely picturesque. At the best-preserved sites like Ephesus and Troy, you'll be among many visitors marveling at the ruins, but at places that are more off the beaten path, you'll be free to wander around and explore with virtually no one else around.

Travel Around the Country by Bus

Taking an intercity bus in Turkey is a lot like taking an airplane in other countries. Since most Turks travel this way, bus terminals are as heavily trafficked as airports, and house a myriad of different companies with buses departing around the clock for every corner of the country. Seats are assigned, with unrelated males and females usually not seated together. During the ride, a uniformed bus attendant will regularly come around distributing snacks, water, and tea and coffee for no extra charge; he'll also offer you lemon-scented cologne to refresh your face and hands. To entertain passengers, films are shown en route—though don't necessarily expect subtitles.

Experience and Appreciate Different Religions

Turkey is a cultural crossroads where the world's three major religions have coexisted for centuries, and one of the most surprising things for many visitors is the way these religions are juxtaposed. Particularly in Istanbul, but in other places as well, you'll see ancient churches and synagogues right around the corner from mosques. This is an excellent opportunity to learn about different religious traditions as you listen to the Muslim call to prayer, visit Istanbul's Jewish Museum, or gaze at Eastern Orthodox iconography in a Byzantine church.

QUINTESSENTIAL TURKEY

Tea

Visitors who come to Turkey expecting to be served thick Turkish coffee at every turn are in for a surprise—tea is the hot beverage of choice and you'll be offered it wherever you go: when looking at rugs in the Grand Bazaar or when finishing your meal in even the humblest restaurant. Tea, called *çay*, is grown domestically along the slopes of the Black Sea coast. Flavorful and aromatic, it's not prepared from tea bags, a concept that horrifies most Turks; instead, it's made in a double boiler that has a larger kettle on the bottom for heating up the water and a smaller kettle on top where a dark concentrate is made using loose tea leaves. The resulting brew—strong and rust-colored—is usually served in a small, tulip-shaped glass, with two or more cubes of sugar (but never, Allah forbid, with milk or lemon). If you want your tea weak (light), ask for an *açık çay*.

Most teahouses will also carry a range of herbal teas, which are also very popular, especially *ada çayı* (sage tea) and *ıhlamur çayı* (linden flower tea). *Elma çayı* (apple tea), usually made from a synthetic powder, is often served to tourists.

Mezes

Good things come in small packages, and the Turkish tradition of serving appetizers known as *mezes*—Turkey's version of tapas—is proof. *Mezes* originated when simple dishes—usually a slice of tangy feta cheese with honeydew melon and fresh bread—were brought out to accompany *rakı*, the anise-flavored spirit that is Turkey's national drink. From its humble origins, though, the *meze* tradition has developed into something quite elaborate. Today, in the *meyhanes* (literally "drinking places") of Istanbul and other restaurants throughout Turkey, waiters will approach your table with a heavy wooden tray loaded down with sometimes more

For many Westerners, visiting Turkey is an exotic experience, but it's incredibly easy to get drawn into the everyday rituals that make life here such a pleasure. Eat, drink, shop . . . you'll quickly understand the allure of the country and why the Turks are renowned for their hospitality.

than 20 different kinds of small dishes—smoky eggplant puree, artichoke hearts braised in olive oil, slices of cured fish, perhaps—for you to choose from. Just point at whatever looks good and the dish will be placed on your table.

Markets and Bargaining

A highlight of any trip to Turkey is a stroll through one of the country's markets; they provide the chance to experience the country at its most vibrant and colorful. The granddaddy of them all is, of course, Istanbul's Grand Bazaar, a must-see simply for its size and historical significance. Though touristy, this is the most convenient place to stock up on the souvenirs—inlaid wood backgammon sets, colorful ceramic bowls, and of course, rugs.

Remember, in all of Turkey's markets, bargaining is the norm. Every vendor (and every buyer, as you will soon discover) has his or her own style, but some general rules govern the interaction. The seller

will undoubtedly offer you a high initial price, so don't feel embarrassed to come back with a price that's much lower—try half, for starters. And remember, it's your money that's being spent, so feel free to walk out at any time—though it's both bad manners and bad business to bargain aggressively or to decline to buy once the seller has accepted your offer. And don't shop in a rush: bargaining takes time.

IF YOU LIKE

Ancient Sites

Turkey, a sort of bridge between Europe and Asia, has been a cultural crossroads for thousands of years. Numerous civilizations—Greeks from the west and Mongols from east—settled or moved through the (vast) area at one point or another, leaving lasting and impressive reminders of their sojourns. As a result, virtually every region in Turkey has a bounty of stunning ancient ruins.

Mt. Nemrut: At the top of a desolate mountain, this 2,000-year-old temple—a collection of larger-than-life statues facing the rising and setting sun—is a testament to the vanity of an ancient king.

Ani: The abandoned former capital of a local Armenian kingdom, this haunting city in the middle of nowhere is filled with the ruins of stunning churches.

Ephesus: This remarkably well-preserved Roman city has a colonnaded library that seems like it could still be checking out books and an amphitheater that appears ready for a show.

Termessos: This impregnable ancient city is set dramatically high up in the mountains above Antalya; even Alexander the Great and the Romans found it too difficult to attack.

Cappadocia's underground cities: A marvel of ancient engineering, these subterranean cities—some reaching 20 stories down and holding up to 20,000 people—served as a refuge for Christians under siege from Arab raiders.

Beaches

With 8,000 km (5,000 mi) of coastline, it's no wonder that Turkey is home to several world-famous beaches, and you can find all kinds: from pristine, remote coves to resort hotel beaches with water sports and all sorts of amenities.

With its frigid waters and sometimes rocky shores, the Black Sea is not usually considered a beach destination, but it has some stretches of lovely, sandy shoreline. The beaches at **Kilyos** just outside Istanbul, are among the nicest and are easy to get to, although you may find them crowded on the weekends.

The Aegean has crystal clear waters and a mix of resorts and quieter seaside spots, although its beaches tend to be pebbly. An exception to that is **Altınkum**, near Çeşme, a series of undeveloped coves with glorious golden sand beaches.

Turkey's Mediterranean coast has turquoise waters that stay warm well into October and an abundance of picture-perfect beaches, although overdevelopment has become a problem in some parts. Thankfully, there are still a good number of unspoiled beaches left. Dalyan's **İztuzu Beach** (a nesting ground for sea turtles) stretches for 5 sandy kilometers (3 mi), with a fresh water lagoon on one side and the Mediterranean on the other. Near Fethiye is **Ölüdeniz**, a stunning lagoon of azure waters backed by white sand. The beach at **Patara** is one of Turkey's best, an 11-km (7-mi) stretch with little but fine white sand and dunes.

Olympos, near Antalya, is another top spot, with a long crescent-shaped beach that is backed by spectacular mountains and ancient ruins.

Castles

The Byzantine and Ottoman empires may be long gone, but they left behind some truly striking monuments: churches, mosques, and palaces that still hold the power to take your breath away.

As the former capital of both empires, Istanbul has the lion's share of Turkey's most famous structures, but there are also impressive ones to be found in every other part of the country. **Aya Sofya**, the monumental church built by the emperor Justinian some 1,500 years ago, continues to be an even more awe-inspiring site— arguably the most impressive one in Istanbul or Turkey. The **Kariye Museum**, in what was the Kariye Cami, is much smaller and not as famous as the Aya Sofya, but this 12th-century Byzantine church, located on the periphery of Istanbul's old city, is filled with glittering mosaics and stunning frescoes that are considered among the finest in the world.

Topkapı Palace, the former home of the Ottoman sultans, is a sumptuous palace with stately buildings, tranquil gardens, and the must-see Harem. Also in Istanbul is the **Blue Mosque**: with its cascading domes and shimmering tiles, this exquisite mosque is one of the Ottomans' finest creations.

Edirne, not far from Istanbul, was the Ottoman capital before Istanbul. It's home to **Selimiye Cami**, the mosque that was the real masterpiece of the sultans' favorite architect, Mimar Sinan. It's massive dome has made many a jaw drop.

In Turkey's far east, near the legendary Mt. Ararat, is **Ishak Paşa Sarayı**, an 18th-century palace that seems like it was transported straight out of a fairy tale.

Museums

The country's wealth and depth of history guarantee that Turkey has lots of artifacts for its museums—even if there has been a problem with other countries shipping the booty off to foreign lands. The best and biggest museums are in Istanbul, where you can spend your days hopping from one fascinating exhibit to the other. The sprawling **Archaeology Museum**, near Topkapı Palace, holds finds from digs throughout the Middle East. Nearby is the excellent **Museum of Turkish and Islamic Art**, housed in an old Ottoman palace, which displays carpets, ceramics, paintings, and folk art. For a taste of something more up-to-date, visit the stylish **Istanbul Modern**, which has a good collection of modern Turkish art and a stunning waterfront location. Also worth visiting is the **Rahmi M Koç Industrial Museum**, an old factory that is now used to display a quirky collection of cars, trains, ships, airplanes, and other industrial artifacts that will pique the interests of children and adults.

Istanbul doesn't have a monopoly on the museum business, though. The **Gaziantep Museum**, in Turkey's southeast, is one of the country's best, with a world-class collection of Roman-era mosaics. Ankara's **Museum of Anatolian Civilizations**, found in a restored 15th-century covered market, holds masterpieces spanning thousands of years of local history. Konya, in central Turkey, is home to the fascinating **Mevlâna Museum**, dedicated to the the founder of the whirling dervishes and located inside what used to be a dervish lodge. The unusual **Museum of Underwater Archaeology**, in a 15th-century castle in Bodrum on the Aegean coast, displays booty found in local shipwrecks.

ISLAM

Islam and Muhammad

Islam is an Abrahamic religion—one of the three largest (and somewhat interrelated) monotheistic religions in the world. The prophet Muhammad is believed to be descended from Ishmael, son of Abraham, through a union with his wife Sarah's handmaiden, Hagar. Abraham also sired Isaac, who was one of the patriarchs of Judaism and Christianity. Thus, many of the prominent figures in Judaism and Christianity—Adam, Moses, and Jesus—are also revered as prophets in Islam.

Muhammad was born in Mecca on the Arabian peninsula (near the Red Sea in present day Saudi Arabia). He became a religious figure in 610 AD when, according to Islamic tradition, while meditating in solitude he began to receive visions from the angel Gabriel. The words of these visitations became the shuras (verses) of the Koran, the holy book of Islam. When Muhammad first began preaching the new religion he was met with hostility by pagan tribesmen and forced to flee to Medina (also in Saudi Arabia)—one duty of each Muslim is to make the pilgrimage, or *haj*, from Mecca to Medina on foot, a commemoration of Muhammad's flight.

After converting the people of Medina to Islam, Muhammad returned to Mecca and converted his home town, and by the end of the 6th century, Islam was the dominant religion in Arabia. In the subsequent centuries Muslim armies would sweep across North Africa and into Spain, throughout the Levant and eastward into Central Asia and Persia. Turkic peoples were converted to Islam sometime during their journey across Asia, and when the Seljuks swept through Byzantine territory in Asia minor, they brought Islam with them.

Islam Today

Islam is a comprehensive religion and its tenets touch all aspects of life. Muslims pray five times a day: at sunrise, midday, in the afternoon, at sunset, and in the early evening—exact times are determined by the sun's passage. One of the first things visitors to Istanbul notice is the sound of the call to prayer—called the muezzin—wafting from the minarets of local mosques. At prayer time, Muslims must perform their ritual ablutions, washing their hands and feet, before bowing down in the direction of Mecca (southeast in Istanbul) to pray. The focal point of Muslim prayer is the Sacred Mosque in Mecca, at the center of which is the Kabaa, a black cubical shrine said to have been built by Abraham and rebuilt by Muhammad.

Despite a lot of praying, modern Turks tend to have a relaxed approach to their religion. Many drink alcohol and smoke cigarettes—both of which are forbidden by strict interpretations of Islam. They don't, however, eat pork. While the Koran expressly forbids eating carnivores and omnivores, pigs are a particular source of disgust to Turks. Turkish men can also be shameless flirts and modern women often dress in contemporary and revealing couture, though such behavior is not in keeping with Islamic concepts of personal modesty. There are, however, a great many conservative folks: housewives in headscarves shop for their families at neighborhood bazaars and old men gather at the neighborhood tea house. In the modern Republic of Turkey, the role of religion in society is hotly debated as the political old guard fights with the young, often more religious majority, over Atatürk's definition of secularism.

Islam and Art

Turkey enjoys a proud tradition of contributing to Islamic art. Ottoman mosque architecture incorporated many of the Byzantine design elements that Mehmet II's armies found in Constantinople. Ottoman mosques with their spacious courtyards and mammoth domes, notably Sultanahmet Mosque and the mosque of Suleiman the magnificent (in Edirne), are essentially variations on Aya Sofya. Ottoman art also boasts some of the most elaborate and colorful tile designs in the world. The best Ottoman tiles were created in İznik during the 16th and 17th centuries. Ottoman tiles sport dazzling geometric and floral designs, which adhere to the Islamic prohibition of depicting human figures. This ban (which scholars believe inspired the iconoclastic period during which the Byzantines actually destroyed their own icons), originated out of a desire to discourage idolatry. When Mehmet II conquered Istanbul, the first thing to go were the mosaics and frescoes. The conqueror recognized, however, that the Christian images were works of art rendered in painstaking detail by talented artists and, rather than having the images scratched out, he merely had them painted over. The Sultan's foresight has allowed restorers to uncover many of the Byzantine images that adorned the walls of the city's churches before 1453.

Ramadan

The Islamic holy month of Ramadan, called "Ramazan" in Turkish, lasts for 30 days and is an especially pious time. During it, observant Muslims abstain from eating, drinking, smoking, and sexual relations, from dawn to sunset; this self-denial teaches restraint and humility and is meant to bring one closer to God. Those who are fasting start each day with a predawn meal called *sahur.* At sundown, the fast is broken with a meal called *iftar,* which traditionally includes dates, soup and bread, olives, and other foods. Many restaurants offer special *iftar* fixed menus during Ramadan. In small towns and conservative parts of Turkey it may be hard to find restaurants open during the day during Ramadan, but in most cities and tourist areas it's not an issue. Though it's understood that non-Muslims will not be fasting, it's respectful to avoid eating in public (e.g., on the street or on public transportation) during Ramadan. You should also be prepared for the fact that in many places, even touristy areas like Sultanahmet in Istanbul, it's customary for drummers to walk around in the wee hours of the morning to wake people for the *sahur*—which can make for a rather startling, and early, awakening. The end of Ramadan is celebrated with a three-day holiday called Ramazan Bayramı or *Şeker Bayramı* ("sugar holiday"), during which people visit family and friends and plentifully consume sweets.

Ramazan Bayramı is a national holiday, and schools and most businesses are closed for the duration; museums and other attractions, however, generally close only for the first day of the holiday. In Turkey this is an especially busy time to travel, comparable to Thanksgiving in the United States. Projected dates are as follows. In 2009: Ramadan, Aug. 21 to Sept. 19; Şeker Bayramı, Sept. 20 to 22. In 2010: Ramadan, Aug. 10 to Sept. 8; Şeker Bayramı, Sept. 9 to 11.

FAQS

Is Turkey cheap?

It depends on where you go. Istanbul, coastal towns in high season, and other tourist locations, like parts of Cappadocia, are quite a bit more expensive than elsewhere in Turkey. Hotels, especially, in Istanbul can be expensive—even along the lines of Paris or New York—though there are budget options. Anything imported is also expensive, so a cup of coffee at Starbucks in Istanbul will cost about the equivalent of $2.50 and a burger meal at McDonalds can cost as much as $5. Anything you buy at the Grand Bazaar or on Istiklal Street, in Istanbul, will be much more expensive than the same wares purchased off the beaten track.

How do I change money?
Does Turkey use the euro?

The Turkish word for change office is *doviz*. In Istanbul and most other tourist hubs, they seem to be everywhere. The fees for changing money aren't usually too outrageous, even in tourist locales; however, your best option is to use your ATM card, with which you usually get that day's exchange rage. Turkey doesn't use the euro (and beware sellers that insist you pay in foreign currency, which is illegal). The currency in Turkey is the New Turkish Lira. At the time of printing $1=1.60 TL and €1=2.14 TL. In January 2009 the New Turkish Lira (which replaced the old lira: during an era of rampant inflation it was once counted in the millions) will revert to being simply the Turkish Lira once more.

Will it be hard to find an alcoholic beverage in a Muslim country?

The anise-flavored spirit rakı, Turkey's national drink, is the traditional accompaniment to a meal of mezes and fish. In large cities like Istanbul and İzmir, and in resort towns along the coast, rakı is consumed quite liberally, as is Efes, the national beer. However, in smaller towns and more conservative parts of the country (particularly central Anatolia), don't be surprised if alcohol is not for sale in restaurants or shops. Because of high taxes, alcoholic drinks, particularly those that are imported, are a fair bit more expensive in Turkey than they are in North America or Europe.

Is Turkish food spicy?

Not really. Turkish cuisine is similar to Greek and Hungarian food. Many dishes consist of roasted meat and boiled or roasted vegetable and rice dishes. Turks often add red pepper on the side, but even heaped generously on your food, it generally won't set the mouth afire. The only thing that might take you by surprise is a roasted pepper, which often comes as a side with kebab dishes. Anything food with heat is easily disarmed with a ubiquitous Turkish favorite—yogurt.

Will Ramadan affect my visit?

Ramadan, the month of fasting between sunrise to sunset, is one of the most exciting times to be in Turkey because after sunset, most Turks party down. It's even rumored that your average Istanbullu actually gains weight during the fast. Elsewhere in Turkey, the degree of adherence to the fast increases in proportion to how far east you venture. In Istanbul and other tourist destinations it's not a problem to find restaurants that are open during the day, although in smaller and more conservative towns the profusion of closed eateries and cafés might make it more difficult to get a bite to eat, but it's by no means impossible.

Do I need to cover up?

No man or woman on the street is ever forced to wear a head scarf, turban, or veil, though many Turkish women do. Due to Turkey's strict secularism, there are some government institutions where the covering of women is banned. In mosques, however, all women—including tourists—are expected to wear head scarves and all visitors must remove their shoes. In Istanbul and in many coastal cities women can dress provocatively and even wear bikinis without fear while in more conservative cities such behavior is frowned upon.

Are the people friendly?

Yes! Turks are renowned for their hospitality and any local will gladly tout this reputation. In Istanbul you might find some cosmopolitan snobbishness, depending on the neighborhood, but just about everywhere else throughout the country Turks are friendly, talkative, and passionate, and often sport large grins along with a hidden mischievous side. As long as you are polite and avoid insulting the nation, its symbols or its politics, you'll do just fine and in all probability you'll be awed by how kind and friendly Turkish people are.

What if I don't speak Turkish?

As in any European nation, it benefits salesmen and waiters in tourist hot spots to speak English, and many young professionals and students also make it a priority to learn English. Some schools even have their instruction entirely in English. There's a good chances that the proprietors of your hotel, the taxi drivers, and the restaurant servers that you meet will all speak perfectly adequate English. Outside of these groups, and in more remote locations, your average Turk speaks little to no English but even still you probably won't have too big a problem. Turkish is not a complicated language, and learning a few key phrases is a good idea before traveling (⇨ *see the vocabulary lists at the back of this book*). Turkish is also an easy language to read as it is written in the Latin alphabet and is entirely phonetic. For the most challenging of linguistic tangles, pointing in a dictionary or trying the same word in a few other languages will often suffice.

Should I be afraid of terrorism?

Terrorism does, unfortunately, seem to be a part of the world we live in today and there is a certain amount of risk inherent in traveling anywhere. In Istanbul the risk of being the victim of a terrorist attack is not much higher than in any European capital: London and Madrid have both been host to terrorist attacks far greater in magnitude than anything in Istanbul. Elsewhere in Turkey the threat level depends on where you are. In the tourist friendly cities of the Mediterranean and Aegean regions as well as Cappadocia the risk is negligible. In the east, where the government is still fighting Kurdish separatists, you might be in greater danger. The key thing is to stay informed, keep a low profile, and bear in mind that while terrorist attacks are dramatic you still have better odds of being struck by lightning.

GREAT ITINERARIES

CROSSROADS OF FAITH, 9 DAYS

Once home to powerful Christian and Muslim empires, the area that makes up modern Turkey has played a crucial role in the development of both religions. This tour takes you to some of the most important religious sites in Turkey, places that still poignantly convey spirituality.

Days 1 and 2: Istanbul

Arrive in Istanbul and check into a hotel in Sultanahmet. If you have time, visit two of the quintessential Istanbul sites: the Aya Sofya and the nearby Blue Mosque.

Start your second day with a visit to the Süleymaniye mosque, one of the greatest achievements of Mimar Sinan, the Ottomans' favorite architect. Then head to the western edge of Istanbul's old city walls, where you'll find the Kariye Museum in what was the Byzantine Chora church. It's filled with glittering mosaics and beautiful frescoes that are considered among the finest in the world. End your day in Eyüp Cami, a historic mosque complex on the Golden Horn that is one of the holiest areas in Istanbul.

Day 3: Konya

Take a morning flight from Istanbul to Konya and pick up a rental car at the airport. In Konya you'll see the magnificent Mevlâna Museum and tomb, dedicated to the life and teachings of Rumi Celaleddin, the 13th-century mystic who founded the order of the whirling dervishes. The city's 13th-century Alaaddin Mosque is also worth a visit. In the evening, catch a live dervish performance at the Cultural Center behind the museum if they're performing.

Days 4 and 5: Cappadocia

After Konya, head east toward the lunar landscape of Cappadocia, where the volcanic rock outcroppings and cliffs were used by local Christians for centuries ago as churches, monasteries, and homes. One of the best places to see these unique structures is in the village of Göreme. Spend the night in one of the hotels built into the stone caves. Ürgüp has what is regarded by some as the best collection of boutique hotels in Turkey.

The attractions in Cappadocia are above ground and below it. Under siege from Arab invaders in the 7th through 10th centuries, local Christians built a series of underground cities—some going down 20 stories and capable of holding 20,000 people—where they sought refuge. The ruins in Kaymaklı and Derinkuyu are marvels of ancient engineering. Get an early start if you want to beat the summer crowds, and bring a flashlight.

If you have time, consider a visit to the Ihlara Valley, a deep gorge that has numerous monasteries and churches cut into its cliffs and a lovely green river running through it.

Days 6 and 7: Cappadocia to Antakya

From landlocked Cappadocia, head south to the Mediterranean Sea and the city of Antakya, formerly known as Antioch, which played an important role in the early days of Christianity. It's a long drive of 472 km (293 mi), so plan on spending most of the day on the road. Fortunately, there's a highway for most of the way. If you get to Antakya early enough, head to the Church of St. Peter, in a cave on the outskirts of town. Blackened by 2,000 years' worth of candle smoke, this

is perhaps the oldest church in the world, where the apostle Paul preached to his converts.

The next day, spend the morning walking through the narrow lanes and the lively bazaar of Antakya's old town. Then visit the Archaeological Museum, which has an excellent collection of Roman and Byzantine mosaics and other artifacts. Antakya is famous for its Syrian-influenced cooking, influenced by Syrian cuisine, so have lunch at one of the restaurants serving local dishes (Antik Han or Sultan Sofrası are two good options). After lunch, begin your 333-km (206-mi) drive to Şanliurfa, where you can stay in one of several grand old stone houses that have been converted into small hotels.

Day 8: Şanliurfa

Many Muslims believe the biblical patriarch Abraham was born in Şanliurfa, and a fascinating and peaceful pilgrimage site has developed here, with mosques and a park with spring-fed pools filled with sacred carp. After lunch, make the quick drive to the small village of Harran, 45 km (28 mi) southeast of Şanliurfa. Harran is mentioned in the Bible as a place where Abraham lived for a period, and the village, with its ancient stone walls and unique beehive-shaped houses, has the look of a place that hasn't changed much since biblical times.

Day 9: Şanliurfa and Return to Istanbul

You can fly back to Istanbul from Şanliurfa, or from nearby Gaziantep (138 km [85 mi] away). If you have a flight from Şanliurfa later in the day, take some time to explore Şanliurfa's bustling and authentic bazaar, where coppersmiths hammer and tailors work on foot-powered sewing machines. If your flight is out of Gaziantep, consider driving there in the morning in order to have lunch at one of that city's famous restaurants. Imam Çağdaş, which has great kebabs and heavenly baklava, is your best bet.

BEST BEACHES AND RUINS, 10 DAYS

It's fairly safe to say that the main features that attract visitors to Turkey are the beaches and the magnificent archaeological sites. This itinerary covers the best of both, along the two major coastlines. Adding a couple days in Istanbul at the beginning or end would make a perfect trip.

Days 1 and 2: Arrival, Istanbul

Arrive in Istanbul and head to one of the charming small hotels in Sultanahmet (the Empress Zoe and the Sarı Konak Oteli are two favorites). If you have time, go to see the awe-inspiring Aya Sofya and the nearby Blue Mosque.

The next day, visit Topkapı Palace to get a sense of how the Ottoman sultans lived (make sure to take a tour of the Harem). From there, go to the nearby Archaeological Museum, whose collection of Roman and Greek artifacts comes from many of the sites that you'll soon be visiting. In the evening, head to one of the little neighborhoods along the Bosphorus, such as Ortaköy or Arnavutköy, for a fish dinner by the waterside (take a taxi if you're just going for dinner; the Bosphorus ferries are good if you've got time for a leisurely cruise).

Day 3: Ephesus

On the morning of Day 3, take the roughly one-hour flight to İzmir and rent a car at the airport to make the quick (79-km [50-mi]) drive down to the ancient Roman city of Ephesus. If you get an early flight out, you should be here by lunch. The site is one of the most popular tourist attractions in Turkey, and you'll see why: the buildings and monuments here are remarkably well preserved and easily give you the sense of what life must have been like in this important trading city 2,000 years ago. After Ephesus, visit the nearby Meryemana, a pilgrimage site for both Christians and Muslims where the Virgin Mary is believed to have spent her final years. Spend the night in the pleasant town of Selçuk, which is right on the doorstep of Ephesus. Or better yet, head 9 km (5.5 mi) into the mountains above Selçuk and stay in the tranquil village of Şirince, surrounded by fruit orchards and vineyards.

Day 4: Priene, Miletus and Didyma

Start off your day with a visit to Priene, an ancient Greek city that sits on a steep hill looking out on a valley below—it's about 60 km (38 mi) from Şirince. From there continue 16 km (10 mi) south to Miletus, another Greek city, where a spectacular theater is all that remains of its former glory. Twenty km (12 mi) south of here is Didyma and its magnificent Temple of Apollo, its scale as grand as the Parthenon, with 124 well-preserved columns. To keep yourself from burning out on ruins, continue another 5 km (3 mi) to the white-sand beach of Altıkum (NOTE: This is not the same as the similarly named beach near Çesme) and take a dip in the warm water, then have a meal at one of the numerous fish restaurants lining the shore. Drive back to the busy seaside resort town of Kuşadası, where there are several small *pansiyons* at which you can spend the night.

Day 5: Aphrodisias

Get an early start for the drive to the ruins of Aphrodisias, a Roman city named in honor of the goddess of love, Aphrodite. High up on a plateau and ringed by mountains, Aphrodisias has a spectacular setting and as much to offer as Ephesus, although with significantly fewer crowds. From here work your way down to the coast and the quiet town of Dalyan, where you can spend the next two nights in one of several riverside *pansiyons*.

Day 6: Dalyan, İztuzu Beach and the Rock Tombs of Kaunos

At Dalyan's riverside quay, you can hire a boat (try Dalyan Kooperatifi) to take you on to the ruins of ancient Kaunos, a city dating back to the 9th century BC and famous for its collection of tombs cut into the surrounding cliffs. Watch for the herons and storks idling in the river's reeds when you stop to take a look at the ruins. Continue your day cruise to the famed İztuzu Beach, a 5-km (3-mi) stretch of undeveloped sand that's also a nesting ground for sea turtles. There are a few snack bars at the beach, but you might want to consider bringing a picnic lunch along.

Day 7: Letoon, Patara and Kaş

The mountainous coastal region south of Dalyan is the home of ancient Lycia. An independent and resourceful people, the Lycians built a series of impressive cities whose ruins are sprinkled throughout the area, today also known as the Turquoise Riviera. To get a good glimpse of one of these Lycian cities, drive from Dalyan to Letoön, a UNESCO World Heritage Site with three fascinating temples dating back to the 2nd century BC. From here continue to Patara, another Lycian ruin that has the added bonus of being right next to one of Turkey's finest and longest beaches. You can spend the night in the relaxing little seaside town of Kaş, which has several good lodging and eating options.
■ TIP➜ If you have an extra day, take the three-hour boat trip out of Kaş through the beautiful Kekova Sound and its fascinating underwater Greek and Roman ruins.

Day 8: Olympos

On your eighth day (ninth if you spend an extra day in Kaş), drive to the Lycian ruins of Olympos, which have running through them a small river that ends at a beautiful crescent beach backed by mountains. Stay in the little village of Çıralı, a good spot for an evening visit to the legendary Chimaera, small flames of ignited gas that shoot out of the rocks of a nearby mountain.

Day 9: Antalya/Termessos (or Aspendos)

Spend your last night in the rapidly growing resort city of Antalya, but before going there head up into the rugged mountains above the city to visit the dramatic site of Termessos, an impregnable city that both Alexander the Great and the Romans decided not to attack. (Alternatively, continue 54 km [34 mi] past Antalya to visit Aspendos, a spectacular Roman theater that is still in use today.) Return to Antalya in the afternoon and stay in one of the renovated old Ottoman houses in the Kaleıçı, the city's charming old town.

Day 10: Return to Istanbul

If you have time before your flight back to Istanbul, use the morning to walk around the narrow streets of the Kaleıçı and then visit the city's large archaeological museum. If you need to stock up on souvenirs before your return, head to Antalya's bazaar before going to the airport.

TIPS

Roads are mostly in good condition, though rarely wider than two lanes or lit at night, so we recommend not driving after sunset.

This trip takes you through some of the most popular spots in Turkey, so book lodgings in advance.

Consider doing this itinerary in the fall: prices will be lower, the crowds will be gone, it won't be baking hot, and the ocean will still be warm enough for swimming.

Many towns on this itinerary have fabulous weekly markets, when farmers and craftspeople from the area come to sell their goods; try to time some of your trip around one of them. Most markets are held on Saturday, but check locally.

Istanbul

WORD OF MOUTH

"Istanbul … beautiful city, lots to see, great mixture of modern and old world, wonderful history and sights, great food, among the nicest people of all of my travels."

—risab

WELCOME TO ISTANBUL

TOP REASONS TO GO

★ **Explore the exotic monuments** of the Byzantine and Ottoman empires.

★ **Cruise up the Bosphorus,** past waterfront villages and forested slopes topped with fortresses.

★ **Haggle in the Grand Bazaar** and the Egyptian Bazaar, the ultimate shopping experiences.

★ **Sweat in a hamam** like an Ottoman sultan and discover the soothing effects of a Turkish rubdown.

★ **Luxuriate overnight in a palace**—or an Ottoman house, or even a sumptuously outfitted former prison.

★ **Sip a cup of tea as you watch** boats ply the Golden Horn.

★ **Dine in style** on Turkish delights against a backdrop of domes and minarets.

Ortaköy

1 Sultanahmet: The historic center. The Blue Mosque, the Hippodrome, Topkapı Sarayı, and Aya Sofya are just some of the above-ground attractions in historic Istanbul; below ground, ancient cisterns bring cool and quiet.

2 The Bazaar area and Environs. Haggle your way through the Grand Bazaar and the Egyptian Bazaar, then follow narrow streets down to the docks on the Golden Horn. Just beyond is the Vefa neighborhood, whose streets of traditional old wooden houses hide former Byzantine churches and magnificient Imperial mosques.

Çiçek Pasajı

Black Sea

Kilyos
Rumeli Feneri
← 8 Edrine
Poyaz
Rumeli Kavağı
Bahçeköy
Anadolu Kavağı
Sarıyer
Kefeliköy
Akbaba
Tarabya
Yalıköy
Yeniköy
Paşabahçe
Ayazağa
Boyacıköy
Çubuklu
E80
Rumelihisarı
Anadoluhisar
Arnavutköy
Bebek
Kandilli
E80
Vaniköy
O2
Beşiktaş 6
Ortaköy
Taksim
Beyoğlu
Dolmabahçe Palace
Çamlıca
Galata Bridge
4
5
Ümraniye
2
Istanbul
O4
3 1
Blue Mosque
O2
Sultanahmet
Kazlıçeşme
Kadıköy
Sea of Marmara
Bostancı
D100
KINALIADA
Burgaz
Heybeli
BURGAZADA
HEYBELİADA 7
Büyük
BÜYÜKADA
MADEN
PRINCES' ISLANDS

2

Grand Bazaar

3 **The Western Districts.**
The primarily residential
areas here hide some of the
city's less-visited mosques
and churches. The con-
servative Fatih neighbor-
hood revolves around the
conquering Sultan's mosque
and tomb; down by the
Golden Horn are the Fener
and Balat nabes, former
centers of the Greek and
Jewish communities. Out by
the medieval walls is the
former Chora church, a gem
of Byzantine art.

4 **Beyoğlu: Istanbul's
"New Town."** This is the
place to see for yourself that
new is a relative term in
Istanbul. Ornate 19th- and
early-20th-century apartment
houses crowd the hillside
neighborhood known both
as Pera and Beyoğlu. You
can shop or just watch the
people go by from one of
the countless cafés.

5 **Karaköy and the Lower
Bosphorus.** Modern art
meets ancient mosques,
Jewish history, and the lavish home of the last Ottoman Sultans. In the Fındıklı
neighborhood you can sip
tea and watch the ships go
by, then check out the Dolmabahçe palace.

6 **The Bosphorus and
Beşiktaş.** Ferries zigzag
between two continents
up the the Bosphorus, past
grand palaces, crumbling
castles, fishing villages, and
old-style wooden villas.

7 **Princes' Islands.** This
nine-island archipelago in
the Sea of Marmara has pine
forests, gardens, beaches …
and a welcome absence of
motorized traffic, the perfect
antidote to the noise and
chaos of the big city.

8 **Edirne.** This well-
preserved Ottoman city is a
good side trip from Istanbul.
Sultans competed to build
bigger and more beauti-
ful mosques here but the
Selimiye Cami, the masterpiece of Ottoman architecture, towers above them all.

GETTING ORIENTED

Istanbul is a city divided.
The Bosphorus—the water-
way joining the Black Sea
to the Mediterranean—
separates the European
side from the Asian side,
and the European side is
itself divided by the Golden
Horn, an 8-km-long (5-mi-
long) inlet that lies between
historic Sultanahmet to the
south and the New Town,
known as Beyoğlu, to the
north. In t Beyoğlu, the
14th-century Galata Tower
dominates the hillside that
rises north of the Golden
Horn; just beyond, high-rise
hotels and other landmarks
of the modern city radiate
out from Taksim Meydanı,
above the Bosphorus-side
neighborhood of Beşiktaş.
To the west, the European
suburbs line the western
shore of the Bosphorus.
The Asian suburbs are
on the eastern shore.

Dolmabahçe Sarayı

Cumhuriyet

Kartal

Batı

0   4 mi

0   4 km

ISTANBUL PLANNER

Festivals

The **Istanbul International Film Festival**, one of the city's most popular events is in mid-April, and screens come alive with a multinational array of images.

Late April sees the Istanbul's **Tulip Festival**, when parks all over the city become a riot of color.

Mid-June is the monthlong **Istanbul Arts Festival**, Turkey's premier cultural event.

June is also the month for the **International Bosphorus Festival**, with an eclectic range of dance and music events.

Late June or July is the **Kırkpınar Oil Wrestling Festival** in Edirne, outside Istanbul.

The **International Istanbul Jazz Festival** is usually in the first two weeks of July and showcases major names, new and old, from the Americas and Europe.

How Much Time Do You Need?

Istanbul is one of the most unique cities in the world and with two continents of treasures, three days will hardly do it justice. A week will give you time to enjoy the sites and sounds and smells with a little leisure. Don't miss the main sites like Topkapı, Aya Sofya, and the Bazaar, then seek out more of what you like: there are plenty more Ottoman mosques and Byzantine remnants, or you can just chill out, şay (tea) in hand, by the waters of the Bosphorus.

When to Go

Summer in Istanbul is hot and humid. Winter usually hits around October and lasts until April: all the surrounding water generally keeps temps above freezing, but a cold wind blows off the frozen Balkans and there's an occasional dusting of snow, though not much rain. Autumn and spring are pleasant and the best time to explore, but often very short.

Tour Options

Names of tour companies and their itineraries change so frequently it's best just to make arrangements through a travel agency or your hotel; the offerings are all pretty similar. A "classical tour" of Aya Sofya, the Museum of Turkish and Islamic Arts, the Hippodrome, Yerebatan Sarayı, and the Blue Mosque should cost about $25 for a half-day; the Topkapı Palace, Süleymaniye Cami, the Grand Bazaar or perhaps the Egyptian Bazaar, and lunch in addition to the above sights would be a full day and about $50 ($60–$80 by private car). Bosphorus tours often include lunch at Sarıyer and visits to the Dolmabahçe and Beylerbeyi palaces.

Visitor Information

There are several branches of the Turkish Ministry of Tourism in Istanbul, including at the airport and in Sultanahmet ✉ *Divan Yolu Cad. 3* ☎ *212/518-1802*).

If You Have Limited Time

Here is one way to plan your visit if time is limited: Start your first day off on a whirlwind, visiting the Blue Mosque and Aya Sofya to get a sense of the grandeur of the Byzantine and Ottoman empires. In the afternoon venture out of Sultanahmet to the Kariye Müzesi to see amazing frescoes and mosaics from the Byzantine era. Then check out the Grand Bazaar, where you can wander until closing time at 7 (6:30 in winter) and maybe stop at nearby Rüstem Paşa Cami for a look at the tiles. If you're staying in Sultanahmet, take an evening stroll to see the floodlit domes and minarets of the Blue Mosque and Aya Sofya.

You could spend your second morning at Topkapı Sarayı and have lunch at one of the cafés in the compound or just outside the gates so you can visit the Arkeoloji Müzesi and Eski Şark Eserleri Müzesi in the palace forecourt in the afternoon. After that, you'll have probably reached your quota of treasure- and antiquities-appreciation, so you can immerse yourself in Istanbul street life. Head to Tünel Square in the New Town, and follow İstiklal Caddesi through Galatasaray Meydanı, stopping at the Fish Market and Flower Arcade, to Taksim Meydanı, the center of the modern city.

With another day, you could see more of the Byzantines, descending into the atmospheric underground cistern, Yerebatan Sarayı, then ogling the exquisite mosaics in the Mozaik Müzesi. For even more evidence of Ottoman power, head to the lower Bosphorus to see Domabahçe Sarayı, the naval and military museums, and Yıldız Parkı.

If you want to see the Bosphorus but don't have a whole day, either take the faster Turyol cruise, or take an evening commuter ferry to relax after a hard day's sightseeing.

If you have more time, you can enjoy Istanbul with a little leisure. Think in terms of neighborhoods: you'll want to spend at least three days in the Old City, seeing the Byzantine and Ottoman monuments, and a day heading out to the less-visited Western Districts. Plan a full day around Karaköy, Beşiktaş, and the New Town, and a day cruising up the Bosphorus. You won't have trouble filling additional time: maybe another look at the mosaics and frescoes at the Kariye Müzesi, then a stop to compare them with those in the Mozaik Müzesi. Or another swing through the Grand Bazaar. Perhaps a trip to the Princes' Islands. Or just wander: few cities reward walkers more amply.

Magnificent Mosques

There are a lot of mosques in Istanbul. You won't have time to see them all, but you shouldn't leave the city without taking in the beauty and spirituality of at least several that rank as some of the most stunning architectural achievements in the world:

The Blue Mosque, for the sheer spectacle of domes, semidomes, minarets, and the 20,000 shimmering blue-green İznik tiles that lend the mosque its name.

Rüstem Paşa Cami, for İznik tiles in a magnificent array of colors and patterns.

Süleymaniye Cami, for its size, austere beauty, the enormous dome that seems to be held up principally by divine cooperation, and the tombs of the architect Sinan, his patron Süleyman the Magnificent, and the sultan's wife, Roxelana.

Sokollu Mehmet Paşa Rüstem, for elegance, harmony, and sumptuous tile work.

See It Here

Many of the antiquities on view in Istanbul have been removed from the archaeological sites of Turkey's ancient cities. Seeing them here first, will help you visualize what belongs in the empty niches you'll see elsewhere around the country.

GETTING HERE & AROUND

By Car

If you're entering or leaving Istanbul by car, E80 runs between Istanbul and central Anatolia to the east; this toll road is the best of several alternatives. You can also enter or leave the city on one of the numerous car ferries that ply the Sea of Marmara from the Yenikapi docks. Getting out of the city by car can challenging, as the signs aren't always as clear as you would hope. It's always useful to have a driving map.

Istanbul is notorious for congested traffic, cavalier attitude to traffic regulations, poor signposting, and shortage of parking spaces. In short, don't even think about renting a **car** for travel in the city.

By Ferry

One of the best ways to get in and out of Istanbul is by sea. A number of fast catamaran ferries leave from Yenikapi, which is south of Aksaray and a short taxi trip from Sultanahmet, to various ports on the southern side of the sea of Marmara. The most convenient are those to Yalova for those heading to Bursa.

By Air

Most international and domestic flights arrive at Istanbul's Atatürk Airport, although some domestic flights and an increasing number of charter airlines fly into the newer Sabiha Gokçen Airport on the Asian side of the city.

Exits and taxi stands are well signposted as you emerge from customs. There is a slow metro directly from Atatürk to the Aksaray neighborhood, where you can catch a tram to Sultanahmet, although it is usually quicker and easier to take a taxi or one of the regular shuttle buses operated by the Havaş company ($7). Taxis and the shuttle buses can be found at the main exit from the terminal building. There is no rail link to Sabiha Gokçen Airport, so if necessary take a taxi or a Havaş shuttle bus ($4).

By Bus

Turkey has an extensive system of intercity buses for travel around the country, and Istanbul's large, chaotic Esenler Otogar is the heart of it. Esenler itself is a bit out of the way, though easily accessible by metro from Aksaray and many of the bus companies have offices around the city and shuttle buses, known as a "servis," that collect passengers from the city and take them to their own mini-bus stations on the main freeway, allowing you to avoid the otogar completely.

A second smaller bus station, on the water on the Asian side of the Bosphorus, at Harem, is easily accessible by the car ferries from Eminönü.

By Train

Istanbul has two main train stations: Sirkeci, on the Eminönü waterfront in Old Istanbul, and Haydarpaşa, on the Asian side of the Bosphorus. Trains in Turkey are known for being slow, though new fast rail lines to Ankara and Konya should be ready in 2009 or 2010. The completion of a train line under the Bosphorus will change things dramatically, though the much delayed project is not expected to be ready until at least 2011.

On Foot

Istanbul is a walker's city, and the best way to experience it is to wander, inevitably getting lost—even with a good map, it's easy to lose your way in Istanbul's winding streets and alleyways. When in doubt, just ask. And when your feet get tired it's easy to use public transportation.

By Bus and Metro

Bus service is frequent, and drivers and riders tend to be helpful, so you should be able to navigate your way to major tourist stops like Sultanahmet, Eminönü, Taksim, and Beşiktaş. The fare is about $1.10 and you can purchase tickets at kiosks near major stops or on buses. The Istanbul metro is continually expanding, though the two lines still don't meet and they mostly take people out to the suburbs. One line goes north from Tünel and Taksim, and another connects the Aksaray, west of Sultanhmet, with the airport and the main bus station. The historic Tünel funicular, in operation since 1875, connects Karaköy and Tünel Square: it's a short trip, but if you're walking the hill is steep; a similar funicular takes you up the hill from Kabataş on the tram line to Taksim.

By Dolmuş

A **dolmuş** is a cross between a taxi and a bus: they run set routes, leave when full, and make fewer stops than a bus, so they're faster. In Istanbul, they mostly head out to the suburbs, so visitors may not find many routes useful, except for Beşiktaş-Taksim, for which the fare is about $1.20. Most dolmuş are bright yellow minibuses. Dolmuş stands are marked by signs but you can sometimes hail one on the street. The destination is shown on a roof sign or a card in the front window.

By Taxi

Taxis are easy and relatively cheap—a ride from Sultanahmet to Taksim is usually less than $5. Many drivers don't speak English, so write your destination on a piece of paper. Ask your hotel to call a taxi or find a stand in front of a hotel—you'll be more likely to get a driver who won't take you the long way around or use the more expensive night rate (make sure the meter says "gündüz" before midnight, meaning the day rate).

The Akbil

Istanbul's smart ticket is known as an Akbil, and it works on buses, trams, the metro, and most ferries. It's a small disk on a piece of plastic that you can hang on a key chain; it's useful if you plan to travel a lot by public transport, as fares are slightly cheaper with it, but the main draw is convenience. The initial purchase includes a deposit of about $4—you need the receipt to get the deposit back, so hold on to it. The Akbil can be bought and refilled at all major transport hubs.

By Tram

Tramways run on select routes through Istanbul. The main line runs from Kabataş, below Taksim, through Eminönü to Sultanahmet, then out past the Grand Bazaar and the Aksaray metro station to the west part of the city; the fare is about $1.10 and tickets are sold at the stations. An historic tram runs along İstiklal Caddesi between Tünel and Taksim; you can take the tram up the hill and walk back down. The fare is 50¢, payable onboard.

ISTANBUL STREET FOOD

As much as the Turkish people love to sit down for a leisurely dinner, they're also serious snackers, day and night, so finding a quick bite to eat is never a problem. The only challenge is choosing among the numerous tempting options.

Street food is not an afterthought in Turkey. Turks are quite demanding when it comes to eating on the run, expecting what is served to be fresh and made with care. While McDonald's and other chains have made inroads in Turkey, many people still prefer their country's original "fast food," which sometimes is not so fast at all. Rather, some of Turkey's most popular street food dishes require some tender loving care in preparation, and frequently will be cooked or assembled right before your eyes, though there are also simple things like roasted chestnuts available.

In Istanbul and other large cities, snack bars and food stalls are open from early morning until late into the night. Look for the crowded places: chances are they're the local favorite.

FOR THE ADVENTUROUS

Fancy a grilled intestine sandwich or stomach soup? To make *kokoreç*, seasoned lamb intestines are wound up into a long, fat loaf, grilled over charcoal and then chopped up with tomatoes and served on a half loaf of crusty bread. *Işkembe* is a soup made out of tripe—cow stomach—and flavored with garlic and vinegar. It's usually sold in small eateries that serve nothing but this soup, said to be the ultimate way to prevent a hangover. For many late night revelers in Turkey's big cities, a night out isn't complete without one of these pungent Turkish street food staples.

2

BOREK

This is the name given to a wide range of flaky filo dough pasteries. The windows of borek shops usually display their freshly baked goods, long coils of rolled-up filo dough stuffed with either ground meat, potato, or cheese and baked until golden brown. *Su boreği* is a *borek* made of buttery egg noodles layered over crumbles of tangy white cheese baked in a deep dish.

DÖNER

This cheap and filling sandwich (below) is Turkey's most popular street food. Meat, usually lamb or chicken, is grilled on a rotating vertical spit, shaved off in paper-thin slices, and served in a pocket bread called *pide* or rolled up in a tortilla-like wrap called *dürüm*. For many Turks, a *döner* sandwich, downed with a glass of refreshing *ayran* (a drink made of salted, watered-down yogurt) is a meal in itself.

KUMPIR

Think of this as a baked potato on steroids. At *kumpir* stands, massive spuds are taken hot out of the oven, split open, and filled with an almost overwhelming assortment of toppings. Options include everything from grated cheese or yogurt to chopped up pickles and hot dog bits. Its not unusual for some to ask for six or more ingredients. The *kumpir*-maker then mixes it all up into a glorious mess, and puts it back in the potato skin.

MIDYE

In Turkey, mussels (above) truly deserve to be called street food. They're usually sold by roving vendors carrying big baskets filled with glistening black shells that have been stuffed with a combination of mussels, rice, and herbs and spices. Hungry pedestrians will usually flag down the mussel seller and scarf down a few of the mollusks before continuing on their way. They're served with a squeeze of lemon. There are also specialty snack bars that serve mussels coated in batter and deep-fried.

SIMIT

Sort of the Turkish answer to the bagel, or a New York street pretzel, you'll see these humble ring-shaped, sesame-coated bread all over Turkey. They're the ultimate street food: cheap, satisfying and—when fresh from the oven—delicious. And they're available all day long, from pushcarts found on almost every street corner. The *simit* has gone slightly upscale in recent years, with the appearance in Istanbul and other Turkish cities of several chains that serve *simits* and other baked goods.

Updated by
Scott Newman

Straddling Europe and Asia, Istanbul—once known as Constantinople, capital of the Byzantine and then the Ottoman Empire—has for centuries been a bustling and cosmopolitan crossroads.

For visitors, what will probably be more striking than the meeting of East and West in Istanbul, is the juxtaposition of the old and the new, tradition and modernity. Brash concrete-and-glass hotels and office towers creep up behind historic old palaces, women in jeans or elegant designer outfits pass others wearing long skirts and head coverings, donkey-drawn carts vie with battered old Fiats and shiny BMWs for dominance of the noisy, narrow streets, and the Grand Bazaar competes with Western-style boutiques and shopping malls. At dawn, when the muezzin's call to prayer rebounds from ancient minarets, there are inevitably a few hearty revelers still making their way home from nightclubs and bars while other residents kneel on their prayer rugs facing Mecca. What a wonderful city of contrasts that manage to coexist.

EXPLORING

SULTANAHMET: THE HISTORIC CENTER

The old walled city of Istanbul rises on several hills above the port of Eminönü, and an incredible concentration of art and architecture spanning thousands of years is packed into the narrow, winding streets of this part of town. To appreciate the beauty and magic of the Old City, and for a postcard-worthy overview of its main sights, head to the Galata Bridge at the mouth of the Haliç, also known as the Golden Horn, where this inlet meets the Bosphorus. Nowhere else in Istanbul do you get such a rich feel for the magic of this ancient and mysterious place. At the eastern edge of the Old City, Topkapı Sarayı sits perched on the promontory overlooking the Bosphorus and the mouth of the Golden Horn, while behind the palace rise the imposing domes and soaring minarets of the Blue Mosque and Aya Sofya. To the southeast you can see the sprawl of old buildings that make up Sultanahmet (named after the sultan who built the Blue Mosque), with Yeni Cami close to the waterfront next to the Egyptian Bazaar; to its right, up the hill is the sprawling Süleymaniye mosque complex. Farther west is the line of the city's ancient land walls. When it comes time to see these sights up close, the best way to get around is on foot, and most of the main sites are within a short distance of each other.

MAIN ATTRACTIONS

2 **Arkeoloji Müzesi** *(Archaeology Museum).* Step into this vast repository of spectacular finds, housed in a forecourt of Topkapı Sarayı, for a head-spinning look at the civilizations that have thrived for thousands of years in Turkey. The museum was created in the 1890s, when forward-thinking archaeologist and painter Osman Hamdi Bey campaigned to keep native antiquities and some items from the former countries of the Ottoman Empire in Turkish hands. The most stunning pieces are tombs that include the so-called Alexander Sarcophagus, from Lebanon, carved with scenes from Alexander the Great's battles and once believed, wrongly, to be his final resting place. An excellent exhibit on Istanbul through the ages shows off artifacts from prehistory through the Byzantines and Ottomans, and helps put the city's complex past in context. There is also an extensive collection of classical sculpture and even a model Trojan horse for the kids.

Fodor'sChoice
★

Another building in the courtyard of Topkapı Sarayı houses the **Eski Şark Eserleri Müzesi** (Museum of the Ancient Orient), where you will be transported to even earlier times: The vast majority of the panels, mosaics, obelisks, and other artifacts here, from Anatolia, Mesopotamia, and elsewhere in the Arab world, date from the pre-Christian centuries. A particularly intricate tablet is the Treaty of Kadesh from the 13th century BC, perhaps the world's earliest known peace treaty, an accord between the Hittite king Hattusilis III and the Egyptian pharaoh Ramses II. The **Çinili Köşkü** (Tiled Pavilion) is one of the most visually pleasing sights in all of Istanbul—a bright profusion of colored tiles covers this one-time hunting lodge of Mehmet the Conqueror, and inside are ceramics from the early Seljuk and Ottoman empires, as well as tiles from İznik, the city that produced perhaps the finest ceramics in the world during the 17th and 18th centuries. In summer, you can mull over these glimpses into the distant past as you sip coffee or tea at the café in the garden. ⊠ *Gülhane Park, next to Topkapı Sarayı* ☎ *212/520–7740* ✉ *$8 (total) for the 3 museums* ⊙ *Archaeology Museum: Tues.–Sun. 9:30–5, ticket sales until 4:30.*

NEED A BREAK?

Java Studio, a coffeehouse and art gallery, is the best place in Sultanahmet to find North American–style brewed coffees, milkshakes, and baked goodies that will remind you of home. Owner Jennifer Gaudet, a Canadian expat, donates 20% of her profits to charity and is a great source of information about goings-on in Sultanahmet. ⊠ *Dalbastı Sokak 13, Sultanahmet* ☎ *212/517–2378* ▬ *MC, V.*

3 **Aya Sofya** *(Hagia Sophia, Church of the Holy Wisdom).* This soaring edifice is perhaps the greatest work of Byzantine architecture and for almost a thousand years, starting from its completion in 537, was the

Fodor'sChoice
★

Istanbul: History in Architecture

Byzantium was already 1,000 years old when, in AD 326, Emperor Constantine the Great began to rebuild it as the new capital of the Roman Empire. On May 11, 330, the city was officially renamed "New Rome," though it soon became known as Constantinople, the city of Constantine. Constantine's successors expanded the city and gave it new walls, aqueducts, and churches.

Under the emperor Justinian (ruled 527–65) Constantine's capital reached its apogee, with the construction of the magnificent Hagia Sophia, or Church of the Holy Wisdom (known as Aya Sofya in Turkish) on the site of a church originally built for Constantine. This awe-inspiring architectural wonder still dominates Istanbul's skyline. Constantinople became the largest, wealthiest metropolis the Western world had ever seen.

The Byzantine Empire began to decline toward the end of the 11th century and a devastating blow came in 1204, when the western Europeans of the Fourth Crusade, who were supposed to be on their way to recapture Jerusalem, decided that instead of going another thousand miles to fight a load of Muslims, they'd sack and occupy Constantinople, forcing members of the Byzantine dynasty to flee to Trabzon on the Black Sea coast. The Byzantines eventually regained control, but neither the city nor the Byzantine Empire recovered.

Constantinople was more of a collection of villages set amongst ruins than a city. Byzantine artists set to work, however, to restore and redecorate the damaged churches, and in their work in the mosaics and frescos of the church of the Holy Savior in Chora, we can see the first breath of the renaissance that would be carried west to Italy by artists and intellectuals fleeing the arrival of the Turks.

The Ottoman sultan Mehmet II, known as Fatih (the Conqueror), conquered the much-diminished Constantinople in 1453, rebuilt it, and made the city once again the capital of a great empire. The Turks officially named the new city as Konstantiniyye, but in time ConSTANtinoPLe was shortened to "Stanbul" by the Greeks and westerners, and to "Istanbul," by the Turks.

In 1468 Mehmet II began building a palace on the hill at the tip of the city where the Golden Horn meets the Bosphorus. Later sultans embellished and extended the building until it grew into the fabulous Topkapı Sarayı. Most of the finest Ottoman buildings in Istanbul, however, date from the time of Süleyman the Magnificent (ruled 1520–1566), who led the Ottoman Empire to its highest achievements in art and architecture, literature, and law. Süleyman and his court commissioned the brilliant architect Sinan (1489–1587) to design buildings that are now recognized as some of the greatest examples of Islamic architecture in the world, including such mosques as the magnificent Süleymaniye, the intimate Sokollu Mehmet Paşa, and the exquisitely tiled Rüstem Paşa. The monuments built by these titans, or in their honor, dominate and define the city of Istanbul and lead you into the arms of the past at every turn.

2

world's largest and most important religious monument. Only Saint Peter's in Rome, not completed until the 17th century, surpassed Aya Sofya in size and grandeur. It was the cathedral of Constantinople, the heart of its spiritual life, and the scene of imperial coronations. It was also the third church on this site: the second, which you can see the foundations of at the entrance, was burned down in the antigovernment Nika riots in 532. The Emperor Justinian commissioned the church and, in response to his dictum that Aya Sofya be the grandest place of worship ever built—far greater than the temples whose columns were incorporated in the church—craftsmen devised a magnificent dome. New architectural rules were made up as the builders went along and not all were foolproof, since the dome collapsed during an earthquake just two years after the church was completed. The church stood a shell until a new architect built a steeper dome, and the aged Justinian finally reopened the church on Christmas Eve 563. Subsequent repairs and such structural innovations as flying buttresses remained firmly in place, making it the prominent fixture it is on the Istanbul skyline to this day. Over the centuries Aya Sofya has survived additional earthquakes, looting crusaders, and the city's conquest by Mehmet the Conqueror in 1453.

Mehmet II famously sprinkled dirt on his head before entering the church after the conquest as a sign of humility. His first order was for the blood to be cleaned off the walls and the images plastered over to convert the church into a mosque, and succeeding sultans added its four minarets. Atatürk made the Aya Sofya into a museum in 1936 and a project of restoration, including the uncovering of the mosaics began. In recent years there has been growing pressure for Aya Sofya to be reopened for Muslim worship, and some people gather to pray at the museum at midday on Friday.

As Justinian may well have intended, the impression that will stay with you longest, years after a visit, is the dome; as you enter the half domes trick you before the great space opens up with the immense dome, almost 18 stories tall and more than 30 meters (100 feet) across towering above—look up into it and you'll see the spectacle of thousands of gold tiles glittering in the light of 40 windows. The dome is believed to have originally been decorated with a giant cross, and the apse still displays a mosaic of the Virgin and child from the 9th century, which looks tiny but is actually 16 feet high. To the right of the Virgin is the archangel Gabriel, while Michael, on the left is mostly lost. Ongoing restoration has filled a quarter of the dome with an ugly

A COLUMN OF LUCKY CHARMS

The marble-and-brass **Sacred Column**, in the north aisle of Aya Sofya, to the left as you enter through the main door, is laden with legends. It's thought that the column weeps water that can work miracles, and over the centuries believers have worn a hole as they caress the column to come in contact with the miraculous moisture. It's also believed that if you place your thumb in the hole and turn your hand 360 degrees, any wish you make while doing so will come true.

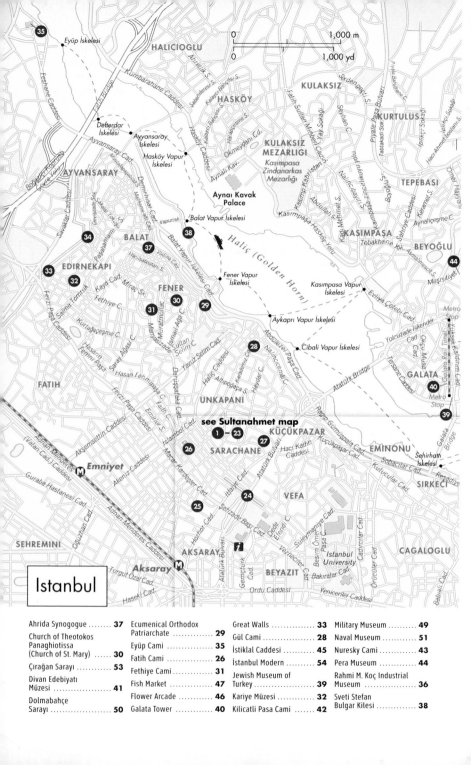

Istanbul

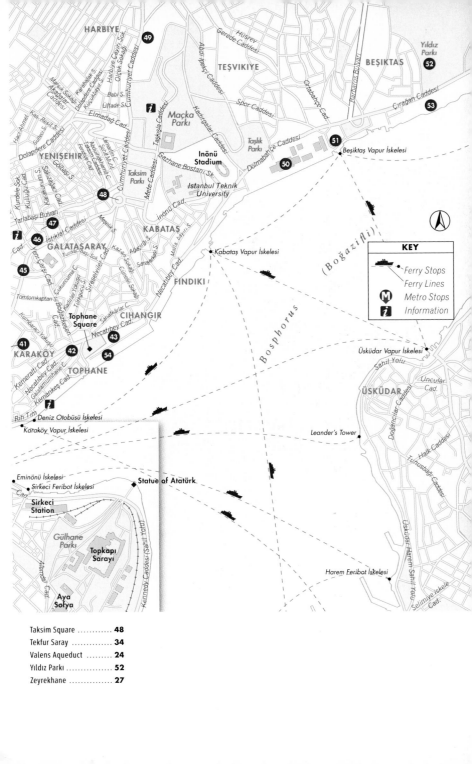

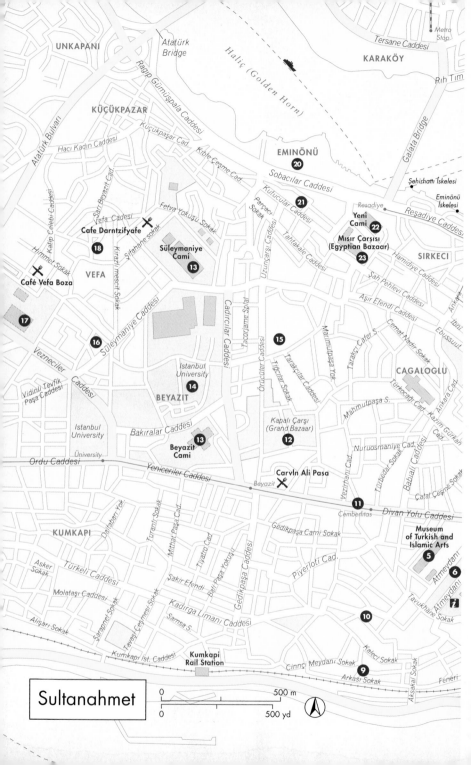

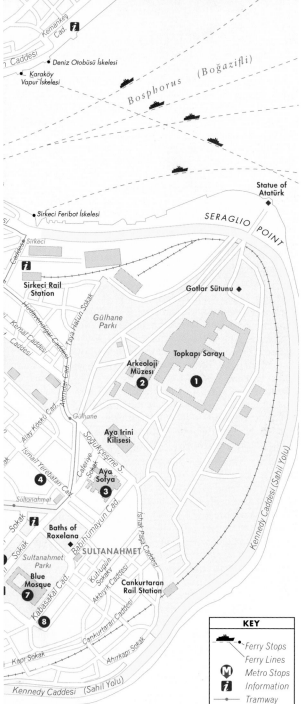

KEY

- Ferry Stops
- Ferry Lines
- Metro Stops
- Information
- Tramway

scaffold for over a decade, and the project seems unlikely to be finished soon. Look for the special round disk on the floor, where the throne of the Byzantine emperors is believed to have stood. Upstairs is a central gallery once used by female worshipers. The north gallery is famous for its graffiti, ranging from Nordic runes to a complete Byzantine galley under sail. At the far end of the south gallery are several imperial portraits, including, on the left, the Empress Zoe, whose husband's face and name were clearly changed as she went through three of them. On the right is the Emperor with his Hungarian wife Irene and their son, Alexius, stuck around the corner. Heading back you will see the great 13th-century Deesis mosaic of Christ flanked by the Virgin and John the Baptist, breathing the life of the early Renaissance that Byzantine artists would carry west to Italy after the fall of the city—note how the shadows match the true light source to the left. On the way out, through the "vestibule of the warriors" a mirror reminds you to look back at the mosaics of Justinian and Constantine presenting the church and the city respectively to the Virgin Mary. ⌧ *Aya Sofya Sq.* ☏*212/522–1750* ⌦*$16* ☉*Tues.–Sun. 9–7, ticket sales until 6:30.*

⑤ Blue Mosque *(Sultan Ahmet Cami).* Only after you enter the Blue Mosque
Fodor'sChoice do you understand why it is so named. Inside, 20,000 shimmering blue-
★ green İznik tiles are interspersed with 260 stained-glass windows; calligraphy and intricate patterns are painted on the ceiling. After the dark corners and stern, sour faces of the Byzantine mosaics in Aya Sofya, this light-filled mosque is positively uplifting. Such a favorable comparison was the intention of architect Mehmet Aga, known as Sedefkar ("Worker of Mother-of-Pearl"), whose goal was to surpass Justinian's crowning achievement (Aya Sofya). At the bequest of Sultan Ahmet I (ruled 1603–17), he spent just eight years creating this masterpiece of Ottoman craftsmanship, beginning in 1609, with the Sultan himself even lending a hand in the construction, and many believe he did indeed succeed in outdoing the splendor of Aya Sofya.

But Mehmet Aga went a little too far when he surrounded the massive structure, studded with domes and semidomes, with six minarets: this number briefly linked the Blue Mosque with the Elharam Mosque in Mecca—and this could not be allowed. So Sultan Ahmet I was forced to send Mehmet Aga down to the Holy City to build a seventh minaret for Elharam and reestablish the eminence of that mosque. Ahmet, his wife, and his three sons are interred in the stunningly tiled *türbe* (mausoleum) at a corner of the complex, which at one time also included such traditional Muslim institutions as an almshouse, an infirmary, and a school. From here—or from the Hippodrome or any other good viewpoint— you can see the genius of Mehmet Aga, who didn't attempt to surpass the massive dome of Aya Sofya but instead created a secession of domes of varying sizes to cover the massive interior space, creating an effect that is both whimsical and uplifting. ⌧*Sultanahmet Sq.* ⌦*Mosque free* ☉*Blue Mosque: daily 9–5, access restricted during prayer times, particularly at midday on Fri.*

❶ Topkapı Sarayı *(Topkapı Palace).* See the highlighted feature in this
Fodor'sChoice chapter.
★

2

❹ Yerebatan Sarnıcı *(Basilica Cistern).* The great problem with the site of
★ Byzantium was the lack of fresh water, and so for the city to grow, a
great system of aqueducts and cisterns was built, the most famous of
which is the Basilica cistern, or Yerebatan Saray, the "sunken palace."
A journey through this ancient underground waterway takes you along
sparsely lit walkways that lead between the 336 marble columns that
rise 26 feet to support Byzantine arches and domes, from which water
drips unceasingly; classical music is usually playing softly in the background. Many of the columns probably come from the original buildings of Constantine, which were built a little too quickly, and soon
started collapsing. The most famous piece features upturned Medusa
heads. The cistern was always kept full as a precaution against long
sieges, and fish, presumably descendants of those that arrived in Byzantine times, still flit through the dark waters. What's the thrill of visiting
what is essentially a municipal waterworks? The cistern is hauntingly
beautiful, an oasis of cool, shadowed, cathedral-like stillness, and a
particularly relaxing place to get away from the hubbub of the Old City
in summer. ⊠ *Yerebatan Cad. at Divan Yolu* ☎ *212/522–1259* ⊕ *www.
yerebatan.com* ✆ *$8* ☉ *Daily 9–4:30.*

ALSO WORTH SEEING

❻ Hippodrome. It takes a bit of imagination to appreciate the Hippodrome,
once a Byzantine stadium for chariot racing, with seating for 100,000.
There isn't much here anymore, but the shape remains, and hundreds
of peddlers selling postcards, nuts, and souvenirs create a hint of the
festive atmosphere that must have prevailed during chariot races and
circuses. Notably absent are the rows and rows of seats that once surrounded the track and the life-size bronze sculpture of four horses that
once adorned the stadium—the Venetians looted the statue, and it now
stands above the entrance to the basilica of San Marco in Venice. You
can, however, see several other monuments that once decorate the central podium. The **Dikilitaş** (Egyptian Obelisk) from the 15th century
BC probably marked the finish line; it has reliefs of the Emperor in his
royal box, which stood opposite, under the Blue Mosque. There is
also the **Örme Sütün** (Column of Constantinos) and the **Yılanlı Sütun**
(Serpentine Column), the latter of which was taken from the Temple
of Apollo at Delphi in Greece, where it was dedicated after the Greek
victory over the invading Persians in the 5th century BC. Views of the
Blue Mosque, just across the way, with its magical cascade of domes,
are quite stunning. Down the hill to the southeast you can see the giant
southern foundations of the Hippodrome. ⊠ *Atmeydanı, Sultanahmet*
✆ *Free* ☉ *Accessible at all hrs.*

❺ İbrahim Paşa Sarayı *(Ibrahim Paşa Palace).* Süleyman the Magnificent
commissioned the great architect Sinan to build this stone palace—the
most grandiose residence in Istanbul—overlooking the Hippodrome,
and the sultan's beloved childhood friend, brother-in-law, and grand
vizier, İbrahim Paşa, took up residence here sometime around 1524 with
his wife, Süleyman's sister (Süleyman lived over in Topkapı). The men
were inseparable, taking all their meals together and watching games
in the Hippodrome from the palace balconies. İbrahim Paşa, however,
didn't have long to enjoy his new home: despite his bonds with the

Most Turkish hamams have separate facilities for men and women.

sultan, he was strangled one night after dinner in Topkapı when he became too powerful for the liking of Süleyman's power-crazed wife, Roxelana, who wanted her son-in law, Sokullu Mehmet Paşa to be grand vizier. The palace now houses the **Türk Ve Islâm Eserleri Müzesi** (Museum of Turkish and Islamic Arts), where you can learn about the lifestyles of Turks at every level of society, from the 8th century to the present. There is an excellent collection of Ottoman arts and crafts here, particularly ceramics and carpets. ⊠ *Atmeydanı 46, Sultanahmet* ☎ *212/518–1385* ✉ *$8* ⊗ *Tues.–Sun. 9–4:30.*

❻ **Mozaik Müzesi** *(Mosaic Museum).* One of Istanbul's more fascinating
★ sights is often overlooked, hidden as it is in the midst of the Arasta Bazaar and overshadowed by such neighbors as the Blue Mosque and Aya Sofya. The **Great Palace** of Byzantium, the imperial residence of Constantine and other Byzantine emperors when they ruled lands stretching from Iran to Italy and from the Caucasus to North Africa stood here, reaching all the way down to the sea; it consisted of several terraces, with various palaces, churches, and parks, almost all of which are gone. Only scant ruins remained by 1935, which was when archaeologists began uncovering what is thought to have been the floor of a palace courtyard, paved in some of the most elaborate and delightful mosaics to survive from the era: many of them have scenes of animals, flowers, and trees, rural idylls far removed from the pomp and elaborate ritual of the imperial court. New excavations, behind the Fours Seasons Hotel are to open as an archaeological park. As you walk the streets of Sultanahmet you will see many fragments of masonry and brickwork that were once part of the palace, and several cisterns have

Continued on page 62

CLOSE UP

Hamams

One of the great pleasures of a visit to Istanbul is spending a lazy afternoon in one of the city's Turkish baths, known as hamams, some of which are in exquisite buildings more than 500 years old. Hamams were born out of necessity: this was how people kept clean before their was home plumbing, but they also became an important part of Ottoman social life, particularly for women. Men had the coffeehouse and women the hamam, a place to gossip and relax.

Now that people bathe at home, hamams are becoming less of a central element in Turkish life. There are still bathhouses dotted throughout Istanbul, but many wouldn't survive without steady tourist traffic.

Most hamams have separate facilities for men and women. Each has a *camekan*, a large domed room with small cubicles where you can undress, wrap yourself in a thin cloth called a *peştemal*, and put on slippers or wooden sandals—all provided. Then you'll continue through a pair of increasingly hotter rooms. The first, known as the *soğukluk*, has showers and toilets and is used for cooling down at the end of your session. Next is the *hararet*, a steamy and softly lit room with marble washbasins along the sides. You can douse yourself by scooping water up from one of the basins with a copper bowl. In the middle of the room is the *göbektaşı*, a marble platform heated by furnaces below and usually covered with reclining bodies. This is where, if you decide to take your chances, a traditional Turkish massage will be "administered."

The masseur, will first scrub you down with a rough, loofa-like sponge known as a *kese*. Be prepared to lose several layers of dead skin. Once you're scrubbed, the masseur will soap you up into a lather, rinse you off, then conduct what will probably be the most vigorous massage you'll ever receive. Speak up if you want your masseuse to use a lighter hand.

Once you've been worked over, you can relax (and recover) on the *göbektaşı* or head back to your change cubicle, where you'll be wrapped in fresh towels and perhaps massaged a bit more, this time with soothing oils. Most cubicles have small beds where you can lie down and sip tea or juice brought by an attendant.

One of the best hamams in Istanbul is **Cağaloğlu Hamamı** (✉ *Prof. Kazı Gürkan Cad. 34, Cağaloğlu* ☎ *212/522–2424*), near Aya Sofya in a magnificent 18th-century building. Florence Nightingale and Kaiser Wilhelm II once steamed here; the clientele today remains generally upscale. Self-service baths cost $20; an extra $18 buys you the Turkish massage. It's open daily 8–8 for women and until 10 PM for men.

Also recommended is the even older **Çemberlitaş Hamam** (✉ *Vezirhan Cad. 8, Çembrelitaş* ☎ *212/522–7974*) which dates back to 1584.

Both of the above cater primarily to tourists. For a more local flavor, try the **Gedikpaşa Hamam** (✉ *Hamam Cad. 65-67, Beyazıt* ☎ *212/517–8956*), which has been in operation since 1457.

2

TOPKAPI

SHOWPLACE OF THE SULTANS

Like Russia's Kremlin, France's Versailles, and China's Forbidden City, Istanbul's Topkapı Sarayı is not simply a spectacular palace but an entire universe unto itself. Treasure house of Islamic art, power hub of the Ottoman Empire, home to more than twenty sultans, and site of the sultry Seraglio, the legendary Topkapı remains a world of wonders.

Astride the promontory of Sultan Point—"the very tip of Europe"—Topkapı Sarayı has lorded over Istanbul for more than 400 years. As much a self-contained town-within-a-town as a gigantic palace, this sprawling complex perches over the Bosphorus and was the residence and center of bloodshed and drama for the Ottoman rulers from the 1450s to the 1850s. At one time home to some 5,000 residents—including a veritable army of slaves and concubines—Topkapı was also the treasure house to which marauding sultans brought back marvels from centuries of conquest, ranging from the world's seventh largest diamond to the greatly revered Mantle of the Prophet Muhammad.

Today's visitors are captivated by the beauty of Topkapı's setting but are even more bewitched by visions of the days of ruby wine and roses, when long-ago sultans walked hand-in-hand with courtesans amid gardens lit by lanterns fastened to the backs of wandering giant tortoises. As privileged as

it was, however, Topkapı was rarely peaceful. Historians now recount horrifying tales of strangled princes, enslaved harem women, and power-mad eunuchs. Not surprisingly, just in front of the main Gate of Salutations (from which decapitated heads were displayed centuries ago) stands the Fountain of the Executioner—a finely carved bit of onyx stonework where mighty vassals once washed the blood of victims from their hands in rose-petaled water. It is history as much as beauty that rivets the attention of thousands of sightseers who stream through Topkapı.

When you've had your fill of the palace's bloody past, venture to one of its marble-paved terraces overlooking the Bosphorus. Islands, mosques, domes, crescents shining in the sun, boats sailing near the strand: here shimmers the water of the Golden Horn, a wonderland as seen by a thousand romantic 19th century travelers—the Constantinople, at last, of our dreams.

Left: Imperial Hall in Harem

FOUR CENTURIES OF BLOOD & POWER

Stretching through times of tragedy and triumph, the story of Topkapı is a saga worthy of Scheherazade. Built between 1459 and 1465 by Sultan Mehmet II, the palace was envisioned as a vast array of satellite pavilions, many topped with cupolas and domes (Turkish architectural conservatism liked to perpetuate the tents of the nomadic past in stone). Over the centuries, sultan after sultan added ever more elaborate architectural frills, until the palace acquired a bewildering conglomeration of buildings extending over four successive courtyards, each more exclusionary than the last.

Sultan Mehmet II

MANSION OR MAUSOLEUM?

While Topkapı became the power center of the Ottoman Empire—it grew to contain the **state mint, the arsenal**, and the *divan* (chamber of the judicial council)—its most fearsome aspect was the **sultan's court.** Many of its inhabitants lived their entire adult lives behind the palace walls, and it was often the scene of intrigue and treachery as members of the sultan's entourage plotted and schemed, sometimes even deposing and assassinating the sultan himself.

A SURFEIT OF SULTANS

Set with stained-glass windows and mother-of-pearl decorations the **Iftariye**, or **"Gilded Cage,"** was where the sultan's closest relatives lived in strict confinement—at least after the old custom of murdering all possible rivals was softened in the 19th century (the greatest number of victims—19 brothers—were strangled in 1595 by order of the mother of Mehmet IV; seven of his father's pregnant concubines were drowned, to boot). House arrest in this golden suite kept the internal peace but deprived the heirs to the throne of interacting with the real world. After Süleyman II spent 39 years in the Gilded Cage he proved so fearful that, in 1687, he nearly refused the sultanate. Indeed, many sultans who ascended the throne were, in effect, ruled by their mothers, the all-powerful *Valide Sultans* (Queen Mothers). The most notorious was Kösem, whose rule over two sultan sons ended in 1648 when she was strangled upon orders of a vengeful daughter-in-law. As much to escape this blood-stained past as to please visiting European royalty, Topkapı was finally abandoned in 1853 when Sultan Mecit I moved his court to Dolmabahçe Palace.

Procession of Constantinople in the Hippodrome (detail)

✉ Babihümayun Caddesi, Gülhane Park, near Sultanahmet Sq.

☎ 212/512-0480

🌐 www.topkapisarayi. gov.tr

🎫 Palace $6; Treasury $6; Harem $6

🕐 Palace & Treasury, Wed.—Mon. 9—7 in summer and 9—5 in winter; Harem: Wed.—Mon. 9:30—3:30 all year.

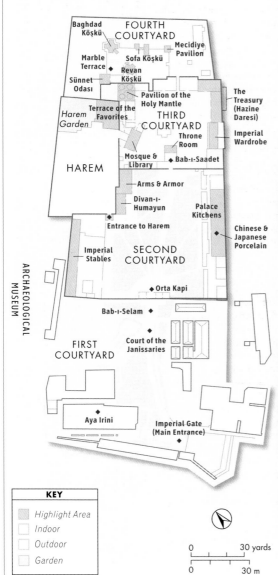

Topkapı Sarayı

Baghdad Köşkü

FOURTH COURTYARD

Mecidiye Pavilion

Marble Terrace

Sofa Köşkü

Revan Köşkü

Sünnet Odası

Pavilion of the Holy Mantle

Harem Garden

Terrace of the Favorites

THIRD COURTYARD

The Treasury (Hazine Daresi)

Throne Room

Imperial Wardrobe

Mosque & Library

Bab-ı-Saadet

HAREM

Arms & Armor

Divan-ı-Humayun

Palace Kitchens

Entrance to Harem

Imperial Stables

SECOND COURTYARD

Chinese & Japanese Porcelain

Orta Kapi

Bab-ı-Selam

ARCHAEOLOGICAL MUSEUM

Court of the Janissaries

FIRST COURTYARD

Aya Irini

Imperial Gate (Main Entrance)

KEY

- Highlight Area
- Indoor
- Outdoor
- Garden

0   30 yards
0   30 m

Imperial Gate

Harem garden

The Tiled Hall

OF RICHES UNTOLD:
TOPKAPI HIGHLIGHTS

THE FIRST COURTYARD

Upon arriving from Istanbul's noisy streets, the magic city of an Oriental tale stretches before you. Also known as the First Courtyard, the **Court of the Janissaries** has always been freely accessible to the public. In the shade of its plane trees, the turbulent Janissaries— the sultan's armed guard—prepared their meals and famously indicated their discontent by overturning the soup kettles: a dreaded protest followed, several times, by the murder of the reigning sultan. Looming over all is the **Aya Irini** church dating from the time of Justinian; it's believed to stand on the site of the first church of Byzantium but, uniquely for Istanbul, has never been converted to a mosque. On the left is the imposing **Archaeological Museum**, housing treasures from Ephesus, Troy, and other ancient sites.

Archaeological Museum

GATE OF SALUTATION

You begin to experience the grandeur of Topkapı when you pass through **Bab-ı-Selam** (Gate of Salutation). Süleyman the Magnificent built the gate in 1524; only a sultan was allowed to pass through it on horseback. Prisoners were kept in the gate's two towers before they were executed next to the nearby executioner's fountain. The palace's ticket office is on the walkway leading to this gate.

Gate of Salutation

THE SECOND COURTYARD

A vast rose garden shaded by cypress trees, the second, or **Divan**, courtyard was once the veritable administrative hub of the Ottoman empire, often the scene of great pageantry when thousands of court officials would gather before the sultan's throne. On the far left is the **Divan-ı-Humayun**, the striking open-air Assembly Room of the Council of State. Occasionally the sultan would sit behind a latticed window, hidden by a curtain, so no one would know when he was listening. Behind the council chamber is **Gülhane Park**, today best known for the **Cinili Kösk**, a charming tiled pavilion dating from Mehmet's time. On the right of the yard are the **Palace Kitchens**, where more than 1,000 cooks once toiled at immense ovens. The cavernous space now displays one of the world's best collections of porcelain, amassed over the centuries by Ottoman rulers. The Yuan and Ming celadon pottery were especially prized for their alleged ability to change color if the dish held poisonous foods.

Gate to the Divan

Kitchen area of the palace

APARTMENTS OF THE SULTANS

The sultan's own apartments are, not surprisingly, a riot of brocades, murals, colored marble, wildly ornate furniture, gold leaf, fine carving, and, of course, the most perfect İznik tiles. Beyond is the open **Courtyard of the Jinns,** above which is the Gilded Cage, where the sultan's relatives were kept under lock and key until they were needed.

THE THIRD COURTYARD

As you walk through the **Bab-ı-Saadet, or Gate of Felicity,** consider yourself privileged, because only the sultan and grand vizier were allowed to pass through this gate. It leads to the palace's inner sanctum, the Third Courtyard, site of the most ornate of the palace's pavilions. Most visitors here only got as far as the audience chamber, the **Arz Odası,** where foreign ambassadors once groveled before the sultan. Here, too, is the fabled **Treasury (Hazine Davesi).**

CHAMBER OF SACRED RELICS

On the courtyard's left side is the Hasoda Koğuşu, or Chamber of Sacred Relics (1578), which comprises five domed rooms containing some of the holiest relics of Islam. Pride of place goes to the Mantel of the Prophet Muhammad, found in a gold casket (exhibited behind shatter-proof glass). Nearby are the Prophet's Standard, or flag; a hair of his beard; his sword; and a cast of his footprint and teeth. Other relics, including the "staff of Moses" and the "cooking pot of Abraham," are also on view.

THE FOURTH COURTYARD

More of an open terrace, this courtyard was the private realm of the sultan, and the small, elegant pavilions, fountains, and reflecting pools are scattered amid tulip gardens overlooking the Bosphorus and Golden Horn. The loveliest of the pavilions, the **Baghdad Kiosk** (covered with İznik tiles), was built by Murat IV in 1638 after his conquest of Baghdad. Just off the wishing-well terrace is the **Pavilion of Circumcision** (Sünnet Odasi), also famed for its lavish tiling.

On the right side of the courtyard are steps leading to the 19th century rococo-style Mecidiye pavilion, now the **Konyali Restaurant** (open Wed.—Mon., lunch only), which serves excellent Turkish food and has a magnificent vista of the Golden Horn. On a terrace below is an outdoor café with an even better view. Go early or reserve a table to beat the tour-group crush.

İznik tiles

Dome atop Gate of Felicity

Interior Baghdad Kiosk

Circumcision Room colonnade

PLEASURE DOMES:
THE HAREM

Evoking all the exoticism and mystery of the Ottoman Empire, the Harem is a bewildering maze of 400 halls, terraces, rooms, wings, and apartments. These were the quarters of the sultan's courtesans, mostly Circassian women from the Caucasus (law forbade Muslim women to be concubines).

Seeing the forty rooms that have been open to the public reminds us that the Harem (the term means "forbidden" in Arabic) was as much about confinement as it was about luxury. Of the 1,000 women housed in the harem, many finished their days here as servants to other concubines.

Imperial Hall

Constructed under the influence of Sultan Süleyman's all-powerful Russian-born wife, Roxlana, the Harem was completed by Murat III in the late 16th century.

Built around grand reception salons—including the beautiful Imperial Hall, the Crown Prince's Pavilions, and the Dining Room of Ahmet III—the Harem was studded with fountains. They not only cooled off torrid days, but the splashes made it hard to eavesdrop on royal conversations.

Ornate ceiling in Harem

WOMEN'S QUARTERS

Adjacent to the Courtyard of the Black Eunuchs (most of whom hailed from Africa's Sudan; their roles were determined by different levels of castration), the first Harem compound housed about 200 lesser concubines in tiny cubicles, like those in a monastery.

As you move deeper into the Harem, the rooms become larger and more opulent, with the four chief wives living in grand suites around a shared courtyard.

Dining Room of Ahmet III

Most concubines were trained in music and poetry, but only those who achieved the highest status were given access to the sultan.

APARTMENTS OF THE VALIDE SULTAN

The true ruler of the Harem was the *Valide Sultan*, the sultan's mother, and her lavish apartments lay at the heart of the Harem complex. For the young women of the Harem, the road to the sultan, quite literally (using a hallway known as the "Golden Way") ran through his mother.

The Harem can only be visited by guided tour ($8). Tickets can be purchased at the separate Harem entrance (located near the Divan-i-Humayun in the Second Courtyard) and are allotted on a first-come, first-serve basis. Be sure to book early after buying general admission tickets to the palace.

DO YOU LOVE EMERALDS?
DON'T MISS TOPKAPI'S TREASURY

If you love jewels, you're in luck—at the **Topkapı Treasury (Hazine Daresi)** you can admire three of the world's most wondrous emerald stones, which are embedded in the hilt of the fabulous Topkapı dagger. Crafted in 1741, it was meant as a gift for the Shah of Persia; he could well have used it but it arrived too late—he was assassinated as the dagger was en route to him. Here also are two of the world's largest extant emeralds: uncut, they each weigh about eight pounds. Now displayed behind glass, they were originally hung from the ceiling as spectacular "lamps." Amazingly, even these mammoth gems were outshone by the 86-carat Spoonmaker diamond which, according to legend, was found by an Istanbul pauper glad to trade it for three wooden spoons. These are but six of the many jewels found here.

Sultan headgear

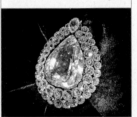
86-carat Spoonmaker diamond

A true cave of Aladdin spilling over four rooms, the treasury is filled with a hoard of opulent objects and possessions, either lavish gifts bestowed upon generations of sultans, or spoils garnered from centuries of war. The largest objects are three imperial thrones, including the gold-plated Bayram throne given to Sultan Murat III by the Khedive of Egypt in 1574. Presiding over the fourth room of the treasury is the throne sent to Istanbul by the same unfortunate shah for whom the Topkapı dagger was intended. All is enhanced by the beautiful display of turban crests and jewel-studded armor, with every possible weapon encrusted with diamonds and pearls—all giving testimony to the fact that, before the 18th century, it was the man, not the woman, who glittered like a peacock.

There are trinkets, chalices, reliquaries, and jewels, jewels, jewels. Ladies, be sure to hide your engagement rings— they will be overwhelmed in comparison!

Topkapi dagger

ROCK STARS

The most glamorous jewel heist film ever, *Topkapi* (1964) is director Jules Dassin's dazzling homage to Istanbul, diamonds, and his famous *Never on Sunday* blonde (and wife), Melina Mercouri. Playing jet-set mastermind Elizabeth Lipp, she seduces a troupe of thieves into attempting to steal the Topkapı dagger. Rooftop high jinks, a script scintillating with wit, the Oscar-winning performance by Peter Ustinov, and an eye-popping credit sequence make for a film almost as intoxicating as a visit to the Treasury itself.

been found under hotels and carpet shops, some of which are open to visitors. Down by the water, there are extensive, very overgrown remains of the facade of the **Bucoleon Palace,** private quarters of the emperors from the 6th to 11th centuries, gradually being shaken apart by the passing train line. ⊠ *Arasta Çarşısı, Kabasakal Cad., Sultanahmet* ☎ *212/518–1205* 🎫 *$3* ⊙ *Tues.–Sun. 9–5.*

TIMING YOUR VISIT TO SULTANAHMET

Check opening times when you plan your outings. Most sights around Sultanahmet, such as the Arkeoloji Müzesi and Aya Sofya are closed Monday, except the Topkapı Sarayı which is closed Tuesday. Places west of the city, like the Kariye Müzesi, and the museums on the Bosphorus are closed on Wednesday.

❾ Küçük Aya Sofya. This church was built by Justinian as the church of Sergios and Bacchus, though it's more commonly known as Küçük Aya Sofya, or "Little Aya Sofya," due to its resemblance to the great church up the hill. In fact, it was built just before Aya Sofya, in about 530, and the architects explored here many of the same ideas of the larger church but on a smaller scale. It was probably built for the rebel "monophysite" priests whom the Empress Theodora was hiding in the nearby Hormisdas palace. In 551 Pope Vigilius was dragged from the altar by the troops of Justinian who had lost patience with the Pope's unwillingness to sign off on the emperor's theological plans. Vigilius was rescued by the shocked mob and escaped the city. The church was converted to a mosque in the 16th century by Hüseyin Ağa Beyazıt II's chief of the white eunuchs. ⊠ *Küçük Aya Sofya Cad.* 🎫 *Free* ⊙ *Daily sunrise–sunset, except during prayer times.*

❿ Sokollu Mehmet Paşa Cami *(Mosque of Mehmet Paşa).* This small mosque, ★ built in 1571, is not as grand as Süleymaniye Cami, but many consider it to be the most beautiful of the mosques that the master architect Sinan built under the direction of Süleyman the Magnificent. Here, Sinan chose not to dazzle with size but to create a graceful, harmonious whole, from the courtyard and porticoes outside, to the delicately carved *mimber* (pulpit), and the gorgeous, well-preserved İznik tiles inside, set off by pure white walls, and floral-motif stained-glass windows. ⊠ *Mehmet Paşa Cad. at Özbekler Sokak, Küçük Ayasofya* ☎ *No phone* 🎫 *Free* ⊙ *Daily sunrise–sunset, except during prayer times.*

THE BAZAAR AREA AND ENVIRONS

The area between the Grand Bazaar and the shore of the Golden Horn teems with people during the day. Even though most of the old Byzantine and Ottoman buildings have long gone, the stalls and peddlers who line the narrow, rather grubby streets winding down the hill from the Grand Bazaar give an impression of what the city must have been like when it was the bustling capital of a vast empire. In addition to the Grand Bazaar and the Egyptian Bazaar, you'll come upon some of the city's most beautiful mosques here.

Safety Concerns?

A true story: A visitor to Istanbul is approached by a friendly young man who is looking for an opportunity to practice his English and would be happy to show the visitor around. The day extends into night and the friendly young man proposes to take his new friend to a club for a drink. At the end of the night, the young man has disappeared and the hapless visitor is left with a bill totaling several hundred dollars for only a few drinks, and surrounded by bunch of goons who are going to make sure the bill is paid.

Stories like this, fortunately, are the exception, not the rule. Istanbul is, for a city of close to 14 million, very safe, especially in the areas frequented by tourists. Still, like any other big city that attracts hordes of travelers, Istanbul also has its share of unscrupulous touts and shills. The busy and crowded areas around Aya Sofya and Taksim Square

seem to especially attract these types. Many of the touts who will approach you, particularly in Sultanahmet, want no more than to steer you toward a harmless carpet shop where they will earn a commission, but the odd few might be less well intentioned. Shoeshine boys love to drop their brush when walking past helpful tourists, then try to massively overcharge for a quick clean. Complicating this is the fact that Turks are by nature exceedingly friendly and will go out of their way to help you—once you approach them. *The key is to be on the lookout for those who approach you first and seem a little too eager to help, and whose English is just a little too polished.* Use your judgment, but don't be embarrassed to say no politely and move on if you feel accosted. You will certainly make many new friends during a visit to Turkey—just make sure you do it on your terms.

When exploring the Bazaar area, you might want to start at the Grand Bazaar and work your way downhill to Eminönü—it's a rather stiff climb the other way. From Sultanahmet, you can take the tram partway down the hill to the Grand Bazaar. It's almost impossible to get lost; just keep walking downhill until you reach the water. These streets can seem like one giant open air bazaar, and are much less touristy the Grand Bazaar itself. Note that the Grand and Egyptian bazaars are closed Sunday; the Beyazıt, Rüstem Paşa, and Süleymaniye mosques are open daily but effectively—if often not officially—closed to non-Muslims at prayer times, particularly Friday midday.

NEED A BREAK?

The Pandelli, up two flights of stairs over the arched gateway to the Egyptian Bazaar, is a tranquil old Greek-owned Istanbul restaurant with impressive tile work; it's a wonderful escape from the bustle and summer heat. A lunch of typical Turkish fare is served; especially good are the eggplant *börek* (pastry) and the sea bass cooked in paper. ⊠ *Mısır Çarşısı 1, Eminönü* ☎ *212/527–3909* ▭ *AE, MC, V.*

MAIN ATTRACTIONS

㉓ Egyptian Bazaar *(Mısır Çarşısı).* See the highlighted Bazaar feature in this chapter.

FodorśChoice
★

❿ Grand Bazaar *(Kapalı Çarşı)*. See the
★ highlighted feature in ths chapter.
It's said that this early version of
a shopping mall is the largest concentration of stores under one roof
anywhere in the world, and that's
easy to believe. Outside the western gate to the bazaar, through a
doorway, is the **Sahaflar Çarşısı**, the
Old Book Bazaar, where you can
buy new editions as well as antique
volumes in Turkish and other lan-
guages. ⊠ *Yeniçeriler Cad. and Fuatpaşa Cad.* 🎫 *Free* ⊙ *Apr.–Oct.,
Mon.–Sat. 8:30–7; Nov.–Mar., Mon.–Sat. 8:30–6:30.*

WORD OF MOUTH

"We did not feel at all threatened
in the Grand Bazaar. Packs of roving
pick pockets...I don't think so...
just take your normal precautions.
We had some great conversations
with some Turkish people in the
Bazaar. Mind you the place is full
of a lot of crap."   —Marko

⓫ The Column of Constantine *(Çemberitaş)*. This column stood at the center
of what was a large circular marketplace or forum, the symbolic heart
of the city, where Constantine formally rededicated the city on May
11, 330. The column is 35 meters (115 feet) high and was once topped
by a golden statue of Apollo to which Constantine added his own
head. According to tradition Constantine placed various relics under
the column, including an ax used by Noah to make the ark, a piece of
the True Cross, and some of the leftover bread from the miracle of the
loaves and fishes. ⊠ *Yeniçeriler Cad. and Vezirhan Cad., on the main
street Divan Yolu, near the entrance to the Bazaar.*

**NEED A
BREAK?**

The **Çorulu Ali Paşa Medrese** has a tea and waterpipe garden that's popular
with tourists as well as students from nearby Istanbul university. It may have
sprouted a few too many carpet and souvenir shops, but it's still a pleasant
place to stop for a glass of tea surrounded by the sweet aroma of the Narghile pipe. The complex was built by Grand Vizier Ali Paşa, and his head was
buried here in 1711 after Ahmet III had it chopped off. ⊠ *Yeniçeriler Cad.
36/5* ⊙ *Open 24 hrs.*

㉑ Rüstem Paşa Cami *(Rüstem Paşa Mosque)*. When you're ready to take a
break from bazaar haggling, follow Uzun Çarşı Sokak, once the major
Byzantine shopping street called the Envelos, to another Sinan masterpiece, tucked away in the backstreets to the north of the Egyptian
Bazaar and built in the 1550s for Süleyman's grand vizier. The mosque,
raised on a high terrace, is unassuming from the outside, but you're in
for a treat when you step into the cool interior, decorated with İznik
tiles in a magnificent array of colors and patterns. ⊠ *Hasırcılar Cad.,
south of Sobacılar Cad.* ⊙ *Daily.*

⓳ Süleymaniye Cami *(Mosque of Süleyman)*. Perched on a hilltop near Istan-
★ bul University, the largest mosque in Istanbul is less arresting visually
than Sokollu Mehmet Paşa Cami and some of the other mosques and
monuments the architect Sinan designed, but a masterful achievement
and grand presence nonetheless. This mosque houses Sinan's tomb,
along with that of his patron, Süleyman the Magnificent, and the sultan's wife, Roxelana. The architectural thrill here is the enormous dome.
Supported by four square columns and arches, as well as exterior walls

SINAN THE ARCHITECT

The master architect Mimar Sinan, the greatest of the Ottoman builders, is said to have designed more than 350 buildings and monuments throughout Turkey. His genius as an architect lay in his use of proportion, and as an engineer he mastered the use of buttresses and other elements to create vast, open spaces. He was born in a Greek or Armenian village in Cappadocia and at age 13 was recruited as a slave for the sultan; all of the sultan's slaves were brought up Muslim and trained to become the backbone of the empire, its army, and bureacracy. Sinan spent most of his life as a military engineer before being appointed chief architect at the age of 50. He then worked into his 90s building nearly 90 mosques, more than 50 in Istanbul alone. Among the buildings attributed to Sinan are the Sokollu Mehmet Paşa, Süleymaniye, and Rüştem Paşa mosques, parts of the kitchens at Topkapı, two of the minarets at Aya Sofya, and Selimiye Cami in Edirne. His tomb is beside his most important Istanbul mosque, the Süleymaniye.

with smaller domes on either side, the soaring space gives the impression that it's held up principally by divine cooperation. Look around the grounds, because the complex still incorporates a hospital, a caravansaray, a huge kitchen, several schools, and other charitable institutions that mosques traditionally operate—and don't miss the wonderful views of the Golden Horn. ⊠*Süleymaniye Cad., near Istanbul University's north gate* ⊙*Daily.*

NEED A BREAK? The old soup kitchen of the Süleymaniye Cami has been returned to its traditional use as the **Darüzziyafe Restaurant**, serving a typical Turkish range of mezes and grilled meats in the leafy courtyard and cool, stone halls. ⊠*Inside Süleymaniye Cami* ☎*212/511–8415* ▭*MC, V.*

ALSO WORTH SEEING

🔞 **Beyazıt Cami.** This domed mosque inspired by Aya Sofya isn't really that interesting in itself; its distinction is being the oldest of the Ottoman imperial mosques still standing in the city, dating from 1504. ⊠*Beyazıt Meyd., Beyazıt* ☜*Free* ⊙*Daily sunrise to sunset; usually closed during prayer times.*

🔞 **Valide Han.** The mass of winding streets between the Grand Bazaar and the Golden Horn contains many old Ottoman commercial buildings. The most important of these was the Valide Han, which was used to store goods coming off the ships anchored in the Golden Horn, and as hotels for passing merchants. The Valide Han was built by the Valide, literally the "Sultan's mother," Kösem Sultan, who as regent to two sons and a grandson legally ruled the Ottoman empire for a generation until her death in 1651 in a coup led by her daughter-in-law. It's still a working building, with porters coming and going with giant weights on their backs, but visitors are welcome to have a look around. Opposite the Valide Han are two more 18th-century hans, the Büyük Yeni Han and Küçük Yeni Han, and the Kürkçü from the 1470s. ⊠*Çakmakçilar Yokusu, Eminönü.*

WORD OF MOUTH

"Wandering the streets of Sultanahmet, with the Blue Mosque in the background, we came across this juice vendor in traditional costume. With the heat of the day the juice was very refreshing!"

—photo by Maureen Barber, Fodors.com member

20 Eminönü. This waterside neighborhood at the south end of the Galata Bridge is the transportation hub of old Istanbul. There are quays for hydrofoil sea buses, the more traditional Bosphorus ferries (including those for the day-long Bosphorus cruises), and the Sirkeci train station and tramway terminal. The main coastal road around the peninsula of the Old City also traverses Eminönü. Thousands of people and vehicles rush through the bustling area, and the many street traders here sell everything from candles to live animals.

> **TEAHOUSES**
>
> Istanbul is filled with teahouses—many with shady gardens—where people spend long hours quietly sipping glass after glass of tea. Sitting down at one of these teahouses, particularly if it has a nice view, like the one in Eminönü's Gülhane Park, is one of the simple pleasures of Turkish life.

14 Istanbul University. You won't find much to do here, other than appreciate the open space—the campus, with its long greensward and giant plane trees, originally served as the Ottoman war ministry, which accounts for the magnificent gateway arch facing Beyazıt Square and the grandiose, martial style of the main buildings. In the garden is the white-marble 200-foot **Beyazıt Tower,** the tallest structure in Old Stamboul, built in 1823 by Mahmut II (ruled 1808–39) as a fire-watch station, although you can no longer ascend. ⊠ *Fuat Paşa Cad., Beyazıt.*

17 Şehzade Cami. This mosque was built for Prince Mehmet, the eldest son of Süleyman the Magnificent, who died of smallpox in 1543 aged 22. This was Sinan's first imperial mosque and he called it his "apprentice work." The result is pleasant looking but a bit plainer than the nearby Süleymaniye. The tranquil gardens contain many grand tombs, which contain some of the best İznik tiles in the city, though these tombs are rarely open. ⊠ *Şehzadebaşt Cad., Vefa* ☉ *Daily sunrise to sunset; usually closed during prayer times.*

16
18 Kalenderhane Cami *(Church the Theotokos Kyriotissa).* It's easy to find this church, converted into a mosque by the Ottomans, located around the corner from Istanbul University, beside the great Valens Aqueduct. It is believed to have been built in the 9th century, and frescos from the Crusader occupation were found and moved to the Istanbul Archaeological Museum. The mosque is usually open; the interior is spacious but a little austere. Nearby, in the backstreets of the poor suburb of Vefa, is the Church of St. Theodore, now known as the **Molla Gürani Cami,** on Molla Şemsittin Sokak off Vefa Cadesi. This former church has an impressive facade, and although it's not often open, inside some mosaics survive in the small domes, with the figures only lightly painted out. ⊠ *16 Mart Şehitleri Cad., Beyazıt* ☉ *Daily sunrise to sunset; usually closed during prayer times.*

NEED A BREAK?

Boza is a mildly alchoholic drink made from fermented wheat that was popular in the Ottoman era: it's a thick beverage, served with a dusting of cinnamon on top, and the whole has a distinctive, slightly bitter taste, and is said to be rich in vitamins B1, B2, C, and E. At the boza shop **Vefa Bozacısı,** which has been in business, little-changed since 1876, you can sample some boza for yourself in this living piece of 19th-century Istanbul. In summer they also serve lemonade, ice cream, and a drink called *shira* made from raisins. ⊠*Katip Çelebi Cad. 104/1, Vefa.*

㉒ **Yeni Cami** *(The New Queen Mother's Mosque).* The most interesting aspect of this mosque is its location, rising out of the Golden Horn on the Eminönü waterfront. The prime spot ensures that the block-ish-looking structure is a dominant feature of the Istanbul skyline—and presented formidable engineering challenges to the student of Sinan who began laying the waterlogged foundations in 1597. Queen Mother Turhan Hattice saw the project through to completion in the middle of the 17th century, and is buried here near her son, Sultan Mehmet IV, along with several succeeding sultans. ⊠*Eminönü waterfront* ⊙*Daily.*

VIEW FROM THE BRIDGE

The Galata bridge, or Galata Köprüsü, connects old Istanbul to the so-called New Town on the other side of the Golden Horn. The bridge opened in 1993, replacing the old pontoon bridge that had been around since 1910, when horse-, ox-, or mule-drawn carriages rattled across it for a fee. The bridge itself isn't much to look at, but you can stand for hours watching ferries chug out on the Bosphorus.

WESTERN DISTRICTS

Constantinople was a huge city, and large western areas are little visited but contain plenty of fascinating pieces of the city's long history. It's predominantly residential, and at times can seem like one giant sea of ugly six-story apartments, but then around a corner you'll find a Byzantine church or Ottoman mosque.

MAIN ATTRACTIONS

㉜ **Kariye Müzesi** *(Kariye Museum or Church of the Holy Savior in Chora).*
Fodor'sChoice The dazzling mosaics and frescoes in the former Church of the Holy
★ Savior in Chora are considered to be among the finest Byzantine works in the world. Most of the mosaics, in 50 panels, depict scenes from the New Testament and date from the 14th century. They are in splendid condition, having been plastered over when the church became a mosque in the 16th century and were not uncovered until the 1940s. A cluster of Ottoman buildings surrounding the former church have also been restored, making this out-of-the-way corner of the city especially atmospheric. "Chora" comes from the Greek word for countryside; the church was originally outside the city walls that were built by Constantine the Great, but at the beginning of the 5th century AD Theodosius built new fortifications to expand the growing city, which brought the church inside the walls. The modern entrance is off to the side of the church, but it's best to head straight to the original front door, in the outer narthex. Here, a large figure of Christ bears the phrase "I am the land (Chora) of the Living." This door leads to the inner narthex, where you can see the mosaic of Theodore Metochites, a kind of Byzantine prime minister, presenting the church to Christ. Metochites was

responsible for the restoration and redecoration of the church after the damage of the fourth crusade. To the left is a series of mosaics depicting the early life of the Virgin Mary: moving clockwise, the series starts at the far end with her parents, Joachim and Anne, her first steps, her service in the temple, her marriage to Joseph, and, finally, the Annunciation. Above in the dome are the ancestors of the Virgin. The story continues back in the outer narthex, at the same far end, with the journey of Mary and Joseph to Egypt. It continues in one long circle of the outer narthex, with the nativity, the wise men before Herod and, at the far end, the massacre of the innocents, continuing gruesomely over several scenes, and finally ending with the return from Egypt and the presentation of the young Jesus in the temple. On the ceiling are various scenes from the ministry of Christ, including his temptation by the devil, the multiplication of loaves, and the transformation of water into wine. These continue into the other side of the inner narthex with scenes of Christ healing the sick and a vast wall mosaic, known as a Deesis, with Christ and the Virgin, and some tiny imperial figures. The church proper is light and airy but has lost most of its decoration, though a mosaic of the Dormition of the Virgin survives over the door. The large chapel was used for burials and contains several large tombs including that of Theodore Metochites, which is surrounded by saints and stories from the Old Testament. In the apse is a forceful image, called the Anastasis or "Resurrection"; it's one of the masterpieces of Byzantine art, with Christ hauling Adam and Eve from their tombs at the end of time. Above, Christ sits enthroned with the saved, whilst the damned are hauled down to hell and an angel rolls up the heavens like a scroll. ⊠ *1 block north of Fevzi Paşa Cad., by Edirne Gate in city's outer walls* ☎ *212/631–9241* ⊠ *$12* ⊙ *Thurs.–Tues. 9:30–4:30.*

> ### WORD OF MOUTH
>
> "I, personally, would rather spend a few hours at Chora to see the fabulous mosaics than see the Blue Mosque or Grand Bazaar."
> —Proenza_Preschooler

㉝ The Great Walls. The walls of Constantinople were the greatest fortifications of the medieval age and stand pretty much intact today, though severely damaged by Sultan Mehmet II's canon in the last great siege of 1453. They were built in the 5th century after the city outgrew the walls built by Constantine and stretch 6.5 km (4 mi) from the Marmara to the Golden Horn. The "wall" is actually made up of a large inner and smaller outer wall, with various towers and gates, as well as a moat. The easiest section to visit is around Edirnekapı, which is a short walk up hill from the Chora church.

㉟ Eyüp Cami. Muslim pilgrims from all over the world make their way to the brightly colored, tile-covered tomb of Eyüp Ensari, the prophet Muhammad's standard-bearer, at this mosque complex on the Golden Horn. Ensari was killed during the first Arab siege, AD 674–78, of what was then Constantinople, and the eternal presence of a man so close to Muhammad makes this the holiest Islamic shrine in Turkey. The grave was visited by Muslim pilgrims in Byzantine times, and was monumentalized in the 15th century by Sultan Mehmet the Conqueror, expanded by his successors, and rebuilt in 1800 after an earthquake. Despite the numbers of visitors, particularly at Friday midday prayer, the plane-tree-shaded courtyards and hundreds of fluttering pigeons imbue Eyüp Cami with a sense of peace and religious devotion not found in many other parts of this often frenetic city. A vast cemetery has grown around the mosque, including some grand tombs of many other distinguished departed. ⊠ *Cami Kebir Cad., Eyüp* ☎ *No phone* ⊙ *Daily.*

NEED A BREAK?

The Pierre Loti Cafe with its sublime view of the Golden Horn toward Aya Sofya and the Topkapı is a favorite of Istanbullus. Ignore the sign at the Eyüp Cami that is actually for people who are driving, and instead walk back toward the water, looking out for the cable car to take you up the hill. The café serves tea and the standard range of drinks and snacks, but the principal attraction is the great view over Golden Horn.

ALSO WORTH SEEING

㉔ Valens Aqueduct. A Roman city needed its aqueduct, and Constantinople, which seriously lacked drinking water, finally got one in 375, under the emperor Valens. The best and most dramatic surviving section are the great arches under which pass the Atatürk Bulavarı highway, beside the Şehzade mosque. The whole system was restored by the architect Sinan and continued to function well into the Ottoman era. **Kız Taşı** *(The Column of Marcian)* sits unexpectedly among the modern buildings. Dating from the 5th century, the tall column has Greek and Latin inscriptions as well as a very battered Winged goddess of Victory on the base, which gives it its Turkish name, "the maidens" column. A statue of the emperor Marcian once stood on top. ⊠ *Kız Taşı Cad. and Dolap Sokak, Fatih.*

㉖ Fatih Cami. This complex of mosque, religious schools, and other pious buildings was the largest in the whole Ottoman empire, and is still the focus of Fatih, Istanbul's most conservative neighborhood. The original mosque, which was destroyed by an earthquake in 1766, was built in 1463 by Mehmet the conqueror on the site of the demolished Church of the Twelve Apostles, the burial church of Byzantine emperors from Constantine on. The 18th-century replacement is pleasant but unexceptional, though it remains culturally one of the most important mosques in the city. Behind it is the reconstructed tomb of Fatih himself and his wife Gülbahar, sometimes said to be a French princess sent to marry the Byzantine emperor. ⊠ *Fevzi Paşa Cad., Fatih* ☎ *No phone* ⊙ *Daily.*

㉛ Fethiye Cami *(The Church of Theotokos Pammakristos).* The 12th-century church, originally part of a nunnery, served as the seat of Orthodox patriarchy from 1456 to 1568 and was then converted into a mosque, the Fethiye Cami, in 1568. The focus now is not on the main church, but the small side chapel that functions as a small museum for its restored mosaics. The mosaics are some of the best anywhere, with a Christ Pantocrator (as "ruler of all") in the dome, with the figures of various saints, angels, and Old Testament prophets on the wall. In this chapel, Mehmet the Conqueror would talk religion and politics with his hand-picked patriarch, Gennadius. ⊠ *Cami Avlusu Sokak off Fethiye Cad., Çarşamba* ☎ *No phone* 🎫 *$4* ⊙ *Thurs.–Tues. 9:30–4.30.*

Anistasis fresco, artist unknown, Kariye Müzesi

❸❹ Tekfur Saray *(The Palace of Blachernae).* After the Byzantines recaptured Constantinople after the crusaders conquered it, they found the old palace uninhabitable, and the emperors took up residence out by the city walls in what became known as the Palace of Blachernae, after the name of the district. The only significant remains are known as the Tefkur Saray, a large three-story building built into the city walls with an impressive facade from the 13th century. The building had an eventful life in Ottoman times, serving as a royal zoo with elephants and giraffes, then as a brothel, and finally as a pottery workshop known for its tiles produced there. ✉ *Hoca Şakir Cad., Edirnekapı.*

❸❽ Sveti Stefan Bulgar Kilesi *(Bulgarian Church of St. Stefan).* One of the most remarkable and odd structures in Istanbul—and that's saying a lot—this neo-Gothic church looks like it's covered with elaborate stone carvings—but when you get up close, you realize that it's all cast iron. It was prefabricated in Vienna, shipped down the Danube on barges, and erected on the western shore of the Golden Horn in 1871. The then-flourishing Bulgarian Orthodox community in Istanbul was eager to have an impressive church of its own to back its demand for freedom from the Greek Orthodox patriarchate; ordering this fancy church was a statement of independence. The dwindling numbers of the Bulgarian community in Istanbul today, though, mean that there isn't always someone on hand to unlock the interior, which is also covered in cast-iron finery. Even if you can't get in, though, it's still an impressive structure to look at, and it's set in neatly tended gardens by the waters of the Golden Horn. ✉ *Mürsel Paşa Cad., Balat.*

37 **The Ahrida Synagogue.** Istanbul's oldest synagogue dates back to at least 1400, when it was founded by Jews from what is today Macedonia. It was extensively restored in the 1990s to the very baroque form of its last major reconstruction in the 1700s. To visit, permission must be obtained in advance from the chief rabbinate (☎212/243–5166 ✉info@musevicemaati.com). ✉Kürkçüçeşme Sokak 9, Balat.

30 **The Church of Theotokos Panaghiotissa** *(The Church of St. Mary of the Mongols).* This rose-red-colored church is the only standing Byzantine church still in Greek hands. It's beside the giant redbrick building of the Fener Greek School for Boys, and while it's usually locked, it's still worth climbing up the hill to look at it from the outside. The church was the center of a nunnery refounded by the Byzantine princess Maria Palaeologina, who spent 16 years in Iran as the wife of the Mongol Khan Halagu in an attempt to form an anti-Muslim alliance. ✉Tevkii Cafer Mektebi Sokak.

29 **Ecumenical Orthodox Patriarchate.** The Greek Orthodox patriarchate, after being kicked out of Aya Sofya, wandered between several churches before settling here in the church of St. George in 1601. The church, rebuilt in 1720, is a relatively small, simple basilica, though the interior—where you'll find sarcophagi with remains of some famous Byzantine saints, a Byzantine-era patriarchal throne, and some mosaics—has a distinctly refined atmosphere. This small church is theoretically the center of the Orthodox world, though the Turks insist that it serves only the dwindling community of Istanbul Greeks. The main front gate is still welded shut after the Turks hung the patriarch Gregory V from it in 1821 as punishment for the Greek revolt. ✉Sadrazam Ali Paşa Cad., Fener ☎212/531–9670 ⊕www.ec-patr.org.

28 **Gül Cami** *(The Church of St. Theodosia).* This large 11th-century former church is a few blocks inland from the water. According to legend, the Turkish name, Gül Cami, or the "rose mosque," comes from the fact that after the conquest the Turks found it filled with roses, left from the previous day of celebrations of the holy day of Saint Theodosia. Another legend has it that the last emperor, Constantine XI, is buried in the crypt. ✉Helvacı Ahmet Sokak 16, Ayakapı.

27 **Zeyrekhane** *(The Church of the Pantocrator).* Standing on a prime site overlooking the Golden Horn, this is the largest surviving Byzantine church in the city, after Aya Sofya itself. Built in about 1230 as a monastery and mausoleum for the ruling Comnenus dynasty, it was once wealthy and sumptuous, though today it's a somewhat sad remnant of its former glory. The church is actually three churches joined end on end, and the middle one held the royal tombs. The southern church functions as a mosque today, and a wooden floor protects the original tile floor. ✉İdabethane Sokak, Zeyrek.

NEED A BREAK? The terrace below the former Zeyrekhane church has been converted into a swish restaurant with spectacular views, serving Ottoman food (open 9 AM– 10 PM, closed Monday). The elegant upmarket dining spot is a distinct contrast to the rather run-down neighborhood of dilapidated wooden houses. At night a taxi would is easiest. ✉İdabethane Arkası sokak, Zeyrek..

2

36 Rahmi M. Koç Industrial Museum. In a foundry that used to cast anchors for the Ottoman fleet, this building is now filled with steam engines, medieval telescopes, planes, boats, a submarine, a tank, trucks, trains, a horse-drawn tram, bicycles, motorbikes, and the great engines that powered the Bosphorus ferries. The wonderful and eclectic collection, on the shore of the Golden Horn, is sponsored by one of Turkey's leading industrialists. Catch one of the Haliç ferries, a bus from Şişhane, or a taxi to get here. ⊠*27 Hasköy Cad., Hasköy* ☎*212/369–6600* ⊕*www.rmk-museum.org.tr* ⊠*$7* ⊙*Tues.–Fri. 10–5, Fri.–Sat. 10–7.*

BEYOĞLU: ISTANBUL'S NEW TOWN

The neighborhood that climbs the Galata Hill is known both as Pera and Beyoğlu, and is often referred to as the "New Town," where the first thing you'll learn is that *new* is a relative term in Istanbul. Much of what you'll see here dates from the 19th century. In the early part of the 20th century, Beyoğlu was one of Istanbul's most fashionable areas, home to large numbers of the city's Greeks, Jews, and Armenians and filled with many grand, European-style apartment buildings. As the decades passed, more people started moving to the greener neighborhoods farther up the Bosphorus and what had once been one of Istanbul's most elegant neighborhoods became crime-ridden and filled with crumbling buildings. Gentrification fever has hit the neighborhood recently, and many Istanbullus are rediscovering the splendid old buildings and incredible views.

Istanbul's New Town clings to the hillside above Karaköy, and the Galata Tower, while only halfway up the hill, dominates the skyline. Tünel Square, just north of the docks, is an appealing gathering spot surrounded by shops and cafés—it also marks the start of İstiklal Caddesi (Independence Street), Istanbul's main pedestrian area. Nearby is the Pera Palace, one of the most famous of Istanbul's hotels, where Agatha Christie wrote *Murder on the Orient Express* and where Mata Hari threw back a few at the bar. From the square, İstiklal Caddesi climbs uphill through Beyoğlu, past consulates in ornate turn-of-the-century buildings, and across Galatasaray Meydanı (Galatasaray Square) to Taksim Meydanı (Taksim Square), the center of modern Istanbul.

As you walk along İstiklal Caddesi, look toward the upper stories and the heavily ornamented facades of the 19th-century buildings. Return your gaze to eye level, and you'll see bookstores, boutiques, kebab shops, movie theaters, and every element of modern Istanbul's vibrant cultural melting pot. The impressive building behind the massive iron gates on Galatasaray Meydanı is a high school, established in 1868 and for a time the most prestigious in the Ottoman Empire.

MAIN ATTRACTIONS

45 İstiklal Caddesi. Once known as "Le Grande Rue de Pera," lively İstiklal Caddesi is the heart of modern Istanbul. In the 19th century, palace-like European embassies were built here, away from the dirt and chaos of the old city. The wealthy cityfolk soon followed, with the Tünel built in 1875 to carry them up the hill from their work in the banks and trading houses of Karaköy, and a tram—now restored—to take them home. The area was traditionally Christian, and the churches here—Greek, Armenian, Catholic, and Protestant—are more prominent than the mosques. Today this is a lively pedestrian area, full of shops, restaurants, cafés, and cinemas. Turks love to promenade here, and

WORD OF MOUTH

"The view from the top of the Galata Tower is a must." —Guenmai

at times it can turn into one great flow of humanity; even in the wee hours of the morning it's still alive with people. This is the Istanbul that never sleeps.

❹ Divan Edebiyatı Müzesi *(Divan Literature Museum, also called the Galata Mevlevihane).* This museum houses a small collection of instruments and other dervish memorabilia, but the best time to come here—and if you're in town, it's well worth the effort—is at 3 PM on Sundays for concerts of Sufi music and dance performances by the Sufi mystics known in the West as the whirling dervishes. ⊠ *Galip Dede Cad. 15, southeast of Tünel Sq., off İstiklal Cad., Beyoğlu* ☎ *212/245–4141* 💷 *$1, $23 for the weekly dance performances* ⊙ *Wed.–Mon. 9:30–4:30.*

❹ Galata Tower *(Galata Kulesi).* The area around the Galata Tower was a thriving Italian settlement both before and after the fall of Constantinople, and the Genoese built the tower in 1349 as part of their fortifications, when they controlled the northern shore of the Golden Horn. The hillside location provided good defense, as well as a perch from which to monitor the comings and goings of vessels in the sea lanes below. You can do the same from the viewing gallery, accessible by elevator and open during the day, with panoramic views of the city and across the Golden Horn and Sea of Marmara. The rocket-shaped tower has also served as a jail and, for a time during the 1900s, as a fire lookout. It now also houses a restaurant and nightclub. ⊠ *Galata Tower: Büyük Hendek Cad.* ☎ *212/245–1160* 💷 *$8* ⊙ *Daily 9–8.*

ALSO WORTH SEEING

❹ Pera Museum. This small private museum, in a grand 19th-century mansion, has a diverse collection. The heart of the museum is an interesting collection of mostly 19th-century paintings by European and Ottoman artists, including some panoramas of the city and scenes of daily life. Downstairs are two smaller galleries, one that focuses on the history of weights and measures from the age of the Hittites to the modern republic, the other on Küthaya ceramics. Two more floors house a diverse range of visiting exhibits. ⊠ *Meşrutiyet Cad. 65, Tepebaşı* ☎ *212/334–9900* 💷 *$5.*

NEED A BREAK?

Tepebası Nargile Cafe. Open 24 hours a day, this café on a large open terrace is a popular escape from the crowds of İstiklal. It's basically a tea place, but with also serves various other drinks and snacks; the main attraction is the view over the Golden Horn to the old city.

❹ Flower Arcade *(Çiçek Pasajı).* Curmudgeons swear this lively warren of flower stalls, tiny restaurants, and bars just off Galatasaray Square is a pale shadow of its former self—its original neo-Baroque home collapsed with a thundering crash one night in 1978, and its redone facade and interior feel rather too much like a reproduction. It's still a pretty spot, though, and you can still get a feel for the arcade's bohemian past, especially when street musicians entertain here, as they often do, though the restaurants are a bit on the pricey side. ⊠ *Along the northernmost stretch of İstiklal Cad.*

47 Fish Market *(Balık Pazarı)*. Beside the Flower Passage a bustling labyrinth ★ of stands peddles fish, fruits, vegetables, and spices—with a couple of pastry shops thrown in—all of which makes for great street theater. Nevizade Sokak is a lively strip of bars and fish restaurants in the market, all with outside tables in the summer. At the end of the market, at Meşrutiyet Caddesi, is the **Üç Horan Armenian Church** (⊠ *İstiklal Cad. 288*)—with its crosses and haloed Christs, it's an unexpected sight in Muslim Istanbul.

48 Taksim Square *(Taksim Meydanı)*. This square at the north end of İstiklal Caddesi is the not particularly handsome center of the modern city. It's basically a chaotic traffic circle with an entrance to Istanbul's subway system, a bit of grass, and the Monument to the Republic and Independence, featuring Atatürk and his revolutionary cohorts. Around the square are Istanbul's main concert hall (the Atatürk Cultural Center), the high-rise Marmara Hotel, and, up the stairs, a small grassy park. On Cumhuriyet Caddesi, the main street heading north from the square, are shops selling carpets and leather goods, several travel agencies and airline ticket offices, and a few nightclubs. Cumhuriyet turns into Halâskârgazi Caddesi. When this street meets Rumeli Caddesi, you enter the city's high-fashion district, where Turkey's top designers sell their wares.

29 Military Museum *(Askeri Müze)*. Not surprisingly, given that the Otto- ★ man Empire was built on military might, this collection of swords, armor, and other weaponry is quite fascinating. Anyone with an interest in military history will be riveted, while others will find plenty of remarkable tidbits, too. Most showy are the gorgeously embroidered silk tents used by the Ottoman sultans on campaigns, and fragments of the great chain that the last Byzantine rulers stretched across the Golden Horn in a vain attempt to prevent the Turks from gaining access to the city by sea. Atatürk was educated in this former military academy, and his personal effects from the 1915 Gallipoli campaign are touchingly humble. ■ TIP→ The main attraction though is the *Mehter* (Janissary) military band which performs 17th- and 18th-century Ottoman military music in full period costume in a special auditorium at 3 PM when they are in town. ⊠ *Valikonağı Cad., Harbiye* ☎ *212/233–2720* 💲 *$2* 🕐 *Wed.–Sun. 9–5.*

KARAKÖY AND THE LOWER BOSPHORUS

Karaköy, with its port, trading house, and several banks was the economic hub of the late Ottoman empire. The wealth may be gone now, and only the Kadıköy ferries and big cruise ships currently stop here, but the area still has a number of sights, old and new, including a number of large and small Ottoman mosques that line the Bosphorus, leading to the grand neoclassical palace of the later Sultans: the Dolmabahçe.

The Tophane and Fındıklı neighborhoods are north of Karaköy, on the water. Tophane gets its name from the large former gun foundry just up the hill (the word "top" means "cannonball"). The original foundry was built by Sultan Mehmet the Conqueror in the 15th century, though the current building only dates from 1803 and has recently been restored as an art gallery with temporary exhibits. Below is large grassy area, where the artillery troops once drilled,

WORD OF MOUTH

"While I enjoyed looking at Taksim Square and the Galata Tower on the other side of Istanbul, quite frankly, the Dolmabahçe Palace over there is my most lasting memory. On your second day, it might be interesting to take the tram to the Topkapı Palace (Old World) in the morning, and then hop back on to go over the bridge to the Dolmabahçe Palace (New World) for a sense of how Turkey's interests shifted." —josephina

now dominated by a pretty baroque fountain from 1732. To the south is the mosque of Kılıç "The Sword" Ali Paşa, an Italian who converted to Islam and rose to the rank of admiral of the Ottoman fleet. The mosque was built by the great Sinan, then aged 90, and is virtually a miniature copy of Aya Sofya. In contrast to the mosque is a rather baroque Nusretiye "Victory" Cami, on the north side, built in 1826 by the reforming Sultan Mahmud II to mark his self-coup over the recalcitrant Janissary troops. A little farther to the north in the Fındıklı neighborhood is another, small mosque by Sinan in 1562 known as the Molla Çelebi Cami.

NEED A BREAK? Restaurants and cafés line the Karaköy waterfront by the passenger ferry landing, but for a truly delicious, cheap snack, the no-frills sandwich known as *balik ekmek*—literally "fish in bread"—may be one of your most memorable seafood meals in Turkey. The recipe is simple: take a freshly grilled fillet of fish and serve it in a half loaf of crusty white bread (adding onion and/or tomato slices is about as fancy as it gets). What makes *balik ekmek*, though, is the setting—in Istanbul, the best sandwiches are served alfresco from small boats that pull up to the atmospheric quays near the city's Galata Bridge, smoke billowing from their on-board grills.

MAIN ATTRACTIONS

53 **Çırağan Sarayı** (*Çırağan Palace*). This palace—now Istanbul's most luxurious hotel—was built by the vacuous Sultan Abdül Aziz (ruled 1861–76), in 1863; he was as extravagant as his brother, Abdül Mecit (who built the nearby Dolmabahçe Sarayı), and was soon attempting to emulate the splendors he had seen on travels in England and France. The Çırağan Sarayı is about a third the size of Dolmabahçe Sarayı, and much less ornate, which says a good deal about the declining state of the Ottoman Empire's coffers. ⊠ *Çırağan Cad. 84, Beşiktaş* ☎ *212/326–4646.*

50 **Dolmabahçe Sarayı** (*Dolmabahçe Palace*). The name means "filled-in garden," from the fact that Sultan Ahmet I (ruled 1603–17) had an

FodorśChoice
★

2

imperial garden planted here on land reclaimed from the sea. In 1853, Abdül Mecit, whose free-spending lifestyle (his main distinction) bankrupted the empire, had this palace built as a symbol of Turkey's march away from its past and toward the European mainstream. He gave his Armenian architect, Nikoğos Baliyan, complete freedom and an unlimited budget, the only demand being that the palace "surpass any other palace of any other potentate anywhere in the world." The result, an extraordinary mixture of Turkish and European architecture and interior design, is a riot of rococo—marble, vast mirrors, stately towers, and formal gardens along a facade stretching nearly ½ km (¼ mi). Abdül Mecit's bed is solid silver; the tub and basins in his marble-paved bathroom are carved of translucent alabaster, and Europe's royalty helped contribute to the splendor: Queen Victoria sent a chandelier weighing 4½ tons, Czar Nicholas I of Russia provided polar-bear rugs. The result is as gaudy and showy as a palace should be, all gilt and crystal and silk, and every bit as garish as Versailles. Abdül Mecit's mother founded the nearby Dolmabahçe Cami (Dolmabahçe Mosque) in 1853. After the establishment of the modern republic in 1923, the palace became the home of Atatürk, who died here in 1938. The palace is divided into the public "Selamlik" and the private "Harem," each of which can only be seen on separate oversized guided tours, which together take about 90 minutes. ⊠ *Dolmabahçe Cad., Beşiktaş* ☎ *212/258–5544* ☜ *Selamlik $12, Harem $8, Joint Ticket $16* ☉ *Tues.–Wed. and Fri.–Sun. 9–4 Last joint tickets sold at 3. Closes one hour earlier in winter.*

54 Istanbul Modern. A converted warehouse on the shores of the Golden Horn showcases modern painting, sculpture, and photography, from Turkey and around the world. You can wander around by yourself, though you'll learn a lot about the art scene in Turkey if you join one of the free guided tours (in English and Turkish); you need to call in advance to confirm availability and make a reservation. The gallery also houses a shop, a small cinema, and a restaurant and café with beautiful views toward Topkapı Sarayı and the Sea of Marmara. The permanent collection tells the story of modern Turkish art from its late-19th-century Orientalist beginnings through to the work of contemporary artists. ⊠ *Meclis-i Mebusan Cad. Liman İşletmeleri Sahası, Antrepo No. 4, Karaköy* ☎ *212/334–7300, 212/334–7322 tour reservations* ⊕ *www.istanbulmodern.org* ☜ *$6, free Thurs.* ☉ *Tues., Wed., and Fri.–Sun. 10–6, Thurs. 10–8. Closed Mon.; tours at 1 and 3.*

ALSO WORTH SEEING

39 ★ Jewish Museum of Turkey. The history of the Jews in Istanbul and other parts of Turkey is a lot more extensive and colorful than the size of this small museum in the Zulfaris Synagogue might suggest. Even so, the documents and photos here, most of them donated by local Jewish families, provide a fascinating glimpse into the lives of Turkish Jews, who have been traced to Anatolia as early as the 4th century BC. Their numbers became sizeable in the Middle Ages as Jews were expelled from parts of Europe. In 1492, the Spanish Inquisition drove Sephardic Jews from Spain and Portugal, and Sultan Bayazid II welcomed the refugees to the Ottoman Empire. Many settled in Istanbul, and a large Jewish population thrived here for centuries. Today, 16 active synagogues,

Continued on page 88

Boom *on the* Bosphorus

Adjacent to the beautiful 19th century Ortaköy mosque
at Ortaköy Pier is the modern Bosphorus suspension bridge.

It's hard to talk about Istanbul without talking in riddles. Medieval yet modern, European yet Eastern, secular yet Islamic, Istanbul is—at one and the same time—one of the newest and oldest cities in the world.

In spite of recent instances of instability—1999 brought a major earthquake, 2001 saw the collapse of the Turkish Lira—Istanbul has been booming in terms of population (12 million at last count) and tourists in the past decade. Guardian of the Bosphorus waterway and Turkey's traditional gateway to the West, the city is busy polishing its image in hopes of becoming the easternmost anchor of the European Union. But as any Turk will tell you, Istanbul is not Turkey—it is a unique entity, and even that is an understatement.

City of 1,001 sights, Istanbul is packed with world-famous museums and monuments. The Topkapı Palace, the Grand Bazaar, Aya Sofya (Hagia Sophia), and

the Blue Mosque all render this a dream city, with a skyline of domes, minarets, and marvelous mosques that, at least on a misty morning, rises up like a vision from one of Scheherazade's tales. Thanks to its many startling juxtapositions, the texture of life in Istanbul is an attraction all by itself. To discover the Istanbul that exists underneath and between the famous landmarks, you need simply to venture outside, where you'll become immersed in the city's teeming streets, colorful *meyhane* (taverns), and waterfront neighborhoods. To help visitors discover this elusive city, this 10-page "road map" attempts to chart Istanbul's psychological and cultural avenues.

TWO WORLDS IN ONE

Part Europe and part Asia, Istanbul can fascinate, frustrate, and enchant you all at once. Here old ways mix with modern in tight quarters, yielding out-of-sync images that make you pause and wonder.

Imagine an Armani-clad driver in a Lexus, shouting into a cell phone—and in the next lane, a horse hitched to a cart, taking the daily gridlock philosophically. Picture young women in designer jeans lined up for a new Western flick; passing by are matrons robed to the ankles, bound for evening prayer. This is a city where you can span

five centuries simply by crossing the street, moving from the distant era of the sultans' seraglios to the ultra modernity of a sleek cocktail bar. Skyscrapers and mosques jostle for primacy, physically as well as sociologically.

Outside many houses of worship, rows of black shoes are often lined up. Wait

BRIDGING THE OLD AND NEW TOWNS

There's a story that goes like this: Two families living on opposite shores used to meet in the evenings for a game of cards. Neither much liked crossing the Galata pontoon bridge after nightfall, so they took turns, saying "Tomorrow is your night to bridge." This became the name of the famous card game.

These days, traveling from the historic heart of Sultanhamet

to the modern hub of "new" Istanbul—across the Galata Bridge—is only a trip of two miles, though it often seems like light-years. In some ways the timeless and the trendy

parts of Istanbul rarely merge. In certain circles, it's a mark of distinction for cosmopolitans living in "new" Beyoğlu to never venture into the old districts in Sultanhamet.

a few minutes and you might see their owners emerge in stocking feet, most wearing business suits. More than a few of these men have MBAs from universities in the United States. Watch how many whip out a cell phone as they ease back into Prada loafers, some of which have been split open in the back for easier removal when entering a mosque.

When the rattle of taxi traffic is dimmed by the voices of the muëzzins calling the faithful to prayer, you remember that Istanbul is not just another cosmopolitan area, it's an Islamic city. Such contrasts are part of the makeup of daily life for Istanbullus, many of whom juggle aspects of ancient and modern life as they daily cross the city's Bosphorus Bridge. This is one of the most unique cities in the world; don't be surprised if you catch yourself wondering what continent you're on, or what century you're in.

Top left, Contemplation on the Bosphorus
Top right, Shopping on Istiklal Caddesi
Bottom left, View from Galata Tower
Bottom right, woman wearing headscarf

ISTANBUL UNVEILED

In this city you can often tell what's on women's minds by looking at what's on their heads. Though the reasons why Turkish women wear different forms of clothing are complex, there are some general trends. Years ago, women traditionally wore a loosely tied headscarf called a *başörtüsü* (headscarf). But in recent times, the influence of political Islam has led many religious urban women to adopt what some in secular circles rather disparagingly call the *türban*, a colorful headscarf, held in place by a clip under the chin and tightly tied so that no hair shows. Some of these women take the Islamic prescription towards modesty further and also wear a knee- or ankle-length overcoat. A small minority of women in extremely religious circles wear the *çarşaf*, a floor-length black robe that veils their hair and envelops their entire body.

WHERE PAST IS PROLOGUE:
ISTANBUL'S GREAT ERAS

Thanks to the Greeks, Romans, Byzantines, Crusaders, Venetians, and Turks, Istanbul has been introducing new aspects of civilization for more than two thousand years. The comeback city, Istanbul has reinvented itself more times than Madonna. Here are the three main eras of its past.

BYZANTIUM: THE "NEW ROME"

Originally settled by Mycenaean Greeks in the 5th century BC—it was said to be founded by a man called Byzas in 658 BC—Istanbul was first known as Byzantium until AD 330, when the Roman emperor Constantine moved the capital of his empire here; his minions, not surprisingly, began calling it Constantinople. Constantine converted to Christianity and ushered in a major building campaign for his *Nova Roma* (New Rome), culminating in the magnificent Aya Sofya (AD 347—548).

Mosaic, Aya Sofya

Aya Sofya. Completed in the year 537, the Hagia Sophia (Aya Sofya in Turkish) became the central church of Christendom and the major inspiration for the mosques of Islam. It was designed by the mathematician Anthemius and the scientist Isidorus. Using innovative architectural designs (that weren't always successful), they managed to create a massive dome that is 106 feet in diameter, which was unrivaled until St. Peter's cupola in the 17th century. Mehmet the Conqueror converted the church into a mosque in 1453, and the four minarets were added by succeeding sultans. With the big middle dome resting on two half-domes, Aya Sofya has awed the faithful, and everyone else, too. It's still one of the most prominent buildings on the Istanbul skyline.

Aya Sofya

Yerebatan Sarnıcı. An almost churchlike peacefulness is found in this immense subterranean reservoir, first excavated by Constantine and then completed by Emperor Justinian during the 6th century. Built to keep a steady supply of fresh water for the city in case of a siege, it has more than 330 marble columns rising from the well water. It's a wonderfully atmospheric place to visit, especially with the classical music playing in the background of the dimly lit caverns. On hot summer days, it's also a cool respite. See if you can spot the fish swimming below.

Medusa head pedestal, Yerebatan Sarnıcı

Right: Yerebatan Sarnıcı

DID YOU KNOW?

Before its 1987 restoration, the atmospheric Yerebatan Sarnıcı, also known as the Sunken Palace, could be explored only by boat. James Bond rowed through in *From Russia with Love*.

OTTOMAN EMPIRE: TURKISH DELIGHT

As the seat of Christendom for the next millennium, Constantinople became the object of Ottoman conquest, which was finally achieved on May 29, 1453 by Sultan Mehmet II. Part of his "Islamization" of the city was transforming Aya Sofya into the Great Mosque. Succeeding sultans then lavished the city with mosques and palaces, many built by Sinan (1490–1588), architect to Süleyman the Magnificent.

Topkapı Sarayı. This sprawling complex was the main palace of the sultans. Both the nerve center of the Ottoman Empire and a fabulous treasure house, its riches still encompass the jewels of the Treasury and holy relics from the prophet Muhammad. In a separate wing, visitors cannot help but imagine what pleasures were indulged in the secret world of the Harem.

Topkapı Sarayı

Blue Mosque. A stone mountain of domes, half-domes, and minarets, the Sultan Ahmet Cami was built during the early 17th century by Ottoman ruler Sultan Ahmet, who wanted to prove that Islam could produce a building as impressive as Christendom's Aya Sofya. Inside, thousands of blue tiles create a dazzling symphony of Arabic patterns.

BELLE EPOQUE: WESTERNIZATION

In the 18th century, military defeats led Ottoman rulers to look to Europe for ways to revitalize their society. Court officials returned from Paris raving about Versailles, and the ornate "Turkish Baroque" style was born. Influenced by new commercial ties between France and Turkey in the 19th century, the Grand Rue de Pera (today's Istiklal Caddesi) was touted as the "Champs-Elysées of the Orient" and a flurry of Belle Epoque cafés set the city's sophisticated style.

Dolmabahçe Sarayı

Dolmabahçe Sarayı. Overlooking the Bosphorus, this 1854 palace was built in storybook Turkish-Indian Baroque style. A combination of a Moorish castle, an Italian Baroque palazzo, and a Hindu shrine, it flaunted more than 30,000 pounds of gold, an opulence that expressed the resolve of the sultans to sustain the grandeur of their declining empire in the heyday of European imperialism.

Sirkeci Station. With its pink marble façade, stained-glass windows, and exotic Seljuk-style archways, Istanbul's grand train station (1890) was the last stop of the Orient Express.

Sirkeci Station

Right: Blue Mosque

DID YOU KNOW?

Sultan Ahmet commissioned this grand mosque, nicknamed the Blue Mosque. It's said that he was so enthusiastic about the project that, at times, he worked alongside the hired laborers.

ISTANBUL NOW

Istanbul today is remaking itself—still—a process that has continued for several millennia. The city is constantly evolving, and three new landmarks prove it. They can be toured in one afternoon.

From the Four Seasons Hotel, take the tramway at the Sultanahmet stop towards Kabataş. Get off at the Tophane stop to find the Istanbul Modern on the Bosphorus shore.

After the museum, walk one stop further north along the tram tracks and take the Funicular up to Taksim where a short walk down Istiklal will lead you to Restaurant 360 Istanbul.

Four Seasons

Four Seasons Hotel Sultanahmet. Istanbullus rejoiced in 1996 when the infamous 19th-century Sultanahmet Prison—perched near the Topkapı Palace—was transformed into a luxurious Four Seasons Hotel. What a change from 1977, when Turkey's tourist industry virtually collapsed as Oliver Stone's *Midnight Express* premiered and revealed hell-on-earth to be a Turkish prison. Where criminals once did hard time, now off-duty screen stars chill out in suites decorated in opulent Ottoman taste.

Istanbul Modern. A symbol of the new Turkey, the country's first museum of modern art is housed in an old warehouse. Set next to the Karaköy maritime terminal, this museum has been extolled as a gateway between Turks and "the outsider." Part of a vast industrial space, à la London's Tate Modern, the museum's soaring halls house everything from 19th-century Orientalist masters to avant-garde videographers. But thanks to the adjacent 16th-century Tophane Mosque and the views of the Old City across the water (best seen from the trendy café), historic Istanbul is never far away.

Istanbul Modern

360 Istanbul Restaurant & Bar. Many of Istanbul's hippest denizens hang out at 360 Istanbul, perched atop an historic 8-story apartment building on Istiklal Caddesi, along the Embassy Row of 19th-century Istanbul. Soaring plate-glass windows, giant photo blow-ups, and contemporary furnishings hardly compete with the jaw-dropping views at every quarter of the compass. Take the pulse of the fashionable crowd while enjoying the Society Shish Kebab "Remix" or the Miss Piggy pizza, then stay to dance the night away.

360 Restaurant & Bar

. . . . AND TOMORROW

"The hustle and bustle and energy of Istiklal as the trolley glides past."—photo by salexg, Fodors.com member

Istanbul has always been a city of startling juxtapositions. In the future, however, the constant pull between East and West, between modern and traditional, may create an underlying tension that will erupt to confound Turkish society and politics.

Long famed as the city of carpets, coffee, and Arabian Nights clichés, Istanbul is increasingly international in flavor. Dealers of rare kilims now compete with stores whose rugs are quite possibly milled in China, and the ever-burgeoning Starbucks is busy weaning customers away from traditional Turkish coffee.

With Ali Baba about to be elbowed out of the way by Burger King, it's little wonder that the Nobel Prize winning Turkish novelist Orhan Pamuk has made the leitmotiv of *hüzün*, or melancholic nostalgia, the theme of his work. As Istanbul makes the leap into the 21st century, will the city of myth and legend be left behind?

WHEN CULTURES COLLIDE

The onslaught of immigrants—some 50,000 people relocate to Istanbul every month from the former Soviet Union and eastern Turkey—is changing the face, and psyche, of the city. While glossy photos focus on the skyscrapers being built in the business quarter, Anatolian immigrants erect *gecekondus*—homes "put up overnight"—in the outlying districts of the city. These working-class settlers have brought with them a wave of conservative Islam. For those who are intent on Turkey joining the EU, the rising fundamentalism means falling hopes.

Tolerance definitely has a place in current Turkish society, and most Istanbullus take pride in pluralism: they like to point to the famous mosaics commissioned by Emperor Justinian of Christ and Virgin Mary that still glow on the walls of Aya Sofya, the church that was transformed into a mosque (today officially a museum)—truly a lesson in tolerance. On the other hand, this is the city where the crescent and the cross have battled many times.

one of which dates from the Byzantine period, serve a Jewish community of 25,000, and some older Turkish Jews still speak a dialect of medieval Spanish called Ladino, or Judeo-Spanish. In the Neve Shalom Synagogue, on Büyük Hendek Sokak near the Galata Tower, 22 Sabbath worshipers were shot by Arabic-speaking gunmen in September 1986. ⊠*Meydanı Perçemil Sokak, just off Karaköy Cad. near the foot of the Galata Bridge, the small street on your coming out of the Tünel entrance of the underpass* ⌨*$4* ⊙*Mon. and Thurs. 10* AM–*4* PM, *Fri. and Sun. 10* AM–*2* PM.

▐ NEED A
BREAK?

One of the great pleasures of Istanbul is to sit at one of the many nameless clusters of plastic seats and umbrellas that line the Bosphorus, and watch the ships go by. A favorite is in Fındıklı behind the mosque, where for the price of a tea, you can enjoy one of the best views in town, stretching from Dolmabahçe, Kız Kulesi opposite with and Ayasofya to the right.

⑤ Naval Museum *(Deniz Müzesi)*. The flashiest displays here are the sultan's barges—the long, slim boats that served as the primary mode of royal transportation for several hundred years—though renovations mean they are off-limits until at least late 2009. Otherwise, the main building houses artifacts from the maritime history of the Ottoman Empire and Turkish Republic, mostly old maps and ship models—giving a pretty good scope of the Ottoman Empire's onetime supremacy at sea. Most of the labels are, unfortunately, in Turkish, but you can still appreciate the standouts, such as cannons including a 23-ton blaster built for Sultan Selim the Grim and a copy on an early Ottoman map of the New World—cribbed from stolen maps by Columbus and other western explorers, and dating from 1513, this was the first map of the whole Americas. Just beside the museum is the Tomb of Hayrettin Paşa or "Barbarossa," the admiral of the fleet, who dominated the Mediterranean in the Ottoman glory days of the early 16th century. ⊠*Beşiktaş Cad., Beşiktaş* ☏*212/327–4346* ⌨*$2* ⊙*Wed.–Sun. 9–noon and 1:30–5:30.*

⑤ Yıldız Parkı. The wooded slopes of Yıldız Parkı once formed part of the great forest that covered the European shore of the Bosphorus from the Golden Horn to the Black Sea. In the waning years of the Ottoman Empire, the park was the private garden of Çırağan Sarayı, and the women of the harem would occasionally be allowed to visit. First the gardeners would be removed, then the eunuchs would lead the women across the footbridge from the palace and along the avenue to the upper gardens. Secluded from prying eyes, they would sit in the shade or wander beneath the acacias, maples, and cypresses, filling their baskets with flowers and figs. Today the park is still hauntingly beautiful, particularly in spring when the flowers bloom, and in fall when the leaves of the deciduous trees change color. At the top of Yıldız Park is the relatively modest *Yıldız* Chalet (Yıldız Şale), *where* Sultan Abdül Hamit II, who distinguished himself as the last despot of the Ottoman Empire (ruled 1876–1909) spent most of his time (he also lived in the Çırağan and Dolmabahçe palaces). Visiting dignitaries from Kaiser Wilhelm to Charles de Gaulle and Margaret Thatcher have stayed here as well. The chalet is often blissfully empty of other tourists, which makes a visit all the more pleasurable. ✉ *Çırağan Cad.* ☏ *212/261–8460 for park, 212/259–4570 for chalet* 🖅 *Chalet: $4* ⊗ *Park: daily 9–9; chalet: Wed.–Sun. 9–4.*

THE BOSPHORUS AND BEŞIKTAŞ

As you leave the chaos of the city behind, you'll see wooded hills; villages large and small, modern and old-fashioned; the old wooden summer homes called *yalıs* (waterside houses) that were built for the city's wealthier residents in the Ottoman era.

BOSPHORUS SIGHTS

Anadolu Hisarı *(Anatolian Castle).* Sultan Beyazıt I built this fortress in 1393 at the mouth of the Göksu stream—known in Ottoman times as one of the "Sweet Waters of Asia"—to cut off Constantinople's access to the Black Sea. The castle looks especially romantic at sunset, when its golden stone blends into the surrounding forest and tiny boats bob beneath its walls. A road passes through the outer keep, but the inner keep is now locked, so there is little to see, though the area is pleasant. Just beyond the fortress is the second Bosphorus bridge, officially known as **Fatih Sultan Mehmet Bridge.**

Arnavutköy. This village on the European side is a pleasant place for a stroll. A row of 19th-century wooden houses lines the waterfront, and up the hill from the water, narrow streets are lined with more old wooden houses, some of them with trailing vines.

Bebek. Also on the European side, Bebek is one of the most fashionable suburbs of Istanbul and is especially popular with an affluent expatriate community. There are many upmarket cafés and restaurants, and the area is perfect for a seaside walk. (Bebek is about 20 minutes by taxi from central Istanbul.)

NEED A BREAK?
Mini Dondurma is a tiny ice-cream shop on Bebek's main street that has repeatedly been rated the best in town. Their 18 creamy flavors, include the distinctive *lokum* **(also known as Turkish Delight) ice-cream.** ✉ *Cevdet Paşa 38A, Bebek.*

Beylerbeyi Sarayı *(Beylerbeyi Palace).* Built as a summer residence for Sultan Abdül Aziz in 1865, Beylerbeyi, on the Asian shore, is sort of a mini-Dolmabahçe, though unlike Dolmabahçe, Beylerbeyi is painted a pinkish peach; it's also smaller, less grandiose, and has more of a personal feel. It's filled with marble and marquetry and gold-encrusted furniture, and the central hall has a white-marble fountain and a stairway wide enough for a regiment. You must join a tour to see the palace. ✉ *Çayıbaşı Durağı, Beylerbeyi* ☏ *216/321–9320* 🖅 *$6* ⊗ *Tues.–Wed. and Fri.–Sun. 9:30–5.*

Emirgan. This town on the European shore across the Bosphorus from Kanlıca was named after a 17th-century Persian prince to whom Sultan Murat IV (ruled 1623–40) presented a palace. All that remains are a park with flower gardens and a number of restored Ottoman pavilions. In late April the town stages a Tulip Festival, when many tulips are

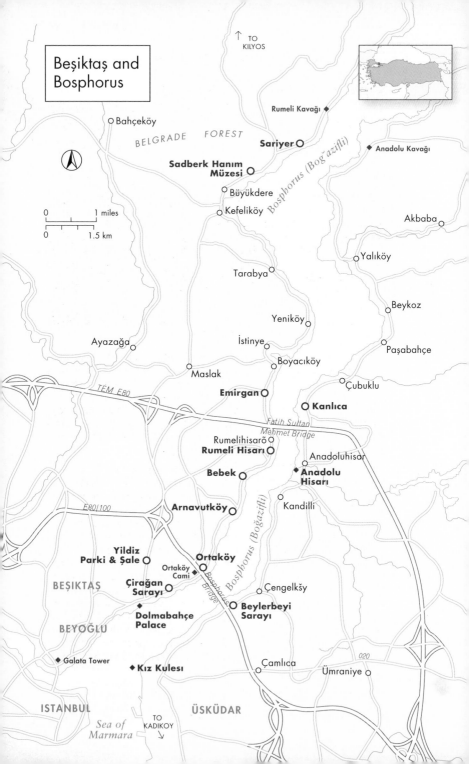

Beşiktaş and Bosphorus

TO KILYOS

BELGRADE FOREST

Rumeli Kavağı ◆

Anadolu Kavağı ◆

Bahçeköy ○

Sarıyer ○

Sadberk Hanım Müzesi ○

Büyükdere ○

Kefeliköy ○

Akbaba ○

Tarabya ○

Yalıköy ○

Beykoz ○

Yeniköy ○

Ayazağa ○

İstinye ○

Paşabahçe ○

Maslak ○

Boyacıköy ○

Çubuklu ○

TEM E80

Emirgan ○

Kanlıca ○

Fatih Sultan Mehmet Bridge

Rumelihisarõ ○

Rumeli Hisarı ○

Anadoluhisar

Bebek ○

◆ **Anadolu Hisarı**

E80/100

Arnavutköy ○

Kandilli ○

Yildiz Parki & Şale ○

Ortaköy ○

Ortaköy Cami ◆

Bosphorus (Boğazifli)

Çengelkšy ○

BEŞİKTAŞ

Çirağan Sarayı ◆

Beylerbeyi Sarayı

BEYOĞLU

◆ **Dolmabahçe Palace**

◆ Galata Tower

◆ **Kız Kulesi**

Çamlıca ○

Ümraniye ○

020

ISTANBUL

Sea of Marmara

TO KADIKOY

ÜSKÜDAR

Bosphorus (Boğ azifli)

0 — 1 miles

0 — 1.5 km

Planning a Bosphorus Day Cruise

This ferry is leaving the Eminönü docks in Sultanahmet to cross the Bosphorus.

One of the most pleasant experiences in Istanbul—and an easy way to escape the chaos of the city—is a trip up the Bosphorus by ferry from the Eminönü docks in the Old Town. Along the way you'll see wooded hills; villages large and small, modern and old-fashioned; the old wooden summer homes called *yalıs* (waterside houses) that were built for the city's wealthier residents in the Ottoman era; and the grand palaces of Beşiktaş.

There are two sorts of ferries: the more popular option is the cruise ferry, which goes up and back, or you can take a commuter ferry; both leave from Eminönü. The third option is the private Turyol tours from the other side of Galata bridge, which whip you up and back in about three hours, costing around $5, with no lunch stop.

Cruise ferries depart daily from Quay 3 (look for the sign reading BOĞAZ HATTI) at 10:35 and 1:35 (times are subject to change, so check first). The round-

trip should cost about $15. These boats zigzag up the Bosphorus with set stops arriving at about noon or 3 PM, respectively, for a three-hour break at either **Rumeli Kavağı** or **Anadolu Kavağı**, two fishing villages near the Black Sea. Then they zigzag back down to Eminönü.

Alternatively, several commuter ferries leave the same dock at around 6 PM for a mere $1, letting you pack more into a day, but it means catching a bus or taxi back, as there are no return ferries until the morning. Numerous buses run up and down both sides; most useful is bus 25, which runs between Sariyer and Eminönü (E) and Taksim (T). On the Asian side several buses run from Uskudar past Beylerbeyi, Anadolu Hisar, and Kanlıca to Beykoz. A final note for planning is that Beylerbeyi is closed Monday and Thursday; Rumeli Hisar and Sadberk Hanım Müzesi are closed Wednesday.

planted. Tulips take their name from the Turkish word *tulbend* (turban); they were originally brought from Mongolia and after their cultivation was refined by the Dutch they were great favorites of the Ottoman sultans. The park contains some pleasant cafés and restaurants.

Kadıköy. On the Asian side of Istanbul, Kadiköy started life as ancient Chalcedon, most famous as the site of the Ecumenical Council of 451 AD that gave the Christian world the creed of Chalcedon. It's the oldest settlement in the area, though it has little to show for it. It's known as one of Istanbul's more relaxed and Bohemian neighborhoods and its car-free market area, up and to the right from the port, is a pleasant place to explore. On Tuesdays, farther inland (beyond the bull statue), there is a giant open-air market, mostly food and clothes.

Kanlıca. This village just north of Fatih Sultan Mehmet Bridge, on the Asian side of the Bosphorus, has been famous for its delicious yogurt for at least 300 years; little restaurants around the plane tree in the square by the quay serve this treat. Nearby, white 19th-century wooden villas line the waterfront.

Kız Kulesi *(Leanders).* Fortified since Byzantine times, this little island off the Asian shore guarded the busy shipping lanes, and now, restored and lit up, it is the star of the lower Bosphorus. The English name associates the island with the legend of Leander, who swam the straits each night guided by the lamp of his lover Hero, though actually this took place in the Dardanelles to the south. The Turkish name comes from a legend associated with several offshore castles: as the story goes, a princess is placed on an island after a prophecy that she will die of a snakebite, but it happens anyway, when a snake comes ashore in a basket of fruit. The castle is now an expensive café and restaurant; there are frequent boats from Kabataş and the adjacent Asian shore.

As you approach the Bosphorus bridge you'll pass the **Ortaköy** neighborhood on the European shore. It's not far from Beşiktaş, but with its cluster of narrow streets it has the feel of a little village, and is quite charming. There are many cafés and restaurants and, during the day, street stalls selling trinkets and jewelry. An open space faces the Bosphorus and it's a lovely spot to spend a summer evening.

Rumeli Kavağı is the end of the line on the Asian side. Another pretty fishing village, it gets enough tourists to have a wide range of seafood restaurants, waffle stands, and ice-cream shops. The main attraction is the dramatically sited Byzantine Castle, a 15-minute walk up from the village through more restaurants and cafés. The hill was once the site of a temple to Zeus Ourios (god of the favoring winds), which dates back, legend has it, to the days when Jason passed in search of the golden fleece. Today there is a large ruined castle, built by the Byzantines and expanded by the Genoese allies. The view over the Upper Bosphoros to the blustery Black Sea is spectacular.

Sadberk Hanım Müzesi *(Sadberk Hanım Museum).* An old waterfront mansion on the European side houses this small but stunning collection of İznik tiles, Ottoman embroidery and calligraphy, and other Islamic and Turkish arts, such as Anatolian antiquities and Byzantine silver. The late billionaire businessman Vehbi Koç amassed the collection and named the museum for his deceased wife. ✉*Piyasa Cad. 27–29, Büyükdere* ☎*212/242–3813* ⊕*www.sadberkhanimmuzesi.org.tr* 💰*$5* ⊗*Thurs.–Tues. 10–5.*

Sariyer. Focused on its little fishing harbor and backed by a row of seafood restaurants, Sariyer still has the feel of a fishing village. There are no sights as such, it's just a great place to sit by the water with the hustle of the big city at arm's length.

Uskudar. Uskudar marks the beginning of the vast Anatolian commuter suburbs, and its waterfront has several interesting old mosques. Sinan's Iskele Cami of 1548 dominates the ferry landing; it's pretty, if a little dark. To the south is the large Yeni Valide Cami of 1710. Beside the water is the small, beautifully located Şemsi Paşa Cami, though it's a bit disfigured by the construction site for the new metro under the Bosphorus. The most important mosque here, though, is Sinan's Atik Valide Cami of 1583, which has one of the best examples of a külliye—the buildings such as the schools, soup kitchens, etcetera, that surrounded an imperial mosque.

WHERE TO EAT

Updated by Vanessa Larson

Istanbul is a food lover's town and restaurants abound, from humble kebab joints to fancy fish restaurants, with lots of excellent options in between. Istanbullus take their food seriously, holding dining establishments to a very high standard: they expect service to be prompt and polite, the restaurant to be spotless, and most importantly, the food to be made with the freshest of ingredients; the places that cater mostly to tourists are the ones that might let their standards slip.

Turkish cuisine varies from region to region, and Istanbul, owing to its location on the Bosphorus, which connects the Black Sea to the Sea of Marmara, is famous for seafood. A classic Istanbul meal, usually eaten at one of the city's rollicking *meyhanes* (literally "drinking places"), starts off with a wide selection of tapas-style small appetizers called mezes and then moves on to a main course of grilled fish, all of it accompanied by the anise-flavored spirit *rakı*, Turkey's national drink. Fish can be expensive, so check prices and ask what's in season before ordering.

While Istanbul's dining scene, though large, was once mostly limited to Turkish cooking, recent years have seen a new generation of chefs successfully fusing local dishes with ingredients and flavors from other parts of the world. Some chefs, trained in the United States and Europe, are bringing home the contemporary cooking techniques they've learned abroad, and the result is a kind of nouvelle Turkish cuisine.

The Sultanahmet area might have most of the city's major monuments and many hotels, but it's lacking in good dining options, save for a few standouts. You'll have better luck if you head across the Golden Horn to the lively Beyoğlu district or to some of the charming, small neighborhoods along the Bosphorus, famous for their fish restaurants. Beyoğlu, with its small backstreets, has everything from hole-in-the-walls serving

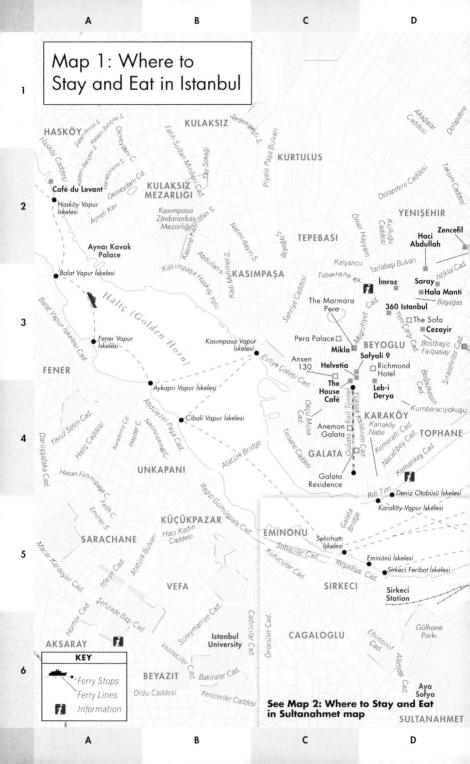

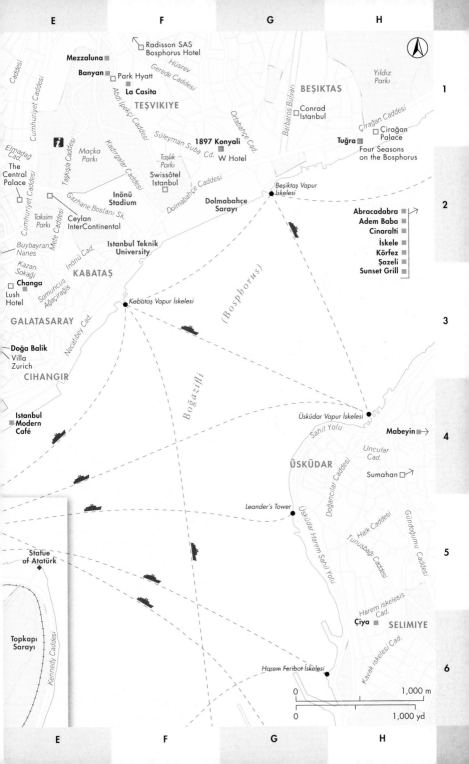

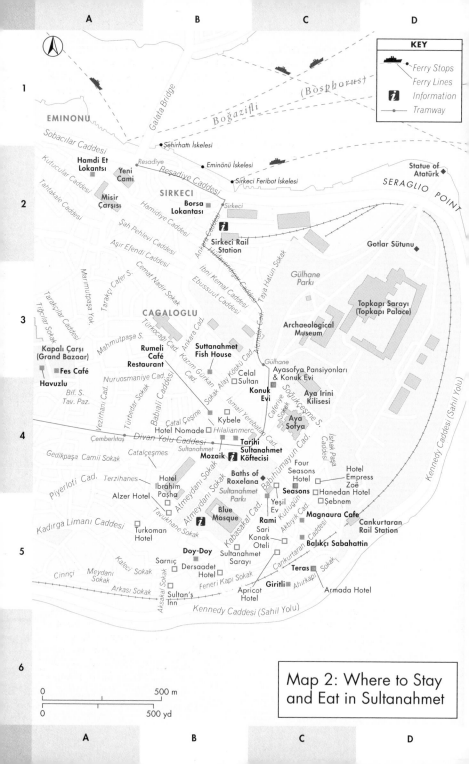

Map 2: Where to Stay and Eat in Sultanahmet

KEY

- Ferry Stops
- Ferry Lines
- ℹ️ Information
- Tramway

A

- EMINONU
- Sobacılar Caddesi
- Kutucular Caddesi
- Tahtakale Caddesi
- Hamdi Et Lokantası
- Yeni Cami
- Mısır Çarşısı
- Şah Pehlevi Caddesi
- Hamidiye Caddesi
- Aşır Efendi Caddesi
- Mahmutpaşa Yok.
- Tığcılar Caddesi
- Tarakçılar Caddesi
- Tarakçı Cafer S.
- Cemal Nadir Sokak
- Kapalı Çarşı (Grand Bazaar)
- Fes Café
- Havuzlu
- Bit. S. Tav. Paz.
- Nuruosmaniye Cad.
- Vezirhanı Cad.
- Türbedar Sokak
- Babıali Caddesi
- Mahmutpaşa S.
- Türkocağı Cad.
- Ankara Cad.
- Rumeli Café Restaurant
- Kazım Gürkan Cad.
- Sokak Alay Köşkü Cad.
- Çatal Çeşme
- Çemberlitaş
- Divan Yolu Caddesi
- Gedikpaşa Camii Sokak
- Çatalçeşmes
- Piyerloti Cad.
- Terzihanes
- Kadırga Limanı Caddesi
- Hotel İbrahim Paşa
- Alzer Hotel
- Tavukhane Sokak
- Turkoman Hotel
- Atmeydanı Sokak
- Kâtcı Sokak
- Cinnçi
- Meydanı Sokak
- Sarnıç
- Doy-Doy
- Dersaadet Hotel
- Aksakal Sokak
- Sultan's Inn
- Arkası Sokak
- Feneri Kapı Sokak
- Kennedy Caddesi (Sahil Yolu)

B

- Galata Bridge
- Boğazıçı
- Şehirhattı İskelesi
- Resadiye
- Eminönü İskelesi
- Resadiye Caddesi
- Sirkeci Feribot İskelesi
- SIRKECI
- Borsa Lokantası
- Sirkeci
- ℹ️
- Sirkeci Rail Station
- Ankara Caddesi
- Hüdavendigar Caddesi
- İbni Kemal Caddesi
- Ebussuut Caddesi
- CAGALOGLU
- Suttanahmet Fish House
- Celal Sultan
- Konuk Evi
- İsmail Yerebatan Cad.
- Kybele
- Hotel Nomade
- Hilalianmerc.
- Sultanahmet
- Tarihi Sultanahmet Köftecisi
- Mozaik
- ℹ️
- Baths of Roxelana
- Sultanahmet Parkı
- Yeşil Ev
- Blue Mosque
- Kabasakal Cad.
- Rami
- Sarı Konak Oteli
- ℹ️
- Sultanahmet Sarayı
- Apricot Hotel
- Giritli
- Ahırkapı
- Taya Hatun Sokak
- Caferiye Cad.
- Yerebatan Cad.
- Kutuğun Cad.
- Akbıyık Cad.
- Cankurtaran Caddesi

C

- (Bosphorus)
- Statue of Atatürk
- SERAGLIO POINT
- Gotlar Sütunu
- Gülhane Parkı
- Archaeological Museum
- Gülhane
- Ayasofya Pansiyonları & Konuk Evi
- Soğukçeşme S.
- Aya İrini Kilisesi
- Aya Sofya
- Four Seasons Hotel
- Seasons
- Hanedan Hotel
- Şebnem
- Magnaura Cafe
- Balıkçı Sabahattin
- Teras
- Hotel Empress Zoë
- İshak Paşa Caddesi
- Cankurtaran Rail Station
- Armada Hotel

D

- Topkapı Sarayı (Topkapı Palace)
- Kennedy Caddesi (Sahil Yolu)

Scale: 0 — 500 m / 0 — 500 yd

delicious home-cooking to some of Istanbul's sleekest restaurants. The Bosphorus restaurants tend to be more upscale and expensive.

Since Istanbullus love to go out, reservations are essential at most of the city's better restaurants. In summer, many establishments move their dining areas outdoors, and reservations become even more important if you want to snag a coveted outside table. For the most part, dining is casual, although Istanbullus enjoy dressing smartly when they're out and about. You may feel terribly underdressed if you show up in a restaurant dressed in shorts and a T-shirt, even in summer.

Despite Muslim proscriptions against alcohol, beer, wine, and the local spirit rakı are widely available, and you can sometimes find cocktails, too, particularly in more upmarket restaurants. Because of high import taxes, however, nonlocal alcoholic drinks will usually be considerably more expensive than in North America or Europe.

WHAT IT COSTS IN U.S. DOLLARS					
	¢	$	$$	$$$	$$$$
Restaurants	under $10	$10–$15	$16–$22	$23–$30	over $30

Prices are per person for a main course at dinner, or a main course equivalent.

ASIAN SIDE

¢–$
TURKISH
Fodor'sChoice
★

✕**Çiya.** Owner and chef Musa Dağdeviren, who hails from the southeastern Turkish city of Gaziantep, is something of a culinary anthropologist, collecting recipes from around Turkey and publishing a journal devoted to Turkish food culture. His no-frills eatery turns out memorable, uniquely seasoned dishes—such as *galye,* a stew of lamb, quince, apricots, and chestnuts. Desserts are equally remarkable and include candied olives, tomatoes, or eggplant, served with sweet clotted cream. The menu is seasonal and changes daily, but always features a variety of vegetarian dishes. Çiya Sofrası is the original restaurant; across the street and a bit farther up, Çiya Kebap has the Sofrası menu as well as a top-notch range of kebabs; Çiya Kebap 2 just does kebabs. ⊠ *Güneşlibahçe Sokak 48B, Kadıköy* ☎ *0216/336–3013* ▤ *MC, V* ✛ *1:6H.*

$$–$$$
TURKISH

✕**Mabeyin.** Though housed in a restored 19th-century mansion and with an elegant interior, Mabeyin features the earthy but intricately spiced food of Turkey's southeast, which has a strong Middle Eastern influence. Kebabs grilled with quince or loquat—a small, succulent fruit only available in late spring and early summer—are some of the unusual items on the menu, but even more interesting are the stews, such as one made with rice and meat dumplings in a warm yogurt broth or another that has two kinds of bulgur dumplings in a tomato-based sauce. Food is served in a splendid garden during warm weather. Mabeyin is a quick cab ride from the Üsküdar ferry terminal. ⊠ *Eski Kısıklı Cad. 129, Kısılı* ☎ *0216/422–5580* ⚄ *Reservations essential* ▤ *AE, MC, V* ✛ *1:4H.*

BEYOĞLU

$$-$$$
ECLECTIC
✕ **360 Istanbul.** Globe-hopping and genre-bending, the food at 360 Istanbul tries to take diners to places they've never been to, although the results sometimes fall flat. The location goes for the same effect, but with more consistency: at the top of a historic building in the heart of the lively Beyoğlu district, the sleek concrete and glass restaurant has lovely views in all directions. Overseen by chef Mike Norman, who worked for several years in the five-star Çırağan Palace Hotel, the kitchen turns out innovative dishes like braised artichokes with sour plums, sesame-crusted Norwegian salmon, and harissa-spiced lamb chops. ⊠ *İstiklal Cad. 311, Beyoğlu* ☏ *212/251–1042* ⌖ *Reservations essential* ▤ *MC, V* ⊘ *No lunch Sat. and Sun.* ✛ *1:3D.*

$$$
FRENCH
✕ **Café du Levant.** Black-and-white floor tiles and turn-of-the-century European furnishings give this café next to the Rahmi M. Koç Industrial Museum the feel of a Paris bistro. And, indeed, the menu is only in French and Turkish. Chef José Alain Perreau turns out superb classic French cuisine, including fillet of turbot with zucchini and tomatoes, and fillet of beef in a red wine sauce. For dessert try the crème brûlée or the soufflé au Grand Marnier with ice cream. ⊠ *Kumbarhane Cad. 2, Hasköy Cad., Hasköy* ☏ *212/369–6607* ⌖ *Reservations essential* ▤ *AE, DC, MC, V* ⊘ *Closed Mon.* ✛ *1:2A.*

$$-$$$
ECLECTIC
Fodor'sChoice
★
✕ **Cezayir.** Cezayir's former chef, Dilara Erbay, spent several years traveling around the world and the restaurant's delicious menu of "new Turkish cuisine" remains largely her creation. Most experimental are the mezes, such as fava bean puree made with a hint of rakı; "Cezayir börek," thin strands of pastrami and fruit paste wrapped in phyllo dough and served with rose-hip sauce; and anchovy ceviche. The main courses, which include lamb shank with spinach roots and tandoori chicken, display the same kind of inventiveness. The restaurant's lounge has wicker chairs, comfortable sofas, and pale yellow walls; it's the perfect place to while the night away. ⊠ *Hayriye Cad. 16, Beyoğlu* ☏ *212/245–9980* ⌖ *Reservations essential* ▤ *AE, MC, V* ✛ *1:3D.*

$$$-$$$$
SEAFOOD
★
✕ **Doğa Balık.** Owner and chef Ibrahim Soğukdağ knows fish—he was a fisherman before he got started in the restaurant business—and this is one of the best places in the city for seafood (the name literally translates as "Nature Fish"). The friendly restaurant usually offers a wide variety of freshly caught options, most often served grilled. This casual spot is also renowned for its extensive selection of mezes, especially lightly cooked, unusual, fresh greens, such as beetroot leaves or samphire, a type of seaweed. On the eighth floor of the Villa Zurich hotel, this open-air restaurant has a commanding view of the Bosphorus and the Istanbul rooftops below. ⊠ *Akarsu Yokuşu Cad. 46, Cihangir* ☏ *212/293–9144* ⌖ *Reservations essential* ▤ *AE, MC, V* ✛ *1:3E.*

¢–$
TURKISH
✕ **Hacı Abdullah.** Tracing its roots back to 1888, this Istanbul institution serves authentic, relatively inexpensive, traditional Ottoman and Turkish cuisine. The places feels a bit touristy (the menu is in multiple languages), but it's also a favorite with locals wishing to enjoy good food in a relaxed atmosphere. Grilled meats, cabbage stuffed with lamb, rice pilaf with pine nuts and currants, and a variety of vegetables stewed in olive oil and served as cold appetizers are among the many

CLOSE UP

Sky-High Dining

2

360 Istanbul

In recent years, Istanbul's newest restaurants have been aiming high, literally, as an increasing number of savvy restauranteurs take advantage of the city's greatest natural asset—its spectacular views—and opened rooftop dining spots. The trend has been especially pronounced in the Beyoğlu neighborhood, which sits on a ridge overlooking the Bosphorus, the Golden Horn, and the sights of Sultanahmet; here you'll have the chance to eat dinner while looking at both Europe and, across the water, Asia. This is real intercontinental dining.

Two restaurants—**360 Istanbul**, atop a historic apartment building, and **Mikla,** at the top of the 18-story Marmara Pera hotel, have spectacular 360-degree views. (If you're choosing between the two, Mikla is, generally speaking, for an older crowd, while 360 Istanbul is a good place to get a glimpse of the city's younger elite.) The open-air (therefore summer only) **NuTeras** is a chic bar that serves excellent mezes and looks out on the Golden Horn. **Leb-i Derya** serves adequate fare on a lovely and breezy terrace bar where you can watch the sunset over the Bosphorus.

offerings. The restaurant, which has several elegant dining rooms done in dark red, faux-Ottoman style, is especially famous for its seemingly inexhaustible range of pickles and homemade fruit compotes. ⊠ *Ağa Cami, Atıf Yılmaz Cad. 9/A, Beyoğlu* ☎*212/293–8561* ▭*AE, MC, V* ✥*1:3D.*

¢ ✕**Hala Mantı.** As its name suggests,
TURKISH   this eatery on busy İstiklal Caddesi
★   specializes in *mantı*, small pockets of pasta filled with ground meat—the Turkish version of ravioli. *Gözleme*, thin pastry shells filled with ingredients such as cheese and spinach, then cooked on huge hot plates as you watch, are also excellent; other options include tasty homestyle vegetable and meat dishes, and desserts. With bare wooden tables and paper napkins, the atmosphere is simple but homey. ⊠ *İstiklal Cad. 131/D, Beyoğlu* ☎*212/292–7004* ▭*AE, MC, V* ✥*1:3D.*

¢ ✕**Helvetia.** Opened by two thirtysomething friends in 2004, this afford-
TURKISH   able, laid-back restaurant serves delicious home-style Turkish food. The menu changes daily, but always features a variety of soups and stewed vegetables, as well as more substantial dishes like zucchini fritters and meatballs in tomato sauce. The red-tiled open kitchen is a hive of constant activity, which occasionally spills into the dining area, so don't be surprised to find one of the cooks shelling peas or peeling an eggplant at the table next to you. The Sunday brunch buffet ($12) is an excellent value and highly recommended. ⊠ *General Yazgan Sokak 12, Beyoğlu* ☎*212/245–8780* ▭*No credit cards* ✥*1:3C.*

$$–$$$ ✕**The House Cafe.** Since the first House Cafe opened in Nişantaşı in 2002,
ECLECTIC   this minichain serving upscale comfort food has successfully expanded to 10 locations, without losing any of its appeal or quality. The eggs Benedict, pancakes, and other breakfast dishes are superb, and the massive burger is a delicious, juicy mess. The salad selection is vast—the warm artichoke and prawn combination is a standout—and the thincrust pizzas are also delicious. With exposed brick walls and tables of solid oak, the place has the right combination of sophistication and hominess. A new branch on İstiklal Caddesi is popular and busy; the older one in Beyoğlu's charming Asmalımescit area is quieter. Ortaköy's branch has a terrace overlooking the Bosphorus, while the one in chic Nişantaşı has a shady garden. ⊠ *İstiklal Cad. Mısır Apt. 163, Beyoğlu* ☎*212/251–7991* ▭*AE, MC, V* ✥*1:4C* ⊠*Asmalı Mescit 9, Beyoğlu* ☎*212/245–9515* ⊠*Atiye Sokak 10, Nişantaşı* ☎*212/259–2377* ⊠*Salhane Sokak 1, Ortaköy* ☎*212/227–2699.*

$–$$ ✕**İmroz.** Among the mostly identical *meyhanes* along Nevizade Sokak,
TURKISH   İmroz stands out for the freshness of its fish and its wide range of tasty
★   mezes such as a creamy and smoky eggplant salad, the spicy cured-meat

---

BEER IN TURKEY

For years, visitors to Turkey basically had one choice when ordering beer: Efes, the locally brewed lager. The situation has started to change, though, and international brands such as Miller, Tuborg, and Foster's are now brewed locally and imports of popular beers such as Corona and Beck's have begun. The most welcome news for beer drinkers, though, may be that Istanbul has entered the microbrew era and Taps, a brewpub in the Istanbul suburbs, has started to distribute its well-made beers to bars and select grocery stores around the city.

pastry *pastırmalı böreği,* and the fried cheese dish called *kaşar pane.* Presided over by the grandfatherly Yorgi Okumuş, a Greek Turk, the restaurant is crowded and friendly, the cigarette smoke is thick, and the rakı flows freely. It's one of the few remaining Greek tavernas in Istanbul—albeit with a Turkish menu. In summer the restaurants and bars on Nevizade have tables outside, giving the street an almost carnival atmosphere. ⊠*Nevizade Sokak 16, Beyoğlu* 🕾*212/249–9073* 🖃*DC, MC, V* ✛*1:3D.*

$–$$
TURKISH
✕**Istanbul Modern Cafe.** With its exquisite waterfront views and stylish industrial-chic decor—exposed air shafts and cement walls—this restaurant has slowly been nudging the exhibits aside as the main attraction of the Istanbul Museum of Modern Art. A sleek, red, rectangular bar dominates the dining room, which looks out onto the busy traffic of Istanbul's harbor. The lunch menu has a variety of pastas, salads, and sandwiches; dinner offers more substantial fare, like thyme-and-rosemary-marinated filet mignon and risotto with grilled shrimp. ⊠*Meclis-i Mebusan Cad., Liman İşletmeleri Sahası, Antrepo 4, Karaköy* 🕾*212/292–2612* ✍*Reservations essential* 🖃*AE, DC, MC, V* ✛*1:4E.*

$$–$$$
ECLECTIC
✕**Leb-i Derya.** It's not easy to find this seventh-floor rooftop restaurant— it's in an apartment building with only a small sign out front—but persevere (ask directions), because the reward is a magnificent view overlooking the Bosphorus and Sultanahmet's historical monuments. The kitchen turns out solid, though unremarkable, versions of international food: nachos, tandoori chicken, and grilled sea bass, as well as desserts like tiramisu and cheesecake; brunch is also served. The furniture is minimalist but stylish, and a greenhouse-like glass roof lets the sun, or the stars, peek in at the hip crowd of locals and expats who frequent the restaurant. ⊠*Kumbaracı Yokuşu 57/6, Beyoğlu* 🕾*212/293–4989* 🖃*AE, MC, V* ✛*1:4D.*

$$$$
TURKISH
★
✕**Mikla.** Mikla is part of the upper echelon of Istanbul restaurants and, on the top floor of the 18-story Marmara Pera Hotel, it has a stunning 360-degree view of Istanbul. American-trained Turkish-Finnish chef Mehmet Gürs brings both Turkish and Nordic influences into his contemporary kitchen, with results such as smoked lamb loin with walnut pesto and white bean puree, and grilled grouper with sun-dried tomato, eggplant puree, and poached artichoke. The decor feels sleek and Scandinavian: black place mats are set on wood tables, complemented with minimalist black and metal chairs. An extensive, though expensive, wine list features gems from Turkey and around the world. ⊠*Meşrutiyet Cad. 167/185, Beyoğlu* 🕾*212/293–5656* ✍*Reservations essential* 🖃*AE, DC, MC, V* ⊘*Closed Sat. lunch and Sun.* ✛*1:3C.*

¢
TURKISH
✕**Saray.** Saray (established in 1935) is best known for its desserts, but it's also an inexpensive place to get a bite to eat. The food is simple and

BEST BETS FOR BUDGET DINING

Çiya, Asian Side

Hala, Beyoğlu

Tarihi Köftecisi, Sultanahmet

Saray, Beyoğlu

Helvetia, Beyoğlu

satisfying: breakfast eggs are served fried or scrambled with cheese and tomatoes, the chicken soup is delicious, and the *döner* (meat carved off a spit) is excellent. Save room so that you can choose from the marvelous assortment of Turkish sweets on offer, from milk puddings to flaky baklava served with *kaymak* (clotted cream), and a glass of Turkish tea. Open late, Saray is a great place to stop off after a night out. ⊠ *İstiklal Cad. 102, Beyoğlu* ☎212/292–3434 ⊟*AE, MC, V* ✛*1:3D.*

$–$$
TURKISH
★ ✕**Sofyalı 9.** On a picturesque backstreet in Beyoğlu's charming Asmalımescit area, this jewel of a restaurant takes classic *meyhane* food several levels above the norm. Mezes, brought to your table on a large tray, are all excellent but standouts include cubes of fried eggplant in a yogurt and tahini sauce and Circassian chicken, a spread made with chicken and ground walnuts. Grilled fish and meat are also served. With Greek music playing in the background and photographs of old Istanbul on the walls, Sofyalı has loads of charm. A limited menu is served during lunch. ⊠*Sofyalı Sokak 9, Beyoğlu* ☎212/245–0362 ⚖*Reservations essential* ⊟*AE, MC, V* ✆*Closed Sun.* ✛*1:3C.*

¢
VEGETARIAN
✕**Zencefil.** The menu at this mostly-vegetarian restaurant includes omelets, salads, and several kinds of quiche and pasta, along with a good assortment of daily specials such as rice with artichoke or chicken with vegetables. There are also homemade breads, fresh-squeezed juices, and cakes and pies baked on the premises. The atmosphere is intimate and café-like, with exposed brick walls and antique floor tiles, and service is friendly and informal. A pleasant garden is open during warm weather. ⊠*Kurabiye Sokak 8–10, Beyoğlu* ☎212/243–8234 ⊟*AE, MC, V* ✆*Closed Sun.* ✛*1:2D.*

BOSPHORUS

$$$–$$$$
TURKISH
✕**1897 Konyalı.** Konyalı, an Istanbul institution, has opened a new restaurant (the main branch is in Topkapı Palace, open for lunch only), named for the year of Konyalı's founding, that takes its signature cuisine a step further. With the aim of recreating authentic Ottoman dishes, the menu includes game as well as fruit-based sauces (fruit was used instead of sugar in the Ottoman kitchen). Try the appetizer of game meat *börek* with apricot sauce, or the entrée of slow-marinated lamb with dried fruits. The restaurant has several smallish rooms decorated with dark woods, mirrors, and original ceramic artwork, while the outdoor patio is a lovely place in summer. Next-door Café Piruhi shares the same kitchen and serves lighter fare. ⊠*Süleyman Seba Cad. 46, Beşiktaş* ☎212/227–4243 ⚖*Reservations essential* ⊟*AE, MC, V* ✛*1:2G.*

$–$$
ECLECTIC
Fodor'sChoice
★ ✕**Abracadabra.** Abracadabra opened in 2008 and has quickly become a hit with Istanbul foodies. Using ingredients that are natural, local, and seasonal—consequently, the menu changes monthly—chef Dilara Erbay (formerly of Cezayir) creates delectable and attractive "traditional-experimental" dishes like salmon tartare with cracked wheat, bulgur-stuffed zucchini flowers served with thick yogurt, and duck confit with purslane and samosas. The four-story restaurant has an open kitchen on the second floor and an eclectic mix of antiques and furniture by Turkish designers throughout; it feels like you're entering the home of your most artistic friends. The top floor has a lovely balcony looking out over

the Bosphorus. ✉*Arnavutköy Cad. 50/1, Arnavutköy* ☎*212/358–6087* 🖃*MC, V* ✛*1:2H.*

$–$$
SEAFOOD
★ ✕**Adem Baba.** This is the Turkish version of a New England fish shack, with nets and crab traps hanging from the ceiling. They even serve a delicious, thick, fish stew that looks and tastes like clam chowder. Families and large groups come here to enjoy simple, fresh, and perfectly prepared fish, at a fraction of what they would pay at some of the fancier restaurants along the Bosphorus. There's no menu, but a refrigerated display at the entrance holds the day's catch. To start, order the fried calamari and the tasty fish *köfte* (fish cakes). It's in Arnavutköy, a low-key Bosphorus neighborhood with several historic wooden Victorian-style villas—perfect for a stroll before, or after, dinner. ✉*Satış Meydanı Sokak 2, Arnavutköy* ☎*212/263–2933* 🖃*MC, V* ✛*1:2H.*

BEST BET FISH RESTAURANTS

Balıkçı Sabahattin, Sultanamet

Adem Baba, Bosphorus

Giritli, Sultanamet

Doğa Balık, Beyoğlu

$$–$$$
TURKISH
✕**Çınaraltı.** Named after the massive sycamore tree growing through the center of the restaurant and shading the upstairs terrace with its branches, Çınaraltı ("under the sycamore") draws a larger number of locals than some of the other, nearly identical, restaurants lining Ortaköy's waterfront square. A refrigerated case inside the restaurant holds the catch of the day—go in and pick out your fish after first sampling some of the mezes. With its relaxed service, spacious feel, and simple but attractive decor, Çınaraltı is refreshingly unpretentious and reasonably priced in a neighborhood known for its trendiness. ✉*İskele Meydanı 28, Ortaköy* ☎*212/261–4616* 🖃*AE, MC, V* ✛*1:2H.*

$$$–$$$$
SEAFOOD
✕**İskele.** In a restored historic ferry terminal on the Bosphorus, İskele's romantic setting is more than matched by a fine range of seafood. After ordering from the selection of mezes, ask the waiter to recommend whatever is especially tasty that day. Eating in the restaurant, with its sliding glass doors that look out onto the Bosphorus, will make you feel like you're dining on the deck of a yacht. Phone ahead for a table by the window or, even better, outside on the terrace in warmer weather. ✉*Yahya Kemal Cad. 1, Rumelihisarı* ☎*212/263–2997* ✍*Reservations essential* 🖃*AE, MC, V* ✛*1:2H.*

$$$$
SEAFOOD
✕**Körfez.** Call ahead and this restaurant in the picturesque village of Kanlıca, on Istanbul's Asian side, can arrange to have you ferried across the Bosphorus from the Rumeli Hisarı neighborhood—a 30-minute cab ride from Taksim Square—in its private boat. Housed in an old *yalı* (waterfront mansion), the restaurant has wonderful views of the Bosphorus. Inside, the look is nautical, and the seafood is fresh and superbly cooked to order. The signature dish is sea bass cooked in salt, and starters such as flying-fish chowder are worth trying, too. It's a bit of a trek, but it's a romantic spot and worth the effort. ✉*Barış Manço Cad. 78, Kanlıca* ☎*216/413–4314* ✍*Reservations essential* 🖃*AE, DC, MC, V* ☯*Closed for lunch Mon.* ✛*1:2H.*

¢–$
TURKISH
✕**Şazeli.** The specialty at this small, family-run kebab house that turns out very tasty food is *dürüm*, kebabs wrapped in a soft, tortilla-like

This Istanbul street vendor is selling freshly roasted chestnuts.

flatbread—but make sure you sample some of the delicious appetizers: perhaps the smoky, grilled eggplant spread mixed with thick yogurt and garlic, or the chopped salad with walnuts in a tangy pomegranate-molasses dressing. Save room for the "Şazeli special dessert," a baklava-like triangle made out of semolina and ground pistachio and pine nuts, and stuffed with butter cream. The restaurant, with an interior dominated by a large copper charcoal grill, is a good low-cost option in the very pleasant neighborhood of Ortaköy. ⊠ *Muallim Naci Cad. 16/C, Ortaköy* ☎ *212/260–6969* ═ *MC, V* ✛ *1:2H.*

$$$$
ECLECTIC
Fodor'sChoice
★

✕ **Sunset Grill & Bar.** On a high hill overlooking the Bosphorus, Sunset seems to be flying over the glittering lights below. In warm weather, tables are set on the garden terrace, affording diners an unforgettable view. The restaurant's interior is sleek yet laid-back; the menu hops from Turkish specialties to California steaks to Asia, and the seafood dishes, such as potato-crusted sea bass, are standouts. With the 2008 arrival of chef Hiroki Takemura, a separate Japanese menu was introduced alongside the terrific sushi bar for which Sunset Grill was already known. The extensive wine and cognac menu features rare and vintage wines and aged cognacs. ⊠ *Yol Sokak 2, Ulus Parkı, Ulus* ☎ *212/287–0357* ⌚ *Reservations essential* ═ *AE, MC, V* ☾ *Sushi bar closed Sun. lunch* ✛ *1:2H.*

$$$$
TURKISH

✕ **Tuğra.** Cookbooks from the Ottoman palace were used to re-create some of the long-lost dishes—such as grilled quail served with noodles and yellow plums, and lamb chops cooked with fennel, chickpeas, pumpkin, and spices in a clay casserole—served at this spacious and luxurious restaurant in the Çırağan Palace. The Bosphorus view is flanked by the palace's marble columns, and the interior, with its soaring ceilings, large mirrors, and ornate chandeliers that hover above, makes you feel like royalty. After dinner, make your way to the hotel's poolside bar and enjoy the breeze. ⊠ *Çırağan Cad. 32 Beşiktaş* ☎ *212/326–4646* ⌕ *Reservations essential. Jacket required* ⊟ *AE, DC, MC, V* ⊘ *No lunch* ✛ *1:1H.*

BEST BETS FOR KEBABS

Çiya, Asian Side

Hamdi Et Lokantası, Eminönü

Mabeyin, Asian Side

Şazeli, Bosphorus

EMINÖNÜ AND THE GOLDEN HORN

¢ ✕ **Borsa Lokantası.** This unpretentious spot, which has been in business since 1927, attracts a hungry crowd that comes to eat wonderful, inexpensive food. Among the options—all served cafeteria-style—the baked lamb in eggplant puree and the stuffed artichokes are especially good. There is also an appealing selection of desserts, so you might want to leave room. Borsa is close to the ferry terminals of Eminönü, making it convenient for a quick meal before or after a boat ride on the Bosphorus or across to the Asian side of the city. ⊠ *Yalıköşkü Cad., Yalıköşkü Han 60–62, Eminönü* ☎ *212/511–8079 or 212/527–2350* ⊟ *AE, MC, V* ✛ *2:2B*

TURKISH ★

$–$$ ✕ **Hamdi Et Lokantası.** An Istanbul institution, Hamdi consistently rates as one of the city's top restaurants for grilled meat. Delicious kebabs of minced lamb mixed with pistachios or poppy seeds are among the more unusual items, while the small *lahmacun* (Turkish pizza topped with spiced ground meat) will make your mouth water. Service is impeccable, with white starched tablecloths and waiters in vests and ties. The four floors can get pretty packed—the place is extremely popular with locals—so make reservations for a table on the restaurant's terrace floor, which has excellent views of the Golden Horn and the Bosphorus. ⊠ *Kalçın Sokak 17, Eminönü* ☎ *212/528–0390* ⌕ *Reservations essential* ⊟ *AE, MC, V* ✛ *2:2A.*

TURKISH ★

GRAND BAZAAR

¢–$ ✕ **Fes Café.** With funky black-and-white Lucite chairs and fresh flowers on the tables, Fes Café provides a shot of modern style and familiar American-style food in the heart of the Grand Bazaar. Squeezed into a former market stall in what's become the hippest section of the market, the small kitchen turns out simple sandwiches, salads, fruit shakes, and homemade cakes and pies. It's a great place to sit back and watch the comings and goings of the bazaar. ⊠ *Halıcılar Cad. 58–62, Grand Bazaar* ☎ *212/528–1613* ⊟ *MC, V* ⊘ *Closed Sun.* ✛ *2:3A.*

CAFE

¢ ✕ **Havuzlu.** Need an escape from the carpet salesmen of the Grand Bazaar? This lunch-only spot, in a quiet corner of the sprawling market, offers just that. A large steam table at the front of the restaurant's open kitchen holds a daily assortment of some 25 dishes, including a variety of meat and vegetable stews. The food is homey, well made, and fresh. After you make your selection, waiters in black vests and ties will swiftly bring the food to your table in

TURKISH

the impressive 500-year-old dining hall, which has large Ottoman-style blown-glass chandeliers hanging from its vaulted ceilings. It closes at 5 PM. ⊠ *Gani Çelebi Sokak 3, Grand Bazaar* ☎ *212/527–3346* ⊕ *No dinner, closed Sun.* ✛ *2:3A.*

BREAKFAST IN ISTANBUL

A Turkish breakfast of fresh bread, *beyaz peynir* (feta-like white cheese), tomatoes, cucumbers, and olives, and often jam or honey, is included at most hotels in Turkey, although not usually at the higher-end properties.

SULTANAHMET

$$$–$$$$
SEAFOOD
★
✕ **Balıkçı Sabahattin.** This Sultanahmet restaurant in a renovated Ottoman house on a quiet backstreet started off more than 40 years ago as a simple fish shack that could barely seat 10 people; it's now known as one of the best places in Istanbul for seafood. Along with the wide assortment of expertly grilled fish, specialties include a pilaf made with mussels, rice, and currants, and a bouillabaisse-like fish stew. It's especially appealing in summer, when tables are set up outside in a shaded, cobblestoned plaza. Expect to pay a fair amount, as the place is a favorite among moneyed Turks. ⊠ *Seyit Hasan Kuyu Sokak 1, Sultanahmet* ☎ *212/458–1824* 🍴 *Reservations essential* ▤ *AE, MC, V* ✛ *2:5C.*

¢
TURKISH
✕ **Doy-Doy.** *Doy-doy* is a Turkish expression for "full" and, unlike many other spots in tourist-filled Sultanahmet, this is a place frequented by locals—and you can indeed fill up here for a reasonable sum. The restaurant serves simple kebabs, chicken and lamb stews, and *pide* (Turkish pizza) baked in a wood-burning oven. A variety of mezes are also available, and the meatless pizzas and salads are excellent options for vegetarians. Service is friendly and personable. The two-level rooftop terrace, open in summer, has fine views of the Blue Mosque and Sea of Marmara. ⊠ *Şifa Hamamı Sok. 13, Sultanahmet* ☎ *212/517–1588* ▤ *MC, V* ✛ *2:5B*

$$$$
SEAFOOD
Fodor'sChoice
★
✕ **Giritli.** Only open since 2003, Giritli has already become an Istanbul classic, and with a prix-fixe only menu of Cretan specialties that includes a generous four courses and unlimited drink (wine or rakı), it's easy to understand why. The food is outstanding, with an enormous selection of delicious appetizers like sea bass ceviche, herb-covered cubes of feta cheese with walnuts and green onion, and perfectly grilled calamari. Starters are followed by a choice of freshly caught fish (there aren't any other options), either grilled or fried. The restaurant garden, with its whitewashed walls and blue trim, feels like a slice of the Greek islands in the middle of Istanbul. ⊠ *Keresteci Hakkı Sokak, Sultanahmet* ☎ *212/458–2270* 🍴 *Reservations essential* ▤ *AE, MC, V* ✛ *2:5C*

$–$$
TURKISH
✕ **Konuk Evi.** A little oasis near Aya Sofya, this inviting restaurant has an outdoor patio with wicker chairs, all shaded by leafy trees. The small menu is comprised of mezes, salads, and grilled meats, as well as an assortment of Turkish desserts. It's a pleasant place to take a break from the hustle and bustle of Sultanahmet. ⊠ *Soğukçeşme Sokak, Sultanahmet* ☎ *212/513–3660* ▤ *AE, MC, V* ✛ *2:4C*

$–$$
TURKISH
✕ **Magnaura Café.** While at first glance Magnaura Café might appear much the same as the other tourist-oriented restaurants on Akbıyık

2

Caddesi, it stands out for its excellent food and service. The menu ranges from Turkish and Ottoman cuisine to international standards. Particularly notable are the steaks—the Marble Steak is grilled and served with flaming cognac, while the Boğaziçi Steak is marinated with vegetables in a terra-cotta pot—and Pasha Tavuk, chicken breast marinated in white wine and cream and served with vegetables. Far greater attention is given to presentation than in most Sultanahmet restaurants. There's also a cozy rooftop terrace with a partial view of the Marmara Sea. ⊠*Akbıyık Cad. 27, Sultanahmet* ☎*212/518–7622* ▤*MC, V* ✛*2:5C*

$$ ✕**Mozaik.** Friendly and accommodating, Mozaik is a delightful refuge
TURKISH in the midst of busy Sultanahmet. In a restored old house on a quiet corner, the charming restaurant's wicker chairs and small, sun-dappled dining rooms give it the feel of a well-worn (and well-loved) bistro. In summer, seating spills out into the alleys beside the restaurant, making for a lively atmosphere. Mozaik has the same owner as Rumeli Café, but its menu is a bit more mainstream and wide-ranging, including Turkish specialties as well as pastas, schnitzel, and even a T-bone steak. There is also an extensive selection of salads. ⊠*Incili Çavuş Sokak 1, Sultanahmet* ☎*212/512–4177* ▤*AE, MC, V* ✛*2:4B*

$–$$ ✕**Rumeli Café Restaurant.** This little eatery on a quiet side street in Sul-
TURKISH tanahmet's main tourist area offers good food at reasonable prices,
★ including a range of salads and meat dishes from a menu that spans Turkey and the globe. Particularly interesting are the dishes from Turkey's Kurdish and Armenian communities, such as *papaz yahnisi*, a Byzantine stew of lamb, potatoes, and pumpkin cooked in a terra-cotta dish. The cozy interior, formerly the site of a book bindery, has Ottoman-style chimneys, Byzantine-style arches, exposed brick walls, and hand-painted frescoes on the walls. In summer you can sit outside at tables on the sidewalk. ⊠*Ticarethane Sokak 8, Sultanahmet* ☎*212/512–0008* ▤*AE, MC, V* ✛*2:4B*

$$$$ ✕**Seasons.** The Istanbul Four Seasons in Sultanahmet is one of the city's
MEDITERRANEAN ritziest hotels, and it's also home to one of the city's finest restaurants, in a delightful gazebo-like glass pavilion in the middle of the hotel's manicured garden. The menu is Ottoman/Mediterranean and features the creations of chef Mehmet Gök. The emphasis is on seafood and lamb, but there are also pastas and risottos. The lunch menu is lighter and more international, with sandwiches, pastas, and salads. On Sundays, the restaurant's brunch buffet ($80) draws crowds from across Istanbul. ⊠*Tevkifhane Sokak 1, Sultanahmet* ☎*212/638–8200* ⌦*Reservations essential* ▤*AE, DC, MC, V* ✛*2:4C*

$–$$ ✕**Sultanahmet Fish House.** This fish restaurant serves good food at some
SEAFOOD of the most reasonable fish prices in Sultanahmet. The mainly seafood mezes include sardines, octopus, and mackerel in olive oil, while the mains include a full range of fish as well as a few meat kebabs. The light blue and yellow walls, multicolored antique lamps hanging from the ceiling, and colorful nomad textiles on the walls make for a vibrant and inviting atmosphere. Run by a husband-and-wife team and their business partner, the restaurant has a friendly, family-oriented feel to it. ⊠*Prof. İsmail Gürkan Cad. 14, Sultanahmet* ☎*212/527–4441* ▤*AE, MC, V* ✛*2:3B*

$$–$$$ ✕ **Teras.** With the Sea of Marmara
TURKISH on one side and the Blue Mosque
★ and Aya Sofya on another, this
open-air restaurant on top of the
Armada Hotel has one of the more
romantic locations in Istanbul. The
view at night, with the lights of
Sultanahmet's historic monuments
reflecting off the sea, is especially
stunning, and the food, a combination of classic Ottoman and modern Turkish dishes such as grilled
lamb with eggplant puree, phyllo
pie stuffed with vegetables, and
a selection of seafood, holds its
own against the dramatic setting.
✉*Ahırkapı Sokak 24, Sultanahmet* ☎*212/455–4455* ⌦*Reservations
essential* ▤*AE, MC, V* ✛*2:5C*

¢ ✕ **Tarihi Sultanahmet Köftecisi.** Like pizza for New Yorkers, humble *köfte*
TURKISH (grilled meatballs) inspire countless arguments among Istanbullus about
who makes them best. This restaurant has a simple menu—meatballs,
piyaz (boiled white beans in olive oil), and salad—that has remained
virtually unchanged since 1920, and it's one of the best places for *köfte*
in the city. Waiters in white coats, marble-topped tables, and framed
photos and letters lining the walls add a touch of class and history to a
budget place that serves essentially nothing but meatballs. Its location, a
few minutes' walk from the Blue Mosque and Aya Sofya, makes it ideal
for a quick and affordable lunch. ■TIP➔ There are several branches of
Tarihi Köftecisi throughout Istanbul, but this one is the original. There are
imitators with similar names, but Tarihi Sultanahmet Koftecisi ("Historic
Sultanahmet Koftecisi") is considered the real deal. ✉*Divan Yolu Cad.
12, Sultanahmet* ☎*212/520–0566* ▤*No credit cards* ✛*2:4B*

TAKSIM AND NIŞANTAŞI

$$–$$$ ✕ **Banyan.** Until recently Istanbul's vibrant dining scene was sorely lack-
ASIAN ing in Asian food, which is why Banyan's arrival in 2003 was so welcome. The restaurant, which has a soothing dining room with long
banquettes, serves traditional Asian fare, including a variety of dim sum
and beef in orange sauce, but the kitchen also makes use of regional
ingredients to create tantalizing modern dishes such as filet mignon
marinated in sake, and octopus satay with a ginger-soy sauce. A branch
in Ortaköy has a terrace that looks out on the Bosphorus and serves
more substantial fare, at higher prices ($$$–$$$$). ✉*Abdi İpekçi Cad.
36, Nişantaşı* ☎*212/219–6011* ⌦*Reservations essential* ▤*AE, MC, V*
✉*Muallim Naci Cad. Salhane Sokak 3, Ortaköy* ☎*212/259–9060*
⌦*Reservations essential* ▤*AE, MC, V* ✛*1:1E.*

$$$–$$$$ ✕ **Changa.** Opened in 1999, Changa has been blazing a culinary path
ECLECTIC in Istanbul that others have only recently started to follow. The menu is
★ overseen by award-winning, London-based chef Peter Gordon, and the
innovative dishes combine flavors and ingredients from around the world,

> ## WORD OF MOUTH
>
> "At the recommendation of our
> guide we chose to try a local place
> for lunch that served sheep intes-
> tine sandwiches. I can honestly say
> it wasn't bad. It was a fried mass on
> a huge roll and as Anthony Bour-
> dain says, 'If it's fried, Americans
> will eat it!' I can say that although it
> didn't taste bad, I probably won't be
> making sheep intestine sandwiches
> for myself here at home!"
> —LowCountryIslander

2

presented with aesthetic flair. Mains include tortellini stuffed with wasabi and salmon and served with a grilled porcini and creamed lemongrass sauce, and grilled beef with greens and a sweet Vietnamese sauce. The restaurant is spread out over three floors of an early-20th-century town house, and a large circular "skylight" cut into the ground floor reveals the bustling basement kitchen below. ⊠*Sıraselviler Cad. 47, Taksim* ☎*212/251–7064 or 212/249–1348* ⚑*Reservations essential* ▭*AE, MC, V* ⊗*No lunch. Closed Sun.* ✥*1:3E.*

$–$$ ✕**La Casita.** Despite its Spanish
TURKISH name, this charming café, which was started a quarter-century ago and is one of three branches in Istanbul, serves Turkish food with a modern twist. La Casita is known for its *mantı*—a ravioli-like Turkish pasta traditionally stuffed with ground meat—and for its own creation: "Feraye" (a name the restaurant has even trademarked), which are *mantı* stuffed with cheese and spinach, potato and cheese, or chicken, and fried. The menu also features creative takes on other Turkish dishes, plus steaks and a variety of salads. The atmosphere is casual, and the decor an eclectic mix of Mediterranean touches and framed vintage records dotting the walls. ⊠*Abdi İpekçi, Atiye Sokak 3, Nişantaşı* ☎*212/327–8293* ▭*AE, MC, V* ✥*1:1F.*

$$–$$$ ✕**Mezzaluna.** This is the place to come for what is probably the best
ITALIAN Italian food in Istanbul. The wide of selection pizzas, baked in a brick oven brought over from Italy, is excellent, but Mezzaluna also turns out antipasti, risottos, and delicious pastas such as linguine with shrimp, calamari, and sun-dried tomatoes. The atmosphere is welcoming and lively: the walls are decorated with artsy photos, the ceiling is painted to look like the sky, and the tables are filled with chatting locals. ⊠*Abdi İpekçi Cad. 38/1, Nişantaşı* ☎*212/231–3142* ⚑*Reservations essential* ▭*AE, MC, V* ✥*1:1E.*

TURKISH COFFEE

Tea might be the beverage of choice in Turkey these days, but those in need of a coffee fix need not worry. Most teahouses serve Turkish coffee, although you may find a better cup by going to a more upscale café, which will probably use better coffee and take the time to prepare it properly. Well-made Turkish coffee should be thick and almost chocolaty, with espresso-like foam on top. Turks drink their coffee three ways: *sade* (plain), *orta* (medium sweet), and *şekerli* (extra sweet). It's usually served with a small glass of water and, frequently, a little piece of *lokum* (Turkish delight).

WHERE TO STAY

With the number of visitors to Turkey growing by about 10% every year, Istanbul's hoteliers have been busy keeping up with the increasing demand. New lodgings, from full-service hotels to smaller boutique inns, are opening all the time, while older establishments are busy renovating and expanding. This means there are plenty more options than there were in the past, but because Istanbul is such a popular destination, it's not the travel bargain it used to be. It's also worth noting that most hotels have started quoting their rates in euros, which makes what might look like a good deal something less than that when paying in U.S. dollars. Most lodgings, save for the five-star hotels, include a full Turkish breakfast with the room rate.

The majority of visitors to Istanbul stay in the Sultanahmet area—the Aya Sofya, Blue Mosque, Topkapı Palace, and most of Istanbul's major sites are in the neighborhood, which has the city's widest selection of hotels, smaller family-run *pansiyons* (guesthouses), and some charming boutique inns. Many of the rooms here tend to be on the small side, and bathrooms often only have showers, but what's lacking in space tends to be more than made up for in character and atmosphere. The downside to Sultanahmet is that at the height of the season, the area is overrun not only with tourists but touts who will try to steer you to their carpet shop. On the upside, stiff local competition means that Sultanahmet usually has the best deals in town; some hotels even offer a 5% to 10% discount for payment in cash.

For a less touristy taste of Istanbul, try the Beyoğlu area across the water, only a 10-minute cab ride or 20-minute tram ride from the sights of Sultanahmet. Once filled with rather grotty low-budget hotels, Beyoğlu has emerged as an attractive alternative to Sultanahmet, particularly in terms of boutiques and more upscale hotels. Staying here puts you closer to Istanbul's best restaurants and nightspots and also gives you a chance to stroll through Beyoğlu's lively backstreets. Istanbul's large modern hotels are mostly clustered around Taksim Square and up along the Bosphorus—the latter is where you'll find the most luxurious, indulgent options.

No matter where you stay, plan ahead: Istanbul, despite adding so many new lodgings, still has a chronic shortage of beds.

WHAT IT COSTS IN U.S. DOLLARS					
	¢	$	$$	$$$	$$$$
Hotels	under $100	$100–$150	$151–$225	$226–$350	over $350

Prices are for two in a standard double in high season, including 18 % tax.

ASIAN SIDE

$$$$
Fodor's Choice
★

Sumahan. Owners Mark and Nedret Butler, both architects, took on the challenge of converting a derelict distillery built in 1875 into a luxury hotel on the Asian side of the Bosphorus; the result is one of Istanbul's most chic and original places to stay. On the water's edge, with an incredible view, the hotel—opened in 2005—has comfortable suites, all with water views and decorated in an unfussy minimalist style. Some rooms have fireplaces; ground-level suites open onto a grassy yard. The hotel has a private launch that makes regular runs across the Bosphorus, but at night you'll need to take ferries or taxis to get back. **Pros:** location on Bosphorus; stylish boutique hotel. **Cons:** far from sights and commercial center. ⊠ *Kuleli Cad. 51, Çengelköy,* ☎ *216/422–8000* ⊕ *www.sumahan.com* ⇄ *7 rooms, 13 suites* ⌂ *In-room: safe, DVD, Internet. In-hotel: restaurant, room service, bar, tennis court, gym,* *laundry service, parking (free), no-smoking rooms* ☐*AE, MC, V* ⦿|*BP* ✛*1:4H.*

BEST BETS FOR BUDGET SLEEPING

Galata Residence, Beyoğlu

Hanedan, Sultanahmet

Hotel Nomade, Sultanahmet

Sarnıç, Sultanahmet

Şebnem, Sultanahmet

BEYOĞLU

$$ 🛏 **Anemon Galata.** With winding cobblestoned streets radiating from a square dominated by a 14th-century Genoese-built tower, the Galata neighborhood is one of Istanbul's most picturesque, least-touristy areas. The Anemon sits in the heart of it, in a meticulously renovated, century-old building just across the street from the Galata Tower. The atmosphere is elegant and Old World, and rooms are plush and comfortable. An upstairs restaurant, where breakfast is served, has wonderful views of the tower and the Golden Horn. Ask for a room away from the street to get a view and avoid noise. **Pros:** historic neighborhood; professional service. **Cons:** though safe, the area can feel a bit abandoned at night; some rooms small. ⊠*Büyükhendek Cad. 5, Galata* ☎*212/293–2343* ⊕*www.anemonhotels.com* ⟿*21 rooms, 7 suites* ⚏*In-room: safe, Wi-Fi. In-hotel: restaurant, room service, laundry service, parking (paid), no-smoking rooms* ☐*AE, MC, V* ⦿|*BP* ✛*1:4C.*

$$$–$$$$ 🛏 **Ansen 130 Suites.** Owner Burak Akkok has lived in New York and ★ Paris, and the Ansen 130 shows it. Stylish and hip, and hosting mostly adult travelers, this small all-suites hotel in a 20th-century building would not seem out of place in either of those cosmopolitan centers. The lobby, which doubles as a café and bar, is updated Art Deco in style, with two-tone wood paneling on the walls and a bar counter topped with dark brown leather. The rooms are spacious, smartly decorated, and have full kitchens. The staff, though dressed in T-shirts, are professional, friendly, and attentive. **Pros:** large, attractive suites; close to nightlife. **Cons:** staff's English is a bit limited. ⊠*Meşrutiyet Cad. 130, Tepebaşı,* ☎*212/245–8808* ⊕*www.ansensuites.com* ⟿*10 suites* ⚏*In-room: safe, kitchen, Wi-Fi. In-hotel: restaurant, room service, bar, laundry service* ☐*AE, MC, V* ⦿|*BP* ✛*1:3C.*

$ 🛏 **Galata Residence.** What was originally an apartment building built ★ in 1881 for the Camondos, one of the leading banking families of the late Ottoman Empire, is now a very appealing residence hotel only a few minutes' walk from the Galata Tower. The large one- and two-bedroom lodgings are decorated with somewhat worn but comfortable period furniture, but they've also been discreetly supplemented with modern conveniences like air-conditioning and full kitchens. The size and price of the apartments make them an especially good value for families or multiple couples. Upper floors have wonderful views across the Golden Horn to the old city. **Pros:** good location; good arrangement for families. **Cons:** steep surrounding streets with stairs make hotel access a bit inconvenient; neighborhood is safe but rather abandoned at night. ⊠*Felek Sokak 2, Bankalar Cad., Galata,* ☎*212/292–4841* ⊕*www.galataresidence.com* ⟿*22 apartments* ⚏*In-room: safe, kitchen, refrigerator, Internet. In-hotel: laundry service* ☐*MC, V* ✛*1:4C.*

$$$$ ⛏ **The Marmara Pera.** Opened in 2004, The Marmara Pera has quickly become one of Istanbul's hippest places to stay, combining the luxury of a full-service hotel with the funky decor of a smaller one. The building doesn't look like much from the outside, but the interior is a treat: think of it as an 18-story boutique hotel. The lobby is done in floor-to-ceiling brown-and-cream tiles and has vintage '50s and '60s furniture. Smallish rooms have large windows overlooking the city. There's a small pool on the roof, and the lobby café has an excellent range of cakes and chocolates. **Pros:** amazing views of city and Golden Horn; great location; good dining options. **Cons:** expensive for the size of the rooms; pool and fitness center are small. ✉ *Meşrutiyet Cad., Derviş Sokak 1 Tepebaşı,* ☎ *212/251–4646* ⊕ *www.themarmarahotels.com* ⇥ *200 rooms, 3 suites* ♿ *In-room: safe, Wi-Fi. In-hotel: restaurant, room service, bar, pool, gym, laundry service, some pets allowed, no-smoking rooms* ⊟ *AE, DC, MC, V* ✚ *1:3C.*

$$$ ⛏ **Pera Palace.** Currently closed for some much-needed renovations, the Pera Palace was built in 1892 to accommodate guests arriving on the *Orient Express.* Everyone who was anyone in the late 19th and early 20th centuries stayed here, from Mata Hari to numerous heads of state, and the rooms once occupied by Kemal Atatürk and Agatha Christie were turned into museums. The hotel has always been full of atmosphere and quirky charm, but although it had been modernized, the facilities and rooms were not in the greatest shape. The Pera is supposed to reopen in late 2009 or the beginning of 2010, but check the Web site for updates. ✉ *Meşrutiyet Cad. 52, Tepebaşı,* ☎ *212/243–0737* ⊕ *www.perapalas.com* ⊟ *AE, DC, MC, V* ✚ *1:3C.*

$$$ ⛏ **Richmond Hotel.** Behind the facade of a turn-of-the-century building on lively pedestrian-only İstiklal Caddesi is this modern hotel. Rooms are comfortable, spacious, and clean, and some have views of the Bosphorus, although beware the ones that look out into a dismal inner courtyard. The top-floor suites are impressive, with lovely water views, full-size desks, and large flat-screen TVs. The rooftop restaurant is a great spot for a sunset drink. The hotel is to receive a complete makeover, intending a more modern, minimalist design and decor and will be closed from June to October 2009 for these renovations. **Pros:** located on main shopping and nightlife drag; professional service. **Cons:** some rooms small; room decor a bit dated (which will no doubt change after renovation). ✉ *İstiklal Cad. 227, Beyoğlu,* ☎ *212/252–5460* ⊕ *www.richmondhotels.com.tr* ⇥ *102 rooms, 2 suites* ♿ *In-room: safe, Wi-Fi. In-hotel: 2 restaurants, room service, bar, laundry service, parking (paid), no-smoking rooms* ⊟ *AE, MC, V* �📶*BP* ✚ *1:3D.*

$$ ⛏ **Villa Zurich.** The quiet Villa Zurich, in the heart of Cihangir, is a good base for exploring this neighborhood and the rest of Istanbul. The lobby is small and rather simple, but the rooms were completely renovated in 2006 (maybe the lobby will be next), with new furniture, carpeting, and bathrooms. The decor is modern and rooms are done in browns, neutrals, and dark blues. The top floor is home to Doğa Balık, one of Istanbul's best fish restaurants, and is also where breakfast is served in summer, with a nice view of the Golden Horn. **Pros:** location in hip residential neighborhood; good value. **Cons:** some rooms and bathrooms have unpleasant odors. ✉ *Akarsu Yokuşu Cad. 44,*

Cihangir, ☎*212/293–0604* ⊕*www. hotelvillazurich.com* ↴*41 rooms* ☖*In-room: safe, Wi-Fi. In-hotel: restaurant, room service, bar, laundry service, parking (paid), no-smoking rooms* ▤*AE, MC, V* ⑩*CP* ✛*1:3E.*

CIHANGIR

Istanbul's Cihangir neighborhood is not on most visitors' maps, but it deserves a look. Long known as a kind of bohemian quarter, it's filled with charming small cafés and restaurants—though not much in the way of historical or cultural sites, or much shopping—and it's far from the bustle of the city, though still walking distance from Beyoğlu's livelier areas. The Villa Zurich hotel, with its Doğa Balık restaurant, is in Cihangir.

BOSPHORUS

$$$$ ⛊**Çırağan Palace Kempinski.** This
★ 19th-century Ottoman palace (pronounced chi-rahn) is Istanbul's most luxurious hotel. There are two buildings: the older palace and a newer addition. The ornate public spaces feel absolutely decadent and the setting, right on the Bosphorus, is breathtaking; the outdoor infinity pool seems to hover on the water's edge. Rooms have Ottoman-inspired wood furnishings and textiles in warm colors; all have balconies, and the views on the Bosphorus side are exceptional (rooms on the other side look out on a park and busy road). Most lodgings are in the new wing, though there are 11 suites in the palace, including the €25,000 per night Sultan's Suite—start saving now. **Pros:** incredible location, service, degree of luxury. **Cons:** exorbitant price of food and drinks. ✉*Çırağan Cad. 32, Beşiktaş,* ☎*212/326–4646* ⊕*www.kempinski-istanbul.com* ↴*280 rooms, 33 suites* ☖*In-room: safe, Wi-Fi. In-hotel: 4 restaurants, room service, bar, pools, gym, spa, children's programs (ages 0–11), laundry service, parking (free), no-smoking rooms* ▤*AE, DC, MC, V* ✛*1:1H.*

$$$–$$$$ ⛊**Conrad Istanbul.** This modern 14-story tower, catering primarily to business travelers, has spectacular views of the Bosphorus and terraced gardens. The busy yet elegant lobby is gleaming white, with furniture covered in golden fabric and a fountain in the center. The rooms, many of which face the Bosphorus, are tastefully furnished and comfortable. The staff is genial and efficient and can help you navigate the hotel's full range of services. Prego restaurant ($$$) serves Italian food in a contemporary setting, while the rooftop Summit Bar has some of the city's finest views. **Pros:** excellent service; Bosphorus views. **Cons:** standard rooms could use sprucing up; atmosphere is that of a business hotel. ✉*Yıldız Cad., Beşiktaş,* ☎*212/227–3000* ⊕*www.conradistanbul.com* ↴*555 rooms, 35 suites* ☖*In-room: safe, Wi-Fi. In-hotel: 2 restaurants, room service, bar, tennis courts, pools, gym, laundry service, parking (paid), no-smoking rooms* ▤*AE, DC, MC, V* ✛*1:1G.*

$$$$ ⛊**Four Seasons Hotel Bosphorus.** The new Four Seasons on the Bosphorus, in a restored 19th-century Ottoman palace with two modern wings added on, has a sumptuous ambience and even more luxurious facilities than its sister in Sultanahmet. Rooms and suites, a quarter of which have Bosphorus views (others have park and city views), are elegant yet understated, with soaring ceilings, muted tones, and Ottoman touches such as handcrafted mirrors. The marble-lined bathrooms, with separate tubs and showers, feel downright palatial. The spa has saunas, steam rooms, and Turkish baths, while the outdoor pool is just steps from the water's edge. Service is impeccable. **Pros:** luxurious accomodations and service; beautiful views. **Cons:** expensive food, drinks, and Internet. ⊠ *Çırağan Cad. 80, Beşiktaş,* ☎ *212/381–4000* ⊕ *www. fourseasons.com/bosphorus* ↩ *141 rooms, 25 suites* ♿ *In-room: safe, DVD, Wi-Fi. In-hotel: restaurant, room service, bars, pools, gym, spa, laundry service, Wi-Fi, parking (free), some pets allowed, no-smoking rooms* ▭ *AE, D, DC, MC, V* ✦ *1:1H.*

$$$$ ⌂ **Radisson SAS Bosphorus Hotel.** Perched on the water's edge, only a few steps from the cobblestoned main square of Ortaköy, one of the prettiest Bosphorus neighborhoods, the Radisson's location is unbeatable. It also earns high marks for its rooms and full range of services. The lobby has a clean, sleek look, with a large, atrium-like glass entrance; rooms are modern and comfortable, with Scandinavian design elements and complimentary snacks. Be sure to ask for a room with a Bosphorus view. The hotel's restaurant has a pleasant open-air terrace looking out on the water. **Pros:** services of a business-class hotel with smaller, more personal feel. **Cons:** somewhat far from tourist destinations. ⊠ *Çırağan Cad. 46, Ortaköy,* ☎ *212/310–1500* ⊕ *www.radissonsas.com* ↩ *111 rooms, 9 suites* ♿ *In-room: safe, Wi-Fi. In-hotel: restaurant, room service, bars, gym, laundry service, parking (free), no-smoking rooms* ▭ *AE, DC, MC, V* ✦ *1:1F.*

$$$$ ⌂ **Swissôtel Istanbul.** In a superb spot just above Dolmabahçe Palace,
★ the Swissôtel was controversial when it was built—nobody liked the idea of such a large, modern structure towering over the palace. The views are magnificent, though: from the water all the way to Topkapı Palace across the Golden Horn. The vast, high-ceiling lobby has terraced levels that seem to cascade down to the Bosphorus and is usually filled with the sounds of a tinkling piano. The overall effect is that of a grand and elegant Old World hotel. Rooms have contemporary if undistinguished furnishings and original art on the walls; service is crisp and efficient. **Pros:** first-class service; extensive dining and fitness options. **Cons:** expensive food and Internet; hotel can only reached by taxi (or on foot); somewhat impersonal atmosphere. ⊠ *Bayıldım Cad. 2, Maçka,* ☎ *212/326–1100* ⊕ *www.swissotel.com* ↩ *497 rooms; 23 suites rooms* ♿ *In-room: safe, Wi-Fi. In-hotel: 6 restaurants, room service, bars, tennis courts, pools, gym, spa, laundry service, parking (no free), no-smoking rooms* ▭ *AE, DC, MC, V* ✦ *1:2F.*

$$$$ ⌂ **W Istanbul.** The first W hotel in Europe combines posh ultramodernity with the property's historic pedigree as an 1870s Ottoman residence, with the extra perk of being surrounded by upscale restaurants and designer shops in the newly redeveloped Akaretler neighborhood. With its sexy—bordering on showy—lighting and chic East-meets-West decor, as well as cool amenities like iPod docks, the hotel attracts hip couples and business travelers looking for pampering. Consistent with the luxury chain's "whatever/whenever" philosophy, service is attentive and personalized. Jean-Georges Vongerichten's Spice Market restaurant offers delectable Southeast Asian cuisine. Eight rooms have outdoor cabanas; some others have tiny gardens. **Pros:** hip, cool atmosphere;

Sumahan   Four Seasons at Sultanahmet

Hotel Empress Zoë   Sarı Konak Oteli

exceptional service; ultra-comfortable beds. **Cons:** some room features so high-tech they are not user-friendly; dim, nightclub-like lighting in public spaces may not suit all tastes. ⊠*Süleyman Seba Cad. 22, Beşiktaş,* ☎*212/381–2121* ⊕*www.whotels.com/istanbul* ⤶*106 rooms, 28 suites* ⏢*In-room: safe, DVD, Wi-Fi. In-hotel: restaurant, room service, bar, gym, spa, laundry service, Wi-Fi, parking (free), some pets allowed, no-smoking rooms* ▭*AE, DC, MC, V* ✛*1:2G.*

SULTANAHMET

$$ ⌘**Alzer Hotel.** This hotel combines friendly service, attractive rooms, and a great location right on the Hippodrome. The wooden floors and old-fashioned furniture are complemented with pastel and cream colors, and antique chandeliers and lamps, along with flat-screen TVs. The three rooms with views of the Hippodrome and the Blue Mosque have cozy bay windows with built-in divans, perfect for taking in the action below. At the hotel's entrance is a pleasant sidewalk restaurant; breakfast is served in an enclosed terrace upstairs that has views of the Blue Mosque, Aya Sofya, and the sea. **Pros:** central location; comfortable rooms. **Cons:** rooms facing Hippodrome can be noisy. ⊠*At Meydanı 72, Sultanahmet,* ☎*212/516–6262* ⊕*www.alzerhotel.com* ⤶*21 rooms, 1 suite* ⏢*In-room: safe, Wi-Fi. In-hotel: 2 restaurants, room service, laundry service, no-smoking rooms* ▭*AE, MC, V* ❍❘*BP* ✛*2:5B.*

¢ ⌘**Apricot Hotel.** This small, cozy, well-run hotel is a good value and the 10 clean, well-maintained rooms are quite ample by Sultanahmet standards, as are the bathrooms. The patterned wallpaper and unique ceiling lamps add some ambience. Four rooms have small balconies and views of the Blue Mosque. Owner and manager Hakan Kocatürk is a licensed tour guide and, besides being extraordinarily friendly, conducts business professionally. Breakfast has traditionally been served in the lobby area but this space is to be turned into two more rooms, while a quiet garden is to be opened in the back. **Pros:** good value; intimate, homey atmosphere; very helpful staff. **Cons:** no elevator; rooms vary in size. ⊠*Amiral Tafdil Sokak 18/2, Sultanahmet,* ☎*212/638–1658* ⊕*www.apricothotel.com* ⤶*10 rooms* ⏢*In-room: Wi-Fi. In-hotel: laundry service, some pets allowed, no-smoking rooms* ▭*MC, V* ❍❘*BP* ✛*2:5C.*

$$
★ ⌘**Armada Hotel.** Only 10 minutes' walk from Istanbul's main tourist sites, the Armada offers spacious, comfortable accommodations with marble-lined bathrooms, lace curtains, and walls painted a soothing shade of green. Most rooms look out either to the sea or over the old city, although one of the best views is at night from the hotel's rooftop Teras Restaurant, from where you can see Aya Sofya and the Blue Mosque. Despite its large size and four-star billing, the hotel has a friendly, even quirky, feel—how many high-end hotels have a pool full of turtles in the middle of the lobby? **Pros:** amazing views of the water; professional service; in quiet area. **Cons:** somewhat steep uphill walk from hotel to the sights of Sultanahmet. ⊠*Ahırkapı Sokak 24, Sultanahmet,* ☎*212/455–4455* ⊕*www.armadahotel.com.tr* ⤶*110 rooms* ⏢*In-room: safe, Wi-Fi. In-hotel: restaurant, room service, bar,*

laundry service, parking (no fee), no-smoking rooms ☰*AE, MC, V* ⑩|*BP* ✛*2:5C.*

$$$ 🏨**Ayasofya Pansiyonları & Konuk Evi.** These accommodations are part of the project undertaken by Turkey's Touring and Automobile Club to restore (or authentically re-create) a movie-set-like street of 19th-century wooden houses along the outer wall of Topkapı Palace. The charming, pastel-colored houses of Ayasofya Pansiyonları have been

WORD OF MOUTH

"We've been to Istanbul 3 times and enjoyed it a lot. We stayed in Sultanhamet two out of the three times and continue to book there rather than other areas in spite of the tourist factor. It's nice to have things lively and a lot going on. that's what makes tourist areas fun."
—JulieVikmanis

turned into *pansiyons* furnished in late Ottoman style. Front rooms have up-close views of Aya Sofya, but the rest do not, so if you want a view, specify when you reserve. The nearby Konuk Evi is an Ottoman mansion that has been restored in similar fashion and has larger rooms. Breakfast is served in the Konuk Evi's shaded garden in summer. **Pros:** unique buildings; location adjacent to Aya Sofya. **Cons:** high room rates because of location. ⊠*Soğukçeşme Sokak, Sultanahmet,* ☎*212/513–3660* ⊕*www.ayasofyapensions.com* ⤵*57 rooms, 5 suites* ♿*In-room: no TV, Wi-Fi. In-hotel: 2 restaurants, room service, laundry service, no-smoking rooms* ☰*AE, DC, MC, V* ⑩|*BP* ✛*2:4C.*

$$$ 🏨**Celal Sultan.** With attentive service and a good restaurant, this hotel successfully straddles the line between the intimacy of a boutique hotel and the comfort of a full-service one. Created out of three restored town houses that were joined together, the Celal Sultan has compact, clean rooms with modern furnishings. The inviting lobby, with its delightful bar, is decorated with colorful kilims and Turkish rugs, and the roof-top terrace provides a fine view of the Aya Sofya. Unusual for Istanbul, the water in the hotel is filtered. The proprietor, Mr. Selami, and his wife are full of good sightseeing and shopping tips. **Pros:** hotel is on a quiet street; personable staff. **Cons:** some rooms small; rates a bit high. ⊠*Salkımsöğüt Sokak 16, Yerebatan Cad., Sultanahmet,* ☎*212/520–9323* ⊕*www.celalsultan.com* ⤵*55 rooms, 2 suites* ♿*In-room: Wi-Fi. In-hotel: restaurant, room service, bars, laundry service, no-smoking rooms* ☰*AE, MC, V* ⑩|*BP* ✛*2:4B.*

$$ 🏨**Dersaadet Hotel.** Dersaadet means "place of happiness" in Ottoman Turkish and this small hotel lives up to its name. Rooms have an elegant, even plush, feel, with colorful rugs on the floor, wood furniture, and ceilings hand-painted with Ottoman ornamental motifs. The top two floors of the hotel have rooms with views, while a cozy terrace, where breakfast is served and classical music plays in the background, looks out on the sea. Deniz Duyar, the hotel's young owner and manager, earned his MBA in New York and runs the place with a high level of professionalism. **Pros:** extraordinary level of service; lovely terrace; good value. **Cons:** some rooms modest in size. ⊠*Küçükayasofya Cad. Kapıağası Sokak 5, Sultanahmet,* ☎*212/458–0760* ⊕*www.hoteldersaadet.com* ⤵*14 rooms, 3 suites* ♿*In-room: safe, Wi-Fi. In-hotel: room service, laundry service, no-smoking rooms* ☰*MC, V* ⑩|*BP* ✛*2:5B.*

$$$$

Fodor'sChoice

★

⚑ **Four Seasons Hotel Sultanahmet.** What a rehabilitation success story: a former prison, this elegant hotel became one of Istanbul's premier accommodations the instant it opened in 1996. This neoclassical building, painted a buttery yellow and decorated with aqua-blue tiles, is steps from Topkapı Palace and Aya Sofya. Rooms and suites overlook the Sea of Marmara, the old city, or a manicured interior courtyard, and are luxuriously outfitted with reading chairs, original works of art, and bathrooms with deep tubs. In 2010, the hotel is to open a new wing—with more rooms, a spa, and swimming pool—built on stilts so as to showcase the archeological site of a Byzantine palace below. **Pros:** historic building surrounded by major tourist attractions; luxurious accommodations; exceptional service. **Cons:** breakfast not included and expensive; high charge for Internet. ⊠*Tevkifhane Sokak 1, Sultanahmet,* ☎*212/638–8200* ⊕*www.fourseasons.com/istanbul* ⤣*54 rooms, 11 suites* ⌂*In-room: safe, DVD, Wi-Fi. In-hotel: restaurant, room service, bar, gym, laundry service, Wi-Fi, parking (paid), some pets allowed, no-smoking rooms* ▭*AE, DC, MC, V* ⊹*2:4C.*

¢

⚑ **Hanedan.** This small, friendly hotel close to the heart of Sultanahmet is one of the area's best values. Rooms are somewhat basic but comfortable, clean, and on the larger side by Sultanahmet standards, as are the bathrooms. The rooftop terrace, where homemade breakfast is served, has a beautiful view of the Sea of Marmara and Aya Sofya. Service is personal and accommodating—the place has the feel of a bed-and-breakfast. **Pros:** good value; personable staff. **Cons:** minimal amenities (no TVs or minibars, etc.); poor soundproofing between rooms; nearby bars can be noisy at night. ⊠*Adliye Sokak 3, Sultanahmet,* ☎*212/516–4869* ⊕*www.hanedanhotel.com* ⤣*10 rooms* ⌂*In-room: safe, no TV, Wi-Fi (some). In-hotel: Wi-Fi, some pets allowed, no-smoking rooms* ▭*MC, V* ⦿*BP* ⊹*2:4C.*

$$

Fodor'sChoice

★

⚑ **Hotel Empress Zoë.** Opened in 1992, this pioneer of Sultanahmet's boutique hotel scene is aging both gracefully and ambitiously. Owner Ann Nevans, an American expat, has in recent years added three new all-suites wings to go along with the hotel's original building, which has small but charming rooms furnished with colorfully canopied four-posters. The new suites are more spacious, some with marble-lined bathrooms done up to look like mini hamams, and there's a two-floor suite with two balconies. The hotel's lush garden, where you can eat breakfast, is an extremely tranquil spot. **Pros:** funky, interesting atmosphere; central location. **Cons:** no elevator and winding staircases in main building; some rooms and bathrooms small. ⊠*Akbıyık Cad., 4/1, Sultanahmet,* ☎*212/518–2504* ⊕*www.emzoe.com* ⤣*14 rooms, 12 suites,* ⌂*In-room: safe, no TV (some), Wi-Fi (some). In-hotel: bar, Wi-Fi, no-smoking room* ▭*MC, V* ⦿*BP* ⊹*2:4C.*

$$

★

⚑ **Hotel İbrahim Pasha.** What was once the home of an extended Armenian family has been turned into a stylish and comfortable boutique hotel. The standard rooms are small but bright, with framed reproductions of Ottoman-era artwork and large windows, most of which look out toward the Blue Mosque. Deluxe rooms have a separate sitting area with a sofa and pillows, and some have walk-in closets and full bathtubs. A new section of the hotel has additional deluxe rooms and an inviting new lobby, as well as a rooftop terrace that has glorious views of Sultanahmet and the Blue Mosque. The personable staff helps ensure a relaxing atmosphere. **Pros:** location just off Hippodrome; ambience and decor; excellent breakfast. **Cons:** the non-deluxe rooms and their bathrooms are small. ⊠ *Terzihane Sokak 5, Sultanahmet,* ☎*212/518–0394* ⊕*www.ibrahimpasha.com* ⤴*24 rooms* ⌂*In-room: safe, DVD, Wi-Fi. In-hotel: room service, bar, laundry service, no-smoking rooms* ⊟*AE, MC, V* ⧫|*BP* ✛*2:5B.*

$ 🏨**Hotel Nomade.** When twin sisters Esra and Hamra Teker opened the
★   Hotel Nomade in 1984, few tourists stayed in Sultanahmet. Today the area is Istanbul's most popular, and the Hotel Nomade remains one of its most appealing and reasonably priced lodgings. A 2004 renovation saw the hotel redone in a stylish (though minimalist) modern-meets-ethnic design: the smallish rooms are painted pastel colors, there are patchwork kilims on the floor, and the bathrooms are lined with mosaic-like tiles. Service is personal and the roof-garden bar and terrace have enchanting views. **Pros:** interesting rooms; gorgeous roof terrace; located right near tram stop. **Cons:** small rooms and very small bathrooms; no view from most rooms. ⊠*Ticarethane Sokak 15, Sultanahmet,* ☎*212/513–8172* ⊕*www.hotelnomade.com* ⤴*16 rooms* ⌂*In-room: safe, Wi-Fi. In-hotel: room service, bar* ⊟*AE, DC, MC, V* ⧫|*BP* ✛*2:4B.*

$$ 🏨**Kybele.** Named after an ancient Anatolian fertility goddess, this
★   charming hotel is one of Sultanahamet's most unusual, thanks to its incredible profusion of antique lamps—4,000 at last count—that hang from the ceilings. The lobby, lit by 1,002 of the lamps, looks like a Victorian parlor, with overstuffed antique furniture and kilims. Rooms are small but imaginatively decorated. There's a little garden in the back (though no view) and a restaurant in the front. Three computers can be used by guests. Alparslan Akbayrak, the gregarious and helpful owner, is as much of a fixture in the hotel as all the lamps. **Pros:** unique decor and atmosphere; friendly staff. **Cons:** no roof terrace or elevator; ornate, lamp-filled rooms may not appeal to everyone. ⊠ *Yerebatan Cad. 35, Sultanahmet,* ☎*212/511–7766* ⊕*www.kybelehotel.com* ⤴*14 rooms, 2 suites* ⌂*In-room: safe, no TV, Wi-Fi. In-hotel: restaurant, room service, laundry service* ⊟*AE, DC, MC, V* ⧫|*BP* ✛*2:4B.*

$ 🏨**Sarı Konak Oteli.** This small, family-run hotel in an Ottoman-style
Fodor'sChoice building provides a very comfortable and pleasant stay. The bright,
★   clean rooms have modern furniture, though the decor also has Turkish and period accents like brass lamps, antique mirrors, and Ottoman-era etchings; some rooms even have original tiled floors. Breakfast is served in a rustic room that opens onto a tiny courtyard; on the rooftop terrace, you can sip a glass of rakı and contemplate the Marmara Sea or the nearby Blue Mosque. If you don't want twin beds, or prefer a bathtub to a shower, request these when making reservations. **Pros:** hotel has cozy rooms and intimate feel; good value. **Cons:** standard rooms a bit small. ⊠*Mimar Mehmet Ağa Cad. 42–46, Sultanahmet,* ☎*212/638–6258* ⊕*www.sarikonak.com* ⤴*21 rooms, 4 suites* ⌂*In-room: safe (some), Wi-Fi. In-hotel: room service, bar, laundry service, no-smoking rooms* ⊟*AE, MC, V* ⧫|*BP* ✛*2:5C.*

$ ☒ **Sarnıç.** This good-value hotel is within walking distance of all the major sites of Sultanahmet, yet far enough from the hustle and bustle that you won't be overwhelmed when you step out the door. Rooms do not have cutting-edge decor, but are clean and comfortable, with carpeting, warm yellow wallpaper, lounge chairs, and each has a small desk. The rooftop terrace has a small restaurant where breakfast is served in summer—it's also a nice place for an evening drink. For an extra fee, the hotel offers Turkish cooking classes, at the end of which guests eat what they've prepared. **Pros:** staff eager to help; good value. **Cons:** rooms somewhat lacking in character; no elevator; small rooms and bathrooms. ☒*Küçük Ayasofya Cad. 26, Sultanahmet,* ☎*212/518–2323* ⊕*www.sarnichotel.com* ⤶*16 rooms* △*In-room: safe, Wi-Fi. In-hotel: restaurant, room service, laundry service, no-smoking rooms* ▭*MC, V* ⵙⵁ*BP* ⊹*2:5B.*

$ ☒ **Şebnem.** This small, laid-back, family-run hotel is well located in Sultanahmet. The clean, bright rooms are simply decorated, with four-post beds that have embroidered canopies, and the recently renovated bathrooms are modern. Two rooms lead out to a small garden patio, while the sought-after Room 18 has a lovely sea view. Breakfast, which includes freshly baked cakes, is served on a comfy terrace with a beautiful sea view. While eating, you can even check your e-mail on one of the three laptops that are free for guests to use. **Pros:** extraordinarily friendly staff; excellent breakfast; lovely terrace. **Cons:** rooms fairly basic, lacks amenities like TVs and shampoo. ☒*Adliye Sokak 1, Sultanahmet,* ☎*212/517–6623* ⊕*www.sebnemhotel.net* ⤶*15 rooms* △*In-room: no TV, Wi-Fi. In-hotel: laundry service, no-smoking rooms* ▭*MC, V* ⵙⵁ*BP* ⊹*2:5C.*

$$ ☒ **Sultanahmet Sarayı.** The sultans meet Las Vegas in this glitzy recreation of an Ottoman palace. A courtyard with a fountain leads to the hotel, the exterior of which is painted a dusty pink and has faux pink granite columns; the lobby has grand marble stairways and a stained-glass atrium. Rooms are also opulent, with marble-lined, hamam-style bathrooms in most (instead of a shower or tub, there's a small marble-lined room with a faucet, a marble ledge to sit on, and a copper bowl; to wash, you fill the bowl with water and pour it over yourself), as well as plush bedspreads, and cushioned divans for reclining and gazing out the windows. Three deluxe rooms have sea views, while eight new standard rooms have tubs instead of hamam baths. A restaurant in back has a terrace looking over the Sea of Marmara. **Pros:** location just behind Blue Mosque; elegant decor and feel. **Cons:** top-floor rooms small; hamam-style bathrooms not for everyone. ☒*Torun Sokak 19, Sultanahmet,* ☎*212/458–0460* ⊕*www.sultanahmetpalace.com* ⤶*45 rooms* △*In-room: safe. In-hotel: restaurant, room service, laundry service, Wi-Fi, parking (paid)* ▭*AE, DC, MC, V* ⵙⵁ*BP* ⊹*2:5B.*

¢–$ ☒ **Sultan's Inn.** This hotel on a quiet backstreet is only a few minutes' walk from the major attractions of Sultanahmet and is a good budget option. It has the atmosphere of a typical Turkish *pansiyon*, with small but cozy rooms, and wooden floors and furniture enlivened by Turkish rugs and embroidered bedspreads. Some rooms have small balconies with a table and chairs. Bathrooms can be a bit run-down, though. An upstairs terrace looks out on the Sea of Marmara and the Blue Mosque. **Pros:** warm atmosphere; nice terrace. **Cons:** some guests report problems with showers; small rooms. ⊠*Mustafapaşa Sokak 50, Sultanahmet,* ☎*212/638–2562* ⊕*www.sultansinn.com* ⤳*17 rooms* ⌂*In-room: Wi-Fi (some). In-hotel: laundry service, Wi-Fi, no-smoking rooms* ☰*MC, V* ⑩*IBP* ⊹*2:5B.*

$ ⌐**Turkoman Hotel.** This restored Ottoman house on a quiet street not far from the Hippodrome and all the major sites has a spacious lobby and simple, clean rooms with brass beds and attractive antique furniture. Rooms in the new annex are larger, and some have views of the Blue Mosque. The two "family suites" each have two bedrooms connected by a short hallway and share a bathroom. The cozy terrace, where breakfast is served in summer, has a fine view over the Sea of Marmara and a fireplace that's lit in the winter. **Pros:** homey atmosphere; good for families; convenient location. **Cons:** bathrooms a bit small and basic; some decor a bit outdated. ⊠*Asmalı Çeşme Sokak 2, Sultanahmet,* ☎*212/516–2956* ⊕*www.turkomanhotel.com* ⤳*17 rooms* ⌂*In-room: DVD (some), Wi-Fi. In-hotel: room service, bar, laundry service, no-smoking rooms* ☰*AE, MC, V* ⊹*2:5A.*

$$$$ ⌐**Yeşil Ev** *(Green House).* A project of the Turkish Touring and Automobile Club, this lovely mansion (built in the early '80s to re-create the site's original historic building) is on the edge of a small park between the Blue Mosque and Aya Sofya. It's been decorated in period Ottoman style, with lace curtains and latticed shutters. Rooms aren't large, but have brass beds and carved wooden furniture upholstered in velvet or silk, and small (but modern) baths. The hotel also has a delightful shady garden courtyard built around a marble fountain, where guests can have breakfast in warmer weather. **Pros:** elegant, historic feel; great location. **Cons:** high room rates reflect location but not amenities. ⊠*Kabasakal Cad. 5, Sultanahmet,* ☎*212/517–6785* ⊕*www.istanbulyesilev.com* ⤳*18 rooms, 1 suite* ⌂*In-room: safe, no TV, Wi-Fi. In-hotel: restaurant, room service, laundry service* ☰*AE, MC, V* ⑩*IBP* ⊹*2:4C.*

TAKSIM AND NIŞANTAŞI

$$$$ ⌐**The Central Palace.** In 2004 the Istanbul municipality took the area behind Taksim Square and turned it into a pedestrian-only zone lined with cobblestones. Since then, a growing number of hotels have sprung up here, all with the advantage of being near Taksim but not in the midst of the noise and commotion. One of the nicer (and pricier) options is the Central Palace, which has large, comfortable rooms decorated in a tasteful, if slightly ornate, Ottoman style: brocaded bedcovers, framed works of *ebru* (marblized paper), and gold trim. The large, marble-lined bathrooms all have Jacuzzi tubs, and some rooms have a foyer and/or small balcony. **Pros:** location right near Taksim and Havaş airport shuttle; spacious rooms; luxurious feel. **Cons:** neighborhood is full of hotels, some of which cater to large tour groups; no alcohol served on hotel and restaurant premises. ⊠*Lamartin Cad. 18, Taksim,* ☎*212/313–4040* ⊕*www.thecentralpalace.com* ⤳*73 rooms, 34 suites* ⌂*In-room: safe,*

Wi-Fi. In-hotel: 2 restaurants, room service, gym, laundry service, parking (free), no-smoking rooms ▤*AE, DC, MC, V* ⦿|*BP* ⊹*1:2E.*

$$$$ ▩**Ceylan InterContinental.** This plush hotel is one of Turkey's premier accommodations, with a broad range of top-class facilities. The 19-floor building sits on a ridge, looking out on Istanbul and the Bosphorus, and the ornate lobby conjures Ottoman splendor: as if the gold-and-glass spiral staircase and fountain weren't enough, potted palm trees are also strategically placed. Rooms are spacious, with attractive if somewhat traditional decor and floor-to-ceiling windows; those on the water side have particularly good views. The spa and gym were completely renovated in 2008, and you can jog on a treadmill while looking out over a breathtaking view of the Bosphorus. **Pros:** high-class service; elegant feel; impressive views. **Cons:** high cost of food, drinks, and Internet; hotel caters primarily to business travelers. ⊠*Asker Ocağı Cad. 1, Taksim,* ☎*212/368–4444, 800/327–0200 in the U.S.* ⊕*www.interconti. com.tr* ⟿*330 rooms, 53 suites* ⊲*In-room: safe, Wi-Fi (fee). In-hotel: 4 restaurants, room service, bars, pool, gym, spa, laundry service, parking (paid), no-smoking rooms* ▤*AE, DC, MC, V* ⊹*1:2E.*

$$$–$$$$ ▩**Lush Hotel.** Quirky-chic Lush Hotel, just a couple blocks from Taksim Square, is ideally located for those looking to be near the city's nightlife. Its 35 rooms are each unique in shape and design, with decor touches ranging from the exposed brick walls of the original building, to black-and-white photos of Istanbul, to modernist furniture and interesting lamps. Most rooms and bathrooms are on the small side, but are clean, comfortable, and make creative use of space (a few have loft beds). The hotel also has a bar/brasserie and a spa with sauna. **Pros:** central location; funky, hip atmosphere. **Cons:** some small rooms and bathrooms; room decor and size vary greatly; street can be noisy at night due to clubs and traffic. ⊠*Sıraselviler Cad. 12, Taksim,* ☎*212/243–9595* ⊕*www.lushhotel.com* ⟿*35 rooms* ⊲*In-room: safe, Wi-Fi. In-hotel: restaurant, room service, gym, spa, laundry service, parking (paid)* ▤*AE, MC, V* ⦿|*BP* ⊹*1:3E.*

$$$$ ▩**Park Hyatt Istanbul–Maçka Palas.** This stylish new hotel is in a restored Italian-style Art Deco 1922 apartment building, in the high-end shopping district. The sophisticated yet inviting lobby has a chic bar with a wine cellar showcasing hundreds of select French and Turkish wines. Spacious rooms are decked out in sleek walnut with modern amenities alongside old-fashioned touches like period chandeliers and black-and-white photographs of Istanbul. Bathrooms have rain showers, free-standing tubs, and heated stone floors. The 25 "spa rooms" also have steam rooms and Turkish baths. **Pros:** luxury hotel with ambiance of a boutique hotel; large rooms; located in trendy shopping and nightlife area. **Cons:** spa rooms are somewhat overwhelmed by their bathrooms; complicated lighting system in rooms. ⊠*Bronz Sokak 35, 34367, Nişantaşı* ☎*212/3151234* ⊕*www.istanbul.park.hyatt.com.* ⟿*80 rooms, 10 suites.* ⊲*In-room: safe, minibar, DVD, Wi-Fi (fee). In-hotel: restaurant, room service, 2 bars, pool, gym, spa, laundry service, concierge, public Wi-Fi (fee), airport shuttle (fee), parking (no fee), no-smoking rooms.* ▤*AE, DC, MC, V* ⊹*1:F1.*

$$$$ ▩**The Sofa.** Nişantaşı is Istanbul's answer to New York's Upper East Side—an upscale neighborhood that has the city's best shopping. It's not an area where tourists usually stay, but the Sofa, a stylish and ambitious hotel that opened in 2006, is starting to change that. The emphasis here is on design, with large rooms that have sleek metal and wood furniture—and the eponymous trademark sofa. The top floor hosts international art exhibits, while the basement has a full-service spa—a subterranean oasis to unwind in after a hard day of shopping at City's, the posh new shopping mall across the street. **Pros:** luxurious rooms; original design and feel. **Cons:** no Bosphorus view from rooms; expensive neighborhood. ☒*Teşvikiye Cad. 45/A, Nişantaşı,* ☏*212/368–1818* ⊕*www.thesofahotel.com* ⤣*65 rooms, 17 suites* ⌂*In-room: safe, DVD, Wi-Fi. In-hotel: 2 restaurants, room service, pool, gym, spa, laundry service, Wi-Fi, some pets allowed, no-smoking rooms* ▭*AE, DC, MC, V* ✛*1:3D.*

NIGHTLIFE AND THE ARTS

Istanbul's nightlife still revolves, in many ways, around its *meyhanes,* tavern-like restaurants where long nights are spent nibbling on mezes and sipping the anise-flavored spirit rakı. The atmosphere at these places—mostly found in the lively Beyoğlu area—is jovial, friendly, and worth experiencing. But there are lots of other options, too, again mostly in Beyoğlu, which has everything from smoky American-style dive bars to sophisticated lounges, performance spaces that host world-class live acts, and discos and dance clubs. In warm weather, much of the city's nightlife action shifts to the Bosphorus shore, where chic (and pricey) summer-only nightclubs play host to Istanbul's rich and famous, and those who want to rub shoulders with them.

For upcoming events, reviews, and other information about what to do in Istanbul, pick up a copy *The Guide,* a reliable bimonthly English-language publication that has listings of hotels, bars, restaurants, and events, as well as features about Istanbul. The English-language *Today's Zaman* is another good resource (better than the recently renamed *Turkish Daily News,* which is now the *Hurriyet Daily News and Economic Report*) for listings and for keeping abreast of what's happening in Turkish and international politics.

NIGHTLIFE

BARS AND LOUNGES

The side streets leading off from İstiklal Caddesi in Beyoğlu are full of small bars. Many cater to a student crowd, with cheap beer and loud music, but there are also several comfortable and inviting lounges. In recent years, the trend in the neighborhood has been literally upward, with the opening of rooftop bars that usually have stunning views and fresh breezes. For more upscale bars, head to the neighborhoods and hotels along the Bosphorus.

BEYOĞLU **5. Kat** (☒*Soğancı Sokak 7, Cihangir* ☏*212/293–3774*) is on the fifth floor of an unassuming building in the quiet Cihangir neighborhood. Once inside, you'll find an excellent view of the Bosphorus, fabulous cocktails, and comfortable couches and chairs that make it feel like you're passing the time in somebody's living room.

Balkon (✉ *Şehbender Sokak 5, Beyoğlu* ☎212/293–2052) is a sixth-floor bar and lounge with views of the Golden Horn and a laid-back outdoor deck. Despite being located in the increasingly trendy Asmalımescit area, drink prices are quite reasonable.

Cezayir (✉ *Hayriye Cad. 16, Beyoğlu* ☎212/245–9980) is an excellent restaurant that also has a *Casablanca*-ish bar, an enclosed garden, and a lounge area—wicker chairs, lazy ceiling fans, and comfortable couches. The bar gets crowded on weekends, when a DJ plays a mix of new and old dance music.

NARGHILES

Narghiles (also known as hookahs) and the billowy smoke they produce have been an integral part of Istanbul's coffeehouses for centuries. Once associated with older men who would spend their days smoking, sipping strong Turkish coffee, and playing backgammon, the narghile is having a renewed popularity with younger Istanbullus. They are often used with a variety of flavored tobaccos, such as apple or strawberry. Because the smoke is filtered through water, it's cool and smooth, though it can make you light-headed if you're not used to it.

KeVe (✉ *Tünel Geçidi 10, Beyoğlu* ☎212/251–4338), in a plant-filled, late-19th-century open-air arcade, has a brasserie kind of feel, and a piano with occasional live music. It's perfect for a quiet drink.

L'Eclipse (✉ *Cezayir Çıkmazı 2, Beyoğlu* ☎212/245–9066), on so-called "French Street," is a café and bar with a rooftop terrace and a nice view of Sultanahmet and the Bosphorus.

NuTeras (✉ *Meşrutiyet Cad. 149, Beyoğlu* ☎212/245–6070) has a striking location—the rooftop of a historic building looking out on the Golden Horn—sleek decor to match, and a fashionable crowd. A kitchen turns out mezes and pizzas from a wood-burning oven, and there's a trendy bar and small dance floor. It's all open-air, so only open in summer.

On Numara (✉ *Galata Köprüsü, Haliç Tarafı 10, Karaköy* ☎212/243–9892), in an arcade below the Galata Bridge, is a good perch from which to view the sun as it sets over the Golden Horn and the minarets of Istanbul. There are cushy beanbag chairs to sit in and a young crowd drinking beer and smoking Narghiles.

BOSPHORUS **Bebek Bar** (✉ *Bebek Hotel, Cevdet Paşa Cad. 34, Bebek* ☎212/358–2000), with a breezy terrace on the Bosphorus and a top-notch restaurant next door, attracts a dressed-up crowd. It's the perfect spot for a drink, before or after dinner.

The W Lounge (✉ W *Istanbul Hotel, Süleyman Seba Cad. 22, Beşiktaş* ☎212/381–2121), the stylish yet comfortable lounge/bar in the W Hotel, has leather divans, low tables, and signature cocktails from the Spice Market restaurant.

SULTANAHMET **Hotel Nomade Bar** (✉ *Ticarethane Sokak 15, Sultanahmet* ☎212/513–8172) is an inviting and laid-back rooftop bar—one of the best options in the Sultanahmet area, not generally known for its nightlife. There are nice views of Aya Sofya and the sea beyond it, and a relaxed vibe.

CABARETS

Surviving strictly on the tourist trade, Istanbul's nightclub shows include everything from folk dancers to jugglers, acrobats, belly dancers, and singers. Rather than being authentically Turkish, the shows are a kitschy attempt to provide tourists with something exotic and Oriental. Typically, dinner is served at about 8, and floor shows start at around 10. Be aware that these are not inexpensive once you've totaled up drink, food, and cover. Reservations are a good idea; be sure to specify whether you're coming for dinner as well as the show or just for drinks.

Kervansaray (⊠*Cumhuriyet Cad. 30, Harbiye* ☎*212/247–1630*) is done up in a style that could be described as Ottoman palace meets wedding hall, with crystal chandeliers, faux-marble columns, and tables that seat 20. It hosts a varied floor show, including belly dancers, folk dances, and medleys of songs from around the world. Dinner and the show will run you about $130; the show and drinks, about $100.

Galata Tower (⊠*Galata* ☎*212/293–8180*) is high atop Beyoğlu, in a round room with fabulous views; the ambience, however, is strictly hotel lounge, and the Turkish food is only average. The fixed prices are around $115 for the show, dinner, and unlimited domestic drinks, or $95 for the show and a drink.

LIVE MUSIC VENUES

As Istanbul's reputation as a hip city continues to grow, the quality of the live acts that come to town has been rising, too. Established and up-and-coming performers now frequently include Istanbul on their European tours, and the city has become a good place to catch a show—for a fraction of what you might pay for the same thing in Paris, London, or New York.

Babylon (⊠*Şehbender Sokak 3, Beyoğlu* ☎*212/292–7368*) is Istanbul's best live music space, hosting world-famous jazz, rock, and world music performers. It's in a converted warehouse and the sound system is excellent—the friendly crowds take their music seriously. It's closed during summer, when Babylon Alaçatı opens in the beach town of Çeşme, near Izmir.

Hayal Kahvesi (⊠*Büyükparmakkapı Sokak 19, Beyoğlu* ☎*212/224–2558*) is a smoky, crowded, late-night hangout for a mostly young crowd that likes live (and loud) rock and blues. The scuffed wood floors are stained with beer—exactly what you might expect from a classic dive bar.

Jolly Joker Balans (⊠*Balo Sokak 22, Beyoğlu* ☎*212/251–7020*), a multi-level bar and live music venue, hosts established and up-and-coming Turkish rock and pop acts and attracts a young and energetic crowd.

Roxy (⊠*Aslanyatağı Sokak 5, Taksim* ☎*212/249–1283*) is a popular bar with a spirited, young crowd and live music—from experimental rock to acoustic folk. The next-door Yan Gastrobar (same owner) serves a good range of tasty food. Roxy is closed during summer.

Going out to hear Turkish music in Istanbul.

JAZZ CLUBS

Istanbul may not be a major spot on the world's jazz map, but this has been changing in recent years. Several top-notch jazz clubs have opened and, as a result, the number of well-known jazz musicians who come to perform in Istanbul is increasing.

Istanbul Jazz Center (⊠ *Çırağan Cad. 10, Ortaköy* ☎ *212/327–5050*), opened in 2005, would not seem out of place in New York or any other big city, with its sophisticated decor, a Steinway concert grand piano on stage, and a program that features well-known musicians from the U.S. and Europe. The club also has a well-regarded restaurant.

Nardis Jazz Club (⊠ *Kuledibi Sokak 14, Beyoğlu* ☎ *212/244–6327*) is a cozy, intimate space that hosts mostly Turkish jazz musicians and the occasional big name from abroad. The club only has room for 120, so reservations are recommended.

TURKISH MUSIC

Going out to listen to Turkish music is, for many Istanbullus, a participatory affair, with many in the crowd clapping and lustily singing along. Live Turkish music in the city can usually be divided into two categories: *fasıl,* which is a raucous but melancholy blend of gypsy, Greek, and classical Middle Eastern music; and Anatolian folk music, which is more subdued but as melancholy, and is usually dominated by a lute-like instrument called the *saz.*

Andon Meyhane (⊠ *Sıraselviler Cad. 89, Taksim* ☎ *212/251–0222*) is on the fourth floor of a renovated 1920s town house and has live Turkish fasıl music every night, along with a traditional meyhane menu. Andon is, in fact, a multivenue, with a disco on the first and second

2

floors, live Turkish pop on the third floor, and a café and a rooftop terrace on the fifth.

Otantik (⊠ *Balo Sokak 1, Beyoğlu* ☎ 212/293–6515) has kilims on the walls, thick cigarette smoke in the air, and a room filled with Turks singing along to folk music being played on a small stage.

DANCE CLUBS

Istanbul has a vibrant dance club scene, though it's not for the faint of heart. Things typically get rolling at about midnight and go until 4 or 5 in the morning. The city's upscale clubs tend to be expensive—admission is generally $20 or more—and there are no guarantees you'll get past the doorman, whose job it is to make sure only Istanbul's best dressed get in. Still, Istanbullus love to party and a good time is assured, if you get in.

360 Istanbul (⊠ *İstiklal Cad. 311, Beyoğlu* ☎ 212/251–1042) is a swank rooftop restaurant (with fabulous views) in the early evening, but becomes a fashionable club after 11 PM, when a well-dressed crowd arrives to dance. Music is provided by a DJ who is sometimes joined by a live percussionist.

Crystal (⊠ *Muallim Naci Cad. 65, Ortaköy* ☎ 212/229–7152) specializes in techno music, often courtesy of well-known European DJs, and attracts a young, energetic crowd. The club has a nice covered garden and is open only on Friday and Saturday nights.

Reina (⊠ *Muallim Naci Cad. 44, Ortaköy* ☎ 212/259–5919), right on the Bosphorus, is Istanbul's most famous and swank club, where the rich and famous come to be seen and where the paparazzi await them. In summer, a half-dozen equally posh open-air restaurants, featuring different types of cuisines, open on the club's terrace.

Sortie (⊠ *Muallim Naci Cad. 54, Ortaköy* ☎ 212/327–8585) is next door to Reina and equally swank, though smaller. Entirely open-air, it's only open in summer.

THE ARTS

Summer is a lively time for the arts in Istanbul. The **Istanbul International Music Festival**, held for the duration of June, attracts renowned artists from around the world performing classical music. Shows take place throughout the city in historic buildings, such as Aya Irini and Rumeli Hisar. The **International Theater Festival** takes place May through early June, and attracts major stage talent from across the globe. The **International Istanbul Jazz Festival** occurs every July and has grown to include much more than just jazz. Recent headliners have included Herbie Hancock, Lenny Kravitz, and members of the Buena Vista Social Club. Tickets for all of these events can be ordered online through Biletix (⊕ *www.biletix.com*) or by contacting the **Istanbul Foundation for Culture and Arts** (⊠ *Istanbul Kültür Sanat Vakfı, İstiklal Cad. 64, Beyoğlu,* ☎ 212/334–0700 ⊕ *www.iksv.org*).

FILM

The strip of theaters along İstiklal Caddesi between Taksim and Galatasaray, a square at the midpoint of İstiklal Caddesi, shows the latest from Hollywood, with a few current European or Turkish movies thrown in. There are also plush, modern theaters at the Cevahir mall in Şişli, and at the Akmerkez shopping center, in Levent. Most foreign films are shown with their original sound track and Turkish subtitles, although many children's films are dubbed into Turkish. Look for the words *Ingilizce* (English) or *orijinal* (original language). Films in languages other than English will have subtitles in Turkish. When in doubt, ask at the ticket office whether the film is dubbed (*dublaj*) or subtitled (*altyazılı*).

The annual **Istanbul International Film Festival,** held the first two weeks of April, presents films from around the world; ask for a schedule at any box office or check the Web site of the IKSV (⊕*www.iksv.org*). Make sure to purchase tickets in advance as the festival is extremely popular. Seats are reserved.

PERFORMANCE VENUES

Akbank Sanat Cultural Center (⊠ *İstiklal Cad., Zambak Sokak 1, Beyoğlu* ☎ *212/252–3500* ⊕*www.akbanksanat.com*) hosts classical and jazz concerts, as well as theater productions and films. It also holds art exhibitions.

Atatürk Kültür Merkezi (⊠ *Taksim Sq.* ☎ *212/251–5600*), in Taksim Square, is Istanbul's main concert hall. The Istanbul State Symphony performs here October through May, and ballet and dance companies have productions year-round. Tickets tend to be almost absurdly cheap.

Cemal Reşit Rey Concert Hall (⊠ *Gümüş Sokak, Harbiye* ☎ *212/232–9830* ⊕*www.crrks.org*), close to the Istanbul Hilton, has just about every kind of entertainment you could want: from chamber and symphonic music to modern dance, rock, folk, and jazz concerts.

Garajistanbul (⊠ *Yeni Çarşı Cad., Kaymakam Reşit Bey Sokak 11A, Galatasaray* ☎ *212/244–4499* ⊕*www.garajistanbul.org*), which opened in 2007 in the basement of a parking lot near Galatasaray Square, is an experimental venue that hosts contemporary dance and theater, as well as musical, literary, and artistic events.

SHOPPING

Istanbul has been a shopper's town for, well, centuries—the sprawling Grand Bazaar, open since 1461, could easily be called the world's oldest shopping mall—but this not to say that the city is stuck in the past. Along with its colorful bazaars and outdoor markets, Istanbul also has a wide range of modern shopping options, from large shopping centers—enormous new malls seem to be sprouting up constantly, and the Cevahir mall in Şişli claims to be the largest in Europe—to small boutiques. Either way, it's almost impossible to leave Istanbul without buying something. Whether you're looking for trinkets and souvenirs, kilims and carpets, brass and silverware, leather goods, old books, prints and maps, or furnishings and clothes (Turkish textiles are among the best in the world), you can find them here. Shopping in Istanbul also provides a snapshot of the city's contrasts and contradictions: from migrants from eastern Turkey selling their wares on the streets, to the leisurely, time-honored haggling over endless glasses of tea in the bazaars and back alleys, to the credit cards and bar codes of the plush, upscale Western-style department stores.

İstiklal Caddesi is a pedestrian-only boulevard with everything from global brands like Levi's and big-name Turkish companies such as Mavi to small shoe stores and bookstores. The high-fashion district is the upscale **Nişantaşı** neighborhood, 1 km (½ mi) north of İstiklal Caddesi— this is where you'll find the best efforts of Turkish fashion designers, such as Özlem Süer, as well as the flagship stores of international brands such as Armani, DKNY, and Hugo Boss. City's, a ritzy mall that opened in 2008, has designer shops like Dolce & Gabbana and Class Roberto Cavalli—though because of the high import taxes, these name brands are usually more expensive in Turkey than they are in the U.S. The **Cevahir** mall, in Şişli, has more than 300 stores selling foreign and local brand-name clothing and is a little easier on the wallet.

MARKETS

In addition to the markets listed below, a flea market is held every Sunday along Çukurcuma Street in the Beyoğlu area; along the Bosphorus in the Ortaköy neighborhood is a Sunday crafts market with street entertainment.

★ The **Arasta Bazaar** (⊠ *Sultanahmet*) is one of few markets open on Sunday; you can find a lot of the same items here as at the Grand Bazaar, but the atmosphere is a lot calmer.

The **Balıkpazarı** (*Fish Market* ⊠ *off İstiklal Cad., Beyoğlu*) sells, of course, fish, as well as everything connected with food, from fresh produce to nuts and candies—though it's not cheap. You can buy the makings of a delicious picnic here.

★ The **Egyptian Bazaar.** See the highlighted feature in this chapter.

Fodor'sChoice The **Grand Bazaar.** See the highlighted feature in this chapter.

★ **Nuruosmaniye Caddesi** (⊠ *Grand Bazaar*), one of the major streets leading to the Grand Bazaar, is lined with some of Istanbul's most stylish shops, with an emphasis on fine carpets, jewelry, and antiques.

Sahaflar Çarşışı (⊠ *Grand Bazaar*), just outside the western end of the Grand Bazaar, is home to a bustling book market, with old and new editions; most are in Turkish, but English and other languages are represented, too. The market is open daily, though Sunday has the most vendors.

SPECIALTY STORES

ANTIQUES

Antiques are a surprisingly rare commodity in this antique land, perhaps because the government, to ensure that Turkish culture is not sold off to richer nations, has made it illegal to export most kinds of antiques that are more than 100 years old. The Grand Bazaar, of course, is a good place to go antique hunting, but an even better option is the Çukurcuma area in Beyoğlu, which is filled with small shops carrying everything from small, Ottoman-era knickknacks to outsized antique marble tubs.

Continued on page 140

SHOPPING IN ISTANBUL
The Grand Bazaar & the Spice Market

Istanbul, historically one of the most important stops on the Silk Road, which linked the East and West through commerce, is today still a fabulous place to shop. You can find everything from the quintessential woven carpet to cheap trinkets, from antique copper trays to faux Prada bags. At the center of it all is the sometimes chaotic Grand Bazaar, also known as the Kapalı Çarşı or "Covered Bazar," which in many ways can be considered the great-grandmother of the modern shopping mall: it's been around since the 15th century, has more than 20 entrances, covers about 65 streets, and is said to have some 4,000 shops. It can be a bit intense, but it's a must-see. The following pages will help you get oriented so the experience will be less daunting. For comparison, check out the Spice Market in Eminönü, it's also several centuries old but specializes in spices and food items and is much calmer. It's great place to find picnic goods and Turkish delicacies to take home (Turkish delight, anyone?).

THE GRAND BAZAAR

This behemoth of a shopping complex was built by Mehmet II (the Conqueror) in the 1450s over several of the main Byzantine shopping streets and expanded over the years. Today it's almost a town unto itself, with its own restaurants, tea houses, mosques, banks, exchange bureaus, post office, police station, health clinic, and several bathrooms nestled among the myriad shops.

Streets in the bazaar are named after the tradespeople who traditionally had businesses there, with colorful names in Turkish like "slipper-makers street," "fez-makers street," and "mirror-makers street." Today, although there's little correspondence between street names and the shops now found on them, the bazaar is still organized roughly by type of merchandise: gold and silver jewelry shops line the prestigious main street, most of the leather stores are in their own wing, carpet shops are clustered primarily in the center, and souvenirs are found throughout. The amazingly polylingual sellers are all anxious to reassure you that you do not have to buy . . . just drink a glass of tea while you browse through leather goods, carpets, fabric, clothing (including counterfeit brand names), brass candelabra, furniture, ceramics, and gold and silver jewelry.

✉ Yeniçeriler Cad. and Fuatpaşa Cad.
🕘 Mon.–Sat. 8:30 – 7

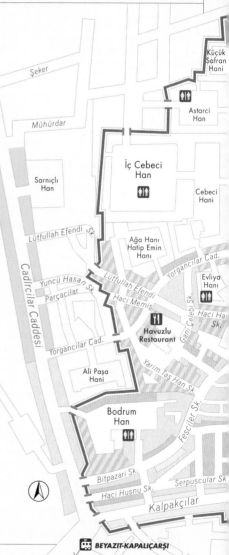

KEY	
▢ Gold	▢ Antiques
▢ Carpets	▢ Silver
▢ Denimwear	◄▮► Main Gates
▢ Copper	🚊 T1 Tram
▢ Fabric	👥 Restroom
▢ Souvenirs	🍴 Restaurant
▢ Leather	

Grand Bazaar Shops

THE BEDESTAN

The domed *iç bedestan* (inner bazaar), once a secure fortress in the heart of the bazaar, is the oldest part of the bazaar and historically where the most valuable goods were kept. The same is still true today: the *bedestan* is filled with tiny shops selling an array of antiques that are of generally better quality than in the rest of the bazaar. In the *bedestan*, you can find anything from pocket watches to vintage cigarette tins, from jewelry to Armenian and Greek religious items. Look for the double-headed Byzantine eagle over the door and you'll know you've found the heart of the bazaar.

Yolgeçen Han

Safran Han

Çukur Han

Mercan Hani Han.

Mercan Hani

Yağlıkçılar Sokağı

Kızlar Ağası Hani

Perdahçı Hani

Tacirler Kapısı

Şahaflar Bedesteni

Kalcilar Han

Zincirli Han

Straodalar Sk.

TO
TOPKAPI

Perdahçılar Sk.

Parçacilar

Terlikciler Sk.

Kavaflar Sk.

Acı Çeşma Sk.

Aynacılar Sk.

Reisoğlu Sk.

Uncuoğlu Sk.

Karakol Sk.

Varakçı Han Sk.

Cuhacı Hani Sk.

Fes Cafe 🍴

Halicilar

Ressam Basmacilar

Orta Kazazlar Sk.

Zenneciler

İç Bedestan
(Inner Bazaar)

Kuyumcular Cad.

Karamanlıoğlu Sk.

Arabacıoğlu Sk.

Ağa Sk.

Muhafazacilar Sk.

Kazazlar Sk.

Takkeciler

Keseciler Caddesi

Sandal Bedesten Sk.

Terzi Başı Sk.

Sandal
Bedestan

Sipahi Caddesi Feraceciler

Kazazlar

Divrilli

Kolancilar

Terziler

Kalpakcilar Caddesi

TO
HAGHIA SOPHIA →
MUSEUM & MOSQUE

Rabia Hani

Yağci Hani

ÇEMBERLITAŞ 🏛→

Sorguçlu Han

Balyaci Han

Kebabçi Han

Kürkcüler Carsisi

Tavuk Pazari Sk.

Yolgeçen Hani

Iskender Boğazi

TO →
BLUE MOSQUE

WHAT TO BUY

JEWELRY

There are over 370 jewelry shops in the bazaar, and you'll find as many locals in them as tourists. Gold and silver jewelry are sold by weight, based on the going market price plus extra for labor, so there's room for bargaining. Sterling silver pieces should have a hallmark. In terms of semiprecious stones, amber and turquoise are especially popular.

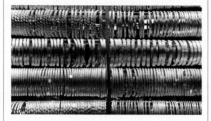

METALWARE (COPPER & BRASSWARE)

Turkey has a long tradition of metalworking, and you can find both new and antique copper and brass items engraved with elaborate designs. Round copper trays can run into the hundreds of dollars for large, intricately worked items if they're new, and into the thousands for antiques. Small serving trays can be acquired for less than $60. Most copper items are plated with tin to make them safe to eat from and therefore appear silver-gray in color. You can find pure copper items but these are suitable for decorative purposes only. Brass items like samovars and pitchers can be shiny if unoxidized or gray-black if oxidized. In general, brass costs more than copper because it's harder to work. Middle Eastern-style lanterns made of worked metal and glass are also neat to check out.

CERAMICS

Turkey's ceramics tradition goes back to Ottoman times. Today, the most important distinction is between İznik and Kütahya designs; traditional İznik designs, recognizable by their blue, red, and green colors on a white background, are more intricate and more expensive. You'll see many gorgeous bowls and plates in both styles, but note that many are coated with lead glazes and are not safe for use with metal utensils or hot food. Medium-size bowls and plates go for between $20-50. Decorative tiles can be made of either ceramic or quartz, with quartz tiles selling for two to three times more than ceramic tiles.

INLAID-WOOD ITEMS

You'll see a lot of wood items at the bazaar, beautifully inlaid with mother-of-pearl and different colored woods. Try to avoid imitation inlay: one clue that the inlay is fake is if the mother-of-pearl sections in the design are too uniform in color. You can also usually tell by weight and touch if a backgammon board is plastic. Price is also a dead giveaway: fake-inlay backgammon boards can be had for around $40, whereas those made of walnut and real mother-of-pearl can go for $130-225 for a medium-size board, with prices varying based on the amount of inlay and intricacy of the workmanship.

LEATHER

Leather is a big industry in Turkey and the Grand Bazaar has no shortage of stores selling leather jackets, bags, wallets, and shoes. When buying leather goods, look carefully at the quality of the workmanship, which can be assessed by examining seams, zippers, and linings. Imitation leather is, unfortunately, fairly widespread, and even dealers say they sometimes can't tell what's fake and what's not—one clue is that real leather is a bit softer than artificial leather. "Genuine fake" designer bags [i.e. imitation designer bags made with (supposedly) real leather], abound in the Bazaar and sell for around $130

SOUVENIRS AND GIFTS

The bazaar is chock-full of trinkets aimed at tourists—including ornaments featuring the ubiquitous evil-eye beads *nazar boncuğu*, Turkish tea sets, and fake designer clothing—but you can also find some nice souvenirs and gift items. Textiles like woven or embroidered pillow covers, and pashmina and silk scarves are inexpensive ($6-15 apiece) and come in many designs and patterns. Tiny jewelry boxes made of camel bone and decorated with Persian-miniature-style paintings sell for about $15. Turkey is also famous for its meerschaum, a mineral that is used primarily to make pipes; prices range from about $30-150 based on the quality of the meerschaum and the intricacy of the carving.

■TIP➔Exporting antiquities from Turkey is forbidden, and the ban is rigorously enforced. If you buy a carpet or other item that looks old, make sure you get certification from the seller that it's not an antique.

BUYING A CARPET

Carpet salesmen in the Grand Bazaar, Kapalı Çarşı

It's almost impossible to visit Istanbul without making a detour into at least one rug shop, and you'll inevitably be poured a glass of tea (or several) while the salesman rolls out one carpet after another on the floor in front of you. Just remember, regardless of how many cups of tea you drink and how persistent the salesman, don't be pressured into making a purchase you don't want.

The vivid colors and patterns of Turkish carpets and kilims, which are flat-woven rugs (without a pile), are hard to resist. Patterns and colors vary by region of origin, and in the case of kilims they often have symbolic meanings.

The Grand Bazaar is, without a doubt, the most convenient place in Istanbul to buy a rug, since the sheer number of rug dealers means there is a wide selection. Also, most of the dealers will pack and ship your purchasse for you. That said, don't go to the Grand Bazaar

looking for bargains—there are enough tourists coming through every day to keep prices out of the bargain basement. ■TIP➡The Arasta Bazaar, near the Blue Mosque, also has several good rug shops in a more relaxed environment and at generally lower prices.

When shopping for a carpet or kilim, the most important thing is to find a dealer you can trust. It's best to look at merchandise at several different shops before buying anything, in order to get an idea of prices and see what's out there. Ask lots of questions, such as what a carpet is made of (wool or silk), what kind of dyes were used, and where it was made (note that many so-called Turkish carpets are now made in countries like India and China). Note that silk carpets are considerably more expensive than wool ones, and kilims are generally less expensive than carpets because they involve less labor.

GRAND BAZAAR TIPS

■ You may want to mentally prepare yourself for being aggressively pursued by merchants who are as shameless about making sales pitches as they are competitive over business; it can be overwhelming at first but underneath the hard sell most of the shop owners are quite friendly.

■ The Grand Bazaar is less crowded earlier on weekday mornings.

■ Once you're in the bazaar, spend some time getting your bearings and comparison shopping before you make any major purchases; this will help you get an idea of prices as well as narrow down what you'd like to buy.

■ Watch out for fakes, be they antique rugs, leather, or jewelry—if a dealer's price seems too good to be true, it probably is.

CARPET AND KILIM TIPS

■ Look for the store's Certificate of Authenticity.

■ Make sure the rug sits flat on the floor when it's laid out, and that its edges are straight and even.

■ Look for breaks in color (streaks where the color seems to fade out) as an indication of a poor quality.

■ Examine the back of a carpet to see how fine the knots are. The more knots per square inch, the finer the knotting will be and the more valuable the carpet.

■ Although the number of knots per square inch is important, it's not the only thing to go by when choosing a carpet. A lower-knot carpet made with high-quality wool and dyes is worth more than a higher-knot carpet made with poor materials.

■ Try to buy the carpet directly from the store owner, and not a solicitor or third party.

BARGAINING AT THE BAZAAR

Prices at the Grand Bazaar are on the high side, due to high rents and the never-ending stream of tourists, but the convenience of the bazaar often makes it a good place to shop. Shop owners will expect you to bargain, so here are some tips.

■ Ask the price of several different items before focusing on the thing you really want, to get an idea of a store's prices and to make your intentions less obvious.

■ After the merchant quotes a price, make a counter-offer that's about half what they asked; then negotiate until you reach a price somewhere in the middle.

■ Do accept a shopkeeper's offer of tea. This gives you the chance to get familiar with the dealer. Accepting tea, however, does not obligate you to buy anything.

■ If you and the merchant can't reach a deal, starting to walk away often results in the merchant lowering the price.

■ The more items you buy from a merchant, the more you can bargain the price down.

DID YOU KNOW?

The Grand Bazaar was ravaged twice by fire in relatively recent years—once in 1954, when it was almost destroyed, and once in 1974, in a smaller conflagration. In both cases, the bazaar was quickly rebuilt in something resembling the original style, with arched passageways and brass-and-tile fountains at regular intervals.

THE SPICE MARKET

MISIR ÇARŞISI, OR THE EGYPTIAN BAZAAR

The Egyptian Bazaar, also known as the Spice Market, in Istanbul's Eminönü neighborhood, is a riot of colors and fragrances. Although some of the spice shops have recently given way to stalls selling tourist souvenirs like you'll find in the Grand Bazaar, the Spice Market, with its mounds of *lokum* (Turkish delight), bags of spices, and heaps of dried fruit and nuts, is still a wonderfully atmospheric place to shop for spices and other delicious edibles.

For the most part prices at the Spice Market are clearly marked. Unlike in the Grand Bazaar, bargaining is discouraged here—if you're buying a lot, you might get the seller to come down by 10%, but don't expect much more.

✉ Yeni Cami Meydam, Eminönü
🕐 Mon.-Sat. 8:30 – 6:30

WHAT TO BUY

Lokum, or **Turkish delight**, in a wide variety of flavors, including rosewater and fruit-essenced, stuffed with pistachios or walnuts, or chocolate-covered. Merchants will enthusiastically ply you with free samples.

Herbs and spices, including cumin, sumac, turmeric, many varieties of pepper, and curry mixes. The best saffron (*safran*) found here comes from neighboring Iran, and although it's still not cheap it's less expensive than in the United States.

Dried fruits, particularly figs, dates, and apricots.

Nuts, including domestically harvested pistachios and hazelnuts.

Black and herbal **teas** and finely ground **Turkish coffee.**

Caviar is also sold here for less than in the U.S. or Europe due to Turkey's proximity to its source, the Caspian Sea. Considering the serious endangerment of sturgeon, however, you might think twice about buying it.

You'll also see a variety of rather questionable-looking concoctions being sold as natural aphrodisiacs or "Turkish Viagra." Draw your own conclusions about their reliability.

Ala Turca (⊠*Faikpaşa Sokak 4, Çukurcuma* ☎*212/245–2933*) is more like a grand private home than a store, filled with a carefully selected (and very expensive) collection of antique rugs and artwork.

Artrium (⊠*Tünel Geçidi 7, Beyoğlu* ☎*212/251–4302*) is a delightful shop located in a historic 19th-century passage. It has a wide range of antiques, including an especially fascinating collection of old prints and paintings, and some interesting handmade crafts and jewelry.

Firuze (⊠*Çukurcuma Cad. Hacıosman Çıkmazı 1, Çukurcuma* ☎*212/245–7245*) is tiny but chock-full of metal objects, trinkets, and other interesting odds and ends.

Levant Koleksiyon (⊠*Tünel Meydanı 188/B, Beyoğlu* ☎*212/293–4394*) has very affordable maps, engravings, and charming old postcards with pictures of Ottoman-era Istanbul. Prices are fair and clearly marked.

Sofa (⊠*Nuruosmaniye Cad. 85, Cağaloğlu* ☎*212/520–2850*), on a pleasant pedestrian boulevard lined with high-end carpet, jewelry, and antique shops, stocks a fascinating collection of old maps and prints, original İznik (blue and white) and Kütahya (variously colored, and with traditional patterns like tulips, paisleys, or fish) ceramics, vintage jewelry, and assorted other treasures.

Ziya Aykaç Antikacı (⊠*Takkeciler Sokak 68–72, Grand Bazaar* ☎*212/527–6082*) has a corner store in the Grand Bazaar filled floor to ceiling with antique fabrics, silverware, ceramics, and other treasures.

CARPETS

Adnan & Hasan (⊠ *Halıcılar Cad. 89–90–92, Grand Bazzar* ☎*212/527–9887*) has a large selection of both old and new carpets and kilims, mostly from Turkey's Anatolia region, and a friendly staff.

Ethnicon (⊠ *Takkeciler Sokak 49–51, Grand Bazaar* ☎*212/527–6841*) sells contemporary kilims made of different-sized squares of fabric, reminiscent of American-style quilts.

Galeri 44 Mozaik (⊠*Arasta Bazzar 163, Sultanahmet* ☎*212/638–1071*) sells a variety of carpets and kilims, including embroidered kilims (*sumaks*), in a friendly atmosphere.

Galeri Cengiz (⊠*Arasta Bazzar 157, Sultanahmet* ☎*212/518–8882*) sells boldly patterned rugs from throughout Turkey and Central Asia.

Şengör (⊠ *Takkeciler Sokak 65–83 and 98, Grand Bazaar* ☎*212/527–2192*) is a long-standing, family-run shop, with a large inventory.

CLOTHING

Istanbullus like to dress smartly and although the city might not be one of Europe's well-known fashion centers, it is certainly not lacking in places to buy clothes, from department stores selling famous international brands to the boutiques of Turkish designers.

Bahar Korçan (⊠*Serder Ekrem Sokak, Seraskerci Sokak 5, Galata* ☎*212/296–9276 or 212/293–6855*) is one of Turkey's most innovative young fashion designers. Her stylish women's clothes, often made using layers of gauzy fabric, have a sense of organic whimsy. The shop is a combination store and atelier.

Beymen (✉ *Abdi İpekçi Cad. 23, Nişantaşı* ☎ *212/373–4800*) is Istanbul's version of Bloomingdale's, with suited doormen and expensive and up-to-date fashions.

Gönül Paksoy (✉ *Atiye Sokak 1/3, Nişantaşı* ☎ *212/236–0209*) is a designer with an elegant and stunning collection of women's clothes that reinterprets Ottoman design and fabrics. The store also has an outstanding selection of jewelry.

The **Mudo** (✉ *Teşvikiye Cad. 149, Nişantaşı* ☎ *212/225–2950*) clothing chain is something like Turkey's Banana Republic, selling affordable smart casual clothing for men and women. Some of the Mudo shops also carry housewares. There are about 20 other locations in Istanbul.

Özlem Süer (✉ *Büyükçiftlik Sokak 12, Nişantaşı* ☎ *212/240–5738*) is one of Turkey's top internationally known fashion designers, with a separate wedding line and an accessories division in addition to her elite fashions.

Vakko (✉ *Abdi İpekçi Cad. 34 [women's clothes], Nişantaşı* ☎ *212/224–3172* ✉ *Abdi İpekçi Cad. 31 [men's clothes],* ☎ *212/234–9218* ✉ *Akmerkez shopping mall, in Etiler* ☎ *212/282–0695* ✉ *Bağdat Cad. 422, in Suadiye [on the Asian side]* ☎ *216/416–4204*) is one of Turkey's oldest and most elegant fashion houses, selling high-end fashions and with an excellent fabric department. Former president Bill Clinton could occasionally be seen sporting one of the Vakko ties presented to him by visiting Turkish delegates.

Yargıcı (✉ *Valikonağı Cad. 34/B, Nişantaşı* ☎ *212/225–2952*), the popular Turkish clothing chain, sells moderately priced but attractive women's clothes that veer between preppy and subtly Oriental. There are a dozen other locations in Istanbul.

Turkish designer **Zeki Triko** (✉ *Tunaman Çarşısı 63/E, Nişantaşı* ☎ *212/233–8279*) sells his own brand of bathing suits and lingerie, completely up-to-date, at his eponymous boutiques.

ENGLISH-LANGUAGE BOOKSTORES

Many of the larger hotels and souvenir shops in Sultanahmet stock some English-language newspapers and books, mostly guides to the more famous sights. A more comprehensive range of reading material can be found at specialty bookstores in Beyoğlu and in the fashionable shopping district of Nişantaşı. Books originally published outside Turkey are marked up anywhere from 15% to 75%. Many newspaper stands throughout the city carry the *International Herald Tribune*. Some

WORD OF MOUTH

"I don't you know your tastes or what you like to bring back but here are some things I liked: The woven bookmarks have been a major hit with everyone who I gave them to…There is pottery. I saw that more inland than along the coast (and in Istanbul). It ranges in price and quality…Cloth purses were also pretty popular with the other women on our tour…. Pashmina and other scarves in a wide selection. Some copper work. Mainly cooking or vase type pots, although I did see a few trays. The Turkish tea glasses were a popular bring back as well…Mosaic lamps in various qualities, but quite striking."

—Diane60030

The centuries old practice of smoking tobacco in a *narghile*, also known as a hookah or water pipe.

of the larger bookstores carrying English-language books include the following.

Galeri Kayseri (✉ *Divanyolu 58 [main store], Sultanahmet* ✉ *11 Divanyolu [a second store], Sultanahmet* ☎ *212/516–3366 or 212/512–0456*) has a very thorough collection of nonfiction books about Turkey in a variety of subject areas, as well as some novels, spread out over their two shops.

Homer (✉ *Yeni Çarşı Cad. 12/A, Galatasaray, Beyoğlu* ☎ *212/249–5902*) is one of Istanbul's best bookstores, carrying an impeccable selection of English-language books, especially ones dealing with the politics and history of Turkey and the Middle East.

Pandora (✉ *Büyük Parmakkapı Sokak 8, Beyoğlu* ☎ *212/243–3503*) carries an impressive selection of books in English and Turkish, with an emphasis on politics and nonfiction.

Robinson Crusoe (✉ *İstiklal Cad. 195/A, Beyoğlu* ☎ *212/293–6968*) is as appealing as a bookstore can get, with two cozy levels lined floor to ceiling with a well-chosen selection of English fiction and nonfiction. It also has an excellent collection of magazines and journals.

USED BOOKS   A number of stores, including the following, specialize in secondhand books, many in English, from dog-eared thrillers to rare old texts about the city. There is also a cluster of antiquarian booksellers in the Sahaflar Çarşısı, just outside the Grand Bazaar.

Aslıhan Sahaflar Çarşısı (✉ *Galatasaray Balık Pazarı, Beyoğlu*) is an underground passage near Beyoğlu's fish market filled with small, disorganized shops that sell used books in various languages, as well as old records and posters.

Librairie de Pera (✉ *Galip Dede Sokak 8, Beyoğlu* ☎*212/243–3991*) is a small shop filled with countless treasures, including old illustrated travelogues, maps, and engravings as well as antiquarian books in French, German, Greek and Armenian.

HANDICRAFTS

Turkey is known for rugs, but there are plenty of other handicrafts to buy that will take up less space in your suitcase—and a smaller bite out of your spending budget.

Abdulla (✉ *Halıcılar Cad. 62, Grand Bazaar* ☎*212/527–3684*) has a simple but immensely appealing and stylish collection of handmade fabrics, tablecloths, and towels made out of all-natural materials, as well as olive-oil soaps and small rugs.

Derviş (✉ *Keseciler Sokak 33–35, Grand Bazaar* ☎*212/514–4525* ✉*Halıcılar Cad. 51, Grand Bazaar*) is run by a former partner at Abdulla and sells similar stock at similar prices.

İznik Foundation (✉ *Öksüz Çocuk Sokak 14, Kuruçeşme* ☎*212/287–3243*), on the Bosphorus, not far from the Bebek neighborhood, is the flagship showroom of a nonprofit group dedicated to reviving and preserving the classic art of İznik ceramic and tile work. Prices are high, but the quality is outstanding.

Kaptan (✉ *Terziler Sokak 30, Grand Bazaar* ☎*212/526–3650*), specializes in handworked copper and bronze items, both old and new, and also sells Middle Eastern lanterns.

SıR (✉ *Serdar Ekrem Sokak 38, Beyoğlu* ☎*212/293–3661*) is the workshop and showroom of a young craftsman who makes both traditional and modern versions of İznik and Küthaya ceramics and sells them at reasonable rates.

JEWELRY

The most common type of jewelry you'll see for sale in Istanbul are amber necklaces and ethnic Turkish silver jewelry threaded with coral and lapis lazuli. Many jewelers are also taking Ottoman-era charms and tile fragments and setting them in silver or gold.

Bagus (✉ *Cevahir Bedestan 42–43 and 133, Grand Bazaar* ☎*212/528–2519*) is located in the Grand Bazaar's Bedestan area and has a large collection of silver handmade jewelry as well as intriguing items imported from around the world.

Horasan (✉ *Terlikçiler Sokak 37, Grand Bazaar* ☎*212/519–3654*) has piles and piles of antique rings, bracelets, and necklaces from Central Asia, as well as walls covered in strands of colorful beads made out of precious and semiprecious stones from which they will help you create your own jewelry. Prices are very fair.

Mor (✉ *Turnacıbaşı Sokak, Sarayhan 10B, Beyoğlu* ☎*212/292–8817*) displays the work of a group of young designers who like to make funky, chunky jewelry that incorporates antique elements into modern design.

Urart (✉ *Abdi İpekçi Cad. 18, Nişantaşı* ☎*212/246–7194*) has chic interpretations of ancient Anatolian designs; there are branches in the Çırağan Palace, Swissotel, and Hilton.

SIDE TRIPS

PRINCES' ISLANDS

20 km (12 mi) off the coast of Istanbul from Sultanahmet.

GETTING HERE AND AROUND

Updated by
Scott Newman

Ferries ($2) and faster Seabuses ($4) depart from Kataba$, and take 90 minutes and 45 minutes, respectively. Schedules change with the seasons, so check beforehand for departure times (⊕*www.ido.com.tr/ en*). In summer the early evening ferries returning to the mainland are often very crowded, particularly on weekends.

Since no cars are allowed on the islands, you'll do most of your exploring on foot. Horse-drawn carriage tours cost $15 to $40. You can rent bicycles ($3 per hour) from one of the shops near the clock tower on Büyükada: definitely a more fun (and more strenuous) way to get around. To get from one of the Princes' Islands to the other, hop aboard any of several daily ferries.

EXPLORING

The Prince's Islands, known simply as Adalar in Turkish, are everything that Istanbul isn't: quiet, green, and car-less. They are primarily a relaxing getaway from the noise and traffic of the big city, though can be quite crowded on sunny weekends. Restrictions on development and a ban on automobiles help maintain the old-fashioned peace and quiet—transportation here is only by horse-drawn carriage or bicycle. There are no real "sights," per se; the attraction is the relaxed peaceful atmosphere. Of the nine islands, four have regular ferry service, but only the two largest, Büyükada and Heybeliada, are of real interest to the general traveler. Both are hilly and wooded, and the fresh breeze is gently pine-scented. They make fun day trips from Istanbul, and with some beautiful hotels, you can even stay overnight. There are frequent ferries—both the atmospheric old boats and the faster, less atmospheric catamarans known as sea buses—from Kataba$, near Taksim at the end of the tram line.

These nine islands of the Sea of Marmara have provided various uses for the people of Istanbul over the years. Back in the days when the city was known as Constantinople, religious undesirables sought refuge here, while in the time of the sultans, the islands provided a convenient place to exile untrustworthy hangers-on. By the turn of the 18th century, well-heeled businessmen had staked their claim and built many of the Victorian gingerbread–style houses that lend the islands their charm. For several years in the 1930s, Büyükada, the largest of the islands, was the home of the exiled Leon Trotsky: the islands were considered to be safer than Istanbul, with its 35,000 hostile white Russian refugees.

From the ferry you can see the two smallest, uninhabited, islands, known in Greek and Turkish as the "pointy" Oxya/Sivri and the "flat" Plate/Yassı. Sivri's main claim to fame was that in the 19th and early 20th centuries Istanbul's stray dogs would be occasionally rounded up and dumped there, while Yassı was the site of the trial and execution of Prime Minister Adnan Menderes after the 1960 military coup. Two of the other inhabited islands are Kınalıada, popular with the city's Armenians, and Burgaz Ada, know to be more Greek, though neither have any significant sights.

2

BÜYÜKADA

Büyükada is the largest of the Princes' Islands and generally the one with the most to offer. To the left as you leave the ferry, you'll see a handful of restaurants and **Yörük Ali Plaj**, the public beach on the west side of the island, is an easy walk from the harbor and also has a little restaurant.

WORD OF MOUTH

"You could get away from the bustle of Istanbul by going to the Prince's Islands, which you can reach by ferry from Istanbul…a peaceful and interesting side trip."
—frogoutofwater

To see the island's splendid old Victorian houses, walk to the clock tower and bear right. The most famous of these is the Izzet Paşa Köşkü, at 55 Çankaya Caddesi, where Trotsky lived while exiled here. To explore the island, carriages are available at the clock tower square or there are many places to hire bikes. The carriage tour winds up hilly lanes lined with gardens filled with jasmine, mimosa, and imported palm trees. After all of Istanbul's mosques and palaces, the frilly pastel houses come as something of a surprise. You can have your buggy driver wait while you make the 20- to 30-minute hike up Yücetepe Hill to the **Greek Monastery of St. George**, a 19th-century church built on Byzantine foundations and with a view that goes on and on. As you walk up the path, notice the pieces of cloth, string, and paper that visitors have tied to the bushes and trees in hope of a wish coming true. This is a popular Orthodox Christian pilgrimage site. The outdoor restaurant next to the monastery, Yücetepe Kir Gazinosu, is known for its homemade wine, once made by the monks themselves, but now made by the family on the Aegean island of Bozcada.

WHERE TO STAY AND EAT

There is little difference from one spot on Büyükada's restaurant row to the next. Generally, the prices are more expensive the closer to the docks. The best bet is to look at a menu and ask to see the dishes on display. Iskele Caddesi, one street behind the shore road, has some cheaper cafés.

$ **Splendid Palace Hotel.** For character, it's hard to beat this wooden turn-of-the-century hotel, with its old-fashioned furniture, large rooms, and Ottoman Victorian styling. The building is topped by twin white domes, copies of those at the Hotel Negresco in Nice. The more expensive front rooms have a stunning sea view. It's difficult to get a room on summer weekends unless you book ahead. **Pros:** romantic; peaceful; charming. **Cons:** a little faded. ⊠ *23 Nisan Cad. 53, Büyükada,* ☎ *216/382–6950* ⊕ *www.splendidhotel.net* ☎ *70 rooms* ⚄ *In-room: no a/c. In-hotel: restaurant, pool* ⊟ *MC, V* ⊘ *Closed Nov.–Apr.*

HEYBELIADA

Heybeliada, the closest island to Büyükada, is similar in appeal, and the quiet, lovely surroundings attract similar boatloads of day-trippers in summer, some hoping to avoid the crowds on the "big island."

The big building to the left of the dock is the **Deniz Kuvvetler** (Turkish Naval Academy). To the right of the dock are teahouses and cafés stretching along the waterfront. You can take a leisurely carriage ride, stopping, if the mood strikes, at one of the island's several small, sandy, and rarely crowded beaches—the best are on the north shore at the foot of **Değirmen Burnu** (Windmill Point) and **Değirmen Tepesi** (Windmill Hill).

Carriage rides also pass the ruined monastery of the **Panaghia**, founded in the 15th century. Though damaged by fires and earthquakes, the chapel and several red-tile-roofed buildings remain. Carriages on Heybeliada do not climb the hills above the harbor, where the old mansions and gardens are, but the walk is not that strenuous.

Up the hill is the 19th-century **Haghia Triada** monastery, built on Byzantine foundations. Once the city's Orthodox seminary, it was shut by the Turks in 1970 and has remained closed despite strong lobbying from the U.S. and Europe.

WHERE TO STAY

$ **Merit Halki Palas.** A member of the Merit chain, the Halki Palas was opened in 1994 after its predecessor, which had been built in the 1850s, burned down. The character of the old hotel has been retained, with white-painted wood and ornate eaves, and the result is an elegant atmosphere that is historic yet crisp and new. The rooms are large and airy, and many have great views, though some of the furniture is starting to show its age. It's one of the most restful hotels in the area of Istanbul, and though the island has few sights of its own, the Old City is only an hour away by ferry. You can dine at the poolside restaurant. **Pros:** elegant and peaceful. **Cons:** out of the way ✉ *Refah Şehitleri Cad. 88, 34973, Heybeliada* ☎ *216/351–0025* ⊕ *www.merithotels.com* ⤶ *36 rooms; 9 suites* ⌂ *In-hotel: 2 restaurants, bar, pool* ▭ *MC, V.*

EDIRNE

235 km (146 mi) northwest of Istanbul.

GETTING HERE AND AROUND

Buses headed for Edirne depart frequently from Istanbul's Esenler Terminal. The trip takes three hours and costs $8. Note that Esenler is a bit out of the way, but many companies have a "servis" minibus into town. In Edirne the bus offices are on the main road between the Selimiye and the Eski Cami. There are also frequent buses from Edirne heading south to Çanakkale.

By car, take the toll road—the E80 TEM, which is faster and much easier than Route 100. The trip takes about 2½ hours.

ESSENTIALS

Tourist information office (✉ *Talat Paşa Cad., near Hürriyet Meyd.* ☎ *284/213–9208* ☾ *Theoretically open every day in summer, although it sometimes closes on Sun. It's generally closed in the off-season*).

Grease Wrestling

The Mediterranean is known for its olive oil, but the Turkish have become famous for using it to lubricate a national sport: Yağlı güreş, known in English as grease or oil wrestling.

The Super Bowl of grease wrestling takes place over three days in late June or July, at Kirkpinar in Edirne. Traditionally, matches lasted until one competitor's strength was sapped (which, in ancient times, could be several days!), but in 1975 official bouts were limited to 30 to 40 minutes. It's still pretty brutal though, with temperatures in Kirkpinar nearing 100°F and no time-outs or water breaks. Broken teeth, bad bruising, and silky-smooth skin are all risk factors.

The wrestlers wear calf-length pants known as kisbet. Kisbet were originally made from the skin of a water buffalo, but are now made from leather or canvas. A wrestler can declare victory in two ways, by pinning his opponent to the ground, or by picking him up and carrying him three steps.

Homer once referred to olive oil as "liquid gold," but these athletes hope to use their physical prowess to turn liquid gold into real gold coins. Champions, known as *baspehlivan* (chief hero),

are in great demand as coaches and trainers. One of the most famous was Ahmet Muhtar Merter, who three-peated his glory in 1957, 1958, and 1959. In Istanbul, the Merter neighborhood is named in his honor.

■ The olive oil used in the match at Kirkpinar is culled from local harvests.

■ Over the course of the three day tournament at Kirkpinar, more than two tons of olive oil is used.

■ The Kirkpinar tournament has been held near Edirne since 1362, making it the world's oldest continual sporting event.

■ In the Ottoman Empire, wrestlers learned the art in spiritual centers, similar to those attended by Japanese Sumo wrestlers.

■ Wrestlers oil each other prior to the match as a demonstration of mutual respect.

■ Wrestlers can perform as many as 42 different moves within a match, and often spend as much as 30 minutes manuevering before trying a paça kazik, or pants grab, which usually ends the match.

EXPLORING

Eastern Thrace (the area historically bounded by the Danube and Nestos rivers, and the Aegean, Marmara, and Black seas) has a harsh climate—sizzling in summer, bitter in winter—and the landscape is unexceptional, but the region has some worthy sights, particularly Edirne, founded in the 2nd century AD as Hadrianopolis by the Roman emperor Hadrian. Edirne was the last great fortress city before Istanbul and was fought over for centuries by every would-be conqueror, including the Bulgars, crusaders, Turks, Greeks, and Russians. It was the Ottoman capital before it was moved to Istanbul, though the rulers often returned, particularly for hunting in the summer, and the many Sultans adorned the city with many magnificent mosques. With the fall of the empire it became something of a picturesque backwater.

Edirne, while no museum town, is a well-preserved Ottoman city; the overhanging balconies of the traditional Ottoman wooden houses shade Edirne's still-cobbled lanes, and its rich collection of mosques and monuments remains mostly unspoiled by the concrete towers so prevalent in Turkey's boomtowns. The rivers and borders have pushed development to the east, allowing the unique feel of an old town still surrounded by fields and greenery. Tourists tend to ignore Edirne, but those who visit appreciate its several remarkable mosques and its covered bazaars. Every summer, Edirne becomes the focus of attention as host of the Kirkpinar, the national grease-wrestling festival.

Hürriyet Meydanı *(Freedom Square)* is Edirne's central square and a good starting point for exploring. Standing in the middle of it is a monument to the city's great passion, wrestling: two enormous wrestlers steal the spotlight from the obligatory Atatürk statue.

Just off the north side of the Hürriyet Meydanı is the **Üç Şerefeli Cami** *(Mosque with Three Galleries)* , built between 1437 and 1447. The galleries circle the tallest of the four minarets, which are notable for their fine brick inlay.

On the grounds of the Üç Şerefeli Mosque is the Sokurlu Hamam, built by Sinan in 1568, and one of the country's more elegant baths. It's open to the public from about 7 AM until 11 PM for men and from 9:30 AM until 6 PM for women and costs $10 for a bath, $16 for a bath with massage.

Walking east from the square along Talat Paşa Caddesi brings you to the **Eski Cami** *(Old Mosque)* . The mosque is appropriately named: completed in 1403, it's the city's oldest. The huge-scale calligraphy of quotes from the Koran and naming the prophets is exceptional in its grace and intricacy. Adjoining it is the **Rüstem Paşa Kervansaray,** restored and reopened as a hotel, just as it was in the 16th century.

Also alongside the mosque is the 14-domed **bedestan** (market), and one block away, the **Ali Paşa Bazaar.** Both are more authentic than Istanbul's Grand Bazaar, as the wares sold—T-shirts, coffeepots, hats, soap shaped like fruits and vegetables, towels, and household ornaments—are meant for locals rather than tourists. ⊠ *Talat Paşa Cad., east from Hürriyet Meyd.* 🕾 *No phone* 🖅 *Free* 🕙 *Daily 9–7.*

FodorsChoice Edirne's **Selimiye Cami** *(Selimiye Mosque)*, not to be confused with Istan-
★ bul's Süleymaniye, is the mosque Sinan described as his masterpiece, and
it's certainly one of the most beautiful buildings in Turkey. It stands out
from afar on the Thracian plain, virtually a symbol of the city. Sinan
was 85 years old when the mosque was completed in 1574, and today
a statue of the architect stands in front, though the mosque remains his
greatest monument. Outside, four identical and slender minarets rise
high, each with three balconies. Inside, the harmony and peacefulness
of the space are immediately striking: The central dome, more than 100
feet in diameter and 148 feet high, rests on eight pillars that have been
set into the walls so as not to disturb the spacious interior, and exter-
nal buttresses help support the weight of 999 windows—legend has it
that Sultan Selim thought 1,000 might be a bit greedy. The minarets
are said to be the tallest in the Muslim world. The *medrese* (mosque
compound) houses Edirne's **Türk-Islâm Eserleri Müzesi** (Museum of
Turkish and Islamic Art), which displays Islamic calligraphy and other
remnants of the city's Islamic past. ⊠ *Hürriyet Meyd.* 🖅 *Free* ⊘ *Daily
sunrise–sunset.*

Edirne Museum. Beyond the Selimiye is a small museum with a collection
of artifacts ranging from Roman tombstones and Thracian jewelry to
folk costumes and kilims. Look in the garden for the large stone-age
dolmen. ⊠ *Kadirpaşa Sokak 7* 🖅 *$4* ⊘ *Tues.–Sun. 9–4:30.*

Muradiye Cami. Continue past the museum down Mimar Sinan Caddesi
and you'll soon see the Muradiye in the distance on the top of a small
hill. This quiet mosque built in 1435 sits peacefully away from everything, and has lovely views over the river valley. It's best to visit around
prayer time as it's usually kept shut at other times because it contains
some of the finest early İznik tiles. ⊠ *Muradiye Bey Sokak.*

The other great mosque in Edirne is the striking **Beyazıt Cami** *(Beyazıt
Mosque)*, on the outskirts of the city across the Tunca River. The
immense complex is about a 20-minute walk (or take a dolmuş from the
square) northwest from Hürriyet Meydanı via the fine-hewn, six-arched
Beyazıt Bridge, which, along with the mosque, dates from the 1480s.
The mosque was built by the Sultan Beyazıt, at the end of the 15th
century, and the complex includes the mosque itself—with a remarkable indented dome and a beautifully fretted mihrab—as well as two
schools, a hospital, a kitchen, and storage depots. In recent years the
complex has been renovated, and it now has permanent exhibitions in
the hospital section, with mannequins in period costumes to re-create
the different forms of treatment for patients in Ottoman times. One section was used as an insane asylum where live musicians performed for
the patients as part of their treatment. The lovely courtyard has benches
and tables set in a neatly tended garden. ⊠ *Head northwest from Hürriyet Meydanı, across Beyazıt Bridge* 🖅 *$8* ⊘ *9 AM–7 PM.*

Sarayiçi, a field with a stadium on one side, is the site of Edirne's famous
wrestling tournament. Usually held in June, it's the best known compe-
tion of those held in villages throughout the country: burly, olive-oil-
coated men have been facing off annually here for more than 600 years,
and thousands of spectators still turn out. Sarayiçi is a 20-minute walk
up the Tunca River from Benazıt Cami.

WHERE TO STAY AND EAT

¢ ✕**Lalezar.** The most popular of a string of restaurants and bars on the
TURKISH   road to Karaağac, Lalezar is an Edirne institution. In summer plastic
tables fill the large garden overlooking the river. The food is a standard
range of Turkish grilled meats and pide and while it may not be as chic
as it would like to think it is, it does have a pleasant atmosphere. The
waiters aren't as helpful as they could be, though. It's a 20-minute walk
or short taxi ride from Hurriyet Meydan. ⊠*Karaağac yol* ☎*283/223–
0600* ⊟*MC V.*

¢ ✕**The London Cafe.** Styled like a London pub, with dark wood furni-
TURKISH   ture and paintings of English rural scenes, this two-story eatery has
an excellent range of large portioned mains, including *köfte* (Turkish
meatballs), grilled meats, and salads. Air-conditioning and a relaxed
atmosphere make it a favorite with locals looking to escape the summer
heat. ⊠*Saraçlar Cad. No. 46* ☎*284/213–8052* ⊟*AE, MC, V.*

¢ ⊡**Efe Hotel.** Tucked away on a side street off the main drag, this hotel's
bright vermilion exterior belies the muted calm of its interior decor—
not that it's going to win any design awards. It's a good midrange hotel,
modern and comfortable, and rooms are relatively large. The staff are
professional and helpful. **Pros:** modern, good value. **Cons:** not much in
the way of atmosphere. ⊠*Maarif Cad. No 13, Kaleiçi* ☎*284/213–6166
or 284/213–6466* ⊕*www.efehotel.com* ⌦*34 rooms* ⌂*In-room: Wi-Fi.
In-hotel: restaurant, bar* ⊟*AE, MC, V.*

$$–$$$ ⊡**Selimiye Taşodalar.** This 15th-century house has recently been restored
as boutique hotel. Rooms are large, and each is distinctively and tastefully decorated with modern wooden furniture and an Ottoman touch.
The suites are especially huge. The building, once the home of Mehmet
the conqueror's wet nurse, is on the far side of Selimiye mosque, with
most rooms looking out onto it. The hotel is aimed more at Turkish
tourists, with little English spoken. **Pros:** large, beautiful rooms. **Cons:**
less central than some of the other hotels. ⊠*Selimiye Arkasi Saray
Hanam Sokak 3* ☎*284/212–3529* ⊕*www.tasodalar.com* ⌂*In-hotel:
restaurant.*

The Sea of Marmara & the North Aegean

WORD OF MOUTH

"If you're into ancient history and wish to enjoy one of the most scenic routes during its best season in April and May . . . there are 3 different places which should not be missed if you can spend an extra night in Çanakkale: these three sites are Gallipoli, Troy, and Pergamum."

—ANATOLIANCRUISER

WELCOME TO THE SEA OF MARMARA & THE NORTH AEGEAN

TOP REASONS TO GO

★ **İznik tiles** Watch the craftswomen engraving on quartz; buy some to take home.

★ **Spend quality time in Bursa** Visit the Yeşil Cami (Green Mosque), stroll the covered bazaar, and make sure to try the local kebab specialty: *İskender kebap.*

★ **Gallipoli** See the battlefields and moving memorials where one of the key campaigns of the First World War was fought.

★ **Explore Mount Ida** Hike among the pine forests and waterfalls, and stay in one of the area's boutique hotels.

★ **Troy** Visit the ruins of this 5,000-year-old city, where more than nine layers of civilization have been uncovered.

★ **Pergamum** Explore this spectacular showcase of the classical period, second in Turkey only to Ephesus.

Ruins of the Temple of Trajan Acropolis of Pergamum

A Canakkale war monument at Gallipoli

1 **Sea of Marmara.** You can still feel the Ottoman spirit in this part of Turkey, where you'll find some of the best examples of early Ottoman architecture, faithfully restored old thermal baths, the surviving arts of tile making and silk-weaving, and wonderful old bazaars. This is also where you'll find Mt. Uludağ, the trendiest ski resort in Turkey.

2 **The Dardanelles.** are the straits southwest of Istanbul running between the Aegean and Marmara seas. Most of the sights are on the Gallipoli Peninsula to the north of the straits and the windswept land is full of moving historical

sites marking the Gallipoli campaign of World War I: beautifully tended cemeteries stretch along the 30 km (19 mi) of land where so many soldiers are buried. Çanakkale is south of Gallipoli.

3 **North Aegean.** The combination of Greek heritage and Turkish rural life, set in an unspoiled natural setting of azure sea, winding coastline, and pine-clad hills, is just starting to attract international tourism. Mount Ida, the home of Greek gods and goddesses, offers a very civilized country experience, and the ruins of Troy, Pergamum, and Behramkale (Assos) aren't far.

GETTING ORIENTED

Tourism to the southern coast of the Sea of Marmara and the North Aegean is taking off as visitors discover this rich area of lovely beaches, wonderful walking country, and impressive range of historical sites dating from the 3rd millennium BC (Troy) to World War I (Gallipoli). The south coast of the Sea of Marmara is close to Istanbul and where you'll find İznik, famed for its beautiful tiles, and the old Ottoman capital of Bursa.

THE SEA OF MARMARA & THE NORTH AEGEAN PLANNER

When to Go

The Southern Marmara and the North Aegean region are considerably cooler than the South Aegean and Mediterranean coasts, but summer is still very hot. In July and August, the national park at Uludağ, in Bursa, remains refreshingly cool, and, with its skiing opportunities, is also an attraction in the winter. If you're here in colder months, Bursa, where you can soak in thermal baths, is a good antidote to the winter blues.

Mount Ida is lovely all year round but is prettiest in spring when nature is awakening.

Çanakkale, Gallipoli, and Troy can be very gusty in late summer and fall. Indeed, Homer refers to Troy as a windy city, and some archaeologists argue that the strong winds are one of the reasons why so many layers of civilization ended up piled on top of one another.

How Much Time Do You Need?

The Sea of Marmara area can be a quick one- or two-day trip from Istanbul: you could do just a day in İznik (make sure you leave Istanbul early), but you'll want to spend an overnight, at least, in Bursa. If you're just planning a day trip or an overnight to the area from Istanbul, the ferry from Istanbul's Yenikapi terminal to Yalova takes about an hour, and then you can catch a bus to İznik or Bursa.

If you have two or three days in the region, visit Gallipoli and Troy, maybe adding a day in the Mt. Ida region. If you have five or six days, you can pretty much see everything in the area, continuing on to Behramkale (Assos) and Ayvalik, with a visit to Cunda, Ayvalik's main island, and the ruins of Pergamum. Be warned, though: Mt. Ida is lovely and has wonderful hiking. Once you get there, you might want to stay longer.

Gallipoli Tours

Touring the battlefields and memorials with a guide is advisable. Tours are conducted all year, daily between April and November, every other day the rest of the year. They run about 5½ hours, starting at noon in summer, 10:30 AM in winter. Good walking shoes or sneakers are advised and, in summer, bring a hat and water.

Hassle-Free Travel Agency. This should be your first choice if you're staying in Çanakkale. They also run a hotel and a hostel in town, which is very practical if you're signed up for the tour. From Çanakkale tours to Gallipoli are about $50 per person including lunch, ferry crossing, and transport. ⌧ Cumhuriyet Meydanı, 5917100, Çanakkale ☎ 286/213–5969 ⊕ www.hasslefreetour.com.

TJ's Tours. TJ's owns a hostel and a hotel in Eceabat. Standard tours to the battlefields cost about $40, including lunch, transport, and admission to the museum. Stay at their hotel and they'll show the film Gallipoli the night before the tour, and the documentary The Fatal Shore on their terrace bar in the morning, to set the mood for the visit. ⌧ Kemalpa Şa Mahallesi, Cumhuriyet Cad. 5/A, Eceabat ☎ 286/814–3121 ⊕ www.anzacgallipolitours.com.

Healthy Aegean Cuisine

Aegean cuisine is in many ways different from Turkish food elsewhere in the country. The shared Turkish and Greek culture of the region's past, the climate and soil suitable for growing a wide range of vegetables, and the prevalence of olive trees and olive-oil production have helped the region develop a much more varied and probably healthier way of eating than elsewhere in Turkey. Olive oil replaces butter and fish replaces meat on most menus. The class of dishes generally called *zeytinyağlı* (literally "with olive oil") mostly comes from this region; it means vegetables cooked in olive oil, mostly with tomatoes and onions, and served cold. Vegetarians will be in heaven.

Local Specialties

Most cities in Turkey claim some kind of fame for their *köfte* (meatballs), but *İegol köfte*—cooked on charcoal—are especially delicious and said to have been invented in Bursa, as was *İskender kebap*, tender beef on pita bread, soaked in tomato sauce, and served with yogurt on the side. And don't let your experience of İskender kebap elsewhere in Turkey put you off trying it in Bursa, where it's far superior.

In the Mt. Ida region you'll find mezes that are made with wild herbs collected in the area and cooked or dressed in olive oil. Cunda island in Ayvalık has an amazing range of seafood and fish mezes and main dishes, enriched by lesser-known Greek dishes and the restaurants' own creations. Fish is always advisable throughout the region if you stick to local and seasonal catches.

Two Days Around the Sea of Marmara

If you leave Istanbul by ferry early enough to be in Yalova by midmorning, you can catch a bus or drive to İznik and have lunch by the lake and visit the Tiles Foundation by the lakeside road. Then head into the center of town to visit Yeşil Cami and Sancta Sophia. If you leave İznik by late afternoon, you'll be in Bursa in the early evening. Spend the second day sightseeing in Bursa—don't miss Yeşil Cami, the Covered Bazaar, the Muradiye Tombs, and the city museum. For lunch, make sure to try the İskender kebap. If you have time, you can take the cable car to Mt. Uludağ and enjoy the view of its pine-clad hills. Return to Yalova in the early evening and catch the last ferry back to Yenikapı terminal in Istanbul.

What It Costs In U.S. Dollars

DINING AND LODGING PRICE CATEGORIES					
	¢	$	$$	$$$	$$$$
Restaurants	under $5	$5–$10	$11–$15	$16–$25	over $25
Hotels	under $50	$51–$75	$76–$150	$151–$250	over $250

Restaurant prices are for one main course at dinner or for two mezes (small dishes). Hotel prices are for two people in a standard double room in high season, including taxes.

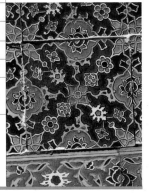

GETTING HERE & AROUND

By Car

The best way to explore this area is by a car, especially in Gallipoli, where the memorials are well signposted, roads are quite good, and parking is available. There are several options for getting out of Istanbul: one is to take the E80 headed for Ankara. At İzmit take Route 130 to Yalova; Route 575 connects Yalova and Bursa.

By Air

There are several airports in the area. Atlas Jet has daily flights between Istanbul and Çanakkale airport. There is also an airport in Edremit, 55 km (35 mi) north of Ayvalık, on the tip of the Gulf of Edremit. Atlas flies here, but only from Istanbul and only three or four times a week; it's a convenient place to fly to if your destination is Ayvalık, the Mount Ida region, or Assos. Bursa, the largest city in the region, currently has a nonoperating airport: every year the possibility of opening it is discussed and then the issue is postponed for another year. Turkish Airlines or private airlines such as Atlas Jet will have the latest info.

By Bus

Buses are a good form of transport in this region, though the frequent stops on some routes, such as between Çanakkale and Edremit, can be frustrating. Most bus companies have branches both in the terminal and the center of town. Several buses make the trip from Istanbul's Esenler terminal to Yalova (about 4 hours) and from there you can travel on to İznik or Bursa. The trip from Istanbul to Çanakkale is about 6 hours and costs $35. From Bursa to Çanakkale is 4½ hours and costs about $14. From Çanakkale buses run almost every hour to İzmir, passing Ezine, Ayvacık, Küçükkuyu, Edremit, Ayvalık, and Bergama on the way. Fares are about $10.

By Boat and Ferry

Fast ferries operate daily between Istanbul's Yenikapı terminal and Yalova and are the quickest way to get to Bursa or İznik. They run every two hours each way between 7:30 AM and 9:30 PM, though on weekends sailings may start later and finish later. The journey takes just over an hour and costs about $10 for passengers and about $55 for a car including driver and passengers. They also operate daily to Bandırma, a good point from which to make your way to the Mount Ida region, Assos, or Ayvalık. Since the Bandırma–Çanakkale road is normally less crowded than Istanbul–Çanakkale, you may want to choose this route when traveling to Gallipoli, though it's not much shorter. Ferries to/from Bandırma/Istanbul run three times daily, take two hours and cost about $25 per passenger and about $100 for a car including driver and passengers. For both ferries reservations are essential during religious holidays and summer weekends, and advisable generally for weekends and between June and August.

By Train

Train journey in this region is not advisable: trains (and tracks) are old and painfully slow. It's also often more expensive than the bus.

3

Updated by
Joel Hanson

The Mediterranean has sun and sand, the south Aegean has lively nightlife and, of course, Ephesus—but if you're interested in fresh air, a cool sea, historic sites, havens in the wilderness, and generally a less touristy experience, then the north Aegean and the area south of the Marmara Sea is for you.

This area doesn't have the high-wattage appeal of the Aegean and Mediterranean regions farther south, but that doesn't mean it should be overlooked. The beaches here tend to be more pebbly and the water a touch colder than in other regions, but they're also frequently less crowded, since the European package-tour crowd has yet to descend. You can see the whole of the region in a week or, if you're based in Istanbul, it can be divided into separate, shorter journeys. Spend at least one evening watching the sun go down over Homer's wine-dark sea, and you'll agree that the north Aegean has a little bit of everything—and a lot you won't find anywhere else.

SEA OF MARMARA

Although quite close to Istanbul, the area around the Sea of Marmara is sometimes overlooked by travelers anxious to get to the beaches of the Aegean coast. There is much here to attract visitors interested in history and beautiful landscapes, though.

İznik, a pilgrimage site for Christians and an important city for the Ottomans, offers historical sights from the Roman, Byzantine, Seljuk, and Ottoman periods, and the town's beautiful tiles are another reason to visit. Bursa, the first capital of the Ottoman Empire, boasts some of the finest examples of Ottoman architecture in its mosques and bazaars. You can visit either city as a day trip from Istanbul, though Bursa deserves at least an overnight stay. Both are, more or less, on the way to the Mediterranean, central Anatolia, or even the north Aegean if you're traveling by ferry across the Marmara Sea. The area's mountain, Uludağ, is Turkey's most popular skiing resort.

İZNIK

190 km (118 mi) from Istanbul.

GETTING HERE AND AROUND
If you're driving, İznik is 190 km (118 mi) from Istanbul via Rte. 100 or E80 to İzmit and Rte. 130 to Yalova; it's 60 km (37 mi) east from Yalova via Route 595. Or take the ferry from Istanbul's Yenikapı terminal to Yalova (1 hour). The ferry trip lops 140 km (87 mi) off the journey.

There are several buses (the 46A and 69 run the most frequently) that run from Cumhuriyet Caddesi (Republic Street) near Taksim Square to Istanbul's Yenikapı terminal.

Once you arrive in Yalova by ferry, if you don't have your own car, exit the ferry port, turn right and walk about 50 meters past the police station to the minibus station on your right. Destinations are clearly displayed in the bus windows, and you'll find the bus to İznik near a series of buildings on your right. The trip from Yalova to İznik costs about $5.

ESSENTIALS
Visitor Information (✉Mahmut Çelebi Mahallesi, S. Demircan [Çiniciler] Sokak 22 ☎224/757-6809).

EXPLORING

İznik has a distinguished past but a faded present. Nobody knows when the city was actually founded, but it was put on the map in 316 BC when one of Alexander the Great's generals claimed the city. It fell under the rule of many subsequent rulers, including the general Lysimachus, who renamed it Nicaea after his wife. The Seljuks made the city their capital for a brief period in the 11th century, and Byzantine emperors in exile did the same in the 13th century while Constantinople was in the hands of Crusaders. The Ottoman Sultan Orhan Gazi (ruled 1326–61) captured it in 1331. The famous İznik tiles, unequaled even today, were created under Ottoman rule.

İznik was an important city in early history, known as the site of the First and Second Councils of Nicaea, the first and seventh Ecumenical Councils, and the Nicene Creed; it was also the capitral of the Byzantine Empire for a short period, between 1204 and 1261. Today, however, it's a fairly average looking city, though with impressive city walls and a lovely lakefront. Nature has been generous to İznik and it's beautifully situated around the east end of İznik Lake, where you can swim (though the water can be chilly) or rent a kayak or paddleboat. The revival of the tile industry draws many travelers—many of whom end up placing huge orders for delivery overseas.

İznik is also an easy place to navigate: the town hasn't grown much, so the classical Roman layout still works. You'll almost certainly come across the city's walls as you explore; the four main gates date back to Roman times, and the city's two main streets intersect each other and end at these gates. Running north–south is Kılıçaslan Caddesi; east–west is Atatürk Caddesi. Sancta Sophia Church is at the intersection of these streets.

WHAT TO SEE

Hacı Özbek Cami. Constructed in 1333 without a minaret, this was was the first Ottoman monument in İzniz. The style is quite primitive and it lacks the ornamentation seen in later buildings in Bursa and Istanbul. The mosque underwent an extensive restoration in 1959 and has a dome made of tiles. ⊠ *Kılıçaslan Cad., east of the Belediye Sarayı (town hall)* ☎ *No phone* ✆ *Free* ⊗ *Daily sunrise–sunset.*

İznik Museum. The building that houses this museum was built in 1388 as a soup kitchen. Such kitchens, serving free food to the poor, were often constructed by the wealthy as demonstrations of Muslim charity. Today the museum contains such artifacts as Greek tombstones, Ottoman weaponry, perfume bottles, and original İznik tiles. If you have time, ask at the museum about a visit to the Byzantine Tomb, the **Yeraltı Mezar**, on the outskirts of town. Discovered in the 1960s, this 5th-century burial place of an unknown family has well-preserved painted murals of peacocks, flowers, and abstract patterns in the Byzantine style. ■ TIP➔ The only way to visit the tomb is by asking at the museum, and they won't take you if they are short of staff. ⊠ *Kılıçaslan Cad., opposite Yeşil Cami* ☎ *224/757–1027* ✆ *$1.50* ⊗ *Daily 8:30–noon and 1:30–5, closed Mon.*

İznik's Tiled Beauty

CLOSE UP

İznik tile makers believe that their tiles have magical properties. There is one fairly sound explanation for this (alongside any number of unsound ones): İznik tiles, made from soil that's found only in the area, have a very high level of quartz, an element believed to have soothing effects. It's not just the level of quartz that makes İznik tiles unique, though. The original tiles also have distinctive patterns and colors: predominantly blue, then green and red, reflecting the colors of precious stones. The patterns are inspired by local flora—flowering trees or tulips. These days artists use different colors and designs as well as the traditional ones.

İznik became a center for the ceramics industry after the 15th-century Ottoman conquest of Istanbul. To upgrade the quality of native work, Sultan Selim I (ruled 1512–15) imported 500 potters from Tabriz in Persia. The government-owned kilns were soon turning out exquisite tiles with intricate motifs of circles, stars, and floral and geometric patterns, in lush turquoise, green, blue, red, and white. Despite their costliness, their popularity spread through the Islamic world, until the industry went into decline in the 18th century.

İznik tiles are expensive—more so than those produced in the rival ceramics center of Kütahya, 120 km (72 mi) farther south. A single tile costs about $20, and the price of a plate varies between $30 and $300. İznik tiles are made of better-quality stone, with a higher quartz content, so they're heavier and more durable, making them ideal for decorating large spaces, from airports to mosques. They're all handmade, with no artificial colors, and the designs tend to be more intricate and elegant. The tile-makers' street, near the city center, has a series of small shops next to each

other. The shops are fun to visit: they're workshops as well as sales points, and you'll usually find someone drawing or painting tiles.

Check out **Cengizhan Çini**, which also functions as a Tourist Information Office. ⊠ *Mahmut Çelebi Mahallesi, S. Demircan (Çiniciler) Sokak 22* ☎ *224/757–6809* ⏱ *10–7.*

Süleyman Paşa Medresesi, the first college of the Ottoman empire, is now a tile workshop with a peaceful courtyard where you can have refreshments. ⊠ *Maltepe Cad. 29* ⏱ *10–7:30 (9 PM in summer).*

The İznik Education and Learning Foundation is a bit out of town along the lake and is a nice place to wander; the garden has displays of the quartz used to make İznik tiles. If you're making a big order for overseas delivery, this is the place; you'll also get a certificate of authencity. ⊠ *Sahil Yolu, Vakıf Sokak 13* ☎ *224/757–6025* ⊕ *www.iznik.com* ⏱ *8–6.*

Lefke Gate *(Lefke Kapısı).* The gray stone eastern gate to the ancient city was built in honor of a visit by the Roman emperor Hadrian in AD 120. Thick, sturdy fortifications like these were what saved many a town from ruin and its old inscriptions, marble reliefs, and friezes remain intact. Outside the gate are the city graveyard and Muslim tombs belonging to a nobleman named Hayrettin Paşa and some lesser luminaries. The oldest is 600 years old.

Roman Theater. The Roman Emperor Trajan asked the governor Plinius to construct this theater in the early 2nd century. Today, despite ongoing excavation, it's mostly a pile of rubble and weeds. Nevertheless, the theater offers a quiet, comfortable place to have a picnic or in-depth conversation with yourself as you wander over the rocks and imagine its former grandeur. On weekdays, you'll have the place entirely to yourself. Like most of the ruins of İznik, it's also easy to find: just head west toward İznik Lake from the bus station. Unfortunately, there are traces of broken glass and plastic soda bottles on the grounds—the remains of weekend partyers—so watch your step.

Sancta Sophia *(Church of the Holy Wisdom).* This church was built in the center of İznik in the 6th century, during the reign of Justinian. Its primitive mosaic floor is believed to date from that time but the wall mosaics were added as part of a reconstruction in the 11th century, after an earthquake toppled the original church. There are some fine fragments of Byzantine fresco here, as well as some mosaics including a mural of Jesus with Mary and St. John the Baptist. ⊠ *Atatürk Cad. and Kılıçaslan Cad.* 🖼 *$4* 🕙 *Daily 9–noon and 1–6.*

Tomb and Mosque of Abdulwahab. If you're looking for a good spot to watch the sunset over İznik Lake, the tomb is an easy 30-minute stroll from the city center and well worth the trip for a sunset view. Take Kılıçaslan Caddesi east through the Lefke Gate and then follow the ruins of the Roman aqueduct along the road on your right. Use the large Turkish flag near the tomb to guide you. On a clear evening, the orange glow of sunset makes the surrounding mountains look like the backs of gigantic serpents sleeping in İznik Lake. The spot attracts couples young and old—and extended families—many of whom often bring dinner along to accentuate the experience.

WHERE TO STAY AND EAT

¢ ✕ **Kenan Çorba.** Just opposite the Sancta Sophia museum, the locals

TURKISH love this restaurant that specializes in soups and beans. Try the fish or chicken soup. İşkembe (tripe soup) is delicious, but probably best for those who are into experimenting: you'll either hate it or love it—although the Turks believe it's the ultimate hangover cure, eaten at the end of a late night of drinking. The beans with sliced Turkish pastrami and rice, accompanied by tiny pickled peppers, are an all-time favorite. The restaurant opens early, at 5 AM. ⊠ *Atatürk Cad., opposite Sancta Sophia* 🕾 *224/757–0235* ▤ *MC, V.*

¢ ✕ **Kofteci Yusuf.** Turks love their köfte (meatballs), and almost every city

TURKISH in the country makes a claim to fame based on its own way of making them. The locals think İznik köfte are the best around, and fill the large canteen-type tables of this casual place at almost all times of the day. Portions are large and served with barbecued tomatoes, peppers, and onions. You might not be able to distinguish these köfte from any other, but the place is its own sort of treat. ⊠ *Atatürk Cad., opposite İznik Lycee* ☎ *224/757–3597* ☰ *V* ⊙ *Open daily 8* AM*–midnight.*

$ ✕⚏ **Çamlık Motel.** On the quiet end of the lakefront, this plain but well established hotel is one of the best places to stay in İznik. Rooms are sparsely furnished but the property has a large, charming garden and it's only about 100 meters from the beach. An extra bonus is satellite TV. The hotel also has the only

> ### DINING IN İZNİK
>
> İznik isn't the place for elaborate restaurants: for dinner and drinks, the lakefront hotels with restaurants are your best bet. While touring the sights, though, eat in the town center in any of the various establishments along Kılıçaslan Caddesi where good *pides* (pizza-like flatbread), *lahmacuns* (flat bread with ground meat on top, literally "meat with dough"), and kebabs are easy-to-find, low-cost options for a quick lunch.

remaining nice fish and meat restaurant on the lake front, open to nonguests: a variety of tasty mezes and fresh lake fish, *yayın*, caught daily, is served in the garden. **Pros:** nice location near the quietest part of the lake; self-service tea and water in the lobby. **Cons:** only four rooms face the lake. ⊠ *Göl Sahil Yolu* ☎ *224/757–1362* ⊕ *www. iznik-camlikmotel.com* ⤳ *24 rooms* ⚭ *In-room: Wi-Fi. In-hotel: restaurant* ☰ *MC, V* ⦿ *BP.*

$ ⚏ **Hotel Aydin.** This clean, simple, and relaxing spot in the center of İznik, is run by a friendly guy named Sertaç. Next door is Aydo Patisserie, an ice-cream business opened by Sertaç's grandfather in 1962 that serves İznik and the surrounding communities with excellent homemade ice cream. Make sure to ask for a room on the south side of the hotel, away from the street noise of Kılıçaslan Caddesi. **Pros:** conveniently located in the center of town near the St. Sofia Museum. **Cons:** lakefront prices without lakefront access; some rooms are close to noisy Kılıçaslan Caddesi. ⊠ *Kılıçaslan Cad. 64* ☎ *224/757–7650* ⊕ *www. iznikhotelaydin.com* ⤳ *18 rooms* ⚭ *In-room: a/c, Wi-Fi. In-hotel: room service, laundry service* ⦿ *BP.*

$$ ⚏ **İznik Çini Vakfı Konukevi.** Right next to, and owned by, the İznik Tiles
★ Education and Learning Foundation, this small hotel has basic comforts but a nice setting and atmosphere. It's in the remote but still easily reachable part of İznik, at the end of the lakefront and a bit inland. The hotel is built partially from dark wood, unlike the concrete of İznik's other hotels, and the garden has displays of quartz stone used to make İznik tiles. The beach is only a 10-minute walk away. **Pros:** location next to the Tiles foundation; quiet. **Cons:** not right on the waterfront. ⊠ *Selcuk Mahallesi, İznik Egitim Ogretim Vakfı Vakıf Sokak 13* ☎ *224/757–6025* 🖷 *224/757–5737* ⤳ *7 rooms* ☰ *V* ⦿ *BP.*

¢ ⚏ **Kaynarca Hotel and Pansiyon.** The clean, well-maintained rooms (two three-bed dorms with shared bathroom; 10 private rooms) are the first choice for budget-conscious backpackers, despite the 10-minute walk from the waterfront. A location plus, however, are the nearby mosques and inexpensive restaurants on Kılıçaslan Caddesi. The proprietor, Ali, has a good command of English and offers a user-friendly map of the city as well as practical information about the various city sites. The hotel also has a shared kitchen area for self-catering, satellite TV, and a large rooftop balcony to relax with other travelers. **Pros:** free city maps; practical travel advice; a good place to meet other travelers. **Cons:** no a/c in rooms; breakfast not included in the room price. ✉*M. Gündem Sokak No. 1* ☎*224/757–1753* ⊕*www.kaynarca.net* ↩*12 rooms* △*In-room: no a/c, Wi-Fi. In-hotel: laundry service* ⏹*EP.*

OFF THE BEATEN PATH

3

Termal (✉*12 km [8 mi] southwest of Yalova on the way to Çınarcık* ⊕*www.yalovatermal.com*), a popular spa since Roman times, is an interesting stop if you're en route between Yalova and either İznik or Bursa. Its springs were used by the Ottomans, refurbished in 1900 by Sultan Abdül Hamid II, and regularly visited by Atatürk in the 1920s and '30s. It's a self-contained resort with two hotels (Çamlık and Çınar), exotic gardens, and three public thermal baths with mineral-rich waters and lockers for clothes. Both hotels also have private baths for guests only. Avoid summer weekends when the area is absolutely packed, and the crowds will probably outweigh any relaxation the baths may give you. The hot baths are more appealing, and the rates cheaper, outside summer, anyway. If you're here when it's overcrowded, consider skipping the soak and opting instead for a walk in the oxygen-rich pine forests, with a packed lunch to eat at the picnic spot.

BURSA

247 km (153 mi) from Istanbul.

GETTING HERE AND AROUND

If you're driving, Bursa is 247 km (153 mi) from Istanbul via Rte. 100 or E80 to İzmit, Rte. 130 to Yalova, and Rte. 575 south from Yalova to Bursa; the Yalova Bursa part of the trip is 60 km (37 mi). Or, take the ferry from Istanbul's Yenikapı terminal to Yalova. Bursa is 85 km from İznik.

From Istanbul, through Yalova, it's a five-hour bus trip to Bursa, including the ferry trip from Darıca to Yalova, and costs about $12. A better option is to take the sea bus to Yalova; near the sea-bus quay in Yalova are buses to Bursa that cost about $5 and take one hour.

ESSENTIALS

Visitor Information (✉*Ulu Cami park, next to Orhan Gazi underpass, No. 1, Heykel* ☎*224/220–1848*).

EXPLORING

Bursa is a large city, stretching out along an east–west axis. The town square, at the intersection of Atatürk Caddesi and İnönü Caddesi, is officially called Cumhuriyet Alanı (Republic Square), but is popularly called **Heykel** (Statue), after its imposing equestrian statue

TAKE THE WATERS

Bursa has been a spa town since Roman times. Rich in minerals, the waters are said to cure a variety of ills from rheumatism to nervous complaints. The thermal springs run along the slopes of the Çekirge region, and mineral baths are an amenity at many hotels in this area.

of Atatürk. East of Heykel, is the Yeşil neighborhood, with Yeşil Cami and Yeşil Türbe. Buses from outside the city center converge on Heykel, from where you can reach most sites. The main bus routes run about every 15 minutes during the day and roughly every 30 minutes at night. There are signs and posted

WORD OF MOUTH

"For mineral hot water springs I would recommend Bursa. Any small guest house or hotel in the Cekirge part of the city has its own thermal baths."   —ANATOLIANCRUISER

schedules at most major stops. Bursa is one of the rare cities that hasn't ceased being important since early Ottoman times. It became the first capital of the nascent Ottoman Empire after the city was captured in 1326 by Orhan Gazi, the empire's first sultan, and the first five sultans of the Ottoman Empire lived here until Mehmet the Conquerer conquered Istanbul and moved the capital. Each of the sultans built his own complex on five different hilltops, and each included a mosque, a *medrese* (theological school), a hamam, a kitchen house, caravansary, and tombs. It was in Bursa that Ottoman architecture blossomed, and where the foundations were laid for the more elaborate works to be found in the later capitals Edirne and Istanbul. More than 125 mosques here are on the list kept by the Turkish Historical Monuments Commission, and their minarets make for a grand skyline.

Present-day Bursa is one of Turkey's more prosperous cities due to its large automobile and textile industries, and the city is a pleasing mix of bustling modernity, old stone buildings, and wealthy suburbs with vintage wood-frame Ottoman villas. Residents proudly call their city Yeşil Bursa (Green Bursa)—for the green İznik tiles decorating some of its most famous monuments, and also for its parks and gardens and the national forest surrounding nearby Mt. Uludağ, Turkey's most popular ski resort.

The city has history, charming villages, sporting opportunities, good food (two local inventions, İskender kebap and İnegöl köfte, made significant contributions to Turkish cuisine), good hotels, and shopping opportunities. Many travelers only spend a half-day here, on the way from Istanbul to the south and west coasts or Cappadocia, but once you're here, there's a good chance you'll want to stay longer, so plan ahead.

WHAT TO SEE

⑩ A 10-minute walk from the Yeşil complex, the **Bursa Kent Muzesi** *(Bursa*
★ *City Museum)* at Heykel, in the city center right behind the statue, is a showcase for Bursa's history and handicrafts. In the basement are impressive re-creations of antique handicraft bazaars like those for silk weavers and knife makers. The lower floor summarizes the history of Bursa and its first five sultans, and touches on Ataürk during the independence war. The second floor displays past and present Bursa clothes, household tools, and re-creations of life at home and in the hamam. The exhibits are in Turkish, so make sure to get English-language headsets at the entrance. ⊠*Atatürk Cad.,* ☎*224/220–2626* ⊕*www. bursakentmuzesi.gov.tr* 🖃*$1* ☉*Daily 9:30–5:30, closed Mon.*

8 The **Emir Sultan Cami** (*Emir Sultan Mosque*) was originally built in 1431 by the daughter of Sultan Yıldırım Beyazıt for her husband, Emir Sultan. It was badly damaged in the 1855 earthquake and was almost totally rebuilt by Sultan Abdülaziz. The single-domed mosque with the two cut-stone minarets for which it is famous—they are considered great examples of rococo—is in a courtyard facing the three-domed arcade that houses the tombs of Emir Sultan, his wife, and children. The setting is quite tranquil, on a quiet hilltop next to a large cemetery among cypress and plane trees overlooking the city. ⊠*Zeytinler Cad.* ☎*No phone* ☑*Free* ☾*Daily sunrise–sunset.*

3

9 The **Kapalı Çarşı** (*covered bazaar*) is a large area with many adjoining
Fodor'sChoice   *hans* (kervansary) and a *bedestan* (the central part of a covered bazaar,
★   which is vaulted and fireproofed). The Bursa sultans built their complexes on different hilltops, but they made sure to divert trade to the same place, adding their own bazaars to existing ones, so as to finance the construction or maintenance of their schools, mosques, or kitchen houses. During the reign of Orhan Sultan the area between the hans was loosely covered by roofs, the earliest form of covered bazaar. Then in the late 14th century Yıldırım Beyazıt perfected the concept by building a bedesten with six woven parts connected by arches and topped by 14 domes. It was flattened by a massive earthquake in 1855, and then parts were badly burned by fire in the 1950s, but it has been lovingly restored, and many of the hans inside still provide wonderful flavor of the past. ■ TIP→ Best buys here include silver and gold jewelry, thick Turkish cotton towels (for which Bursa is famous), and silk goods. ⊠*Between Atatürk and Cumhuriyet Cad. behind Ulu Cami.* ☾*Apr.–Oct., daily 9–8; Nov.–Mar., daily 9–7. Closed Sun.*

3 Dominating the view on Çekirge Caddesi is the refreshingly green **Kültür Parkı** (*Culture Park*), with restaurants, tea gardens, a pond with paddleboats, a sports stadium, and a Ferris wheel. This is also where Bursa's **Arkeoloji Müzesi** (Archaeology Museum) is found; it's pleasant enough, with Roman coins and other artifacts, but there are better ones in Istanbul, Ankara, and elsewhere. The same goes for the nearby **Atatürk Müzesi** (Atatürk Museum), with old-fashioned furniture and a few exhibits on the great leader's life. ⊠*Kültür Parkı: Çekirge Cad. and Stadyum Cad.* ☎*224/234–4918 Archaeology Museum, 224/234–7716 Atatürk Museum* ☑*$4; free for Atatürk museum* ☾*Archaeology Museum: Tues.–Sun. 8:30–12:30 and 1:30–5:30; Atatürk museum: Tues.–Sat. 8–noon and 1–5.*

5 **Muradiye Tombs.** Next to the Sultan Murat mosque, in what is probably
★   the city's most serene resting place, is a fountain ringed by 12 tombs. Among those buried here are Murat himself, Mehmet, and Mustafa, the eldest son of Süleyman the Magnificent, who was strangled in his father's tent. The plainest tomb belongs to Sultan Murad II and was built in accordance with his will, with an open hole in the roof right above the tomb to let the rain in. The most decorated tombs are Celebi Mehmet's and Cem Sultan's (the youngest son of Mehmet the Conquerer), which are kept locked most of the time—ask the caretaker to open them for you. ⊠*Muradiye Mahhallesi. Aralık Sokak 17*

☎224/222–0868 ✉Free ⏱Tombs open daily 9–12:30 and 1:30–5; mosque open dawn–dusk.

❻ The **Sultan Murat II Cami** (Sultan Murat II Mosque) and surrounding complex around the pleasant little park in Bursa's Muradiye neighborhood were built in 1425–26, during the reign of Mehmet the Conqueror, in honor of Murat, Mehmet's father. The mosque is unexceptional, perhaps because Mehmet's attentions were so firmly focused on Constantinople, which he would soon win. On the right side of the mosque and across the street is the kitchen house—once built to give free food to poor people—but now the restaurant Darüzziyafe. It was built without windows by Sultan Murad II, so as not to let the poor be embarrassed by being seen from outside. On Tuesdays there is a street market between the mosque and kitchen house.

⓫ The **Türk İslam Eserleri Müzesi** (Turkish Islamic Arts Museum) is on the site of a former theological school that is part of the complex that includes Yeşil Cami and Yeşil Türbe. The collection includes tile work, inlaid wood, jewelry, books and almanacs, calligraphy work, manuscripts, pottery, traditional clothes with colorful embroidery, and bits of Seljuk architectural decoration. ✉Yeşil Cad., on west side of Yeşil Cami ☎224/327–7679 ✉$2.50 ⏱Mon.–Fri. 8:30–12:30 and 1:30–5:30.

❼ The striking **Ulu Cami** (Grand Mosque) dates from 1399, when Sultan Beyazıt had it built after vowing to build 20 mosques if he was victorious in the battle of Nicopolis in Macedonia; this one mosque with 20 domes was something of a compromise. Its interior is decorated with an elegantly understated display of quotations from the Koran in fine Islamic calligraphy. The fountain, with taps on the sides for ritual washing before prayer, is inside the mosque—an unusual feature. More usual is the fact that the women's section in this huge mosque is rather small and currently also used for other things like dumping construction materials. The sight of several women praying among the men in the main part, rather than in their own designated and inadequate area, is refreshing. ■TIP➔ Ulu Cami draws huge crowds during prayer times, which you'll probably want to avoid. ✉On Atatürk Cad. across from Maksem Cad.

❹ The **Uluumay Müzesi** (Uluumay Ethnography Museum), on the park, ★ opposite the mosque and the tombs, has a fine, though small, collection of Ottoman prêt-a-porter and haute couture costumes along with gorgeous silver jewelry. The building is another medrese, built in 1475 by Şair Ahmet Pasha, whose tomb is in its garden. The models displaying the costumes revolve to allow a thorough study. The costumes are full of colorful embroidery and are in very good condition even though some date back to the 15th century: they were worn only on special occasions and preserved meticulously. On the grounds of the museum is a teahouse opposite the tomb in the garden, overlooking the city. ✉Murad Cad. ☎224/225–4813 ✉$4 ⏱May–Oct., Tues.–Sun. 9–8, Mon. 1:30–7; Nov.–Apr. closes one hour earlier.

⓭ A juxtaposition of simple form, inspired stone carving, and spectacu-
FodorsChoice lar İznik tile work, the **Yeşil Cami** (Green Mosque) is among the finest
★ mosques in Turkey. Work on the mosque began in 1419, during the

Inside Bursa's Yesil Cami (Green Mosque), the array of green and blue tiles is mesmerizing.

reign of Mehmet I Çelebi (ruled 1413–21). Its beauty begins in the marble entryway, where complex feathery patterns and calligraphy are carved in the stone; inside is a sea of blue-and-green İznik tiles. The central hall rests under two shallow domes; in the one near the entrance an oculus sends down a beam of sunlight at midday, illuminating a fountain delicately carved from a single piece of marble. The *mihrab* (prayer niche) towers almost 50 feet, and there are intricate carvings near the top. On a level above the main doorway is the sultan's loge, lavishly decorated and tiled; a caretaker will sometimes take visitors up to see it. ⊠ *Yeşil Cad.* 🎫 *Free* 🕐 *Daily sunrise–sunset.*

NEED A BREAK? Several tea gardens on the west side of the Yeşil Mosque and Yeşil Tomb are pleasant places to have a sandwich or a pastry and take in views of the city. It's a quiet area with colorful, restored Bursa houses whose ground floors are either gift shops or cafés.

⓬ The **Yeşil Türbe** *(Green Mausoleum)* is Mehmet I Çelebi's tomb, built in 1424. The "green" tomb is actually covered in blue tiles, added after an earthquake damaged the originals in the 1800s. Inside, however, are incredible original İznik tiles, including those sheathing Mehmet's immense sarcophagus. The other tombs belong to his children. The tomb has been closed for restoration since 2006 but is expected to reopen by 2009. ⊠ *East end of Yeşil Cad., opposite Yeşil Cami.*

WHERE TO STAY AND EAT

$-$$
TURKISH
★

✕ **Arap Şükrü Yılmaz.** Food is often a family business in Bursa: it's said that an Arab named Şükrü once opened a fish restaurant on Sakarya Caddesi between the center and Çekirge; now the whole area carries his name, and his sons have filled the street with similarly named restaurants, adding their own names to their father's—in this case Yılmaz. The street is a lively destination with tables outside and wandering musicians serenading diners. ⊠*Sakarya Cad. 4, Arap Şükrü* ☎*No phone* ☰*MC, V.*

\$\$\$–\$\$\$\$ ✕**Cumurcul.** In the Çekirge section of town, opposite the Çelik Palas
TURKISH Hotel, this old house that's been converted into a restaurant is a local favorite, serving attentively prepared grilled meats and fish. In addition to the usual cold mezes are hot starters, including the tasty *avcı böreği* (hunter's pie), a deep-fried or oven-baked pastry filled with meat or cheese. Main dishes include international favorites such as filet mignon and chicken Kiev. The upstairs dining room and terrace overlook Kültür Park and the city. ⊠*Cekirge Cad., Ceilk Palas Oteli Karsisi, No. 18* ☎*224/235–3707* ☰*AE, MC, V.*

\$ ✕**Darüzziyafe.**The kitchen house built by Sultan Murad II in the 15th
TURKISH century to help feed the poor is now a restaurant seving Ottoman and
★ Turkish cuisine. It's no longer a charity, but prices are reasonable. *Hünkar beğendi* (tender beef on grilled eggplant mash with bechamel sauce) literally means "the Sultan liked it," and it's hard not to. The place is also known for its köfte, made with lamb, beef, chicken, and pistachios, and for its Ottoman desserts. The terrace is pleasant, but dine indoors and you'll feel like you're eating in the sultan's quarters. No alcohol is served here. ⊠*Muradiye Complex II, Murad Cad. 36, Muradiye* ☎*224/224–6439* ⌚*Reservations essential* ☰*MC, V.*

\$ ✕**Hacı Bey.** Arguments never end over where to find the best İskender
TURKISH kebap, but this downtown stop is always a contender. The setting is basic cafeteria style, but it's the food that matters. If you want a change from the regular İskender, ask for your kebab to be served with grilled eggplant mash. Just opposite there is another restaurant run by one of the inventor's grandsons, which makes equally good İskender. ⊠*Ünlü Cad., Yılmaz İş Han 4C* ☎*224/221–6440* ☰*DC, MC, V.*

\$ ✕**Kebapcı İskender (Oğlu Cevat).** This tiny, central restaurant, with lines
TURKISH outside on the pavement most days, is run by a grandson of the inven-
★ tor of İskender kebab, Mehmet İskenderoğlu—pictured on the wall opposite Atatürk. As is common in the food business in Bursa, more family members opened similar restaurants with similar names all over town, but this one is among the best. It's open daily from 11:30–6:30, so go early. ⊠*Atatürk Cad., Orhan Sokak 60, Heykel* ☎*224/221–1076* ☰*AE, MC, V.*

¢–\$ ✕**Ömür Köftecisi.** Köfte is the thing to order here, served with grilled
TURKISH peppers and tomatoes. Among the salad options, *piyaz* (bean salad with
★ vinegar) accompanies köfte best. In the mornings, the soup is delicious, too. The location is charming, in the covered market by the Ulu Cami—the restaurant has the same architectural features as the hans, with brick and stone walls, and two domes in the ceilings painted in floral patterns. ⊠*Ulu Cami Cad. 7* ☎*224/221–4524* ☰*MC, V.*

\$ ⌂ **Atlas Hotel.** Çekirge is Bursa's posh district, but there are some rea-
sonably priced hotels where you can take advantage of the spring baths at reasonable prices. This is one of the most inviting, with its wood-covered exterior, a small courtyard inside, and cheerful staff. Rooms

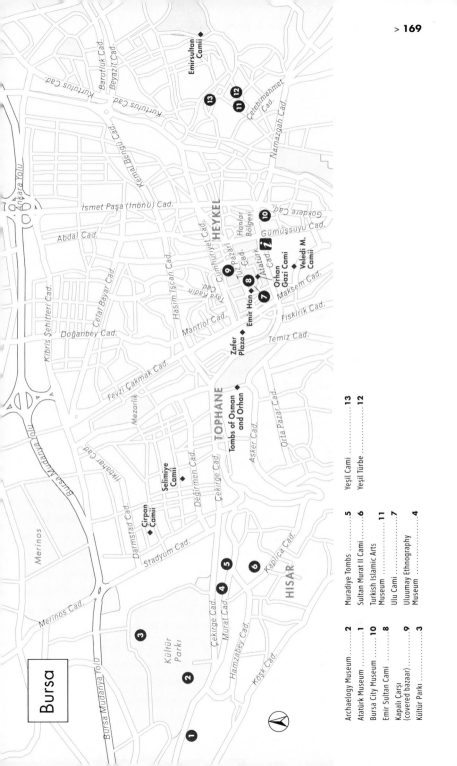

Bursa

Archaelog Museum **2**
Atatürk Museum **1**
Bursa City Museum **10**
Emir Sultan Cami **8**
Kapalı Çarşı
(covered bazaar) **9**
Kültür Parkı **3**

Muradiye Tombs **5**
Sultan Murat II Cami **6**
Turkish Islamic Arts
Museum **11**
Ulu Cami **7**
Uluumay Ethnography
Museum **4**

Yeşil Cami **13**
Yeşil Türbe **12**

are basic but have all modern comforts. There are two thermal baths in the hotel, but the rooms do not get thermal waters. ⊠ *Hamamlar Cad. 24, Çekirge* ☎ *224/234–4100* ⊕ *www.atlashotel.com.tr* ↝ *36 rooms* ⛧⃝ *BP* ⊟ *AE, DC, MC, V.*

Fodor's Choice
★ ⛅ **Çelik Palas.** There are newer, chicer hotels in Bursa, but this one maintains a certain grandeur. The marbled lobby and rooms are old-fashioned but loyally maintained, and the formal service reflects the hotel's pride in its heritage. The Roman-style pool fed by hot springs is a treat—the thermal waters of the Çekirge region were diverted 4 km (2 mi) to get here—and you'll find your fellow guests traipsing through the hallways in their robes, though you can also take the waters in your room. Ask for a room in the historic part overlooking the city; they'll probably oblige, even though it's not supposed to be used unless the newer part is full. **Pros:** excellent service and the opportunity to relax in a spring-fed thermal pool. **Cons:** pricey. ⊠ *Çekirge Cad. 79* ☎ *224/233–3800* ⊕ *www.celikpalasotel.com* ↝ *156 rooms* ⛬ *In-room: safe, Wi-Fi. In-hotel: restaurant, bar, spa* ⊟ *AE, MC, V* ⛧⃝ *BP.*

$$ ⛅ **Hotel Dikmen.** Although less grand than the Çekirge-area hotels, the Dikmen (not to be confused with the Dilmen) is conveniently located downtown, opposite the Ulu Cami; it's popular with business travelers. The rooms are large and plain rooms, but nice touches are the spacious, red-carpeted lobby with a piano, and the sunny garden with a marble fountain. It could use some sprucing up, but the hotel remains a popular choice. ⊠ *Maksem Cad. 78, 16010* ☎ *224/224–1840* ⊕ *www. oteldikmen.com* ↝ *60 rooms* ⛬ *In-room: Wi-Fi. In-hotel: restaurant, bar* ⛧⃝ *BP* ⊟ *MC, V.*

$$$ ⛅ **Hotel Gonluferah.** Ottoman-style decoration is the general rule in most
Fodor's Choice Bursa hotels but this one, recently refurbished, is a good mix of Otto-
★ man and modern: flat-screen TVs and state-of-the-art pressured showers fit in well with the traditional-style high beds, velvet curtains, and ornamental hanging lamps. The hotel claims to have the city's best baths in terms of water quality and decoration, and they're certainly quite nice, though not included in the room price. The rooftop rooms overlooking the city aren't renovated but are the more spacious ones; the low ceilings and plain wood furniture may remind you of a mountain resort. **Pros:** Ottoman elegance at a reasonable price. **Cons:** extra charge for the thermal baths. ⊠ *1 Murad Cad. 24, Çekirge,* ☎ *224/233–9210* ⊕ *www.gonluferahhotel.com* ↝ *70 rooms* ⛬ *In-room: safe, Wi-Fi. In-hotel: restaurant* ⊟ *AE, MC, V* ⛧⃝ *BP.*

$$ ⛅ **Otel Safran.** The best thing about this hotel is its location: within walking distance of the center and most sights, but on a quiet hilltop outside the bustle of the city center, opposite the tombs of Sultans Osman and Orhan. Rooms are comfortable and decorated partly in line with the Ottoman character; ask for one of the more spacious ones on the upper floors, which also get more light. A restaurant next door with the same name serves Turkish cuisine. Breakfast is served in a cozy room downstairs. **Pros:** peaceful elegance close to the city center. **Cons:** difficult to communicate with the non-English-speaking staff. ⊠ *Ortapazar Cad. Arka Sokak 4, Tophane* ☎ *224/224–7216* 🖷 *224/224–7219* ↝ *10*

3

rooms ♿ In-room: refrigerator. In-hotel: restaurant, Internet terminal ▤MC, V ⧀BP.

NIGHTLIFE

The liveliest time for nightlife in Bursa is winter, and the best place for it is out of town in Uludağ. Istanbul's elite fill the hotels of this ski resort on weekends and on longer holidays; there's popular Turkish and Western music, and lots of dancing.

Bursa itself either imitates the Uludağ nightlife scene or sticks to its Ottoman traditions with Turkish *fasıl*, traditional Turkish music, which can be found in restaurants such as Cumurcul or Darüzziyafe during weekend dinners or at the

SHOPPING IN BURSA

Bursa has been a center of the silk industry since the coming of the Ottoman sultans and remains a good place to buy silk scarves, raw-silk fabric by the yard, and other silk products. The price of a silk scarf varies between $3 and $60. The same goes for the famed cotton towels, depending on their thickness and density. Bathrobes are a favorite souvenir, as they're higher-quality and cheaper than those found elsewhere in the country, but they might be a bit bulky to carry overseas.

Turistik Fasıl Bar on Yeşil Caddesi on the way to Yeşil Cami. For nightclubs, try one of the places at the Kültür Park such as Altın Ceylan or a place called simply 224. Vici, 7 km (4 mi) out of town on the way to Mudanya, or Jaz Bar on the way to Uludağ are other clubbing options; both are livelier in winter. Near the center, on Sakarya Caddesi (aka Arap Şükrü), past the restaurants is Café M, which calls itself a pub; it doesn't look much like one, but its shiny lounge and large terrace are among the nicer places to have a few drinks, if you're not averse to Turkish pop music.

SHOPPING

In Bursa the Kapalı Çarşı *(covered bazaar)*, behind the Ulu Cami, is where the action is from 8:30 to 6, Monday through Saturday. As is traditional, each section is dominated by a particular trade: jewelers, silk weavers, antiques dealers. The Koza Han *(Cocoon Caravanserai)* section behind the Orhan Gazi Mosque by the east entrance is the center of the silk trade. It has a lovely courtyard with a tiny mosque and a 150-year-old linden tree under which you can sip your tea. The Emir Han, behind the Ulu Cami, in the southwest section, is an interesting combination of jewelers and a religious books market, and also has a fountain and a courtyard tea garden. Antiques can be found in the small Eski Aynalı Çarşı section of the bazaar, between Koza Han and Emir Han.

Bursa also has many modern shops. The pyramid-shaped glass mall Zafer Plaza at the east end of the Atatürk Caddesi houses many international brands, and instead of the tea gardens of the old bazaars you'll find a large Starbucks. The food court on the top floor offers choices of American and Turkish fast food. A branch of one of the city's famous İskender restaurants can be found here as well as Burger King and McDonald's.

Kuşcenneti National Park. If you're heading on from Bursa to Çanakkale and the Aegean coast, consider stopping at Kuşcenneti (Bird Paradise) National Park, beside Lake Kuş. There are benches and tables for picnics, a viewing tower for bird-watching, and a small information center with exhibits describing the more than 200 species of birds that visit the park. ⊠ *Take Rte. 200 west about 100 km (62 mi) from Bursa; signs for the park appear before the city of Bandırma.*

ULUDAĞ

33 km (20 mi) southeast of Bursa.

Bursa is the jumping-off point for excursions to Uludağ (8,300 feet high), where you will find lush **Uludağ Ulusal Parkı** (Uludağ National Park) and Turkey's most popular ski resort.

To fully appreciate why Bursa is called Green Bursa, take the 30-minute ride up the **teleferik** (cable car) in Bursa to Uludağ's Sarıalan point (5,350 feet) for a panoramic view. This terminus is lively in summer: there are restaurants and picnic areas. In winter, however, the cable car terminus is only a staging point for the hotel area, which is 7 km farther up. In spring or fall, there isn't much activity here, especially when the mist is over the mountain—the cable car runs anyway as the ride itself can be fun. ■ TIP→ Take a sweater or jacket, as temperatures fall dramatically as you climb, even when it's warm downtown. There are also various walking paths up the mountain from Bursa to Uludağ and Uludağ to Bursa; the hike takes about three hours each way. From Uludağ's hotel area you can reach undeveloped spots for blissfully cool hikes in summer.

Uludağ gets most of its attention for its skiing and, lately, snowboarding. There are 30 intermediate and beginner routes, with five chairlifts, and seven T-bars. The season lasts from November until April, though the best conditions are between mid-December and March. The resort is packed on weekends, school holidays, and religious festivals, when prices increase dramatically.

WHERE TO STAY AND EAT

There are 25 hotels in Uludağ. All offer full board and all the modern comforts, and most provide a range of activities and entertainment. Nightlife is becoming almost as important a reason as skiing for the Istanbul elite to go to Uludağ; the more modest hotels do not offer as many amenities but are more likely to attract enthusiastic skiers as opposed to nightclubbers. Akfen Club Hotel, for example, has always been among the favorites. Skiing is a rich man's sport in Turkey, as in the rest of the world, so even the more modest hotels can't really be called budget. Normal winter prices range from $70–$210 for a double room. For information and reservations for all the hotels in the resort, visit ⊕*www.uludaghotels.com* or contact **Icem Tourism Travel Agency** (☎*212/516–7553 or 212/638–1986* ⊕*www.icemtour.com/ uludag_hotels*).

THE DARDANELLES

Dardanelles is the name of the strait that separates Europe from Asia and that connects the Aegean Sea to the Marmara. Controlling these straits meant having substantial commercial and military power, hence its strategic importance. The first historical war took place in the 13th century BC between the Achaeans and Trojans, and the latest was the attack by ANZAC (Australian and New Zealand Army Corps), British, and French troops on Gallipoli during the First World War.

There are several places to base yourself for exploring the area; wherever you are, it's best to arrange a guided tour to visit the battlefields, which are spread along a 35-km (58-mi) stretch of the Gallipoli Peninsula. Çanakkale, on the south side of the straits, is convenient; most tourists stay here rather than in Eceabat on the European side of the Dardanelles, even though the latter is actually closer to the battlefields. Çanakkale is livelier, has more options for accommodation and dining, and is where most of the guided tours start. Ferries making the 25-minute crossing from Çanakkale to Eceabat run every hour until midnight in both directions.

You can visit the region in all times of the year if you're intent is sightseeing but spring may be the best time, when it's cool enough to walk around the sights, and when the area is at its most colorful, with wildflowers dotting the cemeteries and hillsides. Turks commemorate the war on March 18, and British, Australians, and New Zealanders on April 25. The second, in particular, brings many travelers to the region, and offers the visitor the chance to take part in the emotional memorial services; but this is, of course, when reservations for hotels and guided tours are essential well in advance.

GALLIPOLI

310 km (192 mi) southwest of Istanbul.

Tours are an excellent way to see the sites of Gallipoli. See the Planner at the start of this chapter for suggestions.

★ The Gallipoli Peninsula lies to the north of the Dardanelles. Turks call it Gelibolu—though there's also a town of the same name 40 km (25 mi) east. Thirty-one beautifully tended military cemeteries of the Allied dead from World War I line the Gallipoli battlefields. The major battles were in two main areas—along the coast between Kabatepe and Suvla Bay, and at Cape Helles.

Fodor'sChoice
★ The **Australian Memorial at Lone Pine Cemetery** bears the names of the Australian and New Zealand soldiers with unknown graves killed during the war. Some of the most savage hand-to-hand fighting took place here, and more than 3,000 soldiers died. Seven Victoria crosses, the highest award given by British government for bravery and usually quite sparingly distributed, were awarded after the battle. This is the most affecting of all the ANZAC cemeteries, and the epitaphs of the tombstones are very moving.

War & Peace

The Dardanelles have provided the world with many myths and heroes, romances and tragedies. The most recent, and the main reason the region draws visitors today, was the Gallipoli campaign in the First World War. In this offensive, Britain (with soldiers from Australia and New Zealand, then still British colonies) and France tried to breach Çanakkale's defenses in a campaign devised by the young Winston Churchill, at the time lord of the Admiralty. The goal was to capture Istanbul, control the entire waterway from the Aegean to the Black Sea, open up a supply channel to Russia, and pave the way for an attack on Germany from the south. After nine months of bloody fighting that left more than 50,000 Allied and perhaps twice as many Turks dead, the Allies admitted defeat and evacuated, beaten by the superior strategy of Lieutenant-Colonel Mustafa Kemal—later called Atatürk.

Churchill lost his job as a result of the failure in the Dardanelles, and his career suffered until the next world war, two decades later. Mustafa Kemal, on the other hand, became a national hero. He had been an insignificant lieutenant, unpopular among the ruling Committee of Union and Progress, but the fame he earned in this war helped him start and lead the war of independence against the occupying Allies. Soon his enemies were overthrown, and so were the Ottoman sultanate and caliphate. A few years after the Gallipoli campaign, the modern, secular republic of Turkey emerged with Atatürk as president.

For the Australians and New Zealenders, WWI was the first real experience of war overseas, and the shocking losses they sustained left an indelible mark. For the Turks, it was an unexpected defensive victory. It was a war of pride, but also one that left behind many stories of kindness between soldiers on opposing sides. The Anzacs and the Turks came from opposite ends of the earth: there was no history of hostility, or even familiarity between them, until they were told to kill one another, but in some ways the war marked the start of a friendship and thousands of Anzac pilgrims come to visit the battlefields every year. Atatürk's speech, engraved on a Turkish monument in Anzac Cove, seemed to foresee this:

"Those heroes that shed their blood and lost their lives! You are now lying in the soil of a friendly country, therefore rest in peace. There is no difference between the Johnnies and the Mehmets to us, where they lie side by side here in this country of ours. You, the mothers who sent their sons from far-away countries, wipe away your tears. Your sons are now lying in our bosom, and are at peace. After having lost their lives on this land, they have become our sons as well."

At the top of the ridge is **Chunk Bair,** which the Allies aimed to occupy because of its strategic location overlooking the peninsula. They failed, and Mustafa Kemal (Atatürk) became a hero. It was here that he told his soldiers, "I order you not just to fight, but to die." All the men of one of his regiments were wiped out, and he himself was saved miraculously when a bullet hit the pocket watch that was over his heart, but the line held. From this hilltop where there are Turkish trenches, a cemetery, and the New Zealand national memorial, there are good views of the whole peninsula and the strait.

DID YOU KNOW?

The name of Gallipoli's Lone Pine Cemetery comes from a single pine tree which grew on the battlefield. It was destroyed, but the cones were collected and taken to Australia, then sent back to Gallipoli many years later. The lone pine standing there today is said to be the grandson of the original pine tree.

LONE PINE

At **Cape Helles,** on the southernmost tip of the peninsula, is a massive, four-pillared memorial to Turkey's war dead. No one knows how many there were; estimates vary from 60,000 to 250,000. When returning on the ferry to Çanakkale, look for the memorials to the campaign carved into the cliffs. The large one at Kilitbahır reads: "Stop, O passerby. This earth you tread unawares is where an age was lost. Bow and listen, for this quiet place is where the heart of a nation throbs."

Kabatepe Museum and Information Center. This small museum with a poignant exhibit of photographs of soldiers, their uniforms, weapons, and other findings from the battlefield is a good place to start your exploration of the area, thought it's currently closed for renovations. It's unclear when it will reopen, so check before you go. ✉ *Kabatepe* ☎ *286/862–0082* 💲*2$* ⊙ *Daily 9–6.*

ÇANAKKALE

320 km (200 mi) southwest of Istanbul; 303 km (186 mi) from Bursa.

GETTING HERE AND AROUND

By car from Bursa, Route 200 (which becomes E90) runs west toward Çanakkale; the trip is 303 km (188 mi) and takes about 3½ hours. If you're heading for Çanakkale from İstanbul, take E80 west to Tekirda, the E84 to Keşan, and the E87 to Eceabat. From Çanakkale, the E87 goes through Troy, Ezine, Ayvalık, Küçükkuyu, Edremit, and Ayvacık. Ezine is 50 km from Çanakkale, and from there you can take the coast road west to Geyikli, where ferries run to Bozcaada, or to Alexandra Troas, Apollon Sminthion, Babakale, and Assos, all farther south. This is a coastal road that runs through villages; it's a bit rough and winding, but quite scenic and enjoyable.

The bus trip from Istanbul to Çanakkale is about 6 hours and costs $35. From Bursa to Çanakkale is 4½ hours and costs about $14.

ESSENTIALS

Car Rental Info Gezgin Oto (in Çanakkale) car rental (☎ *286/212–2892).*

Visitor Information (✉ *İskele Meydanı, No. 67* ☎ *286/217–1187).*

EXPLORING

West of Bursa, on the southern shore of the Dardanelles, Çanakkale is the largest city of the north Aegean coast. The city itself doesn't have much to offer, other than a decent selection of hotels and bars, but it's a good base for visiting the memorials and battlefields of Gallipolli, a half-hour's ferry journey across the straits.

The heart of Çanakkale is in the docks area, and you really don't need to go inland. An Ottoman clock tower is located between the two halves of the dock. Head toward the sea from this tower and you'll find the ferry that departs for historic Gallipoli. Hotels and restaurants are spread on either side of the docks, along the sea front. Most of the budget hotels, cheap dining options, and bars are in the streets behind the seafront to the left of the tower if you're facing the sea.

The Dardanelles and the North Aegean

If you're in Çanakkale, check out the city's **fortress**, which includes the **Askeri Ve Deniz Müzesi** (*Army and Navy Museum*). The impressive structure was built in the 15th century under the aegis of Mehmet the Conqueror. Inside the high walls all kinds of weaponry are on display, including dozens of cannons, ancient and modern. The real reason to come here, though, is for the sweeping view of the mouth of the Dardanelles and the Aegean. The fortress grounds are good for a nice stroll among the lawns and gardens. ⊠ *On the waterfront, 3 blocks south of ferry dock* ☎ *286/213–1730, 286/213–2641 museum* ✆ *Fortress grounds daily 9 AM–10 PM May–Sept.; daily 9–5 Oct.–Apr.; Museum: 9–noon and 1:30–5, except Mon. and Thurs.* ▨ *$2.50.*

WHERE TO STAY AND EAT

¢–$ ✕ **Doyum Pide Kebap Salonu.** If you like *pide* (Turkish pizza) or kebabs,
TURKISH   try this casual eatery on the right side of the main street going into town from the ferry dock, past the clock tower. The pides are delicious, with mincemeat, cheese, or cubes of lamb as toppings. Try the mixed pide if you want to sample them all. Doyum is popular with locals and tourists, though it's better for a quick meal than an extended evening out. ⊠ *Cumhuriyet Meydani 13* ☎ *286/217–1866* ▭ *MC, V.*

$–$$ ✕ **Maydos Restaurant.** A few minutes' walk from the ferry port, the
TURKISH   Maydos—part of the hotel with the same name—offers more variety

than most other Turkish fish restaurants. The menu isn't quite international, but it does include pasta and steak. Ask for a table outside on the terrace, which has fine views across the Dardanelles. There's another branch across the strait in Eceabat, with a slightly different selection of entrees on the menu, that's also on the seafront. ⊠ *Yali Cad. 12, Merkez, 17100* ☎*286/213–5970* ▤*MC, V.*

$–$$ ✕**Yalova Liman.** The menu at this waterfront restaurant includes appe-
TURKISH tizers and grilled fish or meat. The seafood mezes are all mouthwater-
★ ing: the grilled octopus in vinegar and the sardines wrapped in vine leaves are especially recommended. One of the perks of eating here is the evocative setting: the photographs of old Çanakkale on the walls and the views across the Dardanelles. ⊠ *Yalı Cad., Gümrük Sokak 7* ☎*286/217–1045* ▤*MC, V.*

$$ ⌂**Akol.** If you ask a local to recommend a hotel, most will point you to the Akol—not because it's spectacular, or even one of the city's best, but because it's the longest-established lodging in town. A modern hotel on the Çanakkale waterfront, it has a bright lobby full of cool white marble and brass fixtures. Rooms are spacious and bright. Ask for one overlooking the Dardanelles; you'll be able to see the war memorials in the distance. A perk in summer is the swimming pool. **Pros:** bright, cheerful rooms overlooking the Dardanelles; inviting bar with a pool table. **Cons:** not much English spoken; service can be a bit cold. ⊠ *Kordonboyu,* ☎*286/217–9456* ⊕*www.hotelakol.com.tr* ⇘*138 rooms* ⌂ *In-room: mini-bar, Wi-Fi. In-hotel: laundry service, restaurant, bar, pool, parking (free)* ▤*MC, V* ⧖*BP.*

¢ ⌂**Anzac House.** This hostel, near the clock tower, is the Hassle-Free Travel Agency's budget option, and lures many backpackers. There are rooms for 1, 2, 4, 6, or 15 people. As you'd expect from a hostel, the rooms have nothing but beds and small bedside tables, but they're clean, and fans are provided on request. Internet access in the lobby, and breakfast is available for an extra charge. As with most backpacker establishments, the hotel staff has maps, freely dispenses travel advice, and there's always someone who speaks English. It's also possible to book tours of Troy and Gallipoli from here. **Pros:** great value for the backpacking crowd. **Cons:** lacks character; common area is not very relaxing. ⊠ *Cumhuriyet Meydanı, 59, Çanakkale* ☎*286/213–5969* ⊕*www.anzachouse.com* ⇘*15 rooms* ⌂ *In-hotel: laundry facilities* ▤*AE, MC, V.*

★ ⌂**Kervansaray Hotel.** An old Ottoman house built in 1903, the two-story Kervansaray, with its redbrick walls, large bay window, and white-washed frames and columns, looks very attractive amid the concrete jungle of Çanakkale. In back is a nice courtyard with flowers, fountain, and seating area for breakfast. Rooms are small but elegantly furnished and, on the whole, it's good value. Eight rooms are in the new annex across the courtyard, but the ones in the main building have more character. The affable manager Armağan, who also operates the more modern Anzac Hotel down the street, will do his best to make your stay memorable. **Pros:** a hotel with character in the heart of the city; reasonable prices. **Cons:** the rooms in the Ottoman house outshine those in the new section of the hotel. ⊠ *Kemalpaşa Mahallesi, Fetvane Sokak*

13 (near the clock tower) ☎286/217–9022 *or 286/217–8192* ⊕*www. otelkervansaray.com* ⟿*20 rooms* ⚲*In-room: safe, minibar, Wi-Fi. In-hotel: Internet station, parking* ▤*MC, V* ⑩*BP.*

$$ Maydos Hotel. This is the more upmarket of the Hassle-Free Travel Agency's two hotels. Near the clock tower, it's been turned into a glittering modern block without much character. Rooms are shiny and new, though the size and amount of light in each varies dramatically (as do prices). Request a room overlooking the water if you want one of the better ones and don't mind paying a bit extra. The breakfast buffet includes more than the typical tomato/cucumber fare found in cheaper hotels and you can enjoy it in a bright dining room with views of the boardwalk and harbor. **Pros:** some rooms have excellent views of the harbor; good breakfast buffet included. **Cons:** hotel lacks character. ✉*Yalı Cad. 12,* ☎286/213–5970 ⊕*www.maydos.com.tr/hotel* ⟿*35 rooms, 1 suite* ⚲*In-room: mini-bar, Wi-Fi. In-hotel: restaurant, bar* ▤*MC, V* ⑩*BP.*

NIGHTLIFE

Çanakkale doesn't have the liveliest nightlife, but it's the most exciting place in the area. Fetvane Sokak, on the left of the clock tower if you're facing the sea, is the main bar street: you can choose from spacious open-air bars dominated by pop music, or small, dark dives. The **Telefone Café** is recommended by the locals for coffee or a drink. **Depo** has dancing and a large courtyard with huge cushions and low tables. The historic han at the end of the street called **Tarihi Yalı Hanı** has several bars: you can eat and drink in the ground-floor courtyard, and listen to gypsy music on Thursday nights and live rock on Fridays and Saturdays. In winter there's live music every day. On the waterfront is **Lodos,** similar to Depos in terms of music and crowd but with a nicer location.

ECEABAT

40 km (25 mi) south of Gallipoli Peninsula.

Eceabat, on the Aegean coast, is the closest town to the most-visited battlefields and cemeteries. From where the Eceabat ferry lands on the northern front (car ferries make the 25-minute crossing from Çanakkale to Eceabat every hour until midnight in both directions), it's a 20-minute drive east via the single road skirting the coast and then crossing the peninsula to get to the town itself. The town is small and most of the restaurants and hotels listed here (except for the Hotelu Kum) are along the waterfront.

WHERE TO STAY AND EAT

¢ ✕**Hanımeli.** Serving excellent food at reasonable prices, this restaurant

TURKISH is frequently recommended by the locals and is also a stop for most of

★ the tour bus crowds that stop for lunch before touring the Gallipoli battlefields. The restaurant has a small seating area with views of the Dardanelles and Çanakkale, as well as a large indoor seating area. Old rifles and artillery shells from the WWI era line the walls. Even the straight-up Turkish buffet style fare has a distinctive flavor that sets it apart from most establishments on the waterfront. The lentil soup is excellent, but so is everything else on the menu, including the *mantı*

(Turkish ravioli served with yogurt and dill) and *gözleme* (thin Turkish pastries filled with meat or cheese). ⊠*Iskele Cad. 45/A, Eceabat* ☎*286/814–2345* ⊟*MC, V.*

$$ ✕**Liman Restaurant.** This 35-year-old restaurant is highly respected by
TURKISH locals; there are newer and shinier options on the peninsula but they've
★ failed to tempt the Liman's clientele away. The interior is plain but clean, with white tablecloths and large windows overlooking a small park next to the sea. The fare is fish, meat, and mezes, and all are fresh and tasty. The prawn casserole is especially recommended. Reservations are essential during war anniversaries. ⊠*İsmet Paşa Mahallesi 1/B(67), Eceabat* ☎*286/814–2755* ⊟*MC, V.*

¢ 🏠**The Crowded House.** Like the nearby Eceabat Hotel, the Crowded House is in a nondescript concrete building but the interior is quite charming. It caters to a wide range of travelers: most of the rooms are private, but there are also two six-bed dorms with shared bathrooms. Everything is bright and clean, including the lobby and restaurant. The hotel also offers inexpensive tours of the Gallipoli battlefields as well as snorkeling tours to an Australian ship that sunk during the conflict. **Pros:** great location for touring Gallipoli. **Cons:** Internet access for a price. ⊠*Cumhuriyet Meydanı 15, Eceabat* ☎*286/814–1565* ⊕*www.crowdedhousegallipoli.com* ⤹*27 rooms* ⚴*In-room: no a/c (some), no TV. In-hotel: Internet terminal* ⊟*MC, V* ⦿*BP*

¢ 🏠**Eceabat Hotel.** From the outside, this is a run-down, concrete building, but inside, the rooms are a surprise: there is Ottoman-style furniture hand-carved from 100-year-old wood—including specially ordered extra-large double beds—and lovely old carpets on the wood-floored corridors. The rooftop bar-restaurant's large windows have good views of the Dardanelles. The Australian-Turkish owners, who also run TJ's Tours, are friendly and helpful and do their best to make your Gallipoli experience special. They run a separate building, in the village itself, as a hostel (reservations are taken from the same phone number). **Pros:** friendly, helpful staff; the terrace bar offers a bit of nightlife without having to search the quiet city for it. **Cons:** lots of hustle and bustle. ⊠*Cumhuriyet Meydanı 5, near ferry dock, Eceabat* ☎*286/814–3121* ⊕*www.anzacgallipolitours.com* ⤹*20 rooms* ⚴*In-room: Wi-Fi* ⊟*MC, V* ⦿*BP*

$$ 🏠**Hotel Kum.** On the Aegean coast of the Gallipoli Peninsula, south of the village of Kabatepe, is a beautiful sandy beach, and Hotel Kum is located right in front of it. It's also conveniently located for visits to the memorials on both ends of the peninsula. Rooms are plain and functional, but the hotel is surrounded by open space, with the blue sea in front and green land all around. A buffet-style dinner is included, as is breakfast. **Pros:** large property with lots of activity options, lovely beach and pools. **Cons:** not so much character. ⊠*Kapatepe* ☎*286/814–1455* ⊕*www.hotelkum.com* ⤹*72 rooms, 8 suites* ⚴*In-hotel: restaurant, bar, pools, beachfront* ⊟*MC, V* ⊗*Closed Nov.–Mar.* ⦿*MAP.*

NORTH AEGEAN

The north Aegean offers a different kind of holiday than the south. It's one of the loveliest parts of the Aegean, and all of Turkey, with unspoiled natural landscapes and activities all year round, from swimming and sea sports to trekking, mountain climbing, and horseback riding. You can soak in hot springs or jump in cool waterfalls in the middle of pine forests, visit sleepy fishing villages, or go on safari to see the region's unique fauna and flora. It's not a destination for the big agencies that ship tourists in bulk to huge resorts for sun and sea; it's a more relaxed destination, more rural, where the villages, and the sites, are scattered around. This whole area, so close to Greece, is also where you can see what life was like when the area was Greek, while experiencing its rural Turkish present. Ayvalık is the only large town in the region that can't fairly be called unspoiled, but even it has its own rewards.

TROY (TRUVA)

★ *32 km (20 mi) south of Çanakkale on Rte. E87.*

The wooden horse that stands outside this magnificent site is a modern addition, there to remind us of Homer's epics, but the city walls, layer upon layer of them, date back several millennia. Troy, known as Truva to the Turks and Ilion to the Greeks, is one of the most evocative place names in literature. Long thought to be a figment of the Greek poet Homer's imagination and written about in his epic *Iliad,* the site was excavated in the 1870s by Heinrich Schliemann, a German businessman who had struck it rich in California's gold rush. While scholars scoffed, he poured his wealth into the excavations and had the last laugh: he found the remains not only of fabled Troy but of nine successive civilizations, one on top of the other, dating back 5,000 years (and now known among archaeologists as Troy I–IX). Subsequent excavations during the 1930s revealed 38 additional layers of settlements.

Schliemann found a hoard of jewels that he believed were those of the Trojan War's King Priam, but were more recently been dated to a much earlier era. Adding to the controversy that surrounded his discoveries, Schliemann smuggled the jewels out of the country, and his wife was seen wearing them at fashionable social events. Schliemann later donated them to Berlin's Pergamon Museum, but they disappeared during the Red Army's sack of Berlin in World War II. They reappeared in 1993, when Moscow announced that their State Pushkin Museum of Fine Arts housed what they called the lost "Treasure of Priam." Though Germany, Greece, and Turkey have all claimed the treasures, recent custom dictates that archaeological finds belong to the country in which they were originally found; unfortunately, these have yet to make their way back to Turkey.

What you see today depends on your imagination or the knowledge and linguistic abilities of your guide. You may find the site highly suggestive, with its remnants of massive, rough-hewn walls, a paved chariot ramp, and strategic views over the coastal plains to the sea. Or you

HOMER'S STORY

Because The *Iliad* was written 500 years after the war—traditionally believed to have taken place around 1184 BC—it's hard to say how much of it is history and how much is invention. Nonetheless, it makes for a romantic tale: Paris, the son of King Priam, abducted the beautiful Helen, wife of King Menelaus of Sparta, and fled with her to Troy. Menelaus enlisted the aid of his brother, King Agamemnon, and launched a thousand ships to get her back. His siege lasted 10 years and involved such ancient notables as Achilles, Hector, and the crafty Odysseus, king of Ithaca. It was Odysseus who ended the war, after ordering a huge wooden horse to be built and left outside Troy's gates. Then the Greeks retreated to their ships and pretended to sail away. The Trojans hauled the trophy into their walled city and celebrated their victory. Under cover of darkness, the Greek ships returned, the soldiers hidden inside the horse crept out and opened the city's gates, and the attackers at last gained entry to Troy. Hence the saying: "Beware of Greeks bearing gifts."

may consider it an unimpressive row of trenches with piles of earth and stone. Considering Troy's fame (and the difficulties involved in conquering it), the city is surprisingly small. The best-preserved features are from the Roman city, with its *bouleuterion* (council chamber), the site's most complete structure, and small theater. A site plan shows the general layout and marks the beginning of a sign-posted path leading to key features from several historic civilizations. To make the most of your visit to Troy, hire a guide. Mustafa Aşkin runs the Hisarlık Hotel/Restaurant with his two brothers and gives daily tours of Troy at 9 AM; he grew up in the area, speaks excellent English, and has written books about the fabled city. His 60-minute narrative will illuminate easily overlooked features of the ruins (☎*286/283–0026* ⊕*www.thetroyguide.com*). You can also arrange tours from Çanakkale or Istanbul. ✉*Follow signs from Rte. E87* ☎*No phone* 💲*$8.50; parking: $3.50* ⊗*Apr.–Oct., daily 8–7; Nov.–Mar., daily 8–5.*

WHERE TO STAY AND EAT

$ ⌐ **Hisarlık Otel/Restuarant.** Owned and operated by three brothers, this hotel, about a 10-minute walk from the ruins of Troy, is the only lodging in the immediate area. The rooms are named after characters in the Illiad but they're very basic: essentially just a clean bed and a private bathroom. The large, shared balcony is a plus, although the view is mostly of a parking lot across the street and/or the hordes of people descending from idling tour buses that stop at the restaurant below for lunch before touring Troy. The restaurant itself serves typical buffet style Turkish fare, but the Troy Kebab—a mixture of meat, vegetables, and rice wrapped in a pastry—is especially good. **Pros:** great location for touring Troy. **Cons:** prices are slightly elevated due to a lack of competition in the area; no a/c. ✉*Piri Reis Cad. 13/15 Çanakkule, Truva* ☎*286/283–0026* 📠*286/283–0087* 🛏*11 rooms* ⌂*In-room: no a/c, Wi-Fi.* ▤*MC, V* ⧀*BP.*

The ruins at Troy are not as well-preserved as others in Turkey, but are still atmospheric.

OFF THE BEATEN PATH

If you're heading south from Troy toward Alexandria Troas, you'll pass through Geyikli, where you'll see a signpost for **Bozcaada,** one of the two Aegean islands that belong to Turkey. If you have time, spare a day for this island (though you'll probably then want to spare another) with its unspoiled towns and beautiful old houses, pristine sandy beaches, and lovely country covered with vineyards. The local wine may be the best you'll taste in Turkey without having to spend a fortune. There are two very good hotels here. The **Rengigül Konukevi** (☎286/697–8171 ⊕*www. rengigul.com*), a small B&B in a Greek-style 19th-century house, is a bit cluttered but has a lot of character. It has a large, lovely garden, and serves delicious breakfasts. **Kaikias Hotel** (☎286/697–0250 ⊕*www. kaikas.com*), also a B&B, has elegantly furnished large rooms, a collection of old Greek books and Troy ornaments, and a basement full of wine made by the owners. The **ferries** (☎286/632–0263) run six or seven times a day in summer but only twice daily in winter.

ALEXANDRIA TROAS

32 km (20 mi) from Troy off Rte. E87; 10 km (6 mi) south of Geyikli.

GETTING HERE

The ruins of Alexandria Troas are near the village of Dalyan, which can be reached by bus from Çanakkale or minibus from Ezine. The track leading to the ruins is quite bumpy. You can drive most of the way, but leaving your car at the beginning might be best; from the start of the path it's a 15-minute walk.

EXPLORING

Alexandria Troas was built at the behest of Alexander the Great in approximately 330 BC. It became a wealthy commercial center and the region's main port. The city, called at one point Antigonia, surpassed Troy in its control over the traffic between the Aegean and the Sea of Marmara and was even considered a capital under the Roman and Byzantine empires. The seaside location that won it prosperity also invited plundering by raiders, however, and this led to its demise. St. Paul visited twice on missionary journeys in the middle of the 1st century AD, proceeding by land to Assos at the end of the second trip. In the 16th and 17th centuries, when the city was called Eski Stamboul (Old Istanbul), Ottoman architects had stones hauled from here to Istanbul for use in the building of imperial mosques, the Blue Mosque in particular. Visit today not so much for seeing the scanty remnants of the city's monumental baths and its aqueduct but for the setting: Alexandria Troas is tucked away in a deserted stretch of wilderness that you might very well have all to yourself. The ruins are in the middle of an olive grove, though much of the site itself was damaged by a fire in the summer of 2006, which blackened the stones.

THE APOLLO SMINTHEON

20 km (12 mi) south of Alexandria Troas via the coast road.

GETTING HERE

Apollo Smintheon is down the hill from the center of Gülpınar, which can be reached by bus from Çanakkale or by minibus from Ezine.

EXPLORING

The **Apollo Smintheon** is, as the name suggests, a temple dedicated to the god Apollo. It dates from the 2nd century BC. Smintheus—one of the sun god's many names, meaning "killer of mice"—alludes to a problem that Teucer, the town's founder, had with mice eating his soldiers' bowstrings. The temple has no great historical importance, but it does have some interesting carved pillars and is surrounded by wild pomegranate trees. If you arrive before sunset, watching the sun go down behind the three marble columns makes it well worth the trip here. ☉ *Open 8–5* 🎫 *TL 5.*

BABAKALE

10 km (6 mi) from the Apollo Smintheon on the coast road, south from Gülpınar.

Babakale is a small, sleepy fishing village at the southern tip of the Çanakkale Peninsula. Legend has it that it was originally a pirate's lair, discovered by Sultan Ahmet III on one of his sea voyages in the 18th century. According to the tale, the villagers complained to the sultan about pirates who were stealing their herds, destroying their crops, and disturbing their peace. The sultan ordered a fortress to be built to keep the pirates out and offered to free all prisoners who helped to build it. Working flat-out for three years, the prisoners completed the castle, along with a mosque, hamam, and fountain. It was named

Continued on page 192

TURKEY THROUGH THE AGES

According to an ancient saying, "Turkey is a man running west on a ship heading east." Today this adage is more apt than ever; amid rumblings of a nascent Islamic-headed government, the nation is also eager to join the E.U. The ambivalence here underscores the country's age-old search for identity. Few can deny that Turkey—a country rich in history—is once again trying to remake itself.

Situated at the point where the continents of Europe and Asia come together, Turkey has served as the turntable for sundry migrations of mankind. Hittites, Persians, the armies of Alexander the Great, Romans, Byzantines, and Ottomans all have their place in Turkey's intriguing history, though modern Turks trace their roots to the dawn of man, to a time when ancestors living on the vast Anatolian plain created many of civilization's most enduring myths. Troy, immortalized in Homer's *Iliad*, was located on Turkey's Aegean coast, while in Phrygia, it is said, Alexander the Great split the Gordian knot with his sword, fulfilling the prophecy that this feat would make him king of Asia. These colorful legends are no match for the plain facts of history, but together they make Turkey one of the most fascinating places on earth.

TIMELINE	25,000 BC Paleolithic humans inhabit Karain cave in Anatoli	7000 BC Anatolians begin to grow crops and raise livestock	6500 BC Catalhöyük, the world's first city, is settled

| Prehistory | 7000 BC | 6000 BC | 5000 BC |

Top: Archaeologist discovers obsidian objects in a Catalhöyük house.
Right: Entrance to Karain Cave, Antalya.
Far right: Statues from Hacilar.

25,000 BC–3000 BC

The Earliest Cultures

The history of the lands that comprise modern Turkey began to unfold as long as 25,000 years ago, on the plains of Anatolia (Asia Minor), where bones, teeth, and other evidence of early humans have been unearthed in the Karain cave near Antalya. Some of the most fascinating finds include Göbekli Tepe (in southeast Turkey), the world's oldest known shrine, whose monolithic pillars and templelike structures were erected by hunter-gathers around 9500 BC. Then there are the first signs of agricultural life, from about 7000 BC, which have been found at Hacilar, near Bur-

dur. And Catalhöyük, near Konya, dates from 6500 BC and is often considered to be the world's first city; evidence suggests that as many as 8,000 inhabitants lived in flat-roofed, one-story mud-brick houses, grew crops, and fashioned clay figurines representing a mother goddess. By 3000 BC the residents of many such Anatolian settlements were wielding tools and creating figurines hammered from gold, silver, and copper, and trading them with Mesopotamians to the east and Mediterranean cultures to the west.

■ Sights to see:
Karain cave, Antalya (⇨ Ch. 5).
Catalhöyük (⇨ Ch. 6).

2500 BC–1100 BC

The Hittites

Ushering in the Bronze Age, the Hittites arrived from lands north of the Black Sea around 2000 BC to establish a powerful empire that flourished for almost 800 years. They expanded their holdings as far east as Syria and, in 1284 BC, made an accord with Egypt's great Pharaoh Ramses II—the world's first recorded peace treaty. The Hittites adopted a form of hieroglyphics, developed a pantheon of deities, established a complex civil code, and built shrines and fortifications, many of which been unearthed at such sites as Alişar, Alacahöyük, and Kultepe.

1284 BC Hittites make
the world's first peace accord,
with the Egyptians

| 4000 BC | 3000 BC | 2000 BC | 1000 BC |

3

Top left: Sphinx gate, Alacahöyük.
Center top: Hunat Hatun Mosque,
relief stone, finding from Kültepe.
Above: Roman ruin, Phaselis,
Anatolia.
Bottom left; One of the 13 sun
disks found in tombs in Alacahöyük.
Bottom right: Lycean Rock Tombs.

During this time, colonies were settled on the west coast of modern-day Turkey by Achaeans and Mycenaeans from Greece, who went on to wage a famous war against the Anatolians in Troy (c. 1200 BC), later immortalized by Homer in *The Iliad*. After their victory, not all Achaeans rushed back home.

■ Sights to see:
Troy (⇨ *Ch. 3*).
Kültepe (⇨ *Ch. 6*).
Alacahöyük (⇨ *Ch. 6*).
Museum of Anatolian Civilizations, Ankara (⇨ *Ch. 6*).

1200 BC–600 BC

Invaders & Home-grown Kingdoms

With the passage of time, the Hittite society began to fall to encroaching civilizations. Lycians, Mycenaens, and other early Greeks sailed across the Aegean to establish Ephesus, Smyrna, and other so-called Ionian cities on the shores of Anatolia. The Phrygians also migrated to Anatolia from Thrace, flourishing for a mere century or so, until 690 BC—though long enough to leave the legends of kings Gordias and Midas: Gordias, of the intricate knot that could not be unraveled until Alexander the Great slashed through it with a bold stroke of his sword, and Midas, of

the touch that turned everything to gold. The Lydians emerged as a power in the 7th century BC by introducing the world's first coinage. With their vast gold deposits, they became so wealthy that the last of the Lydian kings has forever since been evoked with the term "rich as Croesus."

■ Sights to see: Lycean tombs at Fethiye and Carian tombs at Dalyan (⇨ *Ch. 5*). Greek ruins at Phaselis (⇨ *Ch. 5*).

Far left: Alexander the Great, King of Macedon, fighting, at Battle of Issus, Mosaic, circa 100 BC.
Top: Arch at Ephesus.
Left: Temple of Trajan, built to honor Trajan, the Roman Emperor (98-117).

550 BC–50 BC
Persians & Alexander the Great

The Persians invaded Anatolia in 546 BC and controlled the area for two centuries, until Alexander the Great swept across Asia. The young warrior's kingdom died with him in 323 BC, and Anatolia entered the Hellenistic Age. Greek and Anatolian cultures mixed liberally amid far flung trading empires. None of these kingdoms were more powerful than Pergamum (present-day Bergama). Adorned with great sculptures such as the Laocoön and an acropolis modeled after that of Athens, it was one of the most beautiful cities of the ancient world.

■ Sights to see:
Pergamum (⇨ Ch. 3).

100 BC–AD 100
Romans & Early Christians

By the middle of the 1st century BC, Roman legions had conquered Anatolia, and Ephesus had become the capital of the Roman province of Asia Minor. As Christianity spread through the empire, it was especially well received in Anatolia. Saint John is said to have come to Ephesus, bringing Mary with him, and both are allegedly buried nearby. Saint Paul, a Jew from Tarsus (on Turkey's coast), traveled through Anatolia and the rest of the empire spreading the Christian word for 30 years, until his martyrdom in Rome in AD 67.

■ Sights to see:
Ephesus (⇨ Ch. 4).

306–563
The Rise of Constantinople

Constantine the Great became Roman emperor in 306 and made two momentous moves: he embraced Christianity and he established ancient Byzantium as the capital of the increasingly unwieldy Roman empire. With the fall of Rome in AD 476, the Byzantine Empire ruled much of the western world from the newly named capital Constantinople. The Byzantines reached their height under Justinian I (527–563), whose accomplishments include the Justinian Code (a compilation of Roman law), and such architectural monuments as the Aya Sofya.

■ Sights to see:
Aya Sofya, Istanbul (⇨ Ch. 2).

Top left: Map of Constantinople.
Above: Wall tiles, Topkapi Palace, Istanbul.
Bottom left: Byzantine mosaic of Jesus, Aya Sophia, Istanbul.
Left: Süleyman the Magnificent.

3

IN FOCUS TURKEY THROUGH THE AGES

The First Turks

1071–1300

Around the 8th century, the nomadic Turkish Seljuks rose to power in Persia and began making inroads into Byzantine lands. The defeat of the Byzantine army in 1071 ushered in the Great Seljuk Empire and Seljuks converted their new subjects to Islam. In turn, Pope Urban II launched the First Crusade to reclaim Byzantium in 1097. Armies from Western Europe clashed with Seljuk forces for the next two centuries. The Mongols, under Genghis Khan, swept down from the north and put an end to the weakening Seljuks.

■ Sights to see:
Mevlana Museum, Konya (⇨ Ch. 6). Hunat Hatun Mosque, Kayseri (⇨ Ch. 6).

The Rise of the Ottomans

1300–1500

By 1300, the Seljuk lands had been divided into independent states, known as the azi emirates. Osman I was one of the leaders, and began to expand what would come to be known as the Ottoman Empire, establishing a capital at Bursa. By the 14th century the Ottomans had extended their rule over most of the eastern Mediterranean. Constantinople, the last Byzantine holdout, fell in 1453 and became the new Ottoman capital, which it would remain for the next six hundred years.

■ Sights to See
Topkapı Palace, Istanbul (⇨ Ch. 2).

The Golden Age of the Ottomans

1520–1566

By the time of the reign of Süleyman the Magnificent, the Ottomans controlled lands stretching east into Persia and Egypt, through Mecca and Medina (Islam's holiest cities), and west into central Europe. The empire entered its Golden Age under Süleyman, himself a poet and author of civil laws. Literature, music, and craftsmanship thrived, while Süleyman's architect, Sinan, built beautiful shrines such as the Süleymaniye Mosque in Istanbul.

■ Sights to see:
Süleymaniye Mosque, Istanbul (⇨ Ch. 2). Blue Mosque, Istanbul (⇨ Ch. 2).

TIMELINE

| 1876 Abdülhamid II becomes Sultan | Late 19th c. Ottoman Empire begins massacre of Armenian populations | 1915 Gallipoli campaign | 1923 Turkish state is established |

1875   1900   1925

1571–early 1900s

The Long Decline

The defeat of the Ottoman navy in 1571 by a coalition of European forces at the Battle of Lepanto, off the western coast of Greece, heralded the end of Ottoman supremacy in the Mediterranean. Incompetent leadership plagued the empire almost continually over the next centuries, and the empire dwindled. Abdülhamid II supported liberal reforms when he became Sultan in 1876, and effectively Westernized many aspects of public works, education, and the economy. He also turned his energies to reinvigorating Islamic identity, aiming to unite the increasingly restive ethnic groups of the empire. Most infamously he surpressed Armenian revolutionary groups and an estimated 300,000 Armenians were killed under his regime. A movement of revolutionary societies grew throughout the country and one in particular, the so-called Young Turks, rose up in revolution in 1908, deposing the Sultan. By the early 20th century, the days of the once great empire—now known as the "Sick Man of Europe"—were clearly numbered.

■ Sights to see:
Battle of Lepanto, Gulf of Patras, Greece

WWI–1938

The Birth of the Republic

World War I, during which the Ottomans sided with the Axis powers, put an end to what was left of the Ottoman Empire. In a key battle in 1915, the Allies landed at Gallipoli but were eventually repulsed with heavy losses. In 1920, the Treaty of Sèvres turned Ottoman lands over to France, Italy, Greece, and other victors, but a nationalist hero had come onto the scene: Mustafa Kemal formed the first Turkish Grand National Assembly at Ankara and led the forces that routed Greek armies, pushing across Anatolia to reclaim lands once part of the Byzantine Empire. In

Top left, opposite: Battle of Lepanto. Bottom left, opposite: Süleymaniye Mosque. Bottom right, opposite: Sultan Abdülhamid II.
Left: Mustafa Kemal Atatürk
Above: Pera Palas Hotel, Istanbul, Turkey: Atatürk's bedroom preserved as a museum.

3

IN FOCUS TURKEY THROUGH THE AGES

1923 the Treaty of Lausanne banished foreign powers and established the boundaries of a Turkish state with its capital in Ankara. Kemal—who took the name Atatürk (literally "Father of the Turks")—reinvented Turkey as a modern nation. Turkey embraced secularism and instituted widespread reforms that replaced religious law with secular jurisprudence, advanced education, implemented universal suffrage, and introduced a Western style of dress, abolishing the fez as a symbol of Ottoman backwardness.

■ Sights to see:
Atatürk's room, Dolmabahçe Palace, Istanbul (⇨ *Ch. 2*).

1938–Present

After Atatürk

Turkey has largely allied itself with the West since Atatürk's death in 1938, though the balance between secularization and the religious right has at times been precarious, with the military often stepping in to ensure the country's western leanings. A military coup in 1960 removed a Democratic party government that had reinstituted the call for prayer in Arabic and instituted other right-wing reforms. The military seized control in two other coups in the 1960s and 1970s, while the government of Turgut Özal from 1983 to 1993 ushered in widespread legal and economic reforms.

The pro-Islamist AKP party has deftly led the country through the first years of the new millennium, steering Turkey through its candidacy for European Union membership, diplomatically denying U.S. requests to launch attacks on Iraq from Turkish airbases, and expanding the rights of the country's sizable Kurdish minority.

■ Sights to see:
The Anıtkabir (Atatürk's Mausoleum), Ankara (⇨ *Ch. 6*).

"Babakale," or Baba Castle ("kale" is the Turkish word for "castle"). Today, Babakale is wonderfully peaceful and spacious, contrasting dramatically with its turbulent past. Four kilometers (2½ mi) before Babakale village, after a right turn toward Akliman, are a long sandy beach and a café up the hill overlooking the pine trees and the beach.

BEHRAMKALE (ASSOS)

★ *20 km (12 mi) southeast of Gülpınar on coast road; 60 km (36 mi) south of Troy; 40 km (24 mi) to Ayvacık on E87 toward south; 20 km (12 mi) toward southwest to Behramkale on coast road.*

GETTING HERE AND AROUND

Buses from Çanakkale in the north and Ayvalık or İzmir in the south stop at Ayvacık, which is the closest (19 km) town to Behramkale. From there, minibuses to Behramkale run every hour. Make sure you get one that also goes down to the port, if that's your final destination.

A minibus runs between the port and the village; it's a five-minute ride, costing TL 1.5. The minibus also goes to Kadırga beach, a 15-minute ride. The lofty ruins of Behramkale, known in ancient times as Assos, provide a panoramic view over the Aegean. As you approach, the road forks, one route leading to the ancient, pretty village atop the hill and the other twisting precariously down to the tiny, charming harbor. There's no particularly logical reason, but nowadays the name "Behramkale" is used for the village at the top and "Assos" for the port area.

EXPLORING

The port is a marvel, pressed against the sheer cliff walls. It's crammed with small hotels that were built of volcanic rock, a fleet of fishing boats, and a small rocky beach at each end. Behramkale village is home to the ruins of Assos: the Acropolis. It has blossomed in recent years and now surpasses the port of Assos in terms of prices—and perhaps in charm as well.

Outside June, July, August, and weekends the rest of the year, the area is less crowded and prices are likely to come down a bit, especially in the port. For more spacious and sandier beaches try Kadırga, on the way to Küçükkuyu.

The **Acropolis** is at the top of a hill, on a site measuring about five square city blocks. Founded about 1000 BC by Aeolian Greeks, the city was successively ruled by Lydians, Persians, Pergamenes, Romans, and Byzantines, until Sultan Orhan Gazi (1288–1360) took it over for the Ottomans in 1330. Aristotle is said to have spent time here in the 4th century BC, and St. Paul stopped en route to Miletus in about AD 55. The carpet and trinket sellers along both sides of the road will show you the way from the village. You're best off leaving your car on one of the wider streets and making your way up the steep, cobbled lanes to the top of the Acropolis, where you'll be rewarded with a sensational view of the coastline and, in the distance, the Greek island of Lesbos, whose citizens were Assos's original settlers.

At the Acropolis are a gymnasium, theater, *agora* (marketplace), and carved into the hillside below the summit of the Acropolis, the site of the **Temple of Athena** (circa 530 BC), which has splendid sea views and is being restored. A more modern addition to the ruins, right before the entrance, is the **Murad Hüdavendigâr Cami,** a mosque built in the late 14th century. The mosque is very simple—a dome atop a square, with little decoration. The Greek crosses carved into the lintel over the door indicate the Ottomans used building material from an earlier church, possibly one on the same site. Back down the slope, on the road to the port, are a parking area for the **necropolis** and city walls stretching 3 km (2 mi). Assos was known for its sarcophagi, made of local limestone, which were shipped throughout the Greek world. Unfortunately, most tombs here are in pieces. ⊙*8–8; closes at 5 PM in winter* ✉*$4.*

WHERE TO STAY AND EAT
Most hotels in Assos port include breakfast and dinner, though some will agree on deals for breakfast only. The fish restaurants are not cheap, but the fish will be fresh, the mezes are tasty, and it's all in a beautiful setting.

$–$$
TURKISH
★
✕**Biber Evi.** Known for its delicious mezes, this small restaurant in the hotel with the same name offers local specialties, international favorites, and fusions like eggplant with tahini sauce, or avocado with chile sauce. The owner, Lütfi, grows many of his own vegetables (including a variety of chilis) and takes pride in offering only the freshest ingredients. Tables are in the hotel courtyard and on the terrace, where the views of the Aegean are mesmerizing. The open carafe wine is fine, but there are better (and more expensive) foreign selections. You won't find a better meal—or more arresting oceans views—in Behramkale. ✉*Behramkale Köyü 46, 17860* ☎*286/721–7410* ▤*AE, DC, MC, V.*

¢–$
TURKISH
✕**Kale Restaurant.** A few minutes' walk from the Acropolis, this casual eatery with stone tables is a welcome stop on the way back from a visit to the ruins, especially on a hot day. The salted *ayran* (a milky yogurt drink) is thirst-quenching and a great restorative. Try the stuffed vine leaves, the *tavuk şiş* (chicken kebap), or the *gözleme,* thin Turkish pastry filled with minced meat, mashed potato, or cheese and cooked on a Turkish wok. It's open for lunch and dinner. ✉*Acropolis road, Behramkale* ☎*543/317–4969* ▤*No credit cards.*

$$
🛏 **Assos Kervansaray.** The best-located of the Assos hotels, at the far end of the harbor, the Kervansaray has an aura of antiquity, probably because of the gray lava stone from which it was built. Having incorporated the Assos Hotel Deluxe across the street, the size and style of the rooms vary depending on the building you stay in: some are small and functional, some contain Jacuzzis, and many have terrific views of the Aegean. The restaurant on the sea serves dressed-up versions of traditional Turkish dishes. There is an indoor and an outdoor swimming pool, as well as a swimming pier, though the beach itself is rocky. **Pros:** romantic setting near the Aegean; impressive array of recreational activities to choose from. **Cons:** different buildings have different size and style of rooms. ✉*Assos Liman (Assos Harbor)* ☎*286/721–7093 or 286/721–7199* ⊕*www.assoskervansaray.com* ⤶*71 rooms, 2 suites*

⚙ *In-room: Wi-Fi. In-hotel: restaurant, pools, beach front, water sports* ⊟*MC, V* ⑃*MAP.*

$$–$$$ ⚏ **Biber Evi.** Literally "Chili House," each of the cozy rooms in this
Fodor's Choice   lovely hotel in the village of Behramkale, a 10-minute walk from the
★   Acropolis, is named after the varieties of peppers grown in the garden
and used in the delicious restaurant (*see listing above*). The hotel is a
150-year-old stone house and each of the six rooms is unique, with
wood paneling, Ottoman decoration, and modern comforts: old wood
furniture, bathrooms with heated floors and walls tiled with pepper
designs. The owner considers himself a whiskey expert and will happily
recommend the finest ones in his selection while you sit on the terrace
and enjoy the spectacular sunsets over the Aegean. ⊠*Behramkale Köyü*
46, 17860 ☎*286/721–7410* ⊕*www.biberevi.com* ⚏*6 rooms* ⚙*In-*
hotel: Wi-Fi. In-hotel: restaurant, bar ⊟*AE, DC, MC, V.*

$$ ⚏ **Eris Pansiyon.** The retirement hobby of an American woman named
Emily who moved to Turkey from New York in the late 1990s, this
250-year-old stone house is on the edge of Behramkale, about 10 min-
utes' walk from the Acropolis. With bookshelves full of English books,
homemade cake and tea in the afternoons, and delicious breakfasts
served on the terrace in nice weather, staying here feels more like you're
at a friend's house than in a *pansiyon*. There's a minimum stay of two
days in high season and the *pansiyon* is open all year, except when
the owner visits the U.S., so call ahead. **Pros:** perhaps the most inti-
mate *pansiyon* in Behramkale; good food. **Cons:** rooms are a bit basic.
⊠*Behramkale Köyü 6, 17864* ☎*286/721–7080* ⊕*www.assos.de/eris*
⚏*3 rooms* ⊟*No credit cards.*

$–$$ ⚏ **Old Bridge House.** Located 1 km from Assos on Ayvacık Road, this is
★   one of the most interesting hotels in the region. Each room has its own
color scheme, elegant local furniture, wood floors, and sophisticated
Jacuzzi and shower. There's also a shaded sitting area outside, with
cushions, a bar, and barbecue. Cabins are available for a more budget
stay. The hotel restaurant uses organic, locally grown vegetables, and
their vegetarian flat balls *köfte* are excellent. The restaurant is open to
nonguests. Can, the convivial owner, is extremely helpful; there is also a
shuttle service to and from Ayvacık. **Pros:** the hotel offers the complete
vacation experience at reasonable prices. **Cons:** location a bit far from
the center of Behramkale. ⊠*Behramkale Köyü 357, next to Ottoman*
Bridge ☎*286/721–7100* ⊕*www.oldbridgehouse.com.tr* ⚏*6 rooms; 3*
cabins ⚙*In-room: minibar, Wi-Fi. In-hotel: restaurant.* ⊟*MC, V.*

NIGHTLIFE

You can have drinks at any of the hotel bar-restaurants or check out the
only actual bar in the Assos Harbor, the **Uzun Ev Bar** (*Long House Bar*
⊠*Behramkale Köyü Sahili, Assos* ☎*286/721–7007*). The whitewashed
stone walls with antique bread-making equipment hanging from them
give the place some character even if it's a bit of a stretch to call the
indoor portion of the bar "long." There are eight tables outside lining the harbor, offering a cool place to relax in summer. The music is
good, too: soft jazz during the day, rock and blues at night. It's open
until 3 AM on weekends.

THE MOUNT IDA REGION (KAZ DAĞLARI)

★ *25 km (15 mi) east along the coast from Behramkale, toward Küçükkuyu.*

GETTING HERE AND AROUND

Küçükkuyu, which is 25 km (15 mi) from Ayvacık and 100 km (62 mi) from Çanakkale, is the setting-off point for the villages of Mount Ida, where a car is especially handy as there is no public transport to some of these villages, which lie to the north of the coastal towns. Edremit is on the eastern stretch of the Mount Ida region: it's the biggest transport hub after Çanakkale in the north Aegean region. It's 25 km (15 mi) from Küçükkuyu and 125 km (78 mi) from Çanakkale on E87.

EXPLORING

The area above the Gulf of Edremit is known as Kaz Dağları in Turkish, but to the Greeks it was Mount Ida, home of ancient gods and goddesses. It was here that Paris, son of King Priam of Troy, was given the fateful task of judging the beauty of three goddesses. He chose Aphrodite, the goddess of love, which ultimately caused the Trojan War.

The Turks have made their own contribution to the region's mythology. Famous for their skilled woodwork, they migrated here at the request of Mehmet the Conqueror in the 15th century to cut and process wood for the new ships needed to expand Mehmet's navy, and these ships were crucial to the conquest of Istanbul.

The 34-km (21-mi) coastal stretch between Küçükkuyu and Edremit is essentially a concrete mess, crammed with holiday homes, and for anyone who doesn't own one, it has little to offer. The mountain area above the coast, however, is a completely different story. Pine trees cover its higher slopes, with olive trees predominating lower down. Delightful unspoiled villages are scattered over the hills; most have managed to keep their original character, with houses made of local stone, narrow cobbled streets, and wide squares in the center, a part of which is usually taken up by the *kahvehane* or coffeehouse, the heart of village life. Hiking here will take your breath away it's so beautiful. Above the villages is Kaz Dağları National Park.

Yeşilyurt, 4 km (2½ mi) northwest of Küçükkuyu, is one of the most popular villages. It is now largely owned by Istanbullus who love the area and have helped preserve and enhance its beauty, though some degree of local character was inevitably lost along the way.

Adatepe, 4 km (2½ mi) north of Küçükkuyu, has a site known as the **Altar of Zeus,** although archaeologists are dubious about its authenticity as there is no reference to it in classical literature—it's a short climb from the village, and the altar itself has splendid views that you'll often have to yourself. Adatepe has been less exposed to the boutique hotel invasion than Yeşilyurt, and so looks more like a real village. A tranquil square at the heart of the Adatepe has chairs and tables under the shade of a giant plane tree. The village is also famous for its olive oil, and down the hill in Küçükkuyu is the **Adatepe Zeytinyağı Müzesi** (Olive Oil Museum), where you can learn how olive oil is made.

MOUNT IDA TOURS

There are few designated walking routes in the area, so a guide can be helpful. Tour guides are still a fairly new concept in the region, though, so while your guide will certainly be good with directions, it's less likely he'll be able to tell you much about regional history or botany. A one-day guided tour costs about TL 40; some include lunch. Visiting the national park is much cheaper with a tour than on your own, as the TL 40 will cover entry to the park and the compulsory guide's fee.

Most hotels in the region organize walking tours and arrange transport; others will at least point out the routes and help you hire a guide. Some will take you to Troy, Assos, or Bergama if you ask. İskender Bey, the owner of the İdakoy, wrote a book on the region showing the various walking routes and the sights to be seen in the park.

There are also several hotels in the area that function as mini-travel agencies, helpful for tours but not optimal as places to stay:

Antandros Tourism Agency (⊠ *Atatürk Cad. 9, Sokak 5, Altınoluk* ☎ *266/396-5511 or 266/395-2277*), in Altınoluk (the largest town between Küçükkuyu and Edremit, though it is not itself worth visiting) has various tours around Mount Ida as well as to Bozcaada, Troy, Assos, and Ayvalık.

Mare & Monte travel agency (⊠ *Fatih Cad. 13, Altınoluk* ☎ *266/396-1730* ⊕ *www.hotelmaremonte.com*) offers tours of Mount Ida and trips to Pergamum (Bergama).

Farther east are less prettified villages, some Turkish and some originally Greek, like **Çamlıbel,** a good base for more ambitious walks.

Tahtakuşlar has an **Etnografya Galerisi** (*ethnographic museum* ☎ *266/387-3340* ⊕ *www.tahtakuslar.8m.com*) boasting the biggest Caretta (a Mediterranean sea turtle) in the world as well as traditional Turkoman clothing, tents, and household tools. Both Tahtakuşlar and Çamlıbel are about 2 km (1 mi) inland from the coast road near **Güre,** a hot-spring bath resort.

For those who can't do without the sea, it's nearby, and it's beautiful. The coast between Küçükkuyu and Edremit is highly developed, but between Küçükkuyu and Assos lies one of Turkey's most delightful swimming seas, and it's clean, calm, and refreshing. Most of the good village hotels have their own private beach somewhere on this route. Alternatively, since the whole of the coast is a protected area, you can park your car among the olive trees almost anywhere along the coast road and jump in—there may not be a sandy beach, but you might feel like you're the first to swim in that exact spot. If you'd rather have the sand, Kadırga Beach is on the same coast closer to Assos.

The **Kaz Dağları National Park** covers 25,000 hectares above the villages, and can only be visited with an official guide—mostly for security purposes, since there are 35 plants and trees unique to the Kaz Dağları and the presence of a guide is a measure against vandalism or smuggling. Make sure you get a guide who speaks English. The Sarıkız peak is 26 km (16 mi) from the entrance: it's a hard day's walk, but most people drive part of the way and walk the rest. There is a series of rivers, pools, and waterfalls, and at the end you'll be rewarded with a magnificent view of the Gulf of Edremit. There are two entrances to the park: one where you can enter with your car and guide; the other is only for special safari tours, as the road is too rough for most cars. You can camp in the park but there's no electricity, toilets, or any other amenities. ⏱ *8–5 daily* 🎫 *TL 17.50 per car, and TL 40 for the compulsory guide.*

SPORTS AND OUTDOORS

HIKING   Trekking is one of the region's main attractions. There are few designated trails, but people from the villages or at the hotels are well informed about routes and happy to help. Several agencies organize tours. The walks are delightful, and there is usually something to see or do on the way, such as bathing in the Bath of Aphrodite or swimming in the pool under the Başdeğirmen waterfall, where you can also picnic on wooden tables set in the middle of the river, and gaze at the Roman bridge that was the only passage to Troy.

WHERE TO STAY AND EAT

The villages of Mount Ida are a haven of boutique hotels; in fact, the region helped introduce the idea of the boutique hotel to Turkey, changing the country's tourism culture. Most hotels claim they offer a genuine countryside experience in modern comfort—no TVs or loud music, but there's a good chance you'll find poetry-reading nights, or organized courses in cooking, philosophy, or yoga. The best place to eat is probably at your hotel, and you're likely to find good international cuisine, as well as local specialties.

$$ 🏠 **Ergüvanlı Ev.** Most of the region's hotels overlook mountainous pine
★   forests, but the Ergüvanlı Ev is right in the middle of one. The gardens are beautiful and the forest beyond keeps summer heat away. Rooms are plain but pleasant, and all nonsmoking. The owner, Suna, gives yoga lessons in the mornings and also offers massages for a fee. The chef is a village woman assisted by the owners; dinner is tasty, but breakfast is a real feast. Try the *menemen* (egg cooked with tomatoes and peppers) with fresh thyme from the garden. Nonguests can call ahead for dinner reservations. **Pros:** beautiful setting; sumptuous breakfast; on-site yoga lessons. **Cons:** rooms are rather austere. ✉ *Yeşilyurt Köyü, Küçükkuyu* ☎ *286/752–5676* ⊕ *www.erguvanliev.com* ⇥ *7 rooms, 1 two-bedroom house* ♿ *In-room: no TV, no a/c (some). In-hotel: restaurant, Wi-Fi, no-smoking rooms* ▤ *MC, V* ⚑ *MAP.*

$$$ 🏠 **Hünnaphan.** This 250-year-old Ottoman mansion has a spacious courtyard and a large, beautiful garden. The open buffet dinner has a rich choice of mezes and local specialties. The owner is also a painter and the walls of the rooms and corridors are hung with her pictures. Rooms are spacious, and plainly but elegantly decorated. There is also a private house for large groups, with its own garden. **Pros:** Ottoman elegance; hotel organizes walking tours and provides guides for its guests. **Cons:** your opinion of the decor depends on what you think of the proprietor's painting skills. ✉ *Adatepe Köyü, Küçükkuyu* ☎ *286/752–6581* ⊕ *www.hunnaphan.com* ⇥ *22 rooms* ♿ *In-room: no TV. In-hotel: restaurant, Wi-Fi* ▤ *MC, V* ⚑ *MAP.*

$$ ⌂ **İdakoy.** This homey hotel looks from the distance like the only house on its hillside, outside the village of Çamlıbel. Its chief attractions are the stunning views of the Gulf of Edremit from the terrace, and owner İskender's deep knowledge of the region: he and his wife Suna cowrote a book on Mount Ida describing otherwise undesignated walking routes. After breakfast, İskender will take his guests out for a walk for an hour or the whole day—it's up to you. The rooms vary in size, and there's no smoking indoors. ⊠ *Camlibel Köyü, 10300 Edremit, Balikesir* ☎ *266/387–3402* 📠 *266/387–3393* ↩ *4 rooms* ⌂ *In-room: no TV.* ⊟ *V* ⏺*MAP.*

$$$
Fodor'sChoice
★

⌂ **Manici Kasrı.** There's a reason why this was chosen Turkey's best small hotel in 2006 by one of Turkey's most influential newspapers: each room is decorated differently but all are elegant and comfortable, with four-poster beds and original paintings on the walls. The garden restaurant overlooks the mountains and serves delicious local and international food. Service overall is flawless. The building is new but it was made from old stones and bricks taken from an old olive oil factory. The hotel has a private beach 5 km (3 mi) down the hill on the Küçükkuyu-Assos road, and a shuttle bus will take you there. A two-day stay is required if you're planning to visit on the weekend. **Pros:** small and intimate feel, a lovely gem in the mountains. **Cons:** beach is not so close. ⊠ *Yeşilyurt village, Küçükkuyu* ☎ *286/752–1731* ⊕ *www.manicikasri.com* ↩ *7 rooms, 3 suites* ⌂ *In-room: Wi-Fi, no TV. In-hotel: restaurant, bar* ⊟ *DC, MC, V* ⏺*MAP.*

AYVALIK

94 km (58 mi) from Edremit, south on Rte. E87, or 75 km (46 mi) from Çanakkale on E87.

ESSENTIALS
Car Rental Duke Tour car rental (☎ *266/373–5807*).

Visitor Information (⊠ *Harbour* ☎ *266/312–2122*).

EXPLORING
Ayvalık is the biggest resort in the region. Like many Turkish seaside towns, it has been somewhat exploited by package tourism in recent years, but its superb geographical setting, stretching onto a peninsula and surrounded by islands, is hard to beat. The setting is lovely, with many bays swirling in and out of its coastline; if you drive up the hill to the Şeytan Sofrası ("the devil's dinner table"), you'll clearly see this. The area also boasts one of Turkey's few blue-flagged (eco-friendly) beaches.

Ayvalık first appears in Ottoman records at the late date of 1770, when an Ottoman naval hero, Gazi Hasan Paşa, was aided by the local Greek community after his ship sank nearby. Soon after, the town was granted autonomy, perhaps as a gesture of gratitude, and the Muslim population was moved to outlying villages, leaving the Greeks to prosper in the olive oil trade. At the close of World War I, the Greeks invaded Turkey and claimed the Aegean coast; in 1922 the Turks ousted the Greek army, and the entire Greek community of Ayvalık was deported. Today the town is mostly Turks, and other than tourism, the main source of income is olive farming and olive oil production.

★ The old Greek quarter of the town has been neglected for decades, though in the last few years policies of protection and restoration have begun to be enforced. Ayvalık has some of the finest 19th-century Greek-style architecture in Turkey. Unlike the typical Ottoman house (tall, narrow, and built of wood, with an overhanging bay window), Greek buildings are stone, with classic triangular pediments above a square box. The best way to explore is to turn your back to the Aegean and wander the tiny side streets leading up the hill into the heart of the old residential quarter (try Talat Paşa Caddesi and Gümrük Caddesi). Several historic churches in town have been converted into mosques. St. John's is now the **Saatlı Cami** (Clock Mosque). St. George's is now the **Çınarlı Cami** (Plane Tree Mosque). There are many mosques converted from churches in Turkey, but these are among the most striking—the elaborate style of Orthodox churches does not suit the plain minimalist style of mosques, and the unimpressive minaret erected later at the Çinarlı mosque looks almost absurd. The pictures of the saints inside are painted over but can still be seen if you look carefully. The **Taxiarchis Church,** currently closed with no set reopening date, is a museum, with a remarkable series of paintings done on fish skin depicting the life of Christ. Barbaros Caddesi on the south end of the pier will take you to **Phaneromeni Church** (Ayazma Klisesi), displaying beautiful stone craftwork, and to **Hayrettin Paşa Cami,** also converted from a church.

In summer, Sarımsaklı Plajı, the 10-km (6-mi) stretch of sandy beach, 7 km (4½ mi) from the center of town, is popular. It's a crowded resort with a mess of concrete hotels right behind the sea front, and traffic and parking can be a problem, but the beach and sea are lovely.

Day or evening cruises to the bays and islands of Ayvalık are enjoyable. The numerous boats in the harbor with desks in front of them will try and sell you a trip as you walk by, and competition makes prices very reasonable—about 13 TL for a day trip including a fish meal. The tours are offered from May until the end of October.

Şeytan Sofrası, a hilltop 9 km (5½ mi) from town, on a right turn on the road from Ayvalık to Sarımsaklı, is the place to get a panoramic view of the islands and the bays. It's lovely at sunset, though there's nothing to see on the hilltop itself since a fire in 2006 burned down all the trees and the café closed.

WHERE TO STAY AND EAT

$$

SEAFOOD

★

✕**Canlı Balık.** This fish restaurant at the end of Ayvalık Pier delivers excellent food in a romantic setting. With its starched white tablecloths and weathered decor, the interior has an air of faded grandeur. In fine weather, opt for the terrace, where local fishing boats sway in the water a few feet away. Start with mezes such as fried squid or mussel salad in local olive oil, then move on to fresh, grilled local fish, perhaps *barbunya* (red mullet), or try *papalina* (small sardines) if you are in town in July and August. ⊠*South of Atatürk Bulvarı, Cumhuriyet Square, on harbor* ☎266/313–0081 ▬*MC, V.*

¢ ✕**Fırat Lokantası.** In the heart of
TURKISH Ayvalık, just north of Saatlı Mosque,
this eatery offers hearty lunches to
hardworking street traders; it's tiny
but almost always full, so you may
have to share one of the half-dozen
tables downstairs (there are a few
more in the even smaller upstairs
section). The decor could not be
plainer but this is typical and delicious Turkish home cooking: rice,
beans, eggplant with minced meat,
and lamb stew. It's the perfect place
for lunch when wandering the historic part of the town. ⊠*Edremit
Cad. 25/A* ☎*266/312–1380* ⊟*No
credit cards* ⊘*No dinner; closed Sun.*

> ### A QUICK TRIP TO GREECE
>
> A trip to the Greek island of Les-
> bos will allow you to see another
> country and culture with a sea
> journey of little more than an hour.
> Ferries depart from Ayvalık pier
> at 6 PM daily and from Lesbos at
> 8:30 AM daily between mid-June
> and mid-November—so a tourist
> from Ayvalık would need to stay at
> least two nights. Fares are about
> $75 return.

$$ ⛩**Ayvalık Beach Hotel.** This hotel, across a causeway toward Şeytan
☺ Sofrası, is actually a cluster of 15 two-story chalets nestled among pine
trees on a wooded slope overlooking a sheltered inlet. Wonderful sea
views more than compensate for the lack of frills in the clean and
comfortable but sparsely furnished rooms. Breakfast and dinner are
buffet-style. There is a pool and a park at the edge of the sea. **Pros:**
arresting ocean views; pool. **Cons:** simple, sparsely furnished rooms.
⊠*Şeytan Sofrası Yolu, Altınkum Mev., Ayvalık,* ☎*266/324–5300*
⊕*www.ayvalikbeach.com* ⌦*70 rooms, 2 suites* ⌂*In-hotel: restau-
rant, bar, pool, beachfront, Wi-Fi* ⊟*MC, V* ⑩*MAP.*

$$$ ⛩**Grand Hotel Temizel.** Away from the other hotels on Sarımsaklı Beach,
this fairly luxurious five-star lodging has a private beach, a casino, a
small Turkish spa, and an elegant marble-and-gleaming-brass lobby.
Rooms are spacious, but they are the least fancy feature of the hotel—
though most have balconies with sea views. The best part is that it's far
from the noise and concrete pollution of the rest of the beach. The large
common areas and the aqua park make it a good choice for families.
Pros: tranquil private beach, casino, tennis court, gym, and beautiful
views of the ocean. **Cons:** rooms are spacious but lacking in character.
⊠*Sarmısaklı Plajı,* ☎*266/324–2000* ⊕*www.temizel.com.tr* ⌦*275
rooms, 12 suites* ⌂*In-room: Wi-Fi In-hotel: 2 restaurants, bar, tennis
court, pool, gym, water sports* ⑩*AP* ⊟*MC, V.*

CUNDA ISLAND (ALI BEY ADASI)

Just off the coast at Ayvalık (connected by a causeway to mainland).

GETTING HERE

There are regular buses to Cunda from Ayvalık, but the best way to
travel is by boat; they run every hour each way, from 10 AM to midnight
in summer (June 15–Sept. 15), and dock at the quay right in the middle
of the restaurants in Cunda. In winter, buses are the only option.

EXPLORING

Like Ayvalık, Cunda Island was once predominantly Greek, and some Greek is still spoken here. The island has a mix of the two cultures in its food, music, and nightlife, and lately has been deliberately cultivating this, having realized the tourism potential.

The fishing town has good seafood restaurants lining its atmospheric quay; they're noted for their grilled *çipura* (a local fish) and for an amazing variety of Turkish and Greek seafood dishes served grilled, fried, baked, or in a cold seafood salad with interesting dressings.

The island's Greek houses are well preserved and varied, and the 19th-century **St. Nicholas Church** (better known as Taksiyarhis, or Taxiarchis, Church to the locals) in the middle of town is a must, even though you can only see it from the outside. With its large cracks, caused by an earthquake in 1924, and the birds flying around its airy domes, the whole place has a ghostly air. You can't go inside anymore because of the danger of a collapse, but peep through the glassless windows and you can see some of the frescoes, several of which have been defaced—the eyes of the apostles have been gouged out. On the left side of the church's quiet courtyard is a small café and *pansiyon*, Zehra Teyze'nin Evi, where you can sit and have a refreshment and enjoy the view of the church.

WHERE TO STAY AND EAT

Cunda has become a popular place for accommodation and nightlife as well as dining. Unlike mainland Ayvalık, it is purely a tourist resort and also attracts weekend escapers all year around, though it's not as built up, and doesn't (yet, at least) attract the big tour groups. Most of the hotels here are quite expensive for what they offer. Waterfront restaurants, on the other hand, while also expensive, are among the best in Turkey. For cheap eating, try Pizza Uno (it's not the American chain) in the center of town. It's the lunchtime favorite of the local shopkeepers and serves kebabs and pides as well as pizza.

$$–$$$
TURKISH
★
× **Lale Restaurant.** Commonly known as Bay Nihat'ın Yeri (literally "the place of Mr. Nihat"), this is the most popular and probably most expensive of the waterfront restaurants in Cunda. The meze selection is a feast for the eyes and stomach, and many options are original creations based on Greek and Turkish cuisine, like local clams with whiskey sauce, and octopus with thyme and pomegranate extract. All are delicious. The seafront part of the restaurant looks similar to its neighbors but a bit sleeker; the indoor winter section is nicely decorated, unlike the scruffy casual interiors of its rivals. ⊠ *The Cunda Quay* ☎ *266/327–1063 or 266/327–1777* ⚏ *Reservations essential* ⊟ *AE, MC, V* ⊙ *Closed for the month of Ramadan.*

$$
⊞ **Zehra Teyze'nin Evi.** This small *pansiyon* hidden among the trees in the courtyard of the Taksiyarhis Church is, literally, the House of Aunt Zehra. She's a straightforward lady who talks with her guests if she feels like it; at other times she can be seen sleeping on the sofa of the *pansiyon*'s garden. There is a cool, quiet garden to relax in. **Pros:** wonderful location, casual and warm atmosphere. **Cons:** rooms are rather plain. ⊠ *Cunda center, next to Taksiyarhis Church* ☎ *266/327–2285* ⊕ *www.cundaevi.com* ⤢ *5 rooms* ⚏ *In-room: Wi-Fi. In-hotel: restaurant* ⊟ *No credit cards.*

NIGHTLIFE

In Sarımsaklı, the beach area in Ayvalık, you'll find discos and clubs that play pop and electronic techno; Cunda has bars that play Turkish and Greek pop music. There are many, and they're easy to find while you're wandering around.

PERGAMUM (BERGAMA)

Fodor'sChoice
★ *54 km (33 mi) from Ayvalık; take Rte. E87 south approximately 44 km (27 mi), then follow signs to Bergama.*

GETTING HERE AND AROUND

If you're coming from Ayvalık, drive 44 km (27 mi) south on the E87 and then turn off following the signs to Bergama, a further 10 km (6 mi).

The Bergama bus terminal is 5 mi out of the city center, but there's a free shuttle service that stops near the post office and basilica in the center of the old town. There's also minibus service for TL 1.5. In other words, if a taxi driver tells you there's no bus service and tries to charge you TL 25 for the short trip, know that there are other options—or bargain with him.

ESSENTIALS

Visitor Information (✉ *Hükümet Konağı, B Blok, Ground Floor* ☎ *232/ 631–2851*).

EXPLORING

The windswept ruins of Pergamum, which surround the modern town of Bergama, are among the most spectacular in Turkey. The attractions here are spread out over several square miles, so if you don't have a car, negotiate with a taxi driver in Bergama (you have to pass through the town anyway) to shuttle you from site to site. Biking is an enjoyable option; some hotels have bicycles on hand for rent or lend them free of charge with the room price.

The run-down but charming old quarter, on the way to the Acropolis, is the best place to stay. It has several clean, economical hotels to choose from and offers good cheap food if you choose to spend a night or two.

Pergamum was one of the ancient world's major powers, though it had a relatively brief moment of glory. Led by a dynasty of maverick rulers, it rose to prominence during the 3rd and 2nd centuries BC. Because he was impressed by the city's impregnable fortress, Lysimachus, one of Alexander the Great's generals, decided this was the place to stow the booty he had accumulated while marching through Asia Minor. Then, when Lysimachus was killed, in 281 BC, Philetaerus (circa 343 BC–263 BC), the commander of Pergamum, claimed the fortune and holed up in the city. He established a dynasty known as the Attalids. After defeating the horde of invading Gauls who had been sacking cities up and down the coast in 240 BC, the Pergamenes were celebrated throughout the Hellenic world as saviors. The Attalids ruled until 133 BC, when the mad Attalus III (circa 170 BC–133 BC) died and bequeathed the entire kingdom to Rome. By a liberal interpretation of his ambiguous bequest, his domain became the Roman province of Asia and transformed Rome's economy with its wealth.

The city was a magnificent architectural and artistic center in its heyday—especially under the rule of Eumenes II (197 BC–159 BC). He built Pergamum's famous library, which contained 200,000 books. When it rivaled the great library in

WORD OF MOUTH

"We were smart enough to stay over night in Pergamum. I have heard others complaining about their tours, mostly looooooong drive, then rush in and rush out."

—WTnow

Alexandria, Egypt, the Egyptians banned the sale of papyrus to Pergamum, which responded by developing a new paper—parchment, made from animal skins instead of reeds. This *charta pergamena* was more expensive but could be used on both sides; because it was difficult to roll, it was cut into pieces and sewn together, much like today's books. The library of Pergamum was transported to Alexandria by Cleopatra, where it survived until the 7th century AD, when it was destroyed by the fanatical Caliph Omar, who considered the books un-Islamic.

The most dramatic of the remains of Pergamum are at the **acropolis.** Signs point the way to the 6-km (4-mi) road to the top, where you can park in the car park across from the souvenir stand—which sells water, film, and reasonably good picture books containing site maps. Buy your ticket at the gate. Broken but still mighty triple ramparts enclose the **upper town,** with its temples, palaces, private houses, and gymnasia (schools). In later Roman times, the town spread out and down to the plain, where the Byzantines subsequently settled for good.

After entering the acropolis through the Royal Gate, there are several different paths. To start at the top, pick the path to the far right, which takes you past the partially restored **Temple of Trajan,** at the summit. This is the very picture of an ancient ruin, with burnished white-marble pillars high above the valley of the Oç Kemer Çayi (Selinos River). On the terraces just below, you can see the scant remains of the **Temple of Athena** and the **Altar of Zeus.** Once among the grandest monuments in the Greek world, the Altar of Zeus was excavated by German archaeologists who sent Berlin's Pergamon Museum every stone they found, including the frieze, 400 feet long, that vividly depicted the battle of the gods against the giants. Now all that's left is the altar's flat stone foundation. There's much more to see of the **Great Theater,** carved into the steep slope west of the terrace, that holds the Temple of Athena: it can seat some 10,000 spectators and retains its astounding acoustics. You can test them by sitting near the top and having a companion do a reading in the stage area. ☎232/631–0778 ✉$8.50 ⊗Apr.–Oct., daily 8:30–6:30; Nov.–Mar., daily 8–5.

Bergama's **Arkeoloji Müzesi** (*Archaeology Museum*) houses a substantial collection of well-presented statues, coins, and other artifacts excavated from the ancient city as well as an ethnography section. The statue of Aphrodite comes from the site of Allianoi, a Roman spa town, which is waiting to be drowned by a dam project. ✉*Cumhuriyet Cad. 10* ☎*232/631–2884* ✉*$5* ⊗*Tues.–Sun. 8:30–5:30.*

The **Asklepion** is believed to have been the world's first full-service health clinic. The name is a reference to Asklepios, god of medicine and recovery, whose snake and staff are now the symbol of modern medicine. In the heyday of the Pergamene Asklepion in the 2nd century AD, patients were prescribed such treatments as fasting, colonic irrigation, and running barefoot in cold weather. The nature of the treatment was generally determined by interpretation of the patient's dreams. The entrance to the complex is at the column-lined **Holy Road,** once the main street connecting the Asklepion to Pergamum's acropolis. Follow it for about a city block into a small square and through the main gate to the temple precinct. Immediately to the right are the **Shrine of Artemis,** devoted to the Greek goddess of chastity, the moon, and hunting, and the **library,** a branch of the one at Pergamum. Patients also received therapy accompanied by music during rites held in the intimate theater, which is now used each May for performances of the Bergama Arts Festival. Nearby are pools that were used for mud and sacred water baths. A subterranean passageway leads down to the sacred cellar of the **Temple of Telesphorus,** where the devout would pray themselves into a trance and record their dreams upon waking; later, the dreams would be interpreted by a resident priest. ⊠*Follow Cumhuriyet Cad. west to Rte. E87; near tourist information office, follow sign pointing off to right 1½ km (1 mi)* ☎*232/631–2886* 🖅*$7* ☉*Apr.–Oct., daily 8:30–6:30; Nov.–Mar., daily 8–5.*

The **Kızıl Avlu** *(Red Basilica)* in Bergama is named for the red bricks from which it's constructed. You'll pass it on the road to and from the acropolis—it's right at the bottom of the hill. This was the last pagan temple constructed in Pergamum before Christianity was declared the state religion in the 4th century. At that time it was converted into a basilica dedicated to St. John. The walls remain, but not the roof. Most interesting are the underground passages, where it is easy to imagine how concealed pagan priests supplied the voices of "spirits" in mystic ceremonies. One of the two towers is closed at the moment for restoration; the other is now used as a mosque. ☎*232/631–2885* 🖅*$3.50* ☉*Apr.–Oct., daily 8:30–5; Nov.–Mar., daily 8–5.*

WHERE TO STAY AND EAT

¢ ✕**Arzu Pide and Corba Salon.** Just down the street from the Odyssey
TURKISH Guest House, Arzu has inexpensive, simple, and satisfying Turkish fare and is typically recommended by the locals. The *pides, lahmacuns,* and lentil soup are especially tasty and the staff is friendly. The restaurant interior is a bit cramped but if you sit inside at lunchtime you can watch the chef roll pide dough while you eat; there are also some tables outside. ⊠*Istiklal Meydanı 37* ☎*232/631–1187* ▭*No credit cards*

¢–$ ✕**Sağlam Restaurant.** This popular spot is a few miles out of town near
TURKISH the bus station, but serves excellent food at reasonable prices. It has two floors and a seating capacity of 250, which is necessary because it's the lunch stop for almost all tour buses to Bergama. The selection is large, but kebabs are the specialty. Try the *beyti sarma,* a lamb kebab dürüm wrap cooked with a variety of spices, or the *kardelen kebabi,* a meat kebab wrapped in naan bread and served with yogurt. ⊠*Atatürk Cad. 111* ☎*232/632–8897* ▭*AE, MC, V.*

DID YOU KNOW?

The city of Pergamum was one of the major powers of the ancient world. The Library (Atheneum) is believed to have contained over 200,000 volumes in the city's heyday, around 175 BC.

$ ✕**Ticaret Odası Lokali.** In a 150-year-old Greek building in a tranquil
TURKISH   part of town, the best thing about this restaurant is the setting; the food
is fine but nothing spectacular. The terrace has views of the acropolis
and basilica, making it a romantic spot for an evening meal. Good, if
unsurprising, mezes, kebabs, and steaks are on the menu and prices
are more reasonable than what the somewhat formal decor and serious
service may imply. ☒*Ulucami Mahalesi, Domuzalanı Mevkii, 35700*
📞*232/632–9641* ▤*MC, V* ⊗*Closed for a month in Ramadan.*

$ 🏨**Akropolis Guest House.** Just 200 yards away from the Red Basilica,
this hotel is on the quiet edge of the old town. Rooms vary in size but
are clean and comfortable. The pool is attractive on a hot day, though
it's not big enough for much swimming. Dinner is served on request:
notify the staff in the morning. Meals are good Turkish home cooking,
with options such as zucchini stuffed with minced meat, and they can
be enjoyed from a small pavilion with views of the acropolis. There are
four bikes available to guests free of charge. **Pros:** near Red Basilica and
Akropolis; good value for the money. **Cons:** the pool and common area
are very close to the rooms. ☒*Kurtuluş Mahallesi, Kayalık Sokak 3*
📞*232/631–2621* ⊕*www.akropolisguesthouse.com* ⤳*9 rooms* ⟁*In-room: Wi-Fi* ▤*MC, V* ��*BP.*

¢   🏨**Odyssey Guest House.** In the heart of the old town in two restored
19th-century Greek houses, the Odyssey is the best budget deal in Bergama, though not all rooms have private baths. It has everything a backpacker could want: large, clean, wood-floored rooms (some with private
sitting areas and balconies), a large breakfast buffet, do-it-yourself laundry facilities, and a book exchange. The friendly proprietor, Ersin, and
his wife also freely dispense travel advice. You can enjoy your breakfast and meet other travelers on the hotel's small terrace from where
there are views of the basilica and the acropolis. **Pros:** excellent value.
Cons: some have shared bathrooms. ☒*Talatpaşa Mahallesi, Abacıhan
Sokak 13, 35700* 📞*232/631–3501* ⊕*www.odysseyguesthouse.com*
⤳*10 rooms* ⟁*In-room: no a/c (some), Wi-Fi* ⓘ*BP.*

The Central & Southern Aegean Coast

WORD OF MOUTH

"If you like archaeology do not miss Ephesus. But also consider Didima, Priene, and Miletus, all of which we did in an easy day's drive between Bodrum and Ephesus . . . Turkey is fabulous, one of our top trips!"

—laurie_ann

WELCOME TO THE CENTRAL & SOUTHERN AEGEAN COAST

TOP REASONS TO GO

★ **Sailing on a Blue Cruise** A *gulet*, a converted wooden fishing boat, is the perfect way to explore the coast, sailing out of Çeşme, Bodrum or other coastal ports and from there gliding across the warm azure waters to secluded coves.

★ **Visit Ephesus** The Library of Celsus, with its tiered facade of columns, and ruins of temples, houses, and shops richly evoke the Greek and Roman worlds.

★ **Wandering through Şirince** This picturesque cluster of two-story houses is set on a lush hill, and villagers sell their handmade crafts.

★ **Swimming and scuba diving in Çeşme and Bodrum** Some of the brightest and bluest waters in the Aegean surround these coastal resorts.

★ **Feasting on fish in Gümüşlük** Escape the tourist crush of Bodrum to enjoy a meal at one this village's waterside restaurants.

Bodrum

Ephesus

1 İzmir and Çeşme. İzmir, in the middle of the Aegean coast, is the region's largest city. Çeşme, a peninsula, is the westernmost tip of the region, and has some of the region's most pristine water. Some of the best beaches are located in Altınkum, southwest of Çeşme.

2 Selçuk, Ephesus and Şirince. Selçuk is the town nearest to the archaeological ruins at Ephesus and the old hill village of Şirince. The slower pace and authentic Turkish feel of both Selçuk and Şirince are a refreshing change from Kuşadası, the overdeveloped port for cruise ships that include Ephesus on their itineraries. The ancient Roman city of Aphrodisias, the layered limestone-travertine terraces and hot springs of Pamukkale, and the ruins of Didyma, Miletus, and Priene can all be visited from Selçuk.

3 Bodrum Peninsula. Bodrum is the southern Aegean coast's other peninsula—its towns are smaller than those on the Çeşme Peninsula, and its coves and bays are great for swimming. Most travelers start at the northeastern tip at the popular town of Gölköy-Türkbükkü and continue counterclockwise along the coast. Bodrum shares an airport with Milas, to its north.

GETTING ORIENTED

Although it's the country's most touristy and developed region, the central and southern Aegean also holds some of Turkey's most fascinating and diverse treasures, from gorgeous white-sand beaches to the ruins of Ephesus. To get a good sense of the region, travel to the smaller, outlying villages and towns, where much of the Aegean's character lives on.

Fishing boat on the Aegean Sea

Aphrodisias
Cine
D550
Yatagan
Mugla   D330
Yerkesik   Gericam
Lake Koycegiz   Koycegiz
Marmaris
Kaunos   Dalaman
Marmaris Limani   D400
Fethiye

St. John's Basillica, Selçuk

4

THE CENTRAL & SOUTHERN AEGEAN COAST PLANNER

Don't Forget to Bring . . .

■ **Sunscreen.** It can be very expensive in the resort towns.

■ **A towel** for sunbathing. Hotels don't like it when you use the in-room towels on the beach.

■ **A hat.** In the summer, temperatures often rise into the 90s. It's amazing what a little shade will do.

■ **Mosquito repellent.** They're fast and furious on the coast!

■ **Tissue packs.** Many public bathrooms do not have tissues or toilet paper.

■ **Sporting gear.** Rental costs can be high, so if you have room in your luggage, try to bring snorkeling gear, wet suits, etc. with you.

Visitor Information

Visitor Information offices are generally open daily from 8:30–12:30 and 1:30–5. Offices are listed in the towns where you can find them.

How Much Time Do You Need?

Given the distances involved and the wealth of alluring sights, ideally, you would need 10 to 12 days to thoroughly explore the region. As a general rule of thumb, if you want to make a lot of stops, it makes more sense to tour as you go along, as driving back and forth between base cities and sights can be tiring. If you are pressed for time, it is best to head straight for İzmir or Selçuk—making either city the base from which you can take in some of the main sights nearby. If you're traveling by car, be sure to leave time to stop and stay in the smaller towns along the coast.

Blue Cruises

Blue Cruises were originally inexpensive boat tours catering to Turkish intellectuals in the 1970s, and they're still one of the most enjoyable and low-key ways to see the coast.

Trips can last two to 14 days between April and October, and most voyages are on *gulets,* converted wooden fishing craft with full crew. The boats' amenities range from modest to luxurious, and prices fluctuate accordingly. You can arrange your trip before you leave home, or on the spot at the docks. Ask a travel agent or someone at your hotel to recommend a reputable company with a good boat and crew. On the Aegean coast, voyages depart from İzmir, Çeşme, Kuşadası, and Bodrum (also see the Blue Cruising" CloseUp box in Ch. 5).

For information try these, contacts: **Cano Yachting** (☎0532/481–6244 or 252/385–3740 ⊕www. canoyachting.com); **Era Tourism** (☎252/316–2310 ⊕www.erayachting.com); **Neyzen Tours** (☎252/316–7204 ⊕www.neyzen.com.tr); **Borda Yachting** (☎252/313–7766 ⊕www.bordayachting.com); **Motif Yachting** (☎252/316–1536 ⊕www.motifyachting.com).

Aegean Seafood

Eating along the Aegean coast is a pleasure, especially if you like seafood. The main course is often the fresh catch of the day, though meat lovers can rest assured that there are always beef and lamb kebabs. Some of the more common fish you'll find are *palamut* (baby tuna), *lüfer* (bluefish), *levrek* (sea bass), *çupra* (sea bream), and *kalkan* (turbot). *(For more about the fish you'll find on the menu in Turkey, see the Seafood Spotlight in Ch. 5.)*

TIPS FOR SEAFOOD RESTAURANTS

Fish is often sold whole (as opposed to fillets) and priced by the kilo. The price and weight are often not listed, so don't hesitate to ask. For example, 1 kilo of sea bream may be equal to two whole fish, and cost $30.

Don't be afraid to bargain for your fish. Many restaurants in touristy areas tend to mark up their prices significantly. Check out the prices offered elsewhere and use those as a reference point. Remember that bargaining is part of Turkish culture.

Don't feel awkward about sharing a main course. This is always acceptable, especially when ordering a large-sized fish.

Make a point of letting your server know if you don't want the fixed-menu option that many restaurants offer. Also, be specific about the exact quantity of the meze, or appetizer, you would like—sometimes waiters will bring you more than one serving of a dish and charge you extra.

Note that there is often an obligatory service charge added to your bill. Some restaurants, regardless of the number of people in your party, also add a gratuity of 10%. Always look at your check to see if it's been added before you leave a tip. The check will say *servis* or *servis ucreti dahildir* if a gratuity has been added.

What It Costs in U.S. Dollars

DINING AND LODGING PRICE CATEGORIES

	¢	$	$$	$$$	$$$$
Restaurants	under $5	$5–$10	$11–$15	$16–$25	over $25
Hotels	under $50	$50–$75	$76–$150	$151–$250	over $250

Restaurant prices are for one main course at dinner or for two mezes (small dishes). Hotel prices are for two people in a standard double room in high season, including taxes.

Off the Beaten Path

Undeveloped areas exist even in this region full of beaten paths. If you want to get away from the hubbub, Lake Bafa would be a good place to start. One hour north of popular Bodrum, the lake offers a peaceful place to swim and to spend time outdoors. There's a beautiful rustic resort here, the ruins at Heraklia are across the lake, and if you start to get bored, Bodrum is just a short bus ride away. Also near Bodrum, Çomakdağı is a beautiful village accessible by car. Although group tours do go there, it has only recently been discovered by locals and tourists, so you should have a pretty authentic experience. Milas and its neighboring sights would also make an enriching trip.

When to Go

July and August are the region's most crowded months. You'll have the beaches pretty much to yourself in June and September, although the water is much cooler than it is during high season. If you're interested in touring the villages and historic sites—and if you've never been to a camel-wrestling match—plan your trip from December through March, when flights and accommodations are inexpensive and camels are competing throughout the region.

GETTING HERE & AROUND

By Air

The quickest way to get to the Central and Southern Aegean is by plane. Daily flights connect Istanbul with airports in İzmir and Milas/Bodrum, and there are direct flights to İzmir and Bodrum from Ankara, Adana, and Antalya as well.

One of the most comfortable and economical ways to get to and from the İzmir and Bodrum airports to their respective downtown areas is Havaş, a modern, spacious shuttle bus service with air-conditioning. The İzmir Havas bus tickets cost about $8 one-way. The Havaş Bodrum ticket costs about $12 one-way. Taxis serve the İzmir and Bodrum airports. Bodrum's fares are known as the most expensive in Turkey, and İzmir is up there as well, so you might want to bargain before agreeing to a ride. Prices go up even more from midnight to 6 AM.

Taxis and Shuttles
Bodrum Tour (☎252/313–3009). **Havaş** (☎212/465–5656 *general, 252/444–0487 for Bodrum* ⊕ *www.havas. net*). **Havalimanı Taksi (İzmir Adnan Airport Taxi)** (☎232/274–2075). **Proper Car Rental (and Airport Transfers)** (✉*Bodrum* ☎252/316–9540 ⊕*www. propercar.com/bodrum-airport-transfer.htm*).

By Boat and Ferry

The Bodrum Ferryboat Association has ferries from Bodrum to Kos and Datça, which are right off its shores. The Bodrum Express Lines Hydrofoil and Ferryboat Services also has ferries from Bodrum to Kos, and they've recently added ferries to Rhodes, Marmaris, and Cleopatra Island from June through August. All trips run about $40 one-way. Reservations are recommended if you're bringing your car. Make sure you bring your passport for ferries to Greece.

Contacts Bodrum Express Lines (☎252/316–2309 ⊕*www.bodrumexpresslines.com*). **Bodrum Ferryboat Association** (☎252/316–0882 ⊕*www.bodrumferryboat. com/time.htm*).

By Bus

A number of bus lines serve the Aegean coast. The ride from Istanbul to İzmir takes around 9 hours, and from Istanbul to Bodrum about 12. Once you're here bus travel is a inexpensive and the towns and attractions are well served by bus, though it's slower and more restrictive than traveling by car. Major bus lines travel between İzmir, Selçuk, Kuşadası, Didyma, Milas, and Bodrum, but you'll have to rely on local, often smaller buses to travel shorter distances to and between smaller towns. Typical travel times are: İzmir to Bodrum, 3½ hours; İzmir to Çeşme, 1½ hours; İzmir to Selçuk, 1½ hours; İzmir to Kuşadası, 80 minutes; and Çeşme to Bodrum, 4½ hours.

For 10-hour-plus journeys, Varan, by far the most luxurious company, and Ulusoy are at the high end, and often make long trips at night. Kamil Koç and Boss are some other good choices. Bus companies offer more trips per day for shorter routes and during high season.

Contacts Boss (☎212/444–0880 *for general inquiries* ☎212/244–6496 *or* 212/244–6497 *Taksim-Istanbul,* 232/472–0094 *İzmir (through Çanakkale Truva office)* ⊕*www.bossturizm.com*). **Çanakkale Truva Bus Company** (☎444–0017 ⊕*www.truvaturizm.com*). **Ulusoy** (☎212/444–1888 *general reservations* ⊕*www. ulusoy.com.tr*). **Varan** (☎212/444–8999 *reservations,* 232/472–0389 *İzmir office* ⊕*www.varan.com.tr*).

By Car

A car is a plus for exploring this region, since it allows you to stop at picturesque towns and track down lesser-known ruins and less-crowded beaches. Except around İzmir, where heavy and hectic traffic requires serious concentration to keep you from getting lost, the highways are generally in good condition, the traffic fairly light, and the main attractions relatively close together. Distances are: Çanakkale to Bergama, 245 km (152 mi); Bergama to İzmir, 98 km (61 mi); İzmir to Ephesus, 79 km (49 mi); Ephesus to Bodrum, 172 km (107 mi).

Portions of the highway that runs down the Aegean coast can be beautiful, especially as you're approaching Çeşme and Bodrum. Sometimes driving within the cities themselves can be tricky, especially in Bodrum, where many important turnoffs are unmarked and many winding roads are still undeveloped. There is a long stretch of multilane highway as you head south toward Bodrum, including the toll highway from İzmir to Çeşme, but by the time you're within 100 mi of the city, single lanes going in every direction take over. Unfortunately, many people still drive as if this weren't the case, and it's common for drivers to pass, even during risky moments and around blind curves.

You're best off picking up a car once you get to the region. It's a long haul from Istanbul to İzmir—565 km (350 mi), an exhausting eight- or nine-hour drive. To make this trip, pick up Route 200 heading west toward Çanakkale. From there the E87 follows the coast south all the way to Kuşadası, where it turns inland toward Antalya. Route 525 continues along the coast, past Priene and Miletus; Route 330 branches off in Bodrum and connects with the main Mediterranean highways.

By Taxi and Dolmuş

Taxi stands, or *taksi durāı*, can be found in every major city and town and can be hailed on the street or called ahead of time; doing the latter is generally more reliable. Cab fares start at around $2 and the rates increase based on distance covered, as well as idle time spent in traffic. They're very expensive in resort towns like Çeşme and Bodrum. In areas with high taxi-to-customer ratios, or when you're traveling long distances, you should definitely use your bargaining skills. In these cases, agree to a fare ahead of time and try to give the driver the exact fare at the end of the trip (in the off-chance that he'll try to renege on your agreement and keep the change). Metered cab prices are fixed and shouldn't change based on number of passengers or pieces of luggage.

The *dolmuş* is a much more economical way to travel, especially in the resort towns. Fares range from $1 to $2 per ride and you can get dropped off anywhere along the driver's route (just say the magic words "eenejek var").

Updated by
Evin Doğu

The central and southern Aegean is a region of rolling hills, mountains surrounded by clear blue seas, and glorious white-sand beaches are just a few of the reasons why. Wandering through historic ruins, boating, scuba diving, basking in the Anatolian sun, and eating fresh fish are just some of the ways you can fill your days.

İzmir, Turkey's third-largest city, can seem very modern and industrial and some of the bigger resort areas like Kuşadasi and Bodrum attract multitudes of package tourists in the busy summer months—this is also where you'll find most of the booming nightlife that the area is becoming known for—yet there are certainly more tranquil spots to be found. Head out to some of the smaller villages, and you'll be amply rewarded.

İZMİR AND ÇEŞME

İZMİR

565 km (351 mi) south of Istanbul; 156 km (97 mi) south of Ayvaık.

GETTING AROUND

While in Izmir, you can travel around by bus or metro (the latter is not very extensive, but plans are underway to extend the route) or bus. The fare is 2 TL per ride.

Taxis are more expensive than in other Turkish cities like Istanbul and Ankara, because they're less in demand, but they're widely available.

ESSENTIALS

Taxi Info **29 Ağustos Taksi (İzmir)** (☎ *232/422–1958*). **Bostanlı Taksi (İzmir)** (☎ *232/362–0300*). **Üçkuyular Terminal Taksi (İzmir)** (☎ *232/278–1538*).

Travel Agencies/Tour operators **Omega Tur** (✉ *Mithatpaşa Cad. 146–148, Karataş, 35260, İzmir* ☎ *232/489–1450–489*). **Ti Amo** (✉ *Gaziosmanpaşa Bulvarı 6/A Alsancak, 35210, İzmir* ☎ *232/446–5060* ⊕ *www.tiamotur.com.tr*).

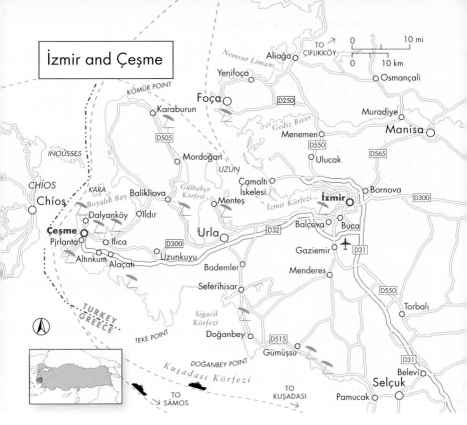

İzmir and Çeşme

TO ÇİFLİKKÖY

0   10 mi
0   10 km

Nemrut Limanı
Aliağa
Yenifoça
Osmançali
KÖMÜR POINT
Foça
D250
Karaburun
Muradiye
Gediz River
Menemen
Manisa
D505
Mordoğan
D550
UZUN
Ulucak
D565
INOÙSSES
Çamaltı
İskelesi
CHÍOS
KARA
Balikliova
Gülbahçe
Körfezi
Bornova
Chíos
Boyalık Bay
Mentes
İzmir Körfezi
İzmir
D300
Dalyanköy
Olldır
Balçova
Buca
Çeşme
Ilıca
Urla
D32
Pirlanta
D300
Gaziemir
D31
Altınkum
Alaçatı
Uzunkuyu
Menderes
Bademler
D550
Seferihisar
Torbalı
TURKEY
GREECE
Sigacil
Körfezi
D31
TEKE POINT
Doğanbey
D515
Belevi
Gümüşsu
Selçuk
DOĞANBEY POINT
Kuşadası Körfezi
TO
KUŞADASI
Pamucak
TO
SÁMOS

Visitor Information (✉Akdeniz Mah., 1344 Sokak 2, Pasaport ☎232/ 483–5117)

EXPLORING

At first glance, this large city on the Gulf of İzmir surrounded by mountains seems modern and industrial—it's the site of many trade expositions and home to NATO's Southeast headquarters—and appears to be more of a hub than a vacation destination.

İzmir may not have immediate appeal, but if you take a few days to explore, you'll come to appreciate the diverse architecture, fascinating ruins, and interesting museums that give the city its edge. Despite the rapid growth of the past few decades, navigating İzmir is still manageable and pleasant. Interconnected piazzas and pedestrian-friendly walkways help ease your travels around the city. You can happily spend a day or two walking along the waterfront promenade, taking time to learn about the city's 7,000-year history, shopping in the outdoor bazaar, or discovering the old churches, synagogues, and other buildings scattered throughout the city are, and there is a lively café culture. The city is also a good base for exploring the southern Aegean region, and there are many outdoor activities nearby—among them bird-watching, skiing, and trekking.

CLOSE UP

History of İzmir

Turkey's third-largest city, with a population of 2 million, İzmir was called Smyrna until 1923. A vital trading port, though one often ravaged by wars and earthquakes, it also had its share of glory. Many believe that Homer was born in Old Smyrna sometime around 850 BC. Alexander the Great favored this city with a citadel atop its highest hill.

İzmir fell into assorted hands after the Romans, starting with the Byzantines and Arabs. From 1097 on, it was a battlefield in the Crusades, passing back and forth between Muslims and Christians. Destroyed and restored successively by Byzantines and Seljuks, Smyrna was held by the Knights of Rhodes in 1402 when the Mongol raider Tamerlane came along, sacked it yet again, and slaughtered its inhabitants. Thirteen years later Sultan Mehmet I Çelebi incorporated it into the Ottoman Empire.

Toward the end of the 15th century, Jews driven from Spain settled in Smyrna, forming a lasting Sephardic community. By the 18th and 19th centuries Smyrna had become a successful, sophisticated commercial port with an international flavor. Its business community included a sizable number of Jews, Italians, Greeks, Armenians, British, and French. This era came to an end with World War I, when Ottoman Turkey allied itself with Germany. In 1918 the Greek army, encouraged by the British and French, landed at the harbor and claimed the city. The occupation lasted until 1922, when Turkish troops under Atatürk defeated the Greek forces and forced them to evacuate. On September 9, 1922, Atatürk made a triumphant entry into the port. The joy of the local Turks was short-lived; a fire shortly thereafter blazed through the city. Fanned by the wind, it burned wooden houses like matches while hidden stores of munitions exploded.

The city was quickly rebuilt—and given the Turkish name İzmir. Like the name, much of the city dates from the '20s, from its wide boulevards to the office buildings and apartment houses painted in bright white or soft pastels. This important industrial center is not particularly pretty, though it has a harborfront promenade and peaceful green Kültür Parkı at its center.

WHAT TO SEE

❶ The sweeping view of the city and its harbor from the windy restored ramparts of the **Kadifekale** *(Velvet Fortress)*, built by Alexander the Great, make this a good spot to orient yourself to İzmir. The name, according to romantics (if not to scholars), alludes to the resemblance of the present-day citadel's walls to rubbed velvet. Rebuilt after various mishaps, and enlarged and strengthened by successive conquerors, the structure looks like a childhood fantasy of a medieval castle, with solid stone blocks (some dating from Alexander's day), Byzantine cisterns, and Ottoman buttresses jutting out to support the walls. ⚠ Locals will warn you (especially women) against going to the Kadifekale alone for fear of being hassled or harassed. The site is near a run-down neighborhood, so to be on the safe side, you may want to go with a guide.

2 The **agora** at the foot of Kadifekale
Hill, just off 816 Sokak (816 Street),
was the Roman city's market. The
present site is a large, dusty, open
space surrounded by ancient columns and foundations. Part has
been closed off for excavations, but
there's still much to see, including

PLANNING AHEAD

Museum opening hours in İzmir
can vary depending on the season.
Always confirm a museum's hours
beforehand.

the well-preserved Roman statues of Poseidon, Artemis, and Demeter
in the northwest corner. To get here from Kadifekale, exit from the fortress's main gate and take the road that descends to the left; when you
see steps built into the sidewalk, turn right and go down. ⊠*Namazgah,
Anafartalar Cad.* ⚄*$1.50* ⊙*Daily 8:30–noon and 1–5.*

10 North of the museum is the neighborhood of **Alsancak.** Now a trendy
spot for İzmir's "high society," during Ottoman times, the neighborhood was predominantly Jewish and Christian, and there are still a
number of synagogues and churches in the area. The pretty two- and
three-story Levantine houses with bay windows are tucked away in
some of the backstreets, which perk up at night with the influx of young
İzmirians drawn to the quaint cafés, bars, and restaurants.

3 The **Arkeoloji Müzesi** *(Archaeology Museum)* contains the 2nd-century
statues of Demeter and Poseidon found when the agora was excavated,
as well as an impressive collection of tombs and friezes and the memorable, colossal statue of the Roman emperor Domitian (AD 51–96,
ruled 81–96). ⊠*Cumhuriyet Bul., Bahribaba Parkı* ☎*232/489–0796*
⚄*$2.50* ⊙*Tues.–Sun. 8:30–5:30.*

4 The **Etnoğrafya Müzesi** *(İzmir Ethnographic Museum),* across the street
from the Archaeology Museum, focuses on folk arts and daily life,
housing everything from period bedrooms to a reconstruction of İzmir's
first pharmacy. ⊠*Cumhuriyet Bul., Bahribaba Parkı* ☎*232/489–0796*
⚄*$2.50* ⊙*Tues.–Sun. 8:30–5:30.*

The **Homa Lagoon (Homa Dalyani)** (☎*232/482–1218),* also known as
kuş cenneti (bird heaven), is a nature reserve protected by the Ministry
of Culture on the Gediz Delta, on the north shore of İzmir Bay near
Çamaltı and a great day trip out of the city. The delta's lagoons, mud-
flats, salt marshes, reed beds, and farmland provide diverse habitats to
more than 230 species of birds, mammals, reptiles, and fish. Tours of
the lagoon can be taken by car or by foot—all tours start at the visitor
center and are free. Unfortunately, few of the staff members at the visitor center speak English. You'll need a car to get here, or you might be
able to hire a taxi for the trip.

8 Just South of the Kültür Parkı is the **İzmir Ahmet Piristina City Archive
and Museum,** a 7,000-year chronicle of the city's history through colorful posters with informative descriptions in English and Turkish. The
museum, housed in the old fire station, has a special section dedicated
to the history of İzmir's multiple fires and its fire brigade. ⊠*Şair Eşref
Bul. 1/A, Çankaya* ☎*232/441–6178* ⚄*Free* ⊙*Daily 9–6.*

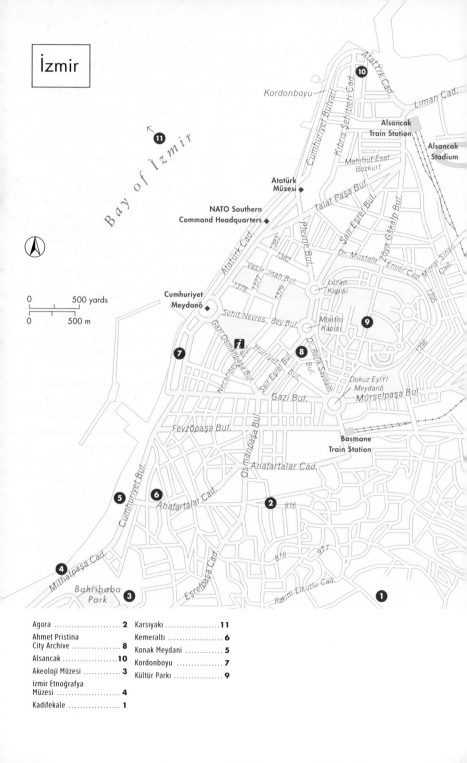

İzmir

Bay of İzmir

Kordonboyu

Alsancak
Train Station

Alsancak
Stadium

Atatürk
Müzesi

NATO Southern
Command Headquarters

Cumhuriyet
Meydanó

Lozan
Kapisi

Montró
Kapisi

Dokuz EylÝl
Meydanó

Basmane
Train Station

Bahríbaba
Park

0   500 yards

0   500 m

⑪ Karsıyaka, the area known as "Opposite Shore" in Turkish, is the purported birthplace of the poet Homer, and was the residence of one of Turkey's most famous contemporary poets, Attila Ilhan. For years, it was a tranquil summer resort for İzmir high society, but has expanded to accommodate İzmir's growing population. On a hot summer day, the 20-minute ferry from Konak to Karsıyaka is a great way to cool off, and once you're here, you can walk along the commercial strip, İzmir's version of Istanbul's İstiklal Caddesi in Taksim. Try some İzmir *lokma* (sweet Turkish donut holes) for which the district is famous. You can catch the ferry at Konak's quay; tickets cost around $1.

⑥ Konak Meydanı marks the start of the modern-day marketplace, **Kemeralt,** a maze of tiny streets filled with shops, covered stalls, and around Fevzipaşa Bulvarı street, cafés and eateries. Anafartalar Caddesi is the bazaar's principal thoroughfare, but try the smaller side streets, too, where you'll find minimarkets dedicated to musical instruments, songbirds, leather, beads, jewelry, and many other treats. Go farther into Kemeralt, and you'll wind up at the **Kestane Pazarı,** a miniature version of Istanbul's Spice Bazaar, which has a decent selection of spices, tea and coffee, fabric stores, and a whole slew of confectioners.

The Hisar Mosque, beyond the bazaar, is the largest and oldest in İzmir, and the nearby **Kızlarağası Hanı** is an 18th-century, recently restored Ottoman kervansaray that houses many vaulted shops that sell quality, although sometimes expensive, Turkish goods like purses, jewelry, miniatures, and rugs.

NEED A BREAK? Making your way through Kemeralt can be exhausting. Stop by Ömer Usta Kahveci (⊠ *905 Sokak 15, Hisar Cami Back Entrance* ☎ *232/425–4706*) for a shot of Turkish coffee brewed in the cup. The atmosphere is pleasant and lively, and if you're traveling during the summer, there are plenty of shaded areas to keep you cool. Be aware that the cups can be scalding hot.

⑤ Konak Meydanı *(Konak Square)*, at the water's edge, is one of the city's two main squares (the other, Cumhuriyet Meydanı, or Republic Square, is to the north along Atatürk Cad.). The **Saat Kulesi** (clock tower) stands out at the center of the plaza, with its ornate, late-Ottoman design. The tower was built in honor of Sultan Abdulhamid in 1901, and the clock itself was sent as a gift from Kaiser Wilhelm II. The small, 18th-century single-domed **Konak Yalı Mosque,** set back from the clock tower, is decorated with colorful tiles and was built by Mehmet Paşa's daughter, Ayşe.

⑦ The **Kordonboyu** *(Cordon)*, the waterfront promenade, is the most fashionable section of town. It starts at the museum complex in **Bahribaba Parkı** and stretches north along the busy harbor, past Konak Meydanı, NATO's Southern Command headquarters, and the small **Atatürk Müzesi** *(Atatürk Museum* ⊠ *Atatürk Cad., Alsancak 248* ☎ *232/421–7026* ⊗ *Tues.–Sun. 8:30–noon and 1–5)*, housed in a pale yellow Levantine building that was originally a house presented to Atatürk as a gift. Along the strip are several good seafood restaurants, all with a few tables outside overlooking the water. You can tour the area ($15 per

A horse-drawn carriage can take you on a tour of İznik's Kordonboyu, the waterfront promenade. Photo by eerkun, Fodors.com member.

ride) by *fayton* (horse-drawn carriages); carriages are stationed in the Cumhuriyet Meydani area of the Kordon.

❾ Kültür Parkı, İzmir's central park, has gardens, a zoo (which will soon be moving to another area), amusement rides, and nightclubs. The park is the site of a major industrial fair from late August to late September. **İzmir Tarih ve Sanat Müzesi** (*İzmir's History and Art Museum*), also in the Kültür Parkı, is a modern compound made up of three buildings showcasing stone objects, ceramic objects, and precious artifacts. The jewelry in the precious artifacts exhibit dates from Hellenistic, Roman, and Byzantine periods. ⊠ *Museum: East of Lozan and Montrö Meyds.* ☎ *232/445-7876* ⊟ *$3* ⊙ *Tues.–Sun. 8:30–5:30.*

WHERE TO EAT

$-$$
FISH
✕ **Balık Pişiricisi Veli.** One of the Kordonboyusm—the waterfront's—many fish restaurants, this one is popular with families and groups of friends alike. The fish, as well as the salads, are seasonal, so you'll always get fresh pickings. Calamari comes either fried or grilled with an old bay seasoning style sauce. The friendly, jovial setting and prompt service are also noteworthy. ⊠ *Atatürk Cad. 212-A 1. Kordon, Alsancak* ☎ *232/464-8090* ⊟ *AE, MC, V.*

$
TURKISH
✕ **Can Döner.** Set at the Saat Kulesii entrance of Kemeraltii, this small *döner* restaurant serves gyro meat Bursa style—in thin, as opposed to chunky, slices. The melted butter and tomato sauce—both high quality—on top of the İskender make this dish the one to try at Can Döner, with a glass of homemade *ayran* (Turkish yogurt drink). The wooden interior make the place feel cozy. ⊠ *Milli Kütüphane Cad. 9 Konak* ☎ *232/484-1313* ⊟ *MC, V.*

$$ ✕**Deniz.** Befitting its bayside location, the main event in this attractive
FISH spot on the ground floor of the İzmir Palas Hotel is the seafood. *Kılıç*
şiş (grilled swordfish kebab) is a house specialty and locals and tourists
alike flock to this popular spot for the *sutlu balik*, or milky fish, which
takes its strange name from its soft and succulent texture. ⊠*Atatürk*
Cad. 188/B, Alsancak ☎*232/422–0601* ▤*DC, MC, V.*

$$ ✕**Koşebaşı.** At this large kebab house, you can savor your kebab from
TURKISH one of the many tables overlooking İzmir's expansive gulf and cascade
★ of mountains. To begin choose from one of the tray full of mezes or start
with a warm, mini *lahmacun* (a thin Turkish pizza). The Beyti kebab,
ground beef and lamb wrapped in thin lavash, served with yogurt, is
hearty and tasty. The tender cubes of meat spiced with oregano are also
particularly flavorful. Note that it'll take a rental car or very expensive
taxi ride to get here. ⊠*Çeşme Çevreyolu, Limontepe Mevkii, Balçova*
☎*232/278–2806* ▤*AE, MC, V.*

¢ ✕**Reyhan Pastanesi.** This patisserie and café in the heart of Alsancak
TURKISH is a favorite among İzmir's denizens. Reyhan is a great place to go for
breakfast or dessert—traditional Turkish baked treats and chocolates
are available as well as Western-style sweets like cheesecake, and an
excellent carrot cake. ⊠*Mustafa Bey Cad. 24* ☎*232/422–2802* ▤*AE,*
MC, V.

$ ✕**Tarihi Kemeraltı Lokantası.** This small, inexpensive eatery is a great place
TURKISH to stop for lunch after exploring the Kemeraltı bazaar. Its main draws
are delicious, coal-fired döner (gyro meat) and traditional Turkish daily
specials. The outside tables are great people-watching. ⊠*Anafartalar*
Cad. 47/A, Veysel Çıkmaz Kemeraltı ☎*232/425–5393 or 232/425–*
5990 ▤*AE, MC, V.*

WHERE TO STAY

$$ ▦**Antikhan.** Rooms in this 200-year-old building in Basmane, one of
İzmir's oldest neighborhoods, surround a pretty courtyard with a large
lemon tree and have low beds and hardwood floors. It's an ideal spot
for travelers looking for a more bohemian, local setting. Kemeraltı
bazaar and the agora are nearby, and the surrounding neighborhood
is quiet and interesting. **Pros:** rooms have nice character; close prox-
imity to tourist sites. **Cons:** a not much going on in the neighborhood
itself. ⊠*Anafartalar Cad. 600, Çankaya,* ☎*232/489–2750* ⊕*www.*
otelantikhan.com ⤵*30 rooms* ⟳*In-room: minibar, Wi-Fi. In-hotel:*
restaurant, bar ▤*AE, MC, V.*

$ ▦**Hotel Baylan.** Rooms spread over four stories are bright, pleasant,
and a good size, with nondescript Scandinavian-style furniture. Views
are over a busy street or parking lot, but rooms are quiet and within an
easy walk of the center. **Pros:** quiet despite the busy area; decent-sized
rooms. **Cons:** old-fashioned decor and ambience; rooms look out onto
a parking lot or the street. ⊠*Anafartalar Cad., Basmane, 1299 Sokak*
8, ☎*232/483–0152* ⊕*www.hotelbaylan.com* ⤵*33 rooms* ⟳*In-hotel:*
restaurant, bar, parking ▤*MC, V.*

$$ ▦**Hotel Kilim.** A central location in the fashionable Kordon neighborhood and modern, bright decor are among the many appealing features
of this hotel, but best of all are the bay and harbor views from most
rooms. Ask for a room on a higher floor, as those close to the street can

be noisy. The somewhat nondescript restaurant Gümüs has sidewalk tables overlooking the harbor in good weather. **Pros:** views; only one floor of the hotel is smoking; good value. **Cons:** small rooms. ⊠*Kazim Dirik Cad. 1, Atatürk Blv.,* ☎*232/484–5340* ⊕*www.kilimotel.com.tr* ⤳*75 rooms* ⌂*In-room: safe. In-hotel: restaurant, bar* ⊟*MC, V.*

$$$ ⌂**Karaca Otel.** Attention to detail stands out in every corner, from the fireplace in the lounge and free in-house cinema to the dark-wood furnishing in the guest rooms. There are live music performances on occasion. **Pros:** helpful staff; smaller and more intimate than many luxury hotels; hotel's cinema is free for guests. **Cons:** ceilings are a bit low; rooms are a little overpriced; there are only a few nonsmoking rooms. ⊠*Necatibey Blv. 1379 Sokak 55 Alsancak* ☎*232/489–1940* ⊕*www. otelkaraca.com.tr* ⤳*73* ⌂*In-room: minibar, Wi-Fi. In-hotel: restaurant, bar* ⊟*AE, MC, V.*

$$$ ⌂**Swiss Hotel–Grand Efes.** Formerly İzmir's Efes Hotel, a recent renovation brings more luxury to the Alsancak/Kordon neighborhood. Rooms are spacious, bright, and beautifully furnished, and many have sea views. **Pros:** many amenities and extra niceties; centrally located in İzmir's Alsancak neighborhood, only a few minutes away from the waterfront promenade. **Cons:** pricey; the hotel is quite large and not very intimate. ⊠*Gaziosmanpaşa Blv. 1 Alsancak 35210* ☎*232/414–0000* ⊕*www.izmir.swissotel.com* ⤳*347 rooms, 55 suites* ⌂*In-room: minibar, Wi-Fi. In-hotel: tennis court, pool, spa* ⊟*AE, MC, V.*

NIGHTLIFE AND THE ARTS

The **State Ballet and Opera House** (⊠*Milli Kütüphane Cad.* ☎*232/484–3692 or 232/484–6445*) offers dance performances, chamber music, and pop and jazz concerts. Tickets can be purchased at the theater on the day of the performance. For outdoor classical music concerts, check out the open-air theater in **Kültür Parkı. The International İzmir Film Festival** takes place in June and July; however, many of the screenings are actually held at Ephesus or Çeşme Castle. The İzmir Foundation for Culture and Arts has festival information on their Web site (⊕*www.iksv.org*). Tickets are usually available at the İzmir Hilton and the State Ballet and Opera House box office.

Rain (⊠*1649 Sokak 79, Karşıyaka* ☎*232/372–2929*) is İzmir's new seaside dining-and-entertainment complex—it has four restaurants (each with its own bar and cuisine), a coffeehouse, and a glamorous nightclub called **En Velo** with a dance floor and DJs that spin club music.

Alsancak has a colorful, lively nightlife and an assortment of bars. **Eko Pub** (⊠*Plevne Bul. 1, Alsancak* ☎*232/421–4459*) is popular with the expatriate and twentysomething crowd. Gazi Kadınlar Sokaği is a great street to check out in general, full of cafés and attractive Levantine homes. For a good beer and a more alternative crowd, head to **Sardunya** (⊠*Muzaffer İzgü Sokak, Alsancak* ☎*232/421–3318*) on one of Alsancak's popular streets, Kıbrıs Şehitleri. For live jazz music, try **Blue.**

SPORTS AND THE OUTDOORS

The most well-known area for hiking and skiing is the 120-km (75-mi) stretch between the Gediz and the Küçük Menderes rivers. **Mount Bozdağ** is 45 km (28 mi) from İzmir. You'll need a car to get there, but the trip is well worth it.

HIKING Summer is a great time for hiking Mount Bozdağ's slopes, with cool, crisp air providing refuge from the city's suffocating heat.

For a less strenuous trip, set out to Gölcük, where there are smaller hills and a beautiful lake ideal for picnics. To get to Gölcük via public transportation, take a bus from İzmir's terminal to Ödemiş; the trip takes about three hours. From Ödemiş, you can get a dolmuş to Gölcük from the corner of Hatay and Namik Kemal streets, near the Ödemiş bus terminal.

SKIING For ski enthusiasts, Mount Bozdağ's 2.16-km-high (1.34-mi-high) summit is a good place to start. Take the chairlift to the top and ski or trek back down (a 2½-hour journey). For less experienced skiers, there are two shorter slopes as well. The pistes are ready for skiers as early as November, when they're covered with artificial snow. The ski resort at Büyük Çavdar, 7 km (4 mi) from the village, has two hotels, as well as bungalows for rent.

SHOPPING

For high-end, brand-name, and designer clothing, the Alsancak neighborhood has it all. In addition, check out the Wednesday **Bostanlı bazaar** in Karşıyakı. It's known for its good-quality, inexpensive clothes. The earlier you go, the better the selection. There's rumor that it might close down, so check before you go.

Dösim (✉ *Cumhuriyet Bulvarı 115, Alsancak* ☎232/483–0789) is run by Turkey's Ministry of Culture. In addition to selling Turkish handicrafts, Dösim preserves and promotes Turkish heritage by maintaining traditional art forms and practices. The fixed prices are very reasonable, and the quality is top-notch.

For a reliable carpet store, check out **Gallery Cetiz** (✉ *Kızlarağası Hanı*), run by the Cetiz family for three generations. Father and son work together and have a wide selection of Turkish kilims and antique and modern Turkish carpets, sold with a certificate of authenticity. Many of the store's workshops are located on the top floor, where you can sit and have a well-prepared cup of Turkish coffee at Acı Kahve overlooking the courtyard of the kervansaray where the shop is housed.

THE WRATH OF ARTEMIS

Artemis, goddess of fertility, was furious when Ares' son, Tmolos, fell in love with the water nymph Arriepe. Angered that a mortal would have the audacity to set his sights this high and blemish the human-divine divide, Artemis sent a bull to trample him to death, with success. Tmolos's son buried his father on the summit of Bozdağ, which subsequently became known as Tmolos.

4

ÇEŞME

81 km (50 mi) west of İzmir on Rte. 300.

GETTING HERE AND AROUND

Çeşme Seyhat Bus Company is the sole bus company for traveling between İzmir and Çeşme. During the summer, buses leave every 20 to 45 minutes or so, often until around 9 PM. Reservations are recommended and especially important for the return trip to İzmir. Tickets cost around $8 one-way and can be bought either at the *otogar* stand or on the bus, in cash.

For getting around the peninsula, most of the coves and bays are accessible by dolmuş, which depart near the entrance of Çeşme's main street and from the tourist office every 30 minutes or when full. Çeşme serves as the main hub, and you may have to make a transfer here if you're traveling from one outlying cove to the other. Dolmuşes cost around $2 per ride; they run less frequently in the off-season.

ESSENTIALS

Bus Info Çeşme Seyahat Bus Company (☎ 232/712–6499 or 232/712–0858 Çeşme central station, 232/472–0051 İzmir central station ⊕ www.cesmeseyahat. com).

EXPLORING

Çeşme, originally a local beach getaway for İzmirians, has now also become a popular summer destination for Istanbul's elite. Despite rapid development, much of the town retains its provincial feel, even if you have to sometimes travel off the beaten path to find it. The location leaves the town exposed to constant winds, making it a hot spot for surfing and windsurfing.

Çeşme is on a bay encircled by small towns that are becoming destinations unto themselves, most of which have better stretches of beach than Çeşme proper. Dalyan is on the northernmost tip of the bay, while the surfer's paradise, Alaçatı, is southeast of Çeşme proper. Ilıca, directly south of Alaçatı, is Çeşme's most popular (and closest) neighboring beach town and the first one you'll arrive at if coming from Izmir.

WHAT TO SEE

The 14th-century **Genoese castle** is very picturesque, with its stone walls lined with sun-basking lizards and its keep often deep in wildflowers. The castle's museum displays weaponry from the glory days of the Ottoman Empire. ☜$2 ⊙ Daily 8:30–11:45 and 1–5:15.

Ayios Haralambos is a large old Greek basilica named after a patron saint. It's worth taking a look at the facade as you stroll down the main street of Çeşme's shopping district. The space is now used as a cultural center that hosts art exhibitions and chess tournaments. ⊠ Inkilap Cad.

BEACHES

The beaches that span 29 km (18 mi) of Çeşme's coastline are the main reason people come here. Each beach has its own distinctive ambience, and you can access most by minibus or dolmuş (to get out to more secluded areas, it helps to have a car). Despite high winds, the aquamarine water is often still and calm, and you can often see to the bottom.

Cesme's beaches attract vacationers from all over the world.

The public beach areas are more crowded and unkempt, so it is often worth paying the $5 to $10 per person to secure a spot with a chaise longue and umbrella. Swimming season starts in April and continues until mid-November—the most popular months are July and August.

Ilıca, once a summer retreat for İzmir's wealthy, fronts one of the peninsula's most popular beaches, with many hotels lined up along the crystal clear water and white sand. It's only 5 km (3 mi) from Çeşme, and dolmuşes leave every half hour or when full. The town has a lot of shops, and is known for its *kumru* (literally translated as "dove" in Turkish), a Turkish-style panini of grilled *kaşar* cheese, *sucuk* (a spicy, Turkish beef sausage), and salami stuffed inside a sesame-seed bread made with chickpea yeast.

Boyalık Bay, slightly west of Ilıca, is on Ayayorgi beach, popular with those who like the beach bar scene. The rest of Boyalık bay is calmer, and you can take a a minibus or cab to quieter beaches.

Alaçatı, a pretty village 2 km (1 mi) south of Ilıca, is very popular in the evening, when its cosmopolitan cafés, restaurants, boutiques, and high-end *pansiyons* serve the hip, urbanite crowd. To avoid the hubbub, spend an afternoon in Alaçatı, when only locals and storeowners are around; buses serving the town leave every half hour from both Ilıca and Çeşme.

The beach at Alaçatı, 2 km (1 mi) south of town, is a prime windsurfing spot, with strong winds and few waves. Disappointingly, there is only a small, public beach here. The water is cooler than it is at other beaches, and the attitude is also a bit frostier. Go for the dozen or so water sports available, including water-skiing, banana boat rides, and windsurfing. At Babylon, a popular summer-only jazz club, you can lay out on wooden decks that extend out over the water and attend concerts at night.

Dalyanköy, 5 km (3 mi) north of Çeşme, is a small fishing village, known for the excellent seafood restaurants that line the small harbor. The beaches are not that noteworthy, so save your trip out here for the evening, when you can wine and dine by the water.

About 5 km (3 mi) south of Çeşme, out along Akburun (White Cape) near the village of Çiflikköy, are several nice stretches and numerous unnamed coves. For lots of waves and wind, try **Pirlanta** beach, just outside of Çiflik to the southwest. The beach has a small section reserved for kiteboarding and another for the public, which is, unfortunately, usually littered with cigarette butts. For a cleaner space, you can rent two chaises and an umbrella for around $7. For lunch, your options are limited to a few beachside cafés. **Altınkum** is a bit farther south of Çiflik, and has calmer, gorgeous water. There is a campsite and a Fun Club, where you can rent kayaks and windsurfers. To steer clear from the crowds, head east along the sand.

WHERE TO EAT

$$ ✕ **Cafe Agrilia.** This Italian restaurant in an old tobacco warehouse was
ITALIAN   around long before the rest of Alaçatı's trendy restaurants came on the
Fodor'sChoice   scene. The homemade tagliatelle with shrimp in a light, garlic sauce is
★   fantastic, and Agrilia also makes creative fresh fruit juice concoctions. ⊠*Kemal Paşa Cad. 75, Alaçatı* ☎*232/716–8594* ⊟*AE, MC, V.*

$$$ ✕ **Cevat'ın Yeri.** An upscale, elegant fish restaurant overlooking Dalyan
TURKISH   bay's marina is an ideal place to spend a summer evening. The menu
★   includes traditional mezes and fresh fish, and all dishes are prepared with attention to taste and presentation. The *gevurdağ* salad is a spicy mix of tomato and onion, and the fresh, crispy calamari with home-made tartar sauce is perfectly cooked. ⊠*Liman Cad., Dalyanköy* ☎*232/724–7045* ⊟*AE, MC, V.*

$ ✕ **Dost Pide.** A great, quick option for lunch, this place has been a local
TURKISH   favorite for 30 years. The specialty is super-long, closed *pides* (Turkish-style calzones), a specialty of the Black Sea region. ⊠*Şifne Cad. 27, Ilıca* ☎*232/723–2059* ⊟*AE, MC, V.*

¢   ✕ **Kumrucu Sevki.** Ilıca has the best *kumru* (Turkish-style panini) around
TURKISH   and Kumrucu Sevki serves the best in town. The sandwich goes well with a bottle of Eker *ayran,* a refreshing yogurt drink. ⊠*Çeşme Ilıca Merkez, Ilıca* ☎*232/723–2392* ⊟*AE, D, MC, V.*

¢   ✕ **L'Apero.** This hilltop café is a perfect place to enjoy an aperitif while
TURKISH   watching the sun set over Dalyan harbor. You might find yourself back
★   at this charming little spot for after-dinner drinks, and light sand-wiches and tasty desserts are served also. ⊠*4227 Sokak, Dalyanköy* ☎*232/724–7034* ⊟*AE, MC, V.*

$$ ✕ **Sahil.** This waterfront eatery across from the Ertan Hotel serves fresh,
TURKISH   tasty appetizers and typical Turkish dishes like lamb kebabs and grilled fish. The terrace has a pleasant but unremarkable view of the bay of Çeşme. Reservations are essential in summer. ⊠*Cumhuriyet Meyd. 12, Çeşme* ☎*232/712–8294* ⊟*MC, V.*

$ ✕**Sevim Café.** The location on a
TURKISH busy corner is less than appealing, but such dishes as the *mantı*
(meat-filled ravioli topped with garlicky yogurt) are delicious, as are
the grilled meats served with salad
on the side. Come early for a good
seat. ✉*Hal Binası 5, opposite Kervansaray, Çeşme* ☎*232/712–9647*
▤*AE, MC, V.*

SWEET SPOT

For dessert, try local favorite **Imren**
(✉*Tokoğlu Mah. Kemalpaşa Cad.,
Alaçatı* ☎*232/716–8356*), where
ice cream comes in many different
flavors, and is served in a homemade waffle cone. *Sakız muhallebe*
is a Turkish gumdrop pudding.

$$ ✕**Yıldız Restaurant.** Yıldız is a good
TURKISH option for a good and reasonably priced lunch in Alaçatı, where pric-
es are skyrocketing. The family-owned spot serves homemade mantı,
Turkish meatballs, and other daily specials. The cool breeze and friendly
service are also a plus. ✉*Kemalpaşa Cad. 51, Alaçatı* ☎*232/716–8090*
▤*AE, MC, V.*

WHERE TO STAY

The prices of most hotels in beach towns peak during the busy sum-
mer months of July and August. Prices drop before and after this time,
and hotels will usually adjust prices for guests staying longer than one
week.

ALAÇATI

$$$ ☖**Alaçatı Beach Resort.** Right on the beach and built of attractive Alaçatı
stone, this small resort is a terribly attractive and quiet getaway. All the
nicely furnished rooms have balconies and well-equipped stone bathrooms, and many clubs and attractions are nearby, though the center is
some distance away. **Pros:** many other activities nearby like windsurfing school, water sports clubs, the jazz club Babylon, and the Alaçatı
windsurf and sailing club. **Cons:** you'll need your own transportation
to visit Alaçatı's center. ✉*Çark Plajı, Liman Mevkii Alaçatı, 35950*
☎*232/716–6161* ⊕*www.alacati.com* ⤶*41 rooms* ⌂*In-room: Wi-Fi.
In-hotel: restaurant, bar, beachfront, tennis courts, pool* ▤*MC, V.*

$$ ☖**Sailors.** The sunny, beautifully decorated rooms smell of fresh pine,
and breakfast is served in the garden at your leisure, beneath pomegran-
ate and jasmine trees. The restaurant, Orta Kahve, offers an excellent
lunch and dinner menu that includes brick-oven pizzas. The beach is a
short bus or dolmuş ride away. **Pros:** rooms are beautifully decorated;
activities such as yoga, pottery, and jewelry design are available. **Cons:**
you'll need transportation to get to the beach. ✉*75 Yıl Cad. Esen
Sokak* ☎*232/716–8765* ⊕*www.sailorsotel.com* ⤶*6 rooms* ⌂*In-
room: Wi-Fi. In-hotel: restaurant* ▤*AE, MC, V.*

$$ ☖**Sakızlı Han.** The restored stone house of a wealthy 19th-century family offers all of the modern amenities with country-style ambience. The
reception area is a pleasant living room. **Pros:** breakfast is served until
noon in a beautiful courtyard garden. **Cons:** you'll need to take some
form of transportation to get to the beach. ✉*Yeni Mecidiye, Mah.
Kemalpaşa Cad. 114* ☎*232/716–6108* ⊕*www.sakizlihan.com* ⤶*8
rooms* ⌂*In-room: no a/c (some), Wi-Fi* ▤*MC, V.*

BOYALIK

$$$ ☒ **HarmoniOtel.** Small but charming rooms open to a little garden, where you can sit among the olive trees and where breakfast is served—this includes such treats as homemade *gözleme* (a Turkish-style crepe), natural honey, and eggs made to order. Some rooms look out to the sea, and the beach is about a five-minute walk away. **Pros:** peaceful atmosphere; delicious food. **Cons:** not right on the beach. ☒ *Gaziosmanpaşa 1, Alsancak* ☏ *232/712–8037 or 232/712–8165* ⊕ *www.harmonibutikotel.com* ⤳ *8 rooms* ⌂ *In-hotel: bar, swimming pool* ▤ *AE, MC, V.*

ÇEŞME

$$ ✕☒ **Kervansaray.** Built in 1528 during the reign of Süleyman the Mag-
★   nificent, this old inn next to Çeşme's medieval castle is decorated in traditional Turkish style, with kilims and low wooden furniture. The in-house restaurant is excellent and in good weather serves in the stone courtyard, surrounded by the ancient stone walls of the Kervansaray; good choices include lamb kebabs with yogurt, cold eggplant salad, and *börek* (deep-fried pastry shells, here filled with goat cheese. **Pros:** historic setting; authentic look and feel. **Cons:** you have to travel to get to a decent beach. ☒ *Kale Yanı* ☏ *232/712–7177 or 232/712–6491* 🖷 *232/712–2906* ⤳ *34 rooms* ⌂ *In-hotel: restaurant, bar* ▤ *AE, DC, MC, V* ⊗ *Closed Nov.–Mar.*

$$ ☒ **Pasifik.** About a 15-minute walk along the waterfront from Çeşme's main square ensures nighttime quiet, though the adjacent beaches are crowded and noisy during the day. Bright, modern rooms have sea views, and the restaurant is well-known for its fresh fish. **Pros:** relatively new, so everything looks very modern and clean; recommended by locals, their restaurant offers fresh fish selections. **Cons:** you'll have to drive or take a public form of transportation to access some of Çeşme's nicer beaches. ☒ *3264 Sokak Tekke Plajı Mevkii 16* ☏ *232/712–2700* ⊕ *www.pasifikotel.com* ⤳ *16 rooms* ⌂ *In-hotel: restaurant.* ▤ *AE, MC, V.*

DALYANKÖY

$$$$ ✕☒ **Dalyan Plaza Hotel.** A private beach, pool, and several restaurants
Fodor's Choice   ensure that you never need to leave this lovely resort. Spacious rooms
★   are full of light, with cool tile floors and guests gather can relax on the terrace where there's an outdoor bar. The hotel also has its own private beach. **Pros:** with several restaurants, you can choose between Aegean, French, and Italian cuisines, and Dalyan's seafood restaurants are within walking distance. **Cons:** without a car, it'll be difficult to travel to the other coves. ☒ *Dalyan Mahallesi, 4227 Sokak 26,* ☏ *232/724–8000* 🖷 *232/724–9252* ⤳ *46 rooms, 10 suites* ⌂ *In-hotel: 3 restaurants, bar, pool, gym* ▤ *AE, MC, V.*

$ ☒ **L'Apero.** There are just two large, tastefully decorated rooms at this small *pansiyon*, one with a kitchen. Either way, you'll get the hospitality of the friendly English-speaking owner, a Belgian who also operates the adjacent café. **Pros:** like a bed-and-breakfast; intimate atmosphere. **Cons:** often booked up. ☒ *4227 Sokak* ☏ *232/724–7034* ⤳ *2 rooms* ⌂ *In-room: no a/c. In-hotel: restaurant, pool* ▤ *AE, MC, V.*

ILICA

$$ 🛏 **Altın Yunus Tatilköyü.** The low, bright white cuboid buildings of this big resort—whose name translates as "golden dolphin"—curve along an attractive white-sand beach edging a cove dotted with sailboats. Rooms are done in Mediterranean style, with lots of white and pale ocean-blue. Everything here feels plusher than is usual for Turkish hotels: carpets are thicker, beds are bigger. **Pros:** with almost every imaginable recreational facility, the resort is a destination unto itself. **Cons:** it's hard to get yourself out to explore Çeşme when staying here. ⊠*Kalemburnu Boyalık Mev., Ilıca* ☎*232/723–1250* ⊕*www.altinyunus.com.tr* ⤴*517 rooms* △*In-hotel: 6 restaurants, bars, tennis courts, pools, gym, beachfront, Internet terminal* ⊟*MC, V.*

$$$ 🛏 **Ilıca Hotel.** Ilıca's newest hotel has elegant, attractive rooms and bungalows, a spa and wellness center, a variety of water-oriented amenities—a private beach, several thermal water pools, and wooden sunbathing platforms that extend out over the sea. Many of the chic rooms have beautiful sea views. Family rooms have upper floors for parents and separate downstairs sleeping area for kids. If you're looking for more privacy, you can opt for one of bungalows a short walk from the main hotel area. **Pros:** great for families; everything you need at the hotel. **Cons:** long walk to Ilıca's nightlife and shopping area. ⊠*Boyalık Mevkii* ☎*232/723–3131* ⊕*www.ilicahotel.com* ⤴*237 rooms, 12 suites, 11 family rooms, 3 bungalows* △*In-room: minibar, Internet. In-hotel: 2 restaurants, bars, tennis court, pools, gym, spa, beachfront, children's programs (ages 4–12)* ⊟*AE, D, MC, V.*

Fodor'sChoice
★

4

NIGHTLIFE AND THE ARTS

The peninsula has a very active nightlife. While the bar and club scene has moved out of Çeşme proper and into the neighboring towns of Ilıca and Alaçatı, many of Çeşme's small eateries stay open 24 hours to accommodate the late-night munchies.

Açık Hava Tiyatrosu, Çeşme's open-air theater, hosts a series of Turkish concerts in summer. **Yıldız Burnu** (⊠*5253 Sokak, No. 1, Yıldızburnu* ☎*232/723–4642*), a trendy part of Ilıca, is made up of fancy waterfront bars and lounges that cater to a young crowd. The entrance is free—the cost is built into the overly expensive drinks.

Ayayorgi's clubs and discos are quite popular with night owls. The 22-year-old **Paparazzi** (⊠*Sakara Mah., Ayayorgi* ☎*232/712–6767*) is still at the top of many people's lists.

The popular Istanbul jazz club **Babylon** (⊠*Çark Plajı, Liman Mevkii, Alaçatı* ☎*232/716–6707*) spends its summer season seaside in Alaçatı. Many weeknight concerts are free, and the club brings in an excellent selection of local and international musicians, covering traditional and pop Turkish music, and jazz.

SPORTS AND THE OUTDOORS

BOAT TOURS During high season, daily boat tours leave from the main harbor in Çeşme and from Ilıca. They cost around $15 per person, including lunch, and stop at several different islands. One of the most popular stops is Donkey Island, where dozens of donkeys will greet you upon arrival. Although a great way to explore Çeşme's waters, many of the boat tours tend to play loud pop music and can sometimes be over-crowded. *Benta,* a smaller boat, is known for being calmer and quieter, whereas *Nirvana* is known as the party boat. The boats operate on a less frequent basis in the spring and fall and won't take off unless their minimum quota is filled. You can just go to the harbor and choose a tour on the day you wish to travel.

WORD OF MOUTH

"I just came home from a 16-day trip to Turkey...Ephesus is simply amazing! I will never forget my first look at the street leading to the library."   —helen63

KITESURFING   Pirlantı Beach has a small kitesurfing site. If you don't have any experience in the sport, you can enroll in a three-day course from the beach's **Kiteschool** (☏536/458–8494 ⊕*www.kitesurfbeach.com*) for $270. Experienced kitesurfers can rent equipment for $75 per day. Use of Kiteschool's facilities (changing rooms, showers, and beach umbrellas) is included in the price of rental or instruction.

SHOPPING

The main street in Çeşme has many gift shops selling trinkets and souvenirs, beachwear, carpets, and leather items. There are also many jewelry stores selling silver and gold, which are marked up a lot, so be sure to bargain. During high season, Ilıca has a weekly antique bazaar Monday through Friday. You can find old furniture, swords, guns, paintings, and dish and glassware from the Ottoman and Selçuk periods. Alaçatı also has an antique bazaar on weekends in summer. Alaçatı's main strip has many little boutiques nestled in between cafés and stone houses.

SELÇUK, EPHESUS AND ŞIRINCE

You can easily spend several days wandering around these three towns. Staying in Selçuk is a convenient, practical, and comfortable way to tour the area. Between the open-air museum of Ephesus and the Archaeology Museum in Selçuk, you'll surely get your share of history, but if you need a break, Şirince is the place to go, with its bucolic views, charming village homes, and deliciously fresh food.

SELÇUK

79 km (49 mi) south of İzmir on Rte. E87.

GETTING HERE AND AROUND

You can take the train from İzmir's Basmane Station to Selçuk's train station in less than two hours (six departures daily). Many bus companies travel to Selçuk from Izmir's main bus terminal.

ESSENTIALS

Bus Information Çanakkale Truva Bus Company (⊠*İzmir Bus Terminal* ☏*232/472–0094/5* ⊕*www.truvaturizm.com*).

Visitor Information (⊠*Atatürk Mah., Agora Çarşısı No. 35* ☏*232/892–6945*).

EXPLORING

Selçuk, the closest city to the archaelogical site of Ephesus, lies beneath an ancient fortress and is unfortunately, often overlooked. The former farming town has interesting sights of its own to offer—St. John the Evangelist was purportedly buried here, and the city has one of the oldest mosques in Turkey. It's also a practical place to base yourself, as it's close to many of the area's attractions. The city is easy to navigate, and there are many friendly, well-run *pansiyons* in the area. The town also hosts an annual camel-wrestling festival every January.

WHAT TO SEE

Fodor's Choice ★ **Ephesus Archaeological Site.**
See the highlighted feature in this chapter.

★ **Ephesus Müzesi** *(Ephesus Museum).*
See the highlighted Ephesus feature in this chapter.

İsa Bey Cami *(İsa Bey Mosque)* is one of the oldest mosques in Turkey, dating from 1375. Its jumble of architectural styles suggests a transition between Seljuk and Ottoman design: like later Ottoman mosques, this one has a courtyard, something not found in Seljuk mosques. The structure is built out of "borrowed" stone: marble blocks with Latin inscriptions, Corinthian columns, black-granite columns from the baths at Ephesus, and pieces from the altar of the Temple of Artemis. ⊠*St. Jean Sokak* ⊙*Daily 9–6.*

Temple of Artemis. See the highlighted Ephesus feature in this chapter.

NEED A BREAK?

Tea and a selection of excellent *lokum* (Turkish delight) are sold at tiny **Tadım** (⊠*In Emlak Bankası arcade*). Hikmet Çeliker's family has been making the confection for the last 250 years and shipping it the world over.

St. John Basilica. See the highlighted Ephesus feature in this chapter.

Meryemana, the House of the Virgin Mary. See the highlighted Ephesus feature in this chapter

WHERE TO STAY AND EAT

¢ ✕ **Ejder Restaurant.** Mehmet, the owner, manages this place within sight of the Selçuk aqueduct, and his wife is the sole cook. It may sometimes take a while to get your food, but the traditional kebabs and Turkish specials are well worth the wait. Mehmet takes much pride in the guestbook filled with customers' comments, so add a few lines. ⊠*Cengiz Topel Cad. 9/E* ☎*232/892–3296* ⊟*AE, MC, V.*

TURKISH

$ ✕ **Eski Ev.** The Ottoman motifs may feel a bit touristy, but the place is done up nicely, with a peaceful, shaded courtyard for outdoor dining attached to an old house. A wide selection of Turkish mezes and main dishes, served on fancy copper plates, include many vegetarian options. ⊠*Cengiz Topel Cad.* ⊟*AE, MC, V.*

TURKISH

¢ ⛱ **Homeros Pansiyon.** The happy-go-lucky owner goes out of his way to make guests feel at home, and fills his rooms with antiques, lace, and other decorations for a cluttered, homey look. The terrace and common rooms are good places to wind down after a day of sightseeing. **Pros:** the owner speaks English well; you feel like you're staying at someone's house; free bicycles for guests. **Cons:** may feel too clustered for some.

Continued on page 243

EPHESUS
CITY OF THE GODS

One would naturally think that the greatest Roman ruins are to be found in Italy. Not so fast! With an ancient arena that dwarfs the one in Pompeii, and a lofty library that rivals any structure in the Roman Forum, Ephesus—once the most important Greco-Roman city of the Eastern Mediterranean—is among the best-preserved ancient sites in the world. Set on a strategic trade route, it first won fame as a cultural and religious crossroads. Here, shrines honored the pagan goddess of fertility, St. Paul did some serious soul-searching, and—legend has it —the Virgin Mary lived out her last days. Today, modern travelers can trace the fault lines of ancient civilization in Ephesus's spectacular landscape of ruined temples, theaters, and colonnaded streets.

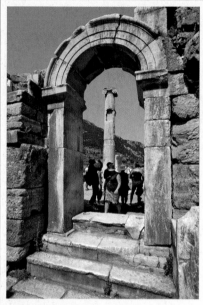

THE AWE-STRUCK ADMIRERS who disembark from cruise ships and tour buses to wander through the largest Roman ruins of the Eastern Mediterranean are not really out of sync with ancient times, since Ephesus was a bustling port of call in the pre-Christian era. Home to upwards of 500,000 people at its height, Efes—to use the Turkish name—drew visitors from near and far with its promise of urbane and sybaritic pleasures, including baths, brothels, theaters, temples, public latrines, and one of the world's largest libraries. Even then, visitors approaching from the harbor could wander under the marble porticos of the Arcadian Way—the ancient world's Rodeo Drive—and visit shops laden with goods from throughout the Mediterranean world.

⊠ Efes (Ephesus), 4 km (2.5 mi) west of Selçuk on Selçuk-Ephesus Rd.

☎ 0232/892-6010 (no official Web site)

🎫 $11; terraced houses, $11; parking: $6.50

🕐 May—Sept., daily 8—7; Oct.—Apr., daily 8—5.

SPIRIT & THE FLESH

Ephesus in pre-Hellenic times was the cult center of Cybele, the Anatolian goddess of fertility. When seafaring Ionians arrived in the 10th century BC they promptly recast her as Artemis, goddess of the hunt. With her three tiers of breasts, this symbol of mother nature was, in turn, both fruitful and barren, according to the season; as such, she was also worshipped by thousands as the goddess of chastity. The riches of her shrines, however, awoke greed; in the 6th century BC, Croesus, king of Lydia, captured Ephesus, but was himself defeated by Persia's Cyrus. The wily Ephesians managed to keep on good terms with everyone by playing up to both sides of any conflict but by the 2nd century BC, Ephesus had become capital of the Roman province of Asia and Artemis had been renamed Diana.

THE GOSPEL TRUTH?

As with other Roman cities, Ephesus eventually became Christian, though not without a struggle. The Gospel of Luke recounts how the city's silversmiths drove St. Paul out of Ephesus for fear that his pronouncements—"there are no gods made with hands"—would lessen the sale of their silver statues. After Paul addressed a gathering of townsfolk in the amphitheater, the craftsmen rioted, but he succeeded in founding an early congregation here thanks to his celebrated "Epistle to the Ephesians." Another tourist to the city was St. John, who visited between 37 and 48 AD (he died here in AD 95 shortly after completing his Gospel); tradition has it he was accompanied by Mary, whom he brought to fulfill a pledge he had made to Jesus to protect her. Whether or not this is true, Ephesus's House of the Virgin Mary—where Mary is reputed to have breathed her last—soon became the earliest pilgrimage site in Christendom.

Top, *Gateway to Odeon;* Right, *The Arcadian Way*

DID YOU KNOW?

When Ephesus became a Roman capital in the 2nd Century BC, numerous shrines were erected to the ancient gods, including Hercules (figure at left). But by the 4th century, the early Christians had become mightier than the fabled hero and Ephesus's pagan temples were plundered for the building of numerous churches.

PRECIOUS STONES: WHAT'S WHERE

"Is there a greater city than Ephesus?" asked St. Paul. "Is there a more beautiful city?" Those who dig ruins can only agree with the saint. Ephesus is the best preserved Helleno-Roman city of the Eastern Mediterranean.

1 Temple of Domitian. One of the largest temples in the city was dedicated to the first-century Roman emperor.

2 Odeon. At this intimate theater, an audience of about 1,500 sat on a semicircle of stone seats to enjoy theatricals and music recitals.

3 Prytaneion. One of the most important buildings in town was dedicated to Hestia, goddess of hearth and home. Priests kept vigil to ensure her sacred flame was never extinguished.

4 Curetes Street. One of the main thoroughfares cuts a diagonal swath through the ancient city and was a processional route leading to the Temple of Artemis; "curetes" are priests of Artemis.

5 Temple of Hadrian. Elegant friezes and graceful columns surround the porch and main chamber of this monument to the 2nd-century Roman emperor. A frieze of Medusa guards the entrance to ward off evil spirits, and, in another, the Christian Emperor Theodosius

is surrounded by pagan gods—a sign that worldly Ephesus was a tolerant place.

6 Slope Houses. The luxurious homes of well-to-do Ephesians of the first to seventh centuries climb the slopes of Mount Koressus. Liberally decorated with frescoes and mosaics this well-heeled enclave is richly evocative of life in the ancient town.

7 Library of Celsus. One of the most spectacular extant ruins of antiquity, this remarkable two-storied building was commissioned in the 2nd century and was destined for double duty—as a mausoleum for Julius Celsus, Roman governor of the Asian provinces, and as a reading room stocked with more than 12,000 scrolls.

8 Brothel. Footsteps etched into the marble paving stones along Curetes Street led the way to one of the busiest businesses in town.

9 Theater. St. Paul preached to the Ephesians in this magnificent space. The largest

outdoor theater of the ancient world was carved out of the flanks of Mount Pion over the course of 60 years and seats as many as 40,000 spectators.

10 Arcadian Way. The grandest street in town, traversing the third of a mile between the harbor and the theater, was flanked by mosaic-floored porticos that were lined with elegant shops and—a luxury afforded by few ancient cities—torch-lit at night. This is where Cleopatra paraded in triumph.

11 Stadium. This 1st-century BC structure accommodated more than 70,000 spectators, who enjoyed such entertainments as chariot races and gladiatorial spectacles.

12 Temple of Artemis. A lone column rising from a swamp is all that remains of one of the Seven Wonders of the World. The largest building in the ancient Mediterranean, once surrounded by 127 columns, was a shrine to the goddess of fertility, abundance, and of womanly concerns, from virginity to child-bearing.

Top Left, *Temple of Hadrian;* Center, *Library of Celsus;* Top Right, *Odeon*

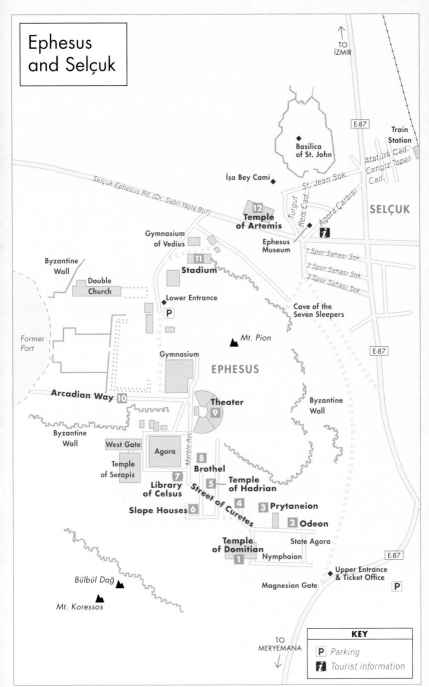

Ephesus and Selçuk

TO
İZMIR

E-87

Train
Station

Basilica
of St. John

İşa Bey Cami

Selçuk-Ephesus Rd. (Dr. Sabri Yayla Bul.)

St. Jean Sok.

Atatürk Cad.
Cengiz Topel
Cad.

Turgut
Reis Cad.

Agora Çarbısı

SELÇUK

12
**Temple
of Artemis**

Gymnasium
of Vedius

Ephesus
Museum

1 Spor Sahası Sok.

11
Stadium

2 Spor Sahası Sok.

3 Spor Sahası Sok.

Byzantine
Wall

Double
Church

P

Lower Entrance

Cave of the
Seven Sleepers

Former
Port

Mt. Pion

E-87

Gymnasium

EPHESUS

Arcadian Way **10**

Theater
9

Byzantine
Wall

Byzantine
Wall

West Gate

Agora

Marble Ave.

8

Temple
of Serapis

Brothel

7

5

**Temple
of Hadrian**

**Library
of Celsus**

Street of Curetes

Slope Houses **6**

4

3 **Prytaneion**

2 **Odeon**

**Temple
of Domitian**

1

State Agora

Nymphaion

Bülbül Dağ

Mt. Koressos

Magnesian Gate

E-87

**Upper Entrance
& Ticket Office**

P

TO
MERYEMANA

KEY

P *Parking*

Tourist information

PLANNING YOUR VISIT

Most people who tour Ephesus (Efes) base themselves in nearby Selçuk. If arriving by car, take the road from Selçuk to Kuşadasi, turning left and following the signs to the archaeological site. There are two public parking lots, at the top and bottom of the site near the two main gates. Note that if you arrive by car you'll have to backtrack the hill one way or the other after walking the site (or opt for an inexpensive cab ride back). It may be best to forgo your car and take taxis to and from Selçuk as the fare is only $6. There is also a dolmuş (shared taxi) that connects with Selçuk.

TIPS FOR TOURING

The main entrance (Lower Gate) is near the turnoff to Selçuk; for the upper Magnesian Gate, follow the signs for the Cave of the Seven Sleepers and House of the Virgin Mary (Meryemana). Since Ephesus is laid out on the slopes of Mounts Pion and Koressos, many opt to begin their tour at the upper Magnesian Gate, visiting the state and religious buildings on the higher reaches before descending to where most of the public arenas and agoras are located.

The main avenue runs about a mile downhill but there are any number of side streets with intriguing detours. Consequently, a minimum visit of two

Top, Amphitheater

EPHESUS GUIDES

Perhaps the easiest way to see all the sights is to take a guided bus tour, which allows you to travel between the Ephesus site, the Ephesus Museum, the House of the Virgin Mary, and the Basilica of St. John stress-free. The day trip (lunch included) usually costs $60–$75. Tour agencies can be found in Izmir and Kuşadası, although the most convenient are located in Selçuk. Here are two recommended outfitters:

■ **Grand Wonders** (✉ Atatürk Mah. 1019 Sok. 6, Selçuk ☎ 232/892-7364 ⊕ www.grandwonders.com).

■ **Peron Tours** (✉ Atatürk Mah. 1006 Sok. 4, Selçuk ☎ 232/892-9547).

As for the one-on-one guides who flock around the entrance gates to the main site, keep in mind they are not particularly knowledgeable (they usually charge around $50 for a two-hour tour for 2 to 10 people). Perhaps the best option—in addition to consulting one of the handy site guidebooks—is to hire the one-hour audio guides ($7) available at the main gates.

DID YOU KNOW?

Begun by the Greek ruler Lysimachus, Ephesus's theater was finished by the Roman emperors Claudius and Trajan in the 2nd century AD. Great vistas reward those who hike to the top of its 66 tiers.

hours can easily stretch to four, not including an hour in the museum and an hour or two at nearby sites like the Cave of the Seven Sleepers and Meryemana.

You'll better appreciate the treasures of Ephesus museum if you tour the ancient city first—knowing where the statuary, mosaics, and other artifacts were located raises them from the dust to life when you visit the museum. As for timing, a visit in early morning or late afternoon might help you skirt the heaviest of the cruise ship crowds from Kuşadası. In summer you'll want to avoid the midday heat and sun. Be sure to bring water.

Above, *Library of Celsus*

WHO'S WHO IN ANCIENT EPHESUS

ALEXANDER THE GREAT

Upon entering Ephesus in triumph after defeating the Persians in 333 BC, Alexander saw the reconstruction efforts of the temple to Artemis underway and offered to pay for the new edifice with the proviso that his name be inscribed over the entrance. The Ephesians, not wanting to offend their goddess, diplomatically informed the noble warrior and mighty king that it would not be right for one divine being to so honor another.

ANDROKLOS

Banished from Athens upon the death of his father, King Kadros, in the 10th century BC, Androklos arrived at the shores of Asia Minor. The oracle at Delphi had told the prince that a fish and a boar would guide him on his way. A fish that Androklos was roasting on the beach leapt from the flames into the bush, and the commotion routed out a wild boar who led him to a fertile valley: the future Ephesus. Androklos, went on to unite the twelve cities of Asia Minor as the Ionian League.

HEROSTRATUS

Stories of all great cities include at least one villain, and in Ephesus the most infamous is Herostratus. One night in 356 BC, the deranged young man burned the most important building in town, the Temple to Artemis. As fate would have it, Alexander the Great was born the same night. The Roman historian Plutarch later observed that the goddess was "too busy taking care of the birth of Alexander to send help to her threatened temple." Ephesian authorities executed Herostratus and tried to condemn him to obscurity by forbidding the mention of his name, but this obviously didn't work.

ST. PAUL

The well-traveled missionary stopped twice in Ephesus, of which he wrote in 1 Corinthians 16, "a great door and effectual is opened unto me, and there are many adversaries." Among them were local merchants, who were infuriated by Paul's proclamation that they should stop selling images of Artemis, lest the practice encourage the worship of pagan idols. Paul may have written his "Epistle to the Ephesians" while being held prisoner in Rome, before his execution in AD 67.

ST. JOHN

Legend has it that the author of the Fourth Gospel arrived in Ephesus with the Virgin Mary and died at age 98. He had his followers dig a square grave, proclaimed "You have called me to your feast," and expired, or so people thought: dust could be seen moving above his grave as if he still drew breath. Emperor Justinian's cathedral—it would be the 7th largest in the world if reconstructed—was built directly over St. John's grave.

Center, Silver tetradrachm issued by Erythrai ca. 200–180 BC, obverse: Alexander the Great as Herakles wearing the lion skin. Above, Tomb of St John in Mezrai, St. John's basilica in Selçuk

BEYOND THE RUINS: OTHER SIGHTS

House of the Virgin Mary

Cave of the Seven Sleepers

THE HOUSE OF THE VIRGIN MARY (MERYEMANA)

Legend has it that the Virgin Mary traveled to Ephesus with St. John and spent her last days in this modest stone dwelling. Such claims were given a boost of credulity in the 19th century when a bedridden German nun had a vision that enabled her to describe the house in precise detail. A hallowed place of pilgrimage, the house has been visited by three popes. John is allegedly buried nearby beneath the now-ruined basilica of St. John in Selçuk. Surrounded by a national park, Mary's house is 7 km (4 mi) southwest of Selçuk, near the entrance to ancient Ephesus. ⊠ *Off Rte. E87* ⊠ *$1.50* ⊙ *Daily 7:30–sunset.*

EPHESUS MUSEUM

While many of the finds from Ephesus were carted off to the British Museum in London and the Ephesus Museum in Vienna, some of the treasures remain in Ephesus, in the small museum in nearby Selçuk. Among the mosaics, coins, and other artifacts are dozens of images of Artemis, including the famous statue of the fertility goddess with several rows of egg-shaped breasts. ⊠ *Agora Carsisi, opposite visitor center in Selçuk* ☎ *232/892–6010* ⊠ *$3* ⊙ *Daily 8:30–noon and 1–5:30.*

CAVE OF THE SEVEN SLEEPERS

Ephesus is awash in legend, but the story associated with this hillside cavern takes the prize. During persecutions ordered by the Roman Emperor Decius in the 2nd century, seven young Christian men were sealed into a cave and left to die. Two centuries later, in the 4th-century era of Christian tolerance, a farmer happened to unseal the cave and found the seven men, now aged, in deep slumber. On awakening, they wandered into Ephesus, as shocked at the sight of crosses affixed to churches as the townsfolk were confused by the sight of these archaically clothed characters, who offered two-centuries-old coinage in an attempt to buy food. After their deaths, a church was erected in their honor. These ancient Rip Van Winkles have found their way into works as diverse as the Koran and the *Golden Legend*, the famous Middle Ages chronicle of the lives of the saints. ⊠ *South of Sor Sahasi Sok. 3* ⊠ *Free.*

Fertility Goddess, Ephesus Museum

Camel Wrestling

While Americans are busy stuffing turkeys and stocking up on Christmas trees, Turkish camels and their owners prepare for an intense season of travel, confrontation, and competition. Every year, around 100 male camels tour the Marmara, Mediterranean, and the Aegean to compete in more than 30 wrestling festivals. Their primary motivation: get the girl. Camels will wrestle only during their mating season, which lasts from November to March, and a female camel is paraded around to provoke them into these contests. The camels' mouths are tied during the match so that they can do no real harm to each other, and between the judges, separaters (*urgancı*), and commentators (*cazgirs*), there are 21 officials (not including the camel owners) moderating the events.

A wrestling camel can expect to compete in 10 to 14 matches per year. The camels begin their wrestling "career" at age four, when they are purchased from Iran. They train for the next four years and spend years eight through 10 coming of age and developing their own strategies. Their right of passage, much like that of Turkish boys' occurs at this age, when the camels receive *havuts*, decorative cloths with their name and the word *maşallah* (may God protect him) sewn on the inside. According to camel owners and those familiar with the sport, wrestling is not a foreign, inhumane practice being imposed on the camels. On the contrary, these *dayluk* (as they're called until age seven, when they become *tülü* or hairy) begin wrestling naturally in the wild during their first years out of the womb, and if trained, can continue until age 25.

People have different theories about camel-wrestling's origins, although many argue it was a nomadic practice and part of the competition between caravan owners. Nomadic or not, these festivals have become a deep-rooted cultural pastime in Turkey. Celebratory events actually begin the day before, during *halı gecesi*, or carpet night, when camels are flaunted around to percussive music, their bells jingling as they amble along. The camel owners, who often get to know one another during the pre-festivities, are also dolled up in cornered caps, traditional neck scarves, and accordion-like boots.

To prevent wearing out the camels, the matches last no more than 10 minutes, and camels compete only once a day. The victor, the camel who gets the most points for outsmarting his rival by swiftly maneuvering and having the most control over the match (which might simply mean not running away), can win anywhere from $2,500–$25,000, depending on the competition. There's usually a wrestling World Cup of sorts at the culmination of the festivals, in which the top camels compete.

The exact dates, times, and locations of the festivals change from year to year, but competitions are always held every Sunday from December to March. The central and southern Aegean cities of Selçuk, İzmir, Bodrum, and Kuşadası host camel-wrestling festivals. Local tourism offices will have specific information about that year's festivals. Tickets cost around $7 per match and can be purchased on-site.

—Evin Dogu

⊠Atatürk mahallesi. 1048 Sokak 3 Selçuk35920 ☏*232/892–3995* ⊕*www.homerospension.com* ⌷*12 rooms* ⌂*In-hotel: restaurant, Wi-Fi* ⊟*AE, MC, V.*

$$ ⌂**Hotel Akay.** Ottoman flourishes abound—including whitewashed walls inside and out, latticed balconies, arched windows and doors, and kilims on the floor. The newest rooms (with TVs) are near the pool, and cost more but are worth it. **Pros:** comfortable, spacious rooms; one of the owners speaks very good English. **Cons:** small bathrooms; a bit pricier relative to other area hotels. *⊠İsa Bey Cami Kar., Serin Sokak 3, Selçuk* ☏*232/892–3172* ⊕*www.hotelakay.com* ⌷*23 rooms* ⌂*In-room: no TV (some). In-hotel: restaurant, bar, pool, laundry service, Wi-Fi* ⊟*AE, MC, V.*

$ ⌂**Hotel Bella.** A spacious terrace with a small library, backgammon
★ boards, and a large-screen TV meeting room are extra pluses at this attractive, cheerfully yellow hotel by the St. John basilica. Some rooms have balconies; all have Turkish carpets and colorful kilims hanging on the walls. **Pros:** large and inviting terrace; prix-fixe dinner is a good value. **Cons:** some rooms are a bit small. *⊠Ataturk Mah. St. John St. No. 7* ☏*232/892–3944* ⊕*www.hotelbella.com* ⌷*12 rooms* ⌂*In-room: no a/c (some). In-hotel: laundry service, Internet terminal* ⊟*AE, MC, V.*

$ ⌂**Kale Han.** These rooms surrounding a walled garden are simple but attractive, with bare whitewashed walls and dark timber beams, and some face the castle behind the hotel. One of the buildings in the garden has a four-bed suite, the swimming pool is most welcome after a day of sightseeing, and simple grilled meats and fish are served in the airy dining room. **Pros:** the pool. **Cons:** some rooms can feel a bit stuffy. *⊠Atatürk Cad. 49, Selçuk* ☏*232/892–6154* ⊕*www.kalehan.com* ⌷*54 rooms, 1 suite* ⌂*In-hotel: restaurant, pool* ⊟*MC, V.*

¢ ⌂**Wallabies Victoria Hotel.** This tidy, cheerful place—named in memory of the owner's time in England—has a comfortable lobby and the smallish rooms, with whitewashed walls set off by honey-colored wood trim, have delightful views of storks nesting on the ancient columns of an aqueduct. **Pros:** many options for dining nearby; friendly and helpful staff. **Cons:** rooms are small. *⊠Cengiz Topel Cad. 4, Selçuk* ☏*232/892–3204* ⊕*www.wallabieshostel.com* ⌷*24 rooms* ⊟*No credit cards.*

SHOPPING

Selçuk's weekly bazaar is held on Wednesday and Saturday in the main square from 9 to 6. There's also a daily market by the İsa Bey Mosque that sells souvenirs and Turkish-themed gifts.

ŞIRINCE

8 km (5 mi) east of Selçuk.

GETTING HERE AND AROUND

You can get to Şirince from Selçuk's small minibus terminal on buses that run all day, either when full or every half hour. The last one usually leaves Şirince around 6 PM. There are also tours from Izmir, Selçuk, and Kuşadası that often include stops at Ephesus and Meryemana as well.

EXPLORING

Şirince, one of Turkey's wealthiest villages, is another worthwhile excursion from Selçuk. Its picturesque cluster of two-story houses is set on a lush hill; the rows of houses create a long string of windows, which have decorative eaves with nature motifs. A former Greek enclave, Şirince has a 19th-century church and a stone basilica, also 19th-century, which has been restored and turned into an art gallery.

The local women's handiwork has become quite popular, and they sell their work along the village paths. Residents also sell fruit wine made from mulberry, quince, and melon, which you can sample over a friendly conversation. Village food is delicious, and there are several inexpensive restaurants scattered around town.

Şrinice attracts many local and foreign visitors, but it is never deluged with tourists. To get to Şirince, take one of the dolmuşes that leave periodically from Selçuk from 8:30AM to 5 PM.

WHERE TO STAY AND EAT

$
TURKISH
×**Arşipel Restaurant.** The dining room of Kırkınca Pansiyon is one of the best restaurants in town, serving such excellent and authentic fare as a delicous cream-based eggplant soup; *şevketi bostan,* a root vegetable cooked with tender pieces of lamb; and the homemade pasta, *erişte,* served in a light cream and almond sauce. Ottoman meat stews and kebabs are also available. ⊠*Şirince Köyü, Selçuk,* ☎*232/898–3216 or 232/898–3133* ▬*MC, V.*

$
TURKISH
×**Artemis.** Artemis's superb setting overlooking a verdant valley and its excellent range of appetizers and meat dishes, particularly its baked lamb, are reason enough to make the trip here from Selçuk. It's also a great place to try the local wine, which is produced by the villagers in their homes. ⊠*Şirince* ☎*232/898–3201 or 232/898–3202* ▬*MC, V.*

¢
TURKISH
×**Köy.** One of the first restaurants in town, Köy is right in the main square. The menu covers a wide spectrum of local cuisine, everything from grilled meats to mezes. ⊠*Across from the bus terminal* ☎*232/898–3120* ▬*AE, MC, V.*

$
☂**Alis Pansiyon.** Follow the red-and-white dove emblem from the main square to get to this cozy bed-and-breakfast on the outskirts of the village. One room has its own private fireplace, and you'll be invited to sit in the garden with the owners, a friendly couple who perform music for their guests on the *ud,* a traditional Turkish instrument. **Pros:** lovely sitting area both indoors and outdoors. **Cons:** rooms can be a bit stuffy. ☎*232/898–3212, 506/734–4665* ⊕*www.sirincealispansiyon.com* ⇖*4 rooms* ⌂*In-hotel: restaurant, Wi-Fi* ▬*No credit cards.*

$$
☂**Kırkınca Pansiyon B&B.** Guest rooms, named after flowers, are elegant in their simplicity and a vine-shaded terrace is delightful. Six restored Greek houses nearby are perfect for families and groups, and more rooms are available at the sister property, Erdem. Free hiking tours are available. **Pros:** helpful, attentive owners who were born and raised in the village. **Cons:** more expensive in relation to other pensions. ⊠*Şirince* ☎*232/898–3133 or 232/898–3140* ⊕*www.kirkinca.com* ⇖*7 rooms, 5 houses* ⌂*In-room: no TV (some), Wi-Fi. In-hotel: restaurant* ▬*AE, MC, V.*

Dried peppers are strung together in an artful manner. Photo by sarabeth, Fodors.com member.

$$–$$$ **Nişanyan Evleri.** The Nişanyans are architects, and their accommo-
Fodors Choice   dations—rooms in a restored mansion, stone cottages at the edge of
★   the village, or old houses in the center—are stunningly designed and
filled with Ottoman antiques. The inn has a pleasant terrace and small
library, and the cottages share a swimming pool and a lovely garden.
Pros: comfortable surroundings; very professional staff. **Cons:** a bit
secluded from the rest of the village and it's a long walk uphill to get
here. ✚ *At the entrance to Şirince, turn right at the hotel's sign and drive
1.2 km (¾ mi)* ☏ *232/898–3208* ⊕ *www.nisanyan.com* ⌂ *5 rooms, 5
cottages, 3 houses* ⌂ *In-room: no a/c, no phone (some), no TV (some).
In-hotel: restaurant, pool, Internet terminal* ▭ MC, V.

KUŞADASI AND ENVIRONS

Kuşadası is a brash, highly touristy place replete with pubs, fish-
and-chips restaurants, and tacky souvenir shops. On a positive note,
Kuşadası is near one of Turkey's most beautiful national parks, as well
as Pamukkale and Aphrodisias and within easy reach of Ephesus.

KUŞADASI

20 km (12 mi) southwest of Selçuk on Rte. 515.

GETTING HERE AND AROUND
The easiest way to get to Kuşadası is by bus or car from Izmir. It's about
a 1½-hour drive from Izmir and a 30-minute drive from Selçuk.

Kuşadasi

Ünlü S.

Atatürk Bul.

Mosque

K. Arikan C.

Seving S.

Kale
Hamami

Bahçearasi S.

Güvercinada C.

Liman C.

1

Kişla S.

50 Yil C.

Kibris C.

Barbaros Hayrettin Paşa Bul.

Town
Hall

İsmet İnönü Blvd.

Rifat Arin S.

Burç Sokak

Zeki Aydinli S.

Bezirgan S.

Bazkurt S.

Saglik C.

Sabucali S.

2

Aydinlik S.

Aslanlar C.

Belediye ◆
Hamami

Barlar S.

Kahramanlar C.

◆ Haci Hatice
Hanim Camii

Friday
Market

Mülgen S.

Candan Tarhan Bul.

Tepe S.

İmam S.

Güzel S.

Anit S.

Altin S.

Yildirim C.

◆ Mosque

Zafer S.

Adnan Menderes Blvd.

Özgür S.

Öztürk S.

Mosque ◆

Sari S.

ESSENTIALS

Visitor Information (✉ *Liman Cad. 13* ☎ *256/614–1103*).

Tour Operators Akdeniz Turizm Omega Tur (✉ *Atatürk Bul. 26, Kuşadası* ☎ *256/ 614–1140*).

EXPLORING

Kuşadası long ago lost its local charm to invasive, sterile buildings and overpopulation, and the huge yacht marina, the largest in the region, has only exacerbated the situation. Kuşadası is also a port for cruise ships. So, what was a small fishing village up until the 1970s is now a sprawling, hyperactive town packed with curio shops and a year-round population of around 60,000, which swells several times over in summer with the influx of tourists and Turks with vacation homes.

If you're looking for beaches, either head north from Kuşadası to Pamucak or travel 33 km (20 mi) south to lovely, wooded **Samsundağ Milli Parkı** *(Samsundağ National Park, also known as Dilek Peninsula National Park)*, which has good hiking trails and several quiet stretches of sandy beach. The İçmeler beach, closest to the entrance, is also the most crowded. Travel 15 minutes to Karaburun for a more low-key atmosphere. To get to the park, take the coast road, marked Güzelçamlı or Devutlar, for about 10 km (6 mi) south of Kuşadası. If you're taking a dolmuş, expect to pay $4 for transportation and entrance into the park. ⌂*Park $2* ⊙*Apr.–Dec.*

There aren't many sights in Kuşadası proper, but the causeway off Kadınlar Denizi, just south of the harbor, connects the town to an ❶ old **Genoese castle** on Güvercin Adası (Pigeon Island). Today the site of a popular disco and several teahouses with gardens and sea views, the fortress was home to three Turkish brothers in the 16th century. These infamous pirates—Barbarossa, Oruc, and Hayrettin—pillaged the coasts of Spain and Italy and sold passengers and crews from captured ships into slavery in Algiers and Constantinople. Rather than fight them, Süleyman the Magnificent (ruled 1520–66) hired Hayrettin as his grand admiral and set him loose on enemies in the Mediterranean. The strategy worked: Hayrettin won victory after victory and was heaped with honors and riches.

❷ Kuşadası's 300-year-old **kervansaray** (⊠*Atatürk Bul. 1*), now the Hotel Club Kervansaray, is loaded with Ottoman atmosphere. Its public areas are worth a look even if you're not staying here.

WHERE TO STAY AND EAT

$$–$$$ ✕**Ali Baba Restaurant.** An appetizing and colorful display of the day's
TURKISH catch meets you at the entrance to this waterside fish house. The decor is simple, the view over the bay is soothing, and the food is fabulous. For starters, try the cold black-eyed pea salad, the marinated octopus salad, or the fried calamari. ⊠*Belediye Turistik Çarşısı 5* ☎*256/614–1551* ⌂*Reservations essential* ═*MC, V.*

¢ ✕**Coşkun Abi.** A mix of locals and tourists come to Coşkun Abi's, a café
TURKISH and narghile (water-pipe) salon, and the atmosphere is very congenial. *Gözleme,* a Turkish-style crepe, is the thing to get here, with fillings of either cheese, spinach, or *ot* (Aegean wild plants). ⊠*Belediye Dugun Salonu Karsisi, Kuşadası* ☎*256/612–8258* ═*No credit cards.*

$$$ ✕**Kazim Usta Restaurant.** Open since 1956, this upscale restaurant made
TURKISH its reputation on its fish dishes, and now serves international cuisine as well. It's right on the water, with a nice lounge and bar inside. ⊠*Scalanuova AVM, Kuşadası* ☎*256/612–2566* ═*AE, MC, V.*

$$ ✕**Özurfa.** The focus at this Turkish fast-food spot is kebabs. The Urfa
TURKISH kebab—spicy, grilled slices of lamb on pita bread—is the house specialty, and the fish kebabs are tasty, too. The location just off Barbaros Hayrettin Caddesi, the main thoroughfare, is convenient to the market and a step away from the crowds. ⊠*Cephane Sokak 7/A* ☎*256/612–9881* ═*AE, MC, V.*

$ ✕**Tarihi Çınar Et.** This popular eatery on the outskirts of town takes
TURKISH its name from the 800-year-old Oriental plane tree (*çınar* in Turkish), whose spreading branches shade the tables. House specialties are lamb and chicken cooked on a spit. There is also a wide range of *mezes* and superb ice cream. ⊠*Davutlar Yolu, Saraydamlı* ☎*256/681–1177* ═*AE, MC, V.*

$ ✕**Yuvam.** Yuvam or "My Nest/Home" is truly that—it offers food
TURKISH you'd find in a Turkish home. During lunch hour, the food runs out quickly, so get there early. Some of their specials include mantı, okra in a tomato-olive oil sauce, meat stew, and baked chicken with rice. ⊠*Kaleici Yedieylül Sokak 4* ☎*256/614–9460* ═*MC, V.*

$ Atınç Otel. What this hotel lacks in style it makes up for with a good location, just a 10-minute walk from the center of town, and a rooftop pool. Guest rooms have balconies, and those in front of the hotel overlook the Aegean. **Pros:** location. **Cons:** rather unattractive building. ✉Atatürk Bul. 42, ☎256/614–7608 ⊕www.hotelatinc.com ⤶75 rooms ⌂In-hotel: 2 restaurants, bars, pool ⊟AE, MC, V.

$$ Hotel Club Kervansaray. A refurbished 300-year-old inn that was once a way station for camel caravans is decorated in Ottoman style. The central courtyard—where the camels were kept—is paved with marble and planted with palm trees, and rooms are decorated with kilims and Turkish folk art. In the dressy Turkish restaurant, there's live entertainment. **Pros:** historic Turkish decor; right across from the port. **Cons:** can be loud on live-music nights. ✉Atatürk Bul. 2, ☎256/614–4115 ⊕www.kusadasihotels.com/caravanserail ⤶26 rooms ⌂In-room: Wi-Fi. In-hotel: restaurant, bar, Wi-Fi ⊟AE, MC, V.

$$ Kısmet. Surrounded by beautifully maintained gardens, the Kısmet
★   is set on a promontory overlooking the marina on one side and the Aegean on the other, and feels almost like a private Mediterranean villa. Each room has a private balcony, most with sea views. Kismet is one of Turkey's best-known hotels and its popularity makes reservations a must. **Pros:** nice view of the harbor; central location. **Cons:** some rooms are small. ✉Akyar Mev., Türkmen Mah., ☎256/618–1290 ⊕www.kismet.com.tr ⤶107 rooms ⌂In-hotel: restaurant, bars, tennis court, beachfront ⊟AE, MC, V ⊗Closed Nov.–Mar.

NIGHTLIFE

The **Club Kervansaray** (✉Atatürk Bul. 2 ☎256/614–4115) has dining, dancing, and a show on most nights, but a younger crowd heads to the vast **Ecstasy Bar** (✉Sakarya Sokak 22 ☎256/613–1391), which plays the latest chart-topping sounds and has an official capacity of 1,000 spread over two floors. On Barlar Sokak, Kuşadası's loud, abrasive bar strip, the spacious and popular **Queen Victoria** (☎No phone) has live music in summer. There are several Irish and British-style pubs farther along **Barlar Sokak.** For a lively night of dancing, young Turks and energetic tourists walk across the causeway to **Pigeon Island** to the "Disco"—there's no other name on the sign, but you can hear its music almost everywhere on this minuscule island.

PAMUKKALE (HIERAPOLIS)

170 km (105 mi) from Selçuk on Rte. E87 (follow road signs after Sarayköy); 200 km (124 mi) from Kuşadası.

★ GETTING HERE AND AROUND

The best way to get to Pamukkale is by bus from Izmir, Selçuk, Kuşadası, or Bodrum; it's about a three- or four-hour drive from any of these cities.

EXPLORING

Pamukkale (pronounced pam-*uck*-al-lay) first appears as an enormous, chalky white cliff rising 330 feet from the plains. Mineral-rich volcanic spring water cascades over basins and natural terraces, crystallizing into white curtains of solidified water seemingly suspended in air. These hot springs are believed to cure rheumatism and other ailments. In the mid-1990s, the diversion of water from the springs to fill **thermal pools** in nearby luxury hotels reduced the volume of water reaching the site to a trickle; that, combined with a huge increase in the number of visitors, discolored the water's once-pristine whiteness. Large sections of the site are now cordoned off, as the authorities strive to conserve and restore a still-striking natural wonder to its former magnificence. Be forewarned that the surrounding area is very commercialized.

WORD OF MOUTH

"Pammukale/Hieropolis is great, but try to go either in the early morning or late afternoon to miss the crowds…Also, at many of the ruins (Pergamum, Priene, Hieropolis), the signs have worn away so if you don't have a guide or guide book, it will be difficult to understand what was there)."   —heasereb

If you have time, spend the night here, as the one-day bus tours from the coast are exhausting and limiting: you'll end up spending more time on the bus than you do at the actual site. One full day at Pamukkale will give you enough time to explore the area.

Hierapolis is an example of how long the magical springs of Pamukkale have cast their spell. The ruins that can be seen today date from the time of the Roman Empire, but there are references to a settlement here as far back as the 5th century BC. Because the sights are spread over about ½ km (¼ mi), prepare for some walking. Between the theater and the Pamukkale Motel are the ruins of a **Temple of Apollo** and a bulky **Byzantine church.** The monumental fountain known as the **Nymphaion,** just north of the Apollo Temple, dates from the 4th century AD. Near the northern city gates is another indication of the town's former popularity, a vast **necropolis** (cemetery) with more than 1,000 cut-stone sarcophagi spilling all the way down to the base of the hill.

The stone building that enclosed Hierapolis's baths is now the **Pamukkale Müzesi,** a museum with a fine display of marble statues found at the site. ☎258/272–2077 for visitor center (for information), 258/272–2034 for museum ⚏$1 ☉ Tues.–Sun. 8–noon and 12:30–6.

WHERE TO STAY AND EAT

$ ✕**Ünal Restaurant.** Good, simple village food, including a delicious
TURKISH   lamb shish, comes at city prices, but that's to be expected in touristic Pamukkale. Meals are served on a patio in warm weather. ⊠Pamukkale Kasabası, Denizli ☎258/272–2451.

$$ ⌆**Grand Sevgi Hotel.** Centered around a large C-shaped swimming pool, this four-story hotel is a small resort in itself. Five bars and a restaurant are scattered about the lounges and terraces, as is a gift shop and fitness center. All that's missing is a view of the travertines, a short walk away. **Pros:** spacious, with more amenities than the other hotels in the area. **Cons:** no view of the travertines; no nonsmoking rooms, though rooms are properly aired out for nonsmokers. ⊠Pamukkale, Denizli, ☎258/272–3000 ⊕www.grandsevgiotel.com ⤶148 rooms ⚏In-hotel: restaurant, bars, swimming pool, gym ⊟AE, MC, V.

DID YOU KNOW?

The stunning white cliffs of Pamukkale were created over several eons as the minerals in the volcanic spring water crystallized into rock.

$ ⌂ **Hal-Tur Hotel.** All of the clean, fresh rooms at this distinctive white stone hotel have balconies overlooking the travertines, and one large family room has its own large terrace with a Jacuzzi. Thoughtful extras, such as candies on the pillows and slippers, make a stay that much more comfortable. **Pros:** staff are knowledgeable about Pamukkale and the surrounding area; rooms have a full view of the travertines in Pamukkale. **Cons:** the family room is large but has low ceilings. ⊠ *Mehmet Akif Ersoy Blv. 45 Pamukkale, Denizli* ☎ *258/272–2723* ⊕ *www.haltur.net* ➘ *11 rooms* ⌂ *In-hotel: bar, pools, gym* ═ *AE, MC, V.*

WORD OF MOUTH

"I am far from an expert, but I... enjoyed Afrodisias very much. I wouldn't say it is as wonderful as Ephesus, but it is truly a fascinating site to visit." —lucy_d

¢ ⌂ **Hotel Pamukkale.** Cheerful rooms surround a pool in a pleasant, motel-like arrangement. The mother-son team make sure the place is spotless and well-run, and serve home-cooked meals on a pleasant terrace in warm weather. **Pros:** good value and quiet; friendly mother-son team run the hotel. **Cons:** not a full view of the travertines, though parts can be seen from the terrace. ⊠ *Pamukkale, Denizli,* ☎ *258/272–2090* ⊕ *www.hotelpamukkale.net* ➘ *12 rooms* ⌂ *In-hotel: restaurant, Wi-Fi* ═ *MC, V.*

APHRODISIAS

80 km (50 mi) from Pamukkale, west on E87 and south on Rte. 585 at town of Kuyucak.

GETTING HERE AND AROUND

You can easily reach Aphrodisias on the way to Pamukkale, or from İzmir, Çeşme, and Selçuk, but the most direct route is from Kuşadası, where a large number of daily tours originate. Many of the tours include Pamukkale as well, since these two sights are only 50 mi apart. You'll need a full day to get a true taste of Aphrodisias, and it may save you much time and energy to rent a car and visit these towns on your own.

EXPLORING

★ **Aphrodisias.** The city of Aphrodite, goddess of love, is one of the largest and best-preserved archaeological sites in Turkey. Though most of what you see today dates from the 1st and 2nd centuries AD, archaeological evidence indicates the local dedication to Aphrodite follows a long history of veneration of pre-Hellenic goddesses, such as the Anatolian mother goddess and the Babylonian god Ishtar. Only about half the site has been excavated.

Aphrodisias, which was granted autonomy by the Roman Empire in the late 1st century BC, prospered as a significant center for religion, arts, and literature in the early 1st century AD. Imposing Christianity on its citizens proved difficult, however, because of Aphrodite's large following. One method used to eradicate remnants of paganism was renaming the city, first Stavropolis (City of the Cross), then simply Caria, which archaeologists believe is the origin of the name of the present-day village of Geyre, which contains Aphrodisias in its borders.

The excavations here have led archaeologists to believe Aphrodisias was a thriving sculpture center, with patrons beyond the borders of the city—statues and fragments with signatures of Aphrodisian artists have shown up as far away as Greece and Italy. The towering Babadağ range of mountains, east of the city, offered ancient sculptors a copious supply of white and delicately veined blue-gray marble, which has been used to stunning effect in statuary, in spiral and fluted columns, and in the delicate reliefs of gods and men, vines, and acanthus leaves on decorative friezes.

The beauty of Aphrodisias rests in its details, and a good place to start absorbing them is the **site museum,** just past the ticket booth. The museum's collection includes several impressive statues from the site, including Aphrodite herself. ■ TIP→ Pick up a guide and a map—you'll need them, as the signage is poor.

From the museum, follow the footpath to the right, which makes a circuit around the site and ends up back at the museum. The **Tetrapylon** is a monumental gateway with four rows of columns and some of the better remaining friezes. The **Temple of Aphrodite** was built in the 1st century BC on the model of the great temples at Ephesus. Its gate and many of its columns are still standing; some bear inscriptions naming the donor of the column. Next to the temple is the fine **Odeon,** an intimate, semicircular concert hall and public meeting room. Farther on is the **stadium,** which once was the scene of footraces, boxing and wrestling matches, and other competitions. One of the best preserved of its kind anywhere, the stadium could seat up to 30,000 spectators. The **theater,** built into the side of a small hill, is still being excavated. Its 5,000 white-marble seats are simply dazzling on a bright day. The adjacent **School of Philosophy** has a colonnaded courtyard with chambers lining both sides where teachers would work with small groups of students. ⌨ *Site $2.50, museum $2.50* ⊘ *Site and museum daily 8:30–5.*

PRIENE, MILETUS AND DIDYMA

GETTING HERE AND AROUND
Tours to these three towns can be arranged in Izmir, Çeşme, Selçuk, Kuşadası, and Bodrum. Pamukkale Bus Company goes from İzmir to Didyma, and minibuses stop at Priene and Miletus.

ESSENTIALS
Visitor Information Didyma (✉ *Eski Kaymakanlık Binası* ☎ *256/811–4529*).

EXPLORING
These three towns make up part of Ancient Ionia. They're all within 40 km (25 mi) of each another, and if you get an early enough start, you can visit them all in one day. If you have more time, and want some time away from the commotion of the Aegean coast, consider staying in Priene, where there's a lovely little *pansiyon.*

★ **Priene** sits spectacularly atop a steep hill above the flat valley of the Büyük Menderes (Maeander River). Dating from about 350 BC, the present-day remains of the city were still under construction in 334, when Alexander the Great liberated the Ionian settlements from Persian rule. At that time it was a thriving port, but as in Ephesus, the harbor silted over, commerce moved to neighboring Miletus, and the city's prosperity waned. As a result, the Romans never rebuilt Priene, and the simpler Greek style predominates as in few other ancient cities in Turkey. Excavated by British archaeologists in 1868–69, it's smaller than Ephesus and far less grandiose.

From the parking area, the walk up to the Priene ruins is fairly steep; because the routes through the ruins are well marked, you won't need a map. After passing through the old city walls, you follow the city's original main thoroughfare; note the drainage gutters and the grooves worn into the marble paving stones by the wheels of 4th-century BC chariots. Continuing west, you come to the well-preserved *bouleterion* (council chamber) on the left. Its 10 rows of seats flank an orchestra pit with a little altar, decorated with bulls' heads and laurel leaves, at the center. Passing through the doors on the opposite side of the council chamber takes you to the **Sacred Stoa,** a colonnaded civic center, and the edge of the **agora,** the marketplace. Farther west along the broad promenade are the remains of a row of **private houses,** each of which typically has two or three rooms on two floors; of the upper stories, only traces of a few stairwells remain. In the largest house a statue of Alexander was found.

A block or so farther along the main street is the **Temple of Athena,** the work of Pytheos, architect of the Mausoleum of Halicarnassus (one of the Seven Wonders of the Ancient World)—the design was repeatedly copied at other sites in the Greek empire. Alexander apparently chipped in on construction costs for the temple, a dwelling for the goddess Athena rather than a place for worshippers to gather; only priests could enter. Walk north and then east along the track that leads to the well-preserved little **theater,** sheltered on all sides by pine trees. Enter through the stage door into the orchestra section; note the five front-row VIP seats, carved thrones with lions' feet. If you scramble up a huge rock known as Samsun Dağı (behind the theater and to your left as you face the seats), you will find the scanty remains of the **Sanctuary of Demeter,** goddess of the harvest; a few bits of columns and walls remain, as well as a big hole through which blood of sacrificial victims was poured as a gift to the deities of the underworld. Since few people make it up here, it is an incredibly peaceful spot, with a terrific view over Priene and the plains. Above this, should you care to go farther, are the remnants of a Hellenistic fortress. ⊠*37 km (23 mi) from Kuşadası, southeast on Rte. 515, south on Rte. 525, west on Rte. 09–55 (follow signs)* ☎*No phone* ☜*$1.50* ⊗*Daily 8:30–6.*

Miletus was one of the greatest commercial centers of the Greek world before its harbor silted over. The first settlers were Minoan Greeks from Crete, who arrived between 1400 BC and 1200 BC. The Ionians, who arrived 200 years later, slaughtered the male population and married the widows. The philosopher Thales was born here in the early 6th century BC; he calculated the height of the pyramids at Giza, suggested that the universe was actually a rational place despite its apparent disorder, and coined the phrase "Know thyself." Miletus was also home to the mathematicians Anaximenes, who held that air was the single element behind the diversity of nature, and Anaximander, whose ideas anticipated the theory of evolution and the concept of the indestructibility of matter. Like the other Ionian cities, Miletus was passed from one ruling empire to another and was successively governed by Alexander's generals Antigonus and Lysimachus and Pergamum's Attalids, among others. Under the Romans the town finally regained some control over its own affairs and shared in the prosperity of the region. St. Paul preached here before the harbor became impassable and the city had to be abandoned once and for all.

The archaeological site is sprawled out along a desolate plain, and laced with well-marked trails. The parking lot is right outside the city's most magnificent building—the **Great Theater,** a remarkably intact 25,000-seat amphitheater built by the Ionians and kept up by the Romans. Along the third to sixth rows some inscriptions reserving seats for notables are still visible, and the vaulted passages leading to the seats have the feel of a modern sporting arena. Climb to the top of the theater for a look at the defensive walls built by the Byzantines and a view across the ancient city.

To see the rest of the ruins, follow the dirt track to the right of the theater. A stand of buildings marks what was once a broad processional avenue. The series begins with the **Delphinion,** a sanctuary of Apollo; a **Seljuk hammam** added to the site in the 15th century, with pipes for hot and cold water still visible; a **stoa** (colonnaded porch) with several reerected Ionic columns; the foundations of a **Roman bath** and **gymnasium;** and the first story of the **Nymphaion,** all that remains of the once highly ornate three-story structure, resembling the Library of Celsus at Ephesus, that once distributed water to the rest of the city.

To the south, the dirt track becomes a tree-lined lane that leads to the **İlyas Bey Cami,** a mosque built in 1404 in celebration of its builder and namesake's escape from Tamerlane, the Mongol terror. The mosque is now a romantic ruin: the ceiling is cracked, dust covers the tiles, and birds roost inside. The path from the mosque back to the parking lot passes a small museum, the **Miletus Müzesi,** containing some finds from the site and the surrounding area. ⊠ *22 km (14 mi) south of Priene on Rte. 09-55* ☎ *No phone* ⌂ *Ruins $1.50, museum $2* ☉ *Tues.–Sun. 8:30–6.*

Didyma (Didim in Turkish), a resort town on the rise, was an important sacred site connected to Miletus by a road of statues. The temple of Apollo is here, as well as some beaches, which are increasingly frequented by Brits who have bought real estate in the area.

Didyma is famous for its magnificent **Temple of Apollo.** As grand in scale as the Parthenon—measuring 623 feet by 167 feet—the temple has 124 well-preserved columns, some still supporting their architraves. Started in 300 BC and under construction for five centuries, the temple was never completed, and some of the columns remain unfluted. The oracle here rivaled the one at Delphi, and beneath the courtyard is a network of underground corridors used by temple priests for their oracular consultations. The corridor walls would throw the oracle's voice into deep and ghostly echoes, which the priests would interpret. The tradition of seeking advice from a sacred oracle here probably started long before the arrival of the Greeks, who in all likelihood converted an older Anatolian cult based at the site into their own religion. The Greek oracle had a good track record, and at the birth of Alexander the Great (356 BC) predicted that he would be victorious over the Persians, that his general Seleucus would later become king, and that Trajan would become an emperor.

The popularity of the oracle dwindled with the rise of Christianity, around AD 385. The temple was later excavated by French and German archaeologists, and its statues are long gone, hauled back to England by Sir Charles Newton in 1858. Fragments of bas-reliefs on display by the entrance to the site include a gigantic head of Medusa and a small statue of Poseidon and his wife, Amphitrite. ⊠ *22 km (14 mi) south of Priene on Rte. 09–55* ☎ No phone ☎ *$1.50* ☉ *Daily 8:30–6.*

For a rest after all this history, continue another 5 km (3 mi) south to **Altınkum.** The white-sand beach, which stretches for a bit less than 1 km (½ mi), is bordered by a row of decent seafood restaurants, all facing the water, and some small hotels.

WHERE TO STAY AND EAT

$$
TURKISH
✕ **Didim Şehir Lokantası.** Though a bit out of the way in Yenihisar, a residential neighborhood, the restaurant offers a complimentary shuttle service and the quality and price of the offerings make the trip worthwhile. The İskender, thin strips of gyro over pita chips, served with a tomato sauce and yogurt, is especially good. ⊠ *Off Cumhuriyet Cad., next to Tedaş, Didyma* ☎ *256/811–4488 or 256/811–4499* ⊕ *www. didimsehirlokantasi.com* ▤ *AE, MC, V.*

$$$
TURKISH
✕ **Kamacı 2.** This is the best restaurant you'll find in Altınkum, located right on the water at the end of the pier away from the noise of Didyma's touristy bars. Evenings here can be very romantic, with the moon often in full view, and the fish is fresh. Prawns, seasoned and cooked to perfection, are a great appetizer to share. ⊠ *Yali Cad. Iskele Karsisi, Altınkum-Didim* ☎ *256/813–2349* ▤ *AE, MC, V.*

$
▨ **Medusa House Pansiyon.** This small, unassuming restored stone house is made for relaxation—the garden and the terrace have plenty of spots for quiet contemplation. It's next to the Temple of Apollo and is one of the nicest accommodations Didyma has to offer. **Pros:** elegantly decorated, best value in the area. **Cons:** not much in the way of amenities. ⊠ *Next to the Temple of Apollo, Didyma* ☎ *256/811–0063* ⊕ *www. medusahouse.com* ⤳ *7 rooms, 2 houses* ⌂ *In-room: no a/c, no phone, no TV* ▤ *AE, MC, V.*

¢
▨ **Priene Pansiyon.** This *pansiyon* is a pleasant getaway in a village near the ruins of Priene, with tidy, bright rooms surrounding a rectangular courtyard. Book in advance in August, when archaeology students fill up the place. **Pros:** provides sanctuary in a very touristy area of Turkey. **Cons:** modest rooms with no amenities. ⊠ *Turunçlar Mh., Güllübahçe* ☎ *256/547–1009* ⤳ *16 rooms* ⌂ *In-room: no a/c* ▤ *AE, MC, V.*

LAKE BAFA

30 km (19 mi) north of Bodrum.

GETTING HERE

Shortly before you reach Milas, along the road to Bodrum, Route 525 skirts the south shore of **Çamiçi Gölü** (Bafa Gölü, or Lake Bafa).

EXPLORING

The lake is relatively small and undeveloped, especially away from the main road. For a change of pace, rent a boat (which will cost you around $45 round-trip) to go across the lake, or drive the rough 10-km (6-mi) road along the eastern shore, to the village of Kapıkiri and the ancient ruins of **Heracleia.** Though a minor town in antiquity, Heracleia has a wonderful setting, surrounded by high mountains. The villagers are Türkmen, descended from the Turkish tribes that settled Anatolia in the 13th and 14th centuries. The ruins, a Temple of Athena and some city walls, are also unusual: they were left by Carians, a native Asian people who adopted the Greek language and culture. On an islet facing the village are the remains of a Byzantine monastery, and huge volcanic boulders are scattered about. The combination of elements is incredibly atmospheric.

WHERE TO STAY AND EAT

$ ✕**Çeri Cafe and Restaurant.** Fresh fish from the lake is the specialty, and TURKISH because the lake is so salty, you'll find sea bream and sea bass, and other denizens of the sea on the menu. You can also just stop by for a drink or snack on the lake, which is beautiful at dusk. ⊠*Off the İzmir-Bodrum road at Lafe Bafa* ☎*252/519–1011* ▤*AE, MC, V.*

¢ ⌂**Club Natura Oliva.** The 24 rooms in several two-story houses have TURKISH fireplaces and views of the Heracleia ruins, the lake, and the Latmos Fodor'sChoice Mountains. Bird-watching is an option, with flamingos and pelicans ★ stopping by, and hiking trails abound. You can go swimming from the club's dock, but make sure you bring swimming shoes during the summer, when there's lots of seaweed and mussel shells. The resort can arrange tours to places like Bodrum, Pamukkale, and Iassos. **Pros:** calm and peaceful atmosphere; open buffet with a good selection homemade Turkish food. **Cons:** need transportation to get to nearby cities, there's nothing within walking distance of the resort. ⊠*Kocaorman Mah. 10, Pınarcık Köyü, Bafa Gölü* ☎*252/519–1072* ⊕*www.clubnatura. com* ⇥*24 rooms* ⌂*In-room: no a/c (some), no TV (some). In-hotel: restaurant, bar, Internet terminal* ▤*AE, MC, V.*

MILAS

50 km (31 mi) north of Bodrum.

ESSENTIALS

Visitor Information **Milas** (⊠*Belediye Cad.* ☎*252/513–7770*).

EXPLORING

Milas is one of the underrated stops on the way to Bodrum: it's usually just visited for its airport, the largest in the region, but the town is rich in history and charm and worth an afternoon, if not an overnight.

The **Archaeological Museum,** south of the dolmuş terminal, and the city's newly opened tourism bureau are side by side and would be a good place to start. The staff at the tourism office is friendly and helpful. ✉ *Şair Ulvi Akgün.* Just across the street, the Ulu Cami (The Great Mosque), the largest one in Milas, is made of pillaged material from antiquity and dates from 1378. From the mosque, make your way up to the Baltalı Kapı, or Axed Gate, which dates back to the 1st century BC, and is named after the double-headed ax located on the gate's keystone. The Gümüşkesen Tomb, from the 2nd century AD, is still in good shape and resembles the Mausoleum in Bodrum.

MILAS RUGS

Milas rugs, woven out of wool, are internationally famous—there is one on display at the Metropolitan Museum of Art in New York City. They are currently no longer produced in Milas, but in a dozen surrounding villages. The entire Milas district includes up to 7,000 weavers, some of whom work full-time and others who work only during periods of high demand.

Many Milas houses were built in the 19th and early 20th century, and are entered through courtyards and have bay windows that jut out into the street. The Çöllüölu Hanı is an 18th-century kervansaray where locals continue to keep workshops and use to store the items they sell nearby. They'll let you walk around up top, which feels a bit precarious, as the building has not been restored. One artisan makes 100% goat-hair doormats with colorful animal motifs or geometric patterns. If you continue to head west, you'll end up at one of the most important Menteşoğulları remains, the 14th-century Firuz Āa Cami, built of gray marble.

WHERE TO EAT

There's not much of a dining scene in Milas, but eateries in the Arasta Park neighborhood serve inexpensive local dishes. Note that many are only open for lunch. There's not much in terms of noteworthy accommodations, either, so you're better off spending the night elsewhere.

SHOPPING

The city's **bazaar,** open Tuesday and Friday, stretches along the western part of Hisarbaşı hill. You could easily spend half the day sorting through the clothes, household goods, carpets, leather goods, jewelry, and other handicrafts. The bazaar receives many visitors from nearby towns, including Bodrum.

There's also a very interesting antique shop, **Antik Eşya** (✉ *Hisarbaşı Mah. Belediye Cad. 20* ☎ *252/512–6898*), across from the tourist office that specializes in restoring antique guns. In addition to weaponry, they have an extensive collection of antiques, some purportedly dating back to pre-Ottoman times.

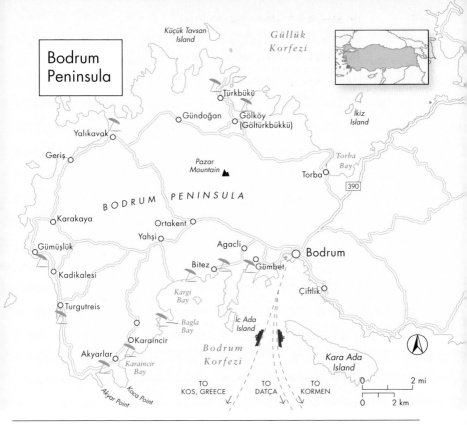

BODRUM AND THE BODRUM PENINSULA

161 km (100 mi) from Kuşadası, southeast on Rte. 515 to Rte. 525, south to Rte. 330 heading southwest; 125 km (78 mi) from Didyma, northeast on town road to Rte. 525 south to Rte. 330 southwest.

GETTING HERE AND AROUND

The Bodrum Ferryboat Assosication has ferries from Bodrum to Kos and Datça, which are right off its shores. The Bodrum Express Lines Hydrofoil and Ferryboat Services also operates ferries from Bodrum to Kos, and to Rhodes, Marmaris, and Cleopatra Island from June through August. Reservations are recommended if you're bringing your car, and make sure you bring your passport for ferries to Greece. You can also fly into the Bodrum-Milas Airport, and all major bus companies serve Bodrum, with direct service from Istanbul and Izmir.

ESSENTIALS

Ferry Info: Bodrum Express Lines (☎ *252/316–2309* ⊕ *www.bodrumexpresslines. com*). **Bodrum Ferryboat Association** (☎ *252/316–0882* ⊕ *www.bodrumferryboat. com/time.htm*).

Visitor Information Bodrum (✉ *Barış Meydanı* ☎ *252/316–1091* ✉ *Bodrum bus station* ☎ *252/316–2637*).

Travel Agencies/Tour Operators Sun Travel Agency (⌧ *Kaynak Sokak 20, Bodrum* ☎ *252/363–7556*). **Neyzen Tours** (⌧ *Kibris Sehitleri Cad. 34, 48400, Bodrum* ☎ *252/316–7204* ⊕ *www.neyzen.com.tr*)

GETTING AROUND BODRUM

Renting a car in Bodrum is only a good idea if you plan on making many day trips outside of the city. Roads are in bad repair and signage is not very good. Instead, hop on one of the minibuses (on average $1.50 per ride) that run all day and, in summer, practically all night.

EXPLORING

Bodrum, known as Halicarnassus in antiquity, is one of Turkey's leading resorts. The modern town stretches along the shores of two crescent-shaped bays and has for years been the favorite haunt of the Turkish upper classes. Today thousands of foreign visitors come here, too, and the area is bursting with hotels, guest houses, cafés, restaurants, and discos. It's still beautiful, though, with gleaming whitewashed buildings covered in bougainvillea and unfettered vistas of the sparkling bays.

Founded around 1000 BC, Halicarnassus was one of the first Greek colonies in Asia. The northern cities of the Aegean formed the Ionian League, but those farther south—Halicarnassus, Kos, Rhodes, Knidos, Lalysos, Lindos, Camiros—joined the Dorian Federation. Halicarnassus reached its height under Mausolus, who ruled from 377 BC to 353 BC as a *satrap* (governor) of what was then a distant outpost of the far-flung Persian Empire. After his death, his wife (who was also his sister), Artemisia, succeeded him. On learning that a woman ruled Halicarnassus, Rhodes sent its fleet to seize the city, only to be promptly—and soundly—defeated.

Artemisia ordered the construction of the great white-marble tomb for Mausolus at Halicarnassus that made the Seven Wonders list and gave us the word *mausoleum*. The **mausoleum** consisted of a solid rectangular base topped by 36 Ionic columns, surmounted by a pyramid, and crowned with a massive statue of Mausolus and Artemisia riding a chariot. The mausoleum has been dismantled, and the site—two blocks north of the bay and indicated by signs on Neyzen Tevfik Caddesi, the shore road ringing the west bay—is not worth the price of admission. ☎ *252/316–1095* ⌧ *$4* ⊙ *Tues.–Sun. 8:30–noon and 1–5.*

The ancient **theater** is one of the few surviving pre-Hellenic theaters in Asia Minor and thus one of the oldest; it's a popular place to take in a sunset. ⌧ *North of mausoleum* ⌧ *Free.*

The **Petronion** (*Castle of St. Peter*) is the most outstanding historic site in modern Bodrum and one of the great showpieces of late-medieval military architecture. The European crusaders known as the Knights of St. John seized Bodrum in 1402 and dismantled the mausoleum, using many of the stones to build the Petronion. The castle and its beautiful gardens, visible from every part of town, look as if they belong in a fairy tale. On the ramparts, you may recognize prominent coats of arms—those of the Plantagenets, d'Aubussons, and others. The five turrets are named after the homelands of the knights, who came from England, France, Germany, Italy, and Spain. Inside is an unusual and interesting

Daily boat cruises from the marina in Bodrum's city center will take you out to various area swimming spots.

Museum of Underwater Archaeology, with treasures recovered from historic wrecks discovered off the Aegean coast. Many artists set up little stands throughout the fortress, including the museum area, where they sell their work. Although some people complain about this addition, the artists have very interesting pieces. One artist, Cem Özakman, has won several awards for his jewelry. ⊠ *Kale Cad.* ☎ *252/316–2516* ✆ *$7* ☉ *Tues.–Sun. 8:30–noon and 1–5.*

WHERE TO STAY AND EAT

Bodrum's city center has a large marina and is on the water, but there's really nowhere to swim. Many daily boat tours leave from the marina and take guests to various coves around the peninsula, which is optimal for swimming. Gümbet, 2 km (1 mi) away from Bodrum, is pretty much considered Bodrum's beach, and as a result, is full of restaurants, bars, and shops, as well as surf schools.

$$$–$$$$ ✕ **Gemibaşı.** This Greek-influenced taverna, a longtime presence in Bod-
TURKISH   rum, is simple and no-frills, focusing on the quality, and freshness of the fish it offers. Batter-coated calamari is a popular starter, while the fresh herbs on the mixed salad taste as though they may have just been picked from the garden. This popular spot fills up at night with locals and Turkish and foreign tourists. ⊠ *Neyzen Teyfik Cad. 176, 48400* ☎ *252/316–1220* ➡ *MC, V.*

$$$–$$$$ ✕ **Körfez.** This lively and popular 50-year-old fish house is noted for
TURKISH   delicious appetizers, such as shrimp cooked in butter and garlic and seaweed (*deniz börülcesi*). ⊠ *Neyzen Tevfik Cad. 2 48400* ☎ *252/313–8248* ⊕ *www.korfezbar.com.tr/_rest* ➡ *AE, MC, V.*

$ ✕ **Öz Sakallı Köfteci.** Turkish shish-style meatballs have made this restau-
TURKISH   rant so popular, but the daily homecooked meals are also very good.
Most of these tend to be stews cooked with seasonal vegetables. ⊠*Çarşı
içi 2. Sokak 11 48400* ☏*252/316–3666* ⊟*MC, V.*

$ ✕ **Sünger Pizza.** This cheap, cheerful, and central spot is popular for its
TURKISH   coal-fired, stone-oven pizza and a Bodrum specialty *Çökertme* kebab,
finely grated french fries topped with thin slices of sirloin and garlicky
yogurt, garnished with lettuce and a few slices of tomato. Ask for a table
on their terrace, where there's a great view of the water and Bodrum
marina. ⊠*Neyzen Tevfik Cad.* ☏*252/316–0854* ⊟*MC, V.*

$$ ⏢ **Manastir Hotel Bodrum.** A former monastery overlooks Bodrum, and
many of the spacious, whitewashed rooms have balconies. With a pool,
restaurants, and bars, this hilltop retreat is a bit of a self-contained
retreat that you may never feel the need to leave. **Pros:** beautiful view
of Bodrum's white houses and the sea; funky building. **Cons:** the long
walk up; not very close to the sea. ⊠*Kumbahçe Mahallesi Mustafa
Pasa Cad. 37* ☏*252/316–2854* ⊕*www.manastirbodrum.com* ⤶*60
rooms* ⚴*In-room: Wi-Fi. In-hotel: 2 restaurants, bars, tennis court,
pool* ⊟*DC, MC, V.*

$ ⏢ **Mylasa Pansiyon.** Proximity to Bodrum sites and nightlife is one of the
main attractions of this simple pension, though the beach is a trek or
bus ride away. Best are the bedrooms with a view of the Aegean, and
the sunny outlook can be enjoyed on the roof terrace as well. **Pros:** the
roof deck and some of the bedrooms have a great view of the Aegean;
within walking distance of many attractions. **Cons:** it can be noisy at
night; you need transportation to get to the beach. ⊠*Cumhuriyet Cad.
Dere Sokak 2,* ☏*252/316–1846* ☏*252/316–1254* ⤶*16 rooms* ⚴*In-
hotel: restaurant, room service, bar* ⊟*MC, V.*

NIGHTLIFE

Nightlife in Bodrum is more sophisticated than elsewhere along the
Aegean. The **Halikarnas Disco** (⊠*Cumhuriyet Cad. 178* ☏*252/316–
8000*) bills itself as "probably the most amazing nightclub in the world."
It is, in fact, rather like discos more commonly found in western Medi-
terranean resorts, complete with fog machines and laser lights.

Hadigari (⊠*Dr. Alım Bey Cad. 37* ☏*252/313–1960*) is one of Bod-
rum's longtime discos that still draws a big crowd. On weekends, they
have female show dancers and a live act featuring a belly dancer with
a snake.

The **Marina Yacht Club** (⊠*Bodrum Marina, Neyzen Tevfik Cad. 5*
☏*252/316–1228*) is the first place both Bodrum locals and Turkish
tourists will recommend for a good night out. The live music is as
diverse as the age groups that come to listen and the dining area on the
second floor has a long bar with a terrific view of the marina. Drinks
are pricey, but there's no cover charge.

Fink and Küba (⊠*Fink: Neyzen Tevik Cad. 32; Küba: Neyzen Tefvık
Cad.*), two upscale lounges within earshot of each other on Bodrum's
harbor, are similar in appearance at first glance. However, Küba also
has an upscale restaurant popular amoung the Bodrum elite, both young

and old, and looks classier. Music ranges from pop-techno to jazz and world.

Mavi Bar (⊠ *Cumhuriyet Cad. 175* ☎ *252/316–3932*) is a venerable mecca in Bodrum drinking circles, attracting Turkish artists, writers, and their numerous hangers-on.

Marine Club Catamaran (⊠ *Next to the Bodrum castle* ☎ *252/313–3600*) is a full-fledged sea party.

THE GREAT INDOORS

If you'd rather just sit back and relax, or if you're recovering from an intensive workout, Bodrum's **hamam** (⊠ *Opposite the bus station on Cevat Şakir Rd.* ☎ *252/313–4129*) is the place. There are separate facilities for men and women.

The catamaran, a floating disco with a transparent, glass-floor disco, sails out to sea after 1 AM, when other nightclubs are required by law to turn the volume down or close up altogether. There are two resident DJs and a choice of five bars.

Each Bodrum cove has its own nightlife, Türkbükkü being the most renowned. The whole quay is covered with lounges, bars, and clubs, each sporting its own deck stretching out over the sea.

The place to see and be seen is **Ship Ahoy** (⊠ *Türkbükkü* ☎ *252/377–5070*), and it's the most crowded spot on any given night.

The chic and sleek **Supper Club** (⊠ *Yalı Mevkii, Gölköy-Türkbükkü*) is the new kid on the block, one of the many bars on the dimly lit slope in Gölköy (coming from Bodrum, it's the neighborhood before you get to Türkbükkü). You'll probably have to ask around to find it.

SPORTS AND THE OUTDOORS

The Bodrum Peninsula has tons of outdoor activities, including scuba diving, sponge diving, horseback riding, hiking, waterskiing, and windsurfing.

DIVING   The sea around Bodrum provides some of the best diving in the Aegean. There are 16 dive spots, with Geriş being the best for sponge divers. At least 10 schools are registered with PADI, the worldwide diving organization. The **Diving Center** (☎ *252/343–1032*) in Aktur/Bitez is one of the most reliable PADI-certified dive operators. Also check out **Motif Diving** (⊠ *Eski Hukumet Sokak 112/C, Bodrum* ☎ *252/316–6252* ⊕ *www.motifdiving.com*). The **Erman Dive Center** (☎ *252/368–9594 or 532/213–5989* ⊕ *www.ermandive.com*) has two locations in Bodrum, in the Hapimag Resort Sea Garden and at the Karada Marina.

HIKING   Yalıkavak, with its mountainous terrain, is the most ideal hiking area. Contact **Bodrum Nature Sport Club** (☎ *252/313–2159*) for more information.

HORSEBACK RIDING   Gündoğan is the best place for horseback riding, with its nice forest trails, although Ortakent and Turgutreis are also good alternatives. Contact **Farilya Farm** (☎ *532/355–9170*) in Gündoğan, **Country Ranch** (☎ *252/382–5654, 533/654–9586 for English*) in Turgutreis, and **Yahşi Riding** (☎ *252/358–6526*) in Yahşi for horseback riding packages.

WINDSURFING   Fener, in the Turgutreis area, is great for windsurfing. **Kempinski Hotel** (☎ *252/311–0303*) in Bodrum has windsurfing rentals and instruction.

SHOPPING

There is a bazaar every day of the week in Bodrum and in the surrounding towns, the most popular being in Turgutreis. The Turgutreis bazaar, held on Saturday, has everything under the Bodrum sun, including leather goods and jewelry. The rest of the bazaars are as follows: Türkbükkü on Monday, Bodrum and Gölköy on Tuesday, Ortakent and Gündoğan on Wednesday, Yalıkavak on Thursday, and Bodrum's fruit, vegetable, and food bazaar on Thursday and Friday.

Bodrum's handmade sandals are renowned. **Ali Güven** (⊠ *Bodrum Sq.*), who once made sandals for Mick Jagger, is the most trusted and well-established of the cobblers; he's been in business for more than 40 years. His lightweight designs are made from specially worked leather, very comfortable for the Mediterranean summer, and aesthetically pleasing as well.

BODRUM'S BEACH TOWNS

Visitors flock to the peninsula for its numerous coves, bays, and multitoned water. Each beach has its own style and ambience, so choose accordingly. You can access many by land, and even more by water, which is why taking a daylong boat trip is an especially good idea. With competition on the rise, there are many different options available.

AKYARLAR/KARAINCIR/TURGUTREIS

Akyarlar and Karaincir, opposite bays, are on the way to Turgutreis near the Aspat Mountains. Some of the peninsula's most picture-postcard waters make up these two beaches. Turgutreis has a more developed coast, with a very popular and lively bazaar. Its marina attracts the yachting crowd and is a bit more touristy than the other bays. After swimming in the pristine sea at Akyarlar and Karaincir, the beaches of Turgutreis don't seem all that enticing.

WHERE TO STAY

$$ ⛺ **Hotel Balkız & Ali.** A restored stone house with a view of Kos Island faces a pretty little beach, and the laid-back ambience and beauty of the natural setting provide a restful retreat. The kitchen serves Italian food, as well as homemade Turkish dishes. **Pros:** beachfront. **Cons:** removed from the center of things in Bodrum. ⊠ *Akyarlar 87, Akyarlar* ☎ *252/393–6025* ⊕ *www.balkizali.com* ⤶ *18 rooms* ⚐ *In-hotel: restaurant, beachfront* ▤ *AE, MC, V.*

$ ⛺ **Hotel Kortan.** Simple elegance is the motif here. Two fancy red swings add flair to the reception area, and many of the tastefully decorated rooms have sea views. The Kortan's private beach stretches in front of the hotel. **Pros:** nice terrace for sunbathing. **Cons:** property is on the main stretch so not very private ⊠ *Atatürk Meydanı Sabancı Cad. 5, Turgutreis* ☎ *252/382–2932* ⊕ *www.kortanotel.com* ⤶ *25 rooms* ⚐ *In-room: Wi-Fi. In-hotel: restaurant, room service, bar, laundry service* ▤ *AE, MC, V.*

BITEZ

The village of Bitez lies 8 km (5 mi) west of Bodrum, and its beach, the longest in Bodrum, is another 2 km (1 mi) to the south. The stone houses in the village were built right on the road to make room for mandarin trees in the backyard. Until several decades ago, residents picked and packed the mandarins onto camels, who then carried them to the nearby ports. Walk along the backroads of Bitez to take in the fresh, citric scent of the mandarins, intermingled with 500-year-old olive trees. The village also has a *kahve* (traditionally, a Turkish café where only men socialize and play backgammon) for women, opened up by the Bitez municipality. The kahve is on Atatürk Caddesi. Most of the sand in this semicircle cove is covered by chaises or plush pillows set up in little, enclosed enclaves. A pedestrian walkway leads through the 2-km (1-mi) stretch of beach, dividing the cafés and hotels from the shore.

> **SWEET SPOT**
>
> People travel long distances for **Bitez Dondurması's** (⊠ *Atatürk Cad., Bitez*) ice cream, which has fresh fruit like mulberries—handpicked in the mountains—mixed in. It may be overpriced, but no doubt delicious.

WHERE TO STAY AND EAT

¢ ✕**Bitez Pidesi.** The *pides* here have been written up in the local papers,
TURKISH and it's no wonder. The crusts are crispy, the fillings delicious, and the prices unbeatable. ⊠*Atatürk Cad. 98, Bitez* ☎252/363–7925 ▤*No credit cards.*

$ ✕**Café Sarnıç.** This trendy beach club has a full-service restaurant. The
TURKISH outstanding homemade mantı, Turkish ravioli, topped with a tomato-yogurt sauce (as opposed to just yogurt, which is what you get at most restaurants), and the stuffed grape leaves make it worth bearing the loud club music that often plays during the day. The best time to come here is when everyone leaves—after dusk. ⊠*Aktur entrance, Bitez* ☎252/343–1433 ▤*MC, V.*

$$ ✕**Daphne.** A garden and a fireplace make this spot ideal in either sum-
TURKISH mer or winter. The fusion menu combines international favorites and seafood. One of the best parts of the meal is the complimentary eggplant, sun-dried tomato, and olive oil spreads you get, served with homemade bread. ⊠*Bitez Yalısı, Bitez* ☎252/363–7722 ▤*MC, V.*

$$ ⌂**Toloman Hotel.** A collection of white houses provide bright, airy accommodations that overlook the water from balconies. Breakfast is served on a waterside terrace, and the beach has chaises and wicker umbrellas. A sense of calm prevails, and the only real distraction, if you could call it that, is the buzzing of the cicadas in summer. ⊠*Bitez Yalısı, Bitez* ☎252/363–7751 ⊕*www.toloman.com* ⤴*33 rooms* ⌂*In-hotel: restaurant, bar, pool* ▤*AE, MC, V.*

GÖLTÜRKBÜKKÜ

The two coastal towns Gölköy and Türkbükkü, 20 km (12 mi) north of Bodrum, recently merged to become Göltürkbükkü, the most glamorous part of the Bodrum peninsula. Türkbükkü, which has been called the "St. Tropez of Turkey," is the summer playground of jet-setting, high-society Turks and foreigners, and its coastline is jam-packed with bars, cafés, restaurants, and boutiques. Gölköy is probably the better place to stay, as it has a slower pace and more stretches of undeveloped waterfront—and you can always head into Türkbükkü to socialize and party. Note that there's not much more to do in Gölköy besides sunbathe, as its layout makes it pretty difficult to walk around. Neither beach has sand, but the water is accessible from wooden decks.

WHERE TO STAY AND EAT

The dining scene in Türkbükkü has faded as the restaurants are not allowed to open out right onto the sea like they used to. As a result, several fish restaurants are no longer in business and the ones that are have lost their cachet. There are many trendy restaurants, but you're better off traveling to one of the other bays for better value and taste.

$
TURKISH
✗**Hocanın Yeri.** Excellent preparation of the Turkish-Tatarian-derived specialty *çiğbörek* (fried dough stuffed with ground beef, onion, and spice) makes this friendly, down-to-earth place popular with locals. ✉*Sahil Yolu* ☎*252/377–5907* ⊟*MC, V.*

$$$
TURKISH
✗**Miam.** A wonderful variety of fish selections includes *balık pastırma* (cured fish seasoned with fenugreek). The filet mignon is also excellent. ✉*Yalı Mevkii51* ☎*252/377–5612* ⊟*MC, V.*

$
TURKISH
✗**Sacide.** In a town full of overpriced meals, this one is a great place to find an inexpensive and delicious home-cooked meal, prepared by a mother and daughter team. ✉*Atatürk Cad. 44 Türkbükü, Bodrum 48400* ☎*252/377–5154* ⊟*MC, V.*

$$
Fodor'sChoice
★
✗🏨**Karianda B&B.** A father-and-daughter team built and expanded run this place with care, ensuring the modestly decorated rooms are spic and span and paying a great deal of attention to food. A wood-fire brick oven supplies *pides* and *lahmacun* (Turkish pizzas) and well-prepared mezes and fish dishes are served on a wooden deck built out over the bay. **Pros:** cozy feel with everything at your fingertips, excellent food. **Cons:** the neighboring pension plays their music a bit loud sometimes but turns it down upon request. ✉*Cumhuriyet Cad. 104–106, Gölköy 48400* ☎*252/357–7303 or 252/357–7819* ⊕*www.karianda. com* ➘*25 rooms* ⌂*In-room: no TV. In-hotel: restaurant, bar, beachfront* ⊟*AE, MC, V.*

$$$$
🏨**Maça Kızı.** The "Queen of Spades" is stylish and sophisticated. Handsome wooden-floored rooms face the bay or a pretty garden, and a long waterside deck is furnished with plush pillows. The restaurant specializes in Mediterranean nouveau cuisine. **Pros:** nice vibe, everything is made of natural stones and woods. **Cons:** expensive ✉*Kesireburnu Mevkii, Türkbükkü* ☎*252/377–6272* ⊕*www.macakizi.com* ➘*37 rooms* ⌂*Inhotel: restaurant, bar, pool, beachfront* ⊟*AE, MC, V.*

GÜMÜŞLÜK

Gümüşlük, 25 km (15½ mi) from Bodrum, is one of the peninsula's more authentic, slower-paced, less-developed villages. It's built on the ancient ruins of Myndos—much of the ruins are submerged underwater, but major land excavations are taking place to recover the ancient city, and an ancient drainage system dating to Myndos's Roman civilization period has already been discovered. The town is popular for its fish restaurants on the water. Its restored church now hosts cultural and artistic events, including an international classical music festival in August. There are also lots of water sports and easy outdoor adventures.

One of the popular things to do is walk through the shallow water to Tavşan Adasıı, Rabbit Island. Glassmakers and other artists reside and keep shop here, and sometimes you can see them at work.

If you have the time, and a car, make the trip up to Karakaya, a village of stone houses perched up on the hillside above Gümüşlük. Development is restricted in this town—no high-rises or large hotels are allowed.

WHERE TO EAT

$$$ ✕**Aquarium.** Excellent starters such as zucchini flower dolma, roasted
TURKISH   eggplant with *tulum* cheese, and rice with shrimp and octopus, are served in two waterside locales on Bodrum's bays, Yalıkavak and Gümüşlük. Whichever one you choose, don't skip dessert—the baklava comes from Antep, known for having the best in Turkey. ⊠*Across from the pier, Gümüşlük; at the pier in Yalıkavak* ☎*252/394–3682 Gümüşlük, 252/385–4151 Yalıkavak* ▭*MC, V.*

$ ✕**Dalgıç.** If you're tired of fish, try these homemade, traditional Turkish
TURKISH   dishes as a refreshing alternative. They are served in pleasant, friendly surroundings. ⊠*Across from the pier, Gümüşlük* ☎*252/394–4229* ▭*MC, V.*

YALIKAVAK

This town is 20 km (12 mi) outside of Bodrum, and is easily identified by the beautiful windmills atop its hill. Once a tiny cluster of houses on the quay, Yalıkavak has recently added a spiffy yacht marina, the peninsula's third. The newly remodeled tourist office is also cheerful and welcoming, and has a number of informative brochures. There are numerous coves to explore around Yalıkavak, and the strong wind makes it ideal for windsurfing. The two most popular beaches here, Dodo and Camel, tend to be overcrowded and host a lively beach club scene. There are also quieter, unnamed stretches of beach. The town is more of a car place, and you'll see a lot more if you have your own transporation.

WHERE TO STAY AND EAT

$$ ✕**Ali Baba.** Food is available from morning into the evening, and the
TURKISH   menu moves from eggs and other breakfast fare into fish, lamb, and the house specialty, the Amphora kebab. ⊠*Atatürk Cad. 42E* ☎*252/385–3194* ▭*AE, DC, MC, V.*

$ ✕**Kavaklı Köfeteci.** A quick and inexpensive meal here includes a serving
TURKISH   of Turkish meatballs, *piyaz* (a cold bean dish), and ayran. The köfte is a little on the greasy side, but very tasty nonetheless. ⊠*Çarşı İçi 24* ☎*252/385–4748* ▭*No credit cards.*

$$★   ⌂**Lavanta Hotel.** Surrounded by well-maintained grounds on a hillside overlooking Bodrum Peninsula just outside the village of Yalikavak, this tranquil retreat breaks the typical mold of bland package tourism. All of the attractive rooms overlook the sea from private terraces and are furnished with tasteful traditional pieces and antiques. Dinner, served to hotel guests only, features traditional Turkish home cooking. **Pros:** panoramic sea view, large rooms, intimate atmosphere. **Cons:** no Wi-Fi. ⊠*Yalikavak-Bodrum,* ☎*252/385–2167* ⊕*www.lavanta.com* ⌐*11*

apartment units and 8 rooms �& *In-hotel: restaurant, bar, pool, laundry service, Internet terminal* ▭*DC, MC, V.*

$$ 🏨 **Yalıkavak Marina Hotel.** Many of the beautiful rooms in this stone building have palm trees right outside their windows, and bamboo chairs, hammocks, and large cushions in the garden invite a lazy afternoon. Rooms are tastefully decorated, but the dark paint on the walls makes them a bit dim. The hotel caters especially to guests docking at the marina, but all are welcome. **Pros:** lovely outdoor area for lounging around. **Cons:** dark paint on the walls makes them a bit dim. ✉*Çokertme Mevkii, Yalikavak* 📞*252/385–3872* ⊕*www.portbodrum.com* ↩*17 rooms* �& *In-hotel: laundry service* ▭*AE, DC, MC, V.*

The Turquoise Riviera

WORD OF MOUTH

"We went to Termessos. Boy was that terrific. Spent the entire day wondering around the ruins on the mountaintop. Our only regret is we did not bring lunch because we thought it would get too hot (but the elevation keeps it cool I think). So starved but didn't leave until 4 . . . One of the best memories."

—Millie64

WELCOME TO THE TURQUOISE RIVIERA

View from the Acropolis of Simena

TOP REASONS TO GO

★ **Take a Blue Cruise.** Sail into the turquoise waters of remote and pristine bays on your own chartered yacht.

★ **Trek the Lycian Way.** Choose a one-day or multiday hike along this long-distance trail that runs parallel to much of the Turquoise Coast, from the coastal mountain forests to untouched beaches.

★ **See spectacular ruins.** Explore the ruins of some of the most spectacular ancient cities in the world—from mountaintop Termessos, to overgrown Olympos, and the extraordinarily intact Roman theater at Aspendos.

★ **Appreciate the landscape.** Rugged pine-clad mountains plunge into a vibrant blue sea that's broken by remote peninsulas and distant Greek islands.

★ **Beaches.** Some of the Mediterranean's most perfect beaches are here; protected from development by national parks, sea turtles sanctuary, and ruins; you can lie on your sun bed or plunge from a floating diving platform, away from the concrete cities.

1 The Datça Peninsula. A yacht chartered in Marmaris or Bodrum is the best way to visit the craggy hills and ancient coves of one of Turkey's most unspoiled stretches of coastline.

2 The Lycian Coast. Rent a car from the Dalaman or Antalya airport and slowly explore the charming ports, boutique hotels, uncrowded beaches, and ancient ruins along the little-developed coastal circuit.

3 Antalya. This vibrant city has everything—an old city, beaches, good restaurants and nightlife—and it's a good place to base yourself for taking in the ancient sites of Aspendos, Perge, Termessos, and Phaselis.

Gulets harbored in Simena

Apollon Temple, Side

GETTING ORIENTED

4 **Pamphylia.** The area from Antalya to Alanya, including the sites of Termessos, Perge, Aspendos, and Alara Han is considered historic Pamphylia. The newly spruced-up centers of Side and Alanya have recovered some of their former charm and benefit from warm spring and autumn seasons.

5 **East of Alanya.** The area east of Alanya is not much traveled but if you're heading to Antakya (Antioch) there are some interesting stops along the way and the drive is quite pretty.

Olüdeniz Beach

The area known as the Turquoise Riviera stretches along the Mediterranean coast from the rugged and unspoiled Datça peninsula on Turkey's southwestern tip to the resort hotels springing up along the Antalya-Alanya strip. The fir-clad mountains rising behind the coastline are punctuated by the ruins of splendid ancient Greek and Roman cities, through which passed the likes of Alexander the Great, Julius Caesar, and St. Paul.

THE TURQUOISE RIVIERA PLANNER

Booking a Local Tour

If you want to book a local tour—anything from boat tours to trekking tours or local spe-cial-interest tours—you're best off wandering through the cen-ter of whatever town you're in. Choose a local travel agency that looks well-kept, and chat with the owner. Don't hesitate to move politely on to another one if you feel hassled or inad-equately served. You can also ask at your hotel: they're likely to recommend the agency that gives them the best commis-sion, and they'll probably add a commission from you, too, but it can be worth the cost for convenience and reliability.

Blue Cruising

A yacht charter in a *gulet*, a wooden motor boat or sail-ing boat, is the quintessential, relaxing way to explore Turkey's coast. For the full effect, plan at least four days and at best a week, perhaps from Anta-lya to Fethiye, or a tour of the Datça peninsula from Marmaris. *For more information, see the Blue Cruising CloseUp in this chapter.*

Specialty Tours

Trekking opportunities abound in this part of Turkey. For serious walkers, the 530-km (331-mi) Lycian Way is the standing challenge. If you prefer to have a guid, individu-ally or as part of a group, contact Middle Earth Travel.

The areas is also great for rafting or trekking trips. The three main areas are around Fethiye and Ölüdeniz, in Köprülü National Park near Antalya, and along Alanya's Dimçay River. You'll pass through soaring canyons and under ancient Roman bridges. The Alraft Rafting and Riding Club, in Alanya, arranges rafting trips, as well as horse-back riding treks. Also in Antalya are Medraft and Trans-Nature, both outdoor-sports specialists. In Fethiye, Aventura specializes in all kinds of activities, including paragliding. In Side, Get Wet can arrange all kinds of outdoor activities such as rafting, trekking, and mountaineering.

History- and religion-oriented tours are not uncommon around the south coast of Turkey area, particularly due to association with **St. Paul,** who evangelized the area. A 400-km (250-mi) trekking route known as the **St. Paul Trail** has takes in some places he is known to have passed through. A guide isn't really necessary and the trekkers are usually independent—but Middle Earth Travel arranges tours. More traditional weeklong bus tours look at Christian sites in the Antalya area and then go on to Ephesus, where St. Paul preached in the theater. More information can be had from Paul's Place in Antalya.

Contacts Alraft Rafting and Riding Club (☎242/513–9155). **Aventura** (☎252/617–0314). **Get Wet** (☎242/753–4071). **Medraft** (☎248/312–0083). **Middle Earth Travel** (☎384/271–2559 ⊕www.middleearthtravel.com). **Paul's Place** (☎242/247–6857). **TransNature** (☎242/324–0011).

How Much Time?

If you just have a weekend or so on the Turquoise Riviera and want to see ancient sites, base yourself in Antalya and drive out to nearby Termessos, Perge, or Aspendos: they're some of the best preserved classical sites in the country.

A road trip around the Lycian coast is beautiful, and full of the ruins of ancient Lycian cities like Xanthos, Patara, and Olympos. Count on about 10 hours' total driving, starting in either Antalya or Dalaman. There are many unspoiled towns and lovely hotels en route. You could spend as few as three days, but five to seven would be more relaxing. A sample six-day tour would have you leave from Antalya and visit Termessos, then cross the mountains to Fethiye. Overnight in the mountains above Ölüdeniz. On Day 2, visit Ölüdeniz, the ghost town of Kaya, and Fethiye; overnight in the same hotel as the previous night. On Day 3, visit the ancient Lycian cities of Pinara, Xanthos, and Letoön, finishing with a swim in Patara. Overnight in Patara or Kalkan. On Day 4, head to Kaş and take a day boat trip to Kekova. Overnight in Kaş. On Day 5, visit St. Nicholas's Basilica in Demre, have lunch in Finike, and visit Arycanda in the afternoon. Overnight in Çıralı and see the burning Chimera. On Day 6, visit Phaselis, then return to Antalya.

About the Local Food

Regional specialties along the coast include mussels stuffed with rice, pine nuts, and currants; *ahtopot salatası,* a cold octopus salad, tossed in olive oil, vinegar, and parsley; and grilled fish. Most of Turkey's tomatoes, cucumbers, eggplants, zucchinis, and peppers are grown along the coast, so fresh salads are delicious. In Lycia, a local home-cooking speciality is stewed eggplant with basil—wonderful if you're offered it. *Semiz otu* (cow parsley) is a refreshing appetizer in a garlic yogurt sauce.

What It Costs in U.S. Dollars

DINING AND LODGING PRICE CATEGORIES

	¢	$	$$	$$$	$$$$
Restaurants	under $5	$5–$10	$11–$15	$16–$25	over $25
Hotels	under $50	$50–$75	$76–$150	$151–$250	over $250

Restaurant prices are for one main course at dinner or for two mezes (small dishes). Hotel prices are for two people in a standard double room in high season, including taxes.

When to Go

The ideal months on the Turquoise Riviera are May–June and September–October. Summers can be hot and humid, especially in July and August, and that's also when the beaches tend to be fuller and waterfront discos pump out their most egregious levels of noise.

Alanya and Side stay warmest longest. They're also best visited when charter tourists are least likely to be about, before or after the high season.

Along the Lycian coast, expect thunderstorms after late-October and an average 12 days of rain per month in December and January, otherwise, while not swimming weather, it can be sunshine and T-shirts. Snow graces mountain peaks well into May, a magnificent site across the ocean from Antalya and Fethiye. While not a winter sun destination, it rarely drops below freezing on the coast. Some hotels stay open between mid-December and March, often with limited facilities.

Festivals

For 4 days in the middle of September, the International Song Contest in Antalya brings open-air concerts to the area around the marina.

5

GETTING HERE & AROUND

By Taxi and Dolmuş

Provincial taxis are somewhat expensive; fares generally work out somewhere near $1 per km traveled. It's best to take a taxi from an established taxi stand, where you see several lined up, since the drivers there will be regulars and if you should have a dispute or lose something, it is much easier to retrace the car that way. It's normal, however, to hail taxis in the street. For longer journeys, you may both wish to settle a price in advance, but normally, within city limits, the taxi driver should automatically switch on the meter when you get in. As elsewhere, if he doesn't, insist upon it.

By Train

There is no train service on the Turquoise Riviera.

By Air

It makes the most sense to fly to the Turquoise Coast if you're coming from Istanbul or elsewhere in Turkey. The main airports here are in Dalaman and Antalya. Antalya is the busiest international airport in Turkey, serving the coast from Alanya to Kaş, including Side, Belek, Olympos, and Finike. Dalaman Airport serves the coast from Kaş to Datça, including Kalkan, Fethiye, Göcek, Dalyan, and Marmaris.

A host of car rental concessions operate at all airports, including all international agencies. Havaş Airport buses also link the two airports to major towns. Major hotels and travel agencies will arrange airport shuttles as well (usually for a fee). Yellow airport taxis are somewhat expensive for individuals but are usually well regulated with a clear legal pricing system prominently displayed, and are a good option if you're sharing.

Taking a bus from Antalya airport into Antalya costs about $8; they're timed to meet all in-coming flights, and leave the city center hourly. Buses to the airport leave the Turkish Airlines building on Cumhuriyet Caddesi (on the clifftop boulevard) once every hour or two. Another bus leaves from nearby **Wing Turizm** (☎ *242/244–2236*) at even more irregular times. Yet another option if you're leaving from Antalya main bus station is to take a bus down the highway east of Antalya, get out at the airport intersection, and take one of the taxis waiting there for the last 2 km (1 mi) into the airport itself, for which the taxi charges about $3—it's a bit of a hassle, but something to consider. A taxi to the airport from the center, by comparison, costs $20.

From Dalaman Airport, airport buses will take airline passengers east via Göcek to Fethiye harbor ($15) and west to Marmaris intercity bus terminal ($19). Theoretically, the buses will leave Marmaris three hours before any flight, and Fethiye 2½ hours before. For more precise information, call Havaş, the Dalaman operating representative.

Contacts Havaş (☎ *212/444-0487 central Turkey call center*).

By Boat and Ferry

There are no longer any long-distance ferries serving the southwestern Turkish coast, though the ferry from Bodrum to Körmen, near Datça, can save a long road trip, and there are a number of ferries linking individual Turkish ports with Greek islands. In general, anyone with a U.S. or European passport, can visit Greece. Note that you need to be at the boats at least an hour before departure time to complete passport formalities. Be aware that shops and museums on Greek islands usually close during the midday heat and do not reopen until late afternoon, so it's sensible to stay a night or two if you are going to take the trouble of making the journey; however, day return tickets are usually significantly cheaper than open returns. There are frequent ferries from Marmaris and Fethiye to Rhodes, Datça to Symi, and Kaş to Kastellorizon.

Contacts **Yesil Marmaris** (☎252/412–2290 ⊕www. yesilmarmaris.com).

By Bus

Inexpensive intercity buses travel between major towns all over Turkey—it's about $40 one way for the 12-hour journey from Istanbul to Antalya. These days, though, that's only about half the price of flying.

Buses and minibuses (*dolmuşes*) are a useful form of short-haul transport within and around the Turquoise Riviera. Every city has an intercity bus terminal, and minibuses to smaller destinations set off from there, too. Major routes, such as Marmaris to Fethiye and Fethiye to Antalya have hourly buses into the early evening, typically charging about $5 per 100 km per person. Minibus schedules depend on the popularity of the route and generally stop anywhere if asked to.

When the intercity bus terminal is outside the city center (as in Antalya), major companies usually provide minibus service from their city center locations to the station: ask for a *servis* (minibus transfer service) when you book your ticket, otherwise, finding your own way to the terminal can be difficult and time-consuming. The Varan Bus Company is more expensive than others, but has better service, no-smoking buses, and its own privately owned and spotlessly clean rest stops.

Contacts **Varan Bus Company** (☎212/551–7474 in Istanbul, 242/331–1111 in Antalya).

By Car

Once here, you'll find renting a car allows you to get around with the most ease; many of the sights you'll want to see are off the main road, and the area is filled with beautiful coastal drives.

Although the highways between towns are well maintained, smaller roads are usually unpaved and rough, and the twisty coastal roads require concentration. To estimate driving times, figure on about 70 km (43 mi) per hour. By car from Istanbul to Marmaris or Antalya is at least a 10-hour, 750-km (470-mi) trek. The speed limit is 90 KPM (56 MPH) on most country roads—120 KPM (75 MPH) on real highways—and for your own safety it's best to stick to it. The police do have radars and they do use them.

All airports have several car rental associations to choose from, and many hotels can arrange car rentals. In general, the smaller and more remote the place, the cheaper the rental, but the more minimal the service.

SEAFOOD ON THE TURKISH COAST

The kebab might be the first thing that comes to mind when you think about Turkish food, but in Istanbul and along Turkey's Aegean, Mediterranean, and Black Sea coasts, fresh fish is readily available.

With its miles and miles of coastline, it's not surprising seafood is an integral part of Turkish cuisine and Turks eat fish at lunch or dinner, usually either grilled or fried, and served with little more than a squeeze of lemon and a side of fresh arugula or slices of raw onion. Varieties might be a bit different from what you're used to, but these are some of the more common ones you'll find.

In winter, hearty fish soups—similar to chowder—are served in many restaurants.

Fresh fish served in restaurants is usually sold by weight, so be sure to ask the price before ordering.

WILD VS. FARMED

Although many of the fish served in Turkey are seasonal, the growth of aquaculture in the country has led to a more dependable supply of certain types of fish, though many diners insist on eating the tastier (and more expensive) wild variety. If you want the open-sea version, ask for the deniz type, which is "from the sea."

BARBUNYA

The tasty small red mullet is popular in Turkey. As the name implies, the *barbunya*'s skin is speckled with glistening reddish spots. The mild-tasting fish, usually only a few inches long, are typically pan-fried whole; an order of them can easily be shared. The prime season for barbunya is spring through early summer.

ÇIPURA

Gilthead bream is the most popular fish caught in the Aegean area. Like *levrek*, it's a mild tasting fish with white, flaky meat, usually grilled whole and served unadorned. Fish farms now supply much of the *Çipura* served in restaurants, but the wild variety, known as *Deniz Çipurasi* is also available.

HAMSI

Size isn't everything. The finger-length anchovy is often referred to in Turkey as the "little prince" of fishes. In the Black Sea area, where *hamsi* are caught, the little fish is used in numerous dishes and forms an important part of the local economy. The most popular way *hamsi* is served is fried in a light coating of corn meal. Another popular recipe is *hamsi pilav*—a rice and anchovy dish infused with an aromatic mix of herbs and spices. *Hamsi* season is fall and winter.

LEVREK

Sea bass is one of the most popular fish in Turkey, prized for its delicate, almost sweet taste and firm white meat. *Levrek* is usually charcoal grilled whole and served with a drizzle of oil and a squeeze of lemon. Or a whole levrek might be encased in sea salt and baked in the oven. Many restaurants serve the cheaper and smaller farmed variety of the fish. Wild levrek is known as *Deniz Levreği*. Both are available all year.

LÜFER

This is the general name for bluefish, which are generally more tasty than the U.S. varieties. Bluefish is popular enough that the different sizes have their own names: small bluefish are *Çinekop*, large bluefish are *Kofana*, and medium bluefish are *Sarıkanat*.

PALAMUT

Also known as bonito, palamut is related to tuna. Unlike *levrek* and *çipura*, it's a strong-tasting, oily fish, similar to mackerel. *Palamut* fillets are often grilled, but another popular—and perhaps tastier—way they are prepared is baked in the oven with an onion and tomato sauce. Palamut appears in Turkey's waters in fall through winter.

The Turquoise Riviera is just as stunning as the name suggests, with luminous blue-green ocean waves lapping at isolated coves and beaches that range from multicolored polished marble pebbles to miles of yellow sand. Spectacular archaeological ruins are never far away.

This part of Turkey's coast is home to some of the country's most iconic beaches—like Ölüdeniz, Patara, and İztuzu—it's also the place to find spectacular ruins from ancient cities of Greek, Roman, and Byzantine origin. Termessos, known as the Eagle's Nest, is said to have defied Alexander the Great because he was daunted by its height, and the Roman theater ins Apsendos rivals the Colisseum in Rome.

THE DATÇA PENINSULA AND MARMARIS

Updated by
Scott Newman

Modernity confronts antiquity in the westernmost portion of the Mediterranean coast. The beaches are gorgeous and the mood is laid back if you don't stay in the resort areas of Datça or Marmaris proper. Datça is quieter than Marmaris, but for even more charming and remote, Eski Datça and Reshadiye are lovely little villages where you can appreciate a calmer way of life.

DATÇA PENINSULA

Datça town is 76 km (47 mi) west of Marmaris and 167 km (104 mi) west of Dalaman on Rte. 400.

GETTING HERE AND AROUND

By air, there are two ways to get to Datça: either fly to Dalaman Airport and make the three-hour drive west to Datça or, more pleasantly, Datça can be reached via Bodrum Airport and then a two-hour car-ferry ride from Bodrum Port to Datça's Körmen Port. In the June–September season, these boats run from both ports at 9 AM and 5 PM. In winter they run only on Monday, Wednesday, and Friday at 9 AM from Datça to Bodrum and at 5 PM from Bodrum to Datça. Regular buses go to

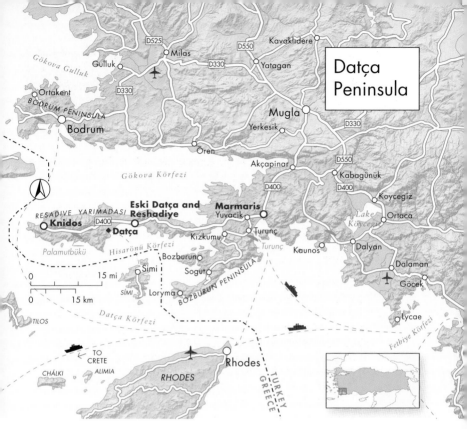

Marmaris from the Pamukkale office in town, and in summer dolmuşes to Yazıköy continue to Knidos.

ESSENTIALS

Official tourist office Datça (⊠ Hük ümet Binası, İskele Mah ☎ 252/712–3163).

EXPLORING

If you make it all the way to the **Datça Peninsula,** you may never want to leave. Winds keep pine forests to sheltered hollows, and habitations are few and far between. Driving along the thin neck of land between the Aegean Sea to the north and the Mediterranean to the south feels like entering the gateway to another, older world. This is not somewhere to drop by for a day or two: you need at least three days to savor the uncluttered joys of this unique destination—it's a place with few pressures, but wide horizons and more than 50 little beaches for inner contemplation. The best time to visit is in spring, when the hills are carpeted in poppies, daisies, and wildflowers, and restaurants offer dishes concocted with wild thyme, rosemary, and other herbs that flourish in the hills and by the sea.

The timeless stone alleys of Eski Datça give a similar sense of being in another, less stressful world. The ancient ruins of Knidos and Loryma, both best reached by boat, are some of the loveliest and most evocative sites along the whole coast.

Datça is a small, little-developed port town with some characterstics of a resort. In itself it's not the best place to stay—Eski Datça and Reşadiye are older and have more charm—but if you're here, it's pleasant to spend an evening wandering around the harbor and sipping a drink at one of the quayside cafés. The weekly market is on Saturday, which is what attracts Greek islanders from nearby Symi. It's also the best place to arrange a boat trip to Knidos. A lovely day out and a meal at an unspoiled beach can also be had at Kargı Koyu, 3 km (2 mi) east of central Datça.

WHERE TO STAY AND EAT

$ ✕**Emek Restaurant.** Everything is made on the premises in the spotless
TURKISH kitchens of this excellent eatery, the best of the bunch overlooking Datça harbor. The owner and chief chef Seyyar Kantarlı says her secret is real olive oil and all fresh ingredients. The fried squid is delicious, and wild Datça herbs make menus interesting in spring. The homemade bread is some of the best on the coast. The menu includes the usual range of seafood and Turkish grills, as well various curries. Call in the morning to reserve a balcony table. ⊠ *Yat Limanı, Datça* 📷252/712–3375 ⊟*MC, V* 🕙*Closed Nov.–Feb.*

$ ✕**Yeşim Bar Restaurant.** One of only two buildings on the pleasant beach
TURKISH at Kargı Koyu, Yeşim has sun beds, umbrellas, and showers at no extra cost to visitors ready to buy at least a glass of tea. A lawn, with trees shading a bar, makes this a cool respite from the sun, and sometimes there's live music. The menu includes pizzas, fish, and meat. ⊠*Follow the southernmost coast road for 3 km (2 mi) east of Datça; stop at the beach where the road ends* 📷252/712–8399 ⊟*MC, V.*

$ 🏨**Bora Hotel.** If you want to stay in town, this simple hotel right behind Datça harbor has clean, bright rooms and new furnishings. Front facing rooms have balconies, and those on the upper floors have sea views. **Pros:** central. **Cons:** the double glazing on the windows may not keep out all the street noise during the high season. ⊠*Street behind the yacht harbor* 📷*252/712–2040* ⊕*www.borahoteldatca.com* 🛏*18 rooms* 🛎*In-room: safe* ⊟*MC, V* 🕙*Oct.–May.*

$$ 🏨**Villa Aşina.** This pretty hotel with a stunning clifftop view over the sea to the Greek islands of Symi and Rhodes opened in 2008. All rooms have a sea view and there's a nice, small pool; a five-minute walk down a steep path leads to the hotel's pebbly beach cove. The hotel is particularly proud of its food, including hearty breakfasts, free afternoon tea, and the owner is a passionate guide to the rare wild fauna of the peninsula. **Pros:** pretty new rooms. **Cons:** a little out of town. ⊠*From Datça harbor, head south along the coast, following the signs to Villa Aşina* 📷*252/712–0443* ⊕*www.villaasina.com* 🛏*14 rooms and 3 suites* 🛎*In-room: safe. In-hotel: pool, Wi-Fi* ⊟*MC, V.*

$$ 🏨**Türk Evi.** This small boutique hotel was built in the style of an Ottoman mansion and, set in a pretty garden just south of the yacht harbor, it's a pleasant and relaxing place to stay. Rooms are decorated in Ottoman style, without being overdone and the hotel has lots of small personal touches, from Ottoman-style paintings in the rooms, to the plants

on the stairs. There is a cozy lounge area, with a TV, and endless tea available. Breakfast is included, and lunch and dinner are available with advance notice. **Pros:** homey. **Cons:** no pool. ⊠*Head west from the Harbour and look for signs* ☎*252/712–4081* ⊕*www.datcaturkevi.com* ⛱*8 rooms* ⛆*In room: no TV, Wi-Fi. In hotel: bar* ▭*MC, V.*

NIGHTLIFE

There are many bars along the yacht harbour. **Sounds Gallus,** just west of the port serves as the main discotheque for Datça; doors don't open until after midnight.

ESKI DATÇA AND RESHADIYE

★ Turkish satirical poet and polemical left-wing social critic Can Yücel retired to a modest old stone house in Eski Datça, setting an artistic tone for this pretty backwater spot, and for nearby Reshadiye. The formerly Greek-populated village, 3 km (2 mi) inland from Datça harbor on the road to Reshadiye, is one of the few in Turkey that has survived intact. It's now experiencing fine restoration efforts that have produced several lovely small houses to rent. Nobody hurries through the stone-paved alleys.

WHERE TO STAY AND EAT

$ ✕**Datça Sofrası.** This is an ideal lunch spot, with a vine-covered terrace
TURKISH and traditional Turkish braised meats emerging from under a brass-hooded charcoal brazier. The menu is also rich in vegetarian dishes and starters concocted from local wild herbs. The speciality is *bademli köfte* (meatballs with almonds). In the hottest summer months, guests can also take refuge in a cool cellar. ⊠*Hurma Cad. 16, Eski Datça* ☎*252/712–4188* ▭*No credit cards.*

$$ ⌂**Dede Pansiyon.** This comfortable stone pansiyon is swathed in bougainvilleas and decorated with curiosities like concrete flagstones set with old bathroom fittings. The large rooms have kitchenettes and themes like "Picasso" or "Theater." It's a good option and has one of the few swimming pools in Eski Datça. The garden area is huge. New owners Mehmet and Yağmur are proud of their art shop where they make and sell their own creations. **Pros:** spacious; with a maximum of eight guests the place will always feel quiet and tranquil. **Cons:** room themes like Chaplin and Picasso aren't Turkish. ⊠*Can Yücel Cad., Eski Datça* ☎*252/712–3951* ⊕*www.dedepansiyon.com* ⛱*4 rooms* ⛆*In-hotel: bar* ▭*No credit cards.*

$$$$ ⌂**Mehmet Ali Ağa Konağı.** A stay in this restored mansion offers the
Fodor'sChoice unique chance to experience the lifestyle and surroundings of a 19th-
★ century Ottoman nobleman. The owners have lovingly re-created five rooms in the main mansion that are works of art in themselves, fitting excellent modern bathrooms behind the original woodwork, restoring old wall paintings, and choosing fine antiques to match. Standard rooms are large but in a modern stone building, though situated around a lovely garden. The details are faultless, right down to the use of nearly one million custom-made iron nails. The hotel's **Elaki Restaurant ($$$)** is a gourmet's delight. Specialties include Mediterranean and Ottoman dishes, and breakfast is delicious. Reserve at least one month in advance

in July and August. The hotel also arranges hikes and trips to ancient sites and has a shuttle to Datça, the beach, and the airport. **Pros:** absolutely beautiful; delicious food. **Cons:** most rooms not in the historic mansion. ⊠*Kavak Meydan, Reshadiye, Datça* ☎*252/712–9257* ⊕*www.kocaev.com* ⌂*15 rooms, 2 suites* ⌂*In-room: no a/c (some), safe, Wi-Fi. In-hotel: bars, pool, bicycles, Internet terminal* ⊟*DC, MC, V* ⊙*Closed Nov.–mid-Apr.* ❖*BP.*

$ ⭐**Yağhane Pansiyon.** If you're in search of help in channeling inner reflection, this comfortable stone-built hotel with a fine English lawn out front specializes in weeklong courses of yoga, meditation, Ayurvedic treatments, and "the search for your inner snake." The owners walked all the way from London until they found Eski Datça and stopped. Home-cooked vegetarian meals are served on a pleasant terrace. Even the locally made forged-iron gates feature the symbols of yin and yang. Reserve well in advance. **Pros:** ommmm. **Cons:** not for everyone. ⊠*Eski Datça* ☎*252/712–2287* ⊕*www.suryaturkey.com* ⌂*4 rooms* ⌂*In-hotel: restaurant* ⊟*No credit cards* ❖*CP.*

KNIDOS

38 km (24 mi) west of Datça.

GETTING HERE AND AROUND

Knidos is most romantic when reached by sea, as the ancients did, and in summer boats leave regularly from Datça, though the trip takes three hours each way. By car, you can reach Knidos from Datça in 40 minutes over bumpy roads. Dolmuşes to Yazıköy go on to the ruins in season.

EXPLORING

Windswept Knidos sits on a headland at the very end of the Datça Peninsula, at the point where the Aegean meets the Mediterranean. A primitive archaeological site, its ruins are scattered amid olive groves and a few hints of modern civilization. The city was founded in the 7th century BC by Dorian Greeks and prospered because of its excellent location on shipping routes between Egypt, Rhodes, Ephesus, the Greek mainland, and other major ports. The center of the site is the large ancient agora or market place, down by the water and the ancient ports. If you continue up the hill on the ancient main street, with its views over the harbour and the modern lighthouse, you'll pass the temple of Apollo and then reach the circular temple of Aphrodite, which used to house a lifelike statue of Aphrodite, one of classical Greece's most famous statues.

Around the back of the site is the Corinthian temple with its ancient sundial; back by the harbor is a small **odeon,** or concert hall. On the promontory with the lighthouse is the rectangular, stone **Lion Tomb.** The sad-eyed lion is in remembrance of a victory over Sparta. The original is now on display in the British Museum with another famous relic from Knidos, a statue of the goddess Demeter. Her **sanctuary,** however, is up the original stairway that leads to the upper portion of the town. ▱*$6.*

There is a small restaurant by the jetty where the tour boats arrive.

Just before Knidos a road heads south to the popular **Palamutbükü Beach,** in a long bay on the south side of the peninsula. It's a popular stopoff after visiting the ruins and behind the beach are a number of restaurants including the **Aylin**; each also serves their own zone of sand.

Southwest of Marmaris is a second peninsula, the Bozburun Peninsula. Most visitors don't make it past the beach at Turunç, but if you do, the village of Bozburn still makes its living by fishing and boatbuilding. Beyond are the little visited ruins of **Loryma.** Large, immaculately cut stones form the walls of a castle that stands guard over lonely Bozuk Bay, making Loryma one of the most beautiful spots on the coast. The citadel dates from Hellenistic times—the late 3rd through 1st centuries BC. Loryma can be reached by road from Bozburun, but approaching from the sea (by boat from Marmaris or Kızkumu) is more dramatic. ⊠ *20 km (12 mi) west of Marmaris, turn south on local road signposted Bozburun and continue to follow signposts to Loryma.*

> **NAKED APHRODITE**
>
> In antiquity Knidos's main claim to fame was its 4th-century-BC statue of Aphrodite. It was the first naked statue of a goddess, and when its commissioners, the people of Kos, saw it they were so shocked that they sent it backed and asked for something a little more respectable. The citizens of Knidos were looking for a statue of Aphrodite at the time, and bought the rejected work, which rapidly became a hit, making Knidos an ancient tourist attraction, drawing travelers from afar, among them Cicero and Julius Caesar.

$
Fodor'sChoice
★
⌂ Sabrina's Haus. This hotel just outside the shipbuilding harbor of Bozburun can be a base for visiting Loryma and is a lovely getaway in any event, especially since it can only be reached by boat or via a 15-minute hike. It's right on the water, and has a gorgeous splash of gardens and palm trees amid the stony mountains of Bozbun Bay. It has an elegant, contemporary feel, and rooms vary from the basic to the spectacular. The Haus is also known for its food, with a chef from the Çırağan Kempinski in Istanbul. This is a wonderful get-away-from-the-rest-of-the-world kind of place. It is a bit of a journey, though, so plan to spend at least two nights. **Pros:** romantic and chic. **Cons:** out of the way. ⊠ *Follow the coast about 1 km (mi) east of Bozburun until the road ends, then call for the hotel boat* ☎ *252/456–2456* ⊕ *www.sabrinashaus.com* ⤶ *17 rooms* ⚭ *In-room: no TV. In-hotel: restaurant, bar, diving, water sports* ☰*MC, V* ☯ *Closed mid-Nov.–mid Apr.* ⃝*MAP.*

MARMARIS

91 km (56 mi) west of the international airport at Dalaman.

GETTING HERE AND AROUND

A series of color-coded minibuses run from the center of town for about $1; light green goes to the bus station, orange to İçmeler, and pink to the Pupa hotel and the "yacht marina." A 60-minute catamaran service to the Greek island of **Rhodes** leaves Marmaris harbor every day at 9 AM, returning at 4 PM, with a single or day return ticket costing $50. It's worth considering spending the night in Rhodes, since Greek island life typically grinds to a halt during the midday hours.

ESSENTIALS

Marmaris Tourist office (✉ *İskele Meyd. 2, by marina* ☎ *252/412–1035* 🖷 *252/ 412–7277*).

EXPLORING

The big, brash resort city Marmaris has two faces, and they're hard to reconcile. From the sea, a thick line of resort hotels stretches around the northern edge of a great bay, the whole encircled by a magical necklace of pine-clad mountains. Behind those same hotels, however, the city has been overwhelmed by boxy concrete development and streets lined with a hundred generically named eateries. An annual horde of European tourists descends on these workaday establishments, but for the international traveler, there is little special about Marmaris that cannot be savored elsewhere in Turkey. It's a very pretty spot, but there is little reason to linger unless you are meeting a yacht, traveling on to the Greek island of Rhodes, or perhaps taking up an unbeatable deal at one of the best resort hotels, some of which are spectacular worlds unto themselves (which is just fine given that you probably won't want to see much else here).

If you're in Marmaris, though, don't miss the city's best achievement, a 10-km [7-mi] **seafront promenade** that stretches all the way from the easternmost marina known as Netsal, past the old fortress, along the palm-lined main boulevard of town, and then out between the beach and the fancy hotels that line the coast, all the way west to the outlying resort of **İçmeler.** Along the way there are any number of cafés at which to pause for refreshment or to take in fine views of sea and mountains. For $5, the footsore can ride back on one of the shared water taxis that run up and down the coast in season (usually April–November).

There are few historic sites in what was until a few decades ago a small, sleepy fishing port. These include a modest 16th-century **citadel**, first built by Süleyman the Magnificent, shelled to bits by the French in the First World War and rebuilt in the 1980s. There is a small museum inside (both are closed on Mondays).

Good day outings from Marmaris include a boat trip from the harbor to **Turunç** on a visit easily arranged by yourself, your hotel, or any of the many travel agencies. Another fine destination is **Sedir Island** (Cedar Island).

This will likely involve a bus ride north to the gulf of Gökova and then a boat. Sedir harbors one of the most perfect beaches in the world—if only one could have it to oneself. The sand is made up of tiny egg-shaped pearls of a luminous white marble, making the water brilliantly clear as you swim before the impressive escarpments of Mt. Kavak over the sea to the north. An hour's bus ride from Marmaris will also take you to the refreshing sulfurous mud baths near **Lake Köyeceğiz** or, on a long but doable day trip, to the town of **Dalyan** and the ruins of ancient Kaunos.

Marmaris Bay is also home to some of Turkey's biggest and busiest marinas, and is one of the main bases from which sailing yachts and wooden gulets can be chartered for Blue Cruises.

WHERE TO STAY AND EAT

Some city blocks in Marmaris appear to be made up entirely of restaurants with a pavement-to-pavement profusion of tables and menus that seem like a catalog of world food. The most striking views can be had from café tables where the seafront promenade curves into the bay around the citadel, and these attract the tourists. The locals, however, prefer the slightly better-prepared food in restaurants that look out onto the Netsel yacht marina just to the east.

$–$$
TURKISH
✕**Antique.** Right next to the Pineapple (*see below*), this establishment is similarly favored by the Turkish residents of the city and it offers a free shuttle to the restaurant from any hotel. The menu mixes pasta, seafood, Turkish grills, and pizza with a side specialty in Chinese dishes. The food is fine, but service is somewhat brusque—rather unusual in Turkey. ⊠*Netsel Marina* ☎252/413–2955 ⊟*MC, V.*

$–$$
ITALIAN
★
✕**Pineapple.** This restaurant in the Netsel marina has a lot more style and dignity than you would guess from the name, and it's a great escape from the mass tourism of Marmaris. The menu is eclectic but mainly Italian-themed. The house specialty is tender Anatolian oven cooked lamb, but the chef also prepares pasta, pizza, steak, and Turkish grills. Above Pineapple is its sister restaurant, My Marina English Pub—not as generic as the name might suggest, and with quite nice views from its balcony. ⊠*Netsel Marina* ☎252/412–0976 ⊟*AE, DC, MC, V.*

$$
TURKISH
✕**Yat Marina Restaurant.** Far from Marmaris's madding crowds, this is where to catch a flavor of the life of international yacht folk. The chefs don't go in for the omnibus menus common in town, preferring to concentrate their considerable talents on getting favorite Turkish dishes just right. There is also pasta and, not surprisingly, a lot of seafood. It's fun to walk around the busy marina where huge rigs pull millionaires' luxury motor cruisers from the water as European pensioners scrub the hulls of their much smaller "pocket" yachts. ⊠*Follow the coast road 8 km (5 mi) east out of Marmaris and park outside the marina gate* ☎252/422–0022 ⊟*MC, V.*

$$$
🛏**Maritim Hotel Grand Azur.** This international resort is one of the few places with any real architectural style in Marmaris and its sleek, curving profile overlooks lush tropical gardens. The resort is a 15-minute walk to the central restaurants and bars, and if you're going to stay in central Marmaris, this is probably the best you'll find. Rooms are on the generic side, but the staff is polite and the beach well maintained. Daily boat trips are availaible from the private jetty to places around the bay. **Pros:** nice private beach area. **Cons:** average rooms for the money. ⊠*Kenan Evren Bulv. 13* ☎252/417–4050 ⊕*www.hotelgrandazur.com* ⤶*257 rooms, 30 suites* ⌂*In-hotel: 2 restaurants, room service, bars, tennis courts, pool, gym, beachfront, water sports, laundry service, no-smoking rooms* ⊟*AE, DC, MC, V* ⊚*MAP*

$$$$
🛏**Martı Resort.** There's not always much differentiating the big resort hotels in Marmaris, but the well-established Martı manages to avoid the often brutal architectural profile of the big hotels. Low, Ottoman-

Blue Cruising

The most charming way to visit the Turquoise Riviera, or the Aegean Coast, is on a Blue Cruise, on a *gulet*—a wooden motor yacht or sailboat. Time has done remarkably little to spoil the crystal clear waters, pine-clad inlets, and limpid lagoons. This will be one of the most unforgettable holidays you've ever had, but there is some organization necessary.

How much will it cost? Gulets come in all shapes and sizes, the majority with between 4 and 12 two-person cabins. To hire your own boat, prices work out to between $80 to $150 per person per day in July and August, about half that in April or October. Most charter on terms that cover all but food and drink. After a discussion with the boat's cook, you and a member of the crew go to the local supermarket and load up. Cabin charters—when you join a group of strangers—are generally on an all-inclusive basis, and start at about $300 per week.

When to go? May is pretty, uncrowded, and charters are cheap, but the water is cooler. June is warm and still not too busy. July and August are hotter, busier, and more expensive. September and early October are often perfect at sea, but the mountainsides are less green.

Other things to consider are how long you have and which port is closest to the sites you want to see. Fethiye is a major jumping-off point, as are Bodrum, Marmaris, and Göcek. Ideally, two weeks are needed to see the whole coast from Bodrum to Antalya, but most travelers only have a week.

Look for a boat with a large area for relaxing in the stern and a good flat space on the foredeck for sleeping outside in hot weather. Don't accept anything too squashed: eight cabins in a boat under 80 feet is too much. If you're out in July and August, look for air-conditioning—and enough power-generation capacity for it. Ask about extras like a windsurfer or kayaks.

The captain is important, too. Make sure you can communicate, and if you're arranging the cruise from abroad, insist on a telephone conversation before sending your deposit. Look for someone who listens to your wishes, and be wary if you are met with a patronizing "leave-it-all-to-me" attitude. If you want to sail rather than motor, you need to be doubly sure you have the right vessel. When you get to the boat, check the captain's license, insist on seeing life vests, and test emergency equipment like radios.

If you're hiring a boat after you've arrived in Turkey, you can walk down the quayside and haggle, but this can be a risky in high season. Most people book months ahead. Look for operators registered with both the Turkish Association of Travel Agencies (TURSAB) and the Chamber of Shipping.

On the Internet there are sites for individual boats, and large agencies operating from major ports. For Marmaris, try ⊕ www.yesilmarmaris.com. Fethiye is popular, with ⊕ www.albatrosyachting.com, ⊕ www.bethereyachting.com, ⊕ www.compassyachting.com, ⊕ www.fethiyeyachting.com, or ⊕ www.alestayachting.com. Antalya is served by ⊕ www.olymposyachting.com.

style tiled roofs with tall chimneys, sweeping pools, and a gorgeous view over a sandy beach toward the mountains of Marmaris Bay make this resort popular among international travelers and Turkish vacationers. Most rooms are pleasant, and have a separate sitting area and balcony, and the food is good, too, though if you're not doing the all-inclusive plan, it can be overpriced. **Pros:** pleasant resort; away from the crowds. **Cons:** avoid the older, 600 block rooms. ⊠*İçmeler, Marmaris* ☎*252/455–3440* ⊕*www.marti.com.tr* ⤸*270 rooms, 2 suites* ⚭*In-room: safe. In-hotel: 3 restaurants, bars, tennis courts, pools, gym, diving, Internet terminal* ⊟*AE, MC, V* ⏐⚋❙*MAP.*

> ### FRANKINCENSE
>
> The area around Marmaris is known for its frankincense forests. On the water's edge, between the city and the Pupa Yacht Hotel, is a lovely national park. In Marmaris market you can buy the frankincense, which is the dried sap of the trees. As incense it's known to be quite soothing.

¢ 📶 **Pupa Yacht Hotel.** This clean, simple hotel east of Marmaris is one of the rare establishments left in Turkey that is peaceful and right on its own little beach. It overlooks its own yacht jetty and the unspoiled, pine-clad mountains beyond. Watching the sun set over the water from the balcony of your room is what a holiday should be all about. A modest restaurant and bar mean you can enjoy a quiet evening by a lawn that leads to a pebbly beach. The rooms are small and pretty basic—but they're not the main reason to come here. As the hotel's name implies, it is an extension of a yacht-charter business, and is popular with the European sea-going crowd, so reserve a month in advance in season. **Pros:** room views any five-star hotel would kill for. **Cons:** rather basic rooms. ⊠*Follow the coast road east of Marmaris for 5 mi, and watch for* PUPA YAT *signs* ☎*252/413–3566* ⊕*www.pupa.com.tr* ⤸*19 rooms* ⚭*In-hotel: restaurant, bar, beachfront, diving, bicycles, Internet terminal* ⊟*AE, MC, V* ⏐⚋❙*BP.*

NIGHTLIFE

Marmaris comes alive at night with a wide selection of bars and dance clubs. European charter tourists display the art of serious drinking on **Bar Street** in the old town and its four solid blocks of drinking establishments. The major clubs here offer seething dance floors, and it's generally an opportunity for excess. The largest open-air club is **Back Street Garden Bar** (⊠*Marmaris Bar Street, Old Town* ☎*252/412–4048*). Another busy club is the **Crazy Daisy.** The party goes on farther west, toward İçmeler, at the restaurant-bar **Malibu Beach** (⊠*Uzunyalı 248 Sokak 9* ☎*252/412–6778*). At İçmeler beach itself are dance clubs and karaoke bars with raucous crowds partying into the night.

For a more upmarket scene, try the **Marmaris Palace Beach Club** (⊠*Marmaris Palace Hotel, Pamucak Mevkii, İçmeler* ☎*252/455–5555*), out on a jetty between Marmaris and İçmeler. It has a restaurant and DJs offering a medley of house, chillout, and trance music.

5

The
Lycian Coast

Guney
Karamanli
Abbas
Tefenni
D 585
D 400 Köyceğiz
Ortaca
Altınyayla
Sögüt
D 350
Korkuteli
D 650
Kávnos
Dalyan
Karain Cave
Termessos
Dalaman
Göcek
D 350
Antalya
see detail
map
İstuzu
Beach
GEMILER
ISLAND
Kargi
Lycae
Imecik
D 400
Fethiye
Elmali
Mt. Olympos
Kaya
Ölüdeniz
L Y K I A
Gonuk
Günlüklü
Beach
D 400
Tlos
Pınara
Saklikent
Xanthos
Arycanda
Altinyaka
Phaselis
D 400
0   15 mi
Letoön
Kalkan
Çirali
Patara
Cyanae
Üçağiz
Myra
Olympos
0   15 km
D 400
Simena
Finike
KEY
Kaş
Demre
(Kale)
Adrasan
Beaches
KASTELORIZO
KEKOVA
Ferry Lines
Komluca

Mediterranean Sea

THE LYCIAN COAST

Lycia is the heart of the Turquoise Coast. It's a beautiful, little-developed area with charming port cities, unique hotels, and uncrowded beaches, not to mention some of Turkey's most fascinating ancient ruins: Xanthos, Pinara, Patara, Olympos, and Phaselis.

DALYAN

25 km (16 mi) west of Dalaman Airport on Rte. 400 and local roads (follow signs).

Dalyan is about 10 mi SW of the highway, and there are regular minibuses to the nearby town of Ortaca.

ESSENTIALS

Official tourist office **Dalyan** (✉ *Cumhuriyet Mey., Maraş Cad. 15* ☎ *252/ 284–4235*).

EXPLORING

Dalyan is a lovely place for a three-day break, especially for those who prefer a quiet vacation in an environment that's been developed in a way that is sensitive to the natural surroundings and the native flora and fauna. The city is on the winding, reed-flanked banks of the

Dalyan River, between the great expanse of Lake Köyeceğiz and the lovely beach of İstuzu. The town is known for its Carian tombs, which are carved into the cliff that rises behind the 15-foot high reeds fringing the undeveloped west bank of the river—an especially fine sight when floodlit at night. Boats lined up along the quayside in the center of town—they're all part of the Dalyan Kooperatifi and fares are regulated; there is no bargaining unless there are many idle boats—will take you on expeditions to the beach, to sulfur baths, on explorations of the lake, to the ruins of the ancient city of Kaunos, and to the pretty bay of Ekincik. If your hotel is on the river, the boatmen will pick you up from there, too. Trekking and footpaths are developing fast, and include walks to Ekincik and elsewhere. Birdwatchers love the lake, where 180 species of bird have been logged. Local markets are also colorful: there's one in Dalyan on Saturdays and one at the local center of Ortaca on Fridays. Dalyan doesn't have much nightlife, and its main-street shops are now no longer rug dealers but estate agents hoping to cash in on the villa-buying boom by British and other European visitors.

5

☾ The unspoiled sands of **İztuzu Beach** stretch for 8 km (5 mi), with the
★ Mediterranean on one side and a freshwater lagoon on the other. In June and July *Caretta caretta* sea turtles lay their eggs here. This is a conservation area, and signs along the beach mark possible nesting places and warn you not to stick umbrellas in the sand or behave in other ways that could disturb the turtles. There are regular boats and minibuses from Dalyan.

The ancient ruins at **Kaunos** can be reached in about 15 to 30 minutes by boat from Dalyan, or find the *geçit*, a rowboat crossing, then walk south for 30 minutes. Up from the port is the agora or market place, with a restored fountain house and a ruined portico dotted with the foundation of statues. Up the hill, past the nice temple terrace is a crumbling Byzantine basilica, a massive Roman bath restored as a site museum, and a well-preserved semicircular theater cut into the hillside in the Greek style. Most date from the 4th century BC, and were carved by a people called the Carians, who dominated the region west of here. The style, however, is that of ancient Lycia, the neighboring region to the east. From the ruins there is a pretty clifftop walk to Ekincik, which takes three to four hours with the possibility of returning by boat. 🎫 $6.

WHERE TO STAY AND EAT

$$ ✕ **Riverside Restaurant.** This excellent open-air restaurant has a prime
TURKISH spot on the river, opposite the tombs, and is known for its seafood.
★ There's a range of starters, including such delicious items as olives with walnuts and garlic; baked eggplant mashed with yogurt, garlic, raisins, pine nuts, and dill; or purslane in a mayonnaise and lemon sauce; for non-fish eaters, these are better than the meat dishes. ⊠ *Sağlık Cad., Maraş District. Follow the Dalyan River bankside walkway 500 m south from the main sq.* ☎ *252/284–3166* ▭ *AE, DC, MC, V.*

$$ 🏨 **Asur Hotel.** With a large swimming pool and gardens overlooking the Dalyan River, this one-story property is a good, less-expensive option. The rooms are clean and pleasant, and free use of bicycles cuts the time taken to cover the kilometer (½ mile) to the center of town. With carved wooded ceilings and a scatter of Ottoman bric-a-brac in the rooms, it

also has a bit more character than an average resort hotel. **Pros:** friendly service; good value. **Cons:** a bit far from town. ☎*252/284–3232* ⊕*www.asurotel.com* ➘*34 rooms, 10 suites* ⚁*In-room: safe, Wi-Fi. In-hotel: restaurant, room service, bar, pool, gym, bicycles* ▤*AE, DC, MC, V* ☾*Closed Oct.–May* ⏇*BP.*

$ ⛨**Beyaz Gül.** This curious hotel is run by an old-fashioned Turkish
☾   lady, and staying here is like living in a fairy-tale cottage. Kids love the rooms decorated with bears, woolen socks, and other knickknacks. A little oasis on the riverfront south of the town center, it has a direct view of the tombs from its garden café and restaurant. **Pros:** not your average hotel. **Cons:** the outdoor grounds are dominated by the restaurant. ✉*Balikhane Cad. 92/93, Maraş* ☎*252/284–2304* ⊕*www. beyazgul.info* ➘*4 rooms* ⚁*In-room: Wi-Fi. In-hotel: restaurant, bar* ▤*No credit cards.*

$$$ ⛨**Dalyan Resort.** This beautifully built hotel opened in 2005 on a bend
★   in the Dalyan River. A bit farther out of Dalyan town center than most other hotels, and more sophisticated, the grounds include wide, well-tended gardens, a tennis court, a large pool, and a bright, well-designed restaurant where even the bread is made in-house. **Pros:** nice pool area. **Cons:** upscale, but not a lot of character. ✉*Kaunos Cad. 50, Maraş, Dalyan—drive south along the river from Dalyan town sq. and follow the many signs* ☎*252/284–5499* ⊕*www.dalyanresort.com* ➘*16 standard rooms, 24 suites, 18 junior suites* ⚁*In-room: safe, Wi-Fi. In-hotel: restaurant, bars, pool, spa* ▤*AE, MC, V* ⏇*BP.*

$ ⛨**Happy Caretta.** This small hotel is in a shady garden on the banks of
Fodor's Choice   the Dalyan River opposite the Kaunos tombs. The rooms are attractive-
★   ly decorated in wood, terra-cotta-style tiles, and white stucco. Guests can swim in the river off a small jetty in front of a splendid row of cypress trees, or wait for a boat to take them to the beach. **Pros:** beautiful riverside gardens; friendly service; altogether lovely. **Cons:** a bit hard to find. ✉*Kaunos Cad. 26, Maraş District; drive south down the Dalyan River and look for signs to the right* ☎*252/284–2109* ⊕*www. happycaretta.com* ➘*10 rooms, 4 suites* ⚁*In-room: Wi-Fi. In-hotel: restaurant, bar* ▤*MC, V* ⏇*BP.*

GÖCEK

22 km (14 mi) east of Dalaman Airport on Rte. 400.

For the visitor who wants a taste of the grandeur of the Turquoise Riviera, but has little time to spare, Göcek is perfect. The tranquil yachting resort town is just a 20-minute drive over the mountains from Dalaman Airport, enjoys gorgeous vistas of sea and mountains, has easy access to the sea, and offers good, upmarket places to eat, sleep, and shop. It has avoided the excesses of package tourism and overdevelopment, and is focused on its pleasant, carless waterfront. Three marinas and an annual regatta make this a major center for Turkey's yachting world, and weekends see it awash with Istanbul *sosyete* (essentially the rich, frequently spoiled, and occasionally glamorous children of the upper classes) on parade. From Göcek, an hour's drive reaches the natural beauties of Dalyan, the sights around Fethiye/Ölüdeniz, or great Lycian

Sea kayaking around the Göcek Islands.

sites like Tlos and Xanthos. There is only one private beach in Göcek itself, so hop on one of the several wooden tour boats that head out each morning to explore elsewhere. The best swimming and snorkeling are around the beaches or in the coves of the **Twelve Islands**, strung out like a necklace across the mouth of the bay.

Göcek is in prime Blue Cruise territory, so you can rent a yacht or a gulet, for as much time and money as you have to spare. The most popular anchorages include Tersane, Kapı Creek, Cleopatra's Bay, the obscure ruins at Lydae, Tomb Bay, or the lovely island of Katrancı.

The **Sundowner Beach** (☎ *252/645–2760*), run privately by Swissotel at the eastern end of Port Göcek marina, is one of the most spectacular—and expensive—on the Turquoise Riviera. It costs $40 for nonguests. For some this is a small price to pay for an excellently maintained beach and bar establishment, and a completely unspoiled, wraparound view of the bay and mountains. The beach is open 10 AM to 6 PM, later if anyone wants to stay; the bar is open in the evening and dinner is served after 7 PM.

WHERE TO STAY AND EAT

$–$$ ⨉**Can.** This busy harborside fish restaurant is popular with Göcek
TURKISH natives because the large interior space is open all year round—and wireless Internet access is free. It's been around for more than 15 years and has the feel of more than just a restaurant but a town institution. In summer, the seating extends out toward the waterfront, under broad tropical trees. Specialities are typical, like fish baked in salt, but the pride of the menu is its selection of 30 starters including tuna with

onion sauce and cheese, served with arugula salad. ⊠ *Western edge of municipal harbor* ☎ *252/645–1507* ⊟*MC, V.*

$$$–$$$$
ECLECTIC
✕**The Galley.** This open wooden chalet with a great view over the masts of the Göcek marina to the mountains beyond is where the visiting yachting elite gathers. The short international menu focuses heavily on seafood. ⊠ *Walk east out of town, restaurant is 100 yards after entrance to Port Göcek just past the security post* ☎*252/645–2760* ⊟*AE, DC, MC, V.*

¢–$
TURKISH
✕**Liman Restaurant Bar.** This traditional Turkish meat restaurant is the locals' choice, since the prices are half that of the seafront establishments. There's no view except of the concrete-built hinterland of Göcek, but the Turkish basics of kebabs and *pide*, are excellent. ⊠*Head north from Yapi Kredi Bank on the main shopping street, Liman is opposite the belediye (city hall)* ☎*252/645–1898* ⊟*MC, V.*

$–$$
★
✕**Özcan.** Cushioned bamboo chairs, attentive waitstaff, and possibly the best grilled octopus you've ever tasted await you at Özcan, a fish restaurant on the wide esplanade that makes up Göcek's main public harborside. The wide range of starters include unusual mushrooms from the mountains out back, fresh seaweed dishes, and squid in garlic, oil, and lemon. An unusual—and delicious—fish is the big-eyed mullet, found in few other places than these waters. The menu is predominatly sea food but there are also excellent kebabs and local lamb dishes. ⊠*Middle of municipal yacht harbor.* ☎*252/645–2593* ⊟*MC, V.*

$$
🛏**The Bay Beach Club.** This pretty hotel, made up of wooden cabins under the chestnut trees, opened in 2008. The standard cabins are nice, and the family ones are huge, with a living room, two bedrooms, and two bathrooms. There is a private section of beach, with a waterfront bar and restaurant and a range of water sports. Massages and a sauna are also on offer, as well as minigolf and a childrens club to take care of the kids. The hotel seems focused on wealthy Turkish families but you may find some English spoken. **Pros:** gorgeous waterfront family cabins. **Cons:** isolated. ⊠*At Gunlüklü Beach, take the right-hand road* ☎*252/633–6310* ⊕*www.thebaybeachclub.com* ⇘*36 cabins* ⌂*In-room: safe, Wi-Fi. In-hotel: restaurant, bars, pools, spa, beachfront, water sports, laundry service* ⊟*MC, V* ⊗*Closed Nov.–Mar.*

$$
★
🛏**Hotel Forest Gate.** This quiet cluster of white two-story villas surrounded by pine trees has generous rooms organized around a pool shaded by a great carob tree, and a friendly atmosphere. It's a good base for exploring the area, but the 10-minute walk back from the center of town is uneven and dark at night. Breakfast is basic but dinners are cooked fresh on demand. **Pros:** nice pool area. **Cons:** out of the way; some rooms are just average. ⊠*From the main road, turn into Göcek at the gas station at the entrance of town and follow signs east* ☎*252/645–2629* ⊕*www.hotelforestgate.com* ⇘*14 rooms, 9 suites* ⌂*In-hotel: restaurant, bar, pool* ⊟*MC, V* ⧖⦿*BP.*

$$
🛏**The Swissotel Göcek Marina and Spa Resort.** The Swissotel has all the luxury and excellent service you'd expect from an international chain. That said, make sure you get one of the cheaper non-attic rooms: the attic rooms really are just that, with very low ceilings. Some rooms have walk-out access to the pool, across the lawn—few, however, have

a real sea view, or much of any view for that matter. The hotel's main selling point is its private, manicured, but expensive Sundowner Beach, a five-minute golf cart ride from the main building. A new wing is due to open 2009, expanding the hotel towards the sea, with new spa facilities. **Pros:** professional and a stylish beach area. **Cons:** rooms are unexceptional with ordinary views. ✉ *Cumhuriyet District, Göcek,* ☎ *252/645–2760* 🌐 *www.gocek.swissotel.com* *119 rooms* *In-room: safe, Wi-Fi. In-hotel: restaurant, pool, gym, spa* ▭ *AE, MC, V* ⏲ *Nov.–mid-Apr.* *BP.*

$$ **Villa Danlin.** On Göcek's main shopping street, this is a good small hotel with rooms shielded from most noise. The location is ideal for access to the harbor, restaurants, and shops. Rooms are a little on the small side and the furniture is of mixed quality; there is a nice, if somewhat claustrophobic, pool area. **Pros:** central. **Cons:** rooms nothing special, you're paying for location. ✉ *Çarşı Içi, Göcek,* ☎ *252/645–1521* 🌐 *www.villadanlin.com* *13 rooms* *In-room: Wi-Fi. In-hotel: pool, laundry facilities* ▭ *MC, V* ⏲ *May–Oct.* *BP.*

EN ROUTE

Gunlüklü Beach. If you get overheated on the main road between Göcek and Fethiye, and need an antidote to the relentless fashionability of Göcek, follow the brown sign south to Gunlüklü Beach. It's a good place to stop for a picnic in a forest of small chestnut trees or to take a swim from a dark sand beach in the unspoiled bay. In season, a shop down by the beach sells basic food. Be forewarned, though: the beach tends to get crowded on weekends with Turkish day-trippers from Fethiye, and the facilities can be a bit rough and ready. The sand is darker than at other Turkish beaches. ✉ *About 10 km (6 mi) from Göcek, 17 km (11 mi) from Fethiye* *$4 per car.*

FETHIYE

50 km (31 mi) east of Dalaman Airport on Rte. 400.

GETTING HERE AND AROUND

Fethiye's modern bus station is a short distance west of the center, and buses to Ölüdeniz run from in front of the Carrefour beside it. Buses running east and west along the coast depart regularly, and several a day cross the mountains for Denizli and Pamukkale. A second bus station a bit closer to the center has minibuses to Göcek and other nearby destinations.

ESSENTIALS

Official tourist office Fethiye (✉ *İskele Karşısı 1* ☎ *252/614–1527*).

EXPLORING

This busy port town is a good base for exploring the ruins of ancient Lycia in the mountains that rise to the east. Fethiye was known in antiquity as Telmessus (not to be confused with Termessos, near Antalya), and was the principal port of Lycia from the Roman period onward. In front of the town hall is one of the finest of several tombs found throughout the city: this one represents a two-story Lycian house, with reliefs of warriors on both sides of its lid.

The small original town was once called Mekri and populated mainly by Greeks before the Greek-Turkish population exchange in 1924. It was renamed in 1934, after an Ottoman pilot called Fethi Bey. He was killed when he crashed in the mountains of Lebanon while attempting a historic flight that was to link all the Middle Eastern provinces of the Ottoman Empire on the eve of the First World War in 1914. Today's town is quite modern, having been substantially rebuilt after an earthquake in 1957. Strolling along the seafront promenade is a pleasant evening outing, and scuba-diving enthusiasts can choose between half a dozen dive boats that collect in the harbor. The town is most fun on Tuesdays, when village folk flock into Fethiye for the weekly market. The harbor has many yachts available for Blue Cruising.

The **Fethiye Museum** (*Fethiye Müzesi*) has some fine statues and jewelry from the glory days of Telmessus, and the labels are in English, but as of late 2008 it was closed for renovations. ⊠ *Off Atatürk Cad. (look for signs)* 🖅 *$3* ⏰ *Tues.–Sun. 8:30–5.*

Impressive ancient Lycian **rock tombs** are carved into the cliff that looms above town. The largest is the **Tomb of Amyntas,** presumably the burial place of a 4th-century-BC ruler or nobleman. Inside are the slabs where corpses were laid out. To reach the tombs, you'll have to climb many steps—the stairway starts at Kaya Caddesi, near the local bus station—but your effort will be well rewarded, particularly at dusk, when the cliffs take on a reddish glow.

Along the crest of the hill overlooking the old town are the battlements of a **castle,** whose foundations date back to antiquity and were later built up by the 12th-century crusader Knights of St. John and the Ottoman Empire.

The main road around the central harbor square of Fethiye also runs past the stage of the antique **theater** of Telmessus, a recent chance rediscovery that gives a sense of history to the modern buildings all around. The rest of the ancient town remains under its urban tomb.

The 16th-century **Hamam** (⊠ *Hamam Cad., close to the main harbor square* 🖀 *252/614–9318* 🌐 *www.oldturkishbath.com*) is still in use, and is a bit touristy. It's a fine way to scrub off the barnacles after a long voyage, and full of atmosphere with 14 domes and six arches.

WHERE TO STAY AND EAT

$–$$ ✕ **Lafiore.** This Italian restaurant in the bazaar was set up by the Meğri
ITALIAN "minichain" beside their main restaurant and provides a rare and welcome change from the "Costa del Kebab." It offers a full Italian experience, replete with faux Italian-villa alfresco—with Turkish grace notes, of course. Just remember, you're not in Italy, so don't expect too much. ⊠ *Eski Cami Ceçidi Likya Cad.* 🖀 *252/612–4046* 🖃 *MC, V.*

$–$$ ✕ **Meğri Lokanta.** The Meğris pretty much rule the restaurant market
TURKISH in Fethiye, but it's a well-deserved hierarchy, at least for now, as their food is quite consistently the best in town. This excellent, straightforward Turkish meat restaurant is on the western edge of the bazaar and much favored by local inhabitants. ⊠ *Western edge of the bazaar* 🖀 *252/614–4047* 🖃 *MC, V.*

Continued on page 299

MEZE: MOUTHWATERING MORSELS

Prepare your taste buds for a Turkish travel experience: tangy yogurt, pungent garlic, fresh herbs, smoky eggplant, marinated salads, and roasted vegetables await.

Whether you're sitting down for dinner along Turkey's coast, in one of Istanbul's historic neighborhoods, or somewhere in the untouristed southeast, your meal will almost certainly begin with meze—the assortment of small dishes that are the heart and soul of Turkish cuisine. Similar to the idea of tapas, meze are more than just a quick snack or an appetizer. For Turks, eating meze is often a meal in itself—a languorous repast made up of countless small plates and an ample supply of raki, the anise-flavored liquor that is Turkey's national drink and the preferred accompaniment to meze.

Dolma

Eating meze is a centuries-old national tradition, influenced by Persian, Arab, and Greek cooking, and you'll find regional differences in what's offered. Dishes in the country's southeast have more of a Middle Eastern influence, while those in Istanbul and the Aegean area have more of a Greek flavor. What they have in common, though, is the Turkish belief that the meze experience is about more than eating and drinking—freewheeling conversation is an essential component. As one famous Turkish saying goes: "The best meze is good table talk."

WHAT'S ON THE MEZE MENU

A typical meze menu includes dozens of mostly meatless dishes, hot and cold, emphasizing freshness and seasonality. In Istanbul's *meyhanes*—rollicking, tavern-like restaurants that specialize in meze—servers arrive at your table with large trays piled high with small dishes. You choose whatever catches your eye.

Left: Octopus salad. Right: A variety of Turkish salads.

TASTES TO EXPECT

When it comes to meze, Turks tend to have a conservative palate. Meze meals, for example, often start with the simplest but most traditional dish of all—a piece of tangy feta cheese accompanied by a slice of sweet honeydew melon and a glass of raki. Meze restaurants (with some notable exceptions) are not trying to outdo one another by inventing ever more creative dishes. Rather, they stick with tried and true meze that have become the classics of Turkish cooking. Here are some of the traditional meze you should be on the lookout for:

COLD (SOGUK) MEZE

BAKLA EZMESI—Dried fava beans that are cooked, mashed with garlic, olive oil, dill, and lemon juice and turned into an earthy paté.

BARBUNYA PILAKI—Barbunya beans (Roman or red beans), usually fresh from the pod, stewed in a garlicky tomato sauce.

ÇERKEZ TAVUĞU—A highlight of classical Turkish cooking, this dish consists of poached chicken that is ground with garlic and walnuts to make a deliciously enticing and flavorful dip.

DENIZ BÖRÜLCESI—A wonderfully fresh-tasting dish made of samphire, a crunchy green that grows by the sea. It's cooked in olive oil and flavored with lemon juice.

ENGINAR—Artichoke hearts stewed in olive oil with onion and carrot, served cold.

EZME—A salad of finely chopped tomatoes and onion, sometimes flavored with pleasantly astringent pomegranate molasses.

HAYDARI—A dip made of thick and creamy strained yogurt, flavored with garlic and dill.

IMAM BAYILDI—Literally "the imam swooned," this dish is one of Turkey's most famous: an eggplant is stuffed with onion, garlic, parsley, and tomato and stewed in olive oil.

KISIR—The Turkish version of tabbouleh, this is a tangy and somewhat spicy salad made out of bulgur wheat and red pepper paste.

LAKERDA—Turkey's take on lox, this is cured mackerel, sliced thick.

MIDYE DOLMASI—In this Istanbul favorite, also sold by street vendors, mussels are cooked with rice, pine nuts, currants, herbs, and spices and then stuffed back into their shell and served with a squirt of lemon.

PATLICAN SALATASI—A salad or dip made out of eggplant, of which there are numerous variations (see the "Ubiquitous Eggplant" sidebar).

SEMIZOTU—When in season, purslane (a variety of green similar to watercress that's rich in vitamins and Omega-3 fatty acids) is mixed with yogurt to make a tangy dip.

YAPRAK SARMA—Grape leaves stuffed with rice, currants, and pine nuts.

ZEYTINYAĞLI—Vegetables such as green beans and artichoke hearts that are stewed in olive oil and served cool or at room temperature. (*Zeytinyağ*, pronounced "zey-teen-yah," is the Turkish name for the oil.)

Kabakli börek (filo pastries with pumpkin).

THE UBIQUITOUS EGGPLANT

According to Turkish culinary lore, there are more than a thousand ways to cook eggplant (*patlican* in Turkish, pronounced "pat-li-jahn"). That may be an exaggeration, but you could certainly lose count of how many dishes feature the humble nightshade—it's even made into a jam! The vegetable certainly plays a starring role on the meze tray: cubes of fried eggplant come covered in a yogurt and tomato sauce; charcoal-roasted eggplant is turned into a smoky puree; and sun-dried eggplants are served stuffed with rice and herbs.

HOT (SICAK) MEZE

ARNAVUT CIĞERI—Cubes of tender lamb's liver, fried with red pepper flakes and served with raw onion.

BÖREK—Filo pastries, sometimes rolled up like cigars and stuffed with cheese, or layered over *pastirma*, which is spicy cured beef.

DOLMA OR SARMA—Stuffed grape leaves and other vegetables, such as chard or cabbage, that are filled with a combination of rice, herbs, spices, and sometimes ground meat.

KALAMAR—Calamari rings batter-fried and served with an addictive sauce made of ground walnuts and garlic known as *tarator*.

KARIDES—Shrimp in a butter or tomato sauce, usually baked in a terra-cotta dish.

MÜCVER—A fried fritter of zucchini and herbs.

PAZI SARMA—Swiss chard stuffed with ground meat and rice, with yogurt on the side.

HELPFUL WORDS TO KNOW

Eating out in Istanbul is often a festive experience.

Being confronted with a tray filled with dozens of little dishes can be daunting, but knowing a few key words will help you navigate the meze maze. Of course, there's nothing wrong with pointing at any mysterious meze and giving your waiter an inquisitive look—most will know a few words in English to help you along. Also remember, there is no need to order everything at once. You can order a few, then call your waiter back when you're ready for more.

Kisir

ACILI—means "spicy."
ACISIZ—literally "not spicy."
DOMATES—tomato.
ET—is meat: *kuzu* is lamb, *dana* is beef, *tavuk* is chicken; you'll rarely see pork, *domuz*, on menus.
IZGARA—grilled.
KIZARTMA—fried.
PEYNIR—cheese; *beyaz peyniris* feta cheese, *kaşar peynir* is a semi-soft yellow cheese.
SALATALIK—cucumber.
SARIMSAK—garlic; a dish with garlic in it is called *sarimsakli.*
SOĞAN—onion; a dish with onions on top is called *soğanli.*

AND TO DRINK?

Although wine and beer are gaining in popularity, anise-flavored raki (similar to Greek ouzo or French pastis) is still the undisputed top choice for a drink to accompany meze. For years, the dependable "Yeni Raki" brand was pretty much the only choice available, although new brands are now becoming popular. Rakis made by the brand Efe are worth seeking out.

Drinking raki, like eating meze, has its own rituals. It's rarely drunk straight because it's so potent: 80 proof or higher. Typically, a shot of raki is mixed with water, turning the drink a milky white. Most raki drinkers also add ice. Even when diluted, raki can be pretty strong, though fans say it goes down smooth with a slight sweetness. They also maintain that a good raki buzz is conducive to entertaining conversation.

$$ ✕**Meğri Restaurant.** Hidden in a side street of the bazaar, the permanent
ECLECTIC part of this restaurant has stone walls, high wood ceilings, and decorative kilims. In summer, most of the large, upscale restaurant spills out into a large courtyard in the middle of the bazaar. A vast menu mixes dishes from Asia, France, Turkey, and the Mediterranean. Portions are large and the food is quite good. ✉*Eski Cami Geçidi Likya Sokak 8–9* ☎*252/614–4046* 🖷*252/612–0446* ▭*MC, V.*

$$$ ✕**MOD Yacht Lounge.** This glass-fronted, pleasingly modern café-restaurant on the harbor-front walkway has a chill-out nautical atmosphere
GERMAN and the tables are moved out to the deck under the trees in summer. The menu is modern and internation, with pasta, seafood, and Turkish grills. With an unimpeded view of the harbor and bay, it's also a great place just to stop in for an evening drink. ✉*Ece Marina, Karagözler* ☎*252/614–3970* ▭*MC, V.*

$$$ 🛎**Ece Saray.** Modeled on the grand hotels of the French Riviera, this is an excellent luxury hotel in a lovely location on the harborfront. Part of the Ece Marina complex, all rooms have full sea views and the fitness center and health spa are particularly impressive. Opened in 2002, its cheaply built plaster-stone facade has crumbled in places, but otherwise the hotel is hard to fault. Rooms are large and tastefully decorated and the waterfront pool area is gorgeous. **Pros:** quality accommodations, with lots of extras. **Cons:** sea but no beach. ✉*Ece Marina, Karagözler* ☎*252/612–5005* ⊕*www.ecesaray.net* ↻*34 rooms, 14 suites* ⌂*In-room: safe, Wi-Fi. In-hotel: 2 restaurants, bars, pool, gym, spa, diving* ▭*AE, MC, V* ⑪*BP.*

$$ 🛎**Yacht Plaza.** This fine medium-size hotel directly on the seafront has its own yacht jetty, waterside bar, and pool. Probably the best of the line of hotels east of the harbor, it's owned by the same family as the older Yacht Hotel (worth considering if the Yacht Plaza is full nearby). Rooms are clean and simple with tile floors, but make sure you're getting a sea view. Note that some signs refer to this as Yeni Yacht. **Pros:** nice waterfront pool area. **Cons:** rooms are fine, but nothing special. ✉*Karagöller, just east of the Ece Marinapro* ☎*252/612–5067* ⊕*www.yachtplazahotel.com* ↻*31 rooms* ⌂*In-room: Wi-Fi. In-hotel: restaurant, bar, pool* ▭*No credit cards* ⑪*BP.*

NIGHTLIFE

Sobe, on the main Fevzi Çakmak Caddesi, is a hip tapas lounge and cocktail bar on a roof terrace overlooking the Ece Marina. Evenings start with chill-out music as the sun sets over the bay, and moves on to house music as things gets going. On weekends there are clubs off Hamam Cad. in the center of Fethiye. **Mango Bar,** a small indoor dance club, sometimes featuring live Turkish music, is also on Hamam Caddesi.

Outside town there is a strip of cheaper, less appealing hotels along Çaliş Beach that stretches west of town—this is where the package tours from northern Europe tend to stay and there are plenty of bars. It's a long way to go for a drink if you're staying in town, but the scene has an appeal for the younger crowd. During the week, nightclubs are busiest in Hisarönü, between Fethiye and Ölüdeniz.

SPORTS AND THE OUTDOORS

You can take one of the boats or water taxis in Fethiye's harbors on a variety of **boat tours,** some including meals, to Göcek, the Twelve Islands, or Ölüdeniz. Itineraries are posted, and there are people on hand to answer questions. Be sure to shop around, as packages vary widely. Costs range from around $20 to $30 per person. Ask to inspect the boat before booking: in theory, for instance, all boats should carry a spare outboard motor in the case of breakdown, yet few do. If Ölüdeniz is your destination, be aware that windy weather can make for heavy waves. Most tours leave about 10 AM, returning about 6 PM.

ÖLÜDENIZ

★ *60 km (38 mi) east of Dalaman Airport.*

Ölüdeniz (it means "dead sea") is one of Turkey's great natural wonders, an azure lagoon rimmed by beaches of white sand. The area, the picture-perfect scene most often featured in Turkish tourism promotion posters, can be reached by day cruise from Fethiye or other ports by car or *dolmuş.* One inland route is through Ovacık (it's the shorter option if you're coming from outside Fethiye) but a prettier one leads past the ruined town of **Kaya,** climbing steeply from a point 1 km (½ mi) west of the harbor. The town itself is a bland package-tourist town, but the position and the natural park beach are stunning.

The water of Ölüdeniz is warm and the setting delightful, even with the crowds. The view is even more splendid from the air, and this is one of Turkey's premier locations for paragliding. Travel agencies in town will organize jeep safaris into the high mountain pastures and villages in the mountains all around for about $40 for the day, with lunch.

Ölüdeniz Natural Park. If you want to bathe at the iconic sandbar that lies across the mouth of the lagoon, then you must enter Ölüdeniz Natural Park—go down to the seafront, turn west, then left at the fork where you can see the toll booth ($7 per car or $4 per person on foot). There's a capacious car park, but even from here, it can be a hot trek of a several hundred yards. The crowds love it here, and the setting is absolutely beautiful, but the beach is still just a beach. Lounge chairs ($3) and umbrellas ($3) can be rented, and there are changing rooms, toilets, and a modest snack restaurant. Just around the corner a concession rents out pedalos and kayaks for $11 to $13 per hour. The water gets deep quickly and there a several diving platforms anchored a short swim out.

Another sand beach can be found behind the park in the shallow, warm waters of the lagoon; this one is popular with families. Although theoretically public property, in practice this beach is run by the campsites and restaurants that line the shore. Use of their facilities, however, is unlikely to be much more expensive than those in the park itself.

The Lycian Way starts in the hills above Ölüdeniz, and one of its most pleasant sections is the 3- to 5-day walk to Patara.

The azure water of Ölüdeniz Bay is surrounded by white sand beaches, attracting beach-goers from around the world.

WHERE TO STAY AND EAT

After two decades of building, the many hotels behind the Ölüdeniz seafront are settled into a relatively pleasant harmony of Mediterranean tiled roofs, growing trees, restaurants, and poolside bars. They're decent enough and all pretty similar—rooms tend to be smallish, having essentially been purpose-built for package tours, but many are block-booked in advance by European agencies for the entire season. Some keep rooms back, and a full list can be seen at ⊕ *www.oludeniztourism. org*, which also has a helpful office on the main road. All the following are reasonably near the sea front and offer pools and air-conditioned rooms. Addresses aren't really necessary: all the hotels are signposted, and it's hard to recommend one of these over another anyway. **Hotel Karbel Sun** (✉ *Ölüdeniz* ☎ *252/617–0173* ⊕ *www.karbelsun.com*); the **Flying Dutchman Hotel** (✉ *Ölüdeniz* ☎ *252/617–0441*), which also has a popular restaurant; or the **Magic Tulip Hotel** (☎ *252/617–0074* ⊕ *www. magictulip.com*).

The campsites by the lagoon, such as **Sugar Beach,** have also sprouted some decent air-con bungalows (☎ *534/414–0949* ⊕ *www.thesugarbeachclub. com*). For a much more enjoyable experience, try one of the hotel/resorts off the beach, listed below.

$$$$ ⊤ **Meri Hotel.** Built in 1973, this hotel was the first—and last—to be allowed by the government to set up shop on the famed Ölüdeniz lagoon. Built on a steep incline amid terraced gardens, overlooking one of Turkey's most beautiful bays, the site is a delight. Rooms are another story: although clean enough, they're small and somewhat down-at-the-heel, and overpriced, though most, but not all, have balconies with

suberb sea views. To reach many of them involves riding up a rickety furnicular lift. The public areas are the main attraction, and there's a pretty pool area with the lagoon beach across the road from the main hotel. **Pros:** location, location . . . location. **Cons:** average rooms. ⊠ *Ölüdeniz, well-signposted* ☎ *252/617–0001* ⊕ *www.hotelmeri.com* ↘ *70 standard rooms, 24 family rooms* ⛄ *In-hotel: 3 restaurants, bar, pools, beachfront* ⊟ *MC, V* ¡○¡*AP.*

$$ ⌐**Montana Pine Resort.** It's not Montana, but it does have a splendid mountain setting, and the Sundowner Bar has a wonderful vista of the sea. Rooms are airy and have balconies. Up above the coast, the air is cooler here but there's a daily shuttle service to the Ölüdeniz beach. This is the place to kick your feet back and celebrate when you've finished the Lycian Way, which officially ends (or starts) close by the Sundowner Bar. **Pros:** professionally run; excellent rooms; many guests return every year. **Cons:** limited beach shuttle service. ⊠ *Ölüdeniz* ☎ *252/616–7108 or 252/616–6366* ⊕ *www.montanapine.com* ↘ *149 rooms with bath, 5 suites* ⛄ *In-room: safe. In-hotel: 2 restaurants, bars, pools, gym* ⊟ *AE, DC, MC, V* ⊘ *Closed Nov.–May.*

$$ ⌐**Ocakköy Holiday Village.** In an abandoned Greek village of stone
★ houses, this 6-acre spread is a delightful retreat. The predominantly English clientele keep coming back for the rural atmosphere and easy access to area sites. Many more of their compatriots, however, are buying apartments and villas that have disfigured the valley below; luckily, the hotel's trees and gardens keep the development at bay. Helpful staff make a stay here pleasurable, and suites have kitchenettes. There is a nice common central area with a pool, Jacuzzi, and restaurants, and a daily shuttle to Ölüdeniz. The hotel can arrange daylong boat excursions. **Pros:** good for families, relaxing, lots of extras. **Cons:** can seem overly resortish. ⊠ *4 km (3 mi) after the end of Fethiye on the Ölüdeniz road, a signpost shows the way at the first turning on the right. Keep right and head for the stone houses higher on the hill, Ocakköy, Fethiye* ☎ *252/616–6156 or 252/616–6157* ⊕ *www.ocakkoey.de* ↘ *8 rooms, 6 studios, 32 cottages* ⛄ *In-room: no phone, refrigerator, no TV, Internet. In-hotel: restaurant, bars, pools, Wi-Fi* ⊟ *AE, DC, MC, V.*

SPORTS AND THE OUTDOORS

A good day out on a boat can be arranged by the skippers of **Ölüdeniz Kooperatif,** who work out of a kiosk halfway between the main body of hotels and the beach. Between May and November, their 15 boats will take groups out to coves with catchy names like Blue Cave, Butterfly Valley, Aquarium Bay, St. Nicholas Island, Cold Water Spring, Camel Beach, and Turquoise Bay. Trips usually run from 11 AM to 6 PM, and cost about $12 per person with lunch (beer and cold drinks extra).

PARAGLIDING Paragliding is a busy industry in Ölüdeniz and a major spectator sport on the beaches; experienced pilots can soar aloft for up to five hours in near-ideal conditions in the summer. The launch point is about 1,700 yards up Mt. Baba, some 20 km (13 mi) by forest tracks from Ölüdeniz—the tour operators drive you up from town. Tourists flying tandem (it will cost around $120) with a pilot generally stay up for 30 to 40 minutes before landing gently on the beach. Full training to internationally recognized certificates in solo piloting is available. Most travel agencies can arrange a flight; in town try **Eftelya Tourism** (✉ *On main road close to Ölüdeniz Beach* ☎252/617–0014).

NIGHTLIFE

On weeknights, the nightlife at Hisarönü, Ölüdeniz, is livelier than in Fethiye itself. Main streets bustle with real estate agents, restaurants, and shops selling jewelry and clothing. After complaints, most of the discotheques have soundproofed their walls although the bass still seeps out. Most operate only in the season between May to October and marquees to look for are **Grand Boozey Bar,** which specializes in satellite TV transmissions of British soccer matches, **Hakuna Matata,** or the more classy **Fez.**

KAYA

5

5 km (3 mi) east of Fethiye, either from the road west of the harbor or through Ovacık and Hisarönü.

Atmospheric Kaya is a ruin of a different order from others along the Mediterranean Coast. It was a thriving Greek community until 1923, when all the village's residents were sent "home"to Greece following a population-exchange agreement between the two countries. Nowadays it's pretty much a deserted ghost town, with some Turkish village settlement on the edges. Spread across three hills, Kaya is atmospheric and eerily quiet and slowly crumbling. You can wander through small cuboid houses reminiscent of those in the Greek Islands, some with a touch of bright Mediterranean blue or red on the walls. In the many churches the murals have been defaced, although Christ and the apostles are visible in one. There is a sign posted for the walk down the hill to Ölüdeniz: it takes two or three hours, and there are lovely views over the lagoon. ✍$5 ⊙*Daily 9–6:30.*

WHERE TO EAT

$$$
ECLECTIC
★

✕**Levissi Garden Wine House and Restaurant.** This fine restaurant is in what was once the house of a prosperous Greek merchant. The specialities are steak and the ultra-tender Anatolian lamb, marinated in wine and slowed cooked in a 400-year-old oven. There is a good range of Turkish wines. In the heat of summer, you can take refuge in the cool basement. The restaurant floodlights the abandoned buildings all around at night, making for a particularly evocative—or spooky, depending on your take—atmosphere. ✉*Kayaköy, Fethiye, near the western ticket office* ☎252/618–0108 ▭MC, V.

$
TURKISH

✕**Oba Kebab Evi.** In a pleasant, spacious garden a few hundred yards from the main slope of Kaya, this is a traditional Turkish meat restaurant where you order your meat, then cook it yourself on a charcoal brazier supplied by the establishment. There are basic salads and appetizers to go with the mains. ✉*Near the center of Kaya, look for the signposted side street.* ☎252/618–0222 ▭MC, V.

GEMILER ISLAND

8 km (5 mi) southwest of Kevya.

This pretty beach is a quieter option to busy Ölüdeniz. An amphitheater of mountains encloses an offshore island with scattered with Byzantine remains dating from the 7th to the 9th centuries AD. To get to the island it's more fun to take one of the boat tours from Fethiye or Ölüdeniz but there are also five buses a day that run from Fethiye to Gemiler in summer, via Kaya, or you can just drive down the road past Kaya until the end. There is a small restaurant and café above the beach and a variety of water sports available.

TLOS

22 km (14 mi) east of Fethiye.

A day expedition to Tlos, a spectacular ancient Lycian city high above the valley of the Xanthos River, can be arranged from any town on the coast from Göcek to Kaş. From the **acropolis** a fine view can be had to the west of the Xanthos Valley—then as now a rich agricultural area—and to the east of the mountains that cradle Tlos's Roman theater. The fortress at the summit is Turkish from the 18th century and was a popular haunt of the pirate Kanlı ("Bloody") Ali Ağa. Below the fortress, off a narrow path, is a cluster of rock tombs. Note the relief here of Bellerophon, son of King Glaucus of Corinth, mounted on Pegasus, his winged steed. The monster he faces is the dreaded Chimera—a fire-breathing creature with a lion's head, goat's body, and serpent's tail. (Famously, Bellerophon had been sent to the King of Lycia with a sealed message saying that he should be put to death on arrival. Unwilling to kill this noble figure outright, the Lycians sent him on apparently fatal tasks like fighting the Chimera. He survived them all with the aid of Pegasus and won half a kingdom. The Chimera's fire can still be seen coming up from the ground near Çirali/Olimpo.) If you have time, hike over to the theater you saw from the fortress; among the ruins are carved blocks depicting actors' masks. Nearby, the old baths provide more good views of the Xanthos Valley. ✉ *From Fethiye take the exit to Rte. 400 and follow the local road east to Antalya, where a yellow sign marks the right turn that leads southwest for 15 km (9 mi)* 🎫*$5* ⊙ *Daily 8:30–sunset.*

Continue up the hill beyond Tlos to the nearby village of Yaka Köyü (it's signposted) and you'll reach the vast but peaceful **Yaka Park Restaurant** (☎252/638–2011), which has become an attraction in its own right (avoid the imitations). On the site of a now-demolished windmill, it has its own trout farm, guaranteeing the fish will always be fresh. The chilly water is everywhere, gurgling around traditional Turkish wooden platforms where diners sit, and there is even a little channel in the bar where fish can swim around your chilled beer.

🍽 **Saklıkent Gorge.** Continue south from Tlos, about 15 km, to reach this spectacular gorge, a popular spot for picnicking and a wonderful place to cool off on a hot summer's day. Children especially love wading up the walkway through the icy stream at the bottom of a deep rock

Ancient Cultures of Lycia & Its Neighbors

Turkey's Mediterranean coast is steeped in 5,000 years of history—so much so that in Side, the hotels, restaurants, and nightclubs are literally built into the ruins of the Greco-Roman city.

Broadly speaking, the geographic divisions of the coastline of ancient times survive today. The westernmost area from from Datça to Dalyan was part of Caria, an ancient Hellenistic kingdom based in nearby Bodrum/Halicarnassus. Caria reached the height of its power in the 4th century BC, and the tomb of its most famous ruler, Mausolus, was such a wonder of the world that it coined the word *mausoleum*. From Dalyan to Phaselis the coast is thought of as Lycia, after a people of very ancient but uncertain origin, some of whom possibly colonized this section of the Anatolian coast from Crete. It now hosts small-scale hotels and harmonious yachting ports. From Antalya to Alanya is the area called Pamphilia, thought to mean "the land of the tribes," much of which is now quite built up and commercial.

Caria, Lycia, and Pamphilia share much the same, rather obscure, history and museums (the best is in Antalya) exhibit relics from Bronze Age settlements that date back to 3000 BC. Our knowledge of indigenous cultures is patchy, but notable in many ways. In Homer's epic, Lycia's Sarpedon memorably declaims that the privileges of the elite must be earned by the elite's readiness to fight for their people. And while not a matriarchal society, Lycians are thought to have been matrilineal and gave women a more equal place than, say, ancient Greece. Some locals were fiercely independent and the people of Xanthos, for example, committed mass suicide rather than submit to the first Persian conquest, and later burned their city (again) rather than pay extra taxes to Rome's Brutus. In addition, the democratic, federal basis of the Lycian League is acknowledged as one source of the U.S. constitution.

Overall, the population of this whole area has long been a mixture of waves of new arrivals, from Greek colonists to Persian administrators, retired Roman legionaries and Turkic shepherds, to today's sun-seekers. Despite wars, plagues, and population exchanges, however, there is some degree of continuity: genetic tests discovered that all two dozen of the local workers on a site north of Antalya were related to the bones that they had just dug out from 1,300-year-old graves.

---

crevasse. The first section is oven a walkway above the torrent to a pleasant leafy tea garden, beyond which the adventurous can cross the glacial water and continue up the canyon. The determined with time to spare can reach a pretty waterfall at the end. The road here continues sout to Çavdir, which is just across the highway from Xanthos, so you continue on. 🎫$5 ⊙ *Daily 8:30–sunset.*

PINARA

40 km (24 mi) southeast of Fethiye; 40 km (25 mi) north of Kalkan, look for sign on Rte. 400

Pınara (it means "something round" in Lycian) is a romantic ruin around a great circular outcrop backed by high cliffs, reachable from most holiday spots in western Lycia. It was probably founded as early as the 5th century BC, and it eventually became one of Lycia's most important cities. You need time and determination to explore, as it's widely scattered, largely unexcavated, and overgrown with plane, fig, and olive trees. You can park in the village of **Minare** and make the half-hour hike up the clearly marked trail. At the top of a steep dirt track, the site steward will collect your admission and point you in the right direction—there are no descriptive signs or good site maps.

The spectacular **Greek theater,** which has overlooked these peaceful hills and fields for thousands of years, is one of the finest in Turkey. It's perfectly proportioned, and unlike that of most other theaters in Turkey, its stage building is still standing. The site also contains groups of rock **tombs** with unusual reliefs, one showing a cityscape, and a cliff wall honeycombed with hundreds of crude rectangular "pigeonholes," which are believed to have been either tombs or food storage receptacles. Nearby villagers volunteer to show tourists this site; it's not a bad idea to accept the offer as they know the highlights. A tip is customary. ⌦*$5* ⊘*Daily 8:30–sunset.*

LETOÖN

63 km (39 mi) southeast of Fethiye; 17 km (11 mi) north of Kalkan on Rte. 400; follow the signposts west.

This site was not a city but a Lycian national religious center and political meeting point for the Lycian League, the world's first democratic federation. It's quite rural and the site can be reached on day tours from western Lycia's main centers—Fethiye, Ölüdeniz, Kaş, or Kalkan. It's a magical site best visited in the late afternoon, perhaps after a visit to nearby Xanthos, which administered the temples in ancient times. Excavations have revealed three temples in Letoön. The first, closest to the parking area, dates from the 2nd century BC and was dedicated to Leto (hence the name, Letoön), the mother of Apollo and Artemis, who was believed to have given birth to the twins here, while hiding from Zeus' jealous wife, Hera. The middle temple, the oldest, is dedicated to Artemis and dates from the 5th or 4th century BC. The last, dating from the 1st century BC, belongs to Apollo and contains a rare Lycian mosaic depicting a bow and arrow (a symbol of Artemis) and a sun and lyre (Apollo's emblems). These are the three Gods most closely associated with Lycia. Compare the first and last temples: The former is Ionic, topped by a simple, triangular pediment and columns with scroll-shape capitals. The latter is Doric, with an ornate pediment with scenic friezes and detailing, and its columns have undecorated capitals. Reerection of some columns of the Temple of Leto has made the site more photogenic. There is also a well-preserved Roman theater, and the frogs chirping from the once-sacred pool lend atmosphere. About 10 km south of Letoön, the road continues to a beach. ⌦*$1* ⊘*Daily 8:30–sunset.*

XANTHOS

★ *61 km (48 mi) southeast of Fethiye; 17 km (10 mi) north of Kalkan on Rte. 400.*

Xanthos, perhaps the greatest city of ancient Lycia, is famed for tombs rising on high, thick, rectangular pillars. Xanthos also earned the region its reputation for fierceness in battle. Determined not to be subjugated by superior forces, the men of Xanthos twice set fire to their own city, with their women and children inside, and fought to the death. The first occasion was against the Persians in 542 BC, the second against Brutus and the Romans in the 1st century BC. Though the site was excavated and stripped by the British in 1838 and most finds are now in London's British Museum, the remains are worth inspecting. Allow at least three hours and expect some company: Unlike the other Lycian cities, Xanthos is on the main tour-bus route.

You can start your exploration across from the parking area, at the 2nd-century AD **theater,** built by Lycians in the Roman style. Inscriptions indicate it was a gift from a wealthy Lycian named Opromoas of Rhodiapolis, who helped restore many Lycian buildings after the great earthquake of 141 AD. Alongside the theater are two much-photographed pillar **tombs.** The more famous of the pair is called the Harpy Tomb—not after what's inside, but because of the half-bird, half-woman figures carved onto the north and south sides. Other reliefs show a seated figure receiving various gifts, including a bird, a pomegranate, and a helmet. This tomb has been dated to 470 BC, although the reliefs are plaster casts of originals in the British Museum. The other tomb consists of a sarcophagus atop a pillar—a rather unusual arrangement. The pillar section is probably as old as the Harpy Tomb, the sarcophagus added later. On the side of the theater, opposite the Harpy Tomb and past the agora (the ancient meeting place), is the Inscribed Pillar of Xanthos, a tomb dating from about 400 BC and etched with a 250-line inscription that recounts the heroic deeds of a champion wrestler and celebrated soldier named Kerei.

Across the road and past the parking area is the ancient agora, or market place, and a large Byzantine **basilica** with its abstract mosaics. Along a path up the hill are several sarcophagi and a good collection of rock-cut house tombs, as well as a welcome spot of shade. Xanthos's center was up on the acropolis behind the theater, accessible by a trail. 🖼️*$2* ☉ *Daily 9–sunset.*

PATARA

70 km (44 mi) southeast of Fethiye; 20 km (13 mi) north of Kalkan, off Rte. 400.

Patara was once Lycia's principal port. Cosmopolitan in its heyday—Hannibal, St. Paul, and the emperor Hadrian all visited, and St. Nicholas, the man who would be Santa Claus, is said to have been born here—the port eventually silted up. The dunes at the edge of the site are now part of one of Turkey's longest and completely unspoiled sand beaches. From here, too, runs one of the best sections of the Lycian

The Lycian Way

Until the 1950s, the only way to reach the Lycian Coast was by boat or via bone-rattling trips through the mountains in antiquated motor vehicles. Even the main roads of today date only from the 1970s, which is is why this was the perfect place to site Turkey's first and most famous long-distance trekking route, the Lycian Way.

The footpath runs for more than 480 km (300 mi), marked by red-and-white painted blazes every 45 to 90 meters (50 to 100 yards) along the sea, following ancient Roman roads, and sometimes clambering up barely visible goat tracks to peaks that rise to nearly 6,500 feet at Mt. Tahtalı, one of many high mountains known as Mt. Olympos in antiquity. The upsides include breathtaking views, innumerable ancient ruins, and a chance to accept hospitality in villages little touched by tourism or time. The downside is that backpacks can be heavy and skills with a compass or satellite positioning devices are essential to avoid becoming lost in regions where few people pass by. Despite government support, the track has no legal status and is subject to adjustments due to landslides and fencing by landowners. If you lose the trail of the markers, go back to the last one you saw and try again. Be aware, too, that the yellow-and-green Lycian Way signposts are not maintained by their original sponsor, an Istanbul bank, and can be misleading.

It would take a month to walk the Lycian Way from end to end, but because it crosses many towns and highways it's easy to break up into sections of as little as one day. You can camp on high pastures, bathe in remote coves, or relax in pansiyons on the way. Kate Clow, the Englishwoman who first designed and mapped the Lycian Way in 2000, recommends several popular day walks near Olympos; her book *The Lycian Way* is the only guide and source of good maps of the route, and the Web site *www.lycianway.com* has updates and satellite grid references. As a trekking agent and mule organizer, Clow recommends **Middle Earth Travel** (⊠ *Gaferli Mah., Cevizler Sokak 20, Göreme, Nevşehir* ☎ *384/271–2558 or 384/271–2559* ⊕ *www.middleearthtravel.com*).

Peak times to trek are February to mid-March (sometimes rainy), early May to mid-July (when spring flowers are out), or September to mid-November (when the seawater is warm and the weather cooler).

Way, a three- to five-day walk to Ölüdeniz. Thanks to the ruins and the turtles that nest on the beach, new development was banned in the modern village, making it a quiet alternative to the style and bustle of nearby Kalkan.

The **ruins** you'll find today are scattered among marshes and sand dunes. The city was famous for a time for its oracle and its still yet-to-be-found temple of Apollo. Herodotus wrote that the oracle worked only part-time, as Apollo spent summers away in Delos (probably to escape the heat!). The heavy stones that make up the front of the monumental **bathhouse** are impressive, and a **triple arch** built by a Roman governor in AD 100 seems a tenth of its age. Beyond are two theaters, several churches, and an impressive section of colonnaded street. Patara is now being excavated by Antalya's Akdeniz University and slowly emerging from the sands. ⌛$2.

Patara Beach, beyond the ruins, is a superb 11-km (7-mi) sweep of sand dunes popular with Turkish families yet never so crowded you need to walk far to find solitude. Umbrellas should only be planted within 20 yards of the sea to prevent disturbance to the nests of *Caretta caretta* turtles. There is a wooden café on the beach that has toilets, changing huts, umbrellas, loungers, drinks, and food.

WHERE TO STAY AND EAT

$
TURKISH

✕**Tlos Restaurant.** This simple little restaurant just off the main intersection is keenly kept by a chef from the town of Bolu, legendarily the hometown of Turkey's best cooks. Individual attention is assured, and alcoholic drinks can be brought over from the Lumière Hotel opposite. There is an extensive menu with many hot and cold starters, seafood, and grilled meats. ⌂ *On the right just off the main street leading to the ruins through the village of Patara* ☎252/843–5135 ▬MC, V ⊘ *Closed Nov.–Apr.*

$ ⌂**Hotel Lumière.** Surrounded by trees, this is a pleasant place to rest after a day's sightseeing has gone on too long to reach the major centers on the coast. Good-size rooms are decorated with old kilims, and mosquito nets are available if you ask. There's a pleasant pool terrace, where you can chill with a drink after a hard day on the beach; the owner will also drive guests the 5 km (3 mi) down to the ruins and beach in her car. **Pros:** cool vibe; good value. **Cons:** rooms are okay, but nothing special. ⌂ *On left in village on way to Patara ruins. On the main street on the left as you come into town* ☎242/317–5399 ⊕*www.hotellumiere.com* ⤴16 *rooms* ⌂ *In-room: no a/c (some), Wi-Fi. In-hotel: bars, pool, laundry facilities* ▬MC, V ⧦BP.

$ ⌂**View Point.** One of the larger hotels in Patara, the View Point sits up on the hill west of town. It's run by a Turkish-English couple, Muzaffer and Anne Louise, who are a good source of information on the area. The rooms are good by Patara standards but nothing exceptional; about half have views over town, but not the ruins or sea. There's a large pool area and an "Ottoman terrace" for meals. Out of season, rooms can be made available on request. **Pros:** friendly; well run. **Cons:** the walk up the hill. ⌂ *Up the hill to the left as you come into town* ☎242/843–5110 ⊕*www.pataraviewpoint.com* ⤴27 *rooms* ⌂ *In-hotel: restaurant, bar, pool* ⊘ *Closed Nov.–Apr.*

KALKAN

80 km (50 mi) southeast of Fethiye; 27 km (17 mi) west of Kaş, on Rte. 400.

Kalkan has two distinct sides: on one hand it has fine restaurants and excellent hotels to match its superb, steep views of the Mediterranean Sea. But it's also a bit overpriced, and regulars complain that the recent explosion of foreign-owned villas has changed the town's character for the worse. The ranks of self catering villas, often rented out on the Internet, are spreading up the mountainsides all around and ensure that tourism seasons are growing longer and more prosperous, though hotel and restaurants complain they are sending them out of business. And still, the old stone alleyways are now positively sleek with whitewash and the small port is crowded with yachts in summer.

Without much archaeology of its own, despite the great Lycian sites nearby, Kalkan is trying hard to develop its tourism offerings and it's an excellent base for touring the area and the surrounding sites. Agencies in town like **Kalamus Travel** (⊠ *Yalıboyu, also doing business as Mavi Real Estate* ☎242/844–2456) can arrange paragliding, diving, horseback riding, jeep safaris, village visits, mountain walks, and guided trips to Lycian ruins.

WORD OF MOUTH

"I think one of the nicest options on the Turquoise Coast is Kalkan—which I much prefered to Kas or Bodrum. If you prefer somewhere quiet, consider Patara—about 30 mins away—which has the longest beach in the Mediterranean, I believe. You should definitely visit Ölüdeniz if you're nearby. It's visually stunning—though it will certainly be crowded." —Steve_James

WHERE TO STAY AND EAT

$$$
TURKISH
★
✕**Aubergine.** This restaurant is an exception to the general rule of avoiding harbor-front eateries. The menu is adventurous and well explained, and includes salmon *en croute*, stuffed sea bass with bacon, extra large steaks, ostrich fillet, and occasionally wild boar shot in the mountains. All the desserts are homemade. ⊠ *On the harbor front* ☎242/844–3332 ▤MC, V.

$$–$$$
TURKISH
✕**Çatı.** At this mid-market Turkish meat restaurant on the slopes above Kalkan, a freshly baked long *lavash* bread is brought to the table when you're seated, along with starters of walnuts and hard white cheese matured in goatskin. The restaurant prides itself on its *acılı ezme,* an appetizer of finely chopped hot chile, tomato, and onion, and the meats that follow are delicious. Thick Turkish *pide* and paper-thin *lahmacun* mincemeat pizzas are also available. ⊠ *Şehitler Cad. 55, Menteşe* ☎242/844–3069 ▤MC, V.

$$$
MEDITERRANEAN
Fodor'sChoice
★
✕**Gironda.** This gourmet restaurant is designed like a rich villa with sumptuous sofas and plaster-of-paris statuary, and the excellent food alone merits a stay in Kalkan. The fare is outstandingly fresh and the dishes are well thought out: even a humble lamb pie topped with phyllo pastry pops with tastes of baby onion, sesame, and mushrooms. Other specialities are pan-seared fish, eggplant with cheese, and fish baked in parchment, as well as a wide variety of pastas. Tables on the terrace upstairs enjoy great views of Kalkan Bay. ⊠ *Two streets up from the harbor in the old town* ☎242/844–3136 ⌂*Reservations essential* ▤MC, V ⊗*Closed Nov.–Apr.*

$$
★
▥**Happy Hotel.** Despite the unimaginative concrete block architecture, this is an attractive hotel and good value. Set against wild olive shrub, on the slopes around Kalamar Bay, the views are stunning and rooms are large, with terra-cotta-style floors and large balconies. An ambitious U.S.-trained manager was hired in 2005 and is improving the already high standards of service in the hotel and its gourmet restaurant. A shuttle is available to get into Kalkan proper. There is a large, pleasant pool terrace, too. **Pros:** giant suites. **Cons:** very limited service into town.

DID YOU KNOW?

Kapıtaş Beach, between Kaş and Kalkan, is dramatically set between the cliffs.

⊠ *Head west of Kalkan to Kalamar Bay, follow the road left as you come over the ridge and follow the signs down the hill* ☎ *242/844–1133* ⊕ *www.happy.com.tr* ⟳ *In-room: safe, DVD (some), Wi-Fi. In-hotel: 2 restaurants, bars, gym* ⊟ *MC, V.*

$$ 🏨 **Hotel Pirat.** This 1986 concrete hotel lacks personality and shows its age in poor design, but the location is great: right on the harbor, and the three pools have superb views over the bay. The hotel is divided into two; the rooms in Pirat II are somewhat better than in Pirat I. Check that your balcony overlooks the water, not the villa sprawl climbing the slopes above town. **Pros:** central location. **Cons:** not much in the way of looks, especially the ugly green carpet. ⊠ *Kalkan harbor* ☎ *242/844– 3178* ⊕ *www.hotelpirat.net* ⟿ *126 rooms, 10 suites* ⟳ *In-room: Wi-Fi. In-hotel: 2 restaurants, bars, pools, beachfront* ⊟ *MC, V.*

$$$ 🏨 **Hotel Villa Mahal.** Clinging to a cliff face with a wraparound view

Fodor's Choice of Kalkan Bay, this immaculate establishment is one of Turkey's most

★ spectacular hotels. A gorgeous pool juts out into the air, making swimming feel like flying, and the beach club at the bottom of the cliff offers many water sports. A hotel boat will run you five minutes across the bay to Kalkan harbor if you want an evening in town. Be ready, however, for the 181 steps from top to bottom, and be aware that the long balcony in front of the picture windows of the standard double rooms also serves as a public walkway. If there is anywhere in the world to splash out on a great room, this is it—try the Sunset Suite with its spacious layout and blue mosaic hot tub and enjoy a second honeymoon. **Pros:** nice rooms; gorgeous location. **Cons:** people walking through your balcony. ⊠ *Patara Evler Yani, about 2 km (1 mi) east of Kalkan. Down and around the signposted road. Take care on the precipitous last approach* ☎ *242/844–3268* ⊕ *www.villamahal.com* ⟿ *4 rooms and 2 suites* ⟳ *In-room: safe. In-hotel: 3 restaurants, bars, Internet terminal, no kids under 9* ⊟ *MC, V* ⊗ *Nov.–Apr.* ⧦ *BP.*

⌐ EN
ROUTE

Kapıtaş Beach. Since neither Kaş or Kalkan have proper beaches this pretty spot between the two is a quite popular. Set in a narrow, steep-sided inlet, a long metal stair takes you down and down to the beach proper. The position between the dramatic cliffs is picturesque, though the beach itself is small and can get crowded in summer.

KAŞ

107 km (67 mi) southeast of Fethiye via Rte 400; 180 km (112 mi) from Antalya via Korkuteli mountain road.

Official tourist office Kaş (⊠ *Cumhuriyet Meyd. 5* ☏ *242/836–1238*).

EXPLORING

In the 1980s, Kaş, with its beautiful wide, island-filled bay, was the main tourist destination on the Lycian coast, but it has since fallen somewhat by the wayside, lacking a real beach and A-list attractions. This has, fortunately, kept away the worst overdevelopment of the last few years, and now Kas is now being rediscovered, with many restaurants and regular visitors migrating from Kalkan. There are excellent hotels and restaurants, the location is relatively central and the size is about right, making it a good stop on your way along the coast.

Kaş was ancient Antiphellus, and has a few **ruins,** including a monumental **sarcophagus** under a massive plane tree, up the sloping street that rises behind the tourist office.

WORD OF MOUTH

"Kaş is a very nice, small fishing village, easily walkable, with a harbor that has small boats for Mediterranean cruises." —Michel_Paris

The tomb has four regal lion's heads carved onto the lid. In 1842, a British naval officer counted more than 100 sarcophagi in Kaş—then called Antifili—but most have been destroyed over the years as locals nabbed the flat side pieces to use in new construction.

A few hundred yards west of the main square, along Hastane Caddesi, is a small, well-preserved antique **theater,** amid the olive trees at the edge of town, with a superb ocean view. Next to the district prefect's office, east of the harbor, is an old wooden barn of the type once universally used as granaries in Lycian villages—and still clearly modeled on old Lycian architectural forms. Even more unusually, ask at Meis discotheque to see their 3rd-century-BC cistern, carved from the solid rock. Kaş makes a good base for boat excursions, and a profusion of scuba-diving boats shows the growing demand for the area's rich underwater sights.

The hour-long boat ride to the Greek Island of **Kastellorizon** (the name of the island is Meis in Turkish—like the Kaş disco) gives you a taste both of Greece and what Kaş must have been like before the 1924 population exchange, when it was mostly populated by Greeks.

All new houses on the island must be built in the traditional manner. Since a day trip only allows one to see the island during exactly the hours most Greeks are having their midday siesta, it's worth trying to arrange to stay the night; there are several hotels and a few *pansiyons.* The island has an impressive 12th- to 16th-century crusader castle with crenellated gray-stone walls, a large cave with fine stalactites, and the 1835 church of St. Konstantine and Eleni, which reused granite columns taken from the Temple of Apollo at Letoön in Lycia.

Other excursion options include Simena and Kekova Sound; Demre, site of the old church of St. Nicholas of Christmas fame; or Patara and Patara Beach. Be aware that high winds can make for a very rough ride, particularly round the cape to Kekova.

WHERE TO STAY AND EAT

$ ✕ **Bahçe & Bahçe Balik.** Bahçe is a courtyard restaurant serving delightful
TURKISH Turkish dishes in a quiet garden setting, just opposite Kaş's iconic 4th-century-BC King's Tomb. The waitstaff is one large family—each taking part in the preparation and serving of food. The starters are famous in Kaş. Especially tasty options are grated carrot with yogurt, mashed walnut, cold spinach, fish balls, and the *arnavut ciğeri* (cold fried liver prepared with chopped nuts). The same family have opened a fish restaurant opposite, Bahçe Balik. ⊠ *Anıt Mezar Karşisi 31* ☎ *242/836–2370* ⊟ *MC, V.*

$$$
FRENCH
★

✕**Chez Evy.** No place in Kaş has more character than this delightful restaurant. Prices might be high, but that's because Evy has a tendency to serve portions that are double the size of anywhere else. The menu is short but varied, including wild boar from the mountains. Dining is in an intimate garden around the back in summer, where shared tables and Evy's big-hearted solicitousness create an atmosphere where everybody is soon talking to everybody else. A digestif is a special treat in the cozy bar with its eccentric decoration and Evy's dancing, cappucino-drinking red parrot. Don't believe rival restaurateurs nearby who claim Evy's has closed. In the November–April off-season, call for a reservation. ⊠*Terzi Sokak 2, in a small street behind the Red Point bar* ☎242/836–1253 ⌾*Reservations essential Nov.–Apr.* ▤MC, V.

$$–$$$
TURKISH
Fodor'sChoice
★

✕**Ikbal.** This new addition to the cluster of restaurants near the Lycian tomb has rapidly earned a reputation for the quality of its food. Run by a German-Turkish couple, it offers a mix of Turkish and Mediterranean dishes. They take great pride in their warm starters, such as the delcious *paçanga börek,* a pastry filled with cheese and dried meat, and the *emücver,* deep-fried eggplant—all of which are cooked fresh rather than reheated as at most other restaurants. For main courses there are the usual range of fish, köfte, lamb, chicken, and steak, and the dessert menu is wide and tempting, including the popular apple pancakes. ⊠*Süleyman Sandıkçı Sokak 6* ☎242/836–3193 ▤MC, V.

$$$–$$$$
TURKISH

✕**Mercan.** With a prime waterfront position, this is one of Kaş's oldest establishments (in business since 1956), and it has a reputation for quality of seafood and steepnees of prices. There is a wide choice of fish, with the day's catch often displayed in a small water-filled boat at the entrance, and a variety of over 30 starters and salads, plus kebabs for those who aren't in the mood for fish. ⊠*Waterfront* ☎242/836–1209 ▤MC, V.

$$$
☾

🏨 **Aquapark Hotel.** On the tip of the peninsula west of Kaş, the Aquapark is a resort with a long-standing reputation for excellent food. Light winds in summer mean that there is less humidity here than elsewhere in Lycia, and grassy terraces under the olive trees beckon anyone who wants to relax, read, or watch the boats go by. There's no beach, but access to the sea is possible from a platform on the rocky point. There is also a disco. Standard rooms are quite large and most have sea views. **Pros:** wow views. **Cons:** the sloping site means lots of stairs. ⊠*Take the road out of Kaş to the Çukurbağ Peninsula, drive 2 km (1 mi) to the farthest point on the road that does a circuit around the point* ☎242/836–1902 ⊕*www.aquapark.org* ⤴*81 rooms, 42 suites* ⌾*In-hotel: 2 restaurants, bars, tennis courts, pools* ▤MC, V ⊗*Closed Nov.–Apr.* ⍩MAP.

$$
★

🏨 **Gardenia.** The first thing you notice here is the art, aquired by the owner on his off-season trips to Asia and South America; it fills the lobby, expands up the stairs, and overflows into the rooms, setting the tone for a boutique, design hotel. The rooms are tastefully furnished, as are the bathrooms with their large cabinet showers. The roof terrace and front rooms have amazing views. **Pros:** stylish. **Cons:** no elevator, and there are lots of stairs to reach the rooftop breakfast terrace. ⊠*Hükmet Cad. 41* ☎242/836–2368 ⊕*www.gardeniahotel-kas.com* ⤴*10 rooms, 1 suite* ⌾*In room: safe. In hotel: restaurant, bar* ⊗*Closed mid-Nov.–Apr.*

$$ ⛯**Hadrian Hotel.** This is a beautifully designed and immaculately kept
Fodor's Choice hotel on the peninsula outside Kaş. There are plenty of hideaways on
★ the property for guests looking for a few days of privacy—if you can
get a room. A platform on the rocks below gives access to the sea, with
a new "moonlight pavilion"—roofed gazebo—beside the water, and
a rare luxury is a generous-sized seawater swimming pool. Reserve
well in advance. **Pros:** gorgeous location; romantic. **Cons:** hotel is 500
yards down a steep hill from the main road, so a rental car is vital if
you plan to do much sightseeing in the area. ⊠*Doğan Kaşaroğlu Cad.
10, south side of Çukurbağ Peninsula, about 500 meters (1,640 feet)
from the tip. Well signposted once on the peninsula* ☎242/836–2856
⊕*www.hotel-hadrian.de* ⇗*10 rooms, 4 suites* ⟳*In-room: safe, Wi-Fi.
In-hotel: 2 restaurants, bar, laundry facilities, Internet terminal* ▤*MC,
V* ⊗*Closed Nov. 15–Apr. 15* �ⓄⓁMAP.

$ ⛯**Medusa Hotel.** This is probably the best-run of the generally good
★ hotels that line the seafront road east of the harbor. Rooms are small,
but most have views and are well-maintained. The hotel has direct
access to local diving schools and its own beach with rock platforms
from which to swim in the sea. Managed since 2006 by a lively archae-
ologist from Belgium and his Turkish wife, whose parents own the
hotel, you can count on the very best advice on which ancient sites to
see. The restaurant is worth a visit in its own right, being reasonably
priced and serving unusual Turkish-Ottoman food like lamb fillet with
cheese sauce. **Pros:** friendly and helpful. **Cons:** rooms nothing special.
⊠*Küçük Çakıl 62* ☎242/836–1440 ⊕*www.medusahotels.com* ⇗*36
rooms, 1 suite* ⟳*In-room: safe, Wi-Fi. In-hotel: restaurant, pool, diving*
▤*AE, MC, V* ⊗*Nov.–Apr.* ⓄⓁBP.

NIGHTLIFE

The **Meis Disco Bar** is a well-run discotheque and venue for live Turk-
ish music performances. This is probably also the only nightclub in
the world to boast a 3rd-century-BC basement cistern carved out of
solid rock, now laid out with tables, and quieter than upstairs. The
ancient basement roof of solid stone slabs is held up by crude pillars
and, according to the owner, sophisticated French glue. The cistern
was discovered by chance when the original building—a high-doored
former stable for camels, which were the main means of transport in
Lycia until just a few decades ago—was being extended. ⊠*On eastern
edge of harbor.*

SIMENA AND KEKOVA SOUND

30 km (19 mi) east of Kaş.

Simena (now known in Turkish as Kaleköy), Kekova Island, and its
surrounding coastline are some of the most enchanted spots in Turkey,
especially as the reflection of the full moon slowly traces its way across
Kekova Sound. Most local transportation is by water, and there are
many day tours from Kaş, but a new road to nearby Üçağız, off Route
400, has eased the overland journey, which has magnificent views.

Kekova Island stands slightly off a shoreline notched with little bays,
whose many inlets create a series of lagoons. Anchoring many are small

fishing communities. The disappearing apse of a Byzantine church backs one beach known as Tersane, whose bay is a favorite swimming spot. It is also famed for its "sunken city" though with swimming now banned there isn't much to see; the main attraction is just exploring the beautiful inlet. The village of Üçağız has small pansiyons and waterside restaurants, and is the base for boat trips across the bay to the island.

Simena, a concrete-free village has the look of the Greek islands before development. Reached by a 10-minute boat ride or half-hour walk from Üçağız, it's a pleasing jumble of boxy houses built up a steep rocky crag alongside layers of history: Lycian tombs, a tiny Greek theater, and the medieval ruins of Simena Castle atop the rocky hill. There are now numerous basic *pansiyons* that are rather expensive for the quality of the rooms, but you're pay for the sublime view from the balconies. All offer boat pickups from Üçağız. Reserve well in advance, in season.

Aperlai & Apollonia. West of Kekova are two small, infrequently visited ruins, linked together by a section of the Lycian way; they make for a good day trip or overnight for those who want to get off the beaten track. Apollonia is on a small hill just south west of the village of Kilicli/Sahilklinigi on the Kaş–Üçağız road 7 km (4½ mi) south of the highway. Take the branch road through the village then head west when you get to the top of the rise. First you'll see a good range of ancient Lycian tombs, scattered east and north of the walled acropolis hill. Continue west for the city proper; there's a small theater and a well-preserved church with views west over the coast towards Kaş. Back on the side road, look for the signed turnoff to the right then walk two hours down the hill to the ruins of Aperlae on a pretty little inlet. The city walls are impressively intact, and inside are a scatter of buildings including a well preserved church, houses, and a bath building by the water, as well the sunken remains of the ancient port, which you can explore with a mask and snorkel from the nearby **Purple House** *pansiyon* and restaurant, in nicely restored stone buildings. From Aperlai a 20-minute walk takes you to another restaurant on the Kekova inlets, and another three hours, first inland, and then along the water, will take you to Üçağız.

WHERE TO STAY AND EAT

$$ ⌐ **Ankh Pansiyon.** This simple hotel is the place to choose if you want to escape from the world and soak up the otherworldliness of Kekova Sound. The wooden rooms are basic but clean, and the family establishment, has a small restaurant, and a bar. The hotel, on the quiet eastern edge of the village, has a charming little jetty on which to sunbathe or from which to dive into the crystal clear water. **Pros:** more private than other places around. **Cons:** rooms lack character. ⊠ *Eastern side of the village, follow the signs through the maze of streets* ☎ 242/874–2171 ⊕ *www.ankhpansion.com* ⌐ *8 rooms* ⌂ *In-room: Wi-Fi. In-hotel: restaurant* ⊟ *MC, V* ⊗ *Closed Nov. 10–Apr.* ⍑ *BP.*

$$ ⌐ **Kale Pension.** In a pretty stone building with lovely old wooden ceilings, this small lodging has a small courtyard on the eastern side of the waterfront. There is a private swimming area, and also a jetty with tables for a sunset dinner. Rooms are basic, but this older building has a bit more character than some of the other nearby options. **Pros:** central

yet separate; family-run; character. **Cons:** ground-floor rooms have less of a view; no Internet. ✉*Just east of the Sahil Pension, follow the signs* ☎242/874–2111 ⊕*www.kalepansiyon.com* ⇆*11 rooms* ⌂*In hotel: restaurant.* ▭*MC, V* ⊘*Closed Nov.–Apr.*

$ ▦**Purple House.** This little *pansiyon* on an idyllic inlet, is the ultimate escape from the mass tourisim of the Turkish coast. Popular with Lycian-way trekkers, the facilities are basic: gas lamps, mountains toilets, and cold showers, but the well-restored rooms in the 200-year-old stone houses will make you feel like you've gone back a hundred years in time. Food and drinks are available, so even if you don't stay, you can take a break here for a bite and a swim—though its best to ring ahead if you want a meal. **Pros:** idylic escape. **Cons:** very basic. ✉*Aperlai* ☎0539/859–9196 ⊕*www.aperlai.com* ⇆*6 rooms* ⌂*In hotel: restaurant.* ▭*No credit cards.*

$$ ▦**Sahil Pension.** This little *pansiyon* above a restaurant and general store is in the middle of things in the center of the Kaleköy waterfront. The rooms share a long balcony with a magnificent view and you can watch the boats coming and going from the nearby port; down by the sea there are deck chairs and pretty tables out on a jetty. **Pros:** central location; great views. **Cons:** less private. ✉*Kaleköy waterfront, look for the shop* ☎242/874–2263 ⊕*www.sahilpension.com* ⇆*4 rooms* ⌂*In hotel: restaurant.* ▭*MC, V.*

DEMRE (KALE)

37 km (23 mi) east of Kaş, 140 km (87 mi) southwest of Antalya on Rte. 400.

Demre is where Saint Nicholas, who later became known as Father Christmas, made his reputation as bishop of the Graeco-Roman diocese of Myra in the first half of the 4th century. Among his good deeds, St. Nicholas is said to have carried out nocturnal visits to the houses of local children to leave gifts, including gold coins as dowries for poor village girls; if a window was closed, said the storytellers, he would drop the gifts down the chimney.

Demre was one of the most important cities along the coast but its remains lie mostly under the concrete and large greenhouses of the modern city between the city center around the Church of St. Nicholas and the hillside to the north, where there is a theater and some rock cut tombs. Demre is, however, primarily an agricultural region, for most tourists a quick stopover on their trip along the coast.

A church was built around the tomb of St. Nicholas in the 6th century, but it was later destroyed in an Arab raid. In 1043 the **St. Nicholas Basilica** was rebuilt with the aid of the Byzantine emperor Constantine IX and the empress Zoë. It now stands near the center of Demre, a couple blocks from the square. St. Nicholas's remains, however, were stolen and taken to Bari, Italy, in 1087, where the church of San Nicola di Bari was built to house them. A few bones remained, so the story goes, and these can be seen in the Antalya Museum. The church in Demre today is mainly the result of restoration work financed by 19th-century Russian noblemen. It's difficult to distinguish between the

DID YOU KNOW?

The top of a submerged Lycian tomb juts out of the water near Kekova.

original church, parts of which may date back to the 5th century, and the restorations, although the bell tower and upper story are clearly late additions. A service is held in the church every year on December 6, the feast day of St. Nicholas, as part of the annual symposium and festival organized by the Father Christmas and Call to World Peace Foundation. 🖃*$7* ⊙ *Daily 8:30–5:30.*

> **A NOTE ON NAMES:**
>
> Demre is also known in Turkish as Kale, not to be confused with Kale, the Turkish name for Simena in nearby Kekova Sound, now usually Kaleköy to avoid the confusion. "Kale" is also Turkish for "castle."

The monuments of ancient **Myra**—a large, well-preserved Roman theater and a cliff face full of Lycian rock tombs—are about 2 km (1 mi) north of Kale, poorly marked by signs. The theater dates from the 2nd century AD and for a time was used for gladiator spectacles involving wild animals. In the cliffs above the theater there are some good reliefs (a stairway leads to a raised viewing platform so you can see them up close) and on the bits of pediments and statuary scattered about the grounds of the site. 🖃*$7* ⊙ *Daily 8:30–5 or 5:30.*

Andriake was the port of ancient Myra and a major stopover on the Egypt-to-Rome route that supplied most of Rome's wheat. St. Paul changed ships here on his journey to Rome in 60 AD. Hadrian built a huge granary here—it's hidden in the bushes south of the road just before you get to the modern port of Demre, and is also clearly visible from the Kaş-Demre road, just west of Demre, as you come around the last bend. If you're willing to ford the waist-deep water of the modern port, Üçağız is about seven hours' walk on the Lycian Way with several pretty costal sections.

Sura was ancient Myra's most important pre-Christian holy site. Priests of Apollo would release holy fish into the sacred pool and then would "read" the future from the movements of the fish as they ate pieces of meat or bread thrown by worshipers. The site is unmarked, just beside the turnoff to Kekova, a few hundred meters north of Andriake. There is a scatter of Lycian tombs and a small acropolis from where you can see the temple of Apollo in the overgrown valley below.

WHERE TO STAY AND EAT

$ ✕**Ipek Restaurant.** One of the best of the group of traditional Turkish
TURKISH   *lokantas* around the church of St. Nicholas, Ipek doesn't look like much and the waiters can be surly, but the kitchen cooks excellent meat dishes that make this the restaurant of choice for many. ✉*As you exit the church, turn left along the pedestrian street. Ipek is 100 yards down, on the left* ☎*242/871–5150* ▭*MC, V.*

$ ✕**Nur Pastaneleri.** After paying your respects to St. Nick, repair here to
TURKISH   enjoy properly arctic air-conditioning and a cold drink or tea accompanied by some of Turkey's freshest *baklava,* the diamond-cut honeyed pastry with nuts. Until early afternoon the café also serves *su böreği,* a salty pastry flavored with feta cheese or mincemeat. ✉*As you exit the St. Nicholas basilica, walk south to the square and on your right is a*

These Lycian rock tombs have been carved into the cliffside of the ancient city of Myra.

*two-story modern shopping center with slim pillars down the facade;
Nur Pastaneleri is on the corner* ☎242/871–6310 ▭MC, V.

FINIKE AND ARYCANDA

111 km (70 mi) southwest of Antalya along Rte. 400.

Finike is a good spot to stop for lunch, or is a jumping-off point for
Arycanda and a series of less glamorous Lycian sites that dot the citrus-
and vegetable-growing coastal plain. The small port town is friendly,
helpful, and inexpensive—and a somewhat unexciting place to stay. A
yacht marina harbors many European boats, but Finike, which makes
most of its money from unglamorous hothouses for growing vegetables,
seems to take their presence unfussily in its stride. A colorful town
market is held every Sunday.

The well-preserved walls and lovely location of **Arycanda,** high in a
mountain valley above Finike, make this ancient Lycian town one of
the most beautiful and least crowded archaeological sites on the Turquoise Riviera. A parking area and easy-to-follow trail lead up to the
acropolis, first passing the monumental **Roman baths,** perhaps Turkey's
best-preserved bathhouse, with intact mosaic floors, standing walls,
and windows framing the valley. The tombs, farther east along the
trail, are more properly Roman rather than Lycian. At the top of the
hills is a pretty ensemble of a sunken agora, or market, with arcades
on three sides and an intimate odeon, or small concert hall, topped by
a Greek-style theater with a breathtaking view of the valley and mountains often capped with snow. Even higher up is the town's stadium or

running track. Farther north is a second, long thin agora, with a small temple above it. From here the official trail scrambles down to some Roman villas, but you may find it easier to backtrack. Back toward the car park are a large church with mosaics and a temple of Trajan with an ancient Roman toilet underneath.To reach Arycanda, drive 35 km (22 mi) north of Finike towards Elmalı, and watch for the Arycanda sign to the right. ☎ *0535/856–6059* 🖭 *$2* ⊙ *Daily 9–7:30.*

WHERE TO STAY AND EAT

$

TURKISH

★

✕**Altın Sofra.** This restaurant in the marina is famed for its lamb and lambs' liver, but it serves a full menu including fish. There is a pleasant garden shaded by plane trees and acacias. Everything here is so fresh the chef refuses to add anything but olive oil and salt to flavor his meats. ✉ *Inside the yacht marina, on the western side, 100 yards past the entrance* ☎ *242/855–1281* ⊟ *MC, V.*

¢–$

TURKISH

★

✕**Anfora Balı Restaurant.** This unassuming-looking restaurant, in a cool basement cavern set into the hillside by the main road above the yatch marina, offers fine seafood and excellent value. Specialties include pots of cooked squid, octopus, and shrimp. The fried squid is famously fresh. ✉ *Main road, just west of the center, 100 yards past the marina entrance on Kordon Cad. (Rte. 400)* ☎ *242/855–3888* ⊟ *MC, V.*

$

🏨**Arikandos Hotel.** A bright and well-furnished commercial hotel just opposite the yacht harbor, the Arikandos is an excellent and inexpensive place to stay, if somewhat unromantic. The hotel has no pool, but a good public beach is a five-minute drive to the west. This is an option if you want to break up your journey, especially if heading up to Arycanda, but not much of a destination in its own right. **Pros:** good value. **Cons:** there's little reason to stay in Finike. ✉ *Center of town on the main road, opposite yacht marina entrance* ☎ *242/855–5805* ⊕ *www. arikandos.com* 🛏 *52 rooms, 4 suites* ⚏ *In-room: safe, Wi-Fi. In-hotel: restaurant, bars* ⊟ *MC, V* ⏐⏐*BP.*

OLYMPOS AND ÇIRALI

★ *Olympos is 89 km (55 mi) southwest of Antalya from Rte. 400. Read signposts carefully—the "Olympos Plaj" leads to Çıralı, not Olympos proper. Adrasan is 10 km (6 mi) southwest from Olympos, 94 km (59 mi) southwest of Antalya; follow Rte. 400 and then signs to Olympos, Çavuşköy, and Adrasan.*

Olympos and its "sister" towns, Çıralı and Adrasan are places unique on the Turquoise Riviera for their natural beauty, ancient ruins, low-rise development, and easygoing culture that mixes international backpackers, ecologically sensitive Turks, and European intellectuals. All three towns are also next to some of the best day walks on the Lycian Way, though the Olympos ruins are the main event in the area. All three are accessed via a secondary road, parallel to the highway.

The ancient city of Olympos is named after a nearby peak that towers above the mountain range behind the beach. A lovely 500-yard walk through the overgrown site gives access to one end of the long sand-and-pebble beach, still unspoiled and backed by an amazing amphitheater of pine-clad mountains. The sights can be seen in a day, but the natural beauty and laid-back atmosphere can prove addictive. One of the hotels has a slogan: "Come for a day, stay for a week," and it's surprising how often that happens. Olympos is, perhaps, a little too beautiful for its own good: it's popular with backpackers and younger Turks, and in summer it can get crowded and noisy, with loud discos at night. Out of season, it returns to bucolic tranquillity. There is a no-concrete rule for development in the region, so accommodation is mostly in wooden cabins, as well as Olympos's famous "tree houses," best described as basic cabins on stilts. A few miles inland, out of the gorge, is a collection of other *pansiyons,* which can be quieter and more upmarket. The nearby town of Çıralı shares the long gorgeous beach and caters more to families and those looking for something quieter; the *pansiyons* here are mostly wooden cabins among the fruit trees. There are few restaurants, and most lodgings include one meal.

> ## WORD OF MOUTH
>
> "Çirali/Olympos is a quiet and peaceful village perfect for families, nature lovers, and for those wishing to get away from the touristic cities or towns…it boasts a beautiful 3.5 km secluded beach, the ruins of Olympos, the flames of the Chimaera, and is a protected area by the WWF for the nesting of the Caretta Caretta sea turtles."
> —brenda66

The ruins of the ancient city of **Olympos,** enshrouded in dense vegetation, have received little excavation and, as a result, are wonderfully atmospheric. Because the ruins are next to a river and shaded by tall firs, flowering oleander bushes, and a mountain gorge, they are also delightfully cool in summer, the perfect time to explore.

Olympos was once a top-voting member of the 2nd-century-BC Lycian League, but most of the buildings viewable today date from Roman times. Roman-era building started in earnest after officers—including the young Julius Ceasar—crushed a two-year-long occupation of the city by invading rebels in about 70 BC. Many tombs are scattered around the ancient city, which is reached by two parallel paths continue down to the beach. In the center of the northern half of the site is the large cathedral complex, once the main temple, which includes a much-photographed 18-foot-high gate, dedicated to Marcus Aurelius in AD 171 and mistakenly referred to by signs as a temple. Note how some walls around the site have clearly been rebuilt in later centuries with narrow arrow slits in the windows as if the city suddenly had to fortify itself. A second side path leads along a water channel to some interesting tombs and a large building perhaps used in funeral ceremonies. At the beach exit is a poetic inscription on a sarcophagus in memory of an ancient ship's captain, along with a carving of his beached boat—not that different from today's gulets. From here you can also climb to a small acropolis and some medieval fortifications where ancients would keep a lookout for ships and pirates.

The southern side of the ancient city is best reached by crossing the riverbed (dry in summer) by the land-side ticket office and heading east toward the beach along a well-beaten path that starts with a remarkable row of tombs with their sliding-stone windows still in place. Farther along are shipping quays, warehouses, a gorgeously overgrown amphitheater, a great bathhouse, and a church whose two great rows of granite columns have collapsed inward toward each other and now lie half-buried in what feels like the floor of a tropical jungle. Farther south along the beach are the walls of a medieval castle variously occupied and improved by crusaders and also used as an outpost of Italian city states. ⌦$3.

The long Olympos beach extends to Çıralı and is one of the wonders of Turkey—not least for how it has managed to escape the ravages of industrial tourism. The beach is mostly smooth white and multicolored marble pebbles mixed with some light gray sand. Float out on your back and marvel at the 5-km (3-mi) sweep of beach, the line of fir trees behind it, and the surrounding amphitheater of mountains that includes the 8,000-foot peak of Mt. Olympos. Several restaurants along the beach front make great places to eat and while away an evening. Olympos and Çıralı are only separated by a short walk along the beach, but it's a long drive around the mountain.

At the far end of Çıralı, a half-hour evening scramble up a sometimes steep path will bring you to the **Chimaera,** named after the ferocious fire-breathing beast of legend. Flames can still be seen rising from cracks in the rock, apparently also burning the gas deep below, since they reignite even if covered. In times past, the flames were apparently more vigorous, even visible by sailors offshore. The Chimaera is inland from the far southern end of of Çıralı; take either of the main roads to the end then head inland. If you're staying in Olympos it's a 7-km (5-mi) 90-minute walk, so you may want to drive to the bottom of the hill, or take a tour. From the parking lot it's a half-hour walk up a lot of stairs. Most hotels in the area will arrange a tour. You can see the flames in the day, but they're best at night. ■TIP➔Bring a flashlight for all those stairs, since there's no lighting, and in peak season go as late as possible to avoid the crowds. ⌦$3 ⌚24 hrs daily.

About 10 mi from Olympos, between Kumluca and Olympos, **Adrasan** is a relaxed little town on a long beach, that's a world away from the flashy resort towns. Don't expect five-star hotels, gourmet restaurants, tour buses or touts, just a great stretch of rarely crowded beach and some decent family *pansiyons*. Boat tours that take you to swim in local coves set off from the beach each morning at about 10 and cost about $25 including lunch. A long, wonderful, and mostly forest-shaded day's walk along the Lycian Way will take you through forests over Mt. Musa to Olympos; another walk will take you to the lighthouse at the point of the Tekke Peninsula; another more difficult route takes seven or eight hours and goes around the peninsula to the wonderful lighthouse at Cape Gelidonya and to the small beach town of Karaöz. Take the official Lycian Way guide book (it comes with a map), adequate water, and preferably a guide for the often lonely pathways. Note that there is very limited public transport to Adrasan, so you're best off if you have a car.

BEYOND OLYMPOS

Why go to Adrasan if you've seen Olympos, you might ask. It's one of Turkey's last quiet, basic, and locally run beachfront holiday spots. Hotels are also up to a third cheaper than those in Çıralı.

The mythical chimera (for which the flame at Olympos is named) was a fire-breathing monster with the body of a goat, the head of a lion, and the tail of a serpent.

SPORTS AND THE OUTDOORS

Olympos is one of Turkey's premier **rock climbing** destinations. Kadirs, a few hundred yards up from the main cluster of buildings in the valley has a climbing center provides support for new and experienced climbers. ☎ *242/892–1316* 🌐 *www.olymposrockclimbing.com.*

WHERE TO STAY

IN THE OLYMPOS VALLEY

¢ **Bayrams.** Bayram is the owner of this extraordinary institution. Some guests come for a beer and stay for a month, though few would say the ample evening-buffet-service food is anything more than adequate; granted, Bayrams is said to have the best breakfast in the valley. Tea is free, the music always seems to be appropriate, a fire pit keeps things warm when nights are cool, and somehow everyone meets and chats here until late on the wooden platforms under the orange and mulberry trees. As with many other *pansiyons* in the Olympos gorge, it offers roofed platforms in the trees, which are the cheapest form of accommodation. There's no pool, but the staff happily hoses guests down as they water the orange trees. Some rooms have shared bathrooms. **Pros:** lively atmosphere. **Cons:** backpacker central. ✉ *About 200 yards from the entrance to the Olympos ruins* ☎ *242/892–1243* 🌐 *www.bayrams.com* *60 bungalows, 10 breehouses, dorms* *In-room: no a/c (some). In-hotel: restaurant, bar, laundry facilities* ▭ *AE, MC, V* *MAP.*

$ **Şaban.** One of the older lodgings in the gorge, Şaban has become one of the most popular places for foreigners of all ages and Olympos regulars say the food here is the best in the valley. It has one of the largest plots of land, too, which means the many cabins aren't jammed in together, as at some of the area options. Space, trees, and a large area with chairs and tables, where you can sit by the fire at night, make this a friendly, hospitable place to stay. **Pros:** friendly and comfortable. **Cons:** Wi-Fi costs extra. ⊠ *Where the road crosses the dry stream, opposite the large, ugly "Turkomens"* ☎ *242/892–1265* ⤶ *50 bungalows, 10 treehouses, 10 dorms* ⌂ *In room: no a/c (some). In hotel: bar, restaurant, Wi-Fi* ⊟ *AE, MC, V.*

ÇIRALI

$$ ☷ **Arcadia.** Real care has been taken with the woodwork, including
★ the elaborate Ottoman style wood ceilings, and these are the prettiest bungalows in the area. At present the five cabins and restaurant occupy a perfect site between the road and the beach, though apparently the local municipality is unhappy with this, and the situation could change. The garden is also a little more formal, than others in Çiralı. The owners offer guided Lycian way walks. **Pros:** lovely cabins; friendly staff. **Cons:** it's a long walk from center of town. ⊠ *Far, southern end of the main beach front road.* ☎ *242/825–7340* ⊕ *www.arcadiaholiday.com* ⤶ *10 cabins* ⌂ *In hotel: restaurant, bar* ⊟ *AE, MC, V.*

$$ ☷ **Myland Nature Hotel.** Relaxed and friendly, this *pansiyon* is across from the beach, about halfway along the beach road. The property is made up of a long row of wooden cabins beside a central garden, and it's run by Istanbul escapees, Engin, who fills the hotel with his photography, and Pinar who teaches the morning yoga classes. There are also bikes to rent. The chef, from the presitigous "kitchen arts center" in Bolu, makes excellent Ottoman-inspired food. **Pros:** friendly; relaxed; close to the beach; good food. **Cons:** cabins are nice, but not exceptional. ⊠ *Halfway along main beach front road, on the left* ☎ *242/825–7044* ⊕ *www.mylandnature.com* ⤶ *13 cabins* ⌂ *In-room: Wi-Fi. In-hotel: restaurant, bicycles, laundry service* ⊟ *AE, MC, V.*

ABOVE THE OLYMPOS VALLEY

$–$$ ☷ **Daphne House.** This hotel outside Olympos gorge opens onto the edge of a pine forest. Owners Bülent and Refiye will lend bikes and, at the guests' own risk, a couple of veteran cars to get to Olympos and the beach. Outside the heat of summer, Bülent is often happy to act as a free guide for local Lycian Way walks. The place has a friendly, alternative atmosphere: all meals are vegetarian, and there is a large rustic, stone living room, with a fire place for the winter months. **Pros:** friendly vibe; tranquil environment. **Cons:** some rooms are small, and accessed by a spiral staircase; carnivores beware. ⊠ *50 yards after the last turning to Olympos, just past the forest-fire fighters station with a very small sign* ☎ *242/892–1133* ⊕ *www.olimpos.org* ⤶ *6 rooms* ⌂ *In-hotel: restaurant, bar, Internet terminal* ⊟ *MC, V* ☉ *Closed Nov.–Apr.* ⋔ *BP.*

$$ ☷ **Kekik Han.** This small, stone hotel outside the gorge, is in a garden with a pool. Along with the Olympos Mitos (with which the Kekik shares facilities), it's one of the nicest lodgings outside the Olympos strip. You'll enjoy your stay more if you have your own car, though the owner will run you down to the ruins of Olympos for the walk to the beach. Kekik guests have access to the more extensive facilities of the new and larger Olympos Mitos next door. **Pros:** very pretty; relaxing. **Cons:** out of the way; smaller than Olympos Mitos. ⊠ *As you descend from Rte. 400, look for the sign down a dirt track about 500 yards before you reach a* *river ford and the final turn for Olympos itself* ☎242/892–1158 ⊕*www. kekikhan.com* ⤢*7 rooms* ⚴*In-hotel: Wi-Fi. In-hotel: restaurant, bar, pool* ▭*AE, MC, V* ⊗*Closed Oct. 15–May 15* †⚭*MAP.*

$ 🏨**Olimpos Mitos.** This new hotel, just above the smaller Kekin Han, with which it shares facilities, is one of the nicest places to stay in the neighborhood. The property is made up of several, pretty two-story wood buildings around a large lawn with cloth-covered pavilions; it has a large pool, and offers a range of activities from mountain biking to yoga and meditation; there's even a small gym. **Pros:** very pretty; relaxing; even nicer than the Kekik Han. **Cons:** out of the way. ⌧*As you descend from Rte. 400, look for the sign down a dirt track about 500 yards before you reach a river ford and the final turn for Olympos itself* ☎242/892–1158 ⊕*www.olimposmitos.com* ⤢*16 rooms, 2 suites* ⚴*In-room: Wi-Fi. In-hotel: restaurant, bar* ▭*AE, MC, V* ⊗*Closed Oct. 15–May 15* †⚭*MAP.*

IN ADRASAN

MEDITERRANEAN

$ ✕**Chill House Lounge.** Chill is the perfect name for this relaxed spot, popular with locals taking a break from the beach or a grabbing a bite. Old record covers hold the menu and Bob Marley is frequently playing on the stereo. Tables are mostly set out in the open area, in a prime spot toward the southern end of the beach. The food ranges from snacks to grilled meat, seafood, and pasta. In the evening, Chill evolves into a bar and the closest thing Adrasan has to a disco. ⌧*Main beach road* ☎532/775–2626.

$ ✕🏨**Ceneviz Hotel and Restaurant.** This hotel and restaurant set back from the beach has modest, clean rooms, some with a sea view. Good Turkish and international food is served in large portions at the pleasant restaurant, which looks out across the sea. **Pros:** great budget option; good central location. **Cons:** rooms are quite basic. ⌧*Deniz Mahallesi, Adrasan (halfway along Adrasan Beach)* ☎242/883–1030 ⊕*www. cenevizhotel.com* ⤢*18 rooms* ⚴*In-hotel: restaurant, bar* ▭*MC, V* †⚭*BP* ⊗*Closed Nov.–Apr.*

$$ 🏨**Ford Hotel.** This basic but small and comfortable hotel is between the sea and a mountain on a prime spot at the southern end of the beach. There is a large spacious terrace with the restaurant, bar, and pool. The two-story main building has good midrange rooms, many with balcony and sea view. **Pros:** location near the beach. **Cons:** at the far end of town. ⌧*Sahil Cad. No. 220, far end of the beach* ☎242/883–1044 ⊕*www.fordhotel.net* ⤢*27 rooms, 2 suites* ⚴*In-hotel: restaurant, bar, pool* ▭*MC, V* †⚭*BP.*

$ 🏨**Ottoman Palace.** This good hotel just inland from the beach is run by an English couple, John and Sue, and makes for a friendly base in Adrasan. The relatively new building is in the middle of a pleasant courtyard, with a nice lawn. Rooms are large and airy with dark wood furniture, and the Turkish tiles used for the room numbers add charm. The owners provide support for trekkers, either as guides or providing drop-off and pick up services for the various walks in the area. They also have their own dive center on the beach. **Pros:** friendly; nice building. **Cons:** not on the beach. ⌧*A few hundred yards in from the beach, look for the yellow second floor* ☎242/883–1462 ⊕*www.jonnyturk. com* ⚴*In-hotel: restaurant, bar, pool* ▭*MC, V* †⚭*MAP.*

EN ROUTE Not far from Olympos and Çirali, midway between Kumluca and Kemer, Rte. 400 passes by the great high spring of Ulupinar, which supplies water to much of this part of the Tekke peninsula. This is a lovely spot to stop and eat in the heat of summer; there are wooden platforms under cool high trees, and water gurgles around you. The speciality is fish, which come from the fish farms at the bottom of the hill. One of the best of the restaurants here is the **Tropik** (☎ *242/825–0098*), where you can dine on a platform over the river or even at a table with your feet right in the cold spring water. Specialities include delicious oven-roasted lamb or, if you give some advance warning, an entire lamb roasted on a spit. A section of the Lycian Way goes from here across the valley to Çiralı, via the Chimaera; it's about a four- or five-hour trek.

PHASELIS

★ *60 km (37 mi) southwest of Antalya on Rte. 400.*

The ruins of Phaselis, the ancient port city majestically located at the edge of three smalls bays, are as romantic as the reputation of its ancient inhabitants was appalling: Demosthenes the Greek called them unsavory, and Roman statesman Cicero called them rapacious pirates. Since the first Greek colonists from Rhodes bought the land from a local shepherd in the 7th century BC for a load of dried fish, classical literature is replete with the expression "a present from the Phaselians," meaning a cheap gift. Still, the setting is beautiful and Alexander the Great spent a whole winter here before marching on to conquer the east. A broad main street, flanked by some remarkably well-preserved buildings, cuts through the half-standing walls of the Roman **agora**. At each end of this main street is a different bay, both with translucent water ideal for swimming. A third bay, to the north, has great harbor stones carved by the ancients, and is less likely to be disturbed by tour boats.

A small **theater** with trees growing among the seats has a majestic view of Mt. Olympos, and fine **sarcophagi** are scattered throughout a necropolis in the pine woods that surround the three bays. The ruins are poetic and impressive, ideal for a picnic or a day at the beach, but weekends and high season days can be crowded and downright depressing when tour yachts from Antalya arrive with loudspeakers blaring. For some reason the refreshment stands at Phaselis are in a legal limbo, so today's pirates of Phaselis are the men selling overpriced drinks under the trees. ⌂*$5 per person* ⊙*June–Sept., daily 8:30–7, Oct.–May, daily 8:30–5.*

WHERE TO STAY AND EAT

$ ⛺ **Sundance Natural Village.** This is a popular green-minded stopover for Lycian way trekkers and arty types taking a break from Istanbul. It's set on a lagoon between the Phaselis beach the rather ugly resort town of Tekirova. The owners zealously guard the property's alternative atmosphere, and there are no direction signs on the highway. Don't expect luxury, but the bungalows are comfortable and the vegetarian food quite decent. There is private beach, horseback riding is available, and the Lycian Way passes through the area, on a pretty, seven-hour coastal section to Çiralı. **Pros:** no pool, TV, or disco. **Cons:** no pool, TV, or disco. ✉ *Between Phaselis and Tekirova, follow the signs to the "eco-park" and keep going* ☎ *242/821–4165* ⊕ *www.sundance.web.tr* ⌂ *26 bungalows* ⌂ *In-room: a/c (some), Wi-Fi. In-hotel: restaurant, bar.*

OFF THE BEATEN PATH

Göynük Gorge. For a cool, memorable day's hiking near Phaselis, pack a picnic and trek up the Göynük Gorge. Drive north of Phaselis to the corner of the coast where Beldibi ends and Göynük begins, a point clearly marked by blue "city limits" signs at the bridge over a riverbed. Turn inland onto the unmarked tarmac and dirt track on the northern bank of the river and follow sporadic signs to the "wasserfall" into the gorge. When you no longer feel comfortable with the rockiness of the track, park by the side of the road and walk on up. Having a guide with you is handy but not essential—red-painted signs from a local café will keep you on the right path, or just keep asking the way. There are usually a number of canyoning tours and individuals from the resort hotels trekking up the gorge. Take note: when the motor road defini-tively ends, take the path up the left hand gorge, following the main river, cross to the far banks, then back again about five minutes later and a forest track carved into the side of the mountain, not the steeper right-hand one. Nearly an hour from the last car park, the road turns into a path, and drops down to the river. You can take a refreshing swim where the cold, clear river flows through a long, deep crevasse carved by the water through the rock. Follow the rope and walk the first sec-tion of the canyon, with chilly waist deep water. With good waterproof "shoes you can continue up some small waterfalls and rocky ledges as far as you feel safe—just observe usual precautions like not canyoning after recent rain. It's an enjoyable half day trip, the valley is beautiful and the canyon fun; take your own drinking water, since there are no vendors anywhere near here.

PAMPHYLIA

When the Greeks migrated from central Turkey to the Mediterranean coast, around the 12th century BC, the area east of Antalya became known as Pamphylia, "the land of the tribes," reflecting the mixed origins of the new inhabitants. The area was remote because the coast was cut off from the main trade routes by the mountains.

Today, Antalya is just one of several good options as a base for excur-sions to the region's major archaeological sites: Termessos, Perge, Aspendos, and Side. The other main options as a base are Belek, which has fancier resort-style hotels, and Side, which has a more intimate atmosphere and is less expensive.

ANTALYA

298 km (185 mi) northeast of Fethiye.

GETTING HERE AND AROUND

The main bus station is north of the city, and a new metro line to the city center is due to open early 2009. Buses to the old city are marked "Kalekapisi." A tram along the Antalya sea front, between Lara and the Antalya museum, it runs every half-hour and costs about $1.

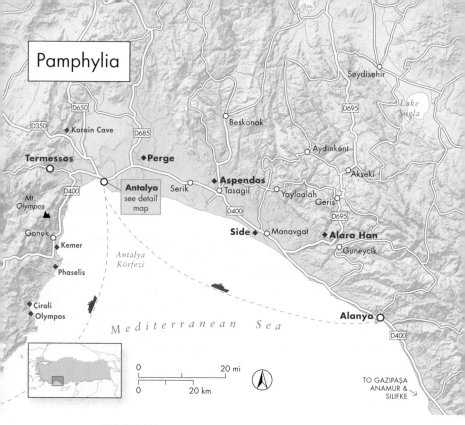

ESSENTIALS

Tourist office **Antalya** (✉ *Cumhuriyet Cad., in booth opposite former offices in tall white official building abandoned after road blasting operations cracked its columns* ☎ *242/241–1747*).

EXPLORING

Antalya is a definite tourist hub, and it's one of Turkey's fastest growing cities; these days the international terminals of Antalya airport are busier even than in Istanbul. Most visitors are on package tours, but Antalya is also a popular destination among Turks. The enormous hotels east of Antalya are themed on Ottoman palaces or the great sights of European capitals and attract increasing numbers of conferences, too.

Antalya has variety, sophistication, and the attraction of having one of Turkey's best museums. It is also quite large. You can happily stay within the winding streets of the atmospheric harbor and old city, known as the Kaleiçi—where there are small houses, restaurants, *pansiyons,* and Mermerli Beach—hardly noticing the big urban conglomeration all around. On the hilltop above the harbor are tea gardens and bars with views that extend south to the Bey Mountains right and around to the Taurus Mountains to the north.

WHAT TO SEE

❶ The first-rate collection at the **Antalya Müzesi** *(Antalya Museum)* includes
Fodor's Choice Turkish crafts, costumes, and artifacts from the Greek and Roman
★ eras (including notable statues of the gods, from Aphrodite to Zeus,
in the Gods Gallery), with bits of Byzantine iconography and some
prehistoric fossils thrown in. Seven fine Roman sarcophagi from the
2nd century AD include a wonderful one illustrating the labors of a
steadily aging Hercules. Don't miss the remains of prehistoric man and
the Seljuks, the children's and ethnographic sections, and the fabulous
open-air sculpture gallery. There is a reasonably priced, good cafeteria
and a gift shop. If you have the time, walk to the museum from the
center of town along the clifftop promenade, which has a fine sea view.
✉ *Konyaaltı Cad., heading west out of town* ☎ *242/241–4528* 💲 *$12*
🕐 *Tues.–Sun. 9–6.*

❽ Shady **Karaalioğlan Parkı** (✉ *Agustos Cad. at Atatürk Cad.*) is a traditional park with trees, grass, and benches, as well as a view of the
Mediterranean. At the northwest end is a stone tower 49 feet tall, called
Hıdırlık Külesi. It dates from the 2nd century AD, and though no one
knows for sure what it is, the best guess is that it was either a combined
lighthouse and fort or a tomb. At sunset, sip a drink at the Castle Bar
next door to enjoy an unforgettable panorama of the Bey Mountains.
There is a path from here down to the old harbor in the heart of the
old town but it's steep and not well lit, so probably best avoided if the
Castle Bar has persuaded you to have one drink too many.

INSIDE THE KALEIÇI (OLD TOWN)

The old town of Antalya lies within the fortified city wall; it's an excellent example of a traditional Ottoman neighborhood. A restoration
project launched in the 1980s saved hundreds of houses, dating mostly
from the 19th century. Most of these were converted into *pansiyons,*
rug shops, restaurants, and art galleries.

❻ One way to enter the old town is via **Hadrian's Gate,** a short walk from
★ Karalioğlan Park along the pleasant palm-lined Atatürk Caddesi outside the eastern edge of the old town walls. The gate was constructed in
honor of a visit by the Roman emperor in AD 130 and has three arches,
each with coffered ceilings decorated with rosettes. Ruts in the marble
road show where carts once trundled through.

❷ Another way to enter the old city is via the **old harbor,** now filled with
★ yachts, fishing vessels, and tourist-excursion boats. If you're in a car,
follow the signs to the *yat limañ,* (harbor) and you'll find a convenient,
free parking lot behind the quaysides. From here you can head up any
of the lanes leading north and east out of the harbor to get to the heart
of the old town.

❹ Several of the old town's cobbled lanes lead north from the harbor to
the old stone **Saat Kulesi** *(Clock Tower),* at the junction known to Anta-
lyans as Kalekapısı, one of the interfaces between the old town and the
new. Just next door you can have your face laser-carved into crystal by
Looxis. ☎ *242/242–4333.*

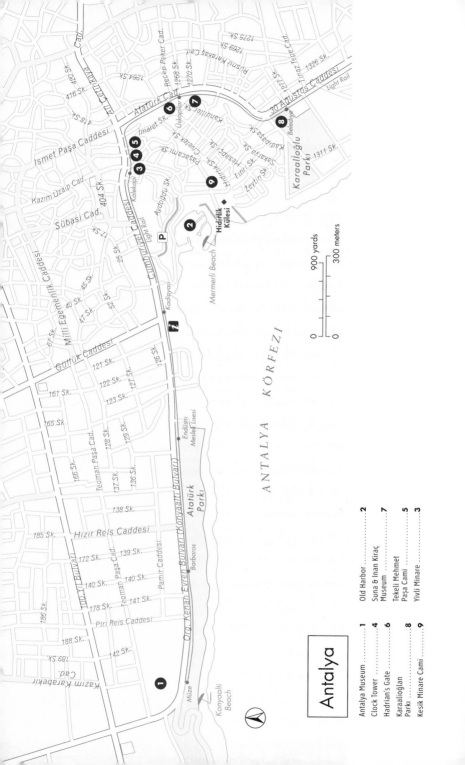

Antalya

Antalya Museum **1**
Clock Tower **4**
Hadrian's Gate **6**
Karaalioğlan
Parkı **8**
Kesik Minare Cami **9**

Old Harbor **2**
Suna & İnan Kıraç
Museum **7**
Tekeli Mehmet
Paşa Cami **5**
Yivli Minare **3**

ANTALYA KÖRFEZI

5 Behind the clock tower, the **Tekeli Mehmet Paşa Cami,** a mosque believed to have been built around the end of the 16th century, is one of the finest surviving Ottoman mosques in the region.

7 Fifty yards inside Hadrian's gate, turn left for the **Suna & Inan Kiraç**
★ **Museum** (⊠*Hadrian's Gate*), a little oasis in a group of restored buildings decorated with an unlikely-looking painted exterior that researchers say was the way most Antalya houses looked in Ottoman times. The museum has an excellent library of books on the region around Antalya—although these are accessible only with special permission—and a good range of guidebooks are on sale in the museum shop. The main display rooms have interesting pictures of Old Antalya and a couple of rooms with waxworks displaying a re-creation of Ottoman wedding scenes. The best part of the museum is the restored church in the garden, where there is a delightful display of historical kitsch from the potteries of the late Ottoman period. ⊠*Kocatepe Sokak 25* ☎*242/243–4274* ⊠*$3* ☉*Thurs.–Tues. 9–noon and 1–6.*

3 Dark blue and turquoise tiles decorate the **Yivli Minare** *(Fluted Minaret),* a graceful 13th-century cylinder commissioned by the Seljuk sultan Alaaddin Keykubat I. The adjoining mosque, named for the sultan, was built on the site of a Byzantine church. Within the complex are two attractive *türbes* (tombs) and an 18th-century *tekke* (monastery), which once housed a community of whirling dervishes. The monastery is now used as an unremarkable art gallery. The Nigar Hatun Türbe (Tomb of Lady Nigar), next to the monastery, though built in Seljuk style, is a 15th-century copy. The *medrese* (theological school) adjacent to the Fluted Minaret has now been glassed in under a bus-station-style roof and is a tourist-oriented shopping center. On offer is the standard tourist fare throughout Turkey—pottery, copperwork, carpets, and tiles—but the prices are better than at most other resorts along the coast. ⊠*Cumhuriyet Cad., south side of Kalekapısı Mey.*

9 **Kesik Minare Cami** or the "Mosque of the Truncated Minaret" on Hıdarlık Sokak, was once the city's cathedral, and dedicated to the Virgin. It was probably built in the 5th century AD. It's usually locked, but you can get a gook look from the outside.

WHERE TO STAY AND EAT

$$–$$$ ✕**Club Arma.** You can't miss this restaurant, which has a spectacular
TURKISH location halfway up the main road from the old harbor. Inside, airy
★ stone arches give it elegant style despite the fact that this was once the port's petroleum depot. Club Arma is Antalya's most luxurious restaurant, serving octopus carpaccio, local *grida* or grouper, lobster, duck, chocolate soufflé, chestnut parfait, and fresh cheesecake, along with a full range of foreign spirits and cigars from a humidor. At 11 PM, the dance club alongside swings into action. ⊠*Kaleiçi Yatlimanı 42* ☎*242/244–9710* ═*MC, V.*

$$–$$$$ ✕**Ekici Restaurant.** This is the most reputable of the harbor-front restau-
TURKISH rants, with a spotless kitchen, good service, and excellent food. Typical
★ specialities are fish stew and fish baked in salt. Fish comes both from the sea and from fish farms (cheaper), and prices vary with the catch and the season. Even here, though, make sure you've agreed on the price of

5

the fish before you order. They also have boats available as floating restaurants, where you can combine dinner with a short cruise. ⊠ *Kaleiçi Yatlımanı 38* ☎ *242/247–8190* ▤ *MC, V.*

$

TURKISH

✕ **Mermerli Restaurant.** This restaurant has an excellent view from the terrace above the eastern end of the harbor, and prices are better than on the waterfront itself. The menu is wide-ranging and they serve breakfast all day. It's a good spot for a meal if you want to relax at Mermerli Beach, down the steps from the restaurant, which controls access to the bathing spot. ⊠ *Banyo Cad. 25* ☎ *242/248–5484* ▤ *MC, V.*

$ – $$

TURKISH

✕ **Parlak Restaurant.** If shopping in the jewelry bazaar behind the clock tower has tired you out, try this long-time Antalya favorite. The speciality is chicken roasted over charcoal, but there's also a full range of fish, meat, and mezes to choose from as well. In summer, tables are spread out under the stars in front of the restaurant. ⊠ *Zincirli Han, Kazım Özalp Cad. 7* ☎ *242/241–9160* ▤ *MC, V.*

$

AMERICAN

✕ **St. Paul's Place.** A clubby retreat on the first floor of a Christian religious center on the eastern edge of the old city, St. Paul's Place serves great coffee, American cakes, and home-cooked lunches (it's only open until 5:30 PM). It also has a library of exchange books and a nice garden. The center organizes religion-oriented tours. ⊠ *Yenikapı Cad.; turn into old city between Karaalioğlan Park and Hadrian's Gate, 100 yards on right* ☎ *242/247–6857* ⊕ *www.stpaulcc-turkey.com* ▤ *No credit cards* ⊗ *Closed the last week of Aug.*

¢

CAFE

✕ **Tophane.** This tea garden overlooks Antalya's harbor and serves inexpensive drinks and snacks along with its priceless views. If you don't feel like walking from here to the museum, you could splurge on a horse-drawn carriage from the top of the harbor road nearby (it's not a cheap method of transportation though). Otherwise, the Antalya tramway leaves the terminus at each end every half hour, arriving at the halfway point in front of the clock tower near Tophane teahouse at about quarter past and quarter to the hour. ⊠ *Cumhuriyet Alanı* ☎ *No phone* ▤ *No credit cards.*

$

⌂ **Atelya Art Hotel.** Inexpensive and friendly, this hotel has larger than usual rooms and a good location in the old town. There is a large central courtyard with trees and tables and the whole place has a pleasingly old-fashioned feel. The art consists of paintings by the owner, hanging in many rooms and corridors. Off season it can seem somewhat dimly lit and musty. In season, book at least one week ahead. **Pros:** good value. **Cons:** a little musty. ⊠ *Kaleiçi Civelek Cad. 21; near the Kesik Minare mosque* ☎ *242/241–6416* ⊕ *www.atelyahotel.com* ↴ *30 rooms* ⌂ *In-hotel: restaurant, bar* ▤ *No credit cards.*

$$

★

⌂ **Doğan Hotel.** Every room is unique and tastefully done in this family-run establishment, made up of three restored old houses. The ceilings are somewhat low but the Ottoman-style wooden decorations help compensate. The best seven or eight rooms on the top floors, like Room 125, have good views of the harbor, but others, like excellent Room 141, have charming views of the gardens. The staff are intelligent, fun, and accommodating. The hotel is only a short walk from the old harbor and Mermerli Beach. There is a lovely pool, too. **Pros:** nice rooms and garden. **Cons:** some of the rooms are a little dark. ⊠ *Mermerli Banyo*

Sok. 5 ☎*242/247–4654 or 241–8842* ⊕*www.doganhotel.com* ⤶*41 rooms* ⌂*In-hotel: 2 restaurants, bars, pool* ▤*MC, V.*

$$$$ 🛏Hillside Su. This resort hotel is unforgettable for its all-white color scheme, from the room TVs to the floors, and it's popular with the weekend crowd that comes in from Istanbul. Everything is designed and run to high and exacting standards—though this might make some travelers feel a little trapped, like the ornamental goldfish in the relentless lines of bowls around the reception area. **Pros:** funky, eclectic atmosphere. **Cons:** maybe too weird to be completely comfortable. ⊠*Dumlupınar Cad., Konyaaltı* ☎*242/249–0700* ⊕*www.hillside.com. tr* ⤶*294 rooms* ⌂*In-room: Wi-Fi. In-hotel: 5 restaurants, pool, gym, beachfront* ▤*AE, MC, V* ⏉|*MAP.*

$$-$$$ 🛏Hotel Alp Paşa. This might be the most atmospheric place to stay in
★ the old city. The center of the hotel is a shady courtyard with a pool, surrounded by the wooden columns of the old mansion and various pieces of antiquity. Rooms vary considerably in size and quality and are decorated with a modern stylish take on historic Ottoman. Each room has a name, rather than number, so don't be surprised if the staff doesn't have a clue where your room is. **Pros:** beautiful and stylish. **Cons:** very small pool for a 60-room hotel; extras are expensive. ⊠*Hesapçi Sokak* ☎*242/247–5676* ⊕*www.alppasa.com* ⤶*60 rooms* ⌂*In-room: safe. In-hotel: restaurant, bars* ▤*AE, DC, MC, V.*

$$ 🛏Marina Hotel. Three vintage Ottoman houses of white stucco with bay windows and dark-wood trim were restored and connected to make this attractive hotel in the historic heart of Antalya. The staff is attentive, and the restaurant serves French-inspired food—no less a personage than former French prime minister François Mitterrand once praised the onion soup. Inside, there are old carpets and kilims, and the pleasant rooms, though on the small side, are done in the same attractive white and dark wood as the facade. A pianist accompanies diners at dinner, and the swimming pool is large. **Pros:** nice pool area. **Cons:** rooms feel a little dated. ⊠*Mermeli Sokak 15* ☎*242/247–5490* 🖷*242/241–1765* ⤶*41 rooms* ⌂*In-room: safe. In-hotel: restaurant, room service, bars, pool* ▤*AE, DC, MC, V* ⏉|*BP.*

$$$ 🛏Talya Hotel. This prime property rises over the cliffs just to the east of
★ Karaalioğlan Parkı, commanding spectacular views of the Bey Mountains (ask for a corner room; these have numbers that end in 17). The hotel has its own bathing platform at the foot of the cliff, and the restaurants all have good views and excellent reputations. One serves international cuisine, the others traditional Turkish fare. **Pros:** modern, professional luxury hotel. **Cons:** rather characterless. ⊠*Fevzi Cakmak Cad. 30* ☎*242/248–6800* ⊕*www.divan.com* ⤶*204 rooms* ⌂*In-room: Wi-Fi. In-hotel: 3 restaurants, room service, bars, pool, gym* ▤*AE, DC, MC, V.*

NIGHTLIFE AND THE ARTS

The perfect start to any evening out in Antalya starts by watching the sun set from the clifftop **Castle Café and Bar** (⊠*Hıdırlık Cad. 48/1* ☎*242/242–3188*), next to Hıdırlık Kulesi—you can accompany your drink with some of their sesame and garlic dip known as *hibeş*. Otherwise, Antalya's bars are centered in three main areas: in Kaleiçi; in the new part of town, on Barlar Caddesi (Bar Street), running off Cumhuri-yet Caddesi; and in Atatürk Park. Most visitors prefer Kaleiçi, where a profusion of bars competes for your attention. For dancing, the smartest place in town is undoubtedly on the harbor road at **Club Arma** (⊠ *Kaleiçi Yatlimanı 42* ☎ *242/244–9710*).

The Atatürk Kulture Merkezi, also known as AKM, is a complex with an exhibition space and several theaters in a cliff-top park about 3 km (2 mi) west of the city center. There are concerts year round—look for fliers posted around the city—and an annual film festival.

SPORTS AND THE OUTDOORS

BEACHES If you didn't know that **Mermerli Beach** (☎ *242/248–5484*) was there, you'd never guess it. This small strip of sand and pebbles outside the harbor wall is reached from the Mermerli Restaurant halfway up the hill east of the harbor. The $5 price of admission to this quiet oasis in the heart of town includes loungers and umbrellas.

For many Turks, Antalya is synonymous with the thick crowds of hol-iday-makers on **Konyaaltı Beach**, and in high season the pebble strand is a hot and somewhat off-putting sight. The city has worked hard to improve the quality of the beach experience, though, with espe-cially impressive results on the 1-km (½-mi) section starting after the museum and ending under Su Hotel. Here, paying an admission charge gives access to a grassy park behind the beach, restaurants, and playgrounds.

RAFTING Rafting has become a major activity from the big hotels, with several agencies offering trips up to various canyons. To avoid the crowds, it's best to get up to the water in the early morning before the package tourists are out of bed. Most companies will pick you up at your hotel. Reputable operators include **Medraft** (☎ *242/312–5770*) and **TransNature** (☎ *242/247–8688*).

SHOPPING

Thanks to its size—in 2006, about 800,000 people lived here—the shopping streets have more variety than anywhere else on the Turquoise Riviera, although the merchandise, in general, is the same sort of stuff you find all over Turkey. East and north of the old town walls are where the less expensive clothing shops are found, including some jewelry arcades. The old town is where to find more decorative souvenirs, travel agencies, boutique hotels, *pansiyons*, cheaper restaurants, and the nice little Mermerli Beach outside the harbor wall. The Kenan Evren bou-levard along the seafront cliffs toward the museum has the concentra-tion of upmarket clothing shops, as well as the offices of airlines that run shuttle buses to the airport. A short taxi ride to the west of town is Antalya's fanciest mall, the Migros Shopping Center, on the main road to Kemer, behind Konyaalti: it has a large supermarket, eight cinemas, a large food court, and branches of almost all of Turkey's big clothing chains like Mavi Jeans, LCW for children's clothes, Derimod for upmar-ket leathers, Bisse and Abbate for shirts, Vakkorama and Boyner for general clothing, and all kinds of international brand-name shops like Swatch, Lacoste, and Tommy Hilfiger among its 100 shops.

EN ROUTE

When driving east on Route 400 from Antalya toward Perge, Aspendos, Side, or Alanya, don't miss one of the region's great culinary experiences: a meal in the strip of restaurants by the highway in Aksu. Turks on business in Antalya will detour for miles just to eat here. Ease off the highway onto the feeder road when you see a pedestrian bridge about 6 km (4 mi) east of the Antalya airport intersection, then park where you can.

$

TURKISH

✕**Öz Şimşek.** Try the superb kumin-flavored köfte meatballs with baked garlic and mild peppers along with a plate of mind-blowingly fresh *piyaz* (white beans in a sauce with sesame paste, tomato, parsley, egg, and olive oil). ✉*Berberoğlu Çarşısı, Çalkaya* ☎242/426–3920 ▬MC, V ⊗6 AM–*11* PM.

$

TURKISH

✕**Ramazan'ın Yeri.** At the southern foot of the pedestrian overpass, this restaurant was one of the first in the strip and offers a remarkable smorgasbord of all animal parts fit to eat. There is a full range of the normal kebabs and stews, but this is the place to experiment. The four daily soups include tripe and *paça*, normally boiled from the head of a calf. In the refrigerator you can select delicacies to follow: ribs, cutlets, liver, kidney, and heart. Calf's brain can be found among the cold appetizers. ☎242/426–3231 ▬MC, V ⊗ *Open 24 hrs.*

TERMESSOS

★ *37 km (23 mi) northwest of Antalya; take E87 north toward Burdur, bear left at fork onto Rte. 350 toward Korkuteli and follow signs to Termessos.*

GETTING HERE AND AROUND

It's easiest to get to Termessos if you have a car, but tours can be arranged by agencies in Antalya, or you can catch any bus from the bus station to Korkuteli and get of at the Termessos intersection where taxis usually wait; one way is around $15. A visit takes at least four hours, and there is no restaurant at the site, so pack water and lunch, and wear sturdy shoes.

Writers in antiquity referred to Termessos as the Eagle's Nest, and when you visit the site, 4,500 feet high in the mountains west of Antalya, and you'll understand why. The city was impregnable and now offers stunning vistas over the beautiful scenery of Termessos National Park. The warlike and fiercely independent people who made their home here launched frequent raids on their coastal neighbors. They were not Greek but a native Asia Minor people who called themselves the Solymians, after ancient Mt. Solymus, which rises above the city. Termessos remained autonomous for much of its history and was quite wealthy by the 2nd century AD. Most of its remains date from this period.

EXPLORING

The attractions in Termessos start right by the parking area, with a monumental **gate,** part of an ancient temple dedicated to Hadrian. The steepness of the path that leads up to the craggy remains of the city walls soon makes it clear just why Alexander the Great declined to attack. Next, on your left, are a **gymnasium,** a **colonnaded street** (half of whose

5

many statue bases once supported likenesses of famed wrestlers), a **bath** complex built of dark gray stone blocks, and then, up and around, is a very ruined colonnaded street and the 5,000-seat **theater,** whose perch at the edge of a sheer cliff has one of the most spectacular settings in Turkey. From this staggering height you can see the sea, the Pamphylian plain, Mt. Solymus, and the occasional mountain goat or ibex. Farther around is the well-preserved bouleterion, where the city council met, surrounded by several temples, the very overgrown market, and some huge underground cisterns. Termessos has one more wonder: several vast **necropolises,** with nearly 1,000 tombs scattered willy-nilly on a rocky hill. A signposted alternate route back to the carpark takes you past several rock-cut tombs, and back at the car park another route from the ticket office takes you to another large collection of tombs. $9 ⊙ *Daily 8–7.*

One kilometer (½ mi) north of the Termessos turnoff from E87 is the **Karain Cave** (follow the yellow signs for Karain). Archaeological digs since 1919 have already proved that it was inhabited as far back as the Paleolithic Age, making it one of the oldest settlements in Turkey. Later it seems to have become a religious center for primitive man. Many of the Karain finds—stone implements, bones of people and animals, and fossilized remains including those of hippopotamuses—are on display in Antalya Museum, but there is also a small museum on the edge of the high meadow where the cave is. Part of the cave itself is also electrically lighted and open to the public, but this is a small site and probably only worth stopping at if you have time after seeing Termessos. $3 ⊙ *Tues.–Sun. 8–5.*

PERGE

22 km (14 mi) from Antalya, east on Rte. 400 to turnoff north at Aksu.

Perge's biggest problem is that it suffers from comparison with its neighbours: it lacks the dramatic location of Termessos and the picture perfect theater of Aspendos. It is, though, one of Turkey's best overall examples of a Roman city. There is a splendid theater amid the **Perge ruins,** unfortunately closed for repairs, but the stadium is one of the best preserved in the ancient world. Beyond that, there are the city's sturdy 3rd-century-BC garrison towers. The vaulted chambers under the stadium bleachers held shops; marble inscriptions record the proprietors' names and businesses.

The rest of the site is about 1 km (½ mi) north. You enter through the old gates, after parking just outside the old city walls. Directly ahead is a fine colonnaded avenue. The slender, sun-bleached columns lining the street once supported a covered porch filled with shops. You can still see floor mosaics in some places, and delicate reliefs of gods and famous citizens decorate the entablatures between some of the columns. The long grooves in the paving are ruts worn by chariot wheels; the unique channel running down the center carried water from a fountain at the far end. St. Paul, who sailed here from Cyprus, preached at the basilica near the end of the street, on the left. $11 ⊙ *Daily 8–7.*

ASPENDOS

★ *49 km (31 mi) east of Antalya on Rte. 400 (follow yellow signs).*

Most experts agree that the **theater** in Aspendos is one of the best preserved in the world. A splendid Roman **aqueduct** that traverses the valley, another superior example of Roman engineering, utilized the pressure of the water flowing from the mountains to supply the summit of the acropolis. The water tower dates from the 2nd century AD, and its stairway is still intact.

Pay your admission to the main site at what was once the actors' entrance to the theater. Built during the reign of Emperor Marcus Aurelius (ruled AD 161–180) by a local architect called Xenon, it is striking for the broad curve of seats, perfectly proportioned porticoes, and rich decoration. The Greeks liked open vistas behind their stages, but the Romans preferred enclosed spaces. The stage building you see today was once covered in marble tiles, and its niches were filled with statues, some now on view in the Antalya Museum. The only extant relief on-site depicts Dionysus (Bacchus) watching over the theater. The acoustics are fine, and the theater is still in use—for concerts and for the Antalya International Opera and Ballet Festival, held every June/July, rather than for the wild-animal and gladiator spectacles as in Roman times. Aspendos is not just a Roman site—the Seljuks used it as an imperial palace in the 13th century, and one of the two towers they added to the structure remains standing. There are traces of the distinctive Seljuk red-and-yellow paint work here and there, too.

Seeing the remainder of the site requires a hike up the zigzagging trail behind the theater, a trek of perhaps an hour or more. The rewards are a tall **Nymphaion**—a sanctuary to the nymphs built around a fountain decorated with a marble dolphin—and the remains of a Byzantine **basilica** and **market hall**. 🎟$11 ⏱Daily 8–7.

SIDE

75 km (47 mi) east of Antalya on Rte. 400.

ESSENTIALS

Official tourist office Side (✉Side Yolu Üzeri, Manavgat ☎242/753–1265 🖷242/753–2657).

EXPLORING

Charter-tour hotels crowding along this stretch of coast threaten to overshadow Side, but at its heart this city's delightful mix of ancient ruins and modern amenities is an underestimated jewel. Sandy beaches run along each side of town, and the area between the harbor and the ruins feels like a real town, not an industrial resort. Side, like Antalya or Alanya, has all sorts of options, from late-night dancing, shopping or kayaking in mountain canyons. It's also close to the major sites of Aspendos and Perge, and less than an hour from Antalya airport. Like its bigger Pamphylian sisters, it's best visited out of the heat of the high season July and August, but weekends can be crowded, too. With the right hotel, it's still possible to experience how Side felt in the 1960s, when the city was off the beaten track, and the likes of dancer Rudolph Nureyev and French intellectual Simone de Beauvoir were visitors.

Side offers plenty of opportunities for shopping. The main street to the harbor is flanked by fancy jewelry shops keen to take in tourist currency. All kinds of souvenir shops abound, as do suppliers of winter furs and leathers, popular with the Russian tourists.

A downside to the influx of tourisms is the spread of large resort complexes that operate on all-inclusive basis: they're killing the restaurants, bars, and nightlife in town.

Follow signs in from Route 400 for *Antik Side* and resist any sense of disappointment—it will dissipate when you suddenly find yourself driving onto the little peninsula through the delightful ruins of the Greco-Roman city. Through a last arch and past a colonnade behind the theater, park your car or, if staying in a hotel inside the town, ask to be let through the barricade that protects the harbor area from traffic. Ruins are all around: there's a lovely theater, with city and sea views from the top row, and 2nd-century-AD temples to Apollo and Athena a few blocks south, on the tip of the peninsula. The town was founded by early Greeks, minting coins from 500 BC, but Side only began to expand when Pompey cleared out the slave-trading pirates in 67 BC. Most of the ruins, laid bare by one of the only systematic excavations of a whole city, date from the prosperous Roman period. One notable feature of the site are the well-preserved Roman communal public latrines.

★ The **Side Müzesi** *(Side Museum)* is near the theater, in the restored Roman baths. The collection of Roman statues is small but one of the best in Asia Minor: it includes a gorgeous group of the marble torsos of the Three Graces, various cherubs, a brilliant satyr, and a bust of Emperor Hadrian. The sculpture garden behind the museum is larger than the museum itself and overlooks the Mediterranean. ⌧$7.

Opposite the Side museum is the city's **theater,** rebuilt in the 2nd century, though the design is more Greek. There are views out over the large agora. ⌧$7.

If you follow Side's main street full of shops selling jewlery and cheap clothes till you reach the water, and then turn left, you reach the beautiful **Temple of Apollo,** built of gleaming white marble that's set off beautifully by the perfect blue ocean behind.

WHERE TO STAY AND EAT

$$–$$$ ✕**Orfoz.** If you want to eat in the harbor area, many would say this is
TURKISH the best restaurant to choose: the bamboo chairs are comfortable, the tables well spaced, there are trees for shade, and the food is excellent. Fresh seafood is the speciality, including a melt-in-the-mouth octopus dish, but there's something for everyone on the international menu, including large, though expensive steaks. The view over the western beach is just right at sunset, the service is good, and if there's a chill in spring or autumn, attentive waiters bring blankets. ⌧*Liman Cad. 58/C* ☎*242/753–1362* ▭*MC, V.*

$$ ✕**Paşaköy Bar and Restaurant.** Paşaköy's has reasonable food, but what
TURKISH differentiates this pleasant restaurant from the rest is its weird and wonderfully kitsch garden, decked out with bizarre mock-classical statuary

DID YOU KNOW?

The Roman theater of ancient Aspendos could seat an audience of about 7,000 people.

and stuffed animals. The grilled meat dishes are good, the waitstaff is friendly and attentive, and the bartender can make a cocktail with a kick. ⊠ *Liman Cad. 98* ☎ *242/753–3622* ⊟ *AE, MC, V* ☉ *Closed Dec.–May.*

$$
MEDITERRANEAN

✕ **Soundwaves Restaurant.** This open-air restaurant on a pedestrian walk overlooking the sea is decked out like a pirate ship but, unlike its piratical neighbors in the harbor, has a long and reliable reputation; it's run by the same management as the nearby Beach House hotel. If you're walking from the harbor, head 500 yards southeast through the temple and around the promontory. Specialities include fish baked in salt, garlic prawns, and thanks to an Australian half-owner, a deep-fried seafood dish called Tasmanian Squid. ⊠ *Barbaros Cad.* ☎ *242/753–1607* ⊟ *MC, V* ☉ *Closed Dec.–Apr.*

$
☺
★

🛏 **Beach House Hotel.** If you want a charmed few days on the Side seafront, this is the place to stay. The rooms are modest, and air-conditioning is only now being added, but the ceiling fans create a breeze. This is where Rudolph Nureyev and Simone de Beauvoir once stayed. The hotel is built on the grounds of a Byzantine villa, whose ruins are used for a garden with lawns and a trampoline. The restaurant overlooks the sea on the east side of the peninsula, southeast of theater. **Pros:** friendly and helpful staff. **Cons:** opposite, rather than on, the beach. ⊠ *Barbaros Cad., Side,* ☎ *242/753–1607* ⊕ *www.beachhouse-hotel. com* ⤶ *23 rooms* ⚭ *In-room: no a/c, Wi-Fi. In-hotel: restaurant, bar* ⊟ *MC, V* �🍽 *BP.*

$$$

🛏 **Hotel Acanthus.** This modest four-story hotel is done in Mediterranean style, with whitewashed walls, dark-wood trim and terraces, a red-tile roof, and direct access to a fine sand beach. It's one of a large cluster of hotels on the beach, just west of central Side. Rooms are comfortable if unimpressive. The same family runs the slightly older Cennet Hotel (an option if you can't get a room at Acanthus), and the two share a garden. The owners also sponsor the Aspendos Opera and Ballet Festival in June, so you may find both hotels full of musicians at that time. **Pros:** good beach location not too far from town. **Cons:** pretty average. ⊠ *Side Köyü, Box 55* ☎ *242/753–3050* 🖷 *242/753–1913* ⤶ *104 rooms* ⚭ *In-room: safe. In-hotel: 2 restaurants, bars, tennis court, pools, beachfront, water sports* ⊟ *MC, V* ⏹ *MAP.*

$

🛏 **Kamer Motel.** This modest, clean hotel in a quiet part of town has a great location on eastern shore, with views of the sea and a private though rocky beach area. The two-story concrete building is no architectural marvel, but the rooms are relatively large and all have sea-view balconies. The restaurant overlooks the sea, too. **Pros:** nice views; good value. **Cons:** uninspired architecture and decor. ⊠ *Barabaros Cad. No. 47, Side,* ☎ *242/753–1007* 🖷 *242/753–2660* ⤶ *26 rooms* ⚭ *In-hotel: restaurant, bar* ⊟ *V* ⏹ *BP.*

$$$

🛏 **Sunrise Queen Hotel.** On its own beach about 3 km (2 mi) northwest from the town center, this is a large and attractive resort made up of one large main building and four additional "blocks." The meal-plan food is quite good here, too. The place is often filled with tour groups, though many Turks also stay here. Suites have whirlpool baths, and there is live music nightly. **Pros:** good facilities. **Cons:** the extras are expensive if you're not doing all-inlusive. ✉*Bingeşi, Kumköy Cad., on main seafront boulevard west of city* ☎*242/753–4783* ⊕*www. sunrisehotels.com* ⤳*312 rooms, 35 suites* ♿*In-room: safe. In-hotel: 4 restaurants, bars, pools, gym* ⊟*AE, MC, V* ⦿*MAP.*

NIGHTLIFE

The evening action begins after sunset as places like the **Royal Castle Bar** (✉*Turgut Reis Cad. 62* ☎*242/753–4373*), just in from the water on the southwest corner—it keeps the Brits happy with its pub-like atmosphere and English football on the TV, and there is also live music most evening in season. **Pegasus Bar,** on the shore west of the theater, almost behind the museum, is a good place to sit with a drink watching the sunset over the ocean; they have a vast range of cocktails, as well as 15 types of coffee, and live music at night. Down by the harbor is the open-air **Lighthouse** discotheque and bar. Somewhat farther afield is **Oxyd,** built like a sub-Saharan adobe palace with a futuristic interior; it's a 3-km (2-mi) drive along the boulevard that serves the resort hotels east of Side.

SPORTS AND THE OUTDOORS

BOAT TRIPS Boat trips along the Manavgat River can be arranged either from the harbor at Side or from the town of Manavgat (on Route 400, 1 km [½ mi] east of the turnoff for Side). Prices vary widely according to the length of the trip and whether food is provided; you should definitely bargain. Times often change, but a boat also usually leaves each morning about 9 AM for Alanya—check the evening before at the sales desk (☎*No phone*) in the middle of the small Side harborfront. Boats stop to let you swim, and some arrange for activities such as jet skiing, waterskiing, or water parachuting; be warned, however, that not all the operators are properly licensed or insured, and serious accidents have occurred.

JEEP SAFARIS Jeep safaris are also popular and can be arranged from one of several travel agencies in Side. One good option is **Unser Tour** (☎*532/413–8431*).

ALARA HAN

118 km (73 mi) east of Antalya or 43 km (26 mi) east of Side, turn north off Rte. 400 onto local road signposted Alara Han; the site is 9 km (6 mi) inland.

The Seljuk Turks fostered the prosperity of their 11th- to 13th-century domains with trade protected by a network of *kervansarays*, or "inns"—called *hans* in Turkish. One of the more romantic of these is Alara Han, built in the early 13th century and now beautifully restored with a fountain, prayer room, unusual lamp stands carved into the stone, and lions' heads on the base of the arches, and a majestic vaulted interior. In summer, the inland countryside location also provides welcome relief from the sweltering coast.

For the energetic ready to scramble with hands and feet, an unusual hand-carved tunnel leads up to the Seljuk fortress built on the crags above the han. To get here, continue to the last stop on the road to the **Alara Cennet Piknik restaurant** (☎*544/260–5520*). A flashlight is essential to make the climb, but if you don't have one, Adem Birdoğan at the Cennet Piknik can lend you one. Ask him for directions across the vegetable fields to the tunnel entrance. Afterward he'll cook you freshly caught trout and you can relax with a cold drink on the river bank, enjoying a cool breeze from the crystal clear snow-fed river.

ALANYA

135 km (84 mi) east of Side on Rte. 400.

ESSENTIALS

Official tourist office Alanya (⊠ *Damlataş Cad. 1* ☎ *242/513–1240* 🖷 *242/ 513–5436*).

EXPLORING

Alanya is Turkey's hottest resort town—literally. Temperatures here are higher than almost anywhere else in Turkey, averaging 106°F (27°C) in July and August, and the waves lapping the long Mediterranean beaches that sweep toward Alanya's great rock citadel are only a degree or two cooler. This makes high summer in Alanya heaven for sun-starved, disco-loving, hard-drinking north Europeans but rather hellish for anyone seeking a quiet holiday surrounded by nature.

That said, Alanya is now home to one of Turkey's biggest year-round expatriate communities, and in spring and autumn it's a pleasantly warm and inexpensive choice for a few days of easily accessible swimming, historic sites, and good food. The city is cleaning up its act, so to speak: former wastelands of concrete-block apartments are now colorfully painted, Ottoman districts around the harbor are well on the way to being restored, and the new and old houses inside the magnificent red-walled citadel are an unspoiled, eclectic jumble. The best swimming place is known as Cleopatra's Beach—yet another accretion to the fables surrounding Mark Antony's courtship of the Egyptian queen—and its yellow sands extend northwest from the rock citadel. Foreign influence has led to improvements like automated touch-screen bike rentals around the center, hundreds of restaurants that can bill in multiple currencies, and a microbrewery called the Red Tower, that serves what many to believe is the best beer in Turkey.

Alanya is famed for its sandy beaches, within walking distance of most hotels. Boats can be hired from the harbor for relaxing day tours to caves around the citadel rock and a view of the only surviving naval arsenal of the 12th and 13th century Seljuks. Alanya, called Kalanaoros by the Byzantines, was captured in 1221 by the Seljuk sultan Alaaddin Keykubad and was the Turkish Seljuks' first stronghold on the

THE SELJUK TURKS AND THE MEDITERRANEAN COAST

The empire of the Roman Seljuks was the first Muslim empire to extend into Anatolia, long before the Ottomans arrived. It reached its height in the 13th century, when the Seljuks established full control of Turkey's Mediterranean and Black Sea coasts. Their capital was at Konya (Iconium), in central Anatolia, where winters were bitterly cold. As a consequence, the Seljuks established Alanya as a secondary winter capital, and there are many Seljuk remains in the area, including the Alara Han.

Mediterranean in their centuries-long migration westward. Several amusing stories explain the Seljuk sultan Alaaddin Keykubad's conquest: one says he married the commander's daughter, another that he tied torches to the horns of thousands of goats and drove them up the hill in the dark of night, suggesting a great army was attacking. Most likely, he simply cut a deal; once settled, he modestly renamed the place Alaiya, after himself, and built defensive walls to ensure he would never be dislodged. The Ottomans arrived in 1471, and gave it its current name, Alanya.

WHAT TO SEE

It's worth dropping by the small **Alanya Müzesi** *(Alanya Museum)*, just to see the perfectly preserved Roman bronze statue of a gleaming, muscular Hercules from the 2nd century AD. Other bronze statues feature Hermes and a graceful woman. There is also a large collection of ancient ceramics and interesting limestone ossuaries and heads from the late Roman period, as well as pictures of some of the less famous sites in the area. Note the Ottoman Greek inscriptions in Karamanli—Turkish written with the Greek alphabet. ⊠ *Azaklar Sokak, south of Atatürk Cad., where the castle hill drops down to Cleopatras beach* ☎ *242/513–1228* ▧ *$2* ⊙ *Tues.–Sun. 8:30–noon and 1:30–5:30.*

Views of the splendid **kale** *(citadel)*, on a mighty crag surrounded on three sides by the sea, dominate all roads into Alanya. The crenellated outer walls are 7 km (4 mi) long and include 146 towers. The road pierces these outer walls through a modern break, and heads up to the summit divided into two, one to the **İç Kale** (inner fortress) and one to the **Ehmediye**; both have places to park. Alternatively there is a regular city bus to the summit, which allows you to walk up or down through the old city's residential area, starting or ending at the **Kızıl Kule**; it's a hot walk in summer, though.

In the center of town are the remains of the original *bedestan* (bazaar), whose old shops are now rooms in a lackluster hotel, with the not very original name, The Bedestan Hotel. Along a road to the top of the promontory, a third wall and a ticket office defends the **İç Kale (Keep).** Inside are the ruins of a Byzantine church, with some 6th-century frescoes of the evangelists. Keykubad probably also had a palace here, although discoveries by the McGhee Center of Georgetown University—itself in a beautiful old Ottoman mansion perched on the cliff-face between the first and second ring of walls—indicates that in times of peace the Seljuk elite probably preferred their pleasure gardens and their hunting and equestrian sports on the well-watered plain below. Steps ascend to the battlement on the summit. A viewing platform is built on the spot where condemned prisoners and women convicted of adultery were once cast to their deaths. The ticket is also valid for the **Ehmediye** area, past the 17th century Suleymaniye Camii, where a small citadel is built on the foundations of classical walls. ⚠ Do not attempt to descend toward ruins including the remains of the monastery on the outer point of the rock, since the mountainside is very treacherous. ☎ *242/512–3304* ▧ *$7 for İç Kale and Byzantine church* ⊙ *Tues.–Sun. 9–7.*

A minor masterpiece of Mediterranean military architecture, the 100-foot-high **Kızıl Kule** *(Red Tower),* was built by the Seljuks in 1225 to defend Alanya harbor and the nearby shipyard known as the **tersane** (arsenal). Sophisticated technology for the time was imported in the form of an architect from Aleppo who was familiar with crusader castle building. The octagonal redbrick structure includes finely judged angles of fire for archers manning the loopholes, cleverly designed stairs to cut attackers off, and a series of troughs to convey boiling tar and melted lead onto besieging forces. Nowadays the Red Tower houses a small but interesting ethnographic museum. A short walk south along the water— or along the castle walls, if you prefer—is another defensive tower rising above the tersane, which is made up of five workshops all under an arched roof. Ships could be pulled up under the vaulted stone arches for building or repairs, and the cover was likely also useful for storing war supplies. ✉*Eastern harbor at south end of İskele Cad.* ✉*$2.*

WHERE TO STAY AND EAT

$$$

MEDITERRANEAN

✕**Filika Restaurant.** On a pretty terrace right on Cleopatra's Beach and looking up to the citadel towering overhead, this fine restaurant is where real-estate agents take new customers before hustling them off to the close-packed fields of villas and apartment blocks mushrooming on the flanks of the mountains north of town. The focus is on meat, steaks, kebabs, and lamb, including lamb with rosemary or, ironically, sprinkled with thyme like that which used to grow where the new developments now stand. There is also a more basic snack menu for lunch. ✉*Güzelyalı Cad., diagonally opposite the museum* ☎*242/519–3227* ▤*MC, V.*

$$$

TURKISH

✕**Güverte Restaurant.** Across from the Kaptan Hotel, this long-standing favorite has a delightful view of the harbor with excellent traditional Turkish fare, focused on fresh seafood. Try the **grida** (grouper) or the fried squid with local "tarator" sauce—a mixture of yogurt, garlic, lemon, walnuts, olive oil, and bread. ✉ *Çarşı Mahallesi, İskele Cad. 70* ☎*242/513–4100* ▤*MC, V.*

$

TURKISH

✕**Özsüt Alanya.** This modern, air-conditioned cake shop is the best place in town for restoring lagging caffeine or blood sugar levels—perhaps before an assault on the citadel above. It's part of a modern chain that has expanded rapidly through Turkish cities thanks to the excellent cakes, pastries, and sweets. ✉*Çarşıı Mah., İskele Cad., Kamburoğlu Apt. No. 84, Alanya* ☎*242/512–2202* ▤*AE, MC, V.*

$$

TURKISH

★

✕**Red Tower Restaurant.** This is one of Turkey's first microbreweries, and the beer here is some of the best you'll find in the country. You have the choice of a traditional pilsner, a light and sweeter Helles, a dark Marzen ale, or a wheat beer. The same management runs the Kale Yolu Et Lokantaı Turkish meat restaurant upstairs, which serves classical Turkish food overlooking the Alanya harbor and the Red Tower fortifications. Both establishments share the terrace across the road. On other floors are a fish restaurant and an international restaurant. On the roof terrace is an open-air Skylounge Bar. All are owned and managed by the same company. ✉*İskele Cad. 80* ☎*242/513–6664* ▤*MC, V.*

$$

▥**Elysée Beach Hotel.** This relatively quiet, clean, and modest hotel is right on Alanya's Cleopatra Beach, a short walk from the center of town. Rooms are on the large side, and the furniture decent but nothing fancy; the nicest rooms are on the ends of the corridors, overlooking the sea. The main attraction here is the beachfront position, and the pool and outdoor terrace. **Pros:** central location and beach. **Cons:** few rooms have real sea views. ⊠*Saray Mah., Atatürk Cad. 145, Alanya* ☎*242/512–8791* ⊕*www.elyseehotels.com* ⤶*60 rooms* ⌂*In-hotel: pool, gym* ▭*MC, V* ⊗*Closed Dec. 15–Mar. 1* ⑂*MAP.*

$$ ⑂**Grand Kaptan Hotel.** For dependable service and facilities, this seafront hotel, 4 km (2 mi) east of town, is the grandest in Alanya. It's frequented by international tour groups as well as visiting Turkish executives, and the main restaurant is geared toward large numbers of people. The outdoor pool is large and has a swim-up bar. A tunnel takes visitors under the highway to a beach where a barbecue restaurant operates in the summer. The beach lacks natural shade—but there are plenty of beach and water sports to occupy guests, from volleyball to jet ski-ing, windsurfing, and waterskiing. The rooms are a bit gloomy, and a few don't have private bath. A shuttle operates between the hotel and the town center nine times a day. **Pros:** professional service; extensive facilities. **Cons:** not *right* on the beach, annex rooms are not as good as the main building. ⊠*Oba Göl Mevkii* ☎*242/514–0101* ⊕*www. kaptanhotels.com* ⤶*412 rooms, including 8 suites, most with bath* ⌂*In-room: Wi-Fi. In-hotel: 3 restaurants, bars, tennis courts, pool, gym, diving* ▭*AE, MC, V.*

$$ ⑂**Iberostar Club Alantur Hotel.** With a white stucco decor theme, wood-panel rooms, and a beachfront location 5 km (3 mi) east of Alanya, Iberostar's pleasant design and 6.5-acre spread raise it above the standard charter tour hotel. The management promises a special effort to look after children, but at the other end of the spectrum, the discotheque, open until 1 AM, can be noisy. **Pros:** prime beachfront location. **Cons:** a bit out of a ways from Alanya proper. ⊠*Dimçay Mevkii, Alanya,* ☎*242/518–1740* ⊕*www.iberostar.com* ⤶*350 rooms* ⌂*In-room: safe. In-hotel: restaurant, 4 bars, tennis courts, pools, diving, water sports, laundry facilities* ▭*AE, MC, V* ⊗*Closed Nov.–Mar.* ⑂*AP.*

¢ ⑂**Kaptan Hotel.** This hotel near the Red Tower was the best in Alanya before tourism development overwhelmed the town. Despite impeccable service and double-glazed windows in all its small rooms, unfortunately it can't be recommended between June and September due to its proxim-ity to Antalya's four loudest harborside open-air discotheques. Owned by the Kaptanoğlu family, the town's more responsible dignitaries still take early evening refuge at its curved and gracious lobby bar. The hotel also has a lively poolside café and the **Kaptan's Güverte Restau-rant** (part of the family domain), across the road. ⊠*İskele Cad. 70* ☎*242/513–4900* ⊕*www.kaptanhotels.com* ⤶*56 rooms* ⌂*In-hotel: restaurant, bars, pools* ▭*AE, DC, MC, V.*

NIGHTLIFE

Alanya's nightlife centers around its harbor and the explosive beat on İskele Caddesi—although there are a few large dance clubs in Dimçay, about 5 km (3mi) outside town. Bars often have extensive menus, and restaurants frequently have live music or turn into impromptu discos after dinner. The Sherwood forest–themed, three-floor **Robin Hood Bar**

(⊠*İskele Cad. 24* ☎*242/511–7692*) is the biggest on the block; it's open all year round and tries to cater to all tastes. Underneath Robin Hood is the **Amalia Bar** (☎*537/796–9289*), run by two Dutchmen. The **James Dean Bar** (⊠*İskele Cad.* ☎*242/512–3195*) is popular and less expensive than some of the other haunts on the strip. **Zapf Hahn** (⊠*İskele Cad.* ☎*242/513–8285*) is the spot to go if you like techno.

Near the seafront on the road to Antalya, the **Summer Garden** offers free transport to five people or more from Alanya to it and its sister **Fresco** restaurant, both part of the same complex. The two large bars among the palm trees have a dance floor cooled with outdoor air-conditioning (really!). Open from 6 PM, the music doesn't stop until about 4 AM. ⊠*Konaklıı Kasabasi, Alanya* ☎*242/565–0059 or 535/768–1326* ⊙*Open mid-May–mid-Nov.*

SPORTS AND THE OUTDOORS

Alanya's main beach, known as Cleopatra's Beach, remains relatively uncrowded except in the height of summer. It's also easy to reach other nearby beaches, coves, and caves by boat. Legend has it that buccaneers kept their most fetching maidens at **Korsanlar Mağarası** (Pirates' Cave) and **Aşıklar Mağarası** (Lovers' Cave), two favorite destinations. Tour boats usually charge from $10 to $20 per person; hiring a private boat, which you can do at the dock near the Red Tower, should cost less than $30 an hour—don't be afraid to bargain.

Organized sporting events are new for sweltering, nightlife-oriented Alanya, but the past few years have seen the advent of **Alanya International Triathlon** (⊕*www.alanya.bel.tr/Triathlon/index.htm*), in the cooler weather of late October. There is also beach volleyball, basketball, handball, and other sporting events, especially in summer.

EAST OF ALANYA

Few tourists continue east of Alanya, though it can be a scenic route to Cappadocia or onward to Antioch and eastern Turkey, and there are some interesting stops along the way. The mountains rise up from the sea and the road winds torturously along the coast, which is pretty in spots, with a long stretch reminiscent of the Amalfi Coast or the French Riviera. Beyond the growing resort town of Gazipaşa the towns are more mostly agricultural, with the occasional cluster of Turkish holiday houses.

ANAMUR

130 km (80 mi) southeast of Alanya on Rte. 400.

Anamur is an uninspiring agricultural town, known throughout Turkey for its bananas. A few resorts are appearing on the coast here, but the main reason to stop are the ruins of ancient Anemurium and the dramatic Marmure Castle.

In the small **Anamur Müzesi** *(Anamur Museum)*, local finds, including earthenware phalluses buried in the fields by farmers as part of a fertility ritual, are on display. This ritual predated the arrival of Christianity but continued well into Christian times; today phalluses still occasionally turn up when farmers are plowing. ✉ *$1* ⊘ *Open 8–5.*

Five kilometers (3 mi) before Anamur is the marked turn off to ancient **Anemurium.** The ruins here are extensive, mostly dating from the late Roman/early Byzantine period and are built out of durable Roman concrete, which makes them better preserved, but less picturesque than the average stone ruins. The Roman bath building is easily the best preserved in the country, with even its great vaulted roof standing. There are also numerous private houses, some with mosaics; a large and a small theater; and a large necropolis. There's also a pebbly beach, where you can take a dip when you've finished.

On the southeast edge of town, on the shore, the highway goes right past the **Mamure Kalesi** *(Mamure Castle, also known as Mamuriye).* Its precise date of construction is uncertain, but it was built in Roman times to protect the city, then known as Anemurium, from seaborne raiders. The castle was renovated and partially rebuilt by the Seljuks, who captured it in the 13th century, and again by the Karamanoğulları, who controlled this part of Anatolia after the Seljuk empire collapsed. Note the inscription to the Karamanoğulları prince, İbrahim Bey II, dating from 1450. The place is so impressively well preserved you'd think it was a modern reconstruction.

SILIFKE

Silifke is 120 km (74 mi) east of Anamur on Rte. 400.

The small town of Silifke is dominated by its Byzantine castle.

In the vicinity of the castle, remains have been found indicating there was a settlement here as far back as the Bronze Age, though most of what can be seen today is from the Roman city known as **Seleuceia Trachea,** or Calycadnos Seleuceia. The ruins include a theater, a stadium, and the Corinthian columns of the 2nd-century-AD Temple of Zeus. Also left are a basilica and tomb dedicated to St. Thecla, St. Paul's first convert and the first female Christian martyr.

Local finds are displayed in the small **Silifke Müzesi** *(Silifke Museum).* ⊘ *Daily 8–5.*

HEAVEN AND HELL

17 km (10 mi) east of Silifke, turn north off Rte. 400 Narlikuyu onto local road signposted "Cennet ve Cehennem Derisi"; the site is 3 km (2 mi) inland.

These two dramatic holes in the ground have been the local attraction since before Roman times. Once you pass through the village you'll see the wall of the Roman Temple of Zeus Corycus, later reused as a church, just past which is a small café and the ticket booth. Beyond you'll see a large completely enclosed valley, caused by an ancient subsidence, sort of a sinkhole. The valley is called the **Valley of Heaven,** "Cennet Deresi." A five-minute walk takes you down to the peaceful green floor and the well-preserved 5th-century-AD Byzantine Church of the Virgin Mary, missing only its roof. The path then leads down into a huge aircraft-hanger-like natural cavern, which may have been the site of a spring known among the ancients as the fountain of knowledge.

Back up the stairs a short walk leads to the **Valley of Hell,** "Cehennem Derisi," which is narrower, with walls too steep to enter, and deep enough for little sunlight to reach the bottom. A dark and gloomy place, pagan, Christian, and Muslim sources all identify it as an entrance to hell. The road continues to a third cavern, the **Cave of Wishes,** "Dilek Mağarası," a peaceful place known to the Romans as an area to find the best crocus, and you may be met by villagers selling bunches of the little flowers.

Down the hill from the highway is the village of Narlikuyu, a picturesque inlet dotted with fish restaurants. This was the site of ancient Corycos, and a small museum includes an excellent mosaic of the "three Graces" part of the Roman bath building.

KIZ KALESI

22 km (14mi) east of Silıfke on Rte. 400.

This small town is easily the best place to stop on the long drive east of Alanya; there's a nice stretch of beach but it's most famous for its picture-perfect castle sitting just off the shore.

WHAT TO SEE

On an island just off the coast is the **Kız Kalesi** *(Maiden's Castle).* The island is known to have been a settlement as early as the 4th century BC, though the castle is nowhere near that old. Several offshore castles in Turkey bear the same name, which comes with a legend of a king, a princess, and a snake: the beautiful princess, apple of her father's eye, had her fortune read by a wandering soothsayer who declared she would die of a snakebite. The king therefore sent her to a castle on a snake-free island. Destiny, however, can never be avoided, and the offending serpent was accidently delivered in a basket of grapes sent as a gift from her father's palace. More prosaicly, the castle was an important part of the row of defenses along the coast that were built and rebuilt over the centuries to stop invaders from Syria entering Anatolia via the coast route to Antalya. What you see is mostly 11th-century Byzantine rebuilding to keep out the Crusaders based in Antioch.

WHERE TO STAY AND EAT

$$ ✕⊡ **Club Barbarossa Hotel.** This modern hotel, right on the Kız Kalesi, has great views of the castle, its own section of beach, and air-conditioning. The rooms are quite nice, with new wooden furniture and balconies, most with sea views. At the center of the property is a large green space, with a pool and piece of ancient stone work, leading down the waterfront. The Barbarossa restaurant serves good, simple Turkish fare. **Pros:** nice modern rooms; great location. **Cons:** hotel building itself is rather dated and old. ⊠ *Head down the peninsula and look for signs on your left* ☎ *324/523–2364* ⊕ *www.barbarossahotel.com* ⇥ *79 rooms* ⌂ *In-hotel: restaurant, bars, pools* ▤ MC, V.

$ ⚏**Yaka Hotel** This is easily the most popular budget option in Kizkalesi. Rooms are spotlessly clean, and at the better end of the budget range. The main attraction is the helpful management and the relaxed atmosphere. **Pros:** popular; friendly. **Cons:** hard to find and not right on the beach. ✉*On your left as you head down the peninsula; you might have to ask* ☎*324/523–2444* ⊕*www.yakahotel.com.tr* ⤳*16 rooms* ⚐*In-room: Wi-Fi* ▭*MC, V.*

VIRANŞEHIR

62 km (39 mi) east of Silifke, turn south off Rte. 400 onto local road signposted Alara Han; the site is 9 km (6 mi) inland.

Just before you reach the large modern city of Mersin are the ruins of ancient Soli, or Viranşehir, which make a good break. This was a colony settled by Rhodes that later became a pirate stronghold. There is a long row of Corinthian columns, part of an ancient colonnaded street; look for the human and animal figures carved into the capitals.

EN ROUTE

Mersin, about 73 km (45 mi) east of Viranşehir, is a large port town, with a reputation as one of Turkey's most modern and secular cities. While archaeologists traced the city's origin back 8,000 years, for the modern visitor there is little appeal. If you're looking for a break in driving, though, the city's waterfront has a nice promenade.

TARSUS

28 km (17 mi) east of Mersin on Route E90.

St. Paul was born some 2,000 years ago in Tarsus, though little sign of the saint remains nowadays in what has become a dusty, sleepy provincial town of no great interest. The only surviving piece of antiquity is the **Gate of Cleopatra Kancık Kapısı** and there is also a 16th-century covered bazaar known as the **Kırkkaşık,** or "40 Spoons."

ADANA

69 km (43 mi) east of Mersin on Rte. E90.

Adana is Turkey's fourth-largest city after Istanbul, Ankara, and İzmir, but it's the least known to tourists because it's a commercial and industrial center, though there are a few first-rate attractions. The **Ulu Camii,** more Arabic in style than Turkish, is one of the prettiest in the country, and its patterned stonework has been well restored. There is also nice courtyard, and the main prayer alcove is filled with some of the best Iznik tiles in existence. Down by the river is the symbol of the city, the impressively long **Taş Köprü** or "stone bridge," built by the Emperor Hadrian in 125 AD and restored by a who's who of Byzantine and Muslim rulers ever since.

There are many castles in the area, mostly dating back to the Armenian rulers of the 12th to 14th centuries AD. The easiest to reach, **Yılan Kalesi,** the "Castle of the Snake," sits unmissably beside the main highway, 40 km (25 mi) east of town: take the marked turn off and drive up to the parking lot, beside the small restaurant and ticket booth. There isn't

The three Graces, or Charities, depicted in this mosaic are said to have linked arms to show that one kindness should lead to another.

a lot to see, but the walls are well preserved and the views of the fertile Çukurova plain from the top are impressive.

WHERE TO STAY AND EAT

$
TURKISH
✕ **Efendi.** In the more upmarket area north of the city center, this is a popular hangout for Adana's young and trendy. The decor is arty minimalist, and the place functions as café, bar, and restaurant all in one, with pizza being the main attraction on the menu. Head through to the back, and you'll find tables with large comfy cusions. It's easiest to get to if you take a taxi from the city center. ⊠ *Cemalpaşa Mah. 6 Sokak 1.*

$–$$
TURKISH
✕ **Yüzevler.** For most Turks Adana means Adana kebab, minced lamb slow charcoal-grilled on a long wide metal skewer. Everyone in Adana has an opinion on where to find the best Adana kebab, but the traditional favourite is Yüzevler, and the photos of a Turkish who's who tucking in proves that this is not your average kebab shop. Obviously, the kebabs are the star of the show, but the *pide* (Turkish pizza) is also good, and this is probably one of the safest places to try the famous raw ground meat *Çiğ Köfte*, literally "raw köfte"; it's "cooked" with spices. ⊠ *Ziyapaşa Bulvarı 25* ☎ *322/454–7513.*

$
🛏 **Doruk Hotel.** This is probably the best of a cluster of hotels right in the center of Adana. Don't expect any more than a decent midrange room, though, and views of the building next door, but the price is good for what you get. **Pros:** good value. **Cons:** dark rooms. ⊠ *İnönü Cad. 89* ☎ *322/363–4343* 📞*82 rooms* ⌂ *In-hotel: restaurant, bar.*

$$$$
🛏 **Seyhan Hotel.** In the heart of the city, this high-rise hotel with a mirrored-glass exterior is a modern Adana landmark. Inside, it lives up to the five-star rating the eccentric Turkish system gives it, though

some of the rooms, while quite large and well-maintained feel a little dated; ask for one of the more modern-décor ones. Therē is a great range of first-class facilities, and the business center points to the hotels main clientele. **Pros:** modern services and atmosphere. **Cons:** large and impersonal; lacks Turkish character. ⊠ *Turhan Cemal Beriker Bul. 18* ☎ *322/455–3030* ⊕ *www.otelseyhan.com.tr* ⤴ *140 rooms, 20 suites, 20 apartments* ⚹ *In-room: safe, Wi-Fi. In-hotel: restaurant, bars, pool, gym, laundry service* ▭ *AE, DC, MC, V.*

ANTAKYA (ANTIOCH)

191 km (118 mi) from Adana, east on Rte. E90, south on Rte. E91.

Antakya is perhaps better known by its old name, Antioch. Founded in about 300 BC by Seleucus Nikator, one of Alexander's generals, the city grew quickly, thanks to its strategic location on the trade routes. After the Roman occupation began in AD 64, Antioch became the empire's third most important city, after Rome and Alexandria. Famed for its luxury and notorious for its depravity, it was chosen by St. Paul as the objective of his first mission to the gentiles. After enduring earthquakes and Byzantine and Arab raids, it fell to the crusaders in 1098; Egyptian raiders nearly leveled it in 1268. A late addition to the Turkish Republic, it was occupied by France after 1920 as part of its mandate over Syria, which still has an outstanding territorial claim on it. Though the city reverted to Turkey just before World War II, it still maintains a distinctive character. The people of Antioch are mostly bilingual, speaking both Turkish and a local dialect of Arabic. In the cobbled streets of the old quarter, on the east bank of the River Orontes, you can also hear Syriac (Aramaic), the language spoken by many of Turkey's Christians.

On the northern edge of town is **Senpiyer Kilisesi** (*Church of St. Peter*), a tiny cave high up on a cliff, blackened by centuries of candle smoke and dripping with water seeping out of the rock. It's here that the apostle preached to his converts and where they first came to be called Christians. The present facade to the cave dates from the 11th and 12th centuries. Mass is celebrated here on the first Sunday of every month. ⊠ *Off Kurtuluş Cad.*

The River Orontes (Asi in Turkish) divides Antioch in two. In the old town you will find the 17th-century **Habib Neccar Cami,** a mosque on Kurtuluş Caddesi, just south of St. Peter's. Just north is the bazaar quarter, a real change of pace: the feel here is more Syrian and Arab than Turkish. On Hürriyet Caddesi, several winding blocks southwest of the mosque, is the loggia of a derelict **Latin monastery**; enter its cloister from the side street.

★ Experts consider the exceptional Roman mosaics of **Hatay Müzesi** (*Hatay Museum*)—portraying scenes from mythology and figures such as Dionysus, Orpheus, Oceanus, and Thetis—among the highest achievements of Roman art. ⊠ *Gündüz Cad. 1, in central square on right bank of Orontes* ☎ *326/214–6167* ⤳ *$1* ☉ *Tues.–Sun. 8:30–12:30 and 1:30–5:30.*

Most mosaics at the Hatay Museum come from villas in **Harbiye,** originally called Daphne, a beautiful gorge of laurel trees and tumbling waterfalls that was said to have been chosen by the gods for the Judgment of Paris and that contained one of the ancient world's most important shrines to the god Apollo (7 km [4 mi] south of Antakya on Route E91). Mark Antony chose it as the venue for his ill-fated marriage to Cleopatra in 40 BC. Daphne was also a favorite resort for wealthy Antiochenes and developed such a reputation for licentiousness, it was put off-limits to the Roman army.

OFF THE
BEATEN
PATH

Samandag and Seleuceia ad Pieria. You'll find a beach at Samandag (also known as Çevlik Beach), as well as tasty but inexpensive fish, 28 km (17 mi) south of Antakya. You'll also find the remains of Antioch's old port, Seleuceia ad Pieria, including an underground water channel, 1,400 meters (1,526 yards) long, which was built entirely by hand. Nearby rock tombs are still used by the local villagers to stable their donkeys.

WHERE TO STAY AND EAT

$$
TURKISH
✕**Antik Han.** The mezes are particularly good at this restaurant with a rooftop terrace, and there's a pleasant courtyard where you can relax and eat. ⊠*Hurriyet Cad.* ☎*No phone.* ▭*No credit cards.*

$
TURKISH
✕**Sultan Sofras.** Tour groups often take up this restaurant, but with good reason: the food is delicious and inexpensive. You'll find all the usual Turkish dishes. ⊠*İstiklal Cad. 20* ☎*No phone.* ▭*No credit cards.*

$$
🛏**Arsuz Hotel.** On its own private beach in Arsuz (also called Uluçınar), outside the city, this clean, bright, and airy hotel has a lush garden leading down to a private beach. **Pros:** beach. **Cons:** rooms are small and basic. ⊠*Arsuz (Uluçınar)* ☎*326/643–2444, 326/643–2445, or 326/643–2447* 🖶*326/643–2448* ⌂*104 rooms, 3 suites* ⌂*In-room: Wi-Fi (some)* ⌂*In-hotel: restaurant, Wi-Fi, bars, beachfront* ☉*Closed Nov.–Apr.* ▭*MC, V.*

$$
🛏**Büyük Antakya.** If you've made it this far, almost to the Syrian border, you deserve the best hotel available, and this is it: a giant, white pyramid of a building with cool marble in the lobby and bright rooms with big windows. All the rooms have balconies, some with views of Eski Antalya. There's also a disco if you need some nightlife. **Pros:** professional and helpful service; old-school ambience. **Cons:** decor is a bit out of date; a bit impersonal; pricey for where you are. ⊠*Atatürk Cad. 8* ☎*326/213–5860* ⊕*www.buyukantakyaoteli.com* ⌂*70 rooms, 2 suites* ⌂*In-room: Wi-Fi, minibar. In-hotel: restaurant, bar, laundry service* ▭*MC, V.*

Central Anatolia

CAPPADOCIA, ANKARA & THE TURKISH HEARTLAND

WORD OF MOUTH

"Cappadocia: go on a hot air balloon excursion. I did and it was the absolute highlight of my trip. I went with Kappadocia Balloon."

—Diane60030

WELCOME TO CENTRAL ANATOLIA

TOP REASONS TO GO

★ **Hike the valleys of Cappadocia** Trails lead past fantastic rock formations and to cave entrances that open on ornately decorated churches.

★ **Balloon over Cappadocia** Dangling high above the forested, rock-littered valleys in a basket, you'll sail past rock cones and fairy chimneys.

★ **Explore underground cities** Kaymaklı, Derinkuyu, and the other subterranean complexes are vast, multistoried, equipped with kitchens, sewage systems, and stables, and once housed tens of thousands of inhabitants.

★ **Luxuriate in a cave** Some of Cappadocia's finest hotels are tucked into elaborately appointed caves, where soft lighting, fireplaces, and even Jacuzzis are common amenities.

★ **See the dervishes whirl** In Konya dervishes whirl in graceful spinning dances as a way to fill themselves with love, the essence of the divine.

Drive from Ürgüp to Göreme, Cappadocia

TO SAFRANBOLU
Kazan
E89
TO HATTUŞA
Kalecik
3
Kabil
★ ANKARA
D200
D200
Baliseyh
Temelli
Golbası
Kirikkale
Keskin
Bala
Haymana
D750
D260
Gokgozsereflisi
Akpinar
Kaman
Karahamzali
Sofular
Hirfanli Baraji
Kerpic
Helvacilar
Kulu
Suluklu
Yeniceoba
Omeranil
Sereflikochisar
Karabiyik
Pinarbasi Yaylasi
Tuz Gölü
Cesmelisebil
Cihanbeyli
Balci
D750
D715
Akorenkisla
Sarayonu
Aksaray
Demirci
Yazibelen
Guzelyurt
D750
Taspinar
Sille
2
Konya
Asakli
TO ÇATAL HÖYÜK
Altinhisar
Goloren

0   30 mi
0   30 km

1 Cappadocia. The weirdest natural landscape you're ever likely to see is a giant outdoor sculpture garden of elaborate cones, needles, pillars, and pyramids. As if these natural phenomena weren't enticing enough, hundreds of caves harbor elaborately frescoed churches from the early days of Christianity.

2 Konya. One of Turkey's most popular pilgrimage sites houses a shrine to the 13th-century philosopher Rumi and is home to the whirling dervishes. Elegant mosques and seminaries enhance the holiness of the place.

3 Ankara and the Hittite Cities. Turkey's capital is home to the enduring legacy of Atatürk, founding father of the secular Turkish Republic. On the barren dusty steppe beyond the city are scattered the ancient ruined sites of the once mighty Hittite Empire. North of Ankara is Safranbolu, one of the best-preserved Ottoman-era towns in Turkey.

GETTING ORIENTED

Central Anatolia stretches across a vast, arid plateau, littered with the ruins of ancient civilizations, slashed by ravines in places and rising to the peaks of extinct volcanoes in others. Think of the region as a triangle, with Ankara, Turkey's sprawling capital, to the northwest; Cappadocia, the land of surrealistic geological formations to the northeast; and Konya, the city where the dervishes whirl, to the south, en route to Antalya and the Mediterranean Coast.

6

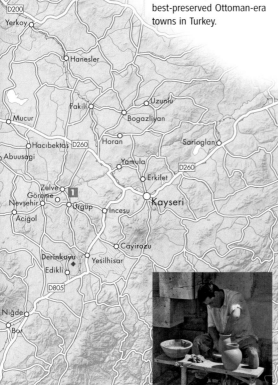

Aritsans at work, Avanos.

CENTRAL ANATOLIA PLANNER

How Much Time Do You Need?

In Cappadocia, you can see the open-air museums and major valleys in two days but you may want to spend several more days just soaking up the enchanting landscapes and enjoying the region's comfortable lodgings. We suggest flying to Nevşehir or Kayseri, and picking up a car (the easiest way to see the region). Avanos, Ürgüp, Göreme, and Uçhisar are all good places to base yourself, with a selection of hotels,

Don't go out of your way to spend vacation time in Ankara, but if you do find yourself here, while away a day in the city's few worthwhile sights, most notably the highly regarded Archaeological Museum, repository of the best archaeological treasures found in Turkey, and Atatürk's Mausoleum, the Anıtkabir. All the Hittite cities can be seen in a day trip from Ankara if you have a car. You can see Konya's famous museums, mosques, and seminaries in half a day, and you may want to use the city as a stopping off point if you're traveling between Cappadocia and Antalya or elsewhere on the Mediterranean coast.

Where to Base Yourself in Cappadocia

Göreme has lodging options ranging from backpacker digs to fancy rock-cut hotels, and it's the easiest base if you don't have a car. It's also near the Göreme Open-Air Museum and many of the most scenic valleys. It's also quite busy and has a rather touristy feel to it.

Ürgüp is more tranquil than Göreme, and a bit farther from the main attractions. Although it doesn't have the delightful fairy chimneys of Göreme, it does have a growing cluster of hotels carved out of the rocks: generally small boutique lodgings that cater to a more upmarket clientele.

Uçhisar: between Nevşehir and Göreme, is central enough to be a good a base and calmer than other nearby towns. High on a rock outcropping, Uçhisar has incredible views of the surrounding valleys. It's popular with French tourists and non-Turkish signs and information are more likely to be written in French than English.

Avanos is at the north end of Cappadocia, is on the banks of the Kızılırmak River; it's quiet but scenic.

Tour Options

In Cappadocia, consider hiring a guide for at least one day. In general, they know the terrain and can lead you to places you might not otherwise find, and fill you in on fascinating details about the geology of the region, early inhabitants, and other info. Expect to pay about $25–$60 a day. Local tourist offices and hotels can make recommendations, or try one of these companies.

Argeus (☎ 384/341–4688 in Ürgüp ⊕ www.argeus.com. tr) is one of Cappadocia's most well-regarded agencies; they work with small groups (maximum eight people) and are on the pricier side. **Argonaut Escapades** (☎ 384/341–6255 in Ürgüp ⊕ www.argonautturkey.com) specializes in individually tailored small-group tours, particularly walking tours.

Anatolian Eating

Central Anatolia is the one region in Turkey that does not touch water, so fish has to be trucked or flown in. Be prepared for a lot of meat; that means kebabs and lamb, often with yogurt and tomato sauce. In Konya you'll encounter *etli ekmek,* flatbread topped with ground lamb and spices, and you'll find *lahmacun,* a kind of flatbread Turkish pizza, throughout the region. Main courses are usually preceded by a delicious array of mezes, which here often include hot humus and *pastırma* (Turkish pastrami).

Restaurants that cater to tourists serve beer, wine (which is produced locally in Cappadocia, with varying results—try the Kalecik Karası or the Öküzgüzü, both reds), and liquor (including rakı). In Konya and other more conservative towns, though, you might be hard pressed to find a drink. Whatever you eat and drink, you'll find it easy to dine in atmospheric surroundings—restored kervansaries, caves, Ottoman mansions, whitewashed courtyards. In many restaurants you'll sit on cushions on the floor, and your meal may well be accompanied by live music.

What It Costs In U.S. Dollars

DINING AND LODGING PRICE CATEGORIES

	¢	$	$$	$$$	$$$$
In Central Anatolia outside Ankara					
Restaurants	under $5	$5–$10	$11–$15	$16–$25	over $25
Hotels	under $50	$50–$75	$76–$150	$151–$250	over $250
In Ankara					
Restaurants	under $8	$8–$12	$13–$20	$21–$30	over $30
Hotels	under $100	$100–$150	$151–$200	$201–$250	over $250

Restaurant prices are for one main course at dinner or for two mezes (small dishes). Hotel prices are for two people in a standard double room in high season, including taxes.

When to Go

Much of Central Anatolia is blazing hot in summer and freezing cold in winter. The best time to visit is early spring (May) before the crowds and heat come, or early fall (September), when the crowds are gone and winter hasn't yet arrived.

Best Walks in Cappadocia

The most memorable experiences you're likely to have in Cappadocia are hikes through the valleys, clambering up tall, soft rock formations that rise in endlessly entertaining forms. You can do these with or without a guide, but a guide's expert knowledge is usually a bonus.

Rose Valley (Güllüdere), where cave entrances lead to multistory, ornately decorated churches.

Güvercinlik Vadisi (Pigeon Valley), a scenic valley dotted with a myriad of dovecotes.

Love Valley (Aşk Vadisi), perhaps named for the preponderance of phallus-looking rock protrusions.

Ilhara Valley, with a cluster of fresco-decorated churches above a river valley.

Soğanlı Kaya Kiliseleri, where you'll likely be alone to explore hundreds of dwellings and churches cut into the cliffs.

GETTING HERE & AROUND

By Air

Air travel isn't much more expensive than the bus, and flying to central Anatolia saves a lot of time. There are direct flights to Ankara's Esenboğa Airport from Europe and New York, as well as many domestic flights. There are also direct flights from Istanbul to the airport at Kayseri, the best option if time is short. The Nevşehir airport is even closer to the towns of Cappadocia but as of this writing there is only one flight a day from Istanbul. Most hotels in Cappadocia will arrange airport shuttles for guests.

By Bus

Cappadocia and Central Anatolia are well served by intercity buses but the distances are long. The 10-hour trip from Istanbul costs about $30. Buses link most towns and cities within the region, and fares are reasonable (less than $15 from Ankara to most anywhere in Central Anatolia). In Cappadocia there are buses connecting the towns, making it easy to get around, at least in summer; bus service is much less frequent in winter.

By Car

Once you're here, renting a car is a good idea since you'll probably be traveling around a lot. The highways in Central Anatolia are generally well maintained and lead to all the major sights. Minor roads, however, are rough and full of potholes. On narrow, winding roads, look out for oncoming trucks, whose drivers often don't stay on their side of the road, and be especially careful at night, when animals and farm vehicles without proper running lights are likely to be on rural roads.

There are good roads between Istanbul and the main cities of Anatolia: Ankara, Konya, and Kayseri. Even so, truck traffic on the main highway from Istanbul to Ankara can be heavy. Two long stretches of toll road (*ücretli geçiş*) linking Istanbul and Ankara—E80 to beyond Düzce and E89 south from Gerede—provide some relief from the rigors of the other highways. You can also reach Central Anatolia on major highways from the Mediterranean coasts: From Ankara, E90 (also known as Rte. 200) leads southwest toward Sivrihisar; continue southwest on E96 to Afyon, where you can pick up highways going south to Antalya or west to İzmir. Route E88/200 leads east out of Ankara and eventually connects with highways to the Black Sea coast.

By Train

Regular rail service connects Ankara to both Istanbul and İzmir, and direct trains also run from Istanbul to Konya (see specific cities for information). Trains generally take longer than buses—often a lot longer—but they do have the advantage of having sleeper cars, which can be quite comfortable. The Istanbul–Ankara corridor, is however, being outfitted with new rails to allow high-speed trains, so the route will be faster in coming years. There is very little train service between small towns in Central Anatolia. The one route that may be of use to tourists is Ankara–Kayseri, but it's generally much quicker to take a bus.

Updated by Vanessa Larson

Some of the oldest known human settlements were established in the hills and valleys of Central Anatolia, but today the main attraction here is the magical landscape of Cappadocia, where wind and rain have shaped the area's soft volcanic rock into a kind of fairytale landscape.

6

The small towns of Ürgup, Göreme, and Uçhisar are good spots to base yourself for exploring the outer-space landscape. You'll discover unimaginable rock formations, spectacular valleys, ancient cave churches, and underground cities that reached 20 stories beneath the surface and could hold up to 20,000 people. The Ihlara valley, a deep gorge that has ancient churches and villages cut into its cliffs and a green river running through it, is another Cappadocian highlight. Southwest of Cappadocia is Konya, home to a fascinating museum and tomb dedicated to the 13th-century founder of the whirling dervishes. Known as Turkey's most religiously conservative city, Konya is not a place for those looking for nightlife (alcohol can be difficult to find in the city) or a dining-out scene. This region's other major city is the Turkish capital, Ankara, a mostly characterless city that ranks fairly low on most visitors' itineraries, though it does have an excellent museum covering Turkey's ancient past and the mausoleum of Atatürk, modern Turkey's founder.

CAPPADOCIA

Cappadocia comprises the triangle of land formed by the towns of Nevşehir to the west, Ürgüp to the east, and Avanos in the north. Inside this triangle is one of the weirdest natural landscapes you're ever likely to see. More than 10 million years ago, three volcanoes in Cappadocia erupted, dropping lava, mud, and ash over the region. Over eons, the explosive products of Mt. Erciyes, Mt. Hasan, and Mt. Melendiz cooled and compressed to form tufa, a soft, porous rock easily worn by erosion. Water poured down, carving and separating giant ridges of rock. Wind whipped around the formations, further shaping them into elaborate cones, needles, pillars, and pyramids. Harder layers of rock like basalt resisted erosion longer, and often ended up perfectly balanced,

Cappadocia

like hats, on top of a tall cone. Oxidation gave the formations color, and then humans began to do their own carving and shaping.

In effect, the region has become a giant outdoor sculpture garden and the valleys here are full of the so-called "fairy chimneys"—rock formations in improbable shapes of cones and enormous spires. Walks through these valleys are unforgettable; you might feel like you're wandering around on another planet. One of the great pleasures of being in Cappadocia is that you still often feel like you're a lone explorer here. Mystical experiences are not uncommon for those hiking across these valleys of wild geological formations.

Indeed, Cappadocia has an undeniable spiritual side, and its natural endowment is only part of the attraction. The region is thought to have been occupied by the Hittites, who worshipped sun gods and first came to power in Anatolia 4,000 years ago. Tiberius claimed Cappadocia as a province of Rome in AD 17, and the early Christians, who more than anyone else have left a human mark on Cappadocia, settled in the region about the same time.

The Christians who established secluded communities here apparently found the otherworldly landscape suitable both to their aesthetic tastes and to their need to hide from persecution. They sat on Cappadocia's rock pillars for years at a time in prayer and carved hundreds of churches into the inside of soft rocks, decorating them with beautiful frescoes. You can still explore these churches, and by the end of a trip you won't be surprised when you duck into a nondescript cave entrance and find carved columns, a domed roof, and vivid frescoes.

Arab raiders also came into the region in the 7th and 8th centuries, forcing the inhabitants underground, where they renovated and expanded subterranean cities left by earlier peoples. It's believed that many sprawling underground complexes have yet to be discovered, and the true extent of some of those that can be explored is still unknown.

Cappadocia remains an exotic place in other ways, too. You'll see local residents traveling between farms and shops in horse-drawn carts. Women drape their houses with strings of apricots and paprika for drying in the sun, and nomadic workers pitch their tents beside sunflower fields and cook on fires that send smoke billowing through the tent tops. In the distance, minarets pierce the sky. Even the hotels are exotic—many occupy caves, and are some of the most delightfully unusual lodgings in which you'll ever stay.

NEVŞEHIR

6

ESSENTIALS
Visitor Information (⊠ Atatürk Bul., next to hospital ☎ 384/213–3659).

EXPLORING
The provincial capital, Nevşehir is not a particularly attractive town but it's an important transportation hub for the Cappadocia region. Although its airport is the closest to Cappadocia, it's much smaller than Kayseri's airport and is served by fewer flights. At the time of writing, aside from charter flights, Turkish Airlines is the only airline serving the airport, with one flight per day. The airport is 30 km (19 mi) northwest of the city, in the village of Tuzköy; public minibuses go from the airport to downtown Nevşehir, but you'll probably want to take a shuttle directly to whatever town you're staying in. Nevşehir is also the transfer point for regional buses, so if you're not traveling around Cappadocia by car, you'll probably end up passing through the town a few times to change buses as you visit the sights (for example, if you are going to Derinkuyu or Kaymaklı from the Göreme area, you'll need to change buses in Nevşehir).

ÜRGÜP

80 km (48 mi) west of Kayseri airport, 300 km (180 mi) south of Ankara, 725 km (435 mi) southeast of Istanbul; 23 km (14 mi) east of Nevşehir.

ESSENTIALS
Visitor Information (⊠ Kayseri Cad. 37, inside park ☎ 384/341–4059).

EXPLORING
With a central location and a busy (for Cappadocia) town center due to its higher population (17,000) than Göreme or Uçhisar, Ürgüp is a logical base for exploring the surrounding area. In recent years it has

CLOSE UP

Ballooning in Cappadocia

"Ballooning over Cappadocia at Sunrise." —photo by rward, Fodors.com member

One of the best ways to appreciate the expansive, diverse landscape of Cappadocia's landscape is from above, in a hot-air balloon. The flights begin just after 5 AM, the safest time to fly because of the calm air, and usually last a little over an hour. A skilled pilot can take you right into a valley, sail through it so the rock cones loom on either side, then climb the edge of a tall fairy chimney. The trip usually ends with a champagne toast, a ballooning tradition. Cappadocia is an ideal place to experience ballooning not only because of its spectacular scenery, but also because the region's microclimate, with calm weather and a high number of flying days per year, makes it one of the best and safest places in the world for ballooning. Balloon trips are offered from April through November.

The oldest and most respected of the Cappadocia balloon companies is Kapadokya Balloons, run by a Swedish-British couple who have been in business since 1991. Göreme Balloons is also very reputable. Ballooning prices are inflated in Cappadocia because hotels and tour agencies make high commissions for booking flights, but booking a flight on your own will not necessarily be cheaper. A typical ride with Kapadokya Balloons will be $315 for a 1½-hour ride and $220 for a 1-hour ride, per person, while Göreme Balloons charges $290 and $200, respectively. Both companies give a small discount if you pay in cash. While other companies may offer cheaper flights, ballooning is not the sort of thing where you really want to be cutting corners.

Contacts Göreme Balloons (✉ Sanayi Cad. Koyunyolu Mevkii 1, Ürgüp ☎ 384/341–5662 ⊕ www.goremeballoons.com).

Kapadokya Balloons (✉ Nevşehir Yolu 14/A, Göreme ☎ 384/271–2442 ⊕ www.kapadokyaballoons.com).

become increasingly known for its boutique hotels, many of which are restored cave houses in the Esbelli neighborhood, a 10-minute uphill walk from the center of town. Hotels in this scenic neighborhood often have breathtaking views of the town and the nearby cliffs dotted with man-made caves. Some beautiful old homes formerly owned by Greeks, who were a significant presence in the town until the Greek-Turkish population exchange in 1923, have also been converted into hotels.

Downtown Ürgüp is a fairly tacky jumble of buildings built up mostly for the tourism industry, but it's a good place to find banks, money exchanges, travel agencies, trinket shops, and even a Turkish bath and a few nightclubs. During the winter months, some of the hotels and restaurants in Ürgüp close, which means fewer options for travelers but a more tranquil atmosphere for those who are around.

Ürgüp's **Turasan Winery,** established in 1943 and one of the region's largest producers, offers tours with wine tastings. Cappadocians have been making wine for thousands of years, though you'll have to judge for yourself how successful they are. In recent years Cappadocian vintners have expanded their range of offerings, and their wines are affordable and omnipresent—and vineyards add even more to the scenery. ⊠ *Çimenli Mevkii, Ürgüp* ☎ *384/341–4961* ⌨ *Tour, 8 TL; tour and tasting, 16 TL* ☉ *Daily 8–sunset.*

WHERE TO STAY AND EAT

$–$$
GREEK
Fodor'sChoice
★

✕ **Old Greek House.** About 5 km (3 mi) from Ürgüp, in the sleepy village of Mustafapaşa, the Old Greek House serves delicious home-cooked specialties, including a variety of mezes, meat dishes like *karnıyarık* (eggplant stuffed with tomatoes and ground meat), and homemade baklava. Portions are generous, and the set menus are a genuine feast. Seating is on cushions on the floor around low, round tables or at regular-size tables in the central courtyard. The building, a 250-year-old Greek mansion, still has original frescoes on the stone walls and original painted wooden ceilings. The house is also an inn, with 13 simple but comfortable rooms. ⊠ *Mustafapaşa, 50420, Ürgüp* ☎ *384/353–5306* 🍴 *Reservations recommended* ⊟ *MC, V.*

$
TURKISH

✕ **Şömine.** Right on the main square, this welcoming lair takes its name from the fireplace in the center that warms guests in winter; in summer, you can dine outside on the rooftop terrace, where there is often live guitar music. In any season, the food is well prepared and well priced. Regional specialties include *testi kebabı,* a meat and vegetable dish cooked in a clay pot, which you break open yourself by whacking it with a large knife, and *kiremit,* a vegetable or meat stew baked on a clay tile. ⊠ *On the main square, Cumhuriyet Meydanı* ☎ *384/341–8442* ⊟ *AE, MC, V.*

$–$$
TURKISH
★

✕ **Ziggy's Cafe.** Ziggy's Mediterranean-inspired menu is refreshingly lighter than the heavy meat-based fare typical of central Anatolia. Creative appetizers include "Ziggy's meze," a tasty mixture of chopped green olives, goat cheese, and walnuts drizzled with spicy olive oil. Among the attractively presented entrées is the unusual but mouth-watering sirloin steak with pumpkin seed sauce, served with bulgur. The atmosphere is cozy, in a sort of Victorian country setting: nice tablecloths and table settings, plush armchairs, dark wood trim, and interesting wrought-iron lamps. An upstairs terrace has sofa-like seats and stone-topped tables. ⊠*Tevfik Fikret Cad. 24, Yunak Mah.* ☎*384/341–7107* ⚓*Reservations essential* ▤*MC, V* ☉*May be closed Jan.–Feb.*

$$ 🏨 **Elkep Evi.** Built into the side of a cliff, the cave rooms at Elkep Evi are large, comfortable and attractively furnished with old-fashioned decor like wooden latticework cabinets, and the cave walls and ceilings have beautiful bas-relief designs. A few rooms have Jacuzzis or a Turkish bath, and all have a private balcony or terrace. The hotel opens onto a large garden, dotted with old wooden artifacts, where guests can relax in hammocks or eat breakfast at small tables with beautiful views overlooking the town and surrounding valley. **Pros:** homey atmosphere; wonderful views; restaurant serving home-cooked food. **Cons:** a lot of stairs to reach some rooms. ⊠*Esbelli Sokak 26, 50400* ☎*384/341–6000* ⊕*www.elkepevi.com* ⌂*18 rooms, 3 suites* ⚑*In-room: no a/c, no TV, Wi-Fi. In-hotel: restaurant, room service, laundry service, some pets allowed, no-smoking rooms* ▤*MC, V* ⑈*BP.*

$$ 🏨 **Esbelli Evi.** Owner Süha Ersöz started buying up a neighborhood of
Fodor'sChoice houses carved into a rocky hillside in 1987, and the inn he created from
★ them is delightful. Large, comfortable, and spotlessly clean cave rooms have homey antique furniture, while suites also have gardens, sitting rooms, and giant bathrooms with double-headed showers and claw-foot tubs. With a kitchen that guests can use, a cozy vaulted-ceiling drawing room with computers and a lovely terrace where breakfast is served, and even laundry facilities, this feels more like someone's house than a hotel. **Pros:** extremely hospitable and attentive staff; good for families; good value. **Cons:** closed in winter. ⊠*Esbelli Sokak 8, Ürgüp* ☎*384/341–3395* ⊕*www.esbelli.com* ⌂*10 rooms, 5 suites* ⚑*In-room: safe, kitchen (some), DVD (some), Wi-Fi. In-hotel: laundry facilities, laundry service, some pets allowed, no-smoking rooms* ▤*AE, MC, V* ☉*Closed Nov. 15–Mar. 1* ⑈*BP.*

$$$ 🏨 **Sacred House.** Each room in this luxurious 250-year-old Greek man-
Fodor'sChoice sion is a veritable work of art and decorated with a theme, with names
★ like "Old Chapel," "Fairies Nest," and "The Byzantium Treasury." There's a strong Gothic flair—ornate candelabras, statues of cupids, carved doors—but rooms are still comfortable. Bathrooms, many with Jacuzzis, are similarly extravagant. The building itself is atmospheric, too, with a central courtyard complete with a fountain and hanging vines. **Pros:** unique, romantic ambience; close to town center; excellent food. **Cons:** no views from most rooms; not good for families with kids; room decor is intense and somewhat dark. ⊠*Dutlucami Mah. Barbaros Hayrettin Sokak 25* ☎*384/341–7102* ⊕*www.sacred-house. com* ⌂*12 rooms* ⚑*In-room: no a/c, no phone, safe, no TV, Wi-Fi. In-hotel: restaurant, room service, bar, laundry service, some pets allowed, no-smoking rooms* ▤*AE, MC, V* ⑈*BP.*

$$–$$$ 🏨 **Serinn House.** Opened in 2007, Serinn House combines stylish con-
★ temporary design with cave accommodations. The spacious rooms, which all look onto a central courtyard, are done in sleek wood and outfitted with hip designer rugs and furniture. Bathrooms have glass-enclosed showers with sand-colored stone tiles that match the cave walls. Despite the trendy decor, the atmosphere is unpretentious and

relaxed, and owner Eren Serpen goes out of her way to make sure guests are comfortable. A delicious breakfast including international foods like focaccia, biscuits, and apple crumble (all baked in-house) is served on the upstairs terrace. **Pros:** sophisticated decor; highly personal service; outstanding breakfast. **Cons:** low lighting in bathrooms. ⊠*Esbelli Sokak 36,* ☎*384/341–6076* ⊕*www.serinnhouse.com* ⟿*5 rooms* ⚏*In-room: no a/c, safe, no TV, Wi-Fi. In-hotel: laundry service, no-smoking rooms* ▤*MC, V* ⊘*Closed Nov. 1–Apr. 1* ⓘⓞⓘ*BP.*

$$ ⓣ**Ürgüp Evi.** At the top of the hill and with wonderful views, Ürgüp Evi has charming, large cave rooms with soft lighting, fireplaces, wooden floors, and big, comfortable beds. The bathrooms are modern and there are tubs in the deluxe rooms (one standard room has a shower) and Jacuzzis in the suites. The grassy lawn with colorful beanbag seats is nice for lounging, while the terrace restaurant is a fine place to enjoy a bottle of wine and watch the sunset. **Pros:** relaxed atmosphere and hospitality; good for families. **Cons:** rather steep uphill walk to hotel. ⊠*Esbelli Mah. 54* ☎*384/341–3173* ⊕*www.urgupevi.com.tr* ⟿*11 rooms, 2 suites* ⚏*In-room: no a/c, no TV (some). In-hotel: restaurant, room service, bar, no elevator, laundry service, public Wi-Fi, airport shuttle (fee), no-smoking rooms* ▤*MC, V* ⓘⓞⓘ*BP.*

$$$ ⓣ**Yunak Evleri.** The cave rooms (and a few stone rooms) at Yunak Evleri are both luxurious and stylish, with wood floors, wrought-iron beds, and Ottoman-themed decorative touches. Equally impressive are the bathrooms, which are large and modern. Rooms have either a private balcony or a terrace shared by several rooms. Alcoholic drinks are available on the honor system, there's a music library with CDs guests can borrow to listen to in their rooms, and meals can be served on request in a private dining room. **Pros:** stylish, luxurious atmosphere; inviting public spaces. **Cons:** views from rooms vary; some rooms rather dark. ⊠*Yunak Mah.* ☎*384/341–6920* ⊕*www.yunak.com* ⟿*23 rooms, 7 suites* ⚏*In-room: no a/c, safe, no TV. In-hotel: restaurant, room service, laundry service, Wi-Fi, no-smoking rooms* ▤*AE, MC, V* ⓘⓞⓘ*BP.*

GÖREME

10 km (6 mi) northeast of Nevşehir; 7 km (4 mi) northwest of Ürgüp.

This bustling town with a cluster of restaurants and numerous hotels is the most convenient base for exploring Cappadocia. Traditionally, Göreme has been more or less inundated with backpackers, who still find plenty of inexpensive lodgings, but recently some mid-range and higher-end hotels have opened, too. There are Internet cafés in the main square, and a used-book shop stocks a surprisingly good collection of foreign titles. You can live cheap and meet other travelers in Göreme, but the reason to be here is to see some of the most spectacular fairy chimney valleys in the region and the open-air museums here and at nearby Zelve, both UNESCO World Heritage Sites. They are the two requisite must-sees of Cappadocia and are normally packed with tourists. Göreme is a fairy-chimney valley famous for its spectacular cave churches. Zelve is a valley filled with rock caves about 6 km (4 mi) away, which provides a glimpse into how people lived in the rock-cut communities.

EXPLORING

Fodor'sChoice   **Göreme Open-Air Museum.** See the highlighted feature in this chapter.

★   **Zelve Open-Air Museum.** See the highlighted Göreme feature in this chapter.

WHERE TO STAY AND EAT

$–$$ ✕**A'laturca.** One of the best restaurants in Göreme, A'laturca serves
TURKISH   a delicious array of mezes, including humus with *pastırma* (Turkish
★   pastrami) and grilled calamari. Main courses are stylishly presented
renditions of such Turkish classics as *ali nazik* (grilled meat served over
eggplant with yogurt), but variations on steak, chicken, and seafood
are all excellent and portions are generous. The decor—terra-cotta tile
floors with kilims—is elegant but not overdone. For dessert, don't miss
the walnut-stuffed dried apricots and figs, served warm with clotted
cream. ⊠*Gaferli Mah.* ☎*384/271–2882* ⊟*MC, V.*

$–$$ ✕**Orient Restaurant.** The menu at the Orient is extensive and diverse,
ECLECTIC   including not just typical mezes and grills but also a range of steak and
lamb options, chicken served with sauces of saffron or spinach, and
even pasta. But what's most impressive is the four-course set menu,
which includes several choices of appetizers, mains, and desserts—it's
excellent food at an unbeatable value. The lanterns hanging from the
traditional wooden ceilings and the carved stone walls decorated with
copper trays create an ambience that's attractive and cozy. ⊠*Adnan
Menderes Cad. 3* ☎*384/271–2346* ⊟*AE, MC, V.*

$$$$ ⌂**Anatolian Houses.** With a beautiful setting among the fairy chimneys,
Anatolian Houses is ideal for travelers looking for romantic, upscale
lodgings. The lobby, with its stone arches, contemporary leather chairs,
and glass staircase lit from below, exudes swankness. Pottery and
antiques are showcased in niches in the stone walls. Rooms combine
plush decor with modern conveniences, and bathrooms are superb,
most with Jacuzzis. For further pampering, there's a small but inviting indoor/outdoor pool, hamam, and sauna. A new wing with an
additional 16 rooms and a gym is planned for mid-2009. **Pros:** luxury;
unique and romantic atmosphere. **Cons:** complicated mood-lighting in
rooms is not user-friendly; a bit over the top. ⊠*Gaferli Mah., 50180*
☎*384/271–2463* ⊕*www.anatolianhouses.com.tr* ⇥*19 suites* ⌂*In-
room: no a/c, safe. In-hotel: restaurant, room service, bar, pool, laundry service, Wi-Fi, parking (free), no-smoking rooms* ⊟*AE, MC, V*
⍾*BP.*

$$$ ⌂**Cappadocia Cave Suites.** This high-end hotel in a cluster of fairy chim-
neys provides luxury without feeling overdone or artificial. Comfortable
rooms, most of which are quirky-shaped cave spaces, combine antiques,
old-fashioned wrought-iron beds, and folk-art bedspreads, with mod-
ern conveniences like satellite TVs, subtle lighting, and Jacuzzis in
most bathrooms (a few have showers instead). Suites are larger and
have additional perks like fireplaces. Rooms are connected by pleasant
open-air patios with wicker chairs arranged around glass-covered coffee
tables. **Pros:** luxurious feel; layout allows for privacy; attentive staff.
Cons: bathrooms with Jacuzzis have no place to mount shower head.

⊠*Gaferli Mah., Ünlü Sokak 19,* ☎*384/271–2800* ⊕*www.cappadociacavesuites.com* ⇖*13 rooms, 7 suites* ⌂*In-room: no a/c, safe, Internet, Wi-Fi (some). In-hotel: restaurant, room service, laundry service, parking (free), no-smoking rooms* ⊟*AE, MC, V* ❍*BP.*

WORD OF MOUTH

"Goreme is a great place to stay. While there I stayed at the Hotel Kelebek (the *pansiyon* part) and enjoyed it immensely. The views are wonderful and you can have a 'cave room' too if you want one."
—Mathieu

$ ⌂**Kelebek Hotel & Pension.** A com-
Fodor'sChoice bined backpacker-type *pansiyon*
★ and rather posh hotel, Kelebek offers accommodations ranging from basic cave rooms to spacious suites. *Pansiyon* rooms are smallish but cozy, while the hotel suites have antique decor and look into a tranquil garden courtyard; most also have Jacuzzis. This lodging has a young feel to it, and great views from the rooftop bar/restaurant. Other highlights are the hamam—free for guests staying in the hotel section—and a small pool. **Pros:** exceptionally helpful staff; good value; excellent breakfast. **Cons:** hotel is a longish uphill walk from town center; some *pansiyon* rooms noisy due to proximity to common areas. ⊠*Aydınlı Mah.* ☎*384/271–2531* ⊕*www.kelebekhotel.com* ⇖*21 rooms, 12 suites* ⌂*In-room: no a/c (some), no phone (some), safe (some), no TV (some). In-hotel: restaurant, pool, laundry service, Wi-Fi, some pets allowed, no-smoking rooms* ⊟*MC, V* ❍*BP.*

$ ⌂**Kısmet Cave House.** In a less touristy neighborhood of Göreme, this hotel stands out for its cozy feel, lovely atmosphere, and friendly and helpful owner. Each of the carefully decorated rooms (three are cave rooms, the others are stone) is named after a different flower, which features in colorful paintings on the room's walls and wooden furniture. Bathrooms are modern and attractive, with walk-in showers and/or Jacuzzis. **Pros:** extraordinary hospitality; beautiful, inspired decor; personal, intimate feel. **Cons:** rooms are not so large; ground-floor rooms receive some noise from surroundings. ⊠*Kağnı Yolu 9* ☎*384/271–2416* ⊕*www.kismetcavehouse.com* ⇖*7 rooms, 1 suite* ⌂*In-room: no a/c, no phone, no TV (some), Wi-Fi (some). In-hotel: restaurant, room service, laundry service, Wi-Fi, no-smoking rooms* ⊟*No credit cards* ❍*BP.*

UÇHISAR

7 km (4 mi) east of Nevşehir or 3 km (2 mi) southwest of Göreme on the Avanos–Nevşehir road.

A beautiful village on a hill, dominated by the Uçhisar Castle, the highest fairy chimney in all the land, Uçhisar has some of the nicest places to stay in Cappadocia. There are some carpet and rug shops here, but most of the town is residential, with clustered stone houses overlooking the valleys. Chickens peck along back streets and are tended to by women who live in nearby caves. From here, it's easy to take off for a walk down Pigeon Valley (Güvercinlik Vadisi), so named for the birds the villagers raise in distinctive-looking cotes lodged in the walls of the valley.

Continued on page 380

WORD OF MOUTH

"Nature is not the same everywhere. A day's hike took us to visit these natural phenomenons—a product of erosion over time."

— julzie49

ROCK OF AGES
UNEARTHING HOLY CAPPADOCIA

A fantasy come true, Cappadocia's phantasmagorical landscape of rock pinnacles, or "fairy chimneys," is one of Turkey's most otherworldly sights. A natural hideout—thanks to Mother Nature's chiseling tools of wind and water—the region became a sort of promised land for Anatolia's earliest Christians. Over the course of the 6th to 12th centuries, these early Cappadocian dwellers incised the fantastic escarpments of Göreme and Zelve with a honeycomb of cave churches. Today you can trace the saga of the early Christians' religious faith by exploring this spectacular setting. As the first monks might have proclaimed: You have to believe it to see it!

Opposite: Cappadocia. Top: Göreme National Park

AN EARLY CHRISTIAN WONDERLAND

Remote and inaccessible, Cappadocia seemed custom-made for early Christian communities, whose members erected their churches in hollowed-out caves and expanded vast underground cities to hide from enemies and live reclusive monastic lives.

The story of Cappadocia begins more than ten million years ago, when three volcanoes began a geological symphony that dropped lava, mud, and ash over the region. Over eons, frequent eruptions of Mt. Erciyes, Mt. Hasan, and Mt. Melendiz covered considerable parts of the land with tufa—a porous rock layer formed of volcanic ash—over which lava spread at various stages of hardening.

Erosion by rain, snow, and wind created soaring stone "fairy chimneys," surrealistic shapes of cones, needles, pillars, and pyramids, not unlike the looming pinnacles of Arizona's Monument Valley. As time went on, earthquakes added valleys and rivers (mostly long-vanished) and slashed rifts into the fragile tufa. Depending on the variable consistency of the rock, the changes occurred more or less violently, with utterly fantastic results.

A REAL RUBBLE-ROUSER

Fast forward some millennia. Persecuted by authorities and often on the run from Arabian armies (Cappadocia was a frontier province), early Christians found the region's cliffs, rock pinnacles, and tufa caves ideal for the construction of their secluded colonies. Within 200 years of the death of Jesus, regional bishoprics had been established in nearby Kayseri and Malatya.

By the 4th century the number-one industry of Cappadocia was prayer, and the early recluses carved dwellings into Cappodocia's malleable stone, their only tools sharpened sticks. The simplicity of construction set a fashion that quickly led to the formation of anchorite colonies. These early monastic communities deftly combined the individuality of meditation with the communal work favored by St. Basil.

Above,: Rock formations (chimneys) in the Göreme Valley

THE WORD MADE ROCK

The worship of God remained of uppermost importance here, and cave chapels and churches proliferated, especially throughout the Göreme Valley. Göreme, a later Turkish name meaning "Can't See," became poignantly justified with the first Arab attack in 642. Large numbers of Christians sought refuge in rocky hide-outs and underground cities like Derinkuyu and Kaymaklı, which grew sufficiently large to house populations of up to 20,000 people.

After the emperors of the Isaurian dynasty repulsed the Arabs 200 years later, hollowed-out churches began to appear aboveground. Reflecting contemporary Byzantine architectural styles, they were decorated with geometrical paintings. Following Empress Theodora's restoration of the use of holy imagery in the 9th century, churches were given increasingly ambitious frescoes. Many of these were painted in color schemes that rivaled the yellow, pink, and russet hues of their rock surroundings.

Top, Göreme Open-Air Museum.
Bottom: Rock homes, Göreme Valley

WHAT CREATED CAPPADOCIA'S "FAIRY CHIMNEYS"?

The volcanoes that formed Cappadocia are inactive now, but the most recent may have erupted just 8,000 years ago; Neolithic humans depicted the eruption in cave dwellings at Çatal Höyük. Nature continues to sculpt the landscape of Cappadocia. In the future, it is likely that some formations now visible will have turned to dust, and other forms will have been separated from the mountains, providing new experiences for tomorrow's travelers.

GÖREME: A ROCKBOUND HEAVEN

A UNESCO World Heritage Site, the Göreme Açik Hava Müzesi (Göreme Open-Air Museum) is a must-see for its amazing landscape and churches. These rock-hewn holy sanctuaries may be *in* the earth but they are not *of* it.

While Cappadocia is sprinkled with hundreds of ancient churches—most built between the 10th and 12th centuries, though some as early as the 6th century—the best are found in the open-air museum at Göreme. Many Göreme churches are built in an inscribed Greek cross plan, a common Byzantine design, wherein all four arms of the church are equal in length.

The central dome almost always features a depiction of Christ Pantocrator ("Omnipotent"). Though dictated in part by Cappadocia's landscape, the small size and intimate feel of Göreme's rock-cut churches was also deliberate: the monastic community living here designed them not as houses of worship for the public but as chapels where members of the community could engage in solitary prayer and worship of specific saints.

EARTH AS ART

Most churches were commissioned by local donors who hired teams of professional artists—some local and some brought from as far away as Constantinople—to paint elaborate frescoes of scenes from the Old and New Testaments and the lives of the saints.

Visible in places where frescoes have peeled off, underlying geometric designs, crosses, and other symbols were painted directly onto the rock walls in red ochre. It is thought that these decorations were made when a church was first carved out of the rock, in order to consecrate the space. Sometime later, professional artists then painted their detailed frescoes on top of these designs. Note that the eyes of some of the figures have been scratched out, probably by Muslim adherents who believed that visually representing human beings was blasphemous.

Above: Göreme Valley. Photo by yversace, Fodors.com member. Opposite: Elmalı Kilise (Church with the Apple).

TIPS FOR VISITING GÖREME

In summer, get an early start to beat the heat and the crowds, or go after 5 PM, when it's cooler and the crowds have thinned. The open-air museum covers a large area, with hundreds of caves and crannies to explore, almost all of which are easily reachable on paved paths. Allow a good two hours to get the most out of your visit. ✉ About 1.5 km (1 mi) southeast of Göreme town center. ☎ 384/271-2167 💰 $8 🕐 Daily 8-7 in summer, 8-5 in winter.

WHAT TO SEE AT THE GÖREME OPEN-AIR MUSEUM

Fresco of St. George and St. Theodorus killing the dragon in Yılanlı Kilise.

1 Convent & Monastery. After you enter the site, you'll see a steep rock to your left: this housed a six-story convent, which had a kitchen and refectory on the lower levels and a chapel on the third; large millstones lay ready to block the narrow passages in times of danger. Opposite is a monastery with the same plan. Unfortunately, in 2007 these structures were deemed unsafe and are now closed to visitors.

2 Elmalı Kilise (Church with the Apple). Accessed through a tunnel, this 11th-century church has wonderfully preserved frescoes of biblical scenes and portraits of saints; red and gray tones predominate. There are an impressive nine domes: eight small and one large; the largest shows Christ Pantocrator "on His heavenly throne." You can see the red-ochre geometric designs and crosses where the frescoes have peeled off.

Elmalı Kilise (detail of fresco)

3 Barbara Kilise (Church of St. Barbara). Above the Elmal Kilise, this chapel has only a few frescoes, including Christ Pantocrator and St. Barbara. Far more interestingly, most of the chapel is decorated with red ochre symbols painted on the rock, including geometric designs and some unusual, almost whimsical, creatures.

4 Yılanlı Kilise (Snake Church/Church of St. Onuphrius). Small but intriguing, this church takes its Turkish name from the scene on the left wall depicting St. George slaying the dragon, which here takes the form of a snake. More unusual is the story of St. Onuphrius, on the right wall of the church: the naked saint is depicted with both a beard and breasts. While the official story says that St. Onuphrius was a pious hermit who lived in Egypt, another version has it that the saint was a loose woman who repented, embraced Christianity, and was given a beard.

5 Refectory/Kitchen. You can still imagine the huge rock-carved dining table packed at mealtimes with priests. The table could seat 40 to 50 people; carved into the opposite wall is the place allotted for wine-making. There are several kitchens at Göreme, but this refectory (near the Yılanhı Kilise) is the largest.

6 Karanlik Kilise (Dark Church). Entrance to this church, which was extensively restored by UNESCO, costs an extra 8 YTL, because of the exceptional group of frescoes. Vibrant scenes, dominated by deep blue colors, decorate the walls and domed ceiling; the frescoes have retained their brilliant colors due to the structure of the church, which lets in little light (hence the name). The frescoes show scenes from the Old and New Testaments; the Crucifixion scene is particularly intense.

7 Çarıklı Kilise (Church of the Sandal). Climb up a metal ladder to reach this church, named after the footprints (some might say indentations) below the Ascension fresco; some believe these to be casts of Jesus' own footprints. The beautiful frescoes in this 11th-century church have been restored and portray a similar narrative cycle to those in the Karanlık Kilise. Note also the geometric and floral patterns between the frescoes.

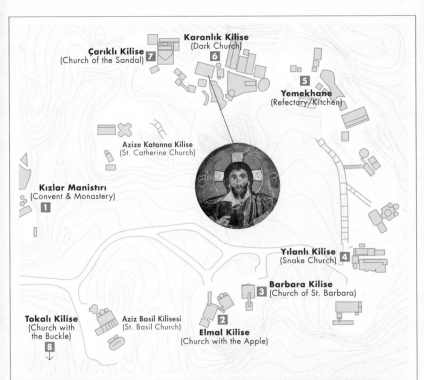

Karanlık Kilise
(Dark Church)
6

Çarıklı Kilise
(Church of the Sandal) **7**

5

Yemekhane
(Refectory/Kitchen)

Azize Katanna Kilise
(St. Catherine Church)

Kızlar Manistırı
(Convent & Monastery)
1

Yılanlı Kilise
(Snake Church) **4**

Barbara Kilise
(Church of St. Barbara) **3**

Tokalı Kilise
(Church with
the Buckle)
8

Aziz Basil Kilisesi
(St. Basil Church)

Elmal Kilise
(Church with the Apple) **2**

8 Tokalı Kilise (Church with the Buckle). Don't miss this church, across from the main museum area and a short way down the road toward Göreme (use the same entrance ticket). The oldest church in the open-air museum, and one of the largest and most impressive, it has high ceilings and brilliant blue colors. It's made up of an "Old Church" and a "New Church." The former was built in the early 10th century, and less than a century later it became the vaulted atrium of the "New Church," which was dug deeper into the rock; both sections have well-preserved frescoes depicting the life of Christ. This is the only church in Göreme in which the narrative scenes take place in chronological order.

Left: Interior of Çarıklı Kilise, Christian murals dating from the 11th century AD.
Right: Murals from Tokalı Kilise

GREAT HIKES

One of the most rewarding walks from Göreme is through the **Rose Valley** (Güllüdere), where cave entrances lead to multi-storey, ornately decorated churches with columns that are two or three stories high. Roman graves, now unreachable, are adorned with Christian crosses and sit high upon eroded fairy chimneys. A hike through the valley often ends up at Paşabaği, the great monastic settlement of fairy chimneys. There are also spectacular hikes through **Love Valley** (Aşk Vadisi), perhaps named for the preponderance of phallus-like rock protrusions.

Though farther afield, the lush **Ihlara Valley** (see the listing in this chapter) also hosts a wealth of rock-carved churches, which are an interesting contrast to those at Göreme because they were carved and decorated not by professional artists, as in Göreme, but by local monks living in the remote valley. The liturgical cycle depicted in the frescoes is somewhat abridged and the style more improvised. There are occasionally even spelling errors, such as in the Kokar Kilise, where the abbreviation of Jesus' name is misspelled with the Greek letters HC instead of IC.

ZELVE'S CAVE DWELLINGS

In approved Cappadocian fashion, man once again combined with nature to create Zelve, a village of rock-hewn houses that even Fred Flintstone would have envied.

While the prizes at Göreme are the fresco-decorated churches, the outdoor museum at Zelve Açik Hava Müzesi (Zelve Open-Air Museum) provides a fascinating look at how people lived in fairy-chimney communities. Zelve was a center of Christian monastic life in the 9th through 13th centuries, and the town was inhabited until the early 1950s, when erosion and cracking began causing slabs of rock to fall and villagers were moved out of the hundreds of cave dwellings.

The site is only about 2,145 feet long, but there's plenty to explore. The valley is made up of several uneven, naturally carved rows of fairy chimneys. These and just about every spare rock-face shelter hundreds of dwellings that vary in size—some are just simple cavelike openings and others are multi-storey houses with rooms on several floors linked by stairs carved deep inside the rocks. There's also a rock-cut mosque and several small churches. Some of the structures have collapsed and giant pieces of carved ceiling lie upside down on the ground.

Be prepared to climb around, and definitely bring a flashlight or you won't be able to explore some of the most interesting and extensive dwellings. You can probably see the whole place in a little over an hour, but you could easily spend more time.

✉ 6 km (4 mi) northeast of the Göreme Open-Air Museum, 3 km (2 mi) off the road to Avanos.

☎ 384/411-7575 💳 $5

🕐 Daily 8-7 in summer, 8-5 in winter

Uçhisar Kalesi *(Uçhisar Castle)* is not so much a castle as the highest fairy chimney in Cappadocia. This striking formation was once a settlement of rock-cut houses where people lived until erosion put everything in danger of collapse and residents moved to houses in the shadow of the giant rock. The hundreds of rooms lend the chimney a Swiss-cheese look. There's a great view

> **TAKE A FLASHLIGHT**
>
> Take a flashlight, or better yet, a headlamp, to explore many of the rock-cut churches, underground cities, and cave dwellings. Small hotels will often lend you, or if you hire a guide, make sure to ask if they can supply one.

of the town and the valleys at the top, but you'll have to walk a lot of stairs to get there. ✉ *Near center of town* 🏷 *$3* ⏱ *Daily 8–sundown.*

WHERE TO STAY AND EAT

$
TURKISH
Fodor'sChoice
★

✕ **Center Restaurant.** It's the opposite of fancy, but locals say this friendly, unpretentious place on the village square is the best restaurant in Uçhisar. It's also reasonably priced. The specialty is a tagine of lamb and artichokes, but even mezes like *cacık* (yogurt with cucumber, herbs, and garlic) and salads like *çoban salatası* (shepherd's salad) are far above average. In warm weather, seating is in a shady garden. ✉ *Belediye Meydanı* ☎ *384/219–3117* 💳 *MC, V.*

$$$
TURKISH

✕ **Elai Restaurant.** A former coffeehouse on the lower slopes of Uçhisar Castle is now an upscale restaurant with a lovely terrace and French flair. The stone walls, Ottoman-style fireplace, and stylish table settings create an elegant atmosphere that complements the sophisticated menu of Turkish and international cuisine. A standout among the mains is the *şaşlık kebabı,* a delicately spiced skewer of lamb served over roasted tomatoes and a phyllo tart filled with pureed eggplant. ✉ *Eski Göreme Cad. 61* ☎ *384/219–3181* ⚭ *Reservations essential* 💳 *AE, MC, V.*

$$$$

🏨 **Cappadocia Cave Resort.** Opened in 2008 and occupying a large swath of Uçhisar's hillside, CCR is truly a resort. With the largest spa in the region—offering every kind of treatment you could want, plus saunas and Turkish baths—and features like a sushi bar, the place could almost make you forget you're in Cappadocia, were it not for the excellent views of the valley below. Decor is plush, veering to over-the-top; some rooms have round beds and Jacuzzis in the bedroom. **Pros:** luxury; extensive spa and dining facilities. **Cons:** Vegas-like decor and lighting in some public areas; room decor and size vary greatly. ✉ *Tekelli Mah. Göreme Cad. 1, 50240* ☎ *384/219–3194* 🌐 *www.ccr-hotels.com* 🛏 *57 rooms, 22 suites* 🛎 *In-room: safe, DVD, Wi-Fi (some). In-hotel: 2 restaurants, room service, bars, pools, gym, spa, laundry service, parking (free), no-smoking rooms* 🍴 *BP.*

$$$
Fodor'sChoice
★

🏨 **Les Maisons de Cappadoce.** French architect Jacques Avizou has restored more than a dozen old houses and turned them into some of the most beautiful places to stay in Cappadocia. The setup is more on-your-own than at a traditional hotel, but all houses (which sleep from four to seven) have a full kitchen; the two- to three-person studios have kitchenettes. The lodgings elegantly blend rustic and modern decor. One house has a beautiful heated swimming pool. **Pros:** lovely atmosphere and magnificent views; houses provide privacy and a less touristy experience; great for families. **Cons:** some studios and their kitchenettes are smallish. ⊠*Belediye Meydanı 24* ☎*384/219–2813* ⊕*www.cappadoce.com* ⤴*16 houses* ⌂*In-room: no a/c, no phone, kitchen, refrigerator, no TV, Wi-Fi. In-hotel: laundry service, some pets allowed* ▤*MC, V* ⋔*BP.*

$$$–$$$$
Fodor'sChoice
★

⛺**Museum Hotel.** The Museum Hotel is a work of art. The owner's impressive collection of antiques, from metalwork to Ottoman caftans to carpets, decorates the rooms and common areas of this luxurious hotel, a cluster of cave and stone buildings connected by labyrinthine passages. Comfortable rooms maintain the contours of the original caves and suites have additional luxuries like Jacuzzis. The showpiece of the terrace is a gorgeous infinity pool with breathtaking views of the valley, and the Lil'a restaurant serves traditional and modern Turkish cuisine. There is talk that they might close the standard rooms and become an all-suites property. **Pros:** unique decor and setting; romantic, luxurious feel; beautiful scenery. **Cons:** rooms vary greatly in size and views, with standard rooms rather small. ⊠*Tekelli Mah. 1* ☎*384/219–2220* ⊕*www.museum-hotel.com* ⤴*14 rooms, 16 suites* ⌂*In-room: no a/c (some), safe, DVD (some). In-hotel: restaurant, room service, bar, pool, laundry service, Wi-Fi, parking (free), some pets allowed, no-smoking rooms* ▤*AE, MC, V* ⋔*BP.*

6

AVANOS

17 km (11 mi) northeast of Nevşehir; 10 km (6 mi) north of Göreme on the Nevşehir–Avanos road; 12 km (7 mi) northeast from Uçhisar.

Avanos is a fun little town on the banks of the Kızılırmak (Red River), so named for the red hue of the clay lining its banks. The town is primarily known for the pottery made from this clay, which vies with tourism as the biggest industry around; the local potters specialize in Hittite shapes and designs inspired by pieces found in archaeological digs across Central Anatolia. Many potters also make ornate pieces in unusual shapes, as well as functional painted items such as wineglasses and tea sets. Pottery is a family affair in Avanos, and as you walk around and check out the local shops selling decorated clay pots and vases, you'll notice family members painting the pieces their fathers and grandfathers make. Almost all of the local potters will demonstrate for free how pottery was made in the old days—with a kick wheel and clay from the river.

Near the lively town square, a wobbly pedestrian bridge crosses the river, the banks of which are lined with cafés. Avanos is also famous for its underground tunnels, some of which may lead to as-yet-undiscovered underground cities or link up with larger ones in Kaymaklı and Derinkuyu. It seems there's a network of secret passages underneath just about every house, which the residents probably once dug in case there was an urgent need to hide or escape. Özkonak, discovered off a dirt road 15 km (9 mi) north of Avanos, may be the largest underground city in Cappadocia, capable of sheltering up to 60,000 people for an extended period of time—it's open for visitors but Derinkuyu and Kaymaklı are by far more interesting.

WHERE TO STAY AND EAT

$
TURKISH

✕ **Bizim Ev Restaurant.** The fanciest restaurant in Avanos has a covered upstairs terrace and a tavernlike interior where local wines are displayed on huge racks. Kilims and pottery hang from the stone walls, and lanterns placed in niches add to the ambience. The delicious but heavy house specialty is *bostan kebabı*, chicken or beef cooked with mushrooms, eggplant, onions, and peppers, topped with cheese, and served in a clay pot. Vegetable appetizers in olive oil and a variety of meat dishes dominate the rest of the menu. ✉ *Orta Mah. Baklacı Sokak 1* ☎ *384/511–5525* ▭ *AE, MC, V.*

¢

▦ **Kirkit Pension.** Four converted Ottoman stone houses comprise this good budget place to stay in Avanos. Clean rooms are decorated with carpets and Uzbek blankets, and some upper-level rooms have nice views of the river. Bathrooms are ample-sized but rather basic. The hotel serves an excellent set-menu dinner, sometimes accompanied by live folk music, which can be enjoyed outside in good weather or, in colder months, in the cozy dining room carved out of the rock. Owner Osman Diler also runs a travel agency and arranges tours for guests. **Pros:** friendly, relaxed atmosphere. **Cons:** bathrooms pretty basic, but European style; some small rooms; no Internet. ✉ *Atatürk Cad. 50 50500, Avanos* ☎ *384/511–3259* ⊕ *www.kirkit.com* ⤺ *15 rooms* ⌂ *In-room: no a/c, no phone, no TV. In-hotel: restaurant, laundry facilities, laundry service, some pets allowed* ▭ *AE, MC, V.*

¢–$
★

▦ **Sofa Hotel.** At the charming Sofa Hotel, rooms are in a complex of 15 Ottoman houses built around a large central courtyard. Sitting areas, labyrinthine passages, and shady outdoor spaces with carpeted floors and long Ottoman-style benches abound. Rooms are unique and are decorated with wood furniture, carpets, and pretty linens. Niches in the stone walls are filled with handicrafts and antiques from the owner's personal collection. Bathrooms are clean, modern, and attractive. **Pros:** excellent value; nice ambience and decor. **Cons:** rooms vary a lot in size, decor, and amenities. ✉ *Orta Mah. Gedik Sokak 9* ☎ *384/511–5186* ⊕ *www.sofa-hotel.com* ⤺ *30 rooms* ⌂ *In-room: no a/c (some), no phone, no TV (some), Wi-Fi (some). In-hotel: restaurant, room service, laundry service, some pets allowed, no-smoking rooms* ▭ *AE, MC, V* ¶⊚¶ *BP.*

POTTERY & THE WORLD'S LARGEST HAIR COLLECTION

Galip Bey's pottery collection is outstanding, though pricey, and his gallery near the post office in the center of Avanos occupies a maze of caverns in the back of the store. Pieces include Hittite-style urns and pots, plates with semipornographic mythological scenes, and copies of famous museum pieces. But hanging from the walls in back is one of the weirdest displays you're likely to see in Turkey, or anywhere: what Galip says is the world's largest collection of human hair. Each lock (he estimates there are now more than 15,000 of them) is clipped to a small card naming the person who gave it to him.

DID YOU KNOW?

In Cappadocia, many of the boutique hotels are built right into the "fairy chimney" caves, with a mix of modern comforts, local handicrafts, and unique rock features.

SHOPPING

The oldest, most famous and by far the funkiest of the pottery shops is **Chez Galip** (☎384/511–4240), which you'll see up a hill near the PTT in the center of town. **Chez Ferhat** (✉*Also near the PTT* ☎384/511–4871) has an excellent array of pieces and will usually let you get a pretty good deal. **Chez Ali Baba** (✉*Fırınbaşı Sokak, up and to the left from the PTT* ☎384/511–3166) is a friendly, family-run store that gives up to 15 days of free pottery-making classes to anyone interested. The shops are generally open seven days a week during tourist season, from 9 to around 6, depending on business.

DERINKUYU AND KAYMAKLI

Kaymaklı is 20 km (12 mi) south of Nevşehir on Rte. 765. Derinkuyu is 9 km (6 mi) south of Kaymaklı on Rte. 765.

The **underground cities** of Cappadocia have excited the imaginations of travelers since the Greek mercenary leader/historian Xenophon wrote about them in the 5th century BC. Some of the cities are merely passages between different dwellings. Others really deserve the title of "city." The impermeable tufa—porous rock—of Cappadocia kept the insides of the cities dry, and interior wells provided water. Some have a special feature—a space above the doorway that came in handy for pouring boiling oil onto would-be attackers. **Derinkuyu**, meaning "deep well," is the most extensive of the known underground cities that have been explored, though it's believed that Özkonak, north of Avanos, might be even larger. Seven floors, reaching to a depth of 55 meters (180 feet), in this subterranean labyrinth are open to the public, though there may be far more floors that are unexplored. There are stables, wineries, a chapel, school, scores of other interconnected rooms, and as many as 600 entrances and air ducts. You'll also see a handful of millstone-like stones used to block off different passageways to protect the city from invaders, plus a ventilation shaft plunging more than 55 meters from ground level. In parts, you'll have to walk doubled over almost in half for a hundred meters (two-thirds of a mile) through a cave corridor. It's an amazing, almost surreal, experience. **Kaymaklı**, about 9 km (6 mi) north of Derinkuyu, was discovered in 1950 and has been opened up to a depth of about 400 feet so far; some believe it is connected to Derinkuyu. Sloping corridors and steps connect the floors of Kaymaklı, with cemeteries and kitchens on every other level. The ceilings are lower here and almost impossible for tall people to navigate. If you're only going to visit one underground city, do Derinkuyu. ☎*Derinkuyu: 384/381–3194, Kaymaklı: 384/218–2500* 🎟*15 TL for each city* ⊙*Daily, summer 8–7, winter 8–5.*

IHLARA VALLEY

★ *About 110 km (66 mi) south of Nevşehir; take Rte. 300 west to Aksaray, then go 42 km (25 mi) southeast past Selime.*

The landscape changes dramatically when you head south through Cappadocia toward Ihlara: the dusty plains turn rich with vegetation, and the Melendiz River carves a rift into the sheer tufa cliffs, which rise up to 490 feet. If you have enough time to spend in Cappadocia, it can be very refreshing to see green—and water—as you hike through the lush valley and explore some of the dozens of churches hidden in nooks above the river. But apart from the churches, this terrain might not really seem like Cappadocia to you, because there are no fairy chimneys.

There are three entrances to the 14-km-long (8½-mi-long) valley: from Selime at the north end, from Belisırma in the middle, and from Ihlara at the south end. Walking the entire valley will take you the better part of a day, but if you just want to get a taste of it, the most interesting section is the Ihlara Vadi Turistik Tesisleri, where a cluster of fresco-decorated churches are within walking distance of one another. You have to walk down more than 400 steps to get there. Belisırma village, inside the valley roughly a three-hour walk from either end, is also an interesting area and has a handful of scenic restaurants. ⊠*Ihlara Vadi Turistik Tesisleri, 2 km (1 mi) from Ilhara village* 🖭*5 TL* 🕓*Daily 8–7 in summer, 8–5 in winter.*

OFF THE BEATEN PATH

You'll need your own transportation and some time to get to the magnificent **Soğanlı Kaya Kiliseleri**, about 80 km (48 mi) southwest of Kayseri on Route 805 toward Niğde; look for the sign off the highway just after Yeşilhisar. You'll likely be alone to explore hundreds of rock dwellings and churches cut into the cliffs. A path follows a little stream past enormous, house-sized boulders and comes to churches with domed ceilings and hundreds of other dwellings and rooms that curve around a wooded canyon. It's completely quiet except for the birds chirping and the frogs croaking. Climb up the cliff face and look around from the top for an awesome experience.

WHERE TO STAY AND EAT

$$ 🍴**Karballa Hotel.** In Güzlyurt, about 10 km (6 mi) from Ihlara village, this hotel is in a graceful 19th-century stone building that was once a Greek monastery. The former refectory has been turned into an attractive vaulted dining room, and a swimming pool is set in beautiful gardens. The rooms—four in the main building, the rest in a secondary building—are rather basic, though there are some pleasant multilevel units that are good for families. **Pros:** atmospheric setting; pool. **Cons:** rooms are rather small and don't live up to the ambience of the building; rates a bit high. ⊠*Çarşıiçi 68500, Güzelyurt/Aksaray* ☎*382/451–2103* ⊕*www.karballahotel.com* ⤢*20 rooms* &In-room: no a/c, no phone, no TV. In-hotel: restaurant, bar, pool, laundry service, Wi-Fi, some pets allowed ⊟*AE, MC, V* 🕓*Closed Nov. 1–Mar. 15* 🍽*BP.*

NIĞDE

126 km (78 mi) southwest of Kayseri on Rte. 805; 85 km (53 mi) south of Nevşehir on Rte. 765.

Niğde is a town with a lot of new factories and old farms, a lot of dust and not a whole lot that's worth seeing. The city flourished under the Seljuks in the 13th century. They built the triple-domed Alaaddin Cami and the neighboring 11th-century fortress. The Ak Medrese, built in 1409, has stone carvings and a small museum and cultural center.

6

The underground city of Derinkuyu is believed to have been home to about 20,000 people.

A little outside of town is the Eski Gümüşler Monastery, probably the only reason to come to Niğde as a traveler.

Eski Gümüşler Manastiri *(Eski Gümüşler Monastery).* The ticket man here says the 11th-century Eski Gümüşler church inside the complex has the only picture of a smiling Virgin Mary in the world. Others say that this is due to an error made during the church's restoration. Whatever the case, the frescoes inside, though dark, are beautiful and amazingly well preserved. (The "smiling" Virgin Mary is in a rock niche in the back left corner of the church.) Parts of the monastery were carved as early as the 7th century but the frescoes, most from around the 11th century, were painted over by local Turkish Muslims, for whom depicting humans was a sin (idolatry). The pictures were cleaned and carefully recovered in the 1960s. In a room above the church are frescoes of animals, thought to be depicting scenes from Aesop's fables—an unusual example of nonreligious art in this region. The monastery also contains a little underground city, a kitchen, and lots of rock-carved rooms around a central courtyard. The sign for the monastery will be one of the first things you'll see at the entrance to Niğde from Kayseri; it's about 3 km (2 mi) down the road from there. ✉ *9 km (6 mi) northeast of Niğde, left off Rte. 805, in village of Gümüşler* 🎫 *3 TL* ☾ *Daily, summer 8–6, winter, 9–5; watchman will unlock bldg. for you.*

HACIBEKTAŞ

46 km (28 mi) north of Nevşehir.

You're likely to find Hacıbektaş a bit boring and unexceptional—unless you're there for the lively festival celebrating the town's spiritual name-sake in mid-August. Hacı Bektaş Veli founded a Muslim sect here in the 13th century that was a synthesis of Sunni and Shiite thought, blended with a touch of Christianity. He became the spiritual leader of the Janissary warriors of the Ottoman Empire and gained a following of dervishes (Bektaşis or Alevis) as well as some considerable political influence. The three-day festival celebrating him begins on August 16th each year and is a colorful, popular affair with Sufi dancing and music in the streets. The souvenir shops sell trinkets with pictures of Atatürk, Hacı Bektaş, and the Imam Ali.

Hacı Bektaş is buried in a tomb inside the **museum,** the main attraction in town. ⊠*In the center of town* ⊕*www.hacibektas.com* ⊠*2.50 TL* ⊙*Tues.–Sun. 8–6.*

KAYSERI

6

80 km (48 mi) east of Ürgüp.

GETTING HERE AND AROUND

Kayseri's airport is 5 km (3 mi) from the city center and is served by several Turkish airlines. Onur Air has its own shuttle from the airport to downtown, but if you fly in on another airline (such as THY or Pegasus) you'll have to take a taxi. In 2007, Kayseri opened a new bus station which is modern, bright, and squeaky clean, but at 10 km (6 mi) from the city center, much less conveniently located than the old one. A taxi from the new bus station into the city center costs around $15 (more at night), but there are also public buses you can take for about $1. Once you're downtown, all the major sites are within walking distance of one another.

ESSENTIALS

Visitor Information (⊠*Zeynel Abidin Türbe Yanı, next to Hunat Hatun complex* ☎*352/222–3903* 🖷*352/222–2581*).

EXPLORING

Kayseri is an old, socially conservative city famous for its Seljuk mosques, an imposing 6th-century citadel, and carpets. The city is now experiencing an industrial boom, which many believe is largely financed by companies with conservative Islamist roots. Hundreds of factories have been constructed here in recent years, and ambitious city plans imply that at least someone believes the boom will continue.

Most visitors these days will see Kayseri only because it has the largest airport serving the Cappadocia region. There's a tourism office in the main square across from the citadel, near the Hunat Hatun Cami, but it may or may not be open when you go. If you have a car and an hour or two to spare, take a whirl through the center of town; check out the citadel, the mosques, and the impressive main square; then hit the road again.

"The predominant practice with wish trees, as can be seen here, is to tie small pieces of fabric or plastic to the branches of the tree, and then to make a wish." —photo by txupham, Fodors.com member

Mt. Erciyes, at 12,922 feet and 26 km (16 mi) south of Kayseri, is the tallest peak in central Anatolia. It's one of three volcanoes whose enormous eruptions over a period of some 10 million years covered Cappadocia with lava and ash, the raw material that eventually gave rise to the region's surreal moonscape. Today, the peak that overlooks Kayseri is covered with snow even at the hottest time of the year. The hour-long drive west out of Kayseri to the villages of central Cappadocia passes through an unattractive landscape that looks something like an abandoned construction site. Hints of more interesting landscapes begin to appear as you approach Ürgüp, when the landscape starts to explode into a surreal valley of giant phallus-like protrusions.

WHAT TO SEE

Arkeoloji Müzesi *(Archaeological Museum)*. The best pieces here are from Kültepe, site of the ancient city of Kanesh, which was settled about 4,000 years ago and comprised the most important trading colony in Anatolia under Assyrians. Merchants from all parts of the reachable world traded metals, foods, spices, and fabrics there and among the findiings shown here are many impressive cuneiform tablets dating from 1920–1840 BC. Greek and Roman artifacts are also exhibited, including a small but touching Roman statue of a pair of lovers. ⊠ *Kışla Cad. 2* ☎ *352/222–2149* 💷 *3 TL* ⏱ *Tues.–Sun. 8–5.*

Within **Atatürk Parkı** is the **Kurşunlu Cami,** built in 1585.

Bedestan. Kayseri's 15th-century *bedestan* (covered market), restored in 1870 after a fire, is noted for its carpets—and there are plenty of exceptional pieces from which to choose. A word on Kayseri and its carpet salesmen: in Turkish folklore the people of Kayseri are renowned for being cunning in business, so keep your wits about you during sales pitches. Accept the tea they offer; this gesture is a normal part of the pitch and carries no obligations. Next to the bedestan is the **covered bazaar,** built in 1859 and now filled with shops selling various necessities of Turkish life. ⊠ *West of the Citadel.*

About 4 km (2½ mi) east of Kayseri is the **Çifte Kümbet** *(Twin-Vaulted Mausoleum).* This Seljuk octagonal tomb was built in 1243 for one of the wives of Keykubat I. ⊠ *Take Sivas Cad. east out of Kayseri.*

Çifte Medrese *(Twin Seminaries).* This complex in Mimar Sinan Parkı may be the oldest medical school in Europe. It's almost certainly the first in Anatolia, built in 1206 from money left by the daughter of a Seljuk sultan, who is entombed on the right side of the courtyard. The two restored seminaries—the Gıyasiye Medrese and Şifaiye Medrese—have been turned into a museum of medical history; of particular interest are the ancient operating room, the carvings of snakes, and the very small rooms for mental patients, which give an idea of how the Seljuks healed their sick and wounded. The museum has been closed since 2008 for restorations and is expected to reopen by the end of 2009, so check open times and admission costs, which may change. ⊠ *Mimar Sinan Parkı* ☎ 352/231–3565 ⊠ *About $1.25* ⊙ *Wed.–Sun. 8–noon and 1–5.*

Hunat Hatun Cami, Medrese ve Türbe *(Hunat Hatun Mosque Complex).* The Hunat Hatun mosque complex is just east of the citadel, and includes a hamam that is still in use, a former religious school, and a tomb. The mosque is named after Hunat Hatun, the wife of the greatest Seljuk Sultan, Alaaddin Keykubat. She was a Georgian princess and is suspected to have poisoned her husband when he was about to disinherit their son from the throne. The *medrese* was constructed in 1237 after the death of her husband and rise of her son. The entrance portals of both the mosque and the medrese are ornately carved, conical half-domes typical of the Seljuks. The mosque and its courtyard can hold some 10,000 people, and are usually full for Friday prayers. The medrese now contains a café and small jewelry and trinket shops. The tiny tomb of Hunat Hatun is reached by going through a shop in the southeast corner of the medrese. ⊠ *Talas Cad. at Cumhuriyet Meyd.* ▨ *Free* ⊙ *Daily 8–5.*

Kayseri Hisarı *(Kayseri Fortress).* Made of forbidding black volcanic stone, this 6th-century fortress is still the most salient prominent landmark in Kayseri. The citadel was built on the orders of the Byzantine Emperor Justinian and substantially repaired by the Seljuks in 1224. Inside, its walls are loads of little bazaar shops, most selling goods that you're unlikely to feel compelled to buy—cheap belts, shoes, cell phone covers, spices, and electronics. A small mosque inside was commissioned by the Ottoman conqueror of Constantinople, Fatih Sultan Mehmet.

Kayseri is known for the **Seljuk tombs** that lie scattered about the town. The most interesting is the **Döner Kümbet,** or Revolving Tomb, on Talas Caddesi. All of its 12 panels have bas-reliefs, including one of the Tree of Life. ⊠ *Talas Cad., 1 km (½ mi) south of citadel.*

Ulu Cami *(Ulu Mosque).* Construction of the twin-domed "Great Mosque," the city's oldest mosque, was begun in 1135 and completed in 1205. ⊠ *Behind the bedestan.*

WHERE TO STAY AND EAT

¢–$ ✕ **Beyazsaray.** If you want to eat with the locals, try this inexpensive spot
TURKISH   where the house specialty is *oltu kebap,* a sandwichlike affair of spit-roasted meat. There's a range of other options, from *pides* to the usual kebabs and grilled meats. The ground level has a convenient take-out counter, while the upper floors progress from borderline tacky decor to a nicer ambience as you go higher up. ⊠ *Millet Cad. 8* ☎ *352/221–0444* ▤ *AE, MC, V.*

¢–$ ✕ **Elmacıoğlu İskender.** Next to the citadel, Elmacıoğlu has been around
TURKISH   since 1959 and is considered the best place in Kayseri for *İskender*
★   *kebap,* thin slices of grilled lamb served over *pide* bread with yogurt and a tomato sauce. If that doesn't sound filling enough, gild the lily by ordering the "Elmacıoğlu İskender kebab," which has meatballs on top. The place feels almost swank, particularly the second floor with its cream-colored leather-covered chairs and dark wood trim. ⊠ *Millet Cad. 5* ☎ *352/222–6965* ▤ *AE, DC, MC, V.*

$$$ ⌂ **Hilton Kayseri.** The huge, white, concave Hilton is smack in the middle of downtown Kayseri, overlooking the city's ancient mosques and citadel. The lobby is refreshingly airy and well lit, though the gold-topped faux marble columns and potted palm trees seem more desert sheik than Kayseri. Rooms are comfortable and bathrooms are modern. The 12th-floor rooftop restaurant has great views of the city and Mt. Erciyes, while the fitness center has a good range of facilities. **Pros:** all the modern amenities and comforts expected of an international luxury hotel. **Cons:** smallish rooms are overwhelmed by king-size beds; expensive Internet. ⊠ *Cumhuriyet Meydanı 1, 38010* ☎ *352/207–5000* ⊕ *www. hilton.com* ⟿ *203 rooms, 9 suites* ⌕ *In-room: safe, Wi-Fi. In-hotel: 2 restaurants, room service, bars, pool, gym, laundry service, parking (free), some pets allowed, no-smoking rooms* ▤ *AE, MC, V.*

$$ ⌂ **Hotel Almer.** This hotel is modern, clean, and conveniently located a few blocks from the main square. Rooms are smallish but comfortable and enlivened by a rather intense red laminate trimming. Bathrooms have a combination shower and half-size tub. There's a lobby bar and a restaurant serving local specialties. **Pros:** location in city center. **Cons:** rooms show small signs of wear and tear; no nonsmoking rooms. ⊠ *Osman Kavuncu Cad. 1, Düvenönü Meyd.* ☎ *352/320–7970* ⊕ *www.almer.com.tr* ⟿ *70 rooms, 7 suites* ⌕ *In-room: Wi-Fi. In-hotel: restaurant, room service, bar, laundry service, parking (no fee)* ▤ *MC, V* ⓘ *BP.*

KONYA

258 km (160 mi) south of Ankara; 142 km (88 mi) southwest of Ihlara.

GETTING HERE AND AROUND

Turkey's major bus companies (Ulusoy, Varan, etc.) don't serve Konya, but Metro, Kontur, and Özkaymak do.

Traveling by train from Istanbul to Konya takes a good bit longer than going by bus. On the upside, not only is it cheaper but you can get a sleeper car. The daily Meram Express costs about $18; it leaves Istanbul at 7:20 PM and arrives in Konya at 10:50 the next morning. From Konya, it departs at 5:40 PM and arrives in Istanbul at 9:20 the next morning. The Toros Express goes three times a week during the daytime, leaving Istanbul at 8:55 AM and arriving in Konya at 10:30 PM. From Konya, it departs at 4:15 AM and arrives in Istanbul at 6 PM. The cost is about $13.

> ### WORD OF MOUTH
>
> "A side trip to Konya from Cappadocia may be an interesting one as the Mausoleum of Rumi is worth visiting especially during the month of Ramadan. It will definitely be a different experience. If you think it is too far, you may go to Hacibektas from Cappadocia for a similar visit."   —ANATOLIANCRUISER

Modern Konya is extremely spread out, but its tourist attractions are all concentrated in the city center near Alaaddin Tepesi (Alaaddin Hill). Konya's bus terminal is about 15 km (9 mi) north of the city center; it's a 30-minute tram ride from the terminal to the Alaaddin tram stop downtown. The airport, 18 km (11 mi) to the northeast, and the train station, 3 km (2 mi) southwest of the city center, are both accessible only by city bus or taxi. Taxis are relatively inexpensive for short distances downtown but can add up if you are going to the bus terminal or airport.

ESSENTIALS
Bus Information Metro (☎ 332/265–0040 ⊕ www.metroturizm.com.tr). **Kontur** (☎ 332/265–0080 ⊕ www.kontur.com.tr). **Özkaymak** (☎ 332/265–0160 ⊕ www.ozkaymak.com.tr).

Visitor Information (✉ Mevlâna Cad. 73, by Mevlâna Museum ☎ 332/351–1074 🖷 332/350–6461).

Tour Information Selene Tour (✉ Aziziye Cad. Ayanbey Sokak 22/B ☎ 332/353–6745 ⊕ www.selene.com.tr).

EXPLORING
Konya is famous for being the location of Rumi's tomb, and is also known throughout Turkey as a very religious and rather conservative city. Its religious attractions draw Muslims on pilgrimages and Turkish schoolchildren on trips, as well as foreign and local tourists. The city is experiencing a boom in popularity that coincides with the surging interest worldwide in the Sufi mystic poet Mevlâna Celaleddin Rumi and the rise to power of a moderate Islamist government in Turkey. During the annual Mevlâna festival that takes place each December (*see the Mevlâna Celaleddin Rumi CloseUp box*), Konya is transformed by an influx of pilgrims—and other curious souls—who come from around the world to honor and observe the anniversary of the Mevlâna's death. At other times of the year, Konya is a fairly quiet and even provincial city, and you can probably see most of the sights in about a day. Note that the dervishes do not whirl regularly outside of festival time, and you're more likely to see them in Istanbul than in Konya. That said,

the Mevlâna Museum, which holds Rumi's tomb, is an impressive site. The city also has a long and interesting history, including its stint as the capital of the Seljuk Empire from the mid-12th through the 13th century, and some notable mosques and other buildings date back to that period.

4 **Alaaddin Cami** *(Alaaddin Mosque).* Completed in 1220 and restored in the 1990s, this graceful mosque crowning Alaaddin Tepesi (Alaaddin Hill) is in the Syrian style—unusual for Anatolia; the architect was Syrian. The pulpit stands in a forest of marble columns taken from Roman temples. Most of the hill is devoted to a park, which contains a café. Below are the scanty remains of a Seljuk palace—two venerable stumps of walls. The city has for some reason deemed it expedient to throw an unsightly concrete shelter over them.

3 **Büyük Karatay Medrese** *(Büyük Karatay Seminary).* Emir Celaleddin Karatay founded this seminary in 1251 and his tomb is in a small room to the left of the main hall. The medrese now houses a ceramics museum, the **Karatay Müzesi** (Karatay Museum), and it's easy to understand why this particular building was selected for that purpose. Its dome is lined with tiles, blue predominating on white, and the effect is dazzling. A frieze beneath the dome is in excellent condition, and the hunting scenes on the rare figurative tiles from the Kubadabad Palace in Beyşehir show the influence of Persia on Seljuk art. Included in the spectacular ceramics collection are figurines of humans and animals, with vine leaves highlighting them with shades of cobalt blue and turquoise. ✉*Alaaddin Bul., at intersection with Ankara Cad.* ☎*332/351–1914* 🖅*2 TL* ⊗*Daily 8–12:30 and 1:30–5.*

5 **İnce Minare Medresesi** *(Seminary of the Slender Minaret).* The minaret at this 13th-century institution is bejeweled with glazed blue tiles. Unfortunately, it is now only half its original height, thanks to a bolt of lightning that struck in 1901. Note also the especially ornate decoration of the building's entry portal. Now a museum, the İnce Minare displays a fine collection of stone and wood carvings. Highlights are the fascinating Persian-influenced Seljuk stone reliefs, which include double-headed eagles, winged angels, and strange creatures that are part human and part bird or beast. ✉*Alaaddin Bul., west side of Alaaddin Tepesi* ☎*332/351–3204* 🖅*3 TL* ⊗*Daily 9–12:30 and 1:30–5.*

2 **Mevlâna Museum.** When Rumi died in 1273, he was buried in Konya beside his father and a great shrine was erected above them. As Rumi's mystic teachings of love and tolerance, ecstatic joy and unity with God spread and his poetry gathered a greater following, his mausoleum drew pilgrims from all parts of the Islamic world. In 1926, three years after the establishment of the Turkish Republic, his shrine was declared a museum, though the Sufi order he founded had been officially banned in 1925 as part of the drastic secularization of Turkish society under Atatürk. Today the museum is one of the most visited sites in Turkey, attracting more than 2 million people a year, the majority of them local tourists. The Sufi dervishes have also been assigned a special status as "Turkish folk dancers," allowing them to perform their mystic whirling without the state overtly recognizing its undeniable religious basis.

Continued on page 398

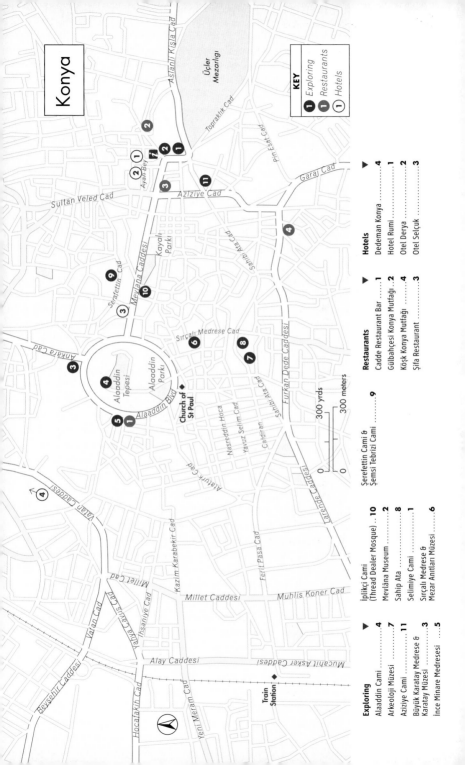

Konya

KEY

- ▶ Exploring
- ▶ Restaurants
- ① Hotels

Exploring ▶

Alaaddin Cami	4
Arkeoloji Müzesi	7
Aziziye Cami	11
Büyük Karatay Medrese & Karatay Müzesi	3
İnce Minare Medresesi	5
İplikçi Cami (Thread Dealer Mosque)	10
Mevlâna Museum	2
Sahip Ata	8
Selimiye Cami	1
Sırçalı Medrese & Mezar Anıtları Müzesi	6
Şerefettin Cami & Şemsi Tebrizi Cami	9

Restaurants ▶

Cadde Restaurant Bar	1
Gülbahçesi Konya Mutfağı	2
Köşk Konya Mutfağı	4
Şifa Restaurant	3

Hotels ①

Dedeman Konya	4
Hotel Rumi	1
Otel Derya	2
Otel Selçuk	3

0 ___ 300 yrds

0 ___ 300 meters

TURKEY'S
WHIRLING DERVISHES

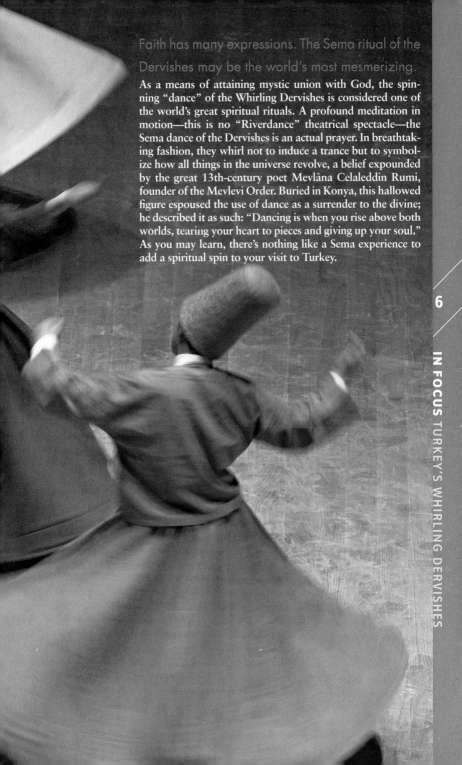

As a means of attaining mystic union with God, the spinning "dance" of the Whirling Dervishes is considered one of the world's great spiritual rituals. A profound meditation in motion—this is no "Riverdance" theatrical spectacle—the Sema dance of the Dervishes is an actual prayer. In breathtaking fashion, they whirl not to induce a trance but to symbolize how all things in the universe revolve, a belief expounded by the great 13th-century poet Mevlâna Celaleddin Rumi, founder of the Mevlevi Order. Buried in Konya, this hallowed figure espoused the use of dance as a surrender to the divine; he described it as such: "Dancing is when you rise above both worlds, tearing your heart to pieces and giving up your soul." As you may learn, there's nothing like a Sema experience to add a spiritual spin to your visit to Turkey.

AROUND THE WHIRL

Extremely detailed and specific directions govern even the slightest pattern and gesture in the ritual dance of the Whirling Dervishes.

1 To help lift themselves into the spiritual realm, the twelve *Semazena* dancers are accompanied by twelve musicians, who play the *ney* (reed flute) and the kettledrum, whose beating signals God's call to "be."

2 First dropping their black cloaks—to signify the shedding of earthly ties—the Dervishes stand with their arms crossed over their chests, a posture that represents the number one, a symbol of God's unity. Their costumes are full of symbolism: the conical hat, or *sikke*, represents a tombstone, the jacket is the tomb itself, and the floor-length skirt, or *tennure*, a funerary shroud. The latter is hemmed with chain to allow it to rise with dramatic effect.

3 The Dervishes' endless spinning—always to the left, counter-clockwise—symbolizes the rotation of the universe. To receive God's goodness, they keep their right hands extended to the sky; to channel God's beneficence to earth, their left hands point toward the floor.

4 The Dervishes usually perform for four *selams*, or musical movements. For the last, they are joined by their Sheikh Efendi—incarnating the figure of Rumi—who stands on a red sheepskin (oriented toward holy Mecca) to represent the channel of divine grace. At the climax, this *semazenashi* (dance master) joins the others and whirls in their midst. At the finale, the Dervishes put their cloaks back on—a symbol of return to the material world.

Above: The Sufi mystic, Mevlâna Celaleddin Rumi, inspired the whirl of the dervishes.

WHERE THE DERVISHES WHIRL

Ever since the days of the Ottoman sultans, the Whirling Dervish rituals have been wildly popular events. In Konya, Dervishes present their spinning dances during the annual, mid-December Mevlâna festival, a week-long series of events dedicated to Rumi. **Konya's Tourism Information Office** (tel. 332/351–1074) can help you find tickets and make hotel reservations for the festival; it is wise to book tickets as far in advance as possible. The Dervishes have been assigned a special status as "Turkish folk dancers," and their presentations are scheduled in many cities around Turkey (in fact, you stand a better chance of catching them in Istanbul than Konya) and, frequently, in cities around the world. Check with local tourist boards and hotel concierges to see if your itinerary might coincide with one of the Whirling Dervish ceremonies.

Mevlâna Celaleddin Rumi

The museum in Konya calls Rumi (also known as Jalal al-Din Muhammed Rumi or simply as "Mevlâna"), a "Turkish theosophic philosopher," though in reality he was born in present-day Afghanistan and wrote his poetry in Persian. Born in the city of Balkh on September 30, 1207, he came to Konya in 1228, when it was a part of the Seljuk Empire. By that time the young Rumi had already been deeply influenced by mystic readings and had made the hajj to Mecca.

Rumi's transformative spiritual moment came in 1248, when his companion, Shams Tabrizi, who initiated Rumi into Islamic mysticism, mysteriously disappeared. Rumi's grief on his beloved friend's disappearance—suspected to be a murder—sparked a prodigious outpouring of searching verse, music, dance, and poetry. After years of searching for his friend and teacher, Rumi found himself in Damascus, where he had a revelation that the universe was one and each person could be his own holy universe. He exclaimed:

"Why should I seek? I am the same as he.

His essence speaks through me.

I have been looking for myself!"

For the rest of his life, Rumi attributed much of his own poetry to Shams, and in a way that would become characteristic

and controversial, mixed his love with his fellow man with his love for God and God's love for man. Rumi became known for his tolerance, his espousal of love, and his use of dance and song to reach spiritual enlightenment. Toward the end of his life, he spent 12 years dictating his master work, the *Masnavi*, to a companion. He died in 1273, and the Mevlevi order of dervishes, famous for their *semas*, or whirling ceremonies, was founded after his death.

The central theme of Rumi's philosophy is a longing for unity—of men, of the universe, with God and with God's spirit. Rumi believed in the use of music, poetry, and dancing as facilitators for reaching God and for focusing on the divine. Through ecstatic dancing, singing, or chanting, Sufi worshippers believed they could negate their bodies and vain selves, becoming empty vessels to be filled with love, the essence of the divine. In Rumi's poetry, he talks of God as one might a lover, and the ecstatic states reached through dancing and singing sometimes border on the erotic. In recent years, Rumi's legacy has been revived, ensuring that his timeless teachings endure. His epitaph suggests he would have been happy with that:

"When we are dead, seek not our tomb in the earth, but find it in the hearts of men."

The shrine is a holy site and, in line with Muslim traditions, women visiting it are required to cover their heads; scarves can be borrowed at the entrance to the museum. Visitors are also required to put plastic covers on over their shoes. You first pass through a courtyard with a large *şadırvan*, or ablutions fountain. At the entrance to the mausoleum are two gorgeous carpets, one from the 17th century and the other from the 18th. The interior of the mausoleum resembles the inside of a mosque, with its intricately painted domes, ornate chandeliers, and Islamic inscriptions on the walls. It is well lit and there is music playing, unusual for a Muslim holy place and a further hint that Rumi was not a proponent of the traditional interpretations of Islam. The room contains many dervish tombs, all of them with carved stone turbans that serve as headstones and beautifully decorated in ornate cloth. Rumi's tomb is the largest and at its head are two massive green turbans. The place is usually filled with Muslim pilgrims standing with their palms outward in prayer, and it is not uncommon to see men and women crying before Rumi's grave.

Rumi was famous for his inclusiveness and would have welcomed you here, no matter what your beliefs. He said:

Come, come, whoever you are.
Wanderer, idolator, worshipper of fire,
Come even though you have broken your vows a thousand times.
Come, and come yet again.
Ours is not a caravan of despair.

The two rooms on the left contain beautifully preserved prayer books; dervish clothing and musical instruments; robes and a *seccade*, or prayer rug, that belonged to Rumi; and a mother-of-pearl box containing hair from the prophet Mohammed's beard.

The former kitchen of the complex (to the right of the main entrance) has a display of mannequins dressed as dervishes carrying out various activities in a kitchen, dining area, and living room, giving an idea of what life was like in the dervish brotherhood. ⊠ *Mevlâna Mahallesi* ☎ *332/351–1215* 🎫 *$1.50* ⊙ *May–Oct., Tues.–Sun. 9–7, Mon. 10–7; Nov.–Apr., Tues.–Sun. 9–5, Mon. 10–5.*

8 7 Sahip Ata. A magnificent portal marks the remains of this complex, a group of structures dating from the late 13th century. Mosque buildings here have been converted into an **Arkeoloji Müzesi** (Archaeological Museum). The most significant room has recent findings from the 7000 BC Neolithic site of Çatal Höyük, including pottery, jewelry, weapons and tools, and the remains of an infant burial; these are accompanied by quite informative explanations. There are also artifacts from the Bronze Age and Greek and Roman periods; the 3rd-century-AD marble sarcophagus depicting the Twelve Labors of Hercules is outstanding. ⊠ *Larende Cad.* ☎ *332/351–3207* 🎫 *3 TL* ⊙ *Tues.–Sun. 9–12:30 and 1:30–5:30.*

1 Selimiye Cami *(Selim Mosque).* Sultan Selim II started this mosque in 1558, when he was heir to the throne and governor of Konya, and the structure was completed after he had become Sultan Selim II. The style is reminiscent of that of the Fatih Cami in Istanbul, with soaring arches and windows surrounding the base of the dome. ⊠ *Opposite Mevlâna Museum on Mevlâna Meyd.*

6 Sırçalı Medrese *(Crystalline Seminary).* Opened in 1242 as a school for Islamic jurisprudence and decorated with lavish blue and black tiles, the seminary provides a dignified home for the **Mezar Anıtları Müzesi** (Tombstone Museum). The Seljuk and Ottoman tombstones with inscriptions in Arabic script are impressive, though unfortunately none have labels or dates. ⊠ *Sırçalı Medrese Cad. 16, south of Mimar Muzaffer Cad.* ☎ *332/353–4031* 🎫 *Free* ⊙ *Mon.–Fri. 8:30–5:30.*

Other mosques. On the way to Konya's ancient acropolis, the Alaaddin Tepesi, heading west from Mevlâna Meydanı, are a few mosques on or just off Mevlâna Caddesi. **Şerefettin Cami** was started by the Seljuks in the 13th century and completed by the Ottomans in 1636. The **Şemsi Tebrizi Cami and Türbe,** north of Şerefettin Cami, off Hükümet Alanı, is dedicated to Mevlâna's mentor and friend and contains his mausoleum. Nearby is Konya's oldest mosque, the **İplikçi Cami** (Thread Dealer Mosque), dating from 1202. **Aziziye Cami** (Sultan Abdül Aziz Mosque), which dates from 1676 and was rebuilt in 1875, flanks the bazaar. The mosque displays a combination of Ottoman and Baroque styles and is known for having windows that are larger than its doors.

WHERE TO STAY AND EAT

$ ✕**Cadde Restaurant Bar.** Across the street from the İnce Minaret Medrese,
TURKISH this is one of the few places in the area where you can get a drink with your meal. The menu has standard mezes and kebabs but what's noteworthy is the atmosphere, with musicians playing Turkish classical and folk music to an appreciative, relaxed crowd. The ambience is a bit more nightlife than restaurant—unadorned wooden tables, low lighting, and a bar along the back wall—but in summer there's also an upstairs terrace for dining. ⊠*Adliye Bulvarı* ▤*No credit cards.*

$ ✕**Gülbahçesi Konya Mutfağı.** Just behind Mevlâna's tomb, this restored
TURKISH old mansion has a terrace with one of the best views you can get of the tomb complex and Selimiye Mosque. In the upstairs rooms, guests sit in traditional Turkish style, crossed-legged on cushions around low, round tables. Specialties include the tasty but heavy *tirit,* a layered concoction of cubed flatbread, yogurt, onions, and chopped lamb, drizzled with melted butter and sprinkled with parsley and ground sumac. There are also variations on *etli ekmek,* such as the "Mevlâna," made with cheese in addition to ground meat. ⊠*Civar Mah. Gülbahçe Sokak 3, Karatay* ☎*332/353–0768* ⌂*Reservations essential* ▤*AE, MC, V.*

$ ✕**Köşk Konya Mutfağı.** In an old mansion down the road from Mevlâna's
TURKISH tomb, this restaurant serves local specialties in a lovely atmosphere.
★ In winter, guests eat in small dining rooms with simple decor but in summer, seating is in the garden. The baby okra soup takes over four hours to prepare and is said to be the best in Konya. There are also excellent meat dishes, but make sure to save room for the *hoşmerim,* an intensely rich local dessert made of pan-fried clotted cream, flour, milk, and sugar, sprinkled with ground pistachio nuts. ⊠*Akçeşme Mah. Topraklık Cad. 66, Karatay* ☎*332/352–8547* ⌂*Reservations essential* ▤*AE, MC, V.*

$ ✕**Şifa Restaurant.** This restaurant on the main drag is far from fancy,
TURKISH but it's been around for a long time and is consistently popular. The menu includes standard Turkish dishes like kebabs and meatballs, plus local specialties *etli ekmek* (flatbread topped with ground meat and spices) and *fırın kebabı* (lamb roasted in the oven in a clay pot). The food is tasty, service is speedy, and you can watch the activity on Mevlâna Caddesi from the floor-to-ceiling windows. ⊠*Mevlâna Cad. 29* ☎*332/352–0519* ▤*AE, MC, V.*

$$$ ⌂**Dedeman Konya.** The towering 18-story Dedeman Konya has filled
TURKISH a gap is the first luxury hotel in downtown Konya. The lobby exudes

opulence, though some may find it a bit overdone. Rooms are spacious, and the state-of-the-art fitness center includes an exercise room, steam bath, sauna, Turkish bath, swimming pools, and a spa. **Pros:** high-class service; multiple dining options; extensive fitness center.

KONYA SPECIALTY

Make sure you try the local specialty, *etli ekmek*, while you're in Konya—flatbread topped with minced meat and spices.

Cons: hotel is 3 to 4 km from Konya's tourist attractions. ⊠ *Özalan Mahallesi, Sille Kavşağı, Selçuklu,* ☎ *332/221–6600* ⊕ *www.dedeman. com* ⌦ *170 rooms, 37 suites* ⚘ *In-room: safe, Wi-Fi. In-hotel: 2 restaurants, room service, bars, pools, gym, spa, laundry service, parking (free), some pets allowed, no-smoking rooms* ▤ *AE, MC, V* ⚑ *BP.*

¢   ▥ **Hotel Rumi.** Just around the corner from Mevlâna's tomb, Hotel Rumi is an excellent option. The lobby, with leather sofas and armchairs, glass-covered coffee tables, and "lucky bamboo" plants, is a breath of contemporary style. Rooms are clean and comfortable and bathrooms are modern and have either tubs or showers. The fifth-floor terrace, where breakfast is served, has excellent views overlooking Mevlâna's tomb. There's also a sauna and hamam in the basement. **Pros:** location; professional service; good value. **Cons:** some rooms smell strongly of smoke. ⊠ *Durakfakih Mah. Durakfakih Sokak 5* ☎ *332/353–1121* ⊕ *www.rumihotel.com* ⌦ *30 rooms, 3 suites* ⚘ *In-room: safe, Wi-Fi. In-hotel: room service, gym, laundry service, parking (free), no-smoking rooms* ▤ *AE, MC, V* ⚑ *BP.*

¢   ▥ **Otel Derya.** Otel Derya is a good budget option on a quiet backstreet. Rooms are basic but clean, and bathrooms are large and modern, with good-sized showers. The lobby is somewhat lacking in character but is spacious and well lit. Note that they sometimes have problems with their Internet, so you might have to make your reservations by fax. **Pros:** good value. **Cons:** limited storage space, as rooms have wall hooks instead of wardrobes. ⊠ *Babı Aksaray Mah. Ayanbey Cad. 18, Karatay* ☎ *332/352–0154* 🖷 *332/352–0155* ⌦ *33 rooms* ⚘ *In-room: Wi-Fi. In-hotel: room service, parking (free)* ▤ *AE, MC, V* ⚑ *BP.*

$$ ▥ **Otel Selçuk.** This is one of Konya's oldest hotels, and though it's not much to look at from the outside, from the moment you step into the lobby you can feel its distinguished, slightly old-fashioned atmosphere. Room decor, in creams and dark greens, feels classic if a bit bland, but nice touches include good-sized closets. Amenities include a sauna and steam room. **Pros:** elegant atmosphere; Western-style service. **Cons:** cramped bathrooms. ⊠ *Mevlâna Cad. M. Babalık Sokak 4* ☎ *332/353–2525* ⊕ *www.otelselcuk.com.tr* ⌦ *77 rooms, 6 suites* ⚘ *In-room: safe, Wi-Fi. In-hotel: 2 restaurants, room service, gym, laundry service, parking (free), some pets allowed, no-smoking rooms* ▤ *MC, V* ⚑ *BP.*

SHOPPING

Konya's **bazaar** was once known for its rug shops, but these now are more likely to be found around Alaaddin Caddesi. The bazaar does have an amazing array of ordinary goods, though interesting antiques and handicrafts can also occasionally be found. ⊠ *Market district, near* *intersection of Selimiye Cad. and Karaman Cad.* ☉*Mon.–Sat. during daylight hrs.*

Horozlu Han and Sille. If you're heading out of Konya in the direction of Ankara, look for the fabulous Seljuk portal at the entrance to the ruined Horozlu Han, a former caravansary near the four-lane beginning of Rte. 715. At Sille, 8 km (5 mi) northwest, St. Helena, mother of Constantine the Great, built a small church in AD 327. Nearby, frescoed rock chapels overlook the shores of a tiny artificial lake.

Karavan Kilim Shop. At this treasure trove down the street from the Mevlâna Museum, thousands of carpets and kilims are piled up in a huge, dark wood old-fashioned showroom that feels like a rich man's bazaar. There are also copper items, handicrafts, and antiques, including an extensive collection of carved wooden doors. ✉*Mevlâna Cad. 71/D* ☎*332/351–0425* ▭*AE, MC, V.*

ÇATAL HÖYÜK

48 km (30 mi) southeast of Konya on Rte. 715 to Çumra and then about 20 km north of Çumra to the site; follow the road signs.

GETTING HERE AND AROUND

A round-trip taxi from Konya to Çatal Höyük will cost between 80 TL and 120 TL, depending on your bargaining skills. Alternatively, you can take a bus to the town of Çumra and then a taxi to the site, for around 30 TL all together. There are also public minibuses labeled Küçükköy/Karkın that leave from Konya's downtown Eski Otogar and go to the village where the site is located. These are infrequent, however, so make sure you inquire before leaving Konya about the time of the last returning bus, so you don't get stranded in the village.

EXPLORING

Çatal Höyük is the site of one of the oldest human settlements ever found, dating back to about 7000 BC, during the Neolithic period. It's believed that as many as 8,000 people lived here at a time, in mud-brick houses that were adjacent to one another. The site was inhabited for some 1,400 years, with new houses being built over old ones, resulting in a buildup of mounds over time. The name Çatal Höyük means "forked mound" and comes from the fact that there are two distinctive mounds separated by an indentation, which you can clearly see as you approach the site.

Çatal Höyük was discovered and initially excavated between 1961 and 1965 by the British archaeologist James Mellaart, who found ancient wall murals, the earliest known pottery, human burials, and many domestic artifacts. He widely publicized his findings, especially a number of female figurines, which are believed to point to the worship of a mother goddess by the prehistoric inhabitants of Çatal Höyük. In the 1990s archaeologists resumed work on the excavations. Since then, other theories have been presented about goddess worship at the site, but the iconic figurines—many of which are on display in the Anatolian Museum of Civilizations in Ankara—remain symbolic of Çatal Höyük.

Summer is the most interesting time to visit the site, when you can watch dozens of archaeologists, comprising several international teams, at work on the excavations, but if you can't visit then, there is still a fair amount to see. Near the entrance area, the "Experimental House" is a recreation of a prehistoric Çatal Höyük adobe home. It has been rendered to look as realistic as possible, with foodstuffs, animal pelts, reed mats on the floor, and murals on the walls. The museum, though small, is modern, attractive, and very informative. However, almost all the artifacts in the museum are recreations, the originals being either in the Ankara Museum of Civilizations or the Konya Archaeology Museum.

The excavations themselves are protected by two open-air hangar-like structures. The South Shelter, built in 2002, covers the deepest excavations, begun by James Mellaart and restarted in 1993. Excavations here have uncovered 13 separate settlement layers, and you can get a good idea of the different layers from the visitor area at the top. Unfortunately, explanations are somewhat minimal. The North Shelter, which opened in 2008, houses several excavation areas and has detailed illustrations and numbered photos explaining what's what. The viewable sections change somewhat from year to year, since the archaeologists sometimes close parts of the excavations sites after they finish their work, in order to protect them. ⊕ *www.catalhoyuk.com* 🖅 *2 TL* ⊙ *Daily 8–5.*

ANKARA AND THE HITTITE CITIES

ANKARA

258 km (160 mi) north of Konya, 454 km (281 mi) southeast of Istanbul.

GETTING HERE

As noted in the chapter Planner, air travel isn't much more expensive than the bus, so flying to central Anatolia saves a lot of time. From the airport, a good option is the Havaş bus service, which generally leaves every half-hour and costs about $6. Board in front of the terminal near flight arrivals, and you will be delivered to the Havaş office in Ulus (19 Mayıs Stadium, B Gate) or the bus station. Havaş buses going to the airport leave from the Ulus office every half-hour between 3:30 AM and 11:30 PM and less frequently at night.

At the time of this writing, traveling between Istanbul and Ankara by train takes between 6½ and 9½ hours, considerably longer than by car or bus. However, this is set to change dramatically with the building of a new high-speed rail line, set to being running sometime in 2009, which should knock several hours off the ride.

As of press time, the Ankara Express runs between Ankara and Istanbul; it leaves both places at 10:30 PM and arriving the next morning at 8. The price is about $38 per person for two people sharing a sleeper compartment or $55 for one person in a compartment, and it is by far the most comfortable train in the country. The Anadolu (Anatolia) Express also runs between Ankara and Istanbul, with simultaneous departures from both cities at 10 PM and arrivals at 7 AM. There are no sleeper cars on this train, just regular seats that cost about $10. The final option between Istanbul and Ankara is the Başkent Express, which leaves Istanbul at 10 AM and arrives in Ankara at 4:50 PM, and leaves Ankara at 10:20 AM and arrives in Istanbul at 4:50 PM. The cost is about $18.

If you're traveling from the Mediterranean coast to Ankara by train, your choice is the 9 Eylül Express, which travels between İzmir and Ankara and leaves İzmir at 7:30 PM and Ankara at 8 PM and arrives in both cities around 9:30 the next morning; the cost is about $27 per person. Another option is the İzmir Mavi, or Blue Train, which departs İzmir at 5:30 PM and from Ankara at 6 PM and arrives in both cities around 8 AM; the cost is the same.

GETTING AROUND
Ankara is a big city with chaotic traffic, and you'll save yourself a lot of grief if you park your car and use public transportation. The main neighborhood encompassing the old part of the city is called Ulus; this is where most of the tourist attractions are, and it's quite compact and walkable.

A car is useful for excursions to the Hittite cities and to Cappadocia. Boğazkale and Hattuşa are about 200 km (124 mi) east of Ankara, Konya is 261 km (162 mi) to the south, and Kayseri is 312 km (194 mi) southeast.

Taxis are more expensive in Ankara than in Istanbul—a taxi from the airport, approximately 35 km (20 mi) from the city center, can cost you about $40. Traveling by taxi to historic sites outside Ankara is usually reasonable ($30 to $60), but always agree on the fare in advance. Cabs can be hailed, or ask your hotel to call one.

There are two subway lines in Ankara: the Metro, which runs north from Kızılay; and the Ankaray, which goes east–west from the AŞTİ bus station in the western suburbs, through Kızılay and on to Dikimevi in the east. It's very easy to get downtown from Ankara's *otogar* (AŞTİ), which connects directly to the Ankaray. Take the Ankaray to the Kızılay stop and then transfer to the Metro (using the same ticket) if you want to continue north to Ulus. Fares are about $1 and trains run between approximately 6 AM and midnight.

ESSENTIALS
Bus Information **Ulusoy** (☎ *312/419–4080 for Ankara* ⊕ *www.ulusoy.com.tr).* **Varan Bus Company** (☎ *312/417–2525 in Ankara* ⊕ *www.varan.com.tr).* **Havaş** (☎ *312/398–0376* ⊕ *www.havas.com.tr).*

Tour Companies **Setur Ankara** (✉ *Kavaklıdere Sokak 5/B, Kavaklıdere* ☎ *312/457–4700* ⊕ *www.setur.com.tr).* **T & T Tourism and Travel** (✉ *Abdullah Cevdet Sokak 22/9, Çankaya* ☎ *312/440–9234* ⊕ *www.tnt-tourism.com).* **Tempo Tour** (✉ *Binnaz Sokak 1/4, Kavaklıdere* ☎ *312/428–2096* 🖨 *312/426–1670* ⊕ *www.tempotour.com.tr).*

Train Information **Ankara train station** (✉ *Talat Paşa Cad., at Cumhuriyet Bul.* ☎ *312/311–0620 for information, 312/311–4994 for reservations).*

Visitor Information (☎ *312/310–8787 Ext. 290* ✉ *Esenboğa Airport* ☎ *312/ 398–0348).*

EXPLORING

Right after the War of Independence, Ankara was made the fledgling Turkish Republic's new capital, in part because it was a barren, dusty steppe city more or less in the middle of nowhere, and therefore considered to be secure. The city still feels that way somewhat, despite being the center of Turkish political activity and having a population of more than 4 million. But although it doesn't come close to having historical richness or vibrancy of Istanbul, Ankara is nonetheless interesting because it's home to the fascinating and enduring legacy of Mustafa Kemal, founding father of the secular Turkish Republic. The capital city is a monument to Atatürk's overpowering will.

For travelers looking to go to Cappadocia and other formerly hard-to-reach parts of Central Anatolia, the emergence of several low-cost airlines with direct flights to Kayseri and Nevşehir means it is no longer necessary to spend a day in Ankara if you don't want to.

If you do chose to visit Ankara, in a day or so you can learn a great deal about Turkey's history, both ancient—at the highly regarded Museum of Anatolian Civilizations, repository of the best archaeological treasures found in Turkey—and modern, by visiting the Anıtkabir, Atatürk's mausoleum. Dining, nightlife, and hotel options are increasingly diverse, and since this is a government and college town, you'll find more relaxed attitudes here than in many other parts of Anatolia. The capital also provides a logical base for exploring the ancient ruined sites of the Hittite Empire, which are contained within a triangle in northeastern Central Anatolia bounded by Hattuşa, Yazılıkaya, and Alacahöyük. All the Hittite cities can be seen in a day trip from Ankara if you have a car.

❷ **Anadolu Medeniyetleri Müzesi** *(Museum of Anatolian Civilizations).* Outside this museum is an impressive announcement—the Ankara Museum of Anatolian Civilizations was voted the European Museum of the Year. Never mind that this was in 1997. Despite the outdated plaudit, the museum is a real gem and one of the two places that you shouldn't miss if you're spending any time in Ankara (the other is the Anıtkabir). Many of the best treasures uncovered from Turkey's ancient past are housed here, making it a great base for understanding the incredible amount of history that has been played out in these lands. The museum is relatively small and has descriptions in English and Turkish, but a guide may be helpful in directing your attention to the most important pieces. Agree on a price in advance.

Fodor'sChoice
★

The museum is in a restored 15th-century bedestan, with exhibits arranged chronologically, starting at the entrance and proceeding counterclockwise. One of the unmistakable highlights is the section on the Neolithic site of Çatal Höyük, one of the oldest human settlements ever discovered. The findings, which date to ca. 7500 BC, include wall frescoes, bull heads, pottery, and the famous mother goddess figurine—a large-breasted woman, giving birth while flanked by two leopards—that has become the symbol of Çatal Höyük.

From Genghis Khan to Atatürk

Tamerlane, the fearsome descendent of Genghis Khan, laid siege to Ankara in 1402 and wrested control of the city away from Beyazit, the Ottoman sultan. Then, perhaps bored with the landscape or seeking greater riches in the abundance of China, Tamerlane and his Mongol horde quickly gave the city back to the Ottomans and turned around and headed back east toward the Mongol plains. Tamerlane died a year later.

Tamerlane's victory in Ankara was but a later scene in the city's long history. Local legend attributes Ankara's foundation to the Amazons, the mythical female warriors, but many archaeologists have factually indentified it with Ankuwash, thought to have been founded around 1200 BC by the Hittites and then taken over by the Phrygians around 700 BC. The city was known to the Greeks and Romans as Ancyra or Ankyra, and later as Angora, famed for its wool. Alexander the Great conquered Ankara centuries before Augustus Caesar annexed the city to Rome in 25 BC.

Over the coming millennia Ankara was attacked and worn down by Persian, Arab, Seljuk, Mongol, and Ottoman invaders. By the early 20th century, Ankara was little more than a provincial town with nice goats and an illustrious past. In 1919, as World War I and the Turkish War of Independence raged, Mustafa Kemal Atatürk made Ankara the headquarters of his secular resistance movement.

When Turkey was declared a republic four years later, Ankara was declared its capital. Atatürk mobilized the young nation's resources to make the city a symbol of a modern and secular Turkish city built on European lines. Tens of thousands of workers streamed in on foot to help build it, with designers intentionally abandoning Ottoman architecture in favor of a symbolic, stark modernism influenced by the Vienna cubist and German Bauhaus schools.

As with most planned cities, Ankara today is mostly convenient and pretty characterless. Despite Atatürk's dreams, it never made a serious bid to overtake Istanbul as the country's cultural capital.

In the later rooms, the Hatti and Hittite artifacts, with their stylized stag and bull sculptures and drawings, are particularly striking. From the Assyrian trade colonies period (1950–1750 BC) come numerous clay cuneiform tablets, the earliest written records found in Anatolia. These palm-sized tablets, some enclosed in their own clay "envelopes" and describing marriage contracts, debt notices, slave trading, and other everyday transactions in minuscule cuneiform script, are fascinating. Also on display are findings from the Phrygian, Urartian, Hellenistic, and Roman eras. ⊠ *Gözcü Sokak 2* ☎ *312/324–3160* ⊕ *www. anadolumedeniyetlerimuzesi.gov.tr* ☎ *15 TL* ⊙ *Daily 8:30–5.*

❾ **The Anıtkabir** *(Atatürk's Mausoleum).* Atatürk's picture is on every
Fodor'sChoice single piece of Turkish currency, his visage hangs in just about every
★ office and official building in the country, and his personality and ideas are the foundations of Turkish political thought. So his vast mausoleum, perched on a hilltop overlooking the capital city he built, is on a scale suitable to his stature in Turkey. A marble promenade flanked

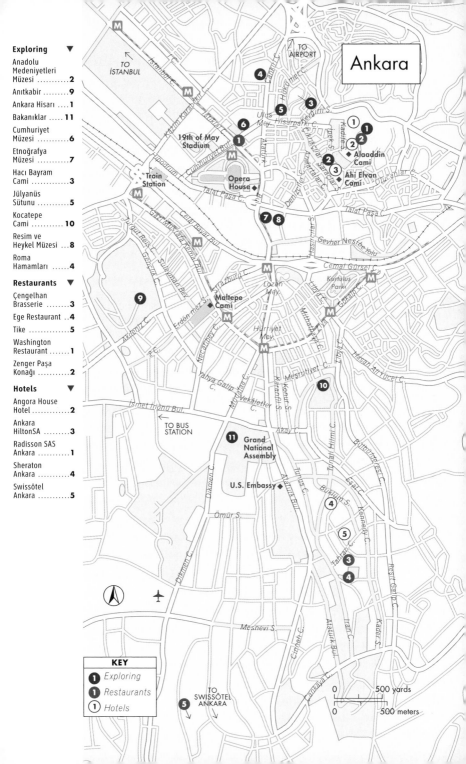

Ankara

TO İSTANBUL

TO AIRPORT

19th of May
Stadium

Train
Station

Opera
House

Alaaddin
Cami

Ahi Elvan
Cami

Maltepe
Cami

Kurtuluş
Parkı

Grand
National
Assembly

U.S. Embassy

TO BUS
STATION

TO
SWISSÔTEL
ANKARA

KEY

❶ Exploring

❶ Restaurants

① Hotels

0   500 yards

0   500 meters

with Hittite-style lions leads to the mausoleum, where the sarcophagus under which the revered man's remains are interred lies beyond brilliant gold mosaics and a colonnade with inscriptions from his speeches. Soldiers march endlessly around the site, and nearly every important foreign dignitary who visits the capital goes to lay a wreath here in tribute to the man who, it is not an exaggeration to say, created modern Turkey.

An adjoining museum contains personal belongings from Atatürk's life, including his clothes, automobiles, and personal library. In the corridors underneath the tomb is an in-depth exhibit on the 1919–1922 War of Independence. An interesting map at the entrance shows Turkey and the territorial claims various other nations were making on it at the time. The focal points of the exhibit are three enormous dioramas, each over 35 meters (100 feet) in length, depicting the three major theaters of war: Çanakkale (1915), Sakarya (1921), and the Great Attack (1922). These are accompanied by rather intense sound effects—explosions, gunfire, etc.—to further dramatize the events. There is also a gift shop selling everything from Atatürk neckties, lapel pins, and watches to posters and books about the man. ⌧ *Anıt Cad., south end* ☎ *312/231–7975* ⊕ *www.tsk.mil.tr/anitkabir/index.html* ⌧ *Free* ⊙ *Daily, summer 9–5, winter 9–4.*

WORD OF MOUTH

"We left the train station and went directly to the Anatolian Civilizations Museum. I'm not a huge museum fan, but this one was pretty good and not so big that it was overwhelming. After about 2 hours at the museum we then made our way to Ataturk's Mausoleum. Wow! What a place, it's gigantic we were there just before noon and it was not very crowded. We did get to see a changing of the guard."   —LowCountryIslander

❶ **Ankara Hisarı** *(Ankara Citadel).* Ankara's main historic sites are clustered around the Hisar, also known as the citadel or castle, high on a hill overlooking the city. The plains on which Tamerlane defeated Beyazıt stretch to the northeast. There's not a lot to see at the crumbling Hisar itself, as the city has grown around and even inside it. The inner walls date to the 7th century, and the best-preserved sections are around the Parmak Kapı. Ankara's oldest mosque, the 12th-century Alaaddin Cami, is also here, and the Ankara Museum of Anatolian Civilizations is within walking distance. ⌧ *Uphill from the Museum of Anatolian Civilizations.*

⓫ **Bakanıklar,** the government district, fills the west side of Atatürk Bulvarı from Hürriyet Meydanı to the Türkiye Büyük Millet Meclisi (Grand National Assembly), the parliament building, at the intersection with İsmet İnönü Bulvarı. Within walking distance, in the Kavaklıdere neighborhood, is Embassy Row, with gardens, fine restaurants, and world-class hotels.

❻ **Cumhuriyet Müzesi** *(Museum of the Republic).* You might think the Museum of the Republic would be one of the best places for a crash course on modern Turkish history—but the descriptions here are all in Turkish, so most non-Turks are confronted with a bunch of pictures of people they don't recognize and documents they can't understand. The museum is in Turkey's first parliament building where, from 1925 to 1960, politicians debated policies that would shape Turkey as a modern, secular nation. Substantial renovations were almost finished at press time, but it's unclear whether there will be more English explanations. ⊠*Cumhuriyet Bul. 22, off Ulus Meyd.* ☎*312/310–5361* 🎫*3 TL* ⊙*Tues.–Sun. 9–noon and 1:30–5.*

7 **Etnoğrafya Müzesi** *(Ethnography Museum).* Atatürk used this Ottoman Revival–style building as an office, and his body lay here for 15 years after his death while his enormous mausoleum was being built. The small but interesting museum houses a rich collection of Turkish carpets, folk costumes, weapons, Islamic calligraphy, ceramics, and woodwork. ⊠*Talat Paşa Cad., Opera* ☎*312/311–3007* 🎫*3 TL* ⊙*Tues.–Sun. 8:30–12:30 and 1:30–5:30.*

3 **Hacı Bayram Cami** *(Hacı Bayram Mosque).* Built in 1427, Hacı Bayram Cami is one of Ankara's most important sacred sites. Built of yellow stone and brick with glazed Kütahya tiles later placed in the interior, it is named after Hacı Bayram, the founder of the Bayrami order of dervishes. Hacı Bayram's tomb is near the entrance to the mosque. If you want religious trinkets to take home, the area surrounding the mosque is a good place to get them. ⊠*Bayram Cad., north of Hisarparkı Cad.* ⊙*Immediately after prayer times.*

5 **Jülyanüs Sütunu** *(Column of Julian).* Now surrounded by Turkish government buildings, the column was erected in honor of Emperor Julian the Apostate (361–363), the last pagan Roman emperor. He won his epithet because he tried to reverse his uncle Constantine's decision to make Christianity the official religion of the empire. The column has 15 fluted drums and a Corinthian top that commemorates a visit by Julian in 362, as he passed through town on his way to death in battle with the Persians. ⊠*Hükümet Meyd., just northeast of Ulus Meyd.*

10 **Kocatepe Cami** *(Kocatepe Mosque).* It took 20 years to build this gigantic neo-Ottoman mosque in the center of Turkey's secular capital. Officially opened in 1987, it is the site of most military and official funerals. The huge, illuminated mosque dominates the city skyline at night. The Kocatepe complex is one of Ankara's most prominent landmarks and also includes a supermarket and department store on its lower floors. ⊠*On Mithat Paşa Cad., Kızılay.*

8 **Resim ve Heykel Müzesi** *(Painting and Sculpture Museum).* These galleries, housed in an ornate marble building next door to the Ethnography Museum, display works by late Ottoman, modern, and contemporary Turkish artists. ⊠*Talat Paşa Cad., Opera* ☎*312/310–2094* 🎫*Free* ⊙*Tues.–Sun. 9–noon and 1–5.*

4 **Roma Hamamları** *(Roman Baths).* You can't bathe at this 3rd-century complex just north of Ulus Square, but you can see how the Romans did it. The bath system includes the frigidarium and caldarium (cold and hot rooms), as well as steam rooms with raised floors. ⊠*Çankırı Cad. 43* ☎*312/310–7280* 🎫*3 TL* ⊙*Daily 8:30–noon and 1–5:30.*

WHERE TO STAY AND EAT

$–$$ ✕**Çengelhan Brasserie.** Perhaps the classiest restaurant on this side of
TURKISH town, the Çengelhan is in the glass-roofed courtyard of the Rahmi M.
★ Koç Museum. The food is presented stylishly, though the marble-topped
tables and soothing sound of a fountain make for a laid-back dining
experience. The menu is modern Turkish and international, with starters like smoked salmon with arugula salad and mains including lamb
shank with dilled pilaf and vegetable ratatouille. The restaurant stays
open in the evening after the museum closes. ⊠*Depo Sokak Güzergahı
1, Ulus* ☎*312/309–6800* ⊟*AE, MC, V* ⊘*Closed Mon.*

$–$$ ✕**Ege Restaurant.** This charming restaurant just off fashionable Tunalı
SEAFOOD Hilmi Avenue specializes in Aegean-style fish dishes (Ege is the Turkish
name for the Aegean Sea) and the decor—painted wood chairs with
simple cushions, blue and white walls with a fish motif—transports
you straight to the Aegean islands. To top it off, a map of the region
is painted on the ceiling. The wide selection of fish comes from both
the Aegean and the Black Sea. ⊠*Büklüm Sokak 54/B, Kavaklıdere*
☎*312/428–2717* ⌇*Reservations essential* ⊘*Closed Sun.* ⊟*AE, DC,
MC, V.*

$–$$ ✕**Tike.** The Istanbul-based upscale kebab chain Tike specializes in tra-
TURKISH ditional mezes and kebabs. Mezes are excellent, with one of the more
Fodor'sChoice unusual but tasty being *mütebbel,* chopped smoked eggplant and gar-
★ licky yogurt topped with ground pistachios. Among the mains, the
"Tike kebab," a version of spicey Adana kebab (skewers of spicy ground
lamb), is delicious, and the *çöp şiş* (diced lamb shish kebab) melts in
your mouth. The decor is contemporary with Turkish touches, the vibe
is trendy, and the glass-roofed back section of the restaurant opens
onto an attractive patio and garden. ⊠*Billur Sokak 17/A, Kavaklıdere*
☎*312/426–0141* ⌇*Reservations essential* ⊟*AE, MC, V.*

$$–$$$ ✕**Washington Restaurant.** Once the de rigueur venue for hosting foreign
TURKISH dignitaries, the Washington remains popular with the diplomatic set and
in-the-know locals. Just inside the citadel and boasting a terrace with
excellent views of the city below, the restaurant serves international
fare—particularly Russian specialties such as borscht, chicken Kiev,
and beef Stroganoff—along with standard Turkish mezes and kebabs.
The decor is white tablecloths, old-fashioned chandeliers, and dark
woods—not cutting edge, but just right for this Ankara institution.
⊠*Doyran Sokak 5/7, Kaleiçi-Ulus* ☎*312/311–4344* ⌇*Reservations
essential* ⊟*MC, V.*

$–$$ ✕**Zenger Paşa Konağı.** At the top of a restored 18th-century Ottoman
TURKISH mansion in the citadel, Zenger Paşa Konağı has excellent panoramic
views of the city. Decor is rustic-traditional, with wooden chairs and kilims. The menu is fairly standard mezes and kebabs, the highlight being
the *saç kavurma,* a meat dish cooked fajita-style over an alcohol flame
as you watch. There is live Turkish music every night and although
the place has an undeniably touristy side, it's also popular with locals.
⊠*Doyran Sokak 13, Kaleiçi, Ulus* ☎*312/311–7070* ⌇*Reservations
essential* ⊟*MC, V.*

¢ 🛏**Angora House Hotel.** The only hotel located inside the walls of Anka-
Fodor'sChoice ra's ancient citadel, Angora House has six charming rooms in a beauti-
★ fully restored Ottoman house—they're good-sized, though slightly dark,

and have original wood floors and ceilings, antique chandeliers and comfortable beds. Bathrooms are modern and spotless, with showers or tubs. The place has the intimate feel of a private home, with breakfast served family-style in the dining room. **Pros:** unique location in historic part of Ankara; old-fashioned yet comfortable furnishings; friendly, helpful staff. **Cons:** neighborhood can be noisy in the early mornings; no elevator or a/c. ✉ *Kale Kapısı Sokak 16, Kale İçi* ☎ *312/309–8380 or 311–1609* ✍ *angorahouse@gmail.com* ⇖ *6 rooms* ♿ *In-room: no a/c, no TV, Wi-Fi. In-hotel: room service, laundry service, no-smoking rooms* ⏰ *Closed Nov. 15–Mar. 25* ▭ *MC, V* ⛍ *BP.*

$$$$ ⌂ **Ankara HiltonSA.** The most senior of Ankara's international luxury hotels, the Hilton has become somewhat old-school, particularly the lobby with its low ceiling, mirrors, and brass trim everywhere. Renovations to be completed by mid-2009, however, are to give the common areas a contemporary makeover. Rooms, already more up-to-date than the public spaces, are large and colorfully-yet-tastefully decorated. The fitness center has an aboveground indoor pool, Jacuzzi, and exercise room pleasantly lit by large skylights. **Pros:** dependable, high-level service. **Cons:** formal, somewhat dated character of public spaces (to change after renovations); hotel feels mostly oriented toward business travelers. ✉ *Tahran Cad. 12, Kavaklıdere* ☎ *312/455–0000* ⊕ *www. hilton.com* ⇖ *315 rooms, 24 suites* ♿ *In-room: safe, DVD (some), Internet (fee). In-hotel: 2 restaurants, room service, bar, pool, gym, laundry service, Wi-Fi, parking (paid), some pets allowed, no-smoking rooms* ▭ *AE, DC, MC, V.*

$ ⌂ **Radisson SAS Ankara.** The 16-story Radisson SAS is the only international chain hotel in Ankara's historic Ulus district. Rooms are comfortable and some of the bathrooms have opaque windows that look from the shower into the room. The roof terrace has excellent views of the city. **Pros:** convenient location near major tourist attractions, next to metro station; predictable Radisson standard of service and amenities. **Cons:** hotel overlooks a loud, busy street; decor feels somewhat generic. ✉ *İstiklal Cad. 20, Ulus* ☎ *312/310–4848* ⊕ *www.ankara. radissonsas.com* ⇖ *183 rooms, 19 suites* ♿ *In-room: safe, Wi-Fi. In-hotel: restaurant, room service, bar, gym, laundry service, parking (free), no-smoking rooms* ▭ *AE, MC, V.*

$$$$ ⌂ **Sheraton Ankara.** Unlike many large international chain hotels, the
★   Sheraton Ankara has personality. The building—tall, white, and round, with a separate convention center adjacent—is an Ankara landmark, while the attractive lobby and chic bar have refreshingly bold textures and lighting. Spacious rooms have similarly contemporary decor, along with modern bathrooms and good views of the city. The fitness center includes a huge exercise room, indoor pool, and steam room. **Pros:** top-notch service; range of dining options; excellent fitness facilities. **Cons:** large hotel/convention center can feel somewhat impersonal; expensive food, drinks, and Internet. ✉ *Noktalı Sokak, Kavaklıdere* ☎ *312/457–6000* ⊕ *www.sheratonankara.com* ⇖ *373 rooms, 41 suites* ♿ *In-room: safe, DVD (some), Wi-Fi. In-hotel: 3 restaurants, room service, bars, tennis court, pool, gym, laundry service, parking (free), some pets allowed, no-smoking rooms* ▭ *AE, DC, MC, V.*

6

$$$$ ⛾ **Swissôtel Ankara.** In Ankara's upscale Çankaya neighborhood, the Swissôtel is the height of luxury, managing to pull off style and sophistication without being overdone. Standard rooms have elegant décor and large bathrooms. The extensive wellness center includes a half-Olympic-size indoor pool, beautiful hamam, sauna, and full spa, along with a large fitness room. **Pros:** posh yet relaxed ambience; excellent service, dining options, and fitness facilities. **Cons:** hotel is located in a residential neighborhood far from major sights and a short drive from nightlife; expensive food, drinks, and Internet. ⊠ *Yıldızlıevler Mah. Jose Marti Cad. 2, Çankaya* ☎*312/409–3000* ⊕*www.ankara.swissotel.com* ⤳*141 rooms, 6 suites* ⟐*In-room: safe, DVD (some), Wi-Fi. In-hotel: 2 restaurants, room service, bar, pool, gym, spa, laundry service, parking (free), some pets allowed, no-smoking rooms* ▤*AE, MC, V.*

SHOPPING

Down the hill south of the Hisar is an area known as **Samanpazarı,** where you can find antiques, rugs, crafts, and copper for sale. There are also a few such shops inside the citadel, geared mostly to tourists but with some interesting merchandise. In the pedestrian area of the district of **Kızılay,** look for books and Turkish music, especially on Konur Sokak. There are also two good shopping malls in central Ankara—Karum (next door to the Sheraton) and Armada—where you can find local Turkish brands.

HATTUŞA AND THE OTHER HITTITE CITIES

★ *Hattuşa is about 200 km (124 mi) from Ankara, east on Rte. E88 and northeast on Rte. 190 until past Sungurlu; then follow road signs.*

The ancient ruined sites of the Hittite Empire are contained within a triangle in northeastern Central Anatolia bounded by Hattuşa, Yazılıkaya, and Alacahöyük. All the Hittite cities can be seen in a day trip from Ankara if you have a car. Otherwise, you'd be best tagging along with a guided archaeological tour.

Hattuşa, east of Ankara in a loop of the Kızılırmak, was the capital of the Hittite Empire. In a beautiful setting of lush green valleys, with steep ravines and rocky hillsides, sheep graze among the ruins of a civilization that was already established here some 6,000 years ago. The entire site, with walls that are 7 km (4 mi) in circumference, was named a UNESCO World Heritage Site in 1986. Though picturesque, the site is extensive and there is little explanation.

Hattuşa dates to the Bronze Age, and by 2300 BC a people called the Hatti were thriving here. The massive walls of the city surrounded a fortress, temples, large administrative buildings, houses, cemeteries, and decorated gateways and courtyards. Around 1800 BC, King Anitta of the as-yet-undiscovered city of Kushar formed an Anatolian confederacy and pronounced himself "Rabum Rabum," or King of Kings.

At about that time, however, a people called the Hittites wandered in. They claimed King Anitta's Hattuşa as their capital and soon began to build their own empire around it. The Hittites, who like the Persians spoke an Indo-European language (unlike the Turks, whose language is Ural-Altaic), apparently entered Anatolia after crossing the Caucasus steppes beyond the Black Sea. They worshipped a storm god and a sun goddess, and had a well-ordered society with written laws. At their height, they conquered Babylon and battled the Egyptian pharaohs. Their reign came to an end after some 600 years, when tribes from the north sacked and burned Hattuşa in 1200 BC. The

> ## GO WITH A GUIDE
>
> When visiting the Hittite cities, guided trips will shed a great deal of light on otherwise unintelligible piles of rocks arranged in squares. The American Research Institute in Turkey, or ARIT (☎ *312/427–2222*), arranges periodic and highly praised guided excursions.

Phrygians then became the dominant people in the region.

One of the most famous finds in Hattuşa is a copy of the Treaty of Kadesh, signed between the Hittite and Egyptian Empires after what might have been the largest chariot-battle ever fought. Some 5,000 chariots are believed to have been involved in one of the best-documented battles of the ancient world, between the Egyptian forces of Ramses II and the Hittite soldiers of Hattusili III. The treaty, written both in Egyptian hieroglyphs and in Akkadian using cuneiform script, declares that both peoples and their gods want peace. It may be the world's first known peace treaty. An original can be seen at the Istanbul Archaeological Museum, and a copy hangs at the entrance to the Security Council chamber in the headquarters of the United Nations in New York.

Once at the site, ignore the awful reconstruction of a castle at the entrance, which looks like it was made out of Legos and covered with clay. The rest of the site consists mostly of huge blocks of ancient cut stones arrayed in rectangular patterns. The first ruins on the right are the **Temple of the Storm God** (Temple I). Inside there used to be statues of the storm god and sun goddess.

Continuing up the hill, you'll pass a series of gates in the city walls. The first is the **Aslankapı**, or Lion Gate. The lions there today are reproductions. Next is the very impressive **Yerkapı**, a long underground tunnel made of stones piled up and leaning into one another to form a triangle above you. Giant stones seem to hover overhead in an impressive display of ancient engineering. It was believed to have been a ceremonial entrance to the city. When the road forks, a left up the hill will take you to Büyükkale, said to be the royal residence of the Hittite kings with a view over the city.

Boğazkale is about 5 km (3 mi) north of Hattuşa. There's not a lot to see there, though the village does have a *pansiyon* and a few restaurants. **Yazılıkaya,** about 2 km (1 mi) east of Hattuşa, is thought to have served as the city's religious sanctuary; its name simply means "rock with writing." The walls here are covered with drawings of Hittite gods, goddesses, and kings from about 1200 BC. On the main shrine, 42 gods march from the left to meet 21 goddesses coming from the right. In the middle is the weather god Teshub with horns in his cap, and the goddess Hepatu riding a leopard. It's thought that funeral rights for kings were performed here.

The Hittite cities are about a two-hour drive east of Ankara. With your own car, you'll be able to do all three in the same day, as well as Alacahöyük. Most visitors will not feel the need to stay the night, though there are a couple of clean but unimpressive hotels around Boğazkale. *4 TL for both cities* 📞*364/452–2200* ⏱*Daily, summer 8–7, winter 8–5* 🌐*www.hattuscha.de/english/english1.htm.*

Alacahöyük, about 25 km (15 mi) from Yazılıkaya, has evidence of human settlement dating back to 5000 BC. All of the signs are in Turkish, but the site is impressive on its own and the small museum makes for a fun half hour or so. On display are bone arrows, some 7,000-year-old pitchers and pots that look like they could still be used, and a broken half-phallus with no explanation.

At the entrance to the site are a couple of sphinxes, a carved gate with scenes of men and animals, and some Early Bronze Age graves. The dead, the sign in Turkish says, were always buried in the northwest corner of the tomb, on their sides with their legs folded toward their chests, and facing south. Silver, gold, and weapons were found inside most of the graves. You'll likely be alone as you explore the site, with roosters crowing from the nearby village. 📞*364/422–7011* *4 TL* ⏱*Daily 8–noon and 1:30–5.*

SAFRANBOLU

225 km (140 mi) north of Ankara.

ESSENTIALS

Visitor Information (✉*On the main square* 📞*370/712-3863*).

EXPLORING

★ Tucked into the hills two hours north of Ankara is one of Turkey's loveliest treasures, a preserved slice of Ottoman past that has been designated a UNESCO World Heritage Site. Once a wealthy trading town, it was known for its golden saffron fields—from which the city derives its name. In the 18th and 19th centuries Safranbolu's merchants built stunning timber and stone mansions, a large number of which remain intact. Great efforts have been put into preserving these houses and their surroundings, and as a result the town's historic atmosphere feels pleasantly authentic.

Safranbolu is essentially divided into three parts: hidden in a wide ravine is the historic center, called Çarşı (bazaar); cars are banned here, artisans ply their crafts in open storefronts, and old Ottoman houses line the cobblestone streets. The modern town, Kıranköy, is just above the valley, while the outlying Bağlar neighborhood, on the slopes of a small mountain overlooking the city, is where the wealthy had their summer homes in Ottoman times. The Çarşı area has the most to see and do, and it's here and in Bağlar that old houses have been turned into charming hotels. The Kıranköy section has little of interest but has modern necessities like banks and bus offices.

Some buildings in the historic center of town are open to the public, among them the **Kaymakamlar Evi** *(Governor's House)*, which has been restored with 200-year-old furnishings. Costumed mannequins

The Temple of the Storm God at Hattuşa.

in the rooms give a good idea of how the house was divided into the *selamlık* (men's quarters, which were open to visitors) and *haremlik* (private women's quarters). ⊠*Hıdırlık Yokuşu Sokak* ☎*370/712–7885* ⏱*Daily, summer 9–8, winter 9–6* 🎫*2.50 TL.*

The nicely restored **Arasta** *(Ottoman Market Hall)* dates back to 1661 and used to house the small shops of shoemakers. Today it's filled with stores selling local handicrafts such as handmade cotton and linen clothes, carved wooden items, and other souvenirs.

South of the Arasta, near the İzzet Mehmet Paşa Cami, is the **Demir-ciler Çarşısı** *(Blacksmiths' Bazaar)*, where blacksmiths, cobblers, saddle makers, and other tradesmen still have shops. With demand for their traditional crafts dwindling, these artisans have begun to cater more towards tourists, and you can pick up interesting items like antique-style wrought-iron door knockers of the sort that grace Safranbolu's old houses. On a hilltop overlooking the old town is the **Eski Hükümet Konağı** *(Old Government Mansion)*, which dates to 1906 and has recently been made into the **Kent Tarihi Müzesi** *(Town History Museum)*. Though small, the museum has some interesting displays on the town's history, includ-ing several ethnographic rooms; moreover, the building itself is rather elegant. On the premises is also a **Saat Kulesi** *(Clock Tower)*, built in 1797 by Sultan Selim III's Grand Vizier, who was from Safranbolu. The views from the top of the tower are excellent, and you can also check out the machinery used to manually wind the clock, which still func-tions. ⊠*Eski Hükümet Konağı* ☎*370/712–1314* 🎫*3 TL* ⏱*Tues.– Sun., 9–7:30 in summer, 9–5:30 in winter.*

If you're in the mood for a scrub-down, head to the historic **Cinci hamam**, where locals have been getting lathered up and massaged since the 17th century. ⊠*Near the main Sq.* ☎*370/712–2103* ⊙*daily 6 AM–11 PM for men, 9 AM–10 PM for women* ⊒*30 TL including massage and scrubdown, 20 TL for entrance only.*

WHERE TO STAY AND EAT

¢
TURKISH
✕**Boncuk Arasta Kahvesi.** In the middle of the Arasta Bazaar, this small café serves simple food like stuffed grape leaves and the Turkish pancakes known as *gözleme.* Chairs and tables are set outside on the market's cobblestones, beneath drooping grapevines. The interior is cozy, with lace curtains and tablecloths. Finish your light meal or snack with an expertly-made Turkish coffee, served in a long-stemmed copper urn with two pieces of Turkish delight on the side. ⊠*Yeminiciler Arastası, Safranbolu* ☎*370/712–2065* ⊟*No credit cards.*

THE SELJUKS

A lot of what you'll see in the area east of Ankara was built by the Seljuks, members of a nomadic Turkic tribe that probably originated in or around Mongolia. The Seljuk Turks converted to Islam in the 10th century and began to push westward. They established their capital in Konya and ruled much of Anatolia from the 12th through 14th centuriesd. Seljuk architecture is recognizable by its similarity to the Gothic architecture that was flourishing in Europe when the Seljuks dominated the Middle East. Many of the mosques, castles, and caravansaries that brood over various Turkish villages were built in this style.

$
TURKISH
✕**Çevrikköprü Restaurant.** A roadside parking lot overflowing with cars will let you know that you've arrived at this popular restaurant some 6 km (4 mi) east of Safranbolu, on the road to Kastamonu. By the side of a small stream, the rustic restaurant has outdoor tables set around a bubbling fountain, shaded by leafy vines. Meals start with a complimentary flatbread served with butter and honey; the house specialty is *kuyu* kebab. The restaurant has two other locations in the old part of town, but this is the original. ⊠*Kastamonu Yolu 6. Km. Safranbolu* ☎*370/737–2461* ⊟*MC, V.*

$-$$
TURKISH
✕**Havuzlu Köşk Restaurant.** To get away from the weekend crowds that sometimes descend on Safranbolu, head up to this restaurant in the mountainside Bağlar district. The food, the usual assortment of kebabs and mezes, is very good; the restaurant is particularly proud of its *saç kavurma,* a lamb and vegetable stew cooked on a griddle. But the location—a 190-year-old house with a Safranbolu-style indoor pool for heating, and a pleasant garden filled with fruit trees, is even better. ⊠*Dibekönü Cad. 32* ☎*370/725–2168* ⊟*AE, MC, V.*

¢-$
TURKISH
✕**Kadıoğlu Şehzade Sofrası.** With low, round tables set around an enclosed courtyard shaded by grapevines, this restaurant is welcoming and laid-back. On the menu are several tasty local specialties, including kuyu kebab and *Şehzade pilavı,* a dish of rice and mushrooms topped with a cheesy crust. Or try the tasty local variation on pide, called *bükme* and filled with spinach and ground meat. Everything is served with fresh-baked flatbread. The same owners also offer lodgings in

DID YOU KNOW?

Craftspeople sell their wares in open store fronts in the bazaar section of Safranbolu, a UNESCO World Heritage Site.

nine different mansions around town. ⊠*Arasta Sokak 8, Safranbolu* ☎*370/712–5091* ▤*V.*

$$
Fodor'sChoice
★

⌨**Gülevi.** Opened in 2006 by a retired Istanbul architect and his wife, these two restored Ottoman houses have lots of style, deftly combining antique and modern touches. The 160-year-old houses have original, built-in divans that run along the walls; they've been upholstered in up-to-date fabrics and the adjoining beds have plush bedspreads. The original wood detailing and floors also remain, while bathrooms have contemporary fittings. On the ground floor, where the stables used to be, is a cozy and inviting bar. **Pros:** exceptional combination of traditional decor and modern style; very gracious hosts; stylish bar. **Cons:** no bedside lamps or TVs in rooms. ⊠*Hükümet Sokak 46, Çarşı, Safranbolu* ☎*370/725–4645* ⊕*www.canbulat.com.tr* ⇩*9 rooms, 1 suite* ⌂*In-room: no a/c, safe, no TV, Wi-Fi. In-hotel: restaurant, room service, bar, laundry service, parking (paid), no-smoking rooms* ▤*AE, MC, V* ⏉*BP.*

$$ ⌨**Havuzlu Asmazlar Konağı.** In three restored, Ottoman-era Safranbolu homes, this hotel is run by the Touring and Automobile Association of Turkey. Painstaking attention has been given to detail, from the embroidered floral motifs on the blinds to the *havuz* (a traditional pool used not for swimming, but for cooling the house) in the breakfast room. The excellent restaurant serves the Safranbolu kebab: grilled lamb, tomato sauce, and yogurt on pita bread, topped with cheese. **Pros:** professional service; good dining. **Cons:** halfway up the slope toward Kıranköy; secondary buildings less atmospheric than the main mansion. ⊠*Çelik Gülersoy Cad. 18, Çarşı* ☎*370/725–2883* ⊕*www.safranbolukonak.com* ⇩*22 rooms, 1 suite* ⌂*In-room: no a/c, Wi-Fi (some). In-hotel: restaurant, room service, laundry service, some pets allowed* ▤*AE, MC, V.*

¢ ⌨**Hotel Selvili Köşk.** Friendly and unassuming, this centrally located hotel is made up of three impressive old houses that have been painted light pastel colors. Large rooms with especially high ceilings feel homey, and some have bathrooms that are cleverly hidden inside old cupboards. There are large common areas with divans to lounge on and a large, pleasant garden where breakfast is served. **Pros:** charming, authentic atmosphere; lovely garden. **Cons:** few amenities; no Internet; no no-smoking rooms. ⊠*Mescit Sokak 23, Safranbolu* ☎*370/712–8646* 🖷*370/725–2294* ⇩*26 rooms* ⌂*In-hotel: laundry service* ▤*MC, V* ⏉*BP.*

SAFRANBOLU SPECIALTIES

One of the local specialties worth trying in Safranbolu is *kuyu* kebab, lamb cooked in an underground pit (*kuyu*). The town is also known for its sweets, particularly its saffron-flavored *lokum* (Turkish delight), which is unique to Safranbolu, and *yaprak helvası*, an extremely sweet and chewy layered concoction of halvah and walnuts.

Excursions to the Far East & Black Sea Coast

WORD OF MOUTH

"We took a boat ride on Lake Van in eastern Turkey to this tiny island [Akdamar], where there is a 10th century Armenian church decorated with marvelous reliefs. I found this ruin of a gravestone outside the church, looking toward the lake."
— photo by nddavidson, Fodors.com member

WELCOME TO THE FAR EAST & THE BLACK SEA COAST

TOP REASONS TO GO

★ **Wandering the bustling bazaars of Şanliurfa and Gaziantep.** Craftsmen in these ancient cities still work the same way they have for centuries.

★ **Float in Lake Van.** As in Israel's Dead Sea, the water is rich in minerals and very alkaline; you'll be remarkably buoyant in the startlingly blue water.

★ **Explore the ruins of the city of Ani,** once the seat of a small Armenian kingdom.

★ **Visit the cliffside monastery of Sümela.** The climb is fairly strenuous, but just seeing this remarkable sight is unforgettable.

★ **Journey up Mt. Nemrut.** The massive stone heads looking out over the horizon are an impressive sight to behold.

Mt. Nemrut

1 **The mountains of the Black Sea coast around Trabzon and the Sümela monastery.** This is the area least like the Turkey that visitors expect to see. With lush green valleys, snow-capped peaks, and small villages with chalet-like homes, it looks like a little piece of Switzerland.

2 **The region between Kars and Van.** This is Turkey's eastern frontier, filled with wide-open vistas, high mountain plateaus, and natural and manmade wonders, all offering a wonderful mix of adventure and history. Here you can see the haunting ancient city of Ani, the majestic Mt. Ararat, and the various sites around Lake Van, especially the island church of Akdamar.

3 **Around Diyarbakır and Mardin.** This area, part of ancient Mesopotamia, is steeped in history. The old cities are filled with honey-colored stone homes and small hillside villages surrounded by vineyards and look something like a Turkish Tuscany.

4 **Gaziantep and Şanliurfa.** Traveling around these cities will give you the flavor of the Middle East, from the bustling bazaars where coppersmiths bang away with hammers, to the spicy local cuisine. This is also the best spot to organize a visit to the huge stone heads atop Mt. Nemrut, also known as Mt. Nimrod.

Climbing Mount Ararat, Doğubeyazit

GETTING ORIENTED

For the visitor who makes it to Turkey's eastern regions, the rewards are plentiful: beautiful scenery, wild nature, countless historic sites, and ancient cities where life has not changed much over the centuries. Turkey's eastern half is so vast that it's possible to divide it into separate regions, each offering something different for travelers.

7

BLACK SEA

Batumi

GEORGIA

Hopa

Ardeşen

Ayder

Trabzon

Of · Rize · 010

Sumela

1

010

Ardahan

010

Kars

950 · 957

Ani

ARMENIA

Horasan

Erzurum

100

Karakose · 100 · **2**

Igdir

Mt Ararat

Hınıs

Dogubayazit

Erciş · 975

IRAN

290

Lake Van

Tatvan

Van

975

965

Diyarbakir · 300

Şiirt

Başkale

950 · **3**

Hasankeyf

Midyat

Hakkari · Yüksekova

Mardin

Akdamar Island

IRAQ

EXCURSIONS TO THE FAR EAST & THE BLACK SEA COAST PLANNER

Getting Here

Getting to eastern Turkey once meant grueling bus rides that sometimes took more than a day. The arrival of budget air travel has changed this dramatically, and several domestic airlines now crisscross Turkey. And feeling the competition, Turkey's national carrier, Turkish Airlines, has started slashing fares on domestic routes. Best of all, Turkey's airlines don't penalize you for buying a one-way ticket, so it's possible to fly into one city and depart from another, which can save a lot of time and money.

Hotels and Dining

With a few notable exceptions, the hotels in the east are basic, with little in the way of the upscale boutique hotels you might find along Turkey's coastline. Food in the Black Sea area relies on dishes made with dairy, corn flour, and seafood, especially *hamsi*, which is locally caught anchovy. Although meat kebabs rule the rest of the east, most restaurants will also offer a variety of delicious vegetable dishes cooked in olive oil, along with stews and other ready-made hot dishes, which are usually meat-based.

Tips for the Excursions

TRABZON AND BLACK SEA

Getting here: Fly to Trabzon from Istanbul.

How much time? Four to five days is enough to see the area, though you could spend an extra night in Ayder.

Getting around: We recommend flying in and renting a car: it's possible to get around with regional buses, but you'll save time and patience with a car

When to go: June–September is the best season. There is less rain, and the area, particularly the Kaçkar mountains, is blissfully cooler than the rest of Turkey.

Top sights: The Aya Sofia in Trabzon, the Sümela monastery complex, mountain summer villages around Ayder.

By yourself or with a guide? It's easy to see most of the area by yourself, though touring the Kaçkar mountains is best done with a guide.

KARS, MT. ARARAT AND LAKE VAN

Getting here: To save time, fly to Kars from Istanbul and then fly back from Van (or the other way around).

How much time? Four or five days is enough. If you have more time, stay an extra night in Van and do one of the side trips along the lake.

Getting around: Intercity buses are a good option, though you might want to rent a car in Van to see the sights around the lake.

When to go: Because of their altitude, Kars and Van are usually pleasant during the summer, though the sun can still be quite strong. May and June, when the area is especially green and covered with wild flowers, are good months to visit. Winter is cold and dreary in Turkey's east, and many places are inaccessible because of snow.

Top sights: The ruins of Ani, Doğubeyazıt's fantastic Ishak Paş Sarayı, the island church of Akdamar in Lake Van.

By yourself or with a guide? You may want a guide for a visit to Ani, the area around Mt. Ararat, and for some of the sites around Lake Van.

DIYARBAKIR, MARDIN, MIDYAT AND HASANKEYF

Getting here: Fly in and out of Diyarbakir from Istanbul.

How much time? Three to four days will give you enough time to see this area. With extra time, spend another night in Mardin.

Getting around: Renting a car in Diyarbakir is the best option, although there are inter-city buses.

When to go: Summer can be oppressively hot, with temperatures over 100°F, and winter is cold and damp, so the best time to visit is in spring (late April through early June) or fall (September to early November).

Top sights: The walls of Diyarbakir, the bazaar and side streets of Mardin, the exquisite stone homes of Midyat and the riverside ruins at Hasankeyf.

By yourself or with a guide? Touring by yourself is a good option, since distances are short and much of the excursion is really about walking around the area's old towns and soaking up the atmosphere.

GAZIANTEP, MT. NEMRUT AND ŞANLIURFA (URFA)

Getting here: Fly in and out of Gaziantep from Istanbul.

How much time? Four or five days is enough time to see thes area; with extra time, spend another night in Gaziantep to try another of the city's great restaurants.

Getting around: We recommend flying, then renting a car, although intercity buses are possible.

When to go: Summer can be oppressively hot, with temperatures over 100°F, and winter is cold and damp, so the best time to visit is in spring (late April through early June) and fall (September-early November).

Top sights: Mount Nemrut, the Gaziantep Museum, the bazaar in Gaziantep, the carp pools in Şanliurfa.

By yourself or with a guide? It's easy to see this area by yourself, though you might want to take a guided tour of Mt. Nemrut from Gaziantep.

What It Costs in U.S. Dollars

DINING AND LODGING PRICE CATEGORIES

	¢	$	$$	$$$	$$$$
Restaurants	under $5	$5–$10	$11–$15	$16–$25	over $25
Hotels	under $50	$50–$75	$76–$150	$151–$250	over $250

Restaurant prices are for one main course at dinner or the equivalent. Hotel prices are for two people in a standard double room in high season, including taxes.

When to Go

Spring and fall are generally the best times to visit these areas, with the exception of the Black Sea coast, which is usually less rainy during the summer but still quite cool compared to the rest of Turkey, which can be sweltering.

Do you speak Turkish?

These areas are less touristy and finding English speakers can sometimes be a challenge, though most hotels will usually have someone on staff who speaks some English. On a pinch, try a combination of hand gestures and key English words nonspeakers are likely to know.

Being Careful?

During the 1980s and '90s, large parts of Turkey's east and southeast (but not the Black Sea area) were the scene of bitter fighting between the separatists of the Kurdistan Workers' Party (PKK) and Turkish security forces. The fighting has largely stopped, which has allowed tourism in the region to get off the ground again, but there have been several isolated incidents recently, particularly near the Turkey–Iraq border. Usually these events have occurred in remote areas where few tourists, let alone Turks, go.

7

Eastern Turkey may not have the resorts, boutique hotels, and upscale restaurants found in the more touristed parts of the country, but the rewards of travel here—impressive sites, both natural and manmade—are many.

The Black Sea area has rocky beaches backed by the majestic Kaçkar mountains—a slice of the Alps in Turkey—where you can hike, relax in picturesque mountain villages, or visit the historic city of Trabzon and the cliffside monastery of Sumela. The remote area between the cities of Kars and Van, in Turkey's far east, has the ancient city of Ani and the towering Mt. Ararat, which some believe is the resting place of Noah's Ark. The walled city of Diyarbakır and beautiful nearby towns of Mardin and Midyat lie in the heart of the ancient region known as Mesopotamia, where you can wander historic neighborhoods and visit churches that date back to the 3rd and 4th centuries AD. The area around the ancient cities of Gaziantep and Şanlıurfa, Turkey's southeast, is especially steeped in biblical history, though bustling local bazaars and scrumptious local cuisine will fortify you before a sunrise visit to the mountaintop temple of Nemrut Dağı.

TRABZON AND THE BLACK SEA COAST

Updated by
Catherine
Marshall

Of all of Turkey's regions, the Black Sea coast least fits the bill of what most visitors imagine to be "Turkish." Instead of long, sandy beaches lined with resorts, the Black Sea's shores are rocky and backed by steep, lush mountains. And instead of sunny days, the area is often shrouded in mist. Culturally, the area has had as much Greek, Georgian, and Armenian influences as it has Ottoman and Turkish. Although less visited than other parts of Turkey, the region is also one of the most rewarding. This excursion will take you to the Black Sea coast's most interesting destinations, from the historic seaside town of Trabzon and the nearby monastery complex of Sümela, clinging dramatically to the side of a cliff in a deep valley, to the Kaçkar mountains, whose 15,000-foot peaks tower over the area.

Trabzon, wedged between the Black Sea and the green mountains that rise behind it, is a city with a long historic pedigree that stretches back to Byzantine times, though today it's quite modern and, like many other cities in the region, is cursed with an overabundance of ugly concrete buildings. A little exploring, though, reveal the city's past, perhaps best represented by the magnificent Byzantine-era Aya Sofya church. Trabzon is also a good base for visiting the fascinating (though defunct) Orthodox monastery complex of Sümela, breathtakingly hidden in a narrow valley and clinging to the side of a steep cliff. Although the monastery, which was functioning until the 1920s, and its beautiful frescoes have over the years been victims to vandalism, an extensive restoration project is under way.

As you head east from Trabzon, toward the border with Georgia, you will pass through Rize, Turkey's tea-growing capital, with hills covered with carefully laid out rows of dark green tea plants. From there you'll soon approach several valleys that lead up into the majestic Kaçkar mountains, dotted with small villages with wooden homes that evoke the Alps. Up in the Fırtına valley is Ayder, a mountain village that serves as a wonderful base for hiking and exploring the area's mountain trails and *yaylas,* the high pasture summer villages where the rhythms of life seems to have changed little over the centuries.

TRABZON

GETTING HERE AND AROUND
There are several daily flights to Trabzon from both Istanbul and Ankara. Fares are competitive, so check with the different airlines to see who has the best. The bus ride from Istanbul to Trabzon takes almost 20 hours, but at around $42 to $58, it can be half as expensive as flying. There is daily service from Istanbul's Esenler bus terminal to the Trabzon bus terminal. There is also daily service from Ankara's AŞTİ bus terminal. Be sure to choose a company with comfortable seats.

Bus service between towns runs frequently and is inexpensive. You can get schedules at the local tourist information office or directly from the bus station in Trabzon. Renting a car, though, is the most convenient way of getting around the Black Sea area. The coast road from Trabzon eastward is currently in the process of being widened and turned into a proper highway, lessening travel time and making the driving experience much safer. Avis has an office in downtown Trabzon, as well as one at the airport. There are also several local companies around Trabzon's main square (Atatürk Alanı).

ESSENTIALS
GUIDED TOURS Eyce Tours in Trabzon can help with arranging tours to Sümela and the region around Trabzon.

Visitor Information (✉ *Ali Naki Efendi Sok. 1/A [near Atatürk Alanı]* ☎ *462/321–4659*).

Tour Information Eyce (☎ *462/326–7174* ⊕ *www.eycetours.com*).

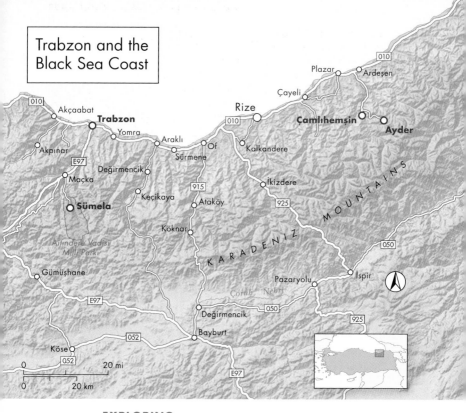

EXPLORING

Trabzon has a dramatic location, perched on a hill overlooking the sea, with lush green mountains behind. Once the capital of the empire founded in 1204 by Alexius Comnene, grandson of a Byzantine emperor, the city was famed for its golden towers and glittering mosaics—probably built with family money diverted from the royal till before the fall of Constantinople.

Today's Trabzon seems far removed from that imperial past: the city is bustling and modern, with a busy port, crowded streets, and seemingly little to distinguish it from many other provincial Turkish towns. It only takes a little digging, though, to get under the modern surface. Byzantine-era churches, such as the lovely Aya Sofya, a smaller version of the similarly named church in Istanbul, can be found not far from modern apartment buildings. The city's old town, meanwhile, with its Ottoman-era houses, pedestrian-only streets, and lively bazaar are a nice break from the concrete and crowds.

You can spend a day exploring the city, which is also a good base for a visit to the Sümela monastery. At night, have a fish dinner by the Black Sea or up in the hills overlooking the city.

The heart of Trabzon's social activity is in its pleasing central square, **Atatürk Alanı** *(also called Taksim Meydanı)*, up İskele Caddesi from

Trabzon's port. It's full of trees and tea gardens and surrounded by most of the city's hotels and restaurants.

The pedestrian-only Kunduracılar Caddesi leads west out of Atatürk Alanı into the maze of the **covered bazaar** (⊠*Just past Cumhuriyet Cad.*), which includes a 16th-century *bedestan*, or market, that has been restored and now houses several cafés and some gift shops selling unremarkable trinkets. The bazaar does have a small but appealing section of coppersmiths, who make a variety of bowls, trays, and pots.

The city's largest mosque, the **Çarşi Cami,** built in 1839, is joined to the market by an archway.

Trabzon's Byzantine-era **citadel,** in between two ravines, is still impos-

TURKISH NUTS & TEA

Economic life on the Black Sea is dominated by two crops: hazelnuts and tea. Near Rize, the hills are covered in row after row of tea plants, tended to by villagers who harvest the leaves in late spring. Every year, over 200,000 tons of tea are harvested in the area, most of it for domestic consumption. Turkey is also the globe's leading producer of hazelnuts, responsible for more than 80% of the world's supply. Hazelnuts, often fresh off the tree and still in their shell, are easy to find in shops and on the street throughout Turkey, especially in late summer and early fall.

ing, though it's pretty much a ruin. Its ramparts were restored after the Ottoman conquest in 1461, although the remains of the Byzantine palace are insignificant. No army ever took Trabzon by force, though many tried. Inside the citadel walls is the 10th-century Church of **Panaghia Chrysokephalos** (the Virgin of the Golden Head), which was the city's most important church for several centuries until the Aya Sofya was built. The Ottomans converted it into a mosque, the **Ortahisar Cami,** in the 15th century. Not much is left of the building's Byzantine glory, although it's soaring basilica and massive columns are still impressive. ⊠*Kale Cad.; from Hükümet Cad. (off Maraş Cad.), follow the Tabakhane Bridge over the gorge, turn left.*

You can get a good view of Trabzon from along **İç Kale Caddesi,** the street south of the citadel. From here you can also make out three other Byzantine monuments, all south of the Atatürk Alanı: the **Yeni Cuma Cami** (New Friday Mosque), built as the Church of St. Eugene in the early 13th century; the 13th-century **Teokephastos Convent,** on the other side of the hill; and the **Kudrettin Cami,** consecrated as the Church of St. Philip in the 14th century. Aya Sofya is visible about 3 km (2 mi) west of Atatürk Alanı.

★ Trabzon's best-known Byzantine monument, the 13th-century **Aya Sofya** *(Church of the Holy Wisdom, or St. Sophia),* sits on a bluff overlooking the Black Sea. The ruined church, known in Greek as Hagia Sofia, has some of the finest Byzantine frescoes and mosaics in existence. It was converted into a mosque in Ottoman times and first opened to the public as a museum in 1963. The west porch houses the real masterpieces: frescoes of Christ preaching in the Temple, the Annunciation, and the wedding at Cana, executed in a style that shows strong Italian influence. As at Istanbul's Aya Sofya, the artworks here were not destroyed by the Ottomans, only hidden under a layer of plaster. There's a shaded tea garden near the entrance. ⊠*Kay-akmeydan Cad.* ☎*462/223–3043* ⊒*$2.30* ⊘*May–Sept., daily 9–6; Oct.–Apr., Tues.–Sun. 8–5.*

Atatürk Köşkü, Atatürk's summer villa (though he didn't spend much time here) is now a museum dedicated to the founder of Turkey. The attractive white gingerbread house, set in a small forest, is pleasant and has a nice view of the city below. ⊠*Soğuksu Cad., 7 km (4 mi) southwest of Trabzon's central square* ☎*462/231–0028* ⊒*$1.50* ⊘*May–Sept., daily 8–7; Oct.–Apr., daily 9–5.*

★ The **Trabzon Museum,** in a 1910 mansion built for a local banker, is intriguing because of the building itself, as well as for its collection. The main floor has incredibly ornate rooms that have been restored and filled with period furniture. The basement holds a variety of archaeological finds from the Trabzon region. ⊠*Zeytinlik Cad. 10* ☎*462/322–3822* ⊒*$2.30* ⊘*Tues.–Sun. 9–5.*

> **BLACK SEA SPECIALTIES**
>
> Size isn't everything, as the miniscule *hamsi* (Black Sea anchovy) proves. Though usually not much longer than your finger, the *hamsi* is often called the prince of the Black Sea fish, and it's found in an almost endless variety of dishes: fried in a coating of cornmeal, served in a fragrant pilaf, baked into bread, or thrown into an omelet (there have even been some attempts at making hamsi ice cream). Also try *muhallema* (a type of Black Sea cheese fondue) and honey made in the high mountain villages of the Kaçkars.

WHERE TO STAY AND EAT

$
TURKISH
✕**Balıçı Dede.** On the western edge of Trabzon, this fish restaurant gets you as close to the water as possible. The sea and mountain views, and the sound of lapping water in the background, make the location a winner, especially at sunset. The fish, served grilled or fried, is fresh, and there is a full selection of well-made mezes to choose from. Alcohol is also served, unlike at many other restaurants in Trabzon. ⊠*Merkez Akyazı Beldesi Devlet Karayolu Üzeri* ☎*462/221–0398* ⊟*MC, V.*

$–$$
TURKISH
✕**Boztepe Aile Gazinosu.** Grilled meat and fish are the specialties at this restaurant with tables in a shady garden and on an outdoor terrace. Above the city in the green Boztepe Park, the restaurant also has a lovely view of the Black Sea and Trabzon's harbor. Finish your meal with tea served in an old-fashioned samovar. ⊠*Boztepe Mahalesi* ☎*462/321–4536* ⊟*MC, V.*

¢–$
CAFE
✕**Brasserie Pera.** On a busy boulevard above Trabzon's main square, a string of cafés tries to create something of a local hip scene. This one, with its striped awning and tables on the sidewalk, has a vaguely European feel to it and always seems to be the most crowded. The menu features sandwiches, salads, and pastas, along with a variety of cakes and ice cream, a nice break from fish and kebabs. ⊠*Yavuz Selim Bulvari 173* ☎*462/326–4696* ⊟*MC, V.*

¢
TURKISH
✕**Murat Balık Salonu.** On the north side of Atatürk Alanı, this small, nononsense restaurant serves perfectly grilled Black Sea. A glass case in the front holds the day's catch: red mullet, mackerel, anchovies, bass, trout, or whatever else is in season. The small dining room, painted an

It's worth the hike to get to the Sümela Monastery. —photo by Brenda Easton, Fodors.com member

electric green, is usually filled with local men who come in for a quick and unceremonious meal. ⊠*Park Karşısı* ☎*462/322–3100* ⊟*No credit cards.*

¢ ✕**Üstad Lokantası.** This homey restaurant on Atatürk Alanı is low on
TURKISH atmosphere, but it's hard to beat the well-made, very affordable food. A steam table at the entrance holds an assortment of dishes, including meat and vegetable stews baked in a large terra-cotta pot, stuffed cabbage, and Turkish-style meatballs. The rice pudding dessert is worth tasting. ⊠*Atatürk Alanı 18/B* ☎*462/321–5406* ⊟*MC, V.*

$ 🛏**Horon Hotel.** One block off the main square, the Horon has spa-
★ cious rooms done up in a slightly tacky peach and green motif. The professional staff is extremely helpful, though, and the parking and valet service are a blessing. On weekends be sure to ask for a room away from the rather loud bar. The rooftop restaurant, which offers a good-value prix-fixe menu, looks out over the sea and the rooftops below. **Pros:** walking distance to the sea; free Wi-Fi; helpful English-speaking staff. **Cons:** no spa/fitness center; not a very tranquil setting. ⊠*Sıramağazalar Cad. 125* ☎*462/326–6455* ⊕*www.otelhoron.com* ⌁*44 rooms* △*In-room: safe, refrigerator, Wi-Fi. In-hotel: restaurant, bar* ⊟*MC, V* ⊺⊚*BP.*

¢ 🛏**Hotel Nur.** With a cheery staff and spotless rooms (though small and painted bright green), this is Trabzon's best budget option. Some of the front rooms on the higher floors even have a sea view. The hotel is conveniently located on a quiet side street just off Trabzon's main square. **Pros:** overlooks the town square; next to a tourist center. **Cons:** the call to prayer from the mosque next door may disturb you in the morning; congested with tour groups. ⊠*Cami Sokak 15, 61100*

☎462/323–0445 🖷462/323–0447 ⏎15 rooms ⚴In-room: refrigerator ▤MC, V ⑩BP.

$$ 🍽**Usta Park Hotel.** Conveniently located off Atatürk Alanı, you can't miss the looming bright red Usta Park Hotel. Rooms are comfortable enough, if somewhat sparsely decorated, but gold-colored bedspreads add warmth. The rooftop restaurant, where breakfast is served, has a nice view of the sea, while the lobby has crystal chandeliers, brown leather lounge chairs, and Greek music playing in the background. Additional perks are the juice bar and patisserie. **Pros:** Turkish bath and sauna; within walking distance to city's main attractions. **Cons:** some rooms face another building across an alley; sauna and fitness rooms are quite small. ✉*Iskenderpaşa Mah. 3, 61100*☎*462/326–5700* ⊕*www.ustaparkhotel.com* ⏎*114 rooms, 6 suites* ⚴*In-room: safe, refrigerator, Wi-Fi. In-hotel: 2 restaurants, bar, gym* ▤*AE, DC, MC, V* ⑩*BP.*

$$$$ 🍽**Zorlu Grand Hotel.** With a marble-lined, atrium-like lobby topped by a stained-glass dome, this is certainly Trabzon's fanciest hotel, with prices to match. Rooms are large, elegant, and comfortably furnished. The staff is courteous and professional and the tranquil lobby, done up in an Art Deco–meets-Moorish style, is a nice refuge from the bustling streets outside. **Pros:** luxury salon and Turkish bath; juice bar; dance bar; concierge can arrange tours for guests; close to city center. **Cons:** expensive spa services; no airport shuttle service; some rooms overlook busy streets. ✉*Maraş Cad. 9, 61100*☎*462/326–8400* ⊕*www.zorlugrand.com* ⏎*143 rooms, 14 suites* ⚴*In-room: safe, refrigerator, Wi-Fi. In-hotel: 3 restaurants, bar, pool, gym, laundry facilities, laundry service, parking (free)* ▤*AE, DC, MC, V* ⑩*BP.*

SÜMELA/MEREYEMANA

47 km (29 mi) south of Trabzon on Rte. 885 to Maçka, and then east on road to Altındere National Park.

★ Set in a dramatic valley and clinging to the side of a sheer cliff, the Sümela monastery (Mereyemana in Turkish) is a spectacular and unforgettable sight. The Orthodox monks who founded the retreat, also known as the **Monastery of the Virgin,** in the 4th century carved their cells right from the rock. Built to house a miraculous icon of the Virgin painted by St. Luke, this shrine was later rebuilt and expanded by Alexius III, who was crowned here in 1340—an event depicted in the frescoes of the main church in the grotto. Where chunks of the frescoes have fallen off—or been chipped away or scribbled over by overly enthusiastic souvenir hunters and graffiti artists—three layers of plaster from repaintings done in the 14th and 18th centuries are clearly visible. Tolerant Ottoman sultans left the retreat alone, but after the Greeks were expelled from Turkey in 1922, the Turkish government permitted monks to transfer the Virgin icon itself to a new monastery in Greek Macedonia. The frescoes here are not as well preserved as those at Trabzon's Aya Sofya, but the setting—a labyrinth of courtyards, corridors, and chapels—is incredible. The monastery and its surrounding rooms are continually being restored, but there's not much hope the job will be finished soon. From the parking lot, you can pick up the well-worn trail that takes you on a rigorous 40-minute hike to the monastery—it's more than 820 feet above the valley floor and disappears completely when the clouds come down. If you're not up for the big hike, a 10-minute drive from the parking lot up a winding gravel road takes you to another trailhead, from where it's only about a 15-minute walk. ⊠*Altındere National Park* ☎*No phone* ⚏*$5 per person, $8 for parking* ☉*Apr.–Oct., daily 9–6; Nov.–Mar., daily 9–4.*

WHERE TO STAY AND EAT

¢ ✕**Sümela Sosyal Tesisleri.** Just below the Sümela monastery, this simple
TURKISH restaurant makes wonderful use of the stunning location—a series of open-air wood patios are spread out along a thunderous rushing stream. You can order köfte or kebabs, or choose from a few regional dishes, such as *kuymak*, the Black Sea version of cheese fondue. The cool air and shade make this an excellent spot to rest after a visit to the monastery. ⊠*Sümela Manastiri* ☎*462/531–1207* ▤*MC, V.*

¢–$ ✕**Sümer Restaurant.** With wooden gazebos set on the edge of a small
TURKISH river, this is a fine spot to have lunch or dinner after visiting Sümela, a 15-minute drive away. There is a wide selection of mezes, along with regional specialties such as *canlı alabalık* (live trout) baked in butter, and *kaygana*, an omlette made with Black Sea anchovies. On the weekends, the restaurant (formerly known as Sümela Ciftlik Restaurant) is filled with families from Trabzon on country outings. ⊠*Maçka Sümela Manastırı Yolu Km 2* ☎*462/512–1581* ▤*MC, V.*

$ ▤**Coşandere Turistik Tesisleri.** Some 2 km (3 mi) from the entrance to Sümela, this is an appealing option if you want to stay near the monastery. The hotel has several bungalows, but most of the rooms are in a four-story, chalet-like wooden building. The cozy rooms have still-fragrant pine furniture. An open-air restaurant by the river serves trout baked in a terra-cotta dish, among other stomach-warming options. In addition to arranging visits to Sümela, the hotel can set up day tours of nearby *yaylas*. **Pros:** great restaurant; ready-made outdoor itineraries available; airport/bus service. **Cons:** a bit secluded; there's not much to do in bad weather; no nightlife. ⊠*Sümela Yolu, Maçka* ☎*462/531–1190* ⊕*www.cosandere.com* ▭*40 rooms, 9 bungalows* ⌂*In-room: refrigerator, Wi-Fi* ▤*MC, V* ☉*Closed Oct.–Apr.* ⋔*BP.*

¢ ▤**Kayalar Pansiyon.** Roughly 3 km (2 mi) before you reach the admission booth to Sümela, this simple family-run *pansiyon* on the side of a grass-covered hill is the best option if you want to stay near the monastery. Run by the friendly Halit and Nereman Kaya (who also does the cooking), the rambling house has simple rooms with kilims covering the pine floors. Five of the rooms have balconies where you can catch a lovely breeze but only two of the rooms have en suite bathrooms. **Pros:** sparse but spacious rooms; gorgeous mountain and sea views; friendly owners; clean kitchen. **Cons:** not every room has a bathroom; off the beaten track. ⊠*Sümela Manastiri Yolu üzeri, Maçka* ☎*462/531–1057* ▭*7 rooms* ▤*No credit cards* ☉*Closed Oct.–Apr.* ⋔*BP.*

EN ROUTE Rize, 75 km (47 mi) east of Trabzon and the capital of the Black Sea's tea-growing region, sits above a small bay but below the foothills of the lush Pontic Mountains. There's not much else to do here but stop for a glass of the local brew in the hilltop **Zıraat Parkı,** a botanical garden near the town's western entrance. There's a small kiosk in the parking lot that sells gift packs of tea.

Morina Balı Lokantası. This unassuming restaurant on the coastal road halfway between Trabzon and Rize serves some of the best fish in the area. There's always a varied selection of freshly caught options—including meaty salmon steaks—cooked over hot coals or fried in a dusting of corn flour. The tomato-based fish chowder is also tasty. A pleasant garden is shaded by creeping vines. This is definitely worth a stop. ⊠ *35 km (22 mi) out of Trabzon in the direction of Rize, Çamburn/ Sürmene* ☎ *462/752-2023.*

Northeast of Rize, several forested valleys lead from the Black Sea into the towering and beautiful Kaçkar Mountains. Dotted with small villages, the cool mountains are a great place for hiking or just kicking back and checking out the alpine views. The mountains are also home to several *yaylas,* high pasture villages that are inhabited only during the summer and are accessible only by footpath.

ÇAMLIHEMŞIN

124 km (77 mi) northeast of Trabzon; 22 km (14 mi) south of Ardeşen.

The small village of Çamlıhemşin, at the junction of two rushing rivers, serves mainly as a gateway to mountain valleys above, particularly to the village of Ayder, but it's a pleasant and quiet overnight stop before heading up into the Kaçkars. There's not much to do here other than look out on the green mountains and listen to the river flowing by.

WHERE TO STAY AND EAT

¢ ✕ **Ibonun Yeri.** Run by friendly Ibrahim Uysal, this riverside restaurant on the road to Ayder serves grilled meats (the veal pan-fried in butter is delicious) and fresh trout. With pine walls and colorful local fabrics hanging from the ceiling, the restaurant is cozy and inviting. Ibrahim's wife works with him and is responsible for the flaky homemade baklava. ⊠ *Merkez Mah.* ☎ *464/651-7288* ▬ *No credit cards.*

TURKISH

$ ⛺ **Fırtına Pansiyon.** The Firtına Pansiyon, in a converted schoolhouse, is the most inviting of the few places to stay in Firtına valley. Run by a local brother and sister, the *pansiyon,* which has six rooms and two bungalows, is nestled between the green mountains in a completely solitary spot. Rooms are small and have shared bathrooms, but the location is beautiful and a good spot for exploring the rest of the valley, which the owners can help you do. **Pros:** beautiful evirons with a quirky style; simple but delicious set menu; assisted tours through the area. **Cons:** quite far from even the nearest store; intermittent hot water; privacy can feel limited in such close quarters. ⊠ *Şenyuva Köyü* ☎ *464/653-3111* ⊕ *www.firtinavadisi.com* 🛏 *6 rooms, 2 cabins* ▬ *No credit cards* ☾ *Closed Oct.–Mar.* ⦿ *MAP.*

**OFF THE
BEATEN
PATH**

Most people take a left out of Çamlıhemşin and continue up to the mountain village of Ayder, but continuing straight on the road takes you into the Fırtına valley, an often mist-shrouded place that sees few visitors and seems forgotten by time. Waterfalls and streams tumble out of the mountains, which are covered by thick stands of green pines. Small villages with peak-roofed two-story wooden houses cling to the mountainsides. As you drive along the road, you'll pass several examples of the elegant Ottoman-era humpback bridges spanning the rivers.

AYDER

90 km (56 mi) northeast of Rize; 17 km (11 mi) southeast of Çamlıhemşin.

At 4,000 feet and surrounded by snow-capped mountains and tumbling waterfalls, the mountain village of Ayder, with its wooden chalets and wandering cows, can seem like a piece of Switzerland transported to Turkey. Once a sleepy yayla, a high pasture village where locals would live in the summer, Ayder has become a popular destination for Turkish tourists and, increasingly, foreign ones. While a few years ago the village's bucolic nature was threatened by overdevelopment, local laws have now ordered all building to be done in the local style, with wooden exteriors and peaked roofs. Despite the summertime crowds that can sometimes fill the small village to capacity, the setting remains magnificent and the nights, when the stars put on a glorious show in the sky above, are still marvelously quiet. The village is also an excellent base for either day hikes or extended treks in the Kaçkars and for visiting some of the less accessible yaylas in the region to see a way of life that has changed little over the centuries.

Ayder has a grassy main square that during the summer frequently plays host to festivals celebrating local Hemşin culture, with music played on a local version of the bagpipe (known as the *bağlama*) and horon dancing, which has men and women dancing together in a big circle.

Ayder is also known for its hot springs, reputed to cure all types of ailments. True or not, the **springs** (☎464/657–210 ⊗ *Mar.–Nov., daily 7–7; Dec.–Feb., daily 10–6* ▨*$5*), housed in a modern, marble-lined building near the village's mosque, are good for a relaxing soak after a day of hiking. There are separate facilities for men and women, as well as private rooms for couples that want to bathe together.

The easiest yayla to visit from Ayder is Yukarı Kavron, about 10 km (6 mi) from the village along a dirt road. A collection of squat stone houses, it's set on a high plateau surrounded by gorgeous mountains. There are several nice hikes leading out of the village. There is regular minivan service in the morning out of Ayder to the yayla, although it's best to check with your hotel or *pansiyon* about the exact schedule.

WHERE TO STAY AND EAT

¢   ✕**Ayder Sofrası.** Run by the owners of the Haşimoğlu hotel, this large
TURKISH restaurant has a nice stone-lined terrace with wooden picnic tables that look over the mountains. The kitchen turns out trout and local dishes such as stuffed cabbage and *muhallama*, the local cheese fondue, and serves an open buffet breakfast every day. ⊠*Ayder Kapalıcaları* ☎464/657–2037 ▤*MC, V.*

¢   ✕**Dört Mevsim.** This low-key restaurant has two things going for it: a
TURKISH great location that looks out on a magnificent waterfall and, a rarity

for Ayder, a liquor license. You can drink your wine or beer along with mezes, kebabs, and muhallama. The outdoor terrace has a view of the waterfall; this is a good spot to rest your legs after a hike around Ayder. ✉ *Şelale Karşısı* ☎ 464/657–2019 ☰ *No credit cards.*

¢   ✕ **Nazlı Cicek.** In a shaded ravine near the entrance to town, the family-
TURKISH run Nazlı Cicek serves tasty trout that is taken fresh from one of the cement pools on the premises. They also serve the usual assortment of grilled meats. You can eat inside the cozy restaurant, which has color-ful Hemşin fabrics on the walls, or outside, near a running stream. The extremely fresh fish, coupled with the relaxing outdoor seating make it a favorite spot. ✉ *Ayder Merkez* ☎ 464/657–2130 ☰ *MC, V.*

$ ⌂ **Fora Pansiyon.** Run by local guide Mehmet Demirci and his wife, this venerable Ayder *pansiyon* is on the top of the hill at the entrance to the village. The wooden house has a rustic feel, with seven simple, cozy rooms lined with wide wooden paneling and shared bathrooms. A stone-lined outdoor terrace, where breakfast and dinner are served, looks out on the forested mountains and the village below. **Pros:** breath-taking views; sauna; hiking itineraries; close to Ayder springs. **Cons:** shared bathrooms; steep walk up to the *pansiyon.* ✉ *Ayder Kaplıcaları* ☎ 464/657–2153 ⊕ *www.turkutour.com* ⇆ *7 rooms, 1 bungalow* ☰ *No credit cards* ⊘ *Closed Dec.–Apr.* ⦿ *MAP.*

$ ⌂ **Kuşpuni Dinlenme Evi.** Set on the edge of a green field, this wooden chalet has comfortable rooms that are larger than those in many of the other local *pansiyons.* With colorful rugs and kilims in the hallways, the place has a homey feel and the owners are very friendly. A nice res-taurant with an outdoor terrace serves local specialties with wonderful views. **Pros:** beautiful terrace; owners are helpful in arranging excur-sions; more peaceful than other *pansiyons.* **Cons:** restaurant is a bit pricey for the quality; off the beaten path; Internet is patchy. ✉ *Yukarı Ambarlik* ☎ 464/657–2052 ⇆ *15 rooms* ⌖ *In-hotel: restaurant* ☰ *MC, V* ⊘ *Closed Oct.–Apr.* ⦿ *BP.*

¢   ⌂ **Serender Pansiyon.** Owner Yusuf Mamuş was born in Ayder but went off to Istanbul to work. He came back in 2000 when he retired, and decided to open the friendly Serender Pansiyon, which is also where he and his wife live. The house, like most of the other *pansiyons* in Ayder, is made of wood. The rooms are simple, but have wonderful views of the mountains and waterfalls; there's the occasional sound of a cow-bell in the distance. A lovely terrace where breakfast is served looks out on pastures and the mountains. **Pros:** peaceful surroundings; own-ers can give great travel advice. **Cons:** only serves breakfast; interior design could use some sprucing up; few amenities. ✉ *Yukarı Ambarlik* ☎ 464/657–2201 ⇆ *14 rooms* ☰ *MC, V* ⦿ *BP.*

KARS, MT. ARARAT AND LAKE VAN

Turkey's east is a region filled with stark contrasts: dusty plains and soaring mountains, simple villages and bustling cities. Near Turkey's border with Armenia and Iran, this remote region is also filled with natural and man-made wonders and, for the visitor, offers the chance to see a part of Turkey that has yet to be invaded by the tourist hordes. While this means that you may not find all the amenities and services

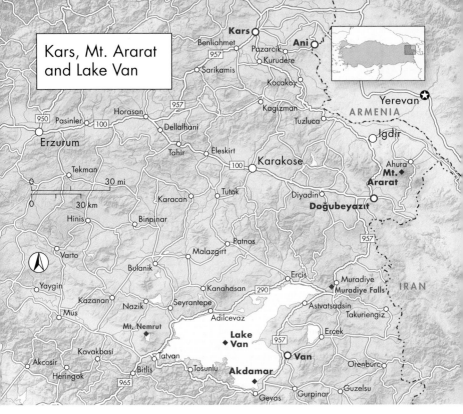

Kars, Mt. Ararat
and Lake Van

available in western Turkey, the friendliness and hospitality of the area's predominantly Kurdish locals will very likely make up for it.

This excursion starts in Kars, which spent the early part of the 20th century under Russian occupation and still looks in places like a small Russian town. More than anything else, though, Kars serves as the base for exploring the haunting Ani, one of Turkey's most important historical sites. Once the capital of an Armenian kingdom that ruled the area more than a thousand years ago and that filled the city with stunning churches, Ani is today more like a ghost town, filled with ruins that still manage to evoke the city's former glory. Its location, at the edge of a windswept gorge with snowcapped mountains in the background and grassy fields stretching out to the horizon, only adds to Ani's mystique.

From Kars continue to Doğubeyazıt, a dusty town not far from the Iranian border. While the town isn't much to look at, it's blessed with being located almost at the foot of the mythical Mt. Ararat, the 16,850-foot peak that some believe is the resting place of Noah's ark. A perfect cone rising to the sky from the flat plains around it, Ararat is quite a sight to behold. Also in Doğubeyazıt is the Ishak Paşa Saray, an 18th-century palace in the hills above town which seems like it was transported straight out of a fairy tale.

Spotlight on the Armenians

Armenians were once an integral part of the ethnic mix in Turkey's east, although today none remain in the region. What happened to them is a topic of sensitive debate in Turkey.

There were various Armenian kingdoms in the region starting in the 3rd century BC and lasting until almost the 11th century AD. After that, the Armenians—who adopted Christianity in AD 301—became the subjects of a succession of rulers, from the Byzantines, to the Persians, and finally the Ottomans. Armenians ended up living in Eastern Turkey throughout the Ottoman Empire, with Istanbul eventually becoming one of their main cultural centers.

During World War I, when the Ottomans came under attack by Russia and the other allied powers, some Armenians in the east saw this as a chance for independence and rose up in revolt. The Armenians claim that the Ottoman response led to the death of hundreds of thousands (some claim even 1.5 million) and have been trying to have

The Armenians were driven east, with only what they could carry

the events of the time recognized as a genocide. The Turks, while admitting that large numbers of Armenians died at the time, say this was the result of war and disease, which also cost the lives of many others living in the region. Some 70,000 Armenians still live in Turkey, mostly in Istanbul.

The next stop is Van, a modern and bustling city that is the economic capital of Turkey's east. Use this city as a base for exploring the area around the nearby Lake Van, one of Turkey's most fascinating natural wonders. Surrounded by mountains, the lake's blue-green waters are rich in minerals and very alkaline, meaning even the poorest swimmer will float with ease. The region around the lake is home to several intriguing historical sites, most importantly the magical island of Akdamar and its 10th-century Armenian church. It's an area that you could easily spend several days exploring.

KARS

The Kars airport is 4 mi out of town.

GETTING HERE AND AROUND

Turkish Airlines, Atlas Jet, and Pegasus have regular flights from Istanbul to Kars.

There are daily buses from Istanbul and Ankara to cities in the east, but it's a long trip and not much cheaper than flying. Kars is about 18 hours from Ankara ($35), 22 hours from Istanbul ($45), and 10 hours from Trabzon ($20). Van is about 20 hours from Ankara ($30), 24 hours from Istanbul ($40), and 12 hours from Trabzon ($20). Van Seyahat makes the trip from Istanbul to Van. Kars Doğu takes passenger from Istanbul to Kars.

The train is not the best option: the trip from Istanbul to Kars (38 hours or more) is brutally slow, though it's cheap.

ESSENTIALS

GUIDED TOURS   The English-speaking guide Celil Ersözoğlu is a good option in Kars. He can arrange for trips to Ani and to some of the Armenian and Georgian monuments in the area.

Tour contacts Celil Ersözoğlu (✉ *532/226–3966* ✎ *celilani@hotmail.com*).

Visitor Information (✉ *Atatürk Cad. next to Süleyman Demirel Parkı, in Milli Eğitim Bldg.* ☎ *474/223–2300* 📠 *474/223–8452*).

EXPLORING

The setting for Turkish novelist Orhan Pamuk's somber novel *Snow,* Kars, not far from Turkey's border with Armenia and Georgia, looks like the frontier town it is: forbidding and grayish, set on a 5,740-foot plateau and forever at the mercy of the winds. The lifting of restrictions on visiting the ancient city of Ani—previously a closed military zone—has meant more tourists are coming through the area, giving locals the incentive to upgrade what Kars has to offer and there are signs of a new breath of life all over town. Some of Kars's Ottoman-era historic buildings are being beautifully restored as part of an ambitious project sponsored by the California-based Global Heritage Fund. A sign of changing times was the opening, in 2006, of the city's first boutique hotel: the Kars Otel.

This mini-revival would be only the latest twist of history in a city that has had at least its own share of ups and downs. Since AD 1064, Kars has been besieged over and over, by various and sundry invaders: from the Akkoyun to the Mongol warriors of Tamerlane. In the 19th century alone, it was attacked three times by czarist armies from Russia. The Turks retook the city in 1920, and Kars was formally ceded to Turkey after the war of independence in 1921. The Russian influence is still obvious in many buildings.

With its low buildings and compact town center, Kars has a relaxed, small-town feeling to it. The city has a reputation as being a liberal and secular-minded outpost, and it certainly has more bars and licensed restaurants than other towns in the conservative east. There is a sense of renewed optimism in Kars today, with locals hoping their position near the border might make the town something of a trade hub and that the tourist traffic to Ani in the summer and the nearby Sarıkamış ski resort in the winter will only increase, further stimulating the city's renewal. For now, though, Kars makes for a nice side dish to the main course that is the nearby mesmerizing site of Ani.

İç Kale *(Kars Castle)* overhangs the town from a high, rocky vantage point. Though it dates from the 10th century, most surviving fortifications were commissioned by Lala Mustafa Paşa in 1579—in 1386

A typical traffic jam in Eastern Turkey. Photo by BrendaE, Fodors.com member

Tamerlane swept violently through the region and razed the original structure. The castle has gone through some restoration in recent years and the panoramic views of Kars merit the 10-minute walk uphill. ⊠*Kale Cad.* ☎*No phone* ✉*Free* ⊙*Daily 9–sunset.*

The **Kümbet Cami** *(Drum-Dome Mosque)*, at the foot of the hill by Kars River, is obviously not Turkish—originally the Armenian Church of the Twelve Apostles, it was built in the 10th century. You can still make out the Apostles on the exterior of the drum-shaped cupola. The mosque is often locked, in which case the only view is through a rusty gate, but the exterior is architecturally interesting.

Just northwest of Kümbet Cami is the **Taşköprü,** known as "the Stone Bridge," a bridge of Seljuk origin dating from the 1400s, built of volcanic rock. ⊠*Kale Cad., at foot of İç Kale*

On either side of the bridge you will be able to see some of the restoration projects being undertaken by the Global Heritage Fund. On the south side is the 300-year-old home of famed poet Nemik Kemal, which is being turned into a cultural center, while on the north side a row of Ottoman-era riverside timber and stone homes has been restored and painted. There are also plans to restore two ancient hamams near the bridge.

Kars Museum *(Kars Müzesi)*, near the train station on the eastern edge of town, is difficult to find—you're best off taking a taxi—but worth the trip. Two floors of displays cover Kars's many rulers—Roman, Greek, Seljuk, and Ottoman—and there are pieces of Armenian churches and a Russian church bell. You can also check out wall-size maps of Ani here, which will help you get your bearings in preparation for visiting the site. ⊠485 *Cumhuriyet Cad.* ☎474/212–2387 💵$2.50 ⊙*Daily 8:30–5:30.*

WHERE TO STAY AND EAT

$
TURKISH
✗**Bistro Kar.** As the name implies, Bistro Kar is trying to bring big-city style to provincial Kars. On a small bluff overlooking a park, the restaurant is in a wooden structure that looks like a big gazebo, with smaller gazebos for outdoor dining. The menu features classic mezes—stuffed eggplants and stewed peppers, for example—along with grilled meat and fish. Roast goose is a local specialty but call ahead to see if it's actually available. The restaurant serves alcohol and has a decent selection of wine. ⊠*Resul Yıldız Cad., Buzhane Üstü* ☎474/212–8050 ▭*MC, V.*

KARS SPECIALTIES

Kars is famous throughout Turkey for its cheese and honey, and you'll see several shops throughout town with sheets of honeycomb and big wheels of the local cheese, known as *kaşar*, on display in their windows.

Büyük Zavotlar (⊠*Halitpaşa Cad. 220* ☎474/223-3138) is a particularly inviting shop that sells an aged *kaşar* that tastes much like an Italian pecorino. You can also do as the locals and stop by in the morning for a takeout breakfast of delicious *"bal* and *kaymak,"* honey with clotted cream.

¢–$
TURKISH
✗**Fasıl Ocakbaşı.** On the second floor of a small shopping center in the middle of town, this kebab restaurant is a bit more relaxed than most other grill houses in town, with less hustle and bustle. It looks very 1970s, with wood paneling all around, but the food—mezes and grilled meat and fish—is well made. And unlike most kebab restaurants, this one has a liquor license. ⊠*Faikbey Cad. 100, Yıl işhanı, Kat 1* ☎474/212–1714 ▭*MC, V.*

¢–$
TURKISH
✗**Ocakbaşı Restoran.** The kebabs are simple and tasty but the restaurant itself has opted for a touch more class than elsewhere, with embroidered curtains, rust-colored tablecloths, and waiters in shiny vests. The lively dining room, which is dominated by a large copper grill, is usually filled with local men eating large meals and having animated conversations. ⊠*Atatürk Cad. 276* ☎474/212–0056 ▭*MC, V.*

¢–$
TURKISH
✗**Şirin Anadolu Mutfağı.** *Şirin* means "cute" in Turkish and this humble restaurant certainly fits the bill. The walls are painted lime and the columns are pink, so it won't win any decor awards, but you'll be won over by the tasty food and friendly staff. Along with kebabs and an assortment of soups, the kitchen also turns out local specialties such as a lamb and chickpea stew called *piti.* Upstairs is a café with wicker chairs and colorful rugs where young locals spend hours chatting over tea and coffee. ⊠*Karadağ Cad. 55* ☎474/212–3379 ▭*MC, V.*

¢
🛏**Güngören Oteli.** This is an excellent budget option. The rooms are comfortable (with full-size tubs, rare for budget hotels in this area) though, for some reason, someone decided that blue and neon green paint, with bedspreads to match, was a good idea. On a quiet side street, the friendly hotel also has a good restaurant, as well as a sauna and hamam in the basement. **Pros:** best bang for your buck in the area; convenient location to town; decent and reasonably priced eats. **Cons:** decor is a throwback to the '80s; no great views. ⊠*Millet Sokak 2*

7

☎474/212–6767 📠474/212–5630 ⤳40 rooms ⌂In-hotel: restaurant, Wi-Fi ▭MC, V ⓘBP.

$$ 🚹 **Hotel Karabağ.** Once one of Kars's top hotels, the Karabağ is a little frayed at the edges these days, with faded carpets and plastic plants in the lobby, but the rooms are good-sized and the staff friendly. It's on a busy main street, so ask for a room in the back. **Pros:** spacious rooms; the helpful staff can advise on half-day/full-day excursions; comfortable lounge and bar. **Cons:** a bit pricey for the services provided; musty smell accompanies the outdated furniture. ✉*Faik Bey Cad. 184, at Atatürk Cad.* ☎474/212–3480 📠474/223–3089 ⤳45 rooms, 5 suites ⌂In-room: refrigerator. In-hotel: restaurant, bar ▭MC, V ⓘBP.

$$$ 🚹 **Kar's otel.** Kars now has not just its first (and, so far, only) boutique hotel, but a very stylish one at that. In a wonderfully restored late-19th-century Russian-built mansion, the hotel has a cool, minimalist white-and-gray color scheme and original art on the walls depicts monuments in Kars. The top two floors of the three-story building have long balconies in the back, where you can sit and order a drink from the hotel's bar. Breakfast is served in a courtyard and there's a very appealing restaurant in the basement. **Pros:** plush and modern rooms; a warm welcome after a day of skiing or sightseeing. **Cons:** luxury treatment but few services. ✉*Halitpaşa Cad. 79* ☎474/212–1616 ⊕*www.karsotel. com* ⤳5 rooms, 3 suites ⌂In-room: Internet. In-hotel: restaurant, bar ▭AE, MC, V ⓘBP.

ANI

Fodor's Choice
★   *42 km (26 mi) east of Kars on Rte. 36–07.*

The ruins at Ani are what draw most people to this remote area of Turkey. Until the Mongol invasion of 1236, Ani (also called Ocaklı) was the chief town of a medieval Armenian kingdom, with 100,000 inhabitants and "a thousand and one churches," according to historical sources. Although it was occupied by the Mongols, Ani still had a large Armenian population well into the 14th century. In 1319 the city was struck by a terrible earthquake, after which the townspeople began to leave. Today, scarcely a half-dozen churches remain, all in various states of disrepair, but even so, the sprawling site is breathtaking, with hundreds of stunning, weather-beaten ruins on a triangular promontory bounded on two sides by steep river gorges. Equally majestic is the surrounding countryside, a mix of severe mountains, tiny Kurdish settlements, and fields of wildflowers. There is a haunted, yet strangely meditative, feeling at the site, an open-air museum holding what are considered some of the finest examples of religious architecture of its period.

The ruins at Ani straddle the Alaçay River, which forms a natural border with Armenia. Until recent years Ani was a restricted military area, but the site is now open to visitors and requires no permits. There is a booth at the main gate where you must buy a ticket to visit the site. Ani has little shade and can get quite hot in the summer, so be sure to bring a hat and water. You should plan on spending several hours at the site if you want to see the highlights, although, depending on your level of interest, you could spend an entire day exploring the various ruins.

Enter through the **Aslan Kapısı** (Lion's Gate), one of three principal portals in Ani's extensive city walls, which stretch for more than 8,200 feet. The 32-foot-tall walls were raised in AD 972 by the Armenian king Smbat II, though the lion relief itself was added by the Seljuk sultan Menuçehr in 1064. A small trail makes a circle through Ani; following it clockwise, the first major ruin you encounter is the **Keseli** (Church of the Redeemer), a huge quadrangular cathedral built in 1035. Its dome (1036) was hit by lightning in the 1950s, which cut the building neatly in half, leaving a surrealistic representation of an Armenian church with the rubble of its former half in the foreground. There are three churches in Ani dedicated to St. Gregory, the Armenian prince who converted his people to Christianity. The best preserved is the **Nakışlı,** built by an Armenian nobleman, Tigran Honentz, in 1215. Nakışlı is the most impressive ruin in Ani, not least because it's at the foot of a ravine with a view over the Arpaçay River. Inside, note the remarkable cycle of murals depicting the Virgin Mary and St. Gregory. If you follow the path into the gorge, you will come to the striking **Kusanatz** (Convent of the Three Virgins), on a rocky outcrop.

The **Menüçehir Camii** (Menüçehir Mosque; 1072), which clings to the heights overlooking the Arpaçay River, but which is not difficult to get to, was originally an Armenian building, perhaps a palace. From here climb to the first citadel and continue to the second at the far edge of town, where the two gorges converge; you'll have a good view of the many cave dwellings in the walls of the western gorge, which once housed the city's poor. The **İç Kale** (Citadel), perched on a rocky plateau at the site's southeast end, is unfortunately off-limits. ☎ *No phone* ✉ *$3 for entire site* ☾ *Daily 9–6.*

DOĞUBEYAZIT AND MT. ARARAT

Doğubeyazıt is 192 km (119 mi) southeast of Kars.

ESSENTIALS

GUIDED TOURS Tour offices in Doğubeyazıt tend to go in and out of business every week, so if you need a guide, you're best off asking at your hotel and/or getting recommendations from other travelers.

EXPLORING

The scrappy frontier town of **Doğubeyazıt** (doh-*oo*-bay-yah-zuht) is a good base from which to enjoy views of Turkey's highest and most famous mountain, the majestic Mt. Ararat (Ağrı Dağı). Not far from the Iranian border, the place seems neglected, if not downright forgotten, with dusty streets and crumbling buildings. But the pace here is laid-back and the locals are friendly. You'll share the town with sheep and Iranian travelers bringing in contraband cigarettes and other cheap goods from Iran. There aren't too many carpet and kilim shops here compared to tourist spots in western Turkey, so you can wander the main street, Çarşı Caddesi, without being bothered too much. A day is probably enough time to spend here, catching an early visit to the sites around Mt. Ararat and then the İshak Paşa Saray at sunset.

★ Doğubeyazıt's only sight, the enchanting **İshak Paşa Saray** *(İshak Paşa Palace),* is in the mountains southeast of town. The fortified palace was

HARK! THE ARK!

The locals around Mt. Ararat have been selling Christian pilgrims old planks reputedly from Noah's ark, since medieval times, and fragments of ancient timber embedded in the ice, have been brought back by various ark-hunting expeditions over the years—though radiocarbon-dating tests have been inconclusive.

Satellite photos showed something embedded in a glacier at 12,500 feet, but further examination proved

it to be nothing more than a freak formation in the strata.

Nevertheless, expeditions by Christian groups are constantly make new claims, and a second Noah's Ark was "discovered" in the 1980s on a hillside 20 km (12 mi) southeast of Ararat. There are organized tours from Doğubeyazıt to visit the site, but to most eyes, this "ark" is nothing more than a pile of rocks.

built in the late 18th century by local potentate Çolak Abdi Paşa and his son İshak. The interior of the building is ornate, a fantastic mixture of Georgian, Persian, and Ottoman styles, though the gold-plated doors were carted off by Russian troops in 1917. Late afternoon is the best time to visit, when the sun casts a deep orange glow over the palace and the ruins of a citadel—carved into the opposite (and inaccessible) mountainside—whose foundations are Urartian but which was rebuilt several times through the centuries. There is a restaurant and teahouse above the palace, otherwise the only hints of civilization are a cluster of Kurdish mud-brick houses and the occasional musician wandering from house to house in search of an audience. ⌧ *6 km (4 mi) southeast of town on road to Göller* ☎*No phone* 🖅*$3* ⊗*Daily 9–5.*

Mt. Ararat *(Ağrı Dağı),* an extinct volcano covered with snow even in summer, soars dramatically 16,850 feet above the arid plateau, dominating the landscape. According to Genesis, after the Great Flood, "the waters were dried up from off the earth; and Noah removed the covering of the ark, and looked, and behold, the face of the ground was dry." The survivors, as the story goes, had just landed on top of Mt. Ararat. Many other ancient sources—Chaldean, Babylonian, Chinese, Assyrian—also tell of an all-destroying flood and of one man who heroically escaped its consequences. The mountain can be easily viewed from Doğubeyazıt, although actually climbing it requires a permit that can only be obtained several months in advance, and the trek must be done with a licensed agency. Local tour offices, though, will take you on a day trip that includes a visit to a village at the base of the mountain, which is the closest you can get to Ararat without a permit.

WHERE TO STAY AND EAT

¢–$ ✕**Evin Restaurant.** A no-frills but friendly restaurant frequented by the

TURKISH   locals—*evin* means "your home" in Turkish—this dining spot has a wide selection of prepared hot dishes, including *mantı* (Turkish ravioli), roast lamb shank, and köfte. They also serve trout, kebabs, and döner. ⌧*Abdullah Baydar Cad. 92* ☎*472/312–6073* ▭*No credit cards.*

¢ ✕**Kadın Destek Kooperatifi Lokantası.** Part of a local cooperative that helps
TURKISH women become financially independent, this is a good place to taste
regional home cooking. Meals are simple and satisfying with options
like chicken stewed in tomato broth or meat sautéed with peppers and
tomatoes. On Saturdays the women make a local specialty called *abig-
dor Koftesi,* a type of poached meatball made with lamb, onion, and
spices. The restaurant is in a somewhat drab and cavernous second-floor
space, but the purple tablecloths and walls hung with kilims made by
the cooperative, makes it a touch cozier. ✉*Ismail Beşikçi Cad., above
the Bosch dealership* ☎472/312–4026 ▭*No credit cards.*

¢–$ ✕**Murat Camping.** Despite the rustic name (there is a small campground
TURKISH on the premises), this restaurant is Doğubeyazıt's only option for a
big night out. Located on a hillside just below the Ishakpaşa Sarayı,
the large space has an outdoor terrace with a commanding view of
Doğubeyazıt and the mountains around it. There is the usual selection
of mezes and kebabs, live Turkish music in the evenings, and wine, beer,
and rakı. ✉*Ishakpaşa Sarayı* ☎472/312–0367 ▭*No credit cards.*

¢–$ ✕**Öz Urfa Kebap.** Looking something like a hunting lodge, with walls
TURKISH of rough wood boards and stools made out of tree stumps, this kebab
restaurant has tons more atmosphere than most other places in town.
There are several kinds of well-made kebabs on offer, as well as an
assortment of *pides* cooked the traditional way in the wood-burning
oven. ✉*Ismail Beşikçi Cad. 34* ☎544/218–0418 ▭*MC, V.*

$ ⌂**Golden Hill Hotel.** This hotel at the entrance to town is hands-down
Doğubeyazıt's best lodging option; the only reason to stay somewhere
else is if you can't get a room here. The eight-story black-granite building has an atrium with a fountain inside, and the rooms are clean and
new, with embroidered curtains. Suites have a separate room with a
couch and a dining table, and are a good value. The rooftop restaurant,
where breakfast is served, has a great view of Ararat. **Pros:** pleasant
decor inside and out; good food. **Cons:** no room service; no pool or
lounge. ✉*Çevreyolu Üzeri* ☎472/312–8717 ⎙472/312–5771 ➦70
rooms, 20 suites* ⌂*In-room: refrigerator, Internet. In-hotel: restaurant*
▭*MC, V* ⎢*BP.*

$ ⌂**Hotel Nuh.** The Nuh has relatively large rooms that are a touch nicer
than the other mid-level hotels in town, though the hotel's greatest
asset is its large rooftop restaurant, which has a smashing view of Mt.
Ararat. Most rooms also have a view of the mountain. **Pros:** great
views of Mt. Ararat or İshakpaşa Palace; hotel arranges excursions
to the mountains or springs; walking distance to city center and markets. **Cons:** no Internet; the American restaurant is not likely to meet
American standards, even for the homesick-for-food traveler; decor
leans toward drab. ✉*Büyük Ağrı Cad. 65* ☎472/312–7232 ⊕*www.
hotelnuh.8m.com* ➦*65 rooms* ⌂*In-hotel: 2 restaurants, bar, parking*
▭*MC, V* ⎢*BP.*

**NEED A
BREAK?** There's not much to see on the road from Doğubeyazıt to Van, so the lovely
Muradiye waterfalls, some 83 km (51 mi) southwest of Doğubeyazıt, come
as a welcome relief. From a small parking lot, a bouncy suspension bridge
crosses a swiftly flowing stream and gives you a good view of the 20-foot

falls. The area is filled with green poplar trees and local families who come here to picnic. A simple teahouse has a lovely view of the tumbling falls and is the perfect spot for taking a rest.

LAKE VAN AND ENVIRONS

171 km (106 mi) from Doğubeyazı, continuing past Muradiye to the town of Van.

GETTING HERE AND AROUND
Atlas Jet has regular flights from Istanbul to Van.

ESSENTIALS
GUIDED TOURS   The Ayanis travel agency in Van can help with travel arrangements and with organizing tours in the Lake Van area.

Tour contacts Ayanis (☎*432/210–1515*).

Visitor Information (✉ *Cumhuriyet Cad* ☎*432/216–2018* 🖨*432/216–3675*).

EXPLORING
The landscape around **Lake Van** *(Van Gölü)* is eerily desolate, a result of winter flash floods and intense summertime heat—in August the average daytime temperature is 38°C (100°F). This is Turkey's largest and most unusual lake, though: 3,738 square km (1,443 square mi) of eerily blue water surrounded by mighty volcanic cones. Lake Van was formed when a volcano blew its top and blocked the course of a river, leaving the newly formed lake with no natural outlet; as a result the water is highly alkaline and full of sulfides and mineral salts, similar to the Dead Sea in Israel, though much less salty. Lake Van's only marine life is a small member of the carp family, the *darekh*, which has somehow adapted to the saline environment. Recreational water sports are limited, and beaches along the rocky shores are few and far between. Swimming in the soft, soapy water is pleasant, but try not to swallow any—it tastes terrible.

The towns of Adilcevaz and Ahlat, on Lake Van's north shore, are worth visiting only if you're in the area; you'll probably want to head instead to Van and the nearby island of Akdamar, along the lake's south shore.

Van. As the commercial center of eastern Anatolia, Van has streets lined with modern shops and choked with traffic. There's a definite sense of bustle to the town, with restaurants and cafés filled with young people, many of them students from the local university. With its collection of rather uniform-looking cement buildings, what Van really lacks is a sense of history, which should not be surprising. The Van of today dates back to the early 20th century, when it was rebuilt some 5 km (3 mi) farther inland from Lake Van after being destroyed in battles with the Armenians and Russians during World War I. Old Van first appears in history 3,000 years ago, when it was the site of the Urartian capital of Tushpa, whose formidable fortress—built on a steep cliff rising from the lakeshore—dominated the countryside. What remains of old Van, in a grassy area near the lake, is a melancholy jumble of foundations

The Armenian Church of Holy Cross, on the uninhabited islet of Akdamar, is a work of art, inside and out.

that cannot be sorted out; only two vaguely restored mosques, one 13th-century, the other 16th-century, rise from the marshland.

An afternoon is enough time to cover the main sights in Van, but the city is a good base for exploring the sites around Lake Van.

Steps—considerably fewer than the 1,000 claimed in local tourist hand-outs—ascend to **Van Kalesi** *(Van Castle)*, the sprawling Urartian fortress on the outskirts of town. A path branches right to Urartian tombs in the sheer south rock face; a cuneiform inscription here honors King Xerxes, whose Persian troops occupied the fortress early in the 5th century BC. The crumbling ramparts are still impressive, but as is often true in these parts, it's the view that makes the steep climb worthwhile. A taxi from the new town should cost no more than $6 one-way. Cheaper *dolmuşes* (shared taxis) depart regularly from Beş Yol, a large intersection two blocks west of the Büyük Urartu Hotel.

The new city's main attraction is the small but well-arranged archaeo-logical and ethnographical **Van Müzesi** *(Van Museum)*, which displays many Urartian artifacts: rich gold jewelry; belts and plates engraved with lions, bulls, and sphinxes; and a carved relief of the god Teshup, for whom their capital was named. The small solarium has a varied col-lection, ranging from prehistoric rock art to Urartian inventory markers to Turkish sarcophagi. If you're interested in local history and archae-ology, the books for sale (some in English) are a wonderful source of information—and a bargain to boot. The museum underwent a com-plete renovation in the summer of 2006. ✉*Cengiz Cad., 1 block east of Cumhuriyet Cad.* ☎*432/216–1139* 🎫*$2.50* ☉*Daily 9–5.*

Fodor'sChoice
★

On the tranquil, uninhabited islet of **Akdamar**, among the wild olive and almond trees, stand the scant remains of a monastery which includes the truly splendid **Church of the Holy Cross.** Built in AD 921 by an Armenian king, Gagik Artzruni of Vaspurakan, it is very much a cousin, architecturally, to the Armenian churches at Ani. Incredible high-relief carvings on the exterior make this church a work of art and one of the most enchanted spots in Turkey. Nearly the entire story of the Bible is told here, from Adam and Eve to David and Goliath. Along the top is a frieze of running animals; another frieze shows a vineyard where laborers work the fields and women dance with bears; and, of course, King Gagik is depicted, offering his church to Christ. The wall paintings in the interior of the church underwent an extensive restoration in 2006. To reach Akdamar from Van, follow Route 300 to Gevaş, which is about 20 mi away. Entering Gevaş, you'll see ferries waiting at the landing (which is near the road and has a sign that says AKDAMAR) to collect the required number of passengers—between 10 and 15—for the 20-minute ride. Depending on how many people board the ferry, the cost is $5 to $8 per person for a round-trip. If other tourists don't turn up, you must pay $35 to $50 to charter the entire boat for a round trip—depending on your ability to bargain. ⊠ *Rte. 300, 56 km (35 mi) west of Van* ☏ *No phone* 🖅 *$3* ⊘ *Daily dawn–sunset.*

> **DID YOU KNOW?**
>
> The kingdom of Urartu (known as Ararat in the Bible) first appeared in this region in the 13th century BC and by the mid–8th century BC ruled an empire extending from the Black Sea to the Caspian Sea. Known as expert builders, stonemasons, and jewelry makers, the Urartian gold necklaces and bracelets, often created with a distinctive lion's head motif, that are some of the most prized holdings in Turkish museums.

OFF THE BEATEN PATH

Çavuştepe and Hoşap Kalesi. From Van, drive 35 km (22 mi) south on the Hakkari road to Çavuştepe, where you can clamber around the stone foundations of the ruined 8th-century-BC Urartian fortress-city Sardurihinli. Nearby are temple ruins and a 6th-century-BC sacrificial altar. Admission to the citadel is $1, though it's sometimes difficult to find the caretaker. If you continue 15 km (9 mi) southeast on the same road, you'll reach Hoşap Castle, a dramatic fortress looming over a river chasm. The 17th-century complex, which was used as a base to "protect" (i.e., ransack) caravans, included a palace, two mosques, three baths, and a dungeon. The great gate, with its carved lions and an inscription in Farsi, is quite a show of strength; a tunnel carved through bedrock leads inside from here. Bring a flashlight, as there are no lights in the castle, which is open daily 9 to 5. Admission is $1.

Mount Nemrut. Across the lake from Van is one of Turkey's loveliest natural wonders, the beautiful and rarely visited crater lakes of Mount Nemrut (Nemrut Dağı, which should not be confused with the more famous Mt. Nemrut farther west). From Tatvan, 146 km (91 mi) west of Van, a rutted road leads up the mountain to the 10,000-foot-high rim of what was once a mighty volcano. From the rim of the crater, you can see down to the two lakes below—a smaller one fed by hot springs and larger "cold" one. A loose dirt road leads down to the lakes, where very simple tea stands have been set up. The inside of the crater has an otherworldly feel to it, with its own ecosystem: stands of short, stunted trees and scrubby bushes, birds and turtles, and cool breezes. Few tourists make it to the lakes, and chances are your only company will be local shephards and their flocks.

WHERE TO STAY AND EAT

¢–$ ✕**Besse.** Van's previously rather
TURKISH   basic dining scene has been shaken up in recent years by the arrival of several restaurants that offer something classier. Besse, on the second floor above a shopping center, is one of the pioneers of this new trend, and it's a refuge from the bustling streets below, with walls painted a warm yellow, dim lighting, and classical music. The restaurant specializes in dishes (lamb, chicken, or trout) baked in terra-cotta pots and also makes a nice Ali Nazik, a kebab served on top of yogurt that's been mixed with garlic and roasted eggplant. ⊠*Melekış Merkezi Kat: 1, Van* ☎*432/215–0050* ═*MC, V.*

¢–$ ✕**Grand Deniz Turizm.** This peaceful lakeside restaurant in Gevaş is a
TURKISH   good spot for lunch or dinner after a visit to Akdamar: the restaurant can arrange a boat to Akdamar (around $30 for a round-trip ride) from their dock, followed by lunch or dinner when you return. Tables are set on a pebbly beach near the water and have an open view of the lake and the mountains. The food, which includes local dishes such as kebabs and trout baked in a terra-cotta dish, is delicious. ⊠*Van-Tatvan Karayolu Km 40, Gevaş* ☎*432/612–4038* ═*MC, V.*

¢   ✕**Imsak Kahvaltı Salonu.** This cheery establishment with only a few tables
TURKISH   has the same menu as its numerous competitors, but the red and white checkered tablecloths and cozy atmosphere are particularly inviting. In addition to the classic Van breakfast, they also serve *menemen,* eggs scrambled with tomatoes and peppers. ⊠*M. Fevzi Çakmak Cad., Bayram Oteli Altı, Van* ☎*432/216–0921* ═*No credit cards.*

¢–$ ✕**Kebabistan.** Filled with mustachioed men sipping tea, this basic eatery
TURKISH   serves the usual kebabs and hot prepared dishes, as well as good *pide* and *lahmacun,* flatbread topped with ground meat and baked. The main dining room is a hive of activity, but upstairs is a comfortable, quieter room. ⊠*Sinemalar Sokak, Van* ☎*432/214–2273* ═*MC, V.*

¢   ✕**Saçı Beyaz.** Another of Van's new upscale restaurants, this spot serves
TURKISH   delicious kebabs in a surprisingly elegant setting. The dining room, on the second floor, has tables covered in crisp white tablecloths and chairs of dark wood. The courteous staff, dressed in white shirts and black ties, seem always poised to bring more plates of freshly baked flatbread to your table. Downstairs is the restaurant's pastry shop, which sells ice cream and good baklava. ⊠*K. Karabekir Cad. Soydan Dağı, Van* ☎*432/214–4016* ═*MC, V.*

BREAKFAST IN VAN

Van is known for, among other things, its delicious local breakfasts—you'll get a variety of locally made cheeses, eggs (usually hard-boiled), and, most important, *kaymak,* a delicious type of thick clotted cream that is eaten on bread with honey. The city is filled with small restaurants that serve breakfast all day long; Imsak Kahvaltı Salonu is particularly good. *Kahvaltı* is the Turkish word for breakfast.

7

¢ ✕**Van Evi.** At the base of Van Castle, this is a good place to taste local
TURKISH dishes, among them *keledoş* (a stew made with meat, chickpeas, lentils,
and butter) and *ekşili* (meat and spinach in a tangy sauce). Two long
wooden pavilions with open sides serve as dining rooms and there is a
large grassy area with tables and chairs for dining alfresco. ⊠*At the
entrance to Van Castle, Van* 🕾*No phone* ⊟*No credit cards.*

$$ 🕾**Büyük Urartu.** This smoothly run hotel, one of the town's best, has
★ reproductions of Urartian art on the walls throughout. Guest rooms
are small but pleasant, with gold-embroidered bedspreads and floral
wallpaper; some face the noisy street—so ask for one in back. Celaled-
din Başak, the friendly front-desk manager, can help arrange tours of
the area. **Pros:** 24-hour room service and information desk; live music
three nights a week; pool and sauna. **Cons:** hotel books up quickly.
⊠*Cumhuriyet Cad. 60* 🕾*432/212–0660* ⊕*www.buyukurartuotel.
com* 🖙*72 rooms, 3 suites* ⚄*In-room: refrigerator, Wi-Fi. In-hotel:
restaurant, bar, pool* ⊟*AE, DC, MC, V* �𝍩*BP.*

$$ 🕾**Merit Şahmaran.** Head to this comfortable, well-run hotel if you want
to stay on Lake Van itself. Located 12 km (7.5 mi) west of Van in the
small town of Edremit, the Merit has large rooms with nice, modern
bathrooms. Ask for one of the lakeside rooms, which have views of the
lake and mountains. There's a terrace restaurant overlooking the water,
where you can watch the sunset and listen to the water lapping against
the rocky shore. A stone pier for swimming juts out into the lake. **Pros:**
great location; full bar and decent restaurant. **Cons:** a lot of what you
pay for is the proximity to Lake Van; since most people come only
for the lake, there aren't great tour options. ⊠*Edremit Yolu Km 12,
Edremit* 🕾*432/312–3060* ⊕*www.merithotels.com* 🖙*90 rooms* ⚄*In-
room: safe, refrigerator, Wi-Fi. In-hotel: restaurant, bar, pool, parking
(free)* ⊟*MC, V* 𝍩*BP.*

¢ 🕾**Otel Akdamar.** The squat Akdamar won't win any architectural prizes,
but the rooms are comfortable and good-sized, with walls painted white
and beds draped in blue bedspreads. The hotel is located on Van's main
drag, so ask for a room in the back. The hotel has one of the city's
nicest bars, too, with comfortable lounge chairs. **Pros:** friendly staff
speaks English; free Wi-Fi. **Cons:** street-side rooms can be noisy. ⊠*K.
Karabekir Cad., Van* 🕾*432/214–9923* 🖷*432/212–0868* 🖙*69 rooms,
3 suites* ⚄*In-room: refrigerator. In-hotel: restaurant, bar* ⊟*MC, V*
𝍩*BP.*

DIYARBAKIR, MARDIN, MIDYAT
AND HASANKEYF

Saying that Turkey's southeast region has a rich history is an understatement. This is, after all, part of the ancient area known as Mesopotamia: the land between the Tigris and the Euphrates rivers, where
modern civilization got its start. This excursion takes you into the heart
of this historic region, to cities that trace their past not over centuries,
but over millennia and through landscapes that seem unchanged with
time. The area is also the historic home of the Assyrian Christians, one

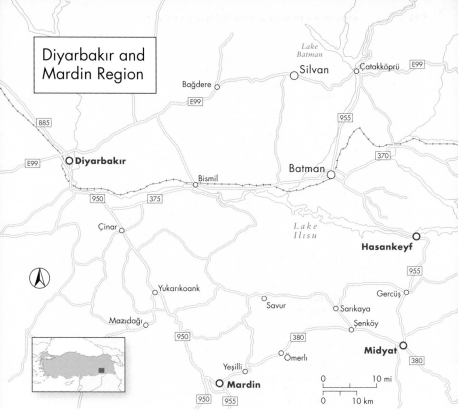

of Christianity's oldest sects, and there are several fascinating Assyrian churches and monasteries that can be visited.

The excursion begins in Diyarbakır, which has long been the region's commercial, cultural, and political center. Surrounded by a thick basalt wall that dates back to Roman times, Diyarbakır's old city has cobblestone lanes that lead to grand old homes hidden behind high stone walls (some of these homes are now open to visitors), intriguing old churches and mosques, and a lively bazaar spread through a maze of narrow lanes.

From here you continue to Mardin, one of the most magical cities in Turkey. Sitting like a crown that looks down on a wide plain below, Mardin is a wonderful place to wander. The narrow streets are lined with old stone homes, gorgeous mosques, and a bazaar where donkeys still carry most of the goods. Spend the day walking around, then relax in the evening at the terrace of one of the local restaurants and look out at the view below and the stars above. Make sure to visit Dayrul Zafran, an ancient Assyrian Christian monastery in the hills just outside of Mardin.

Midyat is one of the best-preserved small towns in Turkey. Once home to a sizable Assyrian Christian community, it's old city is today mostly a ghost town, with many of its former residents now living in Europe.

Spotlight on the Kurds

There are an estimated 20 million Kurds living in the mountainous region that covers parts of Iran, Iraq, Syria, and Turkey. Separated by ethnicity and language from their neighbors, the Kurds have for centuries found themselves the subjects of the area's various rulers.

Turkey has the region's largest Kurdish population, with an estimated 12 million, most of them living in the country's southeast region. When the new Turkish republic was founded in 1923, severe restrictions on Kurdish language and culture were put in place, part of a larger effort to unite the country's various ethnic groups under one national identity. During the 1980s, the Kurdistan Workers' Party (PKK), a militant Marxist group, began a bloody separatist war against the Turkish state that ended up

costing the lives of more than 30,000 and caused great damage to social and economic life in the southeast. The PKK called for a ceasefire in 1999, after its leader was captured by Turkey, and its fighters retreated to the mountains of northern Iraq. In late 2004, though, it resumed its attacks on Turkish troops in the southeast, although the violence is, for the most part, restricted to remote parts of the region and is nowhere near the level of the 1980s and '90s. At the same time, as part of its efforts to join the European Union, Turkey has over the last few years passed legislation aimed at easing the cultural and political restrictions on the Kurds and has promised to revitalize the local economy, bringing a guarded sense of hope to the battle-scarred region.

What they left behind is an incredible collection of honey-colored stone homes with exquisite carvings on their exteriors and several historic churches. As in Mardin, this is a wonderful place to spend a few hours walking around and soaking up the atmosphere. Mor Gabriel, another isolated Assyrian monastery, is worth visiting.

From Midyat, you can make the quick trip to Hasankeyf, a small town that sits in an enchanted spot on the banks of the Tigris River. Spend a few hours exploring Hasankeyf's cliff-top citadel, which dates back to Roman times, and a series of ancient cliff dwellings nearby, and then head down to the river, where you can eat lunch on a veranda that sits on stilts right over the Tigris's gently flowing waters.

DIYARBAKIR

GETTING HERE AND AROUND

Turkish Airlines, Onur, and Pegasus Airlines have flights from Istanbul to Diyarbakır.

There are daily buses from Istanbul to Diyarbakır; the ride takes close to 20 hours and costs about $45. From Diyarbakır, minivans leave regularly from Dağ Kapı for the one-hour trip to Mardin and to Midyat.

The train ride from Istanbul to Diyarbakır is long—more than 35 hours—but scenic, and inexpensive: about $22 (first class) to $44 (sleeper bunk). Time is money, though, and it's much easier to fly.

ESSENTIALS

Visitor Information (✉ *Dağkapi Bureu Giriş Bölmü* ☎ *412/221–2173* 🖷 *412/ 221–1189).*

EXPLORING

On a bluff above the Tigris River, the ancient city of Diyarbakır, one of the oldest cities in the northernmost region of Mesopotamia (the area between the Tigris and Euphrates rivers) is encircled by a 5.5-km (3-mi) stretch of thick, impregnable black-basalt walls. Inside those walls lie twisting alleyways, old stone homes, mosques, and a lively bazaar. The city's long history has meant it's seen quite a succession of rulers, from the Assyrians to the Urartians and Romans, and finally the Ottomans, who took control of the city in 1515. Diyarbakır has been an important regional commercial and cultural center for centuries, and there are some wonderful old houses, mosques, and churches in the cobblestone lanes of the old town.

In the 1980s and '90s, Diyarbakır was forced to absorb a large number of villagers fleeing the fighting in the countryside between Kurdish militants and Turkish security forces, which taxed the city's poor infrastructure and social services and gave the city a grimey feel. In more recent years, though, the local municipality has embarked on several restoration and beautification projects, such as renovating historic homes in the old city and opening them up to visitors, which is helping bring the city's charm closer to the surface.

The Romans left a strong mark on Diyarbakır—not only did they lay the foundations for its famous **city walls**, but they created the basic layout of the old town: a rough rectangle with two main streets that cross and connect the four gates that are found at each compass point. The walls were reconstructed by the Byzantine Emperor Constantius in AD 349 and further restored by the Seljuks in 1088 and again 120 years later by Artakid Turcoman emir al Malik al-Salih Mahmud. On the whole, the walls remain in good shape along their entire length; indeed, if you feel like a bit of an adventure, the best way to appreciate these great walls is to wander along the top. Of the original 72 towers, 67 are still standing, decorated with myriad inscriptions in the language of every conqueror and with Seljuk reliefs of animals and men; you can also explore their inner chambers and corridors. To make a circuit of the city walls on foot, start at the **Mardin Kapısı** (Mardin Gate), on the south side near the Otel Büyük Kervansaray and take the wall-top path west toward the **Urfa Kapısı** (Urfa Gate), also called the Bab er-Rum. About halfway you will come to the twin bastions **Evli Beden Burcu** and **Yedi Kardeş Burcu**—the latter is also known as the Tower of Seven Brothers and was added to the fortifications in 1209. From here you can see the old Ottoman bridge over the Tigris, called **Dicle Köprüsü** (Tigris Bridge). Continue clockwise along the city wall, and you'll eventually reach another gate, the **Dağ Kapısı** (Mountain Gate), which divides Diyarbakır's old and new towns. Farther east, inside the ramparts, are the sad remains of the **Artakid Saray** (Artasid Palace), surrounded by a dry, octagonal pool known as the **Lion's Fountain.** Not long ago there were two carved lions here, now there's only one; what happened to the other is a mystery.

The ruins of the old town's **İç Kale** *(Inner Fortress)*, a circular and heavily eroded section of the city walls, are notable for the 16th-century **Hazreti Süleymaniye Cami** (Prophet Süleyman Mosque), also known as the Citadel Mosque. It has a tall, graceful minaret and is striped with black basalt and pale sandstone, a favorite design of this city's medieval architects. Its courtyard fountain is fed by an underground spring that has probably supplied cold, clear water to the city for 5,000 years. ✉ *İzzet Paşa Cad.* ☏ *No phone* ⊘ *Daily dawn–sunset.*

In the center of the old city is the **Ulu Cami** *(Great Mosque)*, one of the oldest in Anatolia. Though its present form dates from the 12th century, in an older form it served as a Byzantine basilica; its colonnades and columns are made from bits and pieces of earlier Roman buildings. Note its Arabic-style flat-roofed and rectangular plan, unlike the square-shaped and domed mosques common in Turkey. ✉ *Gazi Cad., opposite Yapı Kredi Bank* ☏ *No phone* ⊘ *Daily 10–sunset.*

Diyarbakır's **bazaar** encompasses the half-dozen streets surrounding Ulu Cami; most stalls are shrines to wrought metal—gates, picks, shovels, plumbing fixtures, plastic shoes, and other things you probably would not want to carry home in your luggage. Across the street from the mosque is the grand 16th-century **Hasan Paşa Hanı,** a photogenic kervansaray now mostly used by carpet and souvenir dealers and which was undergoing an extensive renovation in 2006.

Down a narrow alleyway near the Ulu Cami in the old city, the **Cahit Sıtkı Tarancı Müzesi** is a historic home dating back to 1734 that has been renovated and turned into an ethnographic museum, with rooms displaying scenes of life as it once was in Diyarbakır. The museum, which has a pleasant courtyard with a fountain, offers probably the best opportunity of seeing what an old Diybarbakır house looked like. ✉ *Ziya Gökalp Sokak 3* ☏ *412/223–8958* ⊘ *Daily 9–5* 🎟 *Free.*

Diybarbakır was once home to a large Christian population—Armenians, Chaldeans, and Assyrians—and several churches remain in the city, although the only one that still holds regular services is the Assyrian Orthodox **Meryem Ana Kilisesi,** on the western end of the old city. A peaceful oasis in the midst of the bustling city, the church, built on the site of what was a temple used by sun worshippers, has a large courtyard lined with basalt stones and a lovely chapel dating back to the 3rd century with an impressive wooden altar decorated with golden ornamentation. Services are held every Sunday at 8 AM, although only a few people usually show up. ✉ *Ana Sokak 26* ☏ *No phone* ⊘ *Daily 9–5.*

Diyarbakır's **Arkeoloji Müzesi** *(Archaeological Museum)*, where the exhibits cover 4,000 years of history, is located in the new city, a short walk from Dağ Kapı, the main entrance to the old town. In a somewhat run-down building, the exhibits include findings from excavations in the Diyarbakır area, from stone-age tools to Byzantine pottery and coins. ✉ *Gazi Cad.* ☏ *No phone* 🎟 *$2.50* ⊘ *Mon.–Sat. 8:30–4:30.*

The old town's most recognizable mosque is the **Kasım Padişah Cami** (1512), famous for its Dört Ayaklı Minare (Four-Legged Minaret), which appears to be suspended in the air—the minaret balances on four basalt columns, a marvel of medieval engineering. Legend has it that your wish will come true if you pass under the minaret seven times. ⊠ *Yenikapı Cad.* ☎ *No phone* ⊙ *Daily 10–sunset.*

OFF THE
BEATEN
PATH

Gazi Koşku. If you need a break from Diyarbakır's heat and crowds, head to the Gazi Koşku a restored stone house high above the Tigris River on the outskirts of town. The house is surrounded by shady trees and there is a flower-filled tea garden where you can cool off. It's a kilometer (½ mi) south of the Mardin gate along the river road. ⊙ *9 AM–midnight* ▢ *50¢.*

WHERE TO STAY AND EAT

$ ✕**Asmin.** This is Diybarbakır's only real upscale restaurant, the place
TURKISH   where well-to-do locals come for a break from kebabs and to have a more sophisticated dining experience, at least by local standards. The menu features such nonlocal items as schnitzel, beef Stroganoff, and filet mignon, and there's a surprisingly decent wine list. The food is good and the softly lit dining room, with its comfortable armchairs and solicitous bow-tied waiters, is a nice change from the usual. ⊠ *Selahattin Yazıcıoğlu Cad.* ☎ *412/224–3197* ▭ *MC, V.*

$ ✕**Çarşı Konağı.** You have to pass through a small door off one of
TURKISH   Diybarbakır's narrow old city lanes to get to this simple restaurant, in a restored historic stone home with a shaded courtyard—ask for directions. The small menu is made up of kebabs and delicious *sac tava,* chunks of beef sautéed in a woklike pan with tomatoes and green peppers; it's served in the pan, with a mound of flatbread to soak up the tasty juices. It's also a pleasant spot to cool off with a cup of coffee or tea. ⊠ *Gazi Cad. Çarşı* ☎ *412/228–4673* ▭ *No credit cards.*

¢–$ ✕**Çemçe Diyarbakır Mutfağı.** Head here if you want to sample authentic
TURKISH   local dishes, such as *perde pilaf* (chicken and rice baked inside a pastry shell) or for the more adventurous, *mumbar* (lamb intestines stuffed with rice and ground meat). The food, served buffet style, is well made and the setting—an old stone house with several small dining rooms decked out with rugs and antiques—is charming. ⊠ *Kuçuk Kavas Sokak (behind the Class Hotel)* ☎ *412/229–4345* ▭ *MC, V.*

¢–$ ✕**Emre Ocakbaşı.** Diyarbakır is filled with small grill stands that serve
TURKISH   sizzling kebabs to hungry diners who polish them off sitting on stools at outdoor tables. This one, near the Dağ Kapı, the main access point to the old city, has both outdoor and indoor dining areas and serves excellent kebabs, including ones made with the local specialty, liver. Kebabs are served with flatbread, bulgur pilaf, and a tangy salad made with tomatoes, cucumber, parsley, and pomegranate molasses. ⊠ *Kıbrıs Cad., Çelenk Apt. Altı 1/A* ☎ *412/228–7238* ▭ *MC, V.*

¢   ✕**Ka-Mer'in Mutfağı.** Good food for a good cause. This restaurant is
TURKISH   run by a local organization that offers social services for women and the proceeds help fund the group's activities. Staffed by the women the group helps, the kitchen turns out tasty local dishes, like *içli köfte* (ground meat inside a bulgur shell), *mantı* (the Turkish equivalent of ravioli), and a variety of stuffed vegetables. The dining room, with simple wood furniture and walls painted a soft yellow, is tranquil and pleasant. ⊠ *Ali Emiri Sokak 3* ☎ *412/229–0459* ▭ *No credit cards.*

7

$ ✕**Selim Amcanın Sofra Salonu.** Diybarbakır's best-known restaurant
TURKISH is an excellent place to try the delicious regional specialty *kaburga*
★ (lamb stuffed with a fragrant rice pilaf and slowly roasted). This labor-
intensive dish usually needs to be ordered a day in advance, but SASS
(as the restaurant is known) is one of the few restaurants that offers
kaburga on demand, served with flair by waiters who divide the dish
up tableside. With walls covered with mirrors and pink paint, the restaurant has a rather kitschy look; it's a local institution nonetheless.
✉*Ali Emiri Cad. 22/B* ☎*412/224–4447* ▬*MC, V.*

$$$ ⊞**Class Hotel.** Although the lobby and rooms are somewhat character-
less, the Class Hotel is certainly Diyarbakır's fanciest place to stay, with
prices to match. Rooms are large and comfortable, all with desks and
some with small couches. There's a Turkish bath in the basement, a
small pool in the back, and a gym. **Pros:** well-equipped fitness room; cute
nightclub has great atmosphere on packed nights; chefs create special
twists on traditional cuisines. **Cons:** for the price, rooms are a bit lack-
ing. ✉*Gazi Cad. 101* ☎*412/229–5000* ⊕*www.diyarbakirclasshotel.*
com ⇱*107 rooms, 7 suites* ⚏*In-room: refrigerator. In-hotel: 2 restau-*
rants, bar, pool, gym ▬*AE, MC, V* ¶⊙|*BP.*

¢ ⊞**Hotel Birkent.** This budget hotel has surprisingly large rooms that
are comfortable and well maintained. Walls are painted a light lav-
ender, complemented by maroon carpets; bathrooms are small but
spotless. The staff is friendly and helpful. **Pros:** 24-hour hot water;
breakfast included. **Cons:** Internet is spotty (but free). ✉*İnönü Cad. 26*
☎*412/228–7131* 🖶*412/228–7145* ⇱*30 rooms* ⚏*In-room: refrigera-*
tor. In-hotel: Internet. ▬*MC, V* ¶⊙|*BP.*

$$ ⊞**Otel Büyük Kervansaray.** This attractive inn is inside a 16th-century
★ kervansaray with sandstone walls, vaulted ceilings, and kilims that are
used as curtains. Rooms are on the small side, but you're really paying
for the atmosphere and the location, next to the Mardin Kapısı, inside
the city walls. Rooms on the ground floor don't have air-conditioning,
though they stay quite cool, even in summer. There is a lovely courtyard
with a fountain where you can eat dinner or have a drink, and the hotel
pool is a welcome sight in Diyarbakır's heat. **Pros:** indoor and outdoor
restaurants offer international cuisines; pool; trekking nearby. **Cons:**
rooms are a bit small; food is a bit lackluster. ✉*Gazi Cad.* ☎*412/228–*
9606 🖶*412/228–9606* ⇱*31 rooms, 14 suites* ⚏*In-room: refrigerator.*
In-hotel: restaurant, bars, pool ▬*AE, MC, V* ¶⊙|*BP.*

MARDIN

★ *96 km (60 mi) southeast of Diyarbakır.*

GETTING HERE AND AROUND

Turkish Airlines, Onur, and Pegasus Airlines have flights from Istanbul
to Mardin.

EXPLORING

With historic stone houses clinging to a citadel-topped mountain that
overlooks a vast plain below, Mardin has a magical setting. It was hit
hard by the violence of the 1980s and'90s, and the city, which is populated by a mix of Arabic and Kurdish speakers, slid off Turkey's tourist

map, but the return of calm to the region has meant that travelers are rediscovering this enchanted city's maze-like old town, intricately decorated homes, and lively bazaars. Mardin also now has two of the nicer hotels in the region, as well as one of the area's best restaurants.

Mardin was once the seat of a local dynasty, the Artukids, who ruled the area between the 13th and 14th centuries and left the city with several notable mosques and *medreses* (Islamic schools). The best of these are the Lâtifiye Camii (Lâtifiye Mosque, 1371) and the Sultan İsa Medrese (Sultan İsa Seminary, 1385), the latter renowned for its exquisite stone carvings. The Seljuk Ulu Cami (Seljuk Ulu Mosque), which dates from the 12th century and has a ribbed dome that looks like an intricate lemon squeezer, is also worth a visit.

At the city's main square is the small **Mardin Museum,** set in a grand old stone house that used to be the home of an Assyrian Christian patriarch. The stone relief carvings on the exterior are quite exquisite. The museum's collection includes displays from archaeological digs around Mardin, with pieces from the Roman, Byzantine, Seljuk, and other periods. One floor has an ethnographic exhibit showing life in old Mardin. ⊠*Cümhurriyet Meydanı* ☎*482/212–1664* ⚞*$2.50* ⊙*Mon.–Sat. 8–5:30.*

Mardin was once home to a large Christian community and several churches still remain in the city, although only a few are functioning. The **Kirklar Kilisesi** *(Church of the 40s),* an Assyrian Orthodox church, is usually open and worth visiting. It's down a narrow lane near the museum. The church dates back to the year 569 and has beautiful stone carvings and a shady courtyard. Neighborhood children will offer to take you there, which is probably a good idea, since it can be hard to find. It's not far from the Mardin Museum. ⊠*217 Sağlik Sokak 8* ☎*No phone* ⚞*Free* ⊙*Daily 8–5.*

Mardin's lively **bazaar** runs parallel to the old town's main street, Birinici Caddesi, and is refreshingly free of the stalls selling the usual tourist gifts. This is the place to come if you're looking to buy a new saddle for your donkey or a copper urn—or as is more likely, if you just want to get the feel of an authentic town bazaar. There are also spice shops, fresh fruit and vegetable stands with the produce of the season piled high, and assorted other shops catering to local needs.

One of the big pleasures in Mardin is simply walking the old town's narrow cobblestone lanes and seeing what you come across. Although there are many ugly cement homes that have been built in recent years, there are enough historic homes remaining to give the city a great deal of charm. The stone used to build the old homes is the color of golden sand and looks especially beautiful at sunset.

One of the best examples of an old Mardin home is the current **post office** (⊠*On Birinci Cad., across the street from an open-air teahouse, in the center of town*).

OFF THE
BEATEN
PATH

Just 10 km (6 mi) southeast of Mardin is the Syrian **Orthodox Dayrul Zafran** *(Saffron Monastery).* Dating to perhaps as early as the 6th century and partially restored in the 19th, the monastery is still in use. One of the brothers will give you a tour of the building, which sits like a golden jewel nestled in the scrubby hills around it, and perhaps introduce you to one of the *rahip* (priests) who still speak and teach Aramaic, the language of Christ. ⊠ *Off the road from Mardin to Nusaybin* ☎ *No phone* 🖅 *Free* ⊙ *Daily 9–11:30 and 1–4:30.*

WHERE TO STAY AND EAT

$

TURKISH

Fodor'sChoice

★

✕ **Cercis Murat Konağı.** This is certainly Mardin's best restaurant, if not one of the most outstanding in the region. In a gorgeous, restored stone house with a modern kitchen in the basement, the restaurant has several terraces with spectacular views of the plain that unfolds below Mardin. Dishes served are authentic local ones, such as lamb braised in a tangy green plum sauce. There is also a full spread of tantalizing cold and hot mezes, including tasty chickpea fritters and, owing to the Arab influence on Mardin, humus and falafel. ⊠ *Birinci Cad. 517* ☎ *482/213–6841* ⊟ *MC, V.*

¢

TURKISH

✕ **Erdoba Sofra Salonu.** This bright, comfortable eatery is on the second floor of a building on Mardin's main drag. Serving the usual kebabs along with prepared stews, the restaurant has lavender walls and tables with benches covered in colorful fabrics. If you order ahead of time, they can prepare the local specialty kaburga, lamb stuffed with rice. ⊠ *Birinci Cad. 233/A* ☎ *482/212–8849* ⊟ *No credit cards.*

¢

TURKISH

✕ **Kebabçı Yusuf Ustanın Yeri.** This outdoor restaurant in the heart of Mardin serves tasty kebabs and frothy village *ayran*, a salted yogurt drink you can find bottled around the country, but here it's drunk the traditional way: with a ladle from metal bowls. The kebabs are served with fresh flatbread, so you can make your own wrap. It's across the street from the post office, one of the loveliest old buildings in Mardin. ⊠ *Birinci Cad. Üçyol Mevkii* ☎ *482/212–7985* ⊟ *No credit cards.*

$$

🛏 **Artuklu Kervansarayi.** Entering this hotel, in a kervansaray that dates back to 1275, will make you feel like you're taking a trip back in time: the walls are thick stone and the narrow corridors seem like something out of a medieval castle. The hotel itself is dimly lit, though decorated with colorful rugs and antiques. Standard rooms, built in a new addition connected to the old structure, are on the small side, with unadorned stone walls and kilims on the floor. There is a terrace with a panoramic view and an "oriental"-style reading room with rugs and pillows where you can sit back and relax. **Pros:** small bedrooms still feel like a palace; delicious food; great prices. **Cons:** no alcohol permitted at the hotel. ⊠ *Birinci Cad. 70* ☎ *482/213–7353* ⊕ *www.artuklu.com* 🛏 *40 rooms, 3 suites* ⚏ *In-room: refrigerator, Wi-Fi. In-hotel: restaurant, refrigerator, parking (free)* ⊟ *AE, MC, V* ⊙*BP.*

$$

🛏 **Büyük Mardin Oteli.** This modern hotel is on the edge of Mardin and has good views of the old city and the plain below. Rooms are comfortable, with black marble floors, and colorful kilims that serve as curtains. The rooftop terrace has a wonderful view of Mardin, especially at sunset, when the whole city takes on a golden glow. **Pros:** reasonable prices for what you get; authentic Turkish bath offers massages. **Cons:** not a quiet getaway; restaurant is decent but not a highlight. ⊠ *Yeniyol Cad.* ☎ *482/213–1047* ⊕ *www.buyukmardinoteli.com* 🛏 *43 rooms, 11 suites* ⚏ *In-room: refrigerator, Wi-Fi. In-hotel: restaurant, parking (free)* ⊟ *AE, MC, V* ⊙*BP.*

$$ ⚡Erdoba Konakları. A series of historic homes that have been connected,
★ this hotel helped restart Mardin's tourism industry when it opened in
2001. Rooms (ask for one of larger ones) have stone walls and small-
ish bathrooms. A breezy terrace has wicker chairs where you can have
a drink or a meal and take in the fine view. A good restaurant serves
local dishes in a cavernous space below the hotel. **Pros:** vaulted ceilings
and Ottoman decor makes this small hotel feel like a palace; good res-
taurant. **Cons:** some small rooms; the hotel books quickly, so be plan
in advance; pricey, but worth it. ⊠*Birinci Cad. 135* ☎*482/212–7677*
⊕*www.erdoba.com.tr* ⟳*45 rooms, 10 suites* ⌂*In-room: Internet.
In-hotel: restaurant* ▤*AE, MC, V* ⵀⵀ*BP.*

MIDYAT

★ *67 km (42 mi) east of Mardin.*

Not far from Mardin, the lovely old town of Midyat is an architectural
gem that has remained largely untouched by the blight of concrete—
although the new part of the city is dismal. Formerly almost an exclu-
sively Assyrian Christian town, old Midyat is filled with an astonishing
number of beautiful homes built of stone the color of honey or golden
sand. Walking through Midyat's narrow streets reveals house after
beautiful house, many of them with gorgeous ornamental carving work
on their exteriors. Many of Midyat's Christians left during the violence
of the 1980s and '90s, leaving the place feeling a bit like a ghost town
in certain areas, but the homes and churches remain, and now that a
relative calm has returned to the region, some of them are even being
renovated for use as summer homes by Assyrians who used to reside
here but currently have their primary homes in Europe. You can spend
a quiet day exploring Midyat and visiting some of the nearby Assyrian
monasteries; this is also a good base for visiting the historical monu-
ments at the nearby riverside town of Hasankeyf.

With their numbers dwindling, Midyat's Assyrian community rotates
services throughout the old town's churches, so it's hard to know which
one will be open. Your best bet is the **Mor Barsaumo church,** open most
afternoons. It has a beautiful chapel with distinctive locally made art-
work and lovely stonework. ⊠*Şen Cad. 21* ☎*No phone* ▧*Free.*

OFF THE
BEATEN
PATH

Mor Gabriel monastery. Twenty-five kilometers (15.5 mi) southeast of
Midyat is the Mor Gabriel monastery, built on the site of a church that
dates back to 387. The monastery is on the top of a hill in a desolate
area, surrounded by fields and vineyards, a peaceful and tranquil set-
ting. Reopened as a monastery in 1952 after having been closed for
some time, the building is today home to two monks and 14 nuns, as
well as the local patriarch, known as a Metropolitan. An old chapel
and basement grotto hold the graves of monks who lived here through-
out the centuries. There are usually English-speaking guides—young
men who live there as students, who can show you around. ⊠*25 km
(15.5 mi) southeast of Midyat* ☎*482/462–1425* ▧*Free* ☉*Daily
9–11:30 and 1–5.*

WHERE TO STAY AND EAT

¢–$ ✕**Cihan Lokantası.** This basic steam-
TURKISH table restaurant serves the usual
menu but the owners have tried to
add some class by hanging white
lace curtains and putting pots of
plastic yellow flowers on the walls—
your call if it's classy or tacky. Either
way, the food is tasty, the staff is
friendly, and the location, down
the street from the Mor Barsaumo
church, makes it one of the few
decent options near Midyat's old

THE TIGRIS DAM

For the last several years a pro-
posed dam project along the Tigris
has put Hasankeyf in danger of
being submerged. A vocal campaign by environmentalists and
preservationists has currently succeeded in stopping the project, but
there's no telling if this will be successful in the long term.

town. ✉*Cizre Yolu Uzeri, Karakol Karş 52* ☎*482/464–1566* ▭*No credit cards.*

¢ ✕**Tarihi Midyat Gelüşke Hanı.** This grilled-meat restaurant is inside a beau-
TURKISH tifully restored han that served as an inn for traveling traders. You can
eat outside by a fountain in the large courtyard or in one of the small
private dining rooms, where you sit on rugs and eat from low tables,
reclining on pillows when you're done. The kebabs are tasty and served
with a tangy chopped tomato salad and a refreshing cold yogurt soup
that has wheat berries in it. If you call a day in advance, they can prepare the Assyrian speciality, *dobo* (lamb stuffed with rice and pistachios). ✉*Eski Midyat Çarşısı* ☎*482/464–1442* ▭*MC, V.*

¢ ⌂**Midyat Konuk Evi.** Not officially a hotel, this exquisite old stone mansion on a narrow lane was beautifully restored and serves as a guest-
house run by the municipality. The building's six guest rooms are large,
with high vaulted ceilings, big beds, beautiful dark-wood carved furniture, and surprisingly modern bathrooms. The three-story house is on
a hill, and the terrace has a sweeping view of the old town of Midyat.
It's a romantic place to stay, but don't expect much in the way of services beyond a cup of tea in the morning from the friendly attendant.
Pros: very quiet; personable vibe; romantic atmosphere. **Cons:** no in-
room telephone, Internet, or TV. ✉*Güher Sokak* ☎*482/464–0719*
🖶*482/464–2061* ↩*6 rooms* ⌂*In-room: no a/c, no phone, no TV.*

$$ ⌂**Otel Matiat.** This swanky place on the outskirts of Midyat has large
rooms with lounge chairs and spacious bathrooms and profession-
al and courteous service. There is a large, inviting pool. **Pros:** pool,
hamam, and sauna are a perfect way to rejuvenate after a long trip;
fun nightclub. **Cons:** can get crowded with local tourists. ✉*Mardin
Yolu Üzeri* ☎*482/462–5920* ⊕*www.matiat.com.tr* ↩*52 rooms, 8
suites* ⌂*In-room: refrigerator, Wi-Fi. In-hotel: restaurant, bar, pool*
▭*MC, V* ⦿*BP.*

HASANKEYF

43 km (27 mi) north of Midyat.

Just a short drive from Midyat, Hasankeyf makes for a good half-day
trip. Come, explore, have lunch by the Tigris River and then return to
Midyat, Mardin, or even Diyarbakır. This small town has a magical

setting, with stone houses on the banks of the Tigris River, lorded over by a cliff topped with the remains of an ancient citadel.

The **citadel,** which dates back to Roman times, is at the top of a sheer cliff that rises 328 feet above the river. On the backside of the cliff, the citadel looks over a small canyon where several abandoned cave dwellings have been carved into the rock. What remains of the citadel is enough to give a sense of how grand it must have once been. The whole area is extremely atmospheric and worth exploring. ⊠*No address; it's on a dirt road at the edge of town* ☎*No phone* ✆*$2.50* ⊙*Daily 8:30–5:30.*

Just below the citadel, on the way into town, is the **Er Rizk Mosque,** which dates back to the 14th century and has a beautiful minaret that has intricate stone carvings on its exterior. ☎*No phone* ✆*Free* ⊙*During daylight hours.*

Across the river from the citadel is another spot worth visiting, **Zeynelbey Turbesi,** a mausoleum built circa 1480 for a local nobleman. The stylized structure has an onion-dome top and is decorated with still-vivid turquoise-colored tiles set in calligraphy-like geometric patterns. ⊠*On the Batman-Hasankeyf road, near the bridge* ☎*No phone* ✆*Free* ⊙*During daylight hours.*

WHERE TO EAT

¢ ✕**Nehir Çardak.** Do you like dining by the water? How about virtually
TURKISH *in* the water? At this unique restaurant you eating in small thatched-roof pavilions on stilts over the Tigris River. The kitchen is actually in the water and the cook stands in front of the grill with his pants rolled up so they won't get wet. The menu is basic—grilled fish or köfte—but the rustic setting, the river flowing by, and the view of Hasankeyf's cliff are utterly relaxing and wonderful. ⊠*Dicle Kıyısı* ☎*No phone* ▭*No credit cards.*

$ ✕**Yolgeçen Hanı Dinlenme Tesisleri.** There are a number of simple restau-
TURKISH rants along Hasankeyf's riverside, but this one is located in a cool cave just back from the water, which makes it an inviting place for lunch during the hot summer. There are three levels in the large cave, and the floors are covered in kilims and large, colorful pillows for reclining. The restaurant serves kebabs and a flavorful local river fish known as *şabot.* ⊠*Dicle Kıyısı* ☎*488/381–2287* ▭*No credit cards.*

GAZIANTEP, MT. NEMRUT AND ŞANLIURFA

Forget about "George Washington slept here"; in this part of Turkey you're more likely to come across places that claim to have been paid a visit by the biblical patriarch Abraham. This area of southeast Turkey has such depth and richness of history that the cities and monuments trace their roots back to biblical times and beyond. Luckily for the traveler, much of that history hasn't been lost to the sands of time, and the ancient cities and historical sites that are part of this excursion are remarkably well preserved and visitor-friendly.

This excursion begins in Gaziantep, not far from Turkey's border with Syria; it's a vibrant, busy town with a fascinating and well-preserved

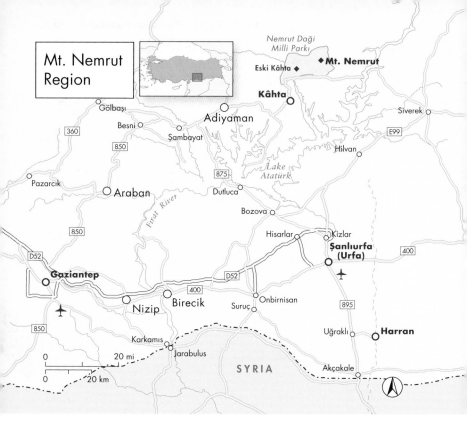

old city and one of the Turkey's most authentic bazaars. Gaziantep also has a fantastic museum featuring a stunning collection of Roman-era mosaics from a nearby archaeological dig and is known among Turks as having some of Turkey's best food and certainly its best baklava.

From Gaziantep you will continue on to Mount Nimrod, a historical site that is something like a Turkish Stonehenge. The fascinating monument, dating back to the 1st century BC, improbably finds a collection of giant sculptures at the top of a lonely mountain—a lasting testament to the vanity of the ruler of a local dynasty.

From here you'll head to Şanliurfa, another of the area's ancient cities and a major pilgrimage site for Muslims. There's a tranquil park with mosques, and ponds with sacred fish built on the spot where many Muslims believe Abraham was born. (Abraham also figures prominently into the history of Harran, a fascinating historic site that's a quick side trip from Şanliurfa.) Not far from the quiet of the park is the city's wonderful bazaar, where tailors work on foot-driven sewing machines and the sound of coppersmiths hammering fills the air. The twisting lanes in the city's old neighborhoods are a wonderful place to wander and admire the beautiful old stone homes.

GAZIANTEP

GETTING HERE AND AROUND

Turkish Airlines and Onurair fly to Gaziantep and Şanlıurfa.

There are daily buses from Istanbul to Gaziantep: the ride takes about 18 hours and costs about $40 to $56. There are regular minivans that make the quick run from Gaziantep to Urfa and from Urfa to Adiyaman, where you can catch a minivan to Kahta. There's an *otogar* (bus station) in each of the main towns.

Train service from Istanbul to Gaziantep has been temporarily suspended due to the construction of a high-speed Istanbul-Ankara line, which was set to be completed in October 2008, but at publication, has not been.

GUIDED TOURS The knowledgable Ayşe Nur Arun at Gaziantep's Arsan travel agency can arrange for tours in Gaziantep, around the region, and to Mt. Nemrut.

ESSENTIALS

Tour Essentials Arsan (☎ *342/220–6464* ⊕ *www.arsan.com.tr*).

EXPLORING

Gaziantep, the economic capital of Turkey's southeast, has an inviting mix of modern vitality and ancient tradition. Responsible for a good chunk of Turkey's industrial output, from bulgur wheat and pistachios to car parts and textiles, the city's modern part is lined with wide boulevards and ever-expanding housing tracts. At the literal and figurative heart of the city, however, lies a narrow-laned old town lined with graceful stone houses, a bustling bazaar filled with the sound of hammering coppersmiths, and a collection of restaurants and baklava bakeries that are considered among the best in Turkey. Only 65 km (40 mi) from the Syrian border, Gaziantep also has a distinctive Middle Eastern feel to it, from the historic homes with their large interior courtyards to the red-pepper paste and cumin used in the local dishes. You could easily spend two days exploring the city and its sites.

Like many cities in the region, Gaziantep's historic center is dominated by an ancient **citadel**, originally Roman but later further fortified by the Byzantines and the Selçuks. It's a pretty steep walk up, but the view from the top of the citadel over the Gaziantep bazaar district is fabulous. ⌗*Free* ☉ *Tues.–Sun. 8:30–4.*

Fodor'sChoice Not far from the citadel is the spiffy **Gaziantep Museum**, one of the city's
★ highlights. The collection used to be just the regular mix of antiquities from throughout the area's long history, but since 2005 it has also been host to a stunning collection of Roman-era mosaics rescued from a nearby archaeological site called Zeugma, which is slowly being submerged under the waters of a man-made lake. The intricate mosaics, some portraying scenes from Roman mythology, others more artistic geometric designs, are dazzling to behold. The fragment of a mosaic depicting a young woman with an enigmatic gaze (called "The Gypsy Girl") is quickly earning Mona Lisa–like iconic status in the area, with signs pointing visitors to her and with reproductions of the mosaic for sale throughout Gaziantep and even the rest of Turkey. ⊠ *Kamil Ocak*

DID YOU KNOW?

Mardin's mountain perch provides breathtaking views over
the plains of Syria.

CLOSE UP

Rediscovering Turkish Food in Gaziantep

Turks can be fiercely proud of the food in their region of the country, but even those from other places will easily admit that Gaziantep has perhaps Turkey's best food. Drawing on culinary influences from Turkish and Arab cooking, the earthy cuisine in Gaziantep is assertively spiced and flavorful. If you've grown tired of kebabs during your time in Turkey, be ready to rediscover them in Gaziantep, where kebab making is seen as both an art and a science. Among some of the best kinds of kebabs you can try here are *sebzeli kebab* (a skewer of lamb, tomato, green peppers, parsley, and garlic minced together) and *Ali Nazik* (cubes of grilled lamb taken off their skewer and served on a heavenly bed of smoky roasted eggplant and garlicky yogurt). Other specialties include *mercimek koftesı* (small ovals made out of red lentils mixed with bulgur wheat, fresh herbs, red pepper paste, and spices) and *yuvalama* (tiny dumplings made out of rice flour and ground meat, served in a yogurt broth).

Most of all, though, Gaziantep is famed for its flaky and buttery baklava, which incorporates with great success one of the area's leading crops, pistachios. It is, without a doubt, the preferred ending to any meal in Gaziantep.

Gaziantep is rightfully known as Turkey's baklava capital and there are several shops incorporating the tongue-twister family name "Güllüoğlu," all of which vie for the title of being the city's best maker of the flaky sweet. One of the best is Baklavacı Güllüoğlu.

Stat karşısı 1–2 ☎*342/324–8809* ☜*$3* ☉*May–Oct., daily 8:30–noon and 1–6; Nov.–Apr., daily 8:30–noon and 1–4:30.*

Hasan Suzer Ethnographic Museum, inside the warren of streets in the city's historic district, is a beautiful traditional Gaziantep house that's been restored and opened up to the public. The rooms of the house, which is built around a central courtyard, are done up with period furniture and somewhat stricken-looking mannequins dressed in traditional local costume. It's an excellent way to see the inside of a local old-style home, and the shady courtyard is a nice place to escape the Gaziantep sun. ☒*Hainfioğlu Sokak 64* ☎*342/230–4721* ☜*$2.50* ☉*Mon.–Sat., 8–noon and 1–5:30; closed Sun.*

You could spend a whole day losing yourself in Gaziantep's lively and sprawling **bazaar,** just south of the citadel. Gaziantep is known for copper work, and the sound of coppersmiths banging away is ubiquitous in the part of the market aptly known as the Coppersmiths' Bazaar. You'll also see saddle makers, woodworkers, spice vendors, and stalls selling everything from housewares and meat grinders to rugs with the image of Princess Diana on them! ☉*Mon.–Sat. 9–6; closed Sun.*

WHERE TO STAY AND EAT

¢

TURKISH

✕**Baklavacı Güllüoğlu.** This little shop, located inside a spice bazaar, is considered by many Turks nationwide to have the best baklava in the country. Run by a fifth-generation baklava maker, this humble store turns out a delicious version of the classic dessert, as well as other phyllo-and-nut-based sweets. ☒*Elmacı Pazarı 4* ☎*342/231–2105* ☏*No credit cards* ☉*Closed Sun.*

$ ✕**Çavuşoğlu.** This place is a touch more refined than many of the other
TURKISH kebab houses in Gaziantep, with its comfortable chairs, beige walls with
dark wood accents, and large photographs of local street scenes. The
food is top-notch, with perfectly grilled kebabs and small *lahmacun*,
round flatbreads topped with minced meat, and with just a touch of
spicy heat. ✉*Eski Saray Cad. 11/B* ☎*342/231–3069* ▬*MC, V.*

$ ✕**Imam Çağdaş.** Open since 1887, Imam Çağdaş is certainly doing some-
TURKISH thing right, and the crowds pack this restaurant in the bazaar district
Fodor'sChoice day and night. The food is earthy and sublime, from the Ali Nazik,
★ minced meat kebab served on puree of roasted eggplant, garlic, and
yogurt, to the *sebzeli* kebab, a skewer of lamb minced with garlic and
parsley. Finish your meal with the restaurant's terrific syrupy baklava.
✉*Kale Civarı Uzun Çarşı* ☎*342/220–4545* ▬*MC, V.*

$ ✕**Incilpinar Antep Sofrası.** Another of the city's top restaurants, this laid-
TURKISH back place is in the middle of a green park, and its several rooms are
decked with kilims and low tables. There is also a shady courtyard.
Along with very good kebabs, you can order various dishes that are
baked in a terra-cotta pot. The restaurant also makes excellent *yuvalama*, a stew made with yogurt and small meat and rice flour dumplings.
✉*100. Yıl Atatürk Kültür Parkı İçi* ☎*No phone* ▬*MC, V.*

¢ ✕**Papirus Cafeteria.** The real attraction at this simple café that serves light
CAFE fare such as pressed sandwiches and pizzas is the incredible old stone
house it's located in. Down a narrow alleyway in one of Gaziantep's
historic quarters, the building once belonged to an Armenian family.
Its large courtyard is covered by leafy vines, while the interior has walls
covered with incredible fresco-like decorative painting. ✉*Noter Sokak
10* ☎*342/220–3279* ▬*MC, V.*

$ ✕**Yörem.** Head here for a break from kebabs and get a taste of clas-
TURKISH sic Gaziantep home cooking. Run by a local woman who returned
★ to Gaziantep after living in Europe for several years, Yörem's menu
rotates on a regular basis, but the food is consistently good. Dishes to
try include *yuvalama,* a meat and dumpling stew; *omaç,* a kind of patty
made of bread, tomato, onion, and parsley; and *kezan* kebab, eggplant
stuffed with meat and poached. For dessert try the local specialty *zerde
sutlaç,* rice pudding with a saffron topping. ✉*Incilpinar Mahallesi 3.
Cad. 15. Sokak* ☎*342/230–5000* ▬*MC, V* ☾*Closed Sun.*

$$ ☷**Anadolu Evleri.** Down a narrow alleyway, behind a high wall hides this
Fodor'sChoice gem, a stylish but comfortable boutique hotel in a historic Gaziantep
★ stone house. Rooms have been meticulously restored and are charm-
ingly decorated with quirky antiques like old radios, sewing machines,
and antique telephones. The courtyard is delightful, with a covered seat-
ing area and tables shaded by umbrellas. Owner Tim Schindel, son of
a Turkish mother and an American father, is helpful and a good source
of information about Gaziantep's cultural heritage. **Pros:** romantic set-
ting; friendly staff; owner speaks fluent English. **Cons:** no swimming
pool or hamam, though it's only a few minutes' walk to the best one
in town. ✉*Şekeroğlu Mahallesi Köroğlu Sokak 6, 27600* ☎*342/220–
9525* ⊕*www.anadoluevleri.com* ⇗*10 rooms, 3 suites* ⌂*In-room: no
TV (some). In-hotel: Wi-Fi* ▬*MC, V* ☉*BP.*

7

$
★ 🏨**Antique Belkis Han.** Come to this charming, small hotel run by a local artist if you want to get a taste of what life used to be like in Gaziantep's old stone homes. Built in the 19th century, the gorgeous house has beautiful stone work and a lovely courtyard. Rooms are tastefully decorated with antique furniture and various knickknacks. The charming downstairs breakfast area has a long communal table, a stone floor, and is filled with more antiques. **Pros:** walking distance to bazaars, Turkish hamams, and museums; comfortable reading room with a variety of books. **Cons:** not every room has a private bathroom; only two rooms are spacious. ⊠*Kayacık Ara Sokak 16* ☎*0342/221–1228* ⊕*www. belkishan.com* ↩*6 rooms* ⊟*No credit cards* ⏉*BP.*

KÂHTA

174 km (108 mi) from Gaziantep.

GETTING HERE AND AROUND

GUIDED TOURS Nemrut Tours in Kâhta, which is connected to the Hotel Nemrut, arranges daily trips to Mt. Nemrut.

ESSENTIALS

Tour Essentials Nemrut Tours (☎*416/725–6881*).

The quiet and dusty little town of Kâhta is really nothing more than a good base for exploring Mt. Nemrut, with a few good hotels and places to eat, but nothing else to see.

The construction of the large Atatürk Dam and the resulting rising waters have meant that Kâhta is now a lakeside town, and a number of restaurants have taken advantage of this, opening up near the water, which makes for a pleasant place to have a meal.

WHERE TO STAY AND EAT

¢–$ ✕**Kahta Sofrası.** The pickings might be slim in Kâhta, but this place
TURKISH stands out for its friendly service and well-made food, including freshly baked *pide* as well as kebabs and prepared dishes like roast chicken and lamb stew. The restaurant is decorated with colorful rugs and is bright and open. ⊠*Mustafa Kemal Cad. 15* ☎*416/726–2055* ⊟*MC, V.*

$ ✕**Neşet'in Yeri.** This lakeside restaurant has an outdoor area shaded
TURKISH by an impressive grape arbor where you can eat trout or kebab while looking at the water. It's a nice spot to unwind after a visit to Nemrut. ⊠*Baraj Kenari* ☎*416/725–7675* ⊟*MC, V.*

¢ 🏨**Hotel Nemrut.** Popular with tour groups, this hotel has clean, comfortable rooms, though the public areas are a bit dark and cheerless. The restaurant is on a shady terrace and the hotel can arrange for tours to Mt. Nemrut. **Pros:** tours are inexpensive; staff is friendly and enthusiastic; food is decent and inexpensive. **Cons:** Internet is spotty (but free); no swimming pool or hamam. ⊠*Adıyaman Yolu* ☎*416/725–6881* ⊕*www.hotelnemrut.net* ↩*80 rooms, 4 suites* ⏉*In-room: refrigerator. In-hotel: restaurant, pool* ⊟*AE, MC, V* ⏉*BP.*

$ 🏨**Zeus Hotel.** With a pool and quiet garden, this well-run hotel is a good base for visiting Mt. Nemrut, something the friendly staff can help arrange. Rooms are spacious and comfortable, and each has a small couch. **Pros:** rooms have free Internet; hotel works with a travel company to arrange specialized tours for guests. **Cons:** they can be pushy about organizing a tour. ✉*Mustafa Kemal Cad. 20* ☎*416/725– 5694* ⊕*www.zeushotel.com.tr* ⤶*58 rooms, 8 suites* ♿*In-room: refrigerator, Internet. In-hotel: restaurant, bar, pool* ▤*MC, V* ⦿*BP.*

MT. NEMRUT AND ENVIRONS

228 km (142 mi) northeast of Gaziantep.

Fodor'sChoice **Mt. Nemrut** *(Nemrut Dağı).* See the highlighted feature in this chapter.

★ ### WHERE TO STAY

$ 🏨**Hotel Euphrat.** This hotel on Mt. Nemrut, like the Otel Kervansary next door, is a low stone building with spartan but clean rooms. There is a restaurant decked out in kilims and rugs with a deck that has a spectacular view of the surrounding mountains and of the stars at night. The food is simple but tasty. The hotel also has a pleasant garden with cherry and quince trees. **Pros:** friendly atmosphere; close to the mountain's summit. **Cons:** a little bit drab on outside and inside; can get crowded in tourist season. ✉*Nemrut Dağı, Karadut Köyü, 54 km (34 mi) from Kâhta, Karadut Köyü* ☎*416/737–2175* ⛴*416/737–2179* ⤶*52 rooms* ♿*In-room: no phone, no TV. In-hotel: restaurant, pool, parking (free)* ▤*MC, V* ⦿*MAP.*

$ 🏨**Otel Kervansaray.** One of the few places to stop on Mt. Nemrut itself,
★ the Kervansaray is in a low stone building near a waterfall 8 km (5 mi) from Mt. Nemrut's summit. The location is stunning, the rooms are basic but clean, and the food is simple but good. It's all wonderfully quiet. The pool is small and nothing fancy. **Pros:** like its neighbor, this hotel has amazing views and is close to the summit; this hotel sells wine and beer; free Internet on the terrace; friendly and helpful owners. **Cons:** rooms are simple with only beds and a nightstand; no TV in the hotel. ✉*Nemrut Dağı, Karadut Köyü, 54 km (34 mi) from Kâhta* ☎*416/737–2190* ⛴*416/737–2085* ⤶*16 rooms* ♿*In-room: no TV. In-hotel: restaurant, pool, Internet terminal* ▤*MC, V* ⦿*MAP.*

ŞANLIURFA (URFA)

★ *143 km (89 mi) southeast of Kâhta on Rte. E99, or 135 km (84 mi) east of Gaziantep.*

GETTING HERE AND AROUND
Turkish Airlines flies to Şanlıurfa for $70 to $90.

ESSENTIALS
GUIDED TOURS Harran-Nemrut tours in Urfa is run by the English-speaking Özcan Aslan, who is friendly and helpful. He can arrange trips to Harran and the surrounding region and also offers one- and two-day tours to Mt. Nemrut from Urfa.

EXPLORING
With its golden-colored stone houses, religious shrines filled with visiting pilgrims, and a very authentic bazaar displaying mounds and mounds of the local specialty, crushed red pepper, in various shades and levels of spiciness, Şanlıurfa has a timeless quality to it. The city

Continued on page 474

MEGALOMANIA ON MOUNT NEMRUT

"I, Antiochus, caused this monument to be erected in commemoration of my own glory and of that of the gods."

At the top of remote Mount Nemrut (Nemrut Daği), the monumental tomb of Antiochus, king of the obscure and short-lived kingdom of Commagene, on the Euphrates, is one of the world's most extraordinary archaeology sights. Antiochus fancied himself a ruler on par with the gods of antiquity, so he had this grandiose monument to himself erected, in the company of his peers.

At 2150 m (7,053 ft), Mt. Nemrut is the highest peak in the area, near the Syrian border. At the center of the mountaintop site is a huge tumulus, or burial mound of small stones. To the east and west of the burial mound are two great platforms, each with an identical giant statue of Antiochus seated with his fellow gods, overlooking the desertlike landscape and the Euphrates River to the east. Over the years the statues have fallen and now the disembodied stone heads stand separate from their bodies.

Statue heads on West Terrace

WHAT TO SEE

1 The Tumulus

The center of the site is the giant tumulus, 500 feet in diameter and 150 feet high, made of small pebbles. It's believed that the entrance to King Antiochus's tomb is underneath the rocks, but despite several attempts at tunneling, it has yet to be found.

THE TERRACES

To the east and west of the tumulus, the land was leveled into large terraces where giant statues of Antiochus and the gods were erected. Annual religious ceremonies were performed here.

2 The East Terrace

On the east terrace, the stone bodies of the statues are quite well preserved, giving the best idea of what they originally looked like. The heads are more worn, and are now lined up at the feet of their respective bodies. The head of Tyche is said to have sat on her statue's stone shoulders until as late as the 1960s.

3 The West Terrace

On the west terrace, the statue bodies have crumbled, but the heads, scattered around the area, are well preserved; these are the now classic images of Mount Nemrut.

ENTRANCE

NORTH TERRACE

Ramp

Ditch

Lining of Steps

ENTRANCE

12

Colossal Statues

9
4
5
6
7
8
9

Ditch

EAST TERRACE

2

TUMULUS/ BURIAL MOUND

1

Professional Way

Colossal Statues

WEST TERRACE

3

11

10

Trial Excavations

Trial Excavations

Professional Way

Above: The tumulus

THE GODS

King Antiochus had himself depicted enthroned with his fellow gods in a matching set of 30-ft-tall stone murals on the east and west terraces. The images of the gods are a mix of eastern and western styles, their faces Greek, their clothes Persian.

4 Hercules, Artagnes, and Ares Hercules is bearded, but with a simpler hat than Zeus. Artaganes, or Vahram, was a Persian warrior god, here combined with both the hero Hercules, and Ares, the Greek god of war. On the east terrace, the statue of Hercules bears the symbol of the club.

5 King Antiochus In front of the statues stood a smaller stele of Antiochus posing with his fellow gods. The image of the king was on the left, beardless with a long thin plume-like hat.

6 Zeus-Oromasdes Zeus, mixed with his Persian equivalent Oromasdes or Ahura Mazda, stood in the center of the site, his stone throne slightly higher than the rest. His bearded face is hard to distinguish from Hercules, but look for the circle and diamond pattern on his conical hat.

7 The Tyche of Commagene Tyche, the godess of fortune, is the only female figure here and, therefore, the easiest to spot. As an embodiment of fortune and abundance, her headdress is filled with fruit.

Hercules

8 Apollo, Hermes, Helius, and Mithra Apollo is another beardless male, with a simpler, more conical, hat than that of Antiochos. The ancients apparently weren't sure who was the Greek equivalent of their Persian Mithra, spirit of light, so his image is a mix of Apollo (the sun god), Helios (the sun itself), and Hermes (the messenger god).

9 Animal Protectors On either side of the gods stood a giant lion and eagle, which acted as their protectors. The eagles were built of multiple pieces, as were the gods, and their heads sit together on the west terrace.

10 The Ancestors Antiochus had some of the most royal blood in the ancient world. On the back of his throne is carved his royal pedigree: the kings of Persia and Armenia on his father's side, and the Greco-Macedonian kings who ruled the empire of Alexander the

great on his mother's side. Around the great statues are carved reliefs depicting Antiochus with his ancestors. The best preserved are those of him with the great kings of Persia—Darius and Xerxes—on the south side of the west terrace.

11 The Lion Horoscope On the west terrace, a relief image of a lion has been called the world's oldest horoscope. It depicts a lion (representing the constellation Leo) with the planets Mars, Mercury, and Jupiter from left to right above its back, and the crescent moon at its feet. Archaeoastronomers have identified the date of this horoscope as either July 109 BC, perhaps Antiochus's birthday or the date of the founding of the dynasty, or July 61 BC, perhaps his coronation.

12 THE FIRE ALTAR The sacred fire was a central part of the Persian Zoroastrian religion and the east terrace featured a large fire altar—it's hardly noticed today, although the area is the most popular place for tourists to watch the sunrise.

The Lion Horoscope

DID YOU KNOW?

There's no connection
between Mt. Nemrut
and the Biblical Nimrod
(Nemrut in English), creator
of the Tower of Babel.
Somehow the name
got attached and stuck;
Antiochus must be turning
in his monumental grave.

THE ROAD TO NEMRUT AND WHAT TO SEE ON IT

There are several ancient sites along the road from Kâhta to Nemrut that have become standard stops for visitors to the mountain.

King Antiochus and Hercules at Arsameia

THE BURIAL MOUND OF KARAKUŞ

A second royal tumulus—it lacks the grandeur of the more famous mountaintop monument—was built by Antiochus's son, for his sister, wife, and daughter. The name Karakuş, or black bird, comes from the statue of an eagle, set on a large column beside the tomb.

CENDERE BRIDGE

Photos don't do justice to the scale of this huge bridge, a monument to Roman engineering: three large columns once held statues of the Emperor Septimus Severus, his wife Julia Domna, and their son, the future emperor Caracalla. A fourth was probably for the second son, Geta, who was killed by Caracalla, who also tried to erase all trace of his brother's existence.

ARSAMEIA

Part way up the mountain are the few remains of what is left of Arsameia, the summer home of the kings of Commagene: several carved stelai, the most famous picturing King Antiochus in Persian dress with a very naked Hercules. Above is a long inscription in Greek with a deep tunnel disappearing into the mountain.

ESKI KÂHTA

The small traditional village of Eski (old) Kâhta, is just off the main road where the mountains start. There is a castle here with a view over a dramatic gorge.

GETTING THERE

Kâhta is the most popular place to base yourself for a trip to Mount Nemrut. From here it's a 2-hour drive, plus stops, and while the road is good, it's steep and bumpy in places and can be very windy. We recommend letting someone else take the wheel and booking one of the many tours ($15–$75) offered from Kâhta (there are also tours based in Cappadocia), which will also give you the benefit of having a tour guide. Most tours are timed for sunrise or sunset, when the landscape and its monuments are at their most dramatic, though in summer arriving for sunrise can mean a 2 AM departure. Dress warmly: even in high summer the nights are quite chilly atop the mountain.

lies at the edge of the Syrian desert, not far from the border with Syria and, like Gaziantep, also has a strong Middle Eastern flavor—literally as well as figuratively, because the local food has a distinct Armenian influence. Formerly a sleepy and arid frontier town that underwent a huge boom due to GAP (the Güneydoğu Anadolu Projesi, or Southeast Anatolia Project, a large-scale damming and irrigation program undertaken by the Turkish government), Urfa is most famous as the supposed birthplace of the biblical patriarch Abraham. A half-dozen mosques crowd around the cave where many Muslims believe Abraham was born, and a pool near the cave is filled with what are believed to be sacred carp.

Şanlıurfa is more commonly called Urfa by Turks and in maps and tourism literature; *şanlı*, or "famous," was added by an act of parliament to the city's name in 1984 to commemorate the city's resistance to the French military occupation of the area following World War I. Urfa's old town, at the southern foot of Divan Caddesi, is a remarkable mix of Babylonian, Assyrian, Roman, Byzantine, and Ottoman architecture, albeit heavily eroded over the centuries.

The **Urfa Kale** *(Urfa Fortress)* is a motley collection of pillars, upturned stones, and broken columns at the top of a wide staircase. It's impossible to detect any one architectural intent here, probably because the fortress has been razed and rebuilt at least a dozen times since the 2nd century BC. Climb to the summit for a fantastic view of the city. ⊠ *Kale Cad.* ☎ *No phone* 💲 *$2.50* ⊙ *Daily 9–6.*

Local legend has it that Abraham was born in the **Hazreti İbrahim Doğum Mağarası** *(Prophet İbrahim's Birth Cave)*, a natural cave hidden behind the Hasan Paşa Mosque. As is usual, men and women enter through separate doorways. Most people huddled inside this small, dark cavern, darkened by 2,000 years of candle smoke, have come to pray, not to snap photos. There's not much to see, but the atmosphere is reverential. Tourists are welcome (many of the visitors inside are themselves from out of town), but remember that this is a shrine. ⊠ *Göl Cad.* ☎ *No phone* 💲 *Free* ⊙ *Daily, sunrise–sunset.*

Gölbaşı Parkı, home of the famed carp pools, is a shady oasis on hot days. According to legend, King Nimrod, angry at Abraham's condemnation of the king's Assyrian polytheism, set about immolating the patriarch. God awakened natural springs, dousing the fire and saving Abraham. Historically the story might not, well, hold water, but these gorgeous springs remain, in the form of these sacred pools filled with carp—an incarnation, according to the myth, of the wood from Abraham's pyre. The place has a serene and distinctly spiritual feel to it, with groups of visiting pilgrims and families from Turkey and neighboring countries strolling about and feeding what are probably the most pampered fish in the world.

A short walk east from the park leads to Urfa's **bazaar,** where in summertime merchants wait patiently in the hot sun for the occasional tour group. The bazaar is a wonderful, filled with small *hans*—a collection of stores and workshops built around a central courtyard—that have tailors, coppersmiths, and other artisans working away, using what seem

The gold-colored houses of Şanlıurfa.

like ancient machines and tools. At the literal heart of the bazaar is the wonderful *bedestan,* a large courtyard filled with chatting men playing backgammon or chess and sipping tea. Around the courtyard are the small workshops of tailors sewing inexpensive suits. Urfa's bazaar is a good place to shop for spices and copper items and you can usually find bargains, especially on carpets and kilims.

Urfa's old neighborhoods are filled with lovely stone homes covered with ornamental carving, and several hours exploring will be time well spent. One place worth seeking out is the old Assyrian church complex, **Il Özel Idaresi Vali Kemalettin Gazezoğlu Kultur ve Sanat Merkezi**—it's a mouthful, but neighborhood locals should be able to point you in the right direction—that has been restored and turned into a cultural center. The hours are unpredictable, but the walk there leads you through narrow alleyways and past several beautiful old houses. ⊠ *Kurtuluş Sokak* 🕾 *No phone* 🎫 *Free* ⊘ *Irregular hours.*

Güzel Sanatlar Galerisi, the city's art gallery, right next to the post office, is another restored house that's worth visiting. The art may not be so impressive, but the stone mansion has delightful relief-carving work on its exterior and a lovely indoor courtyard. ⊠ *Sarayönü Cad.* 🕾 *No phone* 🎫 *Free* ⊘ *Mon.–Fri. 8:30–5, Sat. noon–4.*

Urfa also has a small but appealing **archaeological museum.** The displays are thoughtfully laid out and well lit, covering the area's long history. Especially interesting are a series of Hittite sculptures that were dug up in the area, and a collection of antique wooden doors with exquisite carving work. ⊠ *Çamlık Cad.* 🕾 *414/313–1588* 🎫 *$2.50* ⊘ *Mon.–Fri. 8–noon and 1–5:30.*

WHERE TO STAY AND EAT

¢-$ ✕**Altınşiş.** The combination of good food and friendly service makes this
TURKISH low-key restaurant especially appealing. There are kebabs and döner,
along with *pide* and a large selection of prepared foods being kept warm
on a steam table. The *güveç*, a meat and vegetable stew cooked in a large
terra-cotta pot, is worth trying. The dining room is simple and cheery,
with walls painted a light yellow and tables covered with blue cloths.
✉*Sarayönü Cad. 140* ☎*414/216–0506* ▤*MC, V.*

¢-$ ✕**Çardaklı Köşk.** Another old Urfa stone house restored and turned into
TURKISH a restaurant, but this one looks out over the city's citadel and the fish-
pool complex. Sit on the terrace or in one of the several *çardaks*, small
private rooms where you can recline on pillows. The food, the usual
mix of kebabs and pides, is unexciting, but the location makes up for
it. ✉*Balıkgöl Civarı Tünel Çıkışı 1* ☎*414/217–1080* ▤*MC, V.*

$ ✕**Gülizar Konuk Evi.** One of the first restaurants in Urfa to open up inside
TURKISH one of the city's historic stone houses, this is also one of the best. It
serves the usual kebabs, along with some local specialties such as *çöm-
lek*, a meat and vegetable stew slow-cooked in the oven, and *borani*,
a stew made with lamb and spinach. Found down a winding lane, the
old house also has a beautiful open-air courtyard with a fountain and
a pomegranate tree. You can eat outdoors or in one of the "Oriental"-
style private dining rooms filled with rugs and pillows. ✉*Karameydanı
Camii Yanı 22* ☎*414/215–0505* ▤*MC, V.*

$ ✕**Urfa Sofrası.** This dining establishment is a bit more upscale than most
TURKISH of its competitors. An outdoor terrace overlooks a small park and the
busy streets below. You can order kebabs, *pide*, and *lahmacun* and
kaburga (lamb stuffed with rice). The dishes come served with a cold
and refreshing yogurt soup made with chickpeas and wheat berries.
Finish your meal with a small cup of bracing Arab-style bitter coffee,
served by a roving waiter who pours the coffee from his copper urn.
✉*Karakoyun Işmerkezi Kat 1 No. 226* ☎*414/315–6130* ▤*MC, V.*

$ ⛺**Cevahir Konuk Evi.** Formerly a government guest house, this grand
old stone home with a great view from its terrace is now in private
hands. The hallways are lined with colorful rugs and antique furniture, while the rooms have high ceilings, stone walls, and white bedspreads embroidered with flowers. Tidy bathrooms have full tubs.
There's a good restaurant with a large garden, though they often have
live music at night, so ask for a room that doesn't face the courtyard.
Pros: hotel is surprisingly modern and spacious for the price; pleasant
patio for breakfast and dinner are served. **Cons:** slow Internet; those
looking for peace and quiet may not appreciate the live music most
nights. ✉*Büyükyol Selahattin Eyyubi Cami, Karşısı* ☎*414/215–9377*
⊕*www.cevahirkonukevi.com* ↩*6 rooms, 1 suite* ⌂*In-room: refrigerator, Wi-Fi . In-hotel: restaurant* ▤*AE, MC, V* ⛾*BP.*

$ ⛺**Harran Hotel.** Once the city's best hotel, the Harran is looking a little
aged but the rooms are spacious and comfortable and the bathrooms
are decent sized. The hotel is centrally located and staffed by a phalanx
of friendly employees, and there's a nice pool—a definite bonus during
the hot Urfa summer. The restaurant on the top floor, where breakfast
is served, has an unparalleled view of Urfa. **Pros:** the pool and views

are reason enough to stay here in summer; services combined with free breakfast make this place a bargain. **Cons:** parking is at a different hotel; additional costs for sauna, hamam, and pool. ⊠*Atatürk Bul.* ☎*414/313–2860* ⊕*www.hotelharran.com* ⌂*82 rooms* ⌂*In-room: refrigerator, Wi-Fi. In-hotel: restaurant, pool, gym, parking (free)* ⊟*AE, MC, V* ¶⊙|*BP.*

$$ **Hotel El-Ruha.** This sprawling hotel across the street from Urfa's fish-
★ pools is the city's top place to stay. Built of local stone, it has a comfortable lobby with leather couches and antique furniture. Rooms are spacious and comfortable, with large beds, wood furniture, vaulted ceilings, and bathrooms with mosaic-like tiles; most have a view of the fish pool complex. Service is attentive and professional. **Pros:** beautiful design and architecture; across the street from the fish pool; staff and restaurants go the extra mile to accommodate guests. **Cons:** pricey breakfast and dinner compared to local eats; the only thing this luxury hotel is missing is a luxury pool to give relief in Urfa's hot summers. ⊠*Balıklıgöl* ☎*414/215–4411* ⊕*www.hotelelruha.com* ⌂*71 rooms, 11 suites* ⌂*In-room: refrigerator. In-hotel: 2 restaurants, gym, parking (free)* ⊟*MC, V* ¶⊙|*BP.*

HARRAN

50 km (31 mi) southeast of Urfa.

A quick ride from Urfa, the ancient city of Harran is well worth a visit. The Urfa region is rife with dubious biblical legends, but there seems to be almost unanimous agreement that this Harran of modern Turkey is quite likely the Harran mentioned in the Old Testament as a place where Abraham spent some time before heading off to the promised land. True or not, today's Harran stands on the spot of a very ancient settlement, with crumbling fortifications surrounding what is now a simple village and the ruins of what was once the world's first Islamic university, built in the 8th century, just on the edge of town. Called the **Ulu Cami**, all that's left is a distinctive square minaret that can be seen from throughout Harran. Indeed, in Harran visitors get the sense that not much has changed here over the centuries, and some of the pastoral scenes around Harran, of shepherds driving their flocks of sheep along seem, well, almost biblical.

Harran's main claims to fame, besides playing host to Abraham, are its beehive-shaped houses, wondrous structures built of hay and mud, each topped with a conical roof. The small town is filled with them, although many are no longer family dwellings and are now used as stables or are in the process of collapsing.

The Harran Evi is a good reconstruction of a traditional beehive home where you can take a tour of the inside living quarters and hear the guide extol the virtues—cool in summer, warm in winter—of its unique construction. After the tour, you can sit down for tea or a cold drink in the courtyard or in a rug-lined room inside the beehive house itself. ⊠*Ibni Teymiye Mah* ☎*414/441-2020* ▨*Free* ⊙*Daily 8* AM–10 PM.

The Geleneksel Konik Kubbeli Evi, just down the road from the Harran Evi is another reconstruction of a beehive house built by a rival local family. It's also worth visiting. The family that lives there is especially friendly and rather exuberant, literally running up to the entrance gate with broad smiles to greet visitors. ⊠ *Ceşme Sokak 23* ☏ *542/337–8512* ✉ *Free* ⊙ *Daily 8* AM–*10* PM.

UNDERSTANDING TURKEY

BOOKS & MOVIES

Books

Whether Homer's *Iliad* should be classified as fiction or nonfiction is up for debate, but it's still the most evocative reading on the Trojan War and the key players of Turkish antiquity.

Memoirs, Essays and Observations. For keen insight into the ancient ruins that you may encounter on your try George Bean, author of *Aegean Turkey, Turkey Beyond the Meander, Lycian Turkey,* and *Turkey's Southern Shore.* John Julius Norwich's three-volume *Byzantium* chronicles the rise and fall of one of history's great empires, while Caroline Finkel's *Osman's Dream* provides a comprehensive overview of the history of the Ottoman Empire.

Mary Lee Settle provides a vision of Turkey that is both panoramic and personal in *Turkish Reflections.* The book marks Settle's return to the country that was the setting for her novel *Blood Tie,* a 1978 National Book Award winner. Dame Freya Stark chronicles her visits to Turkey in *The Journey's Echo* and *Alexander's Path.* Only a piece of Mark Twain's *Innocents Abroad* is about Turkey, but it offers a witty glimpse of the country as it used to be. Hans Christian Andersen also wrote a memorable travelogue, *A Poet's Bazaar: A Journey to Greece, Turkey and up the Danube. The Letters and Works of Lady Mary Wortley Montagu* is a significant and entertaining book that delightfully documents life in 18th-century Ottoman Turkey—including its much-quoted passages about the harem—through the eyes of the wife of a British consul.

Irfan Orga's exquisite *Portrait of a Turkish Family* is an evocative memoir weaving personal history with modern politics as it addresses the impact of the upheavals of the early 20th century on his own family. Orhan Pamuk's *Istanbul: Memories of a City* interweaves the novelist's memories of his childhood and youth with black-and-white photographs and vignettes from the city's history; many think this nonfiction is much more readable than his fiction.

History. For modern Turkish history and politics, try *Turkey: A Modern History,* by Erik J. Zürcher, or *Turkey Unveiled,* an accessible, journalistic account of Turkish politics by Nicole and Hugh Pope.

More books have been written about Istanbul than about the rest of Turkey. Two of the finest portraits of the city are the excellent *Constantinople: City of the World's Desire 1453–1924,* by Philip Mansel, and *Istanbul: The Imperial City,* by John Freely.

Literature and Fiction. For an introduction to Turkish literature, track down a copy of *An Anthology of Turkish Literature,* by Kemal Silay. If you prefer to plunge into a complete novel, look out for *Anatolian Tales* or *Mehmet, My Hawk,* by Yaşar Kemal, one of the country's most famous modern novelists. Of the younger generation of Turkish writers, the best-known is Orhan Pamuk, whose dense melancholy prose means that his work is often more highly regarded than it is enjoyed. His novels include *My Name Is Red* and the acclaimed *Snow.* Louis de Bernieres's novel *Birds Without Wings* offers a portrayal of rural life in western Anatolia during the final years of the Ottoman Empire.

Agatha Christie's novel *Murder on the Orient Express* provides the proper atmosphere for a trip to Istanbul, and you can still visit Istanbul's Pera Palas Hotel, the terminus of the famous train, where Christie herself stayed. Harold Nicolson's *Sweet Waters* is usually billed as a thriller although it is more of a love story, and the detail draws heavily on the author's years as a junior diplomat in Istanbul in the years leading up to the outbreak of World War I. If you love spy novels, *Istanbul Intrigues,* by Barry Rubin, paints a vivid picture of real cloak-and-dagger intrigues in the city during World War II.

Poetry. *The Penguin Book of Turkish Verse* offers a good selection in English of leading Ottoman and Turkish poets. Nazım Hikmet (1901–63) is generally regarded as Turkey's greatest, if still controversial, poet, and Randy Blasing and Mutlu Konuk have produced excellent English versions of Hikmet's most important poems in *Poems of Nazim Hikmet* and his extraordinary verse epic *Human Landscapes*. (The best English-language biography of Nazım Hikmet is *Romantic Communist*, by Saime Göksu and Edward Timms.)

The poetry of the Sufi mystic Rumi has few rivals in any language, whether for the beauty of his words or for his message of universal love and tolerance. There are several translations of his poetry: the best known include *Rumi: Poet And Mystic*, by Reynold Nicholson, *The Essential Rumi*, by Coleman Barks, and *Rumi: In the Arms of the Beloved*, by Jonathan Star.

Movies

Western movies filmed in Turkey obviously tend to play up Turkey's exotic aspects, for better or worse. Director Joseph L. Mankiewicz's *Five Fingers* (1952), an Ankara-based spy thriller based on the book *Operation Cicero*, by C. L. Moyzisch, is noteworthy both for its action and for its clever dialogue ("Counter espionage is the highest form of gossip"). Peter Ustinov won an Academy Award for best supporting actor for his performance in the Jules Dassin–directed museum-heist film *Topkapi* (1964), which also stars Melina Mercouri and Maximilian Schell.

Alan Parker directed the film version of *Midnight Express* (1978), about Billy Hayes's days in a Turkish prison following a drug conviction. The film's horrific depiction of Hayes's experiences (some of which were not in his memoir) made the Turkish government gun-shy about allowing Western moviemakers into the country. When *Midnight Express* was finally shown on Turkish TV in the mid-1990s, newscasters interviewed people in the street, who wept over the country's portrayal on-screen and the influence they feared the film may have had on perceptions of Turkey in the West.

Peter Weir's *Gallipoli* (1981) follows the exploits of two Australian soldiers preparing for and fighting in the historic battle in the Dardanelles during World War I. Critics generally praise the film, though some have noted a lack of sensitivity to the Turks.

Turkish movies now regularly feature at international film festivals, and an increasing number are available on DVD (although most on sale in Turkey are Region 2, so you will need a multiregion DVD player to be able to play them in the U.S.). Notable ones include: Nuri Bilge Ceylan's *Uzak* (2000), a hauntingly beautiful depiction of loneliness, set in Istanbul, that manages to be simultaneously melancholic, humorous, and uplifting; Yılmaz Erdoğan and Ömer Faruk Sorak's *Vizontele* (2001), a charming and often hilarious portrayal of the effect of the arrival of electricity on a rural community; and Fatih Akın's *Head-On* (*Gegen die Wand*) (2004), a stunning, if frequently brutal, love story of a couple who build a relationship out of their shattered lives. Turkey finally took revenge for *Midnight Express* with Serdar Akar and Sadullah Şentürk's *Valley of the Wolves: Iraq* (2006). Poorly scripted, anti-Semitic, and anti-American in tone, the movie nevertheless lays bare some of the many complexes and conspiracy theories that underpin popular Turkish conceptions of current events; it broke all box office records in Turkey on its release.

TURKISH VOCABULARY

	ENGLISH	TURKISH	PRONUNCIATION
BASICS			
	Hello	Merhaba	mer-**hab**-a
	Yes/no	Evet/hayır	**eh**-vet/**hi**-yer
	Please	Lütfen	**lewt**-fen
	Thank you	Teşekkür ederim	tay-shake-**kur** eh-day-**reem**
	You're welcome	Rica ederim/ Bir şey değil	ree-**jah** eh-day-**reem**/ beer shay **day**-eel
	Sorry	Özür dilerim	oh-**zewr** deel-air-eem
	Sorry	Pardon	**pahr**-dohn
	Good morning	Günaydın	goon-eye-**den**
	Good day	İyi günler	ee-yee gewn-**lair**
	Good evening	İyi akşamlar	ee-yee ahk-shahm-**lar**
	Goodbye	Allahaısmarladık	**allah**-aw-ees-mar-law-deck
		Güle güle	**gew**-leh **gew**-leh
	Mr. (Sir)	Bey	by, bay
	Mrs./Miss	Hanım	ha-nem
	Pleased to meet you	Memnun oldum	**mam**-noon ohl-doom
	How are you?	Nasılsınız?	**nah**-suhl-suh-nuhz
NUMBERS			
	one half	buçuk	byoo-**chook**
	one	bir	beer
	two	iki	ee-**kee**
	three	üç	ooch
	four	dört	doort
	five	beş	besh
	six	altı	ahl-tuh
	seven	yedi	yed-dee
	eight	sekiz	sek-**keez**
	nine	dokuz	doh-**kooz**
	ten	on	**ohn**

ENGLISH	TURKISH	PRONUNCIATION
eleven	onbir	**ohn**-beer
twelve	oniki	**ohn**-ee-kee
thirteen	onüç	**ohn-ooch**
fourteen	ondört	**ohn-doort**
fifteen	onbeş	**ohn**-besh
sixteen	onaltı	**ohn**-ahl-tuh
seventeen	onyedi	**ohn**-yed-dy
eighteen	onsekiz	**ohn**-sek-**keez**
nineteen	ondokuz	**ohn**-doh-**kooz**
twenty	yirmi	yeer-mee
twenty-one	yirmibir	**yeer**-mee-beer
thirty	otuz	oh-**tooz**
forty	kırk	kerk
fifty	elli	ehl-lee
sixty	altmış	**alt**-muhsh
seventy	yetmiş	**yeht**-meesh
eighty	seksen	sehk-san
ninety	doksan	dohk-**san**
one hundred	yüz	yewz
one thousand	bin	bean
one million	milyon	**mill**-ee-on

COLORS

black	siyah	**see**-yah
blue	mavi	**mah**-vee
brown	kahverengi	**kah**-vay-**rain**-gee
green	yeşil	yay-sheel
orange	portakal rengi	poor-tah-kahl rain-gee
red	kırmızı	ker-muz-uh
white	beyaz	**bay**-ahz
yellow	sarı	sah-**ruh**

ENGLISH	TURKISH	PRONUNCIATION

DAYS OF THE WEEK

ENGLISH	TURKISH	PRONUNCIATION
Sunday	Pazar	pahz-**ahr**
Monday	Pazartesi	pahz-**ahr**-teh-see
Tuesday	Salı	sa-**luh**
Wednesday	Çarşamba	char-shahm-bah
Thursday	Perşembe	pair-shem-beh
Friday	Cuma	joom-**ah**
Saturday	Cumartesi	joom-**ahr**-teh-see

MONTHS

ENGLISH	TURKISH	PRONUNCIATION
January	Ocak	oh-**jahk**
February	Şubat	shoo-**baht**
March	Mart	mart
April	Nisan	nee-**sahn**
May	Mayıs	my-us
June	Haziran	hah-zee-**rahn**
July	Temmuz	**tehm**-mooz
August	Ağustos	ah-oos-tohs
September	Eylül	ey-**lewl**
October	Ekim	eh-**keem**
November	Kasım	kah-suhm
December	Aralık	ah-rah-**luhk**

USEFUL PHRASES

ENGLISH	TURKISH	PRONUNCIATION
Do you speak English?	ingilizce biliyor musunuz?	in-**gee**-**leez**-jay bee-lee-**yohr** moo-soo-nooz
I don't speak Turkish	Türkçe bilmiyorum	**tewrk**-cheh **beel**-mee-yohr-um
I don't understand	Anlamıyorum	ahn-**lah**-muh-yohr-um
I understand	Anlıyorum	ahn-**luh**-yohr-um
I don't know	Bilmiyorum	**beel**-meeh-yohr-um
I'm American	Amerikalıyım	ahm-ay-**ree**-kah-luh-yuhm
I'm British	İngilizim	**een**-gee-leez-eem

ENGLISH	TURKISH	PRONUNCIATION
What's your name?	İsminiz nedir?	ees-mee-niz nay-deer
My name is . . .	Benim adım . . .	bay-**neem** ah-duhm
What time is it?	Saat kaç?	sah-aht **kahch**
How?	Nasıl?	**nah**-suhl
When?	Ne zaman?	**nay** zah-mahn
Yesterday	Dün	dewn
Today	Bugün	**boo**-goon
Tomorrow	Yarın	**yah**-ruhn
This morning/ afternoon	Bu sabah/öğleden sonra	**boo** sah-bah/**ol-lay**-den sohn-rah
Tonight	Bu gece	**boo** ge-jeh
What?	Efendim?/Ne?	**eh**-fan-deem/neh
What is it?	Nedir?	**neh**-deer
Why?	Neden/Niçin?	**neh**-den/**nee**-chin
Who?	Kim?	keem
Where is . . .	Nerede . . .	**nayr**-deh
. . . the train station?	. . . tren istasyonu?	tee-**rehn** ees-**tah**-syohn-oo
. . . the subway station?	. . . metro durağı?	metro doo-**raw**-uh
. . . the bus stop?	. . . otobüs durağı?	oh-toh-**bewse** doo-**raw**-uh
. . . the terminal? (airport)	. . . hava alanı?	hah-**vah ah**-lah-nuh
. . . the post office?	. . . postane?	post-**ahn**-eh
. . . the bank?	. . . banka?	**bahn**-kah
. . . the hotel?	. . . oteli?	oh-**tel-lee**
. . . the museum?	. . . müzesi?	mew-zay-**see**
. . . the hospital?	. . . hastane?	hahs-**tah**-neh
. . . the elevator?	. . . asansör?	ah-san-**sewr**
. . . the telephone?	. . . telefon?	teh-leh-**fohn**
Where are the restrooms?	Tuvalet nerede?	twah-**let** nayr-deh

ENGLISH	TURKISH	PRONUNCIATION
Here/there	Burası/Orası	**boo**-rah-suh/**ohr**-rah-suh
Left/right	sag/sol	sah-ah/sohl
Is it near/	Yakın mı?/	yah-**kuhn** muh/
far?	Uzak mı?	ooz-**ahk**muh
I'd like . . .	. . . istiyorum	**ees**-tee-yohr-ruhm
. . . a room	Bir oda. . .	beer oh-**dah**
. . . the key	Anahtarı. . .	**ahn**-ah-tahr-uh
. . . a newspaper	Bir gazete. . .	beer **gahz**-teh
. . . a stamp	Pul. . .	pool
I'd like to buy . . .	. . . almak istiyorum	ahl-**mahk** ees-tee-your-ruhm
. . . cigarettes	Sigara. . .	**see**-gah-rah
. . . matches	Kibrit. . .	**keeb**-reet
. . . city map	Şehir planı. . .	shay-**heer plah**-nuh
. . . road map	Karayolları haritası. . .	**kah**-rah-yoh-lahr-**uh** hah-ree-tah-**suh**
. . . magazine	Dergi. . .	dair-gee
. . . envelopes	Zarf. . .	zahrf
. . . writing paper	Mektup kagıdı. . .	**make**-toop **kah**-uh-duh
. . . postcard	Kartpostal. . .	cart-poh-stahl
. . . ticket	Bilet. . .	bee-**let**
How much is it?	Fiyatı ne kadar?	fee-yaht-uh **neh** kah-dahr
It's expensive/cheap	pahalı/ucuz	pah-hah-**luh**/oo-**jooz**
A little/a lot	Az/çok	ahz/choke
More/less	daha çok/daha az	da-ha choke/da-ha ahz
Enough/too (much)	Yeter/çok fazla	yay-**tehr**/**choke** fahz-lah
I am ill/sick	Hastayım	**hahs**-tah-yum
Call a doctor	Doktor çağırın	dohk-toor **chah**-uh-run
Help!	İmdat!	eem-**daht**
Stop!	Durun!	doo-**roon**

ENGLISH	TURKISH	PRONUNCIATION

DINING OUT

ENGLISH	TURKISH	PRONUNCIATION
A bottle of . . .	bir şişe . . .	**beer** shee-shay
A cup of . . .	bir fincan . . .	beer **feen**-jahn
A glass of . . .	bir bardak . . .	beer **bar**-dahk
Ashtray	kül tablası	kewl tah-blah-**suh**
Beer	bira	**bee**-ra
Bill/check	hesap	heh-**sahp**
Bread	ekmek	ekmek
Breakfast	kahvaltı	kah-**vahl**-tuh
Butter	tereyağı	tay-**reh**-yah-uh
Cocktail/aperitif	kokteyl, içki	cocktail, **each**-key
Coffee	kahve	**kah**-veh
Dinner	akşam yemegi	**ahk**-shahm yee-may-ee
Fixed-price menu	fiks menü	feex menu
Fork	çatal	**chah**-tahl
I am a vegetarian/I don't eat meat	vejeteryenim/et yemem	vegeterian-**eem**/eht yeh-**mem**
I cannot eat . . .	. . . yiyemem	**yee**-yay-mem
I'd like to order . . .	. . . Ismarlamak isterim	us-mahr-lah-**mahk** ee-stair-eem
I'd like . . .	. . . isterim	ee-stair-**em**
I'm hungry/thirsty	acıktım/susadım	ah-**juck**-tum/soo-sah-**dum**
Is service/the tip included?	servis fiyatı dahil mi?	sehr-vees **fee**-yah-tah dah-heel-**mee**
It's good/bad	güzel/güzel degil	gew-**zell**/gew-**zell day**-eel
It's hot/cold	sıcak/soguk	suh-**jack**/soh-**uk**
Knife	bıçak	buh-**chahk**
Lunch	ögle yemegi	**oi**-leh **yeh**-may-ee
Menu	menü	meh-**noo**
Napkin	peçete	**peh**-cheh-teh

ENGLISH	TURKISH	PRONUNCIATION
Pepper	karabiber	kah-**rah**-bee-behr
Plate	tabak	tah-**bahk**
Please give me . . .	lutfen bana . . .verirmisiniz	**loot**-fan bah-nah vair-**eer**-mee-see-niz
Salt	tuz	tooz
Spoon	kaşık	kah-**shuhk**
Tea	çay	chai
Water	su	soo
Wine	şarap	shah-**rahp**

Travel Smart
Turkey

WORD OF MOUTH

Before your trip, be sure to check out what other travelers are saying in Talk on www.fodors.com.

www.fodors.com/forums

GETTING HERE & AROUND

How you get around Turkey depends on your time and budget. The most common way to travel the country, for both Turks and tourists, is by bus. If you don't mind a long bus ride, the extremely popular night buses that connect the major cities inland and on the coast are a comfortable and cheaper alternative to flying. If you have less time or are traveling very long distances, you may want to fly. Once you've arrived at your destination, you can get around by taxi, minibus, *dolmuş* (shared taxi), or rented car. A car gives you more freedom to explore on your own but is more costly and can be more stressful.

■ BY AIR

Flying time to Istanbul is 10 hours from New York, 13 hours from Chicago, and 15 hours from Los Angeles. Flights from Toronto to Istanbul take 11½ hours. London to Istanbul is a 4-hour flight. In Turkey, security checks for travelers to the U.S. mean that you need to be at the airport three hours before takeoff regardless of which airline you are flying, though lines for check-in at Turkish Airlines are generally long regardless. Procedures at Sabiha Gokçen Airport are more straightforward, although at press time all scheduled (i.e., noncharter) international flights currently used Atatürk Airport.

■ AIRPORTS

Turkey's major international airport is **Atatürk Airport,** about 18 km (12 mi) from Istanbul. Adana, Adıyaman, Ankara, Antalya, Batman, Çanakkale, Dalaman, Denizli, Diyarbakır, Edremit, Elazığ, Erzincan, Erzurum, Eskişehir, Gaziantep, İsparta, İzmir, Kars, Kayseri, Konya, Malatya, Muş, Nevşehir, Samsun, Siirt, Sinop, Sivas, Şanlırfa, Tokat, Trabzon, Uşak, and Van all have smaller domestic airports.

Sabiha Gökçen Airport serves the Asian part of Istanbul, although it is currently mainly used by international charters and some domestic flights. Almost all leading international airlines still arrive at Atatürk Airport.

Airports Atatürk Airport (☏ *212/465–5555* ⊕ *www.ataturkairport.com).* **Sabiha Gökçen Airport** (☏ *216/585–5000* ⊕ *www.sgairport. com).*

GROUND TRANSPORTATION FROM AIRPORTS

In major destinations such as Adana, Ankara, Antalya, Bodrum, Dalaman, Istanbul, İzmir, Kayseri, Nevşehir, and Trabzon, the Havaş company operates shuttle buses to the airports. These run at regular intervals in the major cities and in the provinces are timed to coincide with incoming and outgoing flights.

The other alternative is to take a taxi. In the provinces, it is sometimes possible to negotiate with a taxi driver for less than the metered fare. Many hotels will arrange for a driver to collect you from the airport and for someone to take you to the airport. In the provinces, it is not unusual for hotels to offer this transportation free of charge, although the driver will still appreciate being tipped a couple TL.

TRANSFERS BETWEEN AIRPORTS

The only city in Turkey with multiple airports is Istanbul, which has two: Atatürk Airport and Sabiha Gökçen Airport. There is no direct shuttle bus between them and a taxi ride between the two is very expensive. If you have a connection between an international flight and a domestic flight, try to ensure that they both use the same airport in Istanbul, usually Atatürk Airport. Domestic flights to Sabiha Gökçen Airport are usually cheaper than flights into Atatürk Airport (although prices to the latter vary considerably according to the time of day), but if you have a connecting international flight from Atatürk

Airport, any saving would be more than offset by the time (and it could easily take two to three hours at a busy time of day) and expense of transferring between airports.

Contacts Havaş (☎ *212/465–5656* ⊕ *www.havas.com.tr).*

▌FLIGHTS

You'll probably find that THY/Turkish Airlines, the national flag carrier of Turkey, offers the most nonstops and is very comfortable, though an international carrier based in your home country is more likely to have better connections to your hometown and serve a greater number of gateway cities. Third-country carriers (foreign carriers based in a country other than your own or Turkey) sometimes offer the lowest fares. Air France, for instance has flights from the U.S. to Istanbul; it's worth checking.

Turkish Airlines operates an extensive domestic network, with 16 flights daily on weekdays between Istanbul and Ankara alone. In summer many flights to coastal resorts are added. **Note that at provincial airports it is often necessary for checked luggage to be identified by boarding passengers before it is put on the plane,** and all unidentified luggage is left behind and checked for bombs or firearms. If any luggage has not been identified, an announcement will be made on the plane before departure, based on the name on the label on the luggage, but attempts at the pronunciation of foreign names can often mean that they are unrecognizable. Airline staff will always announce whether you need to identify your luggage at some point before boarding but the messages may be difficult to hear or understand. If in doubt, ask a member of the airline staff as they are checking your boarding pass and watch what the other passengers are doing.

Major Airlines From the U.S.: **Air Canada** (☎ *800/776–3000* ⊕ *www.aircanadacom).* **Air France** (☎ *800/237–2747* ⊕ *www.airfrance. com).* **American Airlines** (☎ *800/433–7300*

⊕ *www.aa.com).* **British Airways** (☎ *800/ 247–9297* ⊕ *www.britishairways.com).* **Continental Airlines** (☎ *800/231–0856 for international reservations* ⊕ *www.continental. com).* **Delta Airlines** (☎ *800/241–4141 for international reservations* ⊕ *www. delta.com).* **Lufthansa** (☎ *800/645–3880* ⊕ *www.lufthansa.com).* **Northwest Airlines** (☎ *800/447–4747 for international destinations* ⊕ *www.nwa.com).* **Olympic Airlines** (☎ *800/223–1226* ⊕ *www.olympicairlines. com).* **Onur Air** (*Onur* ☎ *212/444–6687 in Istanbul for information and reservations for flights between Europe and Turkey* ⊕ *www.onurair.com).* **Swissair** (☎ *800/221– 4750* ⊕ *www.swiss.com).* **THY/Turkish Airlines** (☎ *212/339–9650, 800/874–8875, 212/444–0849 in Istanbul for reservations* ⊕ *www.turkishairlines.com).* **United Airlines** (☎ *800/538–2929 for international reservations* ⊕ *www.united.com).* **USAirways** (☎ *800/622–1015 for international reservations* ⊕ *www.usairways.com).*

Within Turkey Atlas Jet (☎ *212/444–3387 for information and reservations* ⊕ *www. atlasjet.com/en/default.asp).* **Pegasus Airlines** (☎ *212/444–0737 for call center and reservations* ⊕ *www.flypgs.com).*

▌BY BOAT AND FERRY

In some regions, particularly the Black Sea and greater Istanbul area, ferries are the most efficient means of getting around. On the Aegean and Mediterranean coasts, boats are used mostly for leisurely sightseeing and yachting.

The state-owned Turkish Maritime Lines used to operate car ferries and cruise ships from Istanbul to various points in the country. It was broken up and privatized, though, in the early 2000s and the new owners of its ships have only recently begun to operate them again. In 2006, the Cruise and Ferry Lines Deniz company, which is owned by the Turkish Chamber of Shipping, began offering cruise ship transportation between Istanbul and İzmir, with ships leaving every other day. The journey takes 15 hours, departing one city at 5:30 PM and arriving in the other city at 8:30 AM. It is expected that this line will operate from May through September. The one-way trip costs from $40 to $45 for a Pullman seat, $110 for a standard cabin, and $460 for a luxury four-berth cabin, plus $120 for a car. Tickets are available from Cruise and Ferry Lines Deniz or from travel agents that are members of the Association of Turkish Travel Agencies. Although Deniz no longer runs along the Black Sea Coast, there are frequent runs between Turkey and the Aegean Islands in the summer. IDO, a subsidiary of Istanbul Metropolitan Municipality, provides regular ferryboat services within Istanbul, as well as to Yalova and Bandirma (both in the Marmara region), and to Bursa.

For information about sailing trips known as "Blue Cruises" (⇨ *Tours*).

FARES AND SCHEDULES
All major credit cards and Turkish Lira (TL) are acceptable forms of payment. In an emergency, a kindly ticket-seller may take dollars or euros but you shouldn't rely on it.

Information **Cruise and Ferry Lines Deniz** (☎ 212/444–3369 *for reservations and information* ⊕ *www.denizline.com*).

IDO (Istanbul sea bus and fast Ferry) (☎ 212/444–4436 *for timetables and information* ⊕ *www.ido.com.tr*).

▮ BY BUS

In Turkey, buses are much faster than most trains and provide inexpensive service almost around the clock between all cities and towns, and they're usually quite comfortable. There is generally no smoking allowed (sometimes with the exception of the driver), and most offer complimentaries like tea, soda, and biscuits. All are run by private companies, each of which has its own fixed fares for different routes and, usually more significantly, their own standards of comfort. Most bus companies, such as Varan, Ulusoy, Kamil, Koç,

and Pamukkale, which go between major cities and resort areas, can be counted on for comfortable air-conditioned service with snacks. There is often quite a close correlation between price and comfort, with the more expensive companies such as Varan also providing the most amenities. Most of the larger companies have their own terminals. In larger cities they run feeder shuttles from a number of different locations around the city to the main terminal. Contact details for the larger companies is listed below.

Note that *express* buses running between major cities are significantly faster and more comfortable than local buses; look for one of these if you're traveling long distances.

By law, all buses are nonsmoking.

FARES AND SCHEDULES
Buses traveling the Istanbul–Ankara route depart either city every 15 minutes, 24 hours a day, and cost $20 to $40. The Istanbul–İzmir fare ranges from $22 to $35. With larger companies, fares usually include *su* (bottled water) and/or *çay* (tea), as well as a snack on longer journeys. For smaller companies you may want to bring your own water in case beverages are not available. All buses will make periodic rest stops along the way.

PAYING
The larger companies have their own terminals and sales offices as well as Web sites and call centers offering e-tickets. For smaller companies, tickets are sold at stands in a town's *otogar* (central bus terminal); the usual procedure is to go to the bus station and **shop around for the best bus.** All seats are reserved. ▮TIP➔ When buying your ticket, tell the ticket agent that you would like to sit on the shady side of the bus; even on air-conditioned buses the sun can feel oppressive on a long trip.

The larger companies will accept cash or major credit cards. Smaller companies will only accept cash. Traveler's checks are not normally accepted.

Information **Kamil Koç** (☎ *444–0562 no code required* ⊕ *www.kamilkoc.com.tr*). **Metro Turizm** (☎ *212/658–1717 or 212/658–3232* ⊕ *www.metroturizm.com.tr*) **Pamukkale** (☎ *444–3535 no code required* ⊕ *www. pamukkaleturizm.com.tr*). **Truva Tourism** (☎ *224/261–5068 in Bursa, 212/444–0017 in Istanbul, 286/212–2764 in Çanakkale, 286/814–1110 in Eceabat*). **Ulusoy** (☎ *444– 3535 no code required* ⊕ *www.ulusoy.com.tr*). **Varan** (☎ *444–8999 for call center, no code required* ⊕ *www.varan.com.tr*).

▌ BY CAR

In Turkey a driver's license issued in most foreign countries is acceptable.

Turkey has one of the world's highest car accident rates. That said, having a car allows you the freedom that traveling by bus, train, or plane does not. The country has 40,000 km (25,000 mi) of paved and generally well-maintained highways, but off the intercity highways, surfaces are often poor and potholes frequent. Most major highways are two lanes, and cars pass each other with some frequency. ⚠ Sometimes roads will have a third lane meant for passing; although the lane is usually labeled with which direction of traffic is meant to use it, drivers don't always follow this rule, so be extremely careful when passing. In general, always expect the unexpected. Don't, for example, always assume that one-way streets are one-way in practice or that because you wouldn't do something, such as trying to pass in a dangerous situation, the other driver wouldn't either.

In major cities it's possible to hire a driver together with a car, and in some places, like the more remote areas of eastern and southeastern Anatolia, the driver will be included in the package with the car and will either be the owner of the car or an employee of the agency renting it. If it's the latter and you're particularly happy with his performance, you may wish to give him a tip in addition to the price you pay to the agency. Around TL 20 for a day's driving is reasonable.

⚠ Driving in Istanbul and other major cities is best avoided. Urban streets and highways are frequently jammed with vehicles operated by high-speed lunatics and drivers who constantly honk their horns. In Istanbul, especially, just because a street is marked one-way, you never know when someone is going to barrel down one of them in the wrong direction. In cities, it's best to leave your car in a garage and use public transportation or take taxis. Parking is another problem in the cities and larger towns.

▌TIP➜ You should also avoid driving on highways after dusk because drivers often drive without turning their lights on. Vehicles may be stopped on the roads in complete darkness. In the countryside watch out for drivers passing on a curve or at the top of a hill, and beware of carts—very difficult to see at night—and motorcycles weaving in and out of traffic while carrying entire families.

Highways are numbered or specified by direction (e.g., the route to Antalya). Trans-European highways have a European number as well as a Turkish number (E6 is the European number for Turkish Route D100, for example). ⚠ Note, however, that route numbers may be inconsistent from map to map.

Archeological and historic sites are indicated by yellow signposts.

EMERGENCY SERVICES

A road rescue service is available on some highways; before you embark on a journey, ask your car rental agency or hotel how to contact it in case of an emergency. Most major car manufacturers in Turkey (for example, Renault, Fiat, and Opel/General Motors) also have roaming 24-hour services. Most rental agencies will ask you to contact them before attempting to have any repairs done and will usually bring you a replacement car. They will almost certainly give you a cell number which you can call 24/7 in the case of any difficulty. If they don't, ask for one.

Turkish mechanics in the villages can usually manage to get you going again, at least until you reach a city, where you can have the car fully repaired. Most Turkish gas stations have at least one staff member with some knowledge of car mechanics who can diagnose problems and provide "first aid" or advice, such as directions to the nearest mechanic. If a gas station attendant fixes a minor problem, it is customary to give him a small tip of about $5 to $10 depending on the time and effort expended.

In urban areas entire streets are given over to car-repair shops run by teams of experts—one specializes in radiators, another in electrical fittings, and another in steering columns. It's not expensive to have repairs done, but it's customary to give a small tip to the person who does the repairs. Make sure to take all car documents with you when you leave the shop.

GASOLINE

Shell, British Petroleum, Total, Elf, and two Turkish oil companies, Petrol Ofisi and Türkpetrol, operate stations in Turkey. Many of those on the main highways stay open around the clock, others from 6 AM to 10 PM. Almost all Turkish gas stations provide full service and have unleaded gas. Many attendants will clean your windows while the car's tank is being filled. Tipping is not obligatory though not uncommon if the attendant has been particularly attentive—TL 1 is usually enough. In the summer in western Turkey some gas stations have sprinklers that you can drive through slowly to get rid of dust. There may be long distances between gas stations in rural areas so, if you're heading off the beaten track, don't allow the tank to run too low. Most gas stations in towns and major highways take credit cards, although you'll need cash in rural areas. Many gas stations also have small shops, or just a cooler, where you can buy chilled drinks.

RENTING A CAR

Car rental rates in Istanbul begin at about $58 a day and $250 a week for an economy car with unlimited mileage. Gas costs about TL 3.4 per liter. The majority of rental cars are stick shift, though it's possible to get an automatic with advance arrangements. Car seats for children are not compulsory and are often difficult to find, although offices of the multinational firms in larger cities may be able to provide them. Check when you make your reservation. A wide variety of mostly European car makes are available, ranging from the locally manufactured Tofaş (a subsidiary of Fiat) to Renault and Mercedes.

In many places, such as Cappadocia and the Turquoise Coast, you may want to rent a car so you can go exploring on your own instead of having to be part of a guided tour. When traveling long distances, however, you may find it easier to take public transportation (either a bus or plane)—unless you plan on sightseeing en route—and renting a car at your destination.

Leave yourself enough time to return your rental when you have a plane to catch. How long it takes depends on the airport and the location of the rental office. In provincial airports the rental offices are inside the terminal building and the procedure can be quite fast. In larger cities allow 30 minutes or more. Of course, it also depends on whether or not others are returning cars at the same time.

It's best to check the Web sites of the major multinationals to see if they have offices at your destination, since no agency has complete national coverage in Turkey. In the provinces there are also local agencies, some of which have offices at the local airport. Only the contacts for the major companies are listed below. Some of local car rental agencies are listed in the relevant chapters of this book.

Hotels often either rent out cars themselves or have an informal relationship with a local agency—the latter also usually means that the local agency is anxious to keep the hotel happy by providing a good service; it's not unusual for the owner of the agency to be a relative of someone at the hotel. The rates for deals done through the hotel, which will include insurance, etc., are often much cheaper than the multinationals.

In Turkey, the rental agency will usually provide you with instructions about what to do if you have a breakdown or accident. They will also give you a contact number at which you can call them—usually the personal cell number of someone working at the agency. In most cases, they'll tell you that if you have a problem you should call them, tell them where you are, and they will come and find you. It's worth remembering that in the case of an accident, Turkish insurance companies usually refuse to pay until they have seen a police report of the accident. This is particularly important if another vehicle is involved, as the driver will need a police report in order to be able to file a claim with his or her insurance company or with your rental agency. In such a situation, call the contact number for your rental agency and allow them to handle all the procedures when they arrive.

Major Agencies Alamo (☎800/522–9696 ⊕www.alamo.com). **Avis** (☎800/331–1084 ⊕www.avis.com). **Budget** (☎800/472–3325 ⊕www.budget.com). **Hertz** (☎800/654–3001 ⊕www.hertz.com). **National Car Rental** (☎800/227–7368 ⊕www.nationalcar.com).

ROAD CONDITIONS

Throughout Turkey signposts are few, lighting is scarce, rural roads are sometimes rough, and city traffic is chaotic. The top speed limit of 120 KPH (about 75 MPH) is rarely enforced on major highways, although it is not unusual for the Turkish police to set speed traps on other roads. It is advisable to drive carefully and relatively slowly, and to be prepared for sudden changes in both road conditions and the behavior of other drivers.

RULES OF THE ROAD

In general, Turkish driving conforms to Mediterranean customs, with driving on the right and passing on the left, but be prepared for drivers to do anything. Seat belts are required for front-seat passengers and a good idea for those in back seats. Using a cell phone while driving is prohibited—but this law is seldom obeyed. Turning right on a red light is not permitted but one is allowed through a flashing red light provided nothing is coming the other way. Speeding and other traffic violations are subject to on-the-spot fines. It is both illegal and unadvisable to drive under the influence of alcohol. Most rental companies do not allow you to cross international borders in a rented car.

ROAD MAPS

Road maps can often be found in tourist areas, although the rental company will usually provide you with one. Remember, though, signposting is erratic and maps are often not very accurate.

▌ BY FOOT

Especially in the big cities, be aware that streetlights and signs are often only suggestions. Accept it as a rule that drivers are quite aggressive and will not slow down for pedestrians, even in designated cross points. A good rule of thumb is to watch the local crowd and cross the street with them; remember, there's safety in numbers.

On the other hand, central parts of major cities are usually extremely well connected by public transportation, with clearly visible signs in English and Turkish, which make exploring by foot easy and affordable.

▌ BY TAXI AND DOLMUS

Taxis in Turkey are yellow and very easy to spot. They cost about $1 for 1 km (about ½ mi); 50% higher between midnight and 6 AM. During the day, make sure the meter says GÜNDÜZ (day rate); otherwise, you'll be overcharged. Be aware that taxi drivers in tourist areas sometimes doctor their meters to charge more. Don't ride in a taxi in which the meter doesn't work. If you have doubts, ask at your hotel about how much a ride should cost. In Istanbul many of the larger hotels will find a cab for you, usually drivers or companies they know and trust. Note that saying the word *direkt* after giving your destination helps prevent you from getting an unplanned grand tour of town. As a tip, it's customary to round up to the next lira. There are no extra charges for luggage. In Istanbul, if you cross one of the Bosphorus bridges, you will be expected to add the TL 3 cost of the toll to the bill regardless of which direction you are going (vehicles only pay going from west to east—the theory is that even if he does not have to pay to take you across, the taxi driver will have to pay to go back). In Ankara, taxi drivers are allowed to charge "night rates" (i.e., 50% higher) for trips to the airport because it's so isolated and often difficult for them to find a fare to bring back. Particularly in Istanbul and Ankara, taxi drivers often have a very limited knowledge of the city and will have to ask bystanders or other taxi drivers for directions.

It's easiest to hail a taxi on the street, or have your hotel call one for you, but the Web site for Online Taksi lists taxi companies all over Turkey.

Dolmuşes (shared taxis) are bright yellow minibuses that run along various routes. You can often hail a dolmuş on the street or at a bus stop and, as with taxis, dolmuş stands are marked by signs (D). The destination is shown on either a roof sign or a card in the front window. Dolmuş stands can be found at regular intervals, and the vehicles wait for customers to climb in. Note that the dolmuş line you stand in is one of few observed lines in Turkey, and others will let you know if you have butted in line. The savings over a private taxi are significant, and the dolmuş are often just as fast. Although dolmuşes only run along specific routes, they generally

WORD OF MOUTH

Did the resort look as good in real life as it did in the photos? Did you sleep like a baby, or were the walls paper thin? Did you get your money's worth? Rate hotels and write your own reviews in Travel Ratings or start a discussion about your favorite places in Travel Talk on www.fodors.com. Your comments might even appear in our books. Yes, you, too, can be a correspondent!

go to tourist destinations, as well as nightlife hot spots. Another advantage to the dolmuş is that they run through the wee hours of the morning. If you're not familiar with your destination, tell the driver when you get in he will usually try to drop you as close as possible to where you're going and will frequently explain how to continue to your destination; although this explanation will almost certainly be in Turkish, they will generally use exaggerated hand gestures to point you in the right direction.

It is not customary to tip dolmuş drivers, and they will probably be confused if you try to hand them something extra on your way out.

Taxi Information Online Taksi (⊕ *www/ onlinetaksi.com*).

▍ BY TRAIN

The train routes in Turkey tend to meander, meaning that train travel is usually much slower than bus travel—sometimes as much as twice as long. Most travelers opt for buses, which can be quite plush and comfortable, or airplanes. Essentially, the term *express train* is a misnomer in Turkey: although they exist, serving several long-distance routes, they tend to be slow. The train does, however, offer a pleasant venue to meet other international travelers. The overnight sleeper from Istanbul to Ankara (*Ankara Ekspres*) is the most comfortable and convenient of the trains, with private compartments, attentive service, and a candlelit dining car. There is also daytime service between Ankara and Istanbul. Trains also run between Istanbul and Edirne and between Ankara and İzmir. Turkish State Railways (*Türkiye Cumhuriyeti Devlet Demiryolları*) is the company that serves the country. The train trip from Istanbul to Ankara takes about 6½ hours nonstop, or roughly 10 hours overnight with stops along the way. Seat61.com is a helpful Web site about train travel in Europe and Turkey.

Dining cars on trains between the major cities usually have waiter service and offer decent and inexpensive food. Overnight expresses have sleeping cars and bunk beds. The Istanbul–Ankara run costs about $30 for a two-bedroom and about $40 for a single-bed room, including tips; though advance reservations are a must, cancellations are frequent, so you can often get a space at the last minute.

Fares are lower for trains than for buses, and round-trip train fares cost less than two one-way tickets. Student discounts are 10% (30% from December through April). Ticket windows in railroad stations are marked GIŞELERI. Some post offices and authorized travel agencies also sell train tickets. It's advisable to book in advance, in person, for seats on the best trains and for sleeping quarters.

There are no different classes on Turkish trains in the sense of first or second class but long-distance trains offer a number of options, such as pullman (first-class type, reclining seats), compartments with six or eight seats, reclining or not; couchette (shared four-bunk compartments), and sleeper (private one- or two-bed compartments). In Turkish, pullman is *pulman,* compartment is *kompartımanlı,* couchette is *kuşetli,* and sleeper is *yataklı.*

Most train stations do not accept credit cards, foreign money, or traveler's checks, so be prepared to pay in Turkish lira.

The TCDD Web site is very helpful; it gives all the information you'll need about how to buy tickets at the station or through the different travel agencies (*listed below*). In addition, it has pictures and maps, so you know what you're getting into beforehand. It's ideal for the European traveler, as the lines connect to cities all over Europe.

Inter-Rail passes can be used in Turkey; Eurail passes cannot.

THE ORIENT EXPRESS

If you have the time—and money—consider the still-glamorous Venice Simplon-Orient Express. The route runs twice a year from Paris to Istanbul via Budapest and/or Bucharest.

Contacts seat61.com (⊕ *www.seat61.com*). **Turkish State Railways** (Türkiye Cumhuriyeti Devlet Demiryolları) (☎ *312/311–0602* ⊕ *www.tcdd.gov.tr*). **Venice Simplon-Orient Express** (☎ *020/7928–6000, 800/524–2420 in the U.S.* ⊕ *www.orient-express.com*).

Authorized Train Travel Agencies Tur-ISTA Tourism Travel Agency (☎ *212/527–7085 or 212/513–7119 erdemir@tur-ista.com*). **Viking Turizm** (☎ *212/334–2600*).

Train Station Information Ankara Tren İstasyonu (☎ *312/311–0620*). **Haydarpaşa Station** (Istanbul, Asian side) (☎ *216/336–0475*). **Sirkeci Station** (Istanbul) (☎ *212/527–0051*).

ESSENTIALS

▪ ACCOMMODATIONS

Accommodations range from the international luxury chain hotels in Istanbul, Ankara, and İzmir to charming inns occupying historic Ottoman mansions and kervansaries, to comfortable but basic family-run *pansiyons* (guesthouses) in the countryside. It's advisable to plan ahead if you'll be traveling in the peak season (April–October), when resort hotels are often booked by tour companies.

Note that reservations should be confirmed more than once, particularly at hotels in popular destinations. Phone reservations are not always honored, so it's a good idea to e-mail the hotel and get written confirmation of your reservation, as well as to confirm again before you arrive. If you want air-conditioning, make sure to ask about it when you reserve.

Asking to see the room in advance is an accepted practice. It will probably be much more basic than the well-decorated reception area. Check for noise, especially if the room faces a street or is anywhere near a nightclub or disco, and look for such amenities as window screens and mosquito coils—small, flat disks that, when lighted, emit an unscented vapor that keeps biting insects away.

Assume that hotels operate on the European Plan (EP, no meals) unless we specify that they use the Breakfast Plan (BP, with full breakfast), Continental Plan (CP, Continental breakfast), Full American Plan (FAP, all meals), Modified American Plan (MAP, breakfast and dinner), or are all-inclusive (AI, all meals and most activities).

The lodgings we list are the cream of the crop in each price category. We always list the facilities that are available—but we don't specify whether they cost extra: when pricing accommodations, always ask what's included and what's not.

Prices in the lodging charts found in each chapter are for two people in a standard double room in high season, including VAT and service charge. Private bathrooms, air-conditioning, room phones, and a TV are assumed unless otherwise noted. ▪TIP➜ In the low season you should be able to negotiate discounts of at least 20% off the rack rate; it never hurts to try.

HOSTELS

There are around 30 youth hostels in Istanbul and student residences in Ankara, Bolu, Bursa, Çanakkale, İzmir, and Istanbul also serve as youth hostels. There has been an increase in the number of inexpensive hotels offering dormitory-style accommodation in recent years; they're aimed very much at young backpackers. A word of warning, though, for families on a tight budget thinking about staying in a hostel: a cheap hotel is generally a better bet unless you want your children (and yourself) woken up at 3 AM by drunken students stumbling into the bunk above them.

Information Hostelling International (☎ *301/495–1240* ⊕ *www.hihostels.com*).

HOTELS

If you're trying to book a stay right before or after Turkey's high season (April–October), you might save considerably by changing your dates by a week or two. Note, though, that many properties charge peak-season rates for your entire stay even if your travel dates straddle peak and nonpeak seasons. High-end chains catering to businesspeople are often busy only on weekdays and drop rates dramatically on weekends to fill up rooms. Ask when rates go down.

Watch out for hidden costs, including resort fees, energy surcharges, and "convenience" fees for such things as unlimited local phone service you won't use and a free newspaper—possibly written in a language you can't read. Always verify whether local hotel taxes are or are not included in the rates you are quoted, so that you'll know the real price of your stay. In some places, taxes can add 20% or more to your bill. If you're traveling overseas look for price guarantees, which protect you against a falling dollar. With your rate locked in, you won't pay more, even if the price goes up in the local currency.

Hotels are officially classified in Turkey as HL (luxury), H1 to H5 (first- to fifth-class); motels, M1 to M2 (first- to second-class); and P (*pansiyons*—guesthouses). These classifications can be misleading, however, as they're based on the number of facilities rather than the quality of the service and decor, and the lack of a restaurant or lounge automatically relegates the establishment to the bottom of the ratings. In practice, a lower-grade hotel may actually be far more charming and comfortable than one with a higher rating.

The standard Turkish hotel room, which you will encounter everywhere throughout the country, is clean, with bare walls, low wood-frame beds (usually a single bed, twin beds, or, less often, a double), and industrial carpeting or kilims on the floor. Less expensive properties will probably have plumbing and furnishings that leave something to be desired. If you want a real double bed (not two singles pushed together), go to a more expensive property, either Turkish or Western style.

These are some Turkish words that will come in handy when you're making reservations: "air-conditioning" is *klima*, "private bath" is *banyo*, "tub" is *banyo küveti*, "shower" is *düş*, "double bed" is *iki kişilik yatak*, and "twin beds" is *iki tane tek kişilik yataklar* ("separate" is *ayrı*; "pushed together" is *beraber*). There is no Turkish word for "queen bed" but they will probably use the English (a direct translation is *kraliçe yatağı*).The same is true for for "king bed" (they will probably use the English, though a direct translation is *kral yatağı*). The advice for noise-sensitive travelers is to ask for a quiet room, *sessiz bir oda*.

PANSIYONS

Outside the cities and resort areas, these small, family-run establishments will be your most common option. They range from charming old homes decorated with antiques to tiny, utilitarian rooms done in basic modern. As a rule, they are inexpensive and scrupulously clean. Private baths are common, though they are rudimentary—stall showers, toilets with sensitive plumbing. A simple breakfast is typically included. A stay in a *pansiyon* is a comfortable money-saver, especially if you plan on spending most of your time out and about.

■ COMMUNICATIONS

INTERNET

More and more hotels are providing some means for guests to get online; ask when you make a reservation. In most cities and tourist destinations, you'll also be able to find a local Internet café. Contact your Internet provider before you go to find out if it has an access number in Turkey. If you have a GSM mobile, you should be able to plug it into your computer and access the Internet while in Turkey. There are some wireless hot spots in major cities, though most require online subscription. A few hotels, restaurants, and cafés offer free Wi-Fi over their own wireless modems; this is usually advertised with a sign in the window.

Most important, remember that the Turkish electricity supply runs on 220 volts. Any equipment set up for U.S. voltage needs a good converter, and you are advised to bring one with you. Many laptops are equipped with built-in converters, but check with your computer dealer before you leave home to make sure you have what you need.

PHONES

The good news is that you can now make a direct-dial telephone call from virtually any point on earth. The bad news?

You can't always do so cheaply. Calling from a hotel is almost always the most expensive option; hotels usually add huge surcharges to all calls, particularly international ones. In some countries, you can phone from call centers or even the post office. Calling cards usually keep costs to a minimum, but only if you purchase them locally. And then there are mobile phones (⇨ *below*), which are sometimes more prevalent—particularly in the developing world—than landlines; as expensive as mobile phone calls can be, they are still usually a much cheaper option than calling from your hotel.

Telephone numbers in Turkey have seven-digit local numbers preceded by a three-digit city code. Intercity lines are reached by dialing 0 before the area code and number. In Istanbul, European and Asian Istanbul have separate area codes: The code for much of European Istanbul is 212 (making the number look like it's in New York City), and the code for Asian Istanbul (numbers beginning with 3 or 4) is 216. Mobile phone codes are often 534, 533, or 532. The country code for Turkey is 90.

CALLING WITHIN TURKEY

Inside Istanbul you don't need to dial the code for other numbers with the same code, but you need to dial the code (0212 or 0216) when calling from the European to the Asian side of the city or vice versa. All local cellular calls are classed as long distance, and you need to dial the city code for every number.

To call long-distance within Turkey, dial 131 if you need operator assistance; otherwise dial 0, then dial the city code and number.

The increase in the use of mobile phones in Turkey means that very few people now use pay phones, but it's still easy to find them. Most are the blue push-button models, although a few older telephones are still in use. Directions in English and other languages are often posted in phone booths, along with other country codes.

Most Turks do not use directory assistance, and even if you are lucky enough to find an English-speaking operator, you are unlikely to be able to find the number you want. Your best chance of success is to tell the staff at your hotel who or what you are trying to find and let them do the rest.

Public phones generally use either phone cards or credit cards. Phone cards come in denominations of 30 (about TL 5), 60 (about TL 10), and 100 (about TL 13) units; buy a 60 or 100 for long-distance calls within Turkey, a 30 for local use. Phone cards can be purchased at post offices and, for a small markup, at most corner stores, newspaper vendors, and street stalls. You will only find public phones that accept credit cards in the major cities. Because they are cheaper and easy to find, it's more practical to use phone cards when making local or long-distance calls. Make sure to ask for a calling card for a public phone, as they also sell calling cards for cellular phones, and you cannot use the two interchangeably.

To make a local call, insert your phone card or credit card, wait until the light at the top of the phone goes off, and then dial the number.

Some kiosks selling newspapers or small stores have phones that you can use to place calls. The cost is usually approximately the same as a standard pay phone. If you want to use one, say "telefon" (Turkish for telephone), and the proprietor will usually either produce a phone or show you where you can find one.

CALLING OUTSIDE TURKEY

The country code is 1 for the United States.

For international operator services, dial 115. Intercity telephone operators seldom speak English, although international operators usually have some basic English. If you need international dialing codes and assistance or phone books, you can also go to the nearest post office or Internet café.

To make an international call from a public phone in Turkey, dial 00, then dial the country code, area or city code, and the number. Internet cafés typically offer international calling service with prices comparable to a phone card but be sure to ask for rates first.

Access Codes AT&T Direct (☎ *00/800–12277 in Turkey followed by the area code and number*). **MCI WorldPhone** (☎ *00/800–11177 in Turkey followed by the area code and number*). **Sprint International Access** (☎ *00/800– 14477 in Turkey followed by the area code and number*).

MOBILE PHONES

If you have a multiband phone (some countries use frequencies other than those used in the United States) and your service provider uses the world-standard GSM network (as do T-Mobile, AT&T, and Verizon), you can probably use your phone abroad. Roaming fees can be steep, though: 99¢ a minute is considered reasonable. And overseas, you normally pay the toll charges for incoming calls. It's almost always cheaper to send a text message than to make a call since text messages have a very low set fee (often less than 5¢).

If you just want to make local calls, consider buying a new SIM card (note that your provider may have to unlock your phone for you to use a different SIM card) and a prepaid service plan in the destination. You'll then have a local number and can make local calls at local rates. If your trip is extensive, you could also simply buy a new cell phone in your destination as the initial cost will be offset over time.

Renting a phone in Turkey is very expensive, and it's not easy to find shops that rent. The best solution is to buy a SIM card and a pay-as-you-go service. There are three mobile phone providers in Turkey. The largest is Turkcell, followed by Vodafone, and Avea. Each has a network of clearly marked stores, where it is possible to buy SIM cards and pay-as-you-go cards. Most sales people speak enough English to conduct business and answer basic questions. All stores post easy-to-understand signs that indicate unit packages and prices. Expect to pay about $10 for 100 units (*kontör*), regardless of the company. An SMS within Turkey is 2 units, and a three-minute conversation will generally set you back 4 units.

▮ CUSTOMS AND DUTIES

Turkish customs officials rarely look through tourists' luggage on arrival. You are allowed to bring in 400 cigarettes, 50 cigars, 200 grams of tobacco, 1½ kilograms of instant coffee, 500 grams of tea, and 2½ liters of alcohol. Items in the duty-free shops in Turkish airports, for international arrivals, are usually less expensive than they are in European airports or in-flight. Pets are allowed into the country provided that they have all the necessary documentation. Full details can be obtained from the Turkish diplomatic representative in your own country.

⚠ The export of antiquities from Turkey is expressly forbidden, and the ban is rigorously enforced. If you buy a carpet or rug which looks old, make sure to obtain certification that it is not antique, usually from a local museum. The seller will usually be able to help you. The ban on antiquities extends to historical artifacts, coins, and even pieces of masonry. There have been several recent cases where tourists, some of them children, have tried to take small pieces of stone home as souvenirs and been arrested at the airport on suspicion of trying to export parts of ancient monuments. A genuine mistake is not considered sufficient excuse. Even where the tourists have been ultimately acquitted, they have still had to spend many months either in detention or, more commonly, out on bail but denied permission to leave the country. Turkish antiquities laws apply to every piece of detritus, so don't pick up anything off the ground at archaeological sites.

Visit the Turkish embassy Web site in Washington, D.C., and the Web site of the U.S. Embassy in Ankara for more information.

U.S. Information U.S. Customs and Border Protection (⊕ *www.cbp.gov*). **Turkish Embassy** (⊕ *www.turkishembassy.org*).

▌EATING OUT

For more information about traditional Turkish food, the availability of alcohol, and dining establishments in Turkey, see the Eating Out in Turkey section of the Understanding Turkey chapter.

For information on food-related health issues see Health below. The restaurants we list are the cream of the crop in each price category. Prices on the restaurant chart (at the front of each chapter) are per main course, or two small dishes, at dinner. A service or "cover" charge (a charge just for sitting at the table, the bread, the water, etc.) of 10% to 15% is usually added to the bill, but you should tip 10% on top of this. If a restaurant's menu has no prices listed, ask before you order—you'll avoid a surprise when the bill comes.

MEALS AND MEALTIMES

Breakfast, usually eaten at your hotel, typically consists of *beyaz peynir* (goat cheese), sliced tomatoes, cucumbers, and olives, with a side order of fresh bread; the menu varies little, whether you stay in a simple *pansiyon* or an upscale hotel. Yogurt with honey and fresh fruit is generally available as well, as are tea and Nescafé.

Breakfast starts early, typically by 7. Lunch is generally served from noon to 3, dinner from 7 to 10. You can find restaurants or cafés open almost any time of the day or night in cities; in villages getting a meal at odd hours can be a problem. Most Turks fast during daylight hours during the Islamic holy month of Ramadan. If you're visiting during Ramadan, be sensitive to locals and avoid eating on public

WORD OF MOUTH

Was the service stellar or not up to snuff? Did the food give you shivers of delight or leave you cold? Did the prices and portions make you happy or sad? Rate restaurants and write your own reviews in Travel Ratings or start a discussion about your favorite places in Travel Talk on www.fodors.com. Your comments might even appear in our books. Yes, you, too, can be a correspondent!

transportation or other places where you might make mouths water. During Ramadan, many restaurants, particularly smaller ones outside the major cities, close during the day and open at dusk.

Unless otherwise noted, the restaurants listed in this guide are open daily for lunch and dinner.

PAYING

Most relatively upscale restaurants, particularly those in western Turkey, take major credit cards. Smaller eateries will often accept only cash.

For guidelines on tipping, see Tipping below.

RESERVATIONS AND DRESS

Regardless of where you are, it's a good idea to make a reservation if you can. In some places, it's expected. We only mention specifically when reservations are essential (there's no other way you'll ever get a table) or when they are not accepted. We mention dress only when men are required to wear a jacket or a jacket and tie.

▌ELECTRICITY AND ELECTRONICS

Consider making a small investment in a universal adapter, which has several types of plugs in one lightweight, compact unit. Most laptops and mobile phone chargers are dual voltage (i.e., they operate equally well on 110 and 220 volts) and so require only an adapter. These days the same is true more of small appliances such as hair dryers. Always check labels and manufacturer instructions to be sure, though. Don't use 110-volt outlets marked FOR SHAVERS ONLY for high-wattage appliances such as hair dryers.

The electrical current in Turkey is 220 volts, 50 cycles alternating current (AC); wall outlets take European-type plugs, with two or three round prongs. Make sure that you have a voltage and a plug converter if you're going to be using U.S. appliances.

VIDEOS AND DVDS

Most Turkish video players use VHS PAL (unlike in U.S. players which use NTSC). Most types of cassettes for camcorders (digital, VHS-C, 8 mm, etc.) are available in Turkey, but prices vary enormously.

For DVDs, Turkey is Region 2 (the same as Europe), while the U.S. is Region 1. As your DVD-player instructions will explain, DVDs for different regions can only be played on multiregion DVD players. Many new computer models are already installed with multiregion DVD players.

Contacts **Steve Kropla's Help for World Travelers** (⊕ www.kropla.com) has information on electrical and telephone plugs around the world. **Walkabout Travel Gear** (⊕ www. walkabouttravelgear.com) has a good discussion about electricity under "adapters."

▮ EMERGENCIES

If your passport is lost or stolen, contact the police and your embassy immediately. If you have an emergency, you're best off asking a Turk to call an emergency number for you because it's unlikely you'll find an English-speaking person at the other end of the telephone, even at the Tourism Police. Bystanders will almost invariably try their utmost to be of assistance and will usually know of nearby hospitals or doctors. The Turkish words for ambulance, doctor, and police—*ambulans, doktor,* and *polis,* respectively—all sound about the same as their English equivalents, as

does *telefon* for telephone. Say whichever is appropriate, and you can feel fairly certain that you'll be understood when you use the words applicable to your emergency. Note that if you call an ambulance don't expect it to arrive immediately since traffic in the larger cities may cause delays.

Embassies **Canadian Consulate (Istanbul)** (⊠ İstiklal Caddesi No. 373, Beyoğlu ☎ 212/251–9838). **U.S. Consulate (Istanbul)** (⊠ İstinye Mahallesi, Kaplıcalar Mevkii No.2, İstinye, Istanbul ☎ 212/335–9000 ⊕ istanbul. usconsulate.gov). **U.S. Embassy (Ankara)** (⊠ 110 Atatürk Bulv., Kavaklıdere, Ankara ☎ 312/455–5555 ⊕ www.turkishembassy.org). General Emergency Contacts **Ambulance** (☎ 112). **Emergency (police, etc.)** (☎ 155). **Tourism Police (Istanbul)** (☎ 212/527–4503).

▮ HEALTH

No serious health risks are associated with travel to Turkey, although you should take precautions against malaria if you're visiting the far southeast. No vaccinations are required for entry. To avoid problems at customs diabetics carrying needles and syringes should have a letter from their physician confirming their need for insulin injections. Travelers are advised to have vaccinations for hepatitis, cholera, and typhoid for trips to the southeast. Rabies can be a problem in Turkey, occasionally even in the large cities. If bitten or scratched by a dog or cat about which you have suspicions, go to the nearest pharmacy and ask for assistance.

Even in areas where there is no malaria, it's a good idea to use something to ward off mosquitoes. All pharmacies and most corner stores and supermarkets stock a variety of oils and/or tablets to burn, as well as sprays and creams which you can apply to exposed skin; it's generally easy to identify these products as the packaging usually includes a picture of a mosquito. If you can't find what you want, try asking using the Turkish word for

LOCAL DO'S & TABOOS

Turks set great store in politeness. No one will expect you to have mastered the intricacies of polite speech in Turkish, but a respectful attitude and tone of voice, combined with a readiness to smile, will often work wonders.

Although Turks are a very tactile people, particularly with friends of the same sex, this physical contact is like a language, full of pitfalls for the unwary. Be very careful about initiating physical contact, as misunderstandings are easy. Overt public physical displays of affection between the sexes are more common in younger generations in big cities, but are still are likely to offend people outside the major cities.

Turks shake hands as a greeting, although this is more common between men than between women. It is quite acceptable, and often very appreciated, if a foreign male initiates a handshake with another male when, for example, leaving a carpet shop. For handshakes between the sexes, unless the Turkish woman is obviously highly Westernized, a foreign male should leave it up to her to initiate any physical contact. It is all right for foreign women to initiate a handshake, but be prepared for a very religious Turkish male to pointedly avoid shaking a woman's hand.

A combination of simultaneously shaking hands and kissing on both cheeks is the usual form of greeting between male friends, while women friends more often kiss without shaking hands, but it's usually a cheek-to-cheek "air-kiss," and it's unusual for the lips to make contact with the skin. On occasion, a Turk will actually kiss the cheek, but such a kiss is considered very forward when given to members of the opposite sex, particularly those of little acquaintance, and if you are a recipient, you should draw your conclusions accordingly. Done appropriately, an air-kiss between two people of the opposite sex will be appreciated. Use your own discretion, as a kiss from a foreign woman may be misinterpreted.

Most Turks consider hospitality both a duty and a source of pride. If you visit Turks in their homes, it is expected that you will take off your shoes on entering. You will not be expected to bring gifts, particularly on a first visit, although a small token, such as fresh nuts or dessert, is always appreciated. Chances are the lady of the house will have gone to considerable trouble to prepare food if she has had prior knowledge of your arrival so you, in turn, should go with an empty stomach and at least try the dishes that are offered to you. In appreciation, it is traditional to say *ellerinize sağlık* ("ell-lair-in-izeh sah-luk"), which translates literally as, "May your hands be healthy." No offense will be taken if you don't manage to say it, but it will be much appreciated if you do.

BUSINESS ETIQUETTE

Business etiquette is a little different from everyday etiquette. In the major cities, many managers of larger companies will have worked or trained abroad, particularly in the United States, and will be familiar with the ways in which Western companies do business. Punctuality is appreciated, but chronic traffic congestion in Istanbul and Ankara means most businesspeople are used to people arriving a little late for appointments. A telephone call to warn of a late arrival is appreciated.

Business negotiations are usually conducted in a relaxed atmosphere, and the business of the day may be padded with friendly conversation and the ubiquitous cups of tea. Provided you eventually get down to business, it is usually a good idea not to force the pace, as the preliminaries are a way for the parties to assess each other and establish mutual trust.

mosquito: *sinek*. It often seems as though mosquitoes favor foreigners, particularly the fair-skinned, so a Turk's assurances that mosquitoes in a particular place are "not bad" can be both sincere and misleading.

Given the high temperatures in summer, dehydration can be a problem in southern and eastern Turkey. Remember to keep sipping water throughout the day rather than waiting until you are very thirsty.

For minor problems, pharmacists can be helpful, and medical services are widely available. Pharmacists at any *eczane,* or pharmacy, are well versed in common ailments and can prescribe antibiotics and other medications for common travelers' illnesses. Doctors and dentists abound in major cities and can be found in all but the smallest towns; many are women. There are also *hastanes* (hospitals) and *kliniks* (clinics). Road signs marked with an H point the way to the nearest hospital. Even if they cannot converse fluently in English, most qualified doctors will have a working knowledge of the English and French for medical conditions.

If you need a dentist, Turkish dentists, or *dişçi,* are unusually good for the developing world. Each works independently, so it's best to ask a local person you trust for the best one around.

FOOD AND DRINK

Tap water is heavily chlorinated and supposedly safe to drink in cities and resorts. It's okay to wash fruits and vegetables in tap water, but it's best to play it safe and only drink *şişe suyu* (bottled still water), *maden suyu* (bottled sparkling mineral water), or *maden sodası* (carbonated mineral water), which are better tasting and inexpensive. △ **Do not drink tap water in rural areas or in eastern Turkey.** Turkish food is generally safe, though you should still be careful and avoid some types of street food, such as chickpeas and rice (*nohut*) and mussels (*midye*), which can host a number of unfriendly bacteria.

OVER-THE-COUNTER REMEDIES

Many over-the-counter remedies available in Western countries can also be found in Turkish pharmacies, which are usually well stocked. Even a Turkish pharmacist who doesn't speak English will often be able to recognize a specific remedy—particularly if you write the name down—and be able to find an appropriate alternative if that medication is not available.

■ HOURS OF OPERATION

BANKS AND OFFICES

Banks in Turkey are normally open weekdays from 8:30 until noon or 12:30, and then from 1:30 until 5, but select branches of some Turkish banks now remain open during the middle of the day, particularly in larger cities. Many banks throughout Turkey, even those in small towns, provide 24-hour service from ATM machines with service in English.

GAS STATIONS

Most gas stations are open from early morning until late evening, commonly from 6 AM to 10 PM, although there are no fixed rules and there can be considerable variation. In the larger cities and along major highways it is usually possible to find gas stations open 24 hours. Look for the sign 24 SAAT AÇIK.

MUSEUMS AND SIGHTS

Museums are generally open Tuesday through Sunday from 9:30 AM until 5 or 5:30 PM and closed on Monday—this is not a rule, though, so do check the times listed in the individual listings. Palaces are open the same hours but are generally closed Thursday. Many museums stop selling tickets 30 minutes before the actual closing time. Sometimes this is explicitly stated in the official times, but very often, particularly away from the major sites, it is unofficial and just a way for museum staffers to make sure they get away on time. To be on the safe side, try to ensure that you arrive at least 45 minutes before closing time.

PHARMACIES

Most pharmacies (*eczane* in Turkish) are open the same hours as shops, and as with shops, there are variations according to the whim of the pharmacist. Typically, they are open 9:30 AM until 7 or 7:30 PM, Monday through Saturday. In larger cities, one pharmacy in each neighborhood is open 24/7 and is called the *nöbetçi eczane*. Even when a pharmacy is closed, there will be a sign in the window or door with details of the location of the nearest *nöbetçi eczane* and your hotel will always be able to help you find the closest *nöbetçi eczane*. If you are not close to your hotel, passersby will usually be able to help with directions.

SHOPS

Shops and bazaars are usually open Monday through Saturday from 9:30 to 7 and vary on open hours on Sunday. Smaller shops often close for lunch between 1 and 2, although all large stores and even most small shops in the major cities remain open throughout the day. In tourist areas, shops may stay open until 9 PM or even 10 PM and all day Sunday.

▌ HOLIDAYS

Schools and many offices often close for a full or half day on major Turkish holidays, which are as follows: January 1 (New Year's Day); April 23 (National Independence Day); May 19 (Atatürk's Commemoration Day, celebrating his birthday and the day he landed in Samsun, starting the independence movement); August 30 (Zafer Bayramı, or Victory Day, commemorating Turkish victories over Greek forces in 1922, during Turkey's War of Independence); October 29 (Cumhuriyet Bayramı, or Republic Day, celebrating Atatürk's proclamation of the Turkish republic in 1923—many businesses and government offices also close at midday, usually either 12:30 or 1, on the day before Republic Day); November 10 (the anniversary of Atatürk's death is not a full-day public holiday but is commemorated by a nationwide moment of silence at 9:05 AM). Many provincial towns also hold celebrations to mark the anniversary of the date that the Greeks were driven out of the area during the Turkish War of Liberation.

Turks also celebrate the two main Muslim religious holidays each year: the three-day Şeker Bayramı, marking the end of Ramadan and the four-day Kurban Bayramı, which honors Abraham's willingness to sacrifice his son to God. Because the Muslim year is based on the lunar calendar, the dates of the two holidays change every year, both moving earlier by 11 to 12 days each year. The precise timing may vary slightly according to the sighting of the moon. Many businesses and government offices close at midday, usually either 12:30 or 1, on the day before the religious bayrams. In 2008, Şeker Bayramı is due to begin at midday on September 30 and last until the evening of October 2; in 2009 it will begin on September 20 and end on the 22nd; in 2010 it will begin on September 9 and end on the 11th. Kurban Bayramı will begin at midday on December 8, 2008, and continue through the evening of December 11; in 2009 it will begin on November 27 and end on the 30th; in 2010 it will go from November 18 to the 19th. A word of note: If a religious holiday takes up three or four days of a working week, the government will often declare the rest of the week an official holiday as well. However, such decisions are usually made less than a month before the holiday actually begins.

▌ LANGUAGE

In 1928, Atatürk launched sweeping language reforms that, over a period of six weeks, replaced Arabic script with the Latin-based alphabet and eliminated many Arabic and Persian words from the Turkish language.

English, German, and sometimes French are widely spoken in hotels, restaurants, and shops in cities and resorts. In villages and remote areas you may have a hard time finding anyone who speaks anything but Turkish or Kurdish, though rudimentary communications are still usually possible. According to Turkey's education system, everyone learns English in primary school and may continue into high school and university but education varies, so try to learn a few basic Turkish words; it will be appreciated. See the vocabulary list at the back of this book (⇨ Vocab).

▌ MAIL AND SHIPPING

The Turkish for "post office" is *postane*. Post offices are painted bright yellow and have PTT (Post, Telegraph, and Telephone) signs on the front. The central post offices in larger cities are open Monday through Saturday from 8 AM to 9 PM, and Sunday from 9 to 7. Smaller ones are open Monday through Saturday between 8:30 and 5. Turks use franking machines in post offices rather than postage stamps. The latter are still available at post offices but are mainly sold to philatelists and nostalgists. Although you shouldn't expect to find the size of envelopes or boxes you want at the post office, a variety is generally sold in a kiosk not far from the post office. You will occasionally see mailboxes away from post offices, these are often not in use. If you want to maximize the chances of your mail actually arriving at its intended destination, use only the boxes at the post offices themselves.

Mail sent from Turkey can take from three to 10 days, or more, to reach its destination. Be warned that the mail service is erratic and that you may arrive home before your postcards are received by friends and family.

Postage rates are frequently adjusted to keep pace with inflation. It generally costs about 50¢ to send a postcard from Turkey to the U.S. Shipping a 10-pound rug home via surface mail will cost about $25 and take from two to six months.

If you want to receive mail in Turkey and you're uncertain where you'll be staying, have mail sent to Poste Restante, Merkez Posthanesi (Central Post Office), in the town of your choice.

OVERNIGHT AND EXPRESS SERVICES

There is no international overnight courier service to and from Turkey. The main couriers (DHL, Federal Express, UPS, etc.) have offices in Istanbul, but even they take three days from Turkey to the United States and United Kingdom.

SHIPPING PARCELS

In general it is not only much quicker but also much safer to carry your purchases with you—even if you have to pay for excess baggage—rather than entrusting them to the postal service. Most parcels from Turkey do eventually arrive at their destination, but be aware there is a risk they may become damaged or lost in transit. Other alternatives, such as courier services or shipping companies, are quicker and more reliable but often very expensive. Some stores and sellers in bazaars will offer to arrange to ship goods for you but where possible, it's still always better to carry your purchases home with you. If you do decide to have someone ship something for you, make sure it is a large and reputable store.

▌ MONEY

Turkey used to be the least expensive of the Mediterranean countries, but prices have risen in recent years. At press time, Istanbul was roughly equivalent to other cities in the Mediterranean in terms of cost, but in the countryside, and particularly away from the main tourist areas, prices are much lower—room and board are not likely to be much more than $50 per person per day.

Coffee can range from about $1.50 to $4.50 a cup, depending on whether it's the less-expensive Turkish coffee or American-style coffee, and whether it's served in a luxury hotel, a café, or an outlet of a multinational chain such as Starbucks or Gloria Jean's. Coffee lovers beware: most coffee listed on menus in a restaurant, unless specified otherwise, is likely to be instant coffee (Nescafé). Tea will cost you about 50¢–$1 a glass, rising to $1–$3 for a cup (the latter is larger). Local beer will be about $4–$6, depending on the type of establishment; soft drinks, $1–$3; lamb shish kebab, $5–$8; and a taxi, $1 for 1 km, about ½ mi (50% higher between midnight and 6 AM).

Prices throughout this guide are given for adults. Substantially reduced fees are almost always available for children, students, and senior citizens. *For information on taxes, see Taxes.*

ATMS AND BANKS

Your own bank might charge a fee for using ATMs abroad; the foreign bank you use may also charge a fee. Extracting funds as you need them is a safer option than carrying around a large amount of cash.

ATMs can be found even in some of the smallest Turkish towns. Many accept international credit cards or bank cards (a strip of logos is usually displayed above the ATM). Almost all ATMs have a language key that enables you to read the instructions in English. To use your card in Turkey, your PIN must be four digits long.

In Turkey, as elsewhere, using an ATM is one of the easiest ways to get money. Generally the exchange rate is based on the Turkish Central Bank or the exchange rate according to your bank.

CREDIT CARDS

Throughout this guide, the following abbreviations are used: **AE**, American Express; **DC**, Diners Club; **MC**, Master-Card; and **V**, Visa.

It's a good idea to inform your credit card company before you travel, especially if you're going abroad and don't travel internationally very often. Otherwise, the credit card company might put a hold on your card owing to unusual activity—not a good thing halfway through your trip. Record all your credit card numbers—as well as the phone numbers to call if your cards are lost or stolen—in a safe place so you're prepared should something go wrong. Both MasterCard and Visa have general numbers you can call (collect if you're abroad) if your card is lost, but you're better off calling the number of your issuing bank since MasterCard and Visa usually just transfer you to your bank; your bank's number is usually printed on your card.

Before you charge something, ask the merchant whether or not he or she plans to do a dynamic currency conversion (DCC). In such a transaction the credit card *processor* (shop, restaurant, or hotel, not Visa or MasterCard) converts the currency and charges you in dollars. In most cases you'll pay the merchant a 3% fee for this service in addition to any credit-card-company and issuing-bank foreign-transaction surcharges.

DCC programs are becoming increasingly widespread. Merchants who participate in them are supposed to ask whether you want to be charged in dollars or the local currency, but they don't always do so. And even if they do offer you a choice, they may well avoid mentioning the additional surcharges. The good news is that you *do* have a choice. And if this practice really gets your goat, you can avoid it entirely thanks to American Express; with its cards, DCC simply isn't an option.

Credit cards are accepted throughout Turkey, especially in larger cities or towns, but many budget-oriented restaurants or hotels in rural areas do not accept them.

Be warned that Turkey has one of the highest rates of credit-card fraud in Europe. Do not let your credit card out of your sight. Since March 2006, Turkey has started using "chip and PIN" as well as "swipe and sign." The chip-and-PIN system is a more secure method than swipe-and-sign and was introduced in parts of Europe several years ago, but is only just now being used in the United States. It refers to the chip in the credit card, which contains identifying information. The card is inserted in the POS terminal, which reads the chip and sends the information down the line. The user is then asked to enter his/her PIN and this information is also sent down the wire; if everything matches, the transaction is completed.

Reporting Lost Cards American Express (☎ 800/992-3404 in the U.S., 336/393-1111 collect from abroad ⊕ www.americanexpress. com). **Diners Club** (☎ 800/234-6377 in the U.S., 303/799-1504 collect from abroad ⊕ www.dinersclub.com). **MasterCard** (☎ 800/ 622-7747 in the U.S., 636/722-7111 collect from abroad ⊕ www.mastercard.com). **Visa** (☎ 800/847-2911 in the U.S., 410/581-9994 collect from abroad ⊕ www.visa.com).

CURRENCY AND EXCHANGE

At the beginning of 2005, Turkey introduced a new currency, the New Turkish Lira (YTL) to replace the Turkish Lira (TL), which at the time was trading at an outrageous TL 1,350,000 to one U.S. dollar. The old Turkish Lira notes and coins were gradually phased out through 2005 although some still occasionally surface. In 2009, the government is changing the name of the currency back to just Turkish Lira. The Turkish Lira is divided into 100 Kuruş, and is issued in denominations of 5, 10, 20, 50, and 100 TL notes, and 5, 10, 25, 50 kuruş, and 1 TL coins.

Although fees charged for ATM transactions may be higher abroad than at home, Cirrus and Plus exchange rates are excellent because they are based on wholesale rates offered only by major banks. You won't do as well at exchange booths in airports or rail and bus stations, in hotels, in restaurants, or in stores, although you may find their hours more convenient.

Hotels and banks will change money, as will larger post offices, but ■TIP➜ in Turkey the rates are usually better at the foreign exchange booths (look for signs saying FOREIGN EXCHANGE or DÖVIZ). Most are now connected online to the currency markets and there will be little difference between them.

Exchange bureaus are found only in big cities, usually in the center, so if you are heading to small towns make sure you change your money before leaving.

Bureaus in tourist areas often offer slightly less attractive rates—rarely more than 2%–3% difference—than bureaus in other places. Almost all foreign exchange bureaus are open Monday–Saturday. Hours vary but are typically 9:30 AM–6:30 PM. In tourist areas it is sometimes possible to find a bureau that is open on a Sunday, but it will usually compensate for the inconvenience by offering a rate 2%–3% worse than those bureaus that close on Sundays.

İş Bankası (İş Bank) is Turkey's largest bank, with many branches in the cities and at least one in each town, usually in the center of town.

■ PACKING AND WHAT TO WEAR

Although Turkey is an informal country, it is often said that Istanbul isn't Turkey—it's Europe. Expect to see the full spectrum in Istanbul when it comes to style and coverage. You may walk down the street next to a girl in a miniskirt, followed by a woman wearing a head scarf or completely covered from head to toe. Istanbul is a cosmopolitan city, so if you plan on a night out on the town, come prepared to dress accordingly. For men, nice jeans coupled with a clean button-down shirt and decent shoes will usually get you in the door; a jacket and tie are only appropriate for top restaurants in Istanbul, Ankara, and İzmir. Women should feel comfortable wearing fashionable styles but, as in any place, consider what kind of attention you want to attract.

Outside major cities, women would do best to avoid overly revealing outfits and short skirts. The general rule is: the smaller the town, the more casual and, at the same time, conservative the dress.

On the beaches along the Mediterranean, topless sunbathing is increasingly common. Although you may see the occasional Turk going topless, it's far more common to see the European tourists that throng the coasts during peak season getting rid of their tan lines. Shorts are acceptable for hiking through ruins, but not for touring mosques. The importance of a sturdy, comfortable pair of shoes cannot be over-emphasized. Whether you are in Istanbul, where "everything is uphill," or you're hiking the ruins at Ephesus, you'll be glad you sacrificed style for comfort.

Light cottons are best for summer, particularly along the coast. If you're planning excursions into the interior or north of the country, you'll need sweaters in spring or fall and all-out cold-weather gear in winter. An umbrella is advisable on the Black Sea Coast, but as anywhere else in Turkey, as soon as rain begins to fall, people will appear almost magically on the streets to sell cheap umbrellas; so if you don't want to bring one with you, it's almost always possible to find one.

Sunscreen and sunglasses will come in handy. It's a good idea to carry some toilet paper and hand sanitizer with you at all times, especially outside the bigger cities and resort areas. You'll need mosquito repellent for eating outside from March through October, a flashlight for exploring in Cappadocia, and soap if you're staying in more moderately priced hotels.

■ PASSPORTS AND VISAS

All U.S. citizens, even infants, need a valid passport and a visa to enter Turkey for stays of up to 90 days. Visas can be issued at the Turkish embassy or consulate before you go, or at the point of entry; the cost is $20 and must be paid in American dollars. If you do not have a visa and need to buy one at the point of entry, look for a sign saying VISAS usually just before passport control.

Even though visas are multiple entry and usually valid for 90 days, they cannot be issued for periods longer than the validity of the passport you present. If your passport has less than a month to run, you may not be given a visa at all. Check the validity of your passport before applying for the visa. Turkish officials may impose stiff fines for an overstay on your visa.

■TIP→ If your trip includes a stopover to the Greek side of Cyprus before you come to Turkey, make sure you don't get your passport stamped in Cyprus. Instead, ask for a slip of paper indicating your legal entry to Cyprus. Otherwise, you may encounter difficulties getting through passport control in Turkey. n.b. This is not an issue if you're coming from Greece proper, however.

■ RESTROOMS

Public facilities are common in the tourist areas of major cities and resorts and at archeological sites and other attractions; in most, a custodian will ask you to pay a fee (ranging from 50 kuruş to TL 2–3). In virtually all public facilities, including those in all but the fanciest restaurants, toilets are Turkish style (squatters) and toilet paper is often not provided (to cleanse themselves, Turks use a pitcher of water set next to the toilet). Sometimes it's possible to purchase toilet paper from the custodian, but you are well advised to carry a supply with you as part of your travel gear. Alas, standards of restroom cleanliness tend to be a bit low compared to those in Western Europe and America.

If you're away from tourist areas, look for a mosque, as many have restrooms as part of the complex of washing facilities for Muslims to perform their ablutions before performing their prayers. Standards of cleanliness at mosque restrooms are usually higher than at public facilities. Most, but not all, restaurants and cafés have restrooms, but the standard is often extremely variable. In general, five-star hotels have the best facilities, and the staff rarely raise any objection if restrooms are used by foreigners not staying at the hotel. Many gas stations have restrooms.

The Bathroom Diaries is a Web site that's flush with unsanitized info on restrooms the world over—each one located, reviewed, and rated.

Find a Loo The Bathroom Diaries (⊕ www. thebathroomdiaries.com).

▌ SAFETY

Distribute your cash, credit cards, IDs, and other valuables between a deep front pocket, an inside jacket or vest pocket, and a hidden money pouch. Don't reach for the money pouch once you're in public.

Violent crime against strangers in Turkey has increased in recent years, but when compared with Western Europe or North America, it's still relatively rare. You should, nevertheless, watch your valuables, as professional pickpockets do operate in the major cities and tourist areas. Bag snatching has increased in recent years, and women should be careful both when walking and when sitting at open-air cafés and restaurants. Bear in mind that organized gangs often use children to snatch bags.

In June 2004, the separatist Kurdish nationalists, the Kurdistan Workers Party (PKK), resumed its armed campaign after a five-year pause. It is currently conducting a two-front campaign: a rural insurgency in southeastern Turkey and a bombing campaign in the west of the country. One of the PKK's key targets is the tourism industry. There were bombings—and foreign fatalities—in 2005 and 2006, but given that only two foreigners were killed in 2005 and three in 2006, out of the approximately 20 million tourists who visit the country each year, the danger is statistically very low. The situation is different in southeastern Turkey. While cities and major highways are relatively safe, you should be extremely cautious about visiting more out-of-the-way villages in the region and using unpaved roads or traveling after nightfall. Despite the country's proximity to Iraq, the ongoing insurgency there has had no noticeable impact on security inside Turkey. The U.S. occupation of Iraq remains deeply unpopular in Turkey, and Turks will often have little hesitation in letting you know how they feel. However, they will invariably distinguish between the actions of the U.S. government and individual Americans. There have been no reports of any visiting Americans experiencing personal hostility or animosity. For an up-to-date report on the situation, check with the State Department Web site or the hot line in Washington, D.C.

GOVERNMENT ADVISORIES

As different countries have different worldviews, look at travel advisories from a range of governments to get more of a sense of what's going on out there. And be sure to parse the language carefully. For example, a warning to "avoid all travel" carries more weight than one urging you to "avoid nonessential travel," and both are much stronger than a plea to "exercise caution." A U.S. government travel warning is more permanent (though not necessarily more serious) than a so-called public announcement, which carries an expiration date.

The U.S. Department of State's Web site has more than just travel warnings and advisories. The consular information sheets issued for every country have general safety tips, entry requirements (though be sure to verify these with the country's embassy), and other useful details.

Consider registering online with the State Department (⊕ https://travelregistration. state.gov/ibrs), so the government will know to look for you should a crisis occur in the country you're visiting.

If you travel frequently, also look into the Registered Traveler program of the Transportation Security Administration (TSA; ⊕ www.tsa.gov). The program, which is still being tested in five U.S. airports, is designed to cut down on gridlock at security checkpoints by allowing prescreened travelers to pass quickly through kiosks that scan an iris and/or a fingerprint. How sci-fi is that?

General Information and Warnings
Australian Department of Foreign Affairs & Trade (⊕ *www.smartraveller.gov.au*). **Consular Affairs Bureau of Canada** (⊕ *www.voyage. gc.ca*). **U.K. Foreign & Commonwealth Office** (⊕ *www.fco.gov.uk/travel*). **U.S. Department of State** (⊕ *www.travel.state.gov*).

LOCAL SCAMS
As Turkey has one of the highest credit card fraud rates in Europe, you should keep your credit cards within sight at all times to prevent them from being copied. In many restaurants waiters will swipe your card at the table. If a waiter takes the card away, you should either ensure that it remains within eyesight or ask to accompany the waiter to the POS terminal (you can always manufacture an excuse such as telling the waiter that your bank sometimes asks for a PIN).

There have been a few cases of tourists traveling alone being given drugged drinks and then being robbed. The doctored drinks are usually soft drinks such as sodas. Turks are naturally anxious to ply guests with food and drink, and in the vast majority of cases, there should be no cause for alarm. However, if, for example, you are traveling alone and someone is particularly insistent on you having a cold soft drink and comes back with one already poured into a glass, treat it with extreme caution. If you have any doubts, do not consume it. Someone who is being genuinely hospitable will probably be confused and maybe a little hurt; both are better than your being robbed. If the drink is drugged, the person giving it to you will probably be suspiciously insistent that you drink it.

In crowded areas be aware of a common scam in which two men stage a fight or similar distraction while an accomplice picks the tourist's pocket.

Before taking a private taxi, it can be useful to ask the information desk at your hotel what route (i.e., past what landmarks) the driver will likely drive, how many minutes the ride usually is, and what the average cost is: this way you will avoid an unwanted, and often lengthy "free tour" of the city. Note that Turkish hospitality is such that if you need directions, a shopkeeper or assistant will often insist on accompanying you part or all the way to your destination. Don't be overly skeptical of this friendliness, and in most cases they don't expect a tip. If plied for money, TL 1 should suffice.

WOMEN IN TURKEY
Turkey is a generally safe destination for women traveling alone, though in heavily touristed areas such as Istanbul's Sultanahmet, Antalya, and Marmaris, women unaccompanied by men are likely to be approached and sometimes followed. In rural towns, where visits from foreigners are less frequent, men are more respectful toward women traveling on their own. In the far east of the country, though, you should be particularly careful; women traveling alone have been known to be harassed in this region.

Some Turkish men are genuinely curious about women from other lands and really do want only to "practice their English." Still, be forewarned that the willingness to converse can easily be misconstrued as something more meaningful. If you are uncomfortable, seek assistance from a Turkish woman or move toward where there are other women present; when it comes to harassment by males, there really is safety in female solidarity. Young blonde women will find they attract considerably more attention than brunettes. This is mainly because many Turkish men tend to associate anyone who fulfills their stereotypical image of a Russian with a sex worker. If a man is acting inappropriately toward you, it is acceptable to be forward and tell them to go away. The phrase *çok ayıp* ("shame on you") will come in handy, as it will also attract attention from passersby. Another phrase, *defol* ("get lost") is more severe and should dispel any persistent men you may encounter. Women who are pregnant or have small children with them are generally treated with such respect as to be virtually immune from harassment.

As for clothing, Turkey is not the place for clothing that is short, tight, or bare, away from the main tourist areas and major cities. Longer skirts, and shirts and blouses with sleeves, are likely to prevent attracting unwanted attention. To gain entrance to mosques, you will be expected to cover your head with a scarf, although you shouldn't feel pressure to don one on the street.

As in any other country in the world, the best course of action is to simply to walk on if approached, and avoid potentially troublesome situations, such as walking in deserted neighborhoods at night. Note that in Turkey, many hotels, restaurants, and other eating spots identify themselves as being for an *aile* (family) clientele, and many restaurants have special sections for women and children. How comfortable you are with being alone will affect whether you like these areas, which are away from the action—and you may prefer to take your chances in the main room (though some establishments will resist seating you there).

When traveling alone by bus, you should request a seat next to another woman. If a man sees that you are traveling alone, he will probably offer up his own seat so that you may sit next to another woman.

▌ TAXES

The value-added tax, in Turkey called Katma Değer Vergisi, or KDV, is 18% on most goods and services. Hotels typically combine it with a service charge of 10% to 15%, and restaurants usually add a 15% service charge.

Value-added tax is nearly always included in quoted prices. Certain shops are authorized to refund the tax (you must ask). Within a month of leaving Turkey, mail the stamped invoice back to the shop, and a check will be mailed to you—in theory if not always in practice.

When making a purchase, ask for a VAT refund form and find out whether the merchant gives refunds—not all stores do, nor are they required to. Have the form stamped like any customs form by customs officials when you leave the country or, if you're visiting several European Union countries, when you leave the EU. After you're through passport control, take the form to a refund-service counter for an on-the-spot refund (which is usually the quickest and easiest option), or mail it to the address on the form (or the envelope with it) after you arrive home. You receive the total refund stated on the form, but the processing time can be long, especially if you request a credit card adjustment.

Global Refund is a Europe-wide service with 225,000 affiliated stores and more than 700 refund counters at major airports and border crossings. Its refund form, called a Tax Free Check, is the most common across the European continent. The service issues refunds in the form of cash, check, or credit card adjustment.

VAT Refunds Global Refund (☎ *800/566–9828 in the U.S., 800/566–9828 in Canada* ⊕ *www.globalrefund.com*).

▌ TIME

Turkey is 2 hours ahead of London, 7 hours ahead of New York, 10 hours ahead of Los Angeles and Vancouver, 11 hours behind Auckland, and 9 hours behind Sydney and Melbourne. Turkey uses daylight saving the same as North America and Europe.

▮ TIPPING

In restaurants, a 10%–15% charge is added to the bill in all but inexpensive fast-food spots. However, since this money does not necessarily find its way to your waiter, leave an additional 10% on the table. In top establishments, waiters expect tips of 10%–15% in addition to the service charge. Although it's acceptable to include the tip on your bill in restaurants that accept credit cards, it's much appreciated if you leave it in cash.

In Turkey, taxi drivers are becoming used to foreigners giving them something; round off the fare to the nearest 50 kuruş. *Dolmuş* drivers do not get tipped. Hotel porters expect about TL 2. At Turkish baths, staff members who attend to you expect to share a tip of 30%–35% of the bill: don't worry about missing them—they'll be lined up expectantly on your departure.

Tour guides often expect a tip. Offer as much or (as little) as you feel the person deserves, usually TL 5 to TL 7 per day if you were happy with the guide. If you've been with the guide for a number of days, tip more. Crews on chartered boats also expect tips.

Restroom attendants will not expect a tip in addition to the charge for using their facilities.

▮ TOURS

Guided tours are a good option when you don't want to do it all yourself. You travel along with a group (sometimes large, sometimes small), stay in pre-booked hotels, eat with your fellow travelers (sometimes included in the price of your tour, sometimes not), and follow a schedule. But not all guided tours are an *If This Is Tuesday, It Must Be Belgium* experience. A knowledgeable guide can take you places that you might never discover on your own, and you may be pushed to see more than you would have otherwise. Tours aren't for everyone, but they can

be just the thing for trips to places where making travel arrangements is difficult or time-consuming (particularly when you don't speak the language). Whenever you book a guided tour, find out what's included and what isn't. A "land-only" tour includes all your travel (by bus, in most cases) in the destination, but not necessarily your flights to or even within it. Also, in most cases, prices in tour brochures don't include fees and taxes. And remember that you'll be expected to tip your guide (in cash) at the end of the tour.

The advantages of taking a package to Turkey are that they will be cheaper and less trouble than arranging everything yourself. There are, of course, pros and cons to package tours, one disadvantage being that you'll have less flexibility in being able to choose your hotel.

New York–based **Heritage Tours** is highly recommended as a higher-end, full-service travel company. Heritage can design a trip start to finish, including great hotels, private drivers, and tour guides.

Recommended Generalists Heritage Tours (☎ *800/378-4555 [U.S. and Canada]*, *212/206-8400* ⊕ *www.heritagetoursonline. com*). **Pacha Tours** (☎ *800/722-4288 U.S. and Canada* ⊕ *www.pachatours.com*). **Cappadoccia Tours** (☎ *384/341-7485 in Turkey* ⊕ *www.cappadociatours.com*). **Credo Tours** (☎ *212/254-8175 in Turkey* ⊕ *www.credo. com.tr*).

Turkey Life Tours (☎ *212/511-7556 in Turkey* ⊕ *www.turkeylifetours.org*).

SPECIAL-INTEREST TOUR COMPANIES

Biblical Tours Turkey celebrates Turkey's historic richness as a cultivating ground for some of the world's most prominent religions. Different itineraries will take you to historical churches and pilgrimage sites that are awe inspiring, regardless of your religious affiliation. Bird Paradise organizes a number of tours that vary in length and region, all geared toward learning about Turkey's indigenous bird species. Botanical Tours organizes tours for nature-lovers; tours typically start in one major city and end in another, stopping to enjoy Turkey's remarkably diverse scenery and flora along the way. Breakaway Adventures can help you organize trekking tours of Mount Ararat, guided walking tours, and more. Culinary Expeditions in Turkey arranges tours for professional food critics, chefs, and self-proclaimed gastronomists, in regions famed for their culinary traditions. Istanbul Life runs a variety of tours, including a historical tour of Istanbul, Izmir, Ephesus, Aphrodisias, and Pamukkale; a "Green and Blue" tour, which combines the highlights of the interior of the country (the "green") with the coastal hot spots (the "blue"); single city tours; yacht tours; cooking classes, and more. Kirkit Voyage has tours featuring everything from hiking to biking, kayaking to canoeing, rafting, horseback riding, diving. Peter Sommer Travels is a UK-based company that provides academic, yet friendly, guided archaeological tours of Turkey on *gullet* cruises. Runner Tourism and Travel celebrates Slow Food, as opposed to fast food, and lets the traveler experience cuisine from the very beginning: from the farmers and producers to the markets, and finally to your plate. Tours are designed for groups no larger than 12 people. Turkey Central creates "theme" tours of Turkey, including art, handicrafts, and cuisine.

Contacts **Biblical Tours Turkey** (256/ 618–3268 www.biblicaltoursturkey.com). **Bird Paradise** (256/618–3268 www. birdwatchingtoursturkey.com). **Botanical Tours** (542/413–1293 www.wildflowertours. com). **Breakaway Adventures** (800/567– 6286 U.S. www.breakaway-adventures.com). **Culinary Expeditions in Turkey** (415/ 437–5700 U.S. www.turkishfoodandtravel. com). **Istanbul Life** (212/511–7556 www.istanbullife.org). **Kirkit Voyage** (212/518–2282 www.kirkit.com). **Peter Sommer Travels** (44(0)1600–888–220 www.petersommer.com). **Runner Tourism and Travel** (242/237–9842 www.

runnertourism.com). **Turkey Central** (240/ 645–0729 U.S. www.turkeycentral.com/ tours).

■ VISITOR INFORMATION

There are tourist information offices in most of the main cities in Turkey; check the listings in the individual chapters. These offices can be helpful if you arrive in a destination without a hotel reservation, but you're better off trying to book something in advance.

Contacts **Turkish Culture and Tourism Office** (www.tourismturkey.com). **Turkish Tourist Office** (www.turizm.gov.tr).

ONLINE RESOURCES

There are hundreds of Web sites about Turkey; these are some of the standouts. For everything you'd want to know about Turkey before your trip, from Ataturk history to religious festivals, to sample authentic music and more, check out *www.kultur.gov.tr*. For pictures of what you're about to see live and in-person, try *www.balsoy.com/Turkiye/inpictures*. Beat by beat news on the city life in Istanbul, Ankara, and elsewhere around the country, as well as details about what's going culturally, can be found at *www. mymerhaba.com*.

INDEX

Photo Credits: 1, *DoreenD, Fodors.com member.* 2, *pvd, Fodors.com member.* 5, *Sailorr/Shutterstock.* **Chapter 1: Experience Turkey:** 8-9, *DoreenD, Fodors.com member.* 10 (top), *Fatih Kocyildir/Shutterstock.* 10 (bottom), *Svetlana Kuznetsova/iStockphoto.* 11 (left), *Amer Kapetanovic/iStockphoto.* 11 (right), *Turkey Ministry of Culture & Tourism.* 12, *vacationwhipple, Fodors.com member.* 13 (left), *Siobhan O'Hare.* 13 (right), *LouisaN, Fodors.com member.* 16 (left), *Turkey Ministry of Culture & Tourism.* 16 (top center), *Siobhan O'Hare.* 16 (top right), *rm/Shutterstock.* 16 (bottom right), *Maksym Gorpenyuk/Shutterstock.* 17 (top left), *Fronda, Fodors.com member.* 17 (bottom left), *maza, Fodors.com member.* 17 (top center), *wikipedia.org.* 17 (right), *bartoleq/Shutterstock.* 18, *Bartlomiej K. Kwieciszewski/Shutterstock.* 19 (left), *TravelChic13, Fodors.com member.* 19 (right), *nddavidson, Fodors.com member.* 20, *Miroslava/Shutterstock.* 21, *Micke77023, Fodors.com member.* 22, *rayner, Fodors.com member.* 23 (left), *Zeynep Mufti/iStockphoto.* 23 (right), *Gail2000, Fodors.com member.* 24, *TravelChic13, Fodors.com member.* 25 (left), *Sufi/Shutterstock.* 25 (right), *curiousgal, Fodors.com member.* 26, *dgunbug, Fodors.com member.* 27 (left), *rward, Fodors.com member.* 27 (right), *Micke77023, Fodors.com member.* 30, *Eray Haciosmanoglu/Shutterstock.* 32, *ariena missche/iStockphoto.* **Chapter 2: Istanbul:** 33, *Andoni Canela/age fotostock.* 34 (top and bottom), *Turkey Ministry of Culture & Tourism.* 35 (top), *Mariam_Hosseini, Fodors.com member.* 35 (bottom), *Turkey Ministry of Culture & Tourism.* 36, *lmcflorida, Fodors.com member.* 39, *traveller2007, Fodors.com member.* 40, *Mark Henley/age fotostock.* 41 (top), *sila/Flickr.* 41 (bottom), *Pinguino Kolb/Flickr.* 42, *nexus7/Shutterstock.* 52, *Yadid Levy/Alamy.* 54, *Michele Falzone/age fotostock.* 56 (top and bottom), *wikipedia.org.* 57 (top), *Mediamix photo/Shutterstock.* 57 (center), *dundanim/Shutterstock.* 57 (bottom), *Erik Lam/iStockphoto.* 58 (top), *lmcflorida, Fodors.com member.* 58 (2nd from top), *David Pedre/iStockphoto.* 58 (3rd from top), *murat Şen/iStockphoto.* 58 (bottom), *Gryffindor/wikipedia.org.* 59 (top), *Art Kowalsky/Alamy.* 59 (2nd from top), *Earl Eliason/iStockphoto.* 59 (third from top), *Robert Harding Picture Library Ltd/Alamy.* 59 (bottom), *Images&Stories/Alamy.* 60 (top), *Alex Segre/Alamy.* 60 (center), *Dennis Cox/Alamy.* 60 (bottom), *Sibel A. Roberts/iStockphoto.* 61 (left), *Images&Stories/Alamy.* 61 (top right), *Danilo Donadoni/age fotostock.* 61 (bottom right), *Images&Stories/Alamy.* 66, *queenmab225, Fodors.com member.* 71, *SuperStock/age fotostock.* 78-79, *Michele Fanzone/Joan Arnold Travel/Photolibrary.* 80 (top), *Makin_Bacon, Fodors.com member.* 80 (bottom), *Sailorr/Shutterstock.* 81 (top), *Briget, Fodors.com member.* 81 (bottom), *sarabeth, Fodors.com member.* 82 (top and center), *Turkey Ministry of Culture & Tourism.* 82 (bottom), *Connors Bros./Shutterstock.* 83, *Michele Falzone/age fotostock.* 84 (top and center), *Turkey Ministry of Culture & Tourism.* 84 (bottom), *Faraways/Shutterstock.* 85, *ilker canikligil/Shutterstock.* 86 (top), *Jaime Ardiles-Arce/Four Seasons Hotels & Resorts.* 86 (center), *Deniz Ünlüsü/Shutterstock.* 86 (bottom), *360 Restaurant & Bar, Istanbul.* 87, *salexg, Fodors.com member.* 91, *Crispin Rodwell/Alamy.* 99, *360 Restaurant & Bar, Istanbul.* 104, *Alaskan Dude/Flickr.* 115 (top left), *Sumahan.* 115 (top right), *Jaime Ardiles-Arce/Four Seasons Hotels & Resorts.* 115 (bottom left), *Hotel Empress Zoë.* 115 (bottom right), *Umit Okan.* 126, *sarabeth/Fodors.com member.* 130 (top), *Dennis Cox/age fotostock.* 130 (bottom), *Jason Keith Heydorn/Shutterstock.* 131, *TimTheSaxMan, Fodors.com member.* 133, *Vladimir Melnik/Shutterstock.* 134 (top left), *jonbwe, Fodors.com member.* 134 (bottom left), *Orhan/Shutterstock.* 134 (top right), *ukrphoto/Shutterstock.* 134 (bottom right), *Alvaro Leiva/age fotostock.* 135 (top left), *Johnny Lye/Shutterstock.* 135 (top right), *rj lerich/Shutterstock.* 135 (bottom right), *suzdale, Fodors.com member.* 136 (top), *David Sutherland/Alamy.* 136 (bottom all), *Steve Estvanik/Shutterstock.* 137, *Gavin Hellier/Alamy.* 138, *José Enrique Molina/age fotostock.* 139 (top), *julzie49, Fodors.com member.* 139 (bottom), *hilarieH, Fodors.com member.* 142, *DavidHonlPhoto.com.* 147, *wikipedia.org.* **Chapter 3: The Sea of Marmara & the North Aegean:** 151, *Peter Horree/Alamy.* 152, *infocusphotos.com/Alamy.* 153, *Brian Harris/Alamy.* 154, *Çokeker/Shutterstock.* 155, *Vladimir Wrangel/Shutterstock.* 157, *MaxFX/Shutterstock.* 160, *Rebecca Erol/Alamy.* 167, *Bruno Morandi/age fotostock.* 175, *Carlos Chavez/iStockphoto.* 183, *Sadık Güleç/iStockphoto.* 185, *Sylvain Grandadam/age fotostock.* 186 (top left), *Images&Stories/Alamy.* 186 (bottom left), *Klaus-Peter Simon/wikipedia.org.* 186 (right), *Andreas Praefcke/wikipedia.org.* 187 (top left), *Turkey Ministry of Culture & Tourism.* 187 (bottom left), *Noumenon/wikipedia.org.* 187 (top center), *INTERFOTO Pressebildagentur/Alamy.* 187 (top right), *Robert Harding Picture Library Ltd/Alamy.* 187 (bottom right), *joearena99, Fodors.com member.* 188 (left), *INTERFOTO Pressebildagentur/Alamy.* 188 (top right), *PixAchi/Shutterstock.* 188 (bottom right), *eerkun, Fodors.com member.* 189 (top left), *wikipedia.org.* 189 (bottom left), *Hazlan Abdul Hakim/iStockphoto.* 189 (top right), *Peter M. Wilson/Alamy.* 189 (bottom right and 190 top left), *wikipedia.org.* 190 (bottom left), *jonbwe, Fodors.com member.* 190 (right and 191 left), *wikipedia.org.* 191 (right), *Steve Outram/Photolibrary.* 205, *Alaskan Dude/Flickr.* **Chapter 4: The Central & Southern Aegean Coast:** 207, *Turkey Ministry of Culture & Tourism.* 208, *FAN travelstock/Alamy.* 209 (top), *twelfth/ Fodors.com member.* 209 (center), *hilarieH, Fodors.com member.* 209 (bottom), *Siob-*

han O'Hare. 213, Erhan Dayi/Shutterstock. 214, DavidHonlPhoto.com. 220, eerkun, Fodors.com member. 225, DavidHonlPhoto.com. 232, Jose Fuste Raga/age fotostock. 234, IML Image Group Ltd/ Alamy. 235, FAN/age fotostock. 236 (left), Kitkatcrazy/wikipedia.org. 236 (center), Turkey Ministry of Culture & Tourism. 236 (right), Nikater/wikipedia.org. 238, JTB Photo Communications, Inc./Alamy. 239, Turkey Ministry of Culture & Tourism. 240 (top), Marie-Lan Nguyen/wikipedia.org. 240 (bottom), wikipedia.org. 241 (top left), Connors Bros./Shutterstock. 241 (top right), Michael Harder/ Alamy. 241 (bottom), Dennis Cox/Alamy. 245, sarabeth, Fodors.com member. 250-51, Turkey Ministry of Culture & Tourism. 261, Tulay Over/iStockphoto. **Chapter 5: The Turquoise Riviera:** 269, Demetrio Carrasco/age fotostock. 270 (top), rward, Fodors.com member. 270 (bottom), vacationwhipple, Fodors.com member. 271 (top), FAN travelstock/Alamy. 271 (bottom), Steve Outram/Alamy. 271, Turkey Ministry of Culture & Tourism. 276, John Picken/Flickr. 277 (top), yusuf anil akduygu/iStockphoto. 277 (bottom), TurkeyShoot/Alamy. 278, Andrey Gatash/Shutterstock. 291, Images&Stories/ Alamy. 295 (top), Simon Reddy/Alamy. 295 (bottom), Dominic Whiting/Alamy. 296 (left), Daskalogiannis/IML/age fotostock. 296 (right), Kevin O'Hara/age fotostock. 297 (left), Bon Appetit/Alamy. 297 (right), Deniz Ünlüsü/Shutterstock. 298 (top), Bikem Ekberzade/Alamy. 298 (center), Cenap Refik Ongan/Alamy. 298 (bottom), Rebecca Erol/Alamy. 301, Andrey Gatash/Shutterstock. 311 and 318-19, Turkey Ministry of Culture & Tourism. 321, K. Jakubowska/Shutterstock. 325, Simon Podgorsek/ iStockphoto. 341, ismail hayri ordu/iStockphoto. 352, Turkey Ministry of Culture & Tourism. **Chapter 6: Central Anatolia:** 355, Turkey Ministry of Culture & Tourism. 356, turnip, Fodors.com member. 357 (left), Turkey Ministry of Culture & Tourism. 357 (right), eenusa, Fodors.com member. 361, Siobhan O'Hare. 364, rward, Fodors.com member. 370, julzie49, Fodors.com member. 371, Jon Arnold/ Jon Arnold Travel/Photolibrary. 372, Walter Bibikow/age fotostock. 373 (top), Karsten Dörre/wikipedia.org. 373 (bottom), Travelscape Images/Alamy. 374, yversace, Fodors.com member. 375, Blaine Harrington III/Alamy. 376 (top and bottom), Tolo Balaguer/Photolibrary. 377 (top), Turkey Ministry of Culture & Tourism. 377 (bottom left), Marco Simoni/Robert Harding Travel/Photolibrary. 377 (bottom right), Renato Valterza/Tips Italia/Photolibrary. 378, Turkey Ministry of Culture & Tourism. 379, dgunbug, Fodors.com member. 383, R. H. Productions/Robert Harding Travel/Photolibrary. 386, P. Tomlins/Alamy. 388, txupham, Fodors.com member. 394-95, Bruno Morandi/age fotostock. 396 (bottom), wikipedia.org. 397, Bruno Morandi/age fotostock. 415, Ken Gillham/Robert Harding Travel/ Photolibrary. 417, Tulay Over/iStockphoto. **Chapter 7: Excursions to the Far East & Black Sea Coast:** 419 and 420, nddavidson, Fodors.com member. 421 (top), Images&Stories/Alamy. 421 (bottom), queenmab225, Fodors.com member. 424, Turkey Ministry of Culture & Tourism. 429, BrendaE, Fodors.com member. 436, Library of Congress Prints and Photographs Division. 438, BrendaE, Fodors.com member. 445, Mark Grigorian/Flickr. 462-63, Turkey Ministry of Culture & Tourism. 468-69, Jon Arnold Images/Photolibrary. 470, Ali Kabas/Alamy. 471 (top), Jane Sweeney/age fotostock. 471 (bottom) and 472, Turkey Ministry of Culture & Tourism. 473, Michele Burgess/age fotostock. 475, mehmet selim aksan/iStockphoto.

NOTES

NOTES

NOTES

ABOUT OUR WRITERS

Stephen Brewer first set foot in Turkey two decades ago and has been back many, many times since. He considers two of the world's all-time great travel experiences to be hiking through the valleys of Cappadocia and wandering the streets of Istanbul.

Rich Carriero is originally from New Jersey but has has lived in Istanbul with his wife for the past two years. He works a teacher and is a staff writer with *Time Out Istanbul* magazine as well as a contributor to various freelance projects. In addition to his time in Istanbul, he has travelled through Turkey's Aegean region and Cappadocia.

Evin Doğu was born in Baton Rouge, Louisiana, 28 years ago. Hoping to get in touch with her roots and fulfill her ever-present wanderlust, she moved to Istanbul in 2006 and has lived there ever since. When she's not traveling, Evin teaches English as a foreign language.

Joel Hanson worked as a lead instructor at Bilgi University in Istanbul during the 2007-2008 academic year and traveled extensively in Turkey and the surrounding countries in his free time. Even though he currently calls Casablanca home, Joel remains a regular writing contributor to *Time Out Istanbul* and the *Washington Free Press*. You can read more of his work at www.joelmhanson.com.

Vanessa Larson first visited Turkey in 1998 and returned several times—for study, travel, and an internship at the U.S. Consulate—before moving to Istanbul in 2007. A writer and editor, she has written for *Time Out Istanbul* magazine, *Today's Zaman,* and other publications, and has edited several books about Turkey.

Scott Newman first set foot in Turkey in 1994 as a wandering Australian archaeology undergraduate and has been filling passports with Turkish stamps ever since. He's currently living in Istanbul, again, and when not teaching English and writing for *Time Out Istanbul* magazine, he's out hiking the Lycian Way or hunting for lost ruins.

Yigal Schleifer is a freelance journalist based in Istanbul, where he writes for the Christian Science Monitor and the Jerusalem Report, among other publications. Living in Turkey since 2002, he has traveled extensively throughout the country, particularly in the Black Sea and southeast regions.